THE FAMILIAI

The Familiar Enemy re-examines the lingui
of England and France within the context o.
this war, two profoundly intertwined peoples developed complex strategies for expressing their aggressively intimate relationship. This special connection between the English and the French has endured into the modern period as a model for Western nationhood. This book reassesses the concept of 'nation' in this period through a wide-ranging discussion of writing produced in war, truce, or exile from the thirteenth to the fifteenth century, concluding with reflections on the retrospective views of this conflict created by the trials of Jeanne d'Arc and by Shakespeare's *Henry V.* It considers authors writing in French, 'Anglo-Norman', English, and the comic tradition of Anglo-French 'jargon', including Machaut, Deschamps, Froissart, Chaucer, Gower, Charles d'Orléans, as well as many lesser-known or anonymous works. Traditionally Chaucer has been seen as a quintessentially English author. This book argues that he needs to be resituated within the deeply francophone context, not only of England but the wider multilingual cultural geography of medieval Europe. It thus suggests that a modern understanding of what 'English' might have meant in the fourteenth century cannot be separated from 'French', and that this has far-reaching implications both for our understanding of English and the English, and of French and the French.

The Familiar Enemy

Chaucer, Language, and Nation in the Hundred Years War

ARDIS BUTTERFIELD

OXFORD
UNIVERSITY PRESS

OXFORD
UNIVERSITY PRESS

Great Clarendon Street, Oxford, OX2 6DP,
United Kingdom

Oxford University Press is a department of the University of Oxford.
It furthers the University's objective of excellence in research, scholarship,
and education by publishing worldwide. Oxford is a registered trade mark of
Oxford University Press in the UK and in certain other countries

First published 2009
First published in paperback 2013

British Library Cataloguing in Publication Data
Data available

Library of Congress Cataloging in Publication Data
Library of Congress Control Number: 2009935898

ISBN 978–0–19–957486–5
ISBN 978–0–19–965770–4 (Pbk)

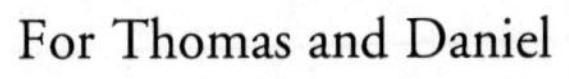

For Thomas and Daniel

Contents

PART II EXCHANGING TERMS: WAR AND PEACE

PART III VERNACULAR SUBJECTS

Acknowledgements

I owe thanks to many people. My first acknowledgement is to the Leverhulme Trust for awarding me a Research Fellowship in 2003–4 which enabled the bulk of the primary research to be carried out. Their generous and unpressured support is a model of its kind, and greatly appreciated. It enabled me to work in a range of libraries: principally the Bibliothèque nationale de France, site François-Mitterand, and the Salle des manuscrits, site Richelieu-Louvois; and at home in London at the UCL Library, the Senate House Library, the Warburg Institute, the Institute for Historical Research, and the British Library. For more specific materials, I gratefully acknowledge the resources and assistance offered at the following libraries: the Bibliothèque municipale d'Arras; the Bibliothèque municipale de Lille; the Bibliothèque municipale de Valenciennes; the Bibliothèque Royale de Belgique in Brussels; the Pierpont Morgan Library in New York; the Rosenbach Museum and Library and the Annenberg Rare Book and Manuscript Library at the University of Pennsylvania, both in Philadelphia; the Charles E. Young Research Library at UCLA, and the Huntington Library in San Marino, California.

Part of Chapter 3 first appeared as 'English, French and Anglo-French: Language and nation in the fabliau', Special Issue of *Zeitschrift für deutsche Philologie: 'Mittelalterliche Novellistik im europaïschen Kontext'*, ed. Mark Chinca, Timo Reuvekamp-Felber, and Christopher Young (Berlin: Erich Schmidt, 2006), 238–59; and part of Chapter 9 as 'Converting Jeanne d'Arc: *trahison* and *nation* in the Hundred Years War', *NML*, 8 (2006), ed. Rita Copeland, Wendy Scase, and David Lawton (Turnhout: Brepols, 2006), 67–97. Both are reproduced with kind permission.

This book was written mostly in Paris, London, and Connecticut, and more of it than I expected on Eurostar. In Paris, various friends, some long-standing, some newer, offered living and working space, cross-channel conversations, Internet access, food, and company: these include Monique Bergeret, Cathérine Axelrad-Bourget and Jean-Loup Bourget, André Crépin, Laura Kendrick, Jean-Pascal Pouzet, Isabelle Ragnard, Luisella and James Simpson, Christina Story, and Céline Surprenant and Jean Demerliac. In Connecticut, Dana English and Tom Whalen, Sam, and Michael offered their warm friendship in a beautiful environment. Much of the immediate stimulus for producing the arguments of the book and the detailed materials to support them came from speaking invitations and the ensuing discussion: I am grateful to colleagues in English, French, and History departments and faculties, in Paris-IV Sorbonne, and L'Académie des Inscriptions et Belles-Lettres in Paris; in Valenciennes, Lille, Metz, and Geneva; at UCE Birmingham, Cambridge, Exeter, Leeds, Kings College London, Oxford, Reading, York; at Harvard, the ICMS at Kalamazoo, NYU, and Penn; as well as to the New Chaucer Society Congresses in Paris, Glasgow, Fordham University, New York, and Swansea. Their hospitality, wide-ranging knowledge, and diverse approaches have been a rich source of collegiality and intellectual debate. Other occasions for conversation have been provided by the London Old and Middle English Research Seminar, under the stimulating leadership of Ruth Kennedy, with the support of other London colleagues; and also the reading group at Kings College London including at different times Sally Burch, Simon Gaunt, Jane Gilbert, Clare Lees, Bob Mills, Karen Pratt, Luke Sunderland, and Marion Turner. Thanks to Elliot Kendall for doing far more than hold the fort at UCL in my absence, along with other UCL colleagues, especially Susan Irvine, Richard North, Henry Woudhuysen, and Rachel Bowlby. Thanks, too, to Danny Karlin for his interest, and to Philip Horne and Greg Dart for their encouragement. More recently, I owe thanks for offprints and references to Peter Ainsworth, Mary Carruthers, Mark Chinca, Joyce Coleman, Helen Cooper, Bradin Cormack, Philippe Contamine, Jane Gilbert, Tony Hunt, Richard Ingham, Hope Johnston, Sarah Kay, Sjoerd Levelt, Serge Lusignan, Brian Merrilees, Marigold Anne Norbye, Richard North, Bob Yeager, and Nicky Zeeman. More detailed comment on individual chapters was provided by Daron Burrows, Olivier Collet, Godfried Croenen, Yolanda Plumley, Jean-Pascal Pouzet, Craig Taylor, and David Trotter. The generosity of these colleagues in sharing their expertise has been humbling. I am particularly grateful to David Trotter, Daron Burrows, Olivier Collet, and Godfried Croenen for their advice on matters of language. None, of course, is responsible for any errors or vagaries of argument. It is also a pleasure to record thanks to the postgraduates in the UCL Department of English MA in Medieval Literature for their fresh and stimulating approach to the topic of 'English and Englishness: the Politics of the Vernacular': in particular to Lisa Arsenieva, Neil Dangerfield, Aditi Nafde, Claire Pascolini-Campbell, and Ruen-Chuan Ma.

Even greater, I fear unpayable, debts of friendship and scholarship are owed to Kevin Brownlee, Rita Copeland, Susan Crane, Simon Gaunt, Derek Pearsall, James Simpson, Paul Strohm, and David Wallace. Derek, *preudomme*, with typical *largesse* and *vaillance*, read the entire manuscript at a late stage. Fortunately, he liked some of it. Andrew McNeillie did not blink as the manuscript grew longer and longer: for which trust I only hope he is somehow rewarded, perhaps in another life. I am grateful to Kathleen Palti for the scholarly care with which she has helped check through the final draft; and to Shanaz Begum and latterly Julie Miles for their friendship and help with the school run. My family has been extraordinarily patient, always encouraging and understanding especially in the last endless stages of footnoting and checking, and full of distractions when I needed them (and sometimes when I thought I didn't). Thanks to my mother for her intrepid linguistic travels in a very full life, first on her own from Switzerland to England via France, and then with my father across several cultures and continents; to my wonderful brother and his family; to Thomas for his huge support and keen interrogations of my ideas and my prose; and to Daniel (taking after his grandmother) for his inspiring interest in languages. Brian has, of course, I confess, done too much to be thanked as such, but I thank him all the same, *de coeur*.

List of Illustrations

Figures

Maps

Bibliographical note

All quotations from Chaucer are taken from *The Riverside Chaucer*, gen. ed. Larry D. Benson, 3rd edn (Oxford: Houghton Mifflin, 1987; pbk repr. Oxford University Press, 1988) and cited by line number, or, in the case of the *Canterbury Tales*, by fragment (in roman numerals) and line number in the text. On Froissart's *Chroniques*: the editorial history is complex. The full editions by Buchon and Kervyn de Lettenhove are each problematic in different ways, since both are variously amalgamated rather than critical texts and Buchon uses, in addition, a modernized spelling. De Lettenhove, however, draws more directly from the manuscripts than Buchon who often uses earlier editions instead. The thorough re-edition by the Société de l'histoire de France is currently still incomplete. Citations to Froissart's *Chroniques* thus use the Société de l'histoire de France edition for Books I, II, and III, supplemented on occasion by de Lettenhove. Citations to Book IV refer to de Lettenhove; I also make use of the excellent newer editions by Diller for the separate versions of Book I in the Rome and Amiens MSS, and by Ainsworth and Varvaro of Book IV (in generous extract).

My principles in translation have been, of necessity, mixed: where (for certain authors) there is a reliable published translation I have used it, though occasionally where interpretation is crucial, providing corrections and alternatives. Given the complex textual state of the *Chroniques*, all citations from Froissart have been freshly translated, however, and all other unattributed translations throughout are also mine.

On the vexed question of names, I have decided not to follow the usual principle in an English-language book of general Anglicization, but to give French names in French style. However, since consistency is impossible, especially in negotiating medieval and modern spellings, I have tried to clarify some cases of alternative nomenclature through cross-references in the index.

List of Abbreviations

AND	Used to refer to the electronic edition of the *Anglo-Norman Dictionary*, at <http://www.anglo-norman.net/>. This incorporates material from the first edition of the *Anglo-Norman Dictionary* (*AND*^{1}), ed. William Rothwell, Louise W. Stone, and T. B. W. Reid (London: Modern Humanities Research Association, 1977–1992), but largely supersedes this with an ongoing substantially revised and expanded second edition (*AND*^{2}), ed. David Trotter et al (2001–).
ANTS	Anglo-Norman Text Society
ATILF	Analyse et traitement informatique de la langue française
BnF	Bibliothèque nationale de France
BoLE	*A Book of London English 1384–1425*, ed. R.W. Chambers and Marjorie Daunt (Oxford: Clarendon Press, 1931)
CFMA	Classiques français du moyen âge
CNRS	Centre national de la recherche scientifique
DMF	*Dictionnaire du Moyen Français* (ATILF-Nancy Université & CNRS), http://www.atilf.fr/dmf
EETS	Early English Text Society
EMH	*Early Music History*
ES	Extra Series
Idea of the Vernacular	*The Idea of the Vernacular: An Anthology of Middle English Literary Theory 1280–1520*, ed. Jocelyn Wogan-Browne, Nicholas Watson, Andrew Taylor and Ruth Evans (Exeter: University of Exeter Press, 1999)
JMEMS	*Journal of Medieval and Early Modern Studies*
MED	Middle English Dictionary, ed. Hans Kurath et al (Ann Arbor, Mich.: University of Michigan Press, 1956–2001), available online at <http://quod.lib.umich.edu/m/med>
MHRA	Modern Humanities Research Association
MLA	Modern Language Association
MLQ	*Modern Language Quarterly*

MLR	*Modern Language Review*
NML	*New Medieval Literatures*
NRCF	*Nouveau Recueil complet des fabliaux*, ed. Willem Noomen and Nico van den Boogaard, 10 vols (Assen: Van Gorcum, 1983–98)
OS	Original Series
PUF	Presses Universitaires de France
PMLA	*Publications of the Modern Language Association*
SAC	*Studies in the Age of Chaucer*
SATF	Société des anciens textes français
SHF	Société de l'histoire de France
TLF	Textes littéraires français
TL	*Altfranzösisches Wörterbuch*, ed. Adolf Tobler and Erhard Lommatzsch, 10 vols (Berlin: Weidmannsche Buchhandlung, 1925–76)

Froissart's *Chroniques*

Amiens	Jean Froissart, *Chroniques. Livre I. Le manuscrit d'Amiens*, ed. G. T. Diller, 5 vols (Geneva: Droz, 1991–8)
KL	Jean Froissart, *Oeuvres de Froissart: Chroniques*, ed. J. B. M. C. Kervyn de Lettenhove, 25 vols in 28 (Brussels: V. Devaux, 1867–77)
Livre I Rome MS	Jean Froissart, *Chroniques, début du premier livre. Edition du manuscript de Rome Reg.lat.869*, ed. G. T. Diller, TLF, 194 (Geneva: Droz, 1972)
SHF	Jean Froissart, *Chroniques, Livre I*, ed. S. Luce, I–VII (Paris: Mme Ve. J. Renouard, 1869–88), *Livre II*, ed. G. Raynaud, VIII–XI (Paris: Mme Ve. J. Renouard, 1894–99), *Livre III*, ed. L. and A. Mirot, XII–XV (Paris: Champion, 1931–75)

Machaut lyrics

Lo	Numbers used in Guillaume de Machaut, *Poésies lyriques*, ed. V. Chichmaref, 2 vols (Paris: Champion, 1909; repr. Geneva, 1973)
Wilk	Numbers used in Guillaume de Machaut, *La Louange des Dames by Guillaume de Machaut*, ed. Nigel Wilkins (Edinburgh: Scottish Academic Press, 1972)

Jeanne d'Arc

Doncoeur	Paul Doncoeur and Y. Lanhers, eds, *La Minute française des interrogatoires de Jeanne La Pucelle d'après le Réquisitoire de Jean d'Estivet et les manuscrits de d'Urfé et d'Orléans* (Melun: Librairie d'Argences, 1952)
Duparc	*Procès en nullité de la condamnation de Jeanne d'Arc*, ed. Pierre Duparc, 5 vols (Paris: Klincksieck, 1977–88)
Hobbins	*The Trial of Joan of Arc*, ed. and trans. Daniel Hobbins (Cambridge, MA: Harvard University Press, 2005)
Quicherat	*Procès de condemnation et de réhabilitation de Jeanne d'Arc dite La Pucelle*, ed. Jules Quicherat, SHF, 5 vols (Paris: Renquard, 1841–9)
Tisset and Lanhers	*Procès de condamnation de Jeanne d'Arc*, ed. Pierre Tisset and Yvonne Lanhers, 3 vols (Paris: Klincksieck, 1960–71)

Preface

The relationship between England and France, *soeurs ennemies*, has been praised, mocked, fought for and resisted, ceaselessly discussed, and self-consciously lived, for longer than any other Western axis. It makes an irresistible claim to be studied for what it can tell us about nation. For over a millennium, in a stable geographical tension either side of a narrow sleeve of sea, the English and the French have provided a model of how people identify with one another while also preserving 'un espace autonome'.[1] The most significant period in this long stretch of time was undoubtedly the Hundred Years War: not only did it bring to the surface the fundamental antagonisms of their familial relationship, it also brought with it a huge experiential and written trace through which the medieval era has uniquely influenced the political constructs of the modern western world. No modern version of nationhood is complete without an understanding of how the English and the French have lived and articulated their mutual history during, and as a result of, the long medieval war. Two images, one verbal and English, one pictorial and French, show the depths of this fraught intimacy. For an Anglophone, its image is overwhelmingly formed by Shakespeare's Henry V crying 'we few, we happy few, we band of brothers' at Agincourt, and the Black Prince watched from on high by his father 'up in the air, crowned with the golden sun' (II, 4: 58). A late fourteenth century illustration (shown on the cover) of the *Chroniques de France*, a history commissioned by Charles V, presents, by contrast, a deeply ambiguous fraternal embrace. Edward III and Philippe VI, at the very moment where Edward swears fealty, are shown locked close and cheek to cheek. This gesture, visually so full of affection, proclaims the start of war.

It seems incumbent on a medievalist to seek to convey that understanding. Many distinguished historians have undertaken that task. Yet, perhaps surprisingly, there still remains space for the literary critic to attempt his or her own explication of the war. For despite its historical and cultural prominence, the Hundred Years War has remained very much on the margins of literary history. Chaucer, the figure who dominates that history from an English perspective, is rarely viewed as a poet of war. 'War and chivalry are not Chaucer's favourite subject,' says his most influential modern biographer, and modern readers of his poetry since the two world wars have (for no doubt complex reasons) tended to walk uneasily away from the topic rather than see it as central to his outlook.[2] The war thus constitutes the strangely undiscussed epicentre of the relationship

[1] F. Braudel, 'Comment l'Angleterre devint une île', in *Le Temps du monde*, 3 vols (Paris: Armand Colin, 1979), III, 302–4 (302).

[2] D. Pearsall, *The Life of Geoffrey Chaucer: A Critical Biography* (Oxford: Blackwell, 1992), 46.

between English and French writers in this period. Anglo-French conflict was not only a constant fact or threat throughout Chaucer's lifetime, but it also shaped the way people thought, conducted business, kept records, sought social rewards, and wrote prose and poetry. One purpose of this book is (still uneasily) to bring war back into view for literary history, but not so much to understand war itself as to grasp how it affected writing and the imaginative intellect.

This purpose is driven, not by a historian's desire to comprehend the events and causes of war, but by thinking about war as literary. The brilliant work of reconstruction and assimilation which began among contemporary medieval historians and continues to our own time has been an essential part of any sense of the war's significance and meaning. A literary perspective, while it depends on such work, is seeking something else, perhaps most readily defined as a concentration on text, particularly of words—their production and effect. War, indeed any sense of broad political context, likewise has meaning through the actions and choices people make in their articulation of experience through language. If we want to learn more of the intangible cultural emotions of allegiance and betrayal, that instinctual spark of fellow feeling or antipathy, that desire to speak on behalf of someone, to voice a principle, to declare a vision, or express a reason for action, then we are interested in the work of words as an index, vehicle, and stimulus for human behaviour. Literary, in this sense, is a broad and inclusive category, a 'dialogue', yes, of 'text and world', but also a social performance of the experience of thinking and reflecting within the 'constant pressures' of the 'material world'.[3]

What has drawn me to this particular conflict is that it has exemplary but also peculiar characteristics. This is not a war of nation-states where the boundaries of aggression are clearly marked, but a feudal and familial one where the two sides are tightly bound by lengthy and intimate identifications, through marriage and territorial possession. Above all, they are linked and separated by language. In order to think through the nature of the Anglo-French relationship we need to take account of this vital fact, that the two cultures shared a language for four centuries, indeed, one might argue, that they share it still. From before the Norman Conquest, when Emma of Normandy was wife first to Ethelred and then Canute, kings of England married French-speaking queens. From William of Normandy to Edward IV, with the single exception of Richard the Lionheart, they did so invariably.[4] In specific but overlapping social and intellectual circles until the 1420s and 1430s, and in some fields such as law for much longer, French in England was the language of jurisdiction, of official and private correspondence, diplomacy, parliamentary petitions, the Privy Seal, guild

[3] P. Strohm, *Theory and the Premodern Text* (Minneapolis: University of Minnesota Press, 2000), xv.

[4] I have included second wives. The range of languages spoken by these consorts (such as Berengaria of Navarre) is, of course, not always certain.

documents, administrative registers, business transactions, the Bible, sermons and moral and devotional treatises, history, biography, satire, romance, lyric, science, and medicine. Before the fifteenth century, the overwhelming majority of books owned and used in England were in Latin and French, a situation which did not change markedly with the development of printing.[5] Among figures associated with the court and Westminster whose booklists survive—Richard II himself, Simon Burley his tutor and later chamberlain, diplomat and Garter Knight, Thomas, Duke of Gloucester (Richard's uncle) and Thomas's wife, Eleanor Bohun—a total between them of some hundred and thirty books are mentioned: of these over ninety were in French and over thirty in Latin: just four were in English.[6] The heart of my study concerns what it means to be English and French in the light of this common possession. Sharing a language and a literature crucially confuses a clear sense of distinction between English and French. The world and work of words from the period is thickly coloured by histories of meaning, speaking, and writing that are both English *and* French, by a use of French that is English as well as French, that is homely *and* foreign. This, I argue, has profound repercussions for thinking about nationhood, and thinking about language.

The Familiar Enemy traces these repercussions through a variety of approaches. If language, and therefore literature, are at the centre, then which literature? Why Chaucer? This is where disciplinary emphases distinguish themselves. For a linguist, non-'literary' language is the best place to investigate how language is changing in a period. The words used by shipbuilders or brewers as recorded in daily professional documents have been shown to yield absorbing information about the *Mischsprache* of late medieval English society whose implications are far more far-reaching for social and literary analyses of the period than it might seem given their specificity.[7] For a historian, and literary historians primarily

[5] A. Pettegree, 'Centre and Periphery in the European Book World', *Transactions of the Royal Historical Society*, 18 (2008), 101–28. See also L. Hellinger and J. B. Trapp, 'Introduction', *The Cambridge History of the Book in Britain*, ed. Hellinger and Trapp, vol. 3: *1400–1557* (Cambridge: Cambridge University Press, 1999), 1–30.

[6] V. J. Scattergood, 'Literary Culture at the Court of Richard II', in *English Court Culture in the Later Middle Ages*, ed. V. J. Scattergood and J. W. Sherborne (London: Duckworth, 1983), 29–43 (32–4); C. M. Meale, 'Patrons, Buyers and Owners: Book Production and Social Status', in *Book Production and Publishing in Britain 1375–1475*, ed. J. Griffiths and D. Pearsall (Cambridge: Cambridge University Press, 1989), 201–38 (202). Richard II inherited thirteen secular works from his grandfather, all French, and mostly romances. Simon Burley owned nine French romances and one in English as well as a few works in French of history, politics, and philosophy and one Latin book. Gloucester owned over ninety altogether, of which Scattergood estimates that forty-eight were in French, twenty-five in Latin and three in English (one probably a Wycliffite Bible) (34). His wife, Eleanor Bohun, had a range of largely religious books: again the majority were in French with some in Latin, and none in English. See further C. Paul Christianson, 'The Rise of London's Book-Trade', 128–47 and J.Boffey and A. S. G. Edwards, 'Literary texts', 555–75, both in Hellinger and Trapp, eds., *The Cambridge History of the Book in Britain.*

[7] See, respectively, D. Trotter, 'Language Contact, Multilingualism and the Evidence Problem', in *The Beginnings of Standardization: Language and Culture in Fourteenth-Century England*, ed.

interested in the political and theological circumstances of vernacular production from the fourteenth century on, the rise of Lollardy and the translation of the Bible into English assume centre stage, together with the increasing amount of devotional and homiletic material that began to be produced and translated into English, such as the *Lay Folk's Catechism* (c.1300), the *Speculum Vitae* (mid-fourteenth century), and the *Prick of Conscience* (1360). In literary studies, however, it is above all Chaucer who dominates. In that sense, Chaucer entitles this book by default: he is there because from the earliest decades of the fifteenth century he has been taken to stand for English literature by his creation of a new literary English, the 'firste fyndere of our faire langage' as Hoccleve puts it.[8] He is crucial, then, in any investigation of nation; like Shakespeare after him, his use of English down the generations has been metonymically collapsed into Englishness in a deep-rooted and still active process of cultural and national symbolism.

A single book cannot reconcile the potentially contradictory implications of these varying emphases: yet it is worth observing that the sheer quantity of writing in insular and continental French in all these areas is a constant and under-researched element. If this study has a presiding genius it is therefore Chaucer, but more as an *eminence grise* than a striding colossus who blocks out other views. In fact, much of the time I argue that he needs to be less visible than we have made him, not at all in order to belittle his extraordinary achievements, but to set those achievements in a wider and more detailed French context than before. This setting, I argue, better represents the multilingual literary perspectives of the time than our own retrospective isolation of English. One of the book's prime purposes is indeed to separate Chaucer from such notions of English and Englishness.

It also seeks to achieve this by looking back at English writing from the continent: an immersion in continental French writing and in modern as well as medieval French history seems vital as a way of understanding Englishness, not merely as a set of insular characteristics but, like Frenchness, as a construct mutually, though not necessarily explicitly, fashioned by both sides. To read Machaut and Deschamps alongside Gower and Usk, the *Chroniques de France* alongside *The Westminster Chronicle*, and figures who are of both sides or neither, such as Jean Froissart, is to learn how subtly perspectives can deny as well as support, ignore as well as over-emphasize, coincide as well as disagree, all in often unexpected places. Encouraged, furthermore, by the spate of important historical work on the Low Countries, and the pioneering efforts of David Wallace to bring 'Flaundres' to Chaucerians' attention, *The Familiar Enemy*, despite my linguistic limitations in Dutch, tries to take account of the powerful contacts between

Ursula Schaefer (Frankfurt: Peter Lang, 2006), 73–90 and L. Wright, *Sources of London English: Medieval Thames Vocabulary* (Oxford: Clarendon Press, 1996).

[8] *Thomas Hoccleve: The Regiment of Princes*, ed. Charles R. Blyth (Kalamazoo, Michigan: Medieval Institute Publications, 1999), line 4978.

England and the Low Countries, and ponder the ways in which this area of the medieval *francophonie* disrupts not only an English but also a Parisian sense of 'French'.

The current sense of how Chaucer used English, 'what his language was' is strongly influenced by a subtle argument put forward by Christopher Cannon. He has suggested that Chaucer was not quite as much of an originator as he seems. Instead, Chaucer manages the pose of being new so successfully that he has been constantly *mistaken* as the inventor of a new English. If you sift through all his words rather than rely on impressionistic judgements—and this even includes the judgements of the earliest editors of the *OED*—he is in truth a deeply traditional writer, employing the English of his often anonymous predecessors much more often than we had thought as well as spinning new words in a greatly expanded linguistic web. He seems new because he so brilliantly stages the choices he makes between words: English emerges as a newly powerful vernacular because it is shown to be a matter of artful selection rather than familiar formulas.[9]

The question that attends such an argument about Chaucer is whether in that case he really affects the course of English or whether he only seems to, and if he only seems to, however important that has been to English literary history, whether other factors and other writers at large were really changing the language. The origins of a distinctive vernacular literary imagination in English, and its periodization, have recently been freshly re-argued by James Simpson.[10] Others have further held that concentration on Chaucer has blinded us to the wider currents flowing in literary English, to the work of Langland, and writers working outside the metropolis.[11] A Chaucer-centred view of medieval writing 'is less pivotal to the development of written English and of theorizing in and about English than is often thought.'[12]

The Familiar Enemy engages with these issues by suggesting that the category of English is itself in need of new investigation. Cannon has done a great service in showing so clearly how retrospective scholarly desires have influenced lexical approaches to Chaucer's English. In this he has been part of a chorus of voices that have perceptively exposed the nature of medievalism and its nineteenth

[9] C. Cannon, *The Making of Chaucer's English* (Cambridge: Cambridge University Press, 1998). I allude also to his contribution 'What Chaucer's Language Is' to the 'Colloquium: Chaucer and the Future of Language Study', *SAC*, 24 (2002), 299–354 (301–8).

[10] J. Simpson, *Reform and Cultural Revolution* (Oxford: Oxford University Press, 2002).

[11] Ralph Hanna, for instance, makes this case repeatedly; see, most recently, *London Literature: 1300–1380* (Cambridge: Cambridge University Press, 2005), 305–13. It is a point made by several of the contributors to the 'Colloquium: Chaucer and the Future of Language Study'.

[12] J. Wogan-Browne, N. Watson, A. Taylor, and R. Evans, eds, *The Idea of the Vernacular: An Anthology of Middle English Literary Theory 1280–1520* (Exeter: University of Exeter Press, 1999) (hereafter *Idea of the Vernacular*), xvi.

century founding impulses.[13] It is possible to go much further. The remarkable transformations of linguistic knowledge demonstrated and facilitated by the ongoing revision of the *Anglo-Norman Dictionary* and the ground-breaking books by the historical linguist Serge Lusignan on the status of French in France *and* England in the later medieval period, have made available material on French that has the potential radically to alter our understanding of England's plural linguistic culture.[14] It is the claim of this study, albeit from a literary point of view, that English needs revaluing as a far less hard-edged object of study than modern dictionaries lead us to believe, and that such notions of categorization lie at the root of modern discourse on the nation. The constant recourse to English in modern debates creates of English an autonomous, distinct, and identifiable entity. Despite all we know of English's plural past there is a presumption of independence, of national character. Chaucer has always worked beautifully as an embodiment of this national character, but in a sense the presumption and the desire that impels it goes deeper: both seek a notion of English that will represent something natural, original, autochthonous; both seek a vindication of the mother tongue.

But the history of language spoken and written in England does not conform to this monolingual model. Modern readers know this very well in theory but it has proved more difficult to bring it into our critical practice. To whatever extent French or Latin has been recognized, through the pioneering work of H. J. Chaytor and subsequently M. T. Clanchy, as a fundamental part of medieval literacy, we still tend to put each language into a separate cultural category and for an Anglophone reader the direction of influence tends to flow into English.[15] English is the end point of borrowings, the capacious destination of other linguistic transformations. And it has been all too tempting to cast this as a triumphant story. Other languages are fought off; English is liberated and isolated. My effort in this book is to try to go back to the medieval period without that conviction of English's separate and separable character. What happens to the story of English if we do not isolate it from French, England's other vernacular? An even longer and better book would bring Latin properly into the picture as well, since in a sense this is the most important linguistic perspective of all. Yet it seems worth starting at least with the vernacular, our own starting point and, for many commentators, the starting point of nation.

[13] See, in particular, Stephanie Trigg's acute study, *Congenial Souls: Reading Chaucer from Medieval to Postmodern* (Minneapolis: University of Minesota Press, 2002) and D. Matthews, *The Making of Middle English, 1765–1910* (Minneapolis: University of Minnesota Press, 1999).

[14] S. Lusignan, *Parler vulgairement: Les Intellectuels et la langue française aux XIIIe et XIVe siècles* (Paris; Montréal: Vrin; Les Presses de l'Université de Montréal, 1986) and S. Lusignan, *La Langue des rois au Moyen Âge: le français en France et en Angleterre* (Paris: PUF, 2004).

[15] H. J. Chaytor, *From Script to Print* (Cambridge: Cambridge University Press, 1945); M. T. Clanchy, *From Memory to Written Record: England 1066–1307*, 2nd edn (Oxford: Blackwell, 1993; 1st edn 1979).

So, which starting point? Although no specialist in the earliest periods of the vernaculars of French and English, I have felt it necessary to attempt to include something of this early history because it has had such a profound, yet confusing effect on subsequent histories of the nation on both sides of the Channel. In one version on the English side, English begins with the Norman Conquest. French is part of the paternity of English through the 'Norman yoke' but finally English overthrows and transcends its continental father in an Oedipal blow that liberates English into a new national condition. Chaucer is usually cast as this rebellious son, and his work passing as a consequence through three stages from French-inspired early poetry, through Italian-influenced mid-career writing, to the truly English articulations of his mature work, the *Canterbury Tales.* In another version, common in the nineteenth and early-twentieth century but still surfacing now, modern English emerges fundamentally as a transition from Old English. In the latter, French appears as a kind of temporary foreign extra, an added luxury which gives the English blend sweetness, sophistication, and cultural cachet (and, in some versions, effeminacy) but ultimately fails to touch its inner Anglo-Saxon core. Carl Horstmann provides a very clear late-nineteenth century example in the introduction to his edition of Richard Rolle's writings. For him, a professor in Berlin, 'England's fatherland' is Germany, and although 'Saxon heaviness has been partly relieved by the immigration of the Normans... the groundwork of the nation remains Saxon.'[16] This narrative connects with arguments about the English nation by scholars of the Anglo-Saxon period that draw attention to the unusually strong status of English in relation to Latin in those centuries and the powerfully unifying military and cultural work achieved by Alfred on a previously fragmented set of peoples.

On the French side, which is (tellingly) not much concerned with English literary history, the earliest surviving instances of French have been sought as evidence of the unbroken continuity of importance that attaches to the French language and French nationhood. The very singularity and hence purity of French linguistic history over so long a period has been vital to many definitions of the French nation over the centuries, including those articulated by the Académie française (founded in 1635) and such founding figures of French medievalism as Gaston Paris and Joseph Bédier.[17]

In working with a plural model of language in England, however, the singularity of French comes under question. If English literary history needs to reckon more fully with the French language, French literary history in turn needs to

[16] C. Horstmann, ed., *Yorkshire Writers: Richard Rolle of Hampole* (London: Swan Sonnenschein; New York: Macmillan, 1895), v. For a very recent instance, see D. Daniell, *The Bible in English: Its History and Influence* (New Haven and London: Yale University Press, 2003), 59–60.

[17] For discussion of Bédier's colonial roots, see M. R. Warren, '"Au commencement était l'île": the colonial formation of Joseph Bédier's *Chanson de Roland*', in *Postcolonial Approaches to the European Middle Ages: Translating Cultures,* ed. A. Jahanara Kabir and D. Williams (Cambridge: Cambridge University Press, 2005), 205–26.

reckon more fully with its part in English culture, indeed with the way English culture took on and took over French. The long history of French in England is as much part of the history of French as continental French is part of the history of English. *The Familiar Enemy* seeks to restore the doubleness of this narrative; in order to write either history, the other history must also be audible. Thus, although it is disheartening to think that conflict with the continent should be the underlying model for an 'English' notion of linguistic change, it is also a positive impetus for enquiry since it provides a fresh, and far more extended way of thinking about the significance of French culture in England that involves the continent with both of England's vernaculars.

This can best be appreciated (on the English side) through the character of English responses to Chaucer. That French was important to Chaucer is perhaps the oldest chestnut in Chaucer criticism. But it is an importance scholars are currently oddly ambivalent and even silent about. This study stands under the light cast by the two great beacons of twentieth century scholarship on Chaucer and France, Charles Muscatine and James Wimsatt. Their perspectives remain dominant even now; while this is a tribute to their powerful scholarship it is also perhaps a less happy reflection of our own reluctance to work dynamically with their legacy. For although 'the French tradition' gains much lip service there is also a certain insouciance, indeed resistance to it. It is taken for granted; it is ignored; it is often claimed that Chaucer moved on from it. As I argue in Chapter 8, Muscatine's very qualities as a critic are partly responsible. His remarkable influence derives, I suggest, from the sense he gives of the vividly respectful intimacy of Chaucer's reading of French literature. The *Roman d'Enéas*, Chretien de Troyes, Guillaume de Lorris, and Jean de Meun, and anonymous fabliaux writers all come alive in Muscatine's descriptions. Yet French literature remains characterized as a fundamentally continental tradition, and the end point, once more, is how Chaucer 'assimilates' French literature 'to his English consciousness' (7). It is important for Muscatine to frame his whole book with an assertion of Chaucer's Englishness: 'I share the conviction of generations of readers that there is nothing so primally English in spirit as the *Canterbury Tales'* and a denial that his book takes Chaucer's Frenchness so far as to forget that.[18] One way in which he achieves this distance from his subject is to restrict French literature to the twelfth and thirteenth centuries. Wimsatt's gift is to allow Chaucer's French contemporaries (dismissed by Muscatine as 'pretty' and 'decorative') also to speak and be given their due. Yet even here, the poems of Guillaume de Machaut

[18] C. Muscatine, *Chaucer and the French Tradition: A Study in Style and Meaning* (Berkeley: University of California Press, 1957), and J. Wimsatt, *Chaucer and the French Love Poets: The Literary Background of The Book of the Duchess'* (Chapel Hill: University of North Carolina Press, 1968), and *Chaucer and His French Contemporaries: Natural Music in the Fourteenth Century* (Toronto: University of Toronto Press, 1992).

and Jean Froissart are kept in their place as sources, as a kind of foreign French credit to which Chaucer was indebted.

While myself enormously indebted to both scholars, the directions of my own engagement with French writing have led to a different focus. Once we take the literature back to its constituent words, we see it as shaped and produced by mutual interactions between French and English cultures over several centuries. French no longer looks like a background or source for Chaucer but an overwhelming, insistent, and conflicted presence. Its character is complex because it is not merely other. In reading French, Chaucer was not acting as the dazzled tourist confronted with exotic foreignness but as a reader of a language that was familiar, daily, domestic, and professional. French, for Chaucer, did not come to England from the continent, it was already here. This is not to say that there was no perceived difference between insular and continental French—although by the late fourteenth century the extent of cross-channel interchange meant that this difference could on occasion be negligible—but that (in a way that was never true in reverse) French was a co-vernacular in England.

The task of *The Familiar Enemy* is to ponder the implications of this double status of French, by considering it to be part of a triangular set of relationships between English, the other English vernacular of Anglo-French, and French. I attempt to follow this triangular conversation in three broadly chronological stages. In the period covered in Part I of the book to the end of the thirteenth century, French is the dominant cultural vernacular of England as well as many other areas of the continent, a familiar language, shared between peoples who were themselves part of more than one culture and landscape. Here I trace some of the comic ironies of this shared condition as well as its more troubling aspects as a way of understanding how the later complex entanglements of war developed. To complement existing work on early Middle English, and to redress the balance of attention towards England's other vernacular, my focus will be on French as an 'English' language. In Part II, relating largely to the fourteenth century, sameness is not the same, and this starts to matter in the context of war where tricky issues of shifting dominance begin to surface. What, people ask, is 'our' language? How does one possess, or assert rights over a language? The language was changing as people spoke and wrote it and not in ways that they necessarily liked or felt able to control. But the mechanisms of control are fascinating to watch in the use of envoys and diplomats to argue, press, resist, deny, and claim. In these debates and negotiations about English and French territorial and political possessions there is a political dialogue about Englishness and about Frenchness that is expressed through concerns about language. Charges and counter-charges about each side's linguistic competence enter into the larger diplomatic and poetic tussles—*how* they speak is part of what they are speaking about. The realization *from the other side*, once the English soldiers started to dominate at Crécy and Poitiers, that 'French' as a political and linguistic category now meant 'English' (at least to the English) was one of the crises of the period.

Part III re-examines the rise of English by taking all these arguments into account. There is no doubt that English gains more of a presence and cultural force from the late-fourteenth century and into the fifteenth than it had before. But how much? And how do we gauge it? English and French now have huge pressures on them, in several directions: political, economic, cultural, social, and linguistic. The political pressures were particularly volatile: English transcendence was often transient or even illusory, and things always looked different from home. Thus English as a political force was sometimes very strongly dominant in relation to French and sometimes hesitant and stuttering. Culturally, it was exactly the reverse. French had an international dominance that English entirely lacked. Nonetheless, the moments of English supremacy in terms of military and political strength caused continental anxiety about the capacity of French to articulate French resistance to English subjugation.

The last stages of the Hundred Years War provide a platform for viewing language and nation together. Taking account of French as well as English, and of English as well as French, prompts a rethinking of how nation is claimed and identified. Realizing the entanglements of identity, the treachery and factionalism within as well as without the case of Jeanne d'Arc, and the profound bi-vernacular humour of *Shakespeare's Henry V*, makes one doubt whether asserting nation even in the sixteenth century has much meaning beyond the local claim. In this *The Familiar Enemy* goes against the grain of most current discussions of nationhood in the medieval and early modern periods. Derek Pearsall is one of the few medieval scholars to resist an 'idea of Englishness' in the medieval period.[19] In general, there has been an understandable desire to defy modernist insistence that the nation is a concept born in the Enlightenment. Although I have learnt much from Thorlac Turville-Petre's important study of English national identity from 1290 to 1340 and the richly intelligent collection of essays edited by Kathy Lavezzo, the long view of an intertwined English and French culture has impelled me into a different approach.[20]

The slightly awkward locution 'nation', used often in this book, is part of this approach. It is difficult to avoid terms that yoke past to present with unexamined ease. Versions of what V. H. Galbraith called 'the sentiment of nationality' are often invoked as a way of talking about nation transhistorically whereas 'nationalism' or the nation-state jut out as uncomfortably period-specific.[21] Yet, as we

[19] D. Pearsall, 'The Idea of Englishness in the Fifteenth Century', in *Nation, Court and Culture: New Essays on Fifteenth-Century English Poetry*, ed. H. Cooney (Dublin: Four Courts Press, 2001), 15–27 (17); 'Chaucer and Englishness', *Proceedings of the British Academy*, 101 (1999 for 1998), 77–99.

[20] T. Turville-Petre, *England the Nation: Language, Literature and National Identity 1290–1340* (Oxford: Clarendon Press, 1996); K. Lavezzo, ed., *Imagining a Medieval English Nation* (Minneapolis: University of Minnesota Press, 2004). Turville-Petre modifies some of the claims of his book in his 'Afterword' to Lavezzo's collection.

[21] V. H. Galbraith, 'Nationality and Language in Medieval England', *Transactions of the Royal Historical Society*, 23 (1941), 113–28.

well know, national sentiment is in danger of being reclaimed as fascism, even as it pretends to vaguely emotive universality. David Wallace has shown through ideas of polity, place, and memory, in sympathy with Pearsall but with a different, inimitably imaginative methodology, that European relationships are endlessly interweaving and mutually shaping in their reach in ways that preclude 'a progressivist logic' of nation.[22] In the long journey of this book I have sought to avoid claiming 'the' nation in favour of re-examining the medieval uses of *natio, nation, nascioun* as a description of birth and its implications for social, political, and cultural identity. Rather than see Chaucer anticipating national discourses, I have tried to see him in a wider and longer *durée* of Anglo-French identifications and distinctions. The result may seem to diminish Chaucer only if we think that an exclusive approach to Chaucer is the best way of granting his incomparable poetic skill and stature. I have risked embedding his writing so thoroughly in French that it may appear at times submerged. But there is such a large accretion of retrospective 'English' assumption about his poetic achievements that there is much work to do in re-finding his genius in a far thicker—and absorbingly rich—linguistic environment than we have usually allowed ourselves to see. Chaucer is more than an English author; he is a cross-channel author, continental as well as insular, committed to a plural linguistic texture and an international imagination that speaks directly to our own.

My effort has been to keep returning to the assertions, the comments made by medieval writers on issues of identity through language, to find their context, to unravel their significance to us from their significance then. It has seemed important not to locate retrospectively a generalizing impulse of nation, but to try to understand cultural likeness and unlikeness. This book purposively seeks to pause and work over those moments where the modern desire to generalize can often seem irresistible. In the process it seeks to develop both a postmodern and a pre-modern approach to nation by arguing that in this period, nation is less assertively clear as a concept. May it then be itself a means of reassessing more recent notions of nationhood? Seeing Chaucer in a much broader European literary history rather than constituting a history all by himself is liberating rather than diminishing. It shows us a way forward from the past. For this reason, the book aims to maintain its dialogue between Englishness and Frenchness alongside a second dialogue with past and present. Rather than presume upon cultural difference, and—even more so—rather than claim some priority of one perspective over the other, my aim is to follow through their tightly interwoven historical and cultural threads. The notion that Europe's vernaculars produced nation states by bursting out in sudden atomized individuality against the oppressive

[22] D. Wallace, *Chaucerian Polity: Absolutist Lineages and Associational Forms in England and Italy* (Stanford: Stanford University Press, 1997, and *Premodern Places: Calais to Surinam, Chaucer to Aphra Behn* (Oxford: Blackwell, 2004); for the citation see p. 18, n. 23 and also *Chaucerian Polity*, 55 on the dangers of conceiving of the text of Chaucer 'as an insular, medieval text'.

stranglehold of a homogenized Latin Western culture is an old model of nationhood, not a current one. What we need is a recognition that these models are currently falling apart, and what we see now around us has much more in common than is usually granted with the highly plural, contested, and reticulated identities of medieval culture(s).

I hope in pausing over such moments to show them to be revealing rather than opaquely assertive, perceptive of their entanglement rather than crudely declamatory. Perhaps only by refusing to indulge in that terrible desire to assume dominance over one's partner, English or French, past or present, will a post-national perspective catch up with a pre-national one.

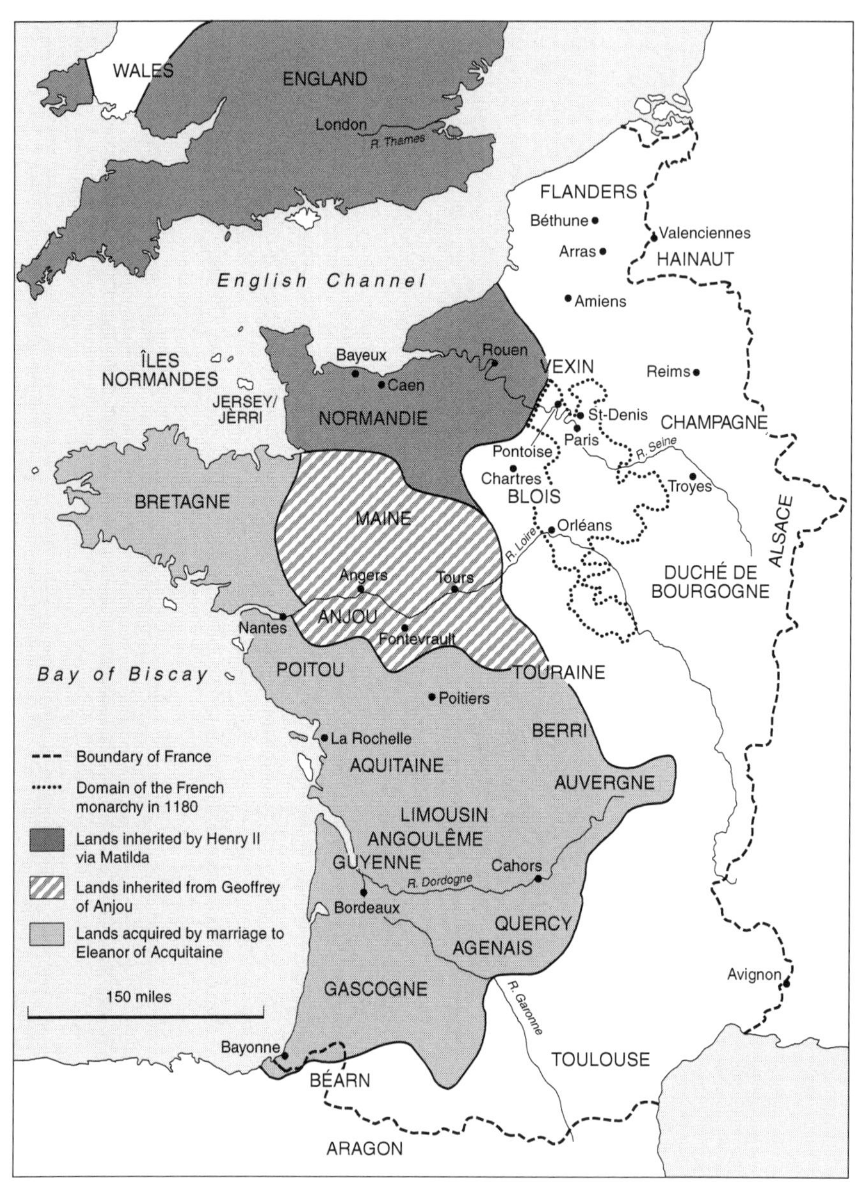

Map 1. France in 1157

PART I
NATION AND LANGUAGE

Part I of *The Familiar Enemy* attempts to introduce a double act on double grounds: it wants to set the two histories of English and Englishness, French and Frenchness within the same overarching narrative, and to tell each from its own perspective. The absorbing and often comic tensions involved in telling the same story from both sides of the Channel point towards the central argument of this book, that each side is crucially involved in each other's history, but that this cannot be grasped until the linguistic intricacies of that history are unravelled. The prehistory of the Hundred Years War is traced in the belief that war is not merely the cause of Anglo-French separation but the symptom of its fundamental likeness. The section as a whole aims to substantiate and develop the approach towards language outlined in the Preface in order to establish the density and variety of meaning of 'French' and 'English' as cultural and linguistic categories in the earlier medieval period.

The introductory chapter sets out the double perspective of the book through the eyes of two Jersey writers, Wace and Victor Hugo. Each raises the issue of language as both a unifying and divisive factor in their apprehensions of identity; each gives written life to the ways in which notions of identity are entangled between past and present. The chapter then considers the role Chaucer has played as 'father' to English and Englishness, and argues that decoupling Chaucer from 'English' may help us to grasp both Chaucer and Englishness more clearly. Two further threads in this chapter, on 'England's vernaculars' and the constant presence of war, are unwound to give context to the wide range of English and French writings that are discussed throughout the book as a whole. The chapter concludes by pondering the connections between nation and modernity: where does the medieval belong in a construction of nation as modern—for instance in the well-known formulations of Benedict Anderson? It suggests that there might be much to connect current 'post-national' anxieties about ideologies of nation and the 'pre-national' Middle Ages.

Chapter 2, 'Origins and Language', continues this debate by revisiting the symbolic importance attached to language and stories of national origin in some of the earliest examples of written 'English' and 'French'—the former, on Hengist and Horsa, actually written retrospectively in French, and the latter, the so-called

Strasbourg Oaths, in a hybrid mixture of Latin and vernacular. It then considers the linguistic mobility of French in England and on the continent in the thirteenth century. In line with, and drawing upon, the most recent linguistic research, the grounds for using the term Anglo-French rather than Anglo-Norman are explored in some detail. Once we look at French more broadly across both sides of the Channel, in England and in different areas of France, older, rigid models of dialect and linguistic change seem inadequate to describe the ways in which both 'French' and 'Anglo-French' fragment under scrutiny into shifting, porous and, most importantly, shared forms and instances of language variation.

Chapter 3, 'A Common Language?', carries this through into an exploration of how certain writings represent people interacting across language differences. This involves trying to gain a sense of how people thought about their own language use, what they understood by linguistic barriers, and what significance they attached to them. When they heard one another speak, what did they hear? How did an English speaker of French hear continental French, and how did a continental French speaker hear Anglo-French? Through close reading of a collection of fabliaux, variously 'Anglo-French', and other 'textes en jargon franco-anglais' in which writers display a self-conscious humour about the differences between kinds of French, I argue that issues of identity are performed through differences in pronunciation. With subtle comedy, these writers show that sharing a language can be a rich source of social distinction, yet also an unreliable means of wielding power.

1

Pre-nation and Post-nation

ENGLAND AND FRANCE: PERSPECTIVES

> Tant al soleil, tant as esteilles,
> Tant as avirons, tant as veilles,
> A Toteneis en Dertremue
> Est tute la flote venue:
> Ço est l'ille dunt la deuesse
> Lur fist el sunge la premesse.
> Des nés a terre fors eissirent;
> Mult firent lied, grant joie firent.
> De la terre qu'il unt trovee
> Que tant une quise e desirree,
> Unt tuz les travailz ubliez
> E les Deus en unt merciez.
>
> (Wace, *Roman de Brut*, 1051–62)[1]

[Travelling partly by sunlight, partly by starlight, partly with oars, partly with sails, the whole fleet arrived at Totnes in Dartmouth. This was the island the goddess had promised them in the dream. They disembarked, and were very happy and joyful. They forgot all their suffering for the land they had found, so long sought and desired, and gave thanks to the gods.]

Writing in the twelfth century, on the island of Jersey, the poet Wace creates an astonishingly moving and lyrical image of what it was like for Brutus and his men to arrive in Britain. The description is suffused with emotion and ecstasy: like Aeneas, like Odysseus, the seafarers are overcome with joy at the sight of an island which turns out to be the long-desired haven of their dreams. Using carefully balanced phrases, the poet's understated concision gives the journey an epic serenity of scale: passing through sunlight and starlight, with oars and sails, their landing is a release and a gift. Never mind that the island is teeming with giants, Brutus, aided by his heroic henchman Corineus, tosses them off the cliffs into the sea and claims the land as his own, as Britain.

It is easy to smile at the extravagant romance of this account. Totnes was not the nearest point they could have chosen to land from the French coast, yet

[1] Citations for this work are taken from *Wace's Roman de Brut: A History of the British*, ed. and trans. J. Weiss, rev. edn (Exeter: University of Exeter Press, 2002).

getting there could hardly have been an epic journey.[2] Fresh from routing the French, Brutus and his army arrive not war-weary so much as in their fighting prime, ready and able to colonize the discovered land with violent glee. In terms of plot, they are beginning a narrative, not reaching the blissful and hard-earned end of one. Wace even admits before the conclusion of the same paragraph in which Brutus names his new land after himself, that the Britons were quickly ousted by the Saxons, who, having renamed the land England, ensured that the Britons 'unches puis ne redrescerent' ['never regained power'] (1200).[3] Yet the power of the description derives not from its geographical or historical accuracy, but from its poetic, even rapturous charge. Wace at this early date invests the image of Britain with many of its enduring symbols: the island approached by sea, the safe and separate haven, the formidable cliffs, the fertile and varied landscape.[4] All these symbols have weight because of the extra narrative resonance of past stories of national suffering and triumph, both classical (Aeneas and the founding of Rome) and biblical (the Jewish search for the promised land). Wace lightly and unobtrusively calls on these rich stores of narrative memory, producing a golden and mythologized perspective of the island that permeates his whole work.

From what perspective was Wace writing? This glorious description of Britain was not written by a Briton or an Englishman or even, properly speaking, a Frenchman. Jersey at this date was owned by the ducs de Normandie: Wace was apparently born there around 1110, spent time in Caen as a child learning Latin, and for further study proceeded to the Île de France. The sketchy details he provides of his life do not make clear when he went to England or how long he stayed there; rather, the hints we have indicate how thoroughly a Jersiais could make his home as much on the continent as on the islands of Jersey or Britain. He seems to have lived in Bayeux as well as Caen, and spent a long time studying 'en France', which probably means Paris or perhaps Chartres.[5] During his lifetime, Henry, duc d'Anjou et de Normandie, married Eleanor of Aquitaine and in 1154 became Henry II, King of England, ending a period of civil war between his mother, Matilda, and Stephen of Blois. Both Wace's verse histories were thus written against a context of war and more particularly of doubts about

[2] He casts it indeed more as a kind of reverse epic in which they journey from Greece to England.

[3] On the complexity of the gradual annexing of 'Britain' for the purposes of an 'English' identity, see R. R. Davies, *The First English Empire: Power and Identities in the British Isles 1093–1343* (Oxford: Oxford University Press, 2000), especially ch. 2, 'Island Mythologies'.

[4] See the celebrated descriptions of the land of Britain in Gildas, *De Excidio Britonum*, ed. and trans. M. Winterbottom (Chichester: Phillimore, 2002; 1st pub.1978); ch. 3, 89–90 (trans. 16–17); and Bede, *Bede's Ecclesiastical History of the English People*, ed. B. Colgrave and R. A. B. Mynors (Oxford: Clarendon Press, 1979; 1st pub.1969), I, 1.

[5] See his *Le Roman de Rou de Wace*, ed. A. J. Holden (Paris: Picard, 1970–73), *Troisième Partie*, 5305–12. For discussion, see *The History of the Norman People: Wace's Roman de Rou*, trans. G. S. Burgess (Woodbridge: Boydell, 2004), xiii–xvii and *A Companion to Wace*, ed. F. H. M. Le Saux (Cambridge: D. S. Brewer, 2005), 1–10.

possession and identity: although 'Norman' proved to be a more persuasive category than any of the others that were claiming recognition in and around the British Isles—Angevin, Français, Blois, Breton, Engleis, Jersiais—it was not a national one.

Looking at Britain through the eyes of Wace and his Trojan seafarers gives us an insight into the entangled character of British identity in the earlier medieval period. As I have just implied, to talk of it as a matter of contention between 'England' and 'France', or even between England and the Normans, is misleading. Quite apart from the question of how England related to Britain, or rather of how English peoples related to the Scots, Irish, and Welsh,[6] these varieties of identity in the British Isles came up against an even more factional collection of continental 'French' identities.[7] But Wace in particular reminds us that the boundary between 'continental' and 'insular' is itself more fluid than we often allow. His vantage point on an island offshore from both mainlands perhaps explains his special gift for writing about the sea, but it also makes us ponder the importance of perspective. Free from the partisan rootedness of either an insular or a continental birth, Wace shows how identity is not just a matter of historical fact but of carefully cultivated perception. The Channel does not simply divide two countries; it provides an imaginative space between them. This space may be represented in countless different ways; each side has a different name and image for the sea that lies between them as well as for each other.

The importance of perspective as a theme for this book can be seen through the eyes of another Jersey writer, Victor Hugo. Unlike Wace, Hugo was not born in Jersey but rather exiled there from France, only to be exiled once more to Guernsey three years later. Already an icon of French literary greatness before he left France, 'French of the French' as Tennyson described him, Hugo's favourite image of himself during this period of estrangement was the pose of the poet looking back to France.[8] He would look out from his bedroom window across the sea to France, and in Jersey would climb the great rock, 'Le Rocher des Proscrits', most days for solitary (but also carefully photographed) contemplation of the distant French shore.[9] An island in La Manche, for Hugo, was clearly a troubling location since the Channel marked an impassable boundary between his sense of national belonging and France itself. Yet over the nineteen years of his enforced stay it just as clearly became a powerful stimulus to his cultural and

[6] Davies, *The First English Empire.*

[7] Characterized satirically by Defoe in his poem, 'The True-Born Englishman', cited in B. Anderson, *Imagined Communities* (London and New York: Verso,1983; rev. edn 1991), x, and, from there, L. Colley, *Britons: Forging the Nation 1707–1837* (New Haven and London: Yale University Press, 1992), 15.

[8] 'To Victor Hugo', *The Poems of Tennyson,* ed. C. Ricks (London and Harlow: Longmans, 1969), 1240, line 3.

[9] An important collection of photographs of Hugo, taken by his sons, looking out to France from the rock is held in the Maison de Victor Hugo in Paris.

philosophical imagination. His great *roman*-in-exile, *Les Travailleurs de la mer*, together with his deft and often wryly comic commentary on the Channel Islands, *L'Archipel de la Manche*, uses the intervening seascape between these varied insular communities to draw a subtle and often self-undermining portrait of his own complexities of reaction to a world that struck him as oddly in between other worlds.

He gives expression to this in his famous remark that 'les îles de la Manche sont des morceaux de France tombés dans la mer et ramassés par l'Angleterre' ['the Channel islands are fragments of France fallen into the sea and picked up by England'].[10] The ambivalent sense of possession in this, hinting at a kind of English appropriation of property perhaps accidentally, perhaps carelessly, lost by the French, develops in the next comment into a deeply perceptive analysis of the way the appropriation has, with continuing ambivalence, taken root:

> Les Jersiais et les Guernesiais ne sont certainement pas anglais sans le vouloir, mais ils sont français sans le savoir. S'ils le savent, ils tiennent à l'oublier. Cela se voit un peu au français qu'ils parlent.[11]

> It is certain that the Jersiais and the Guernesiais are not English without wishing it, but it is also true that they are French without knowing it. If they know it, they make every effort to forget it. One can see that a little from the French that they speak.

English, at least not unwillingly; French, but only unconsciously; to the quintessential French man of letters the Channel islanders become less French the more they open their mouths. Hugo registers here not only the islanders' imperfect control over their unwitting Frenchness, but his own delicately phrased impatience at their betrayal. He notes with sociological gusto list after list of phrases, idioms, and vocabulary that strike him as distinctive or, even more, in need of translation. Often he cannot help a faint note of mockery, as when he comments that '*noble* est un des mots les plus usités dans ce français local' ['noble is one of the most commonly used words in this local French'],[12], but he can also turn the humour in another direction such as the anecdote he tells of an old Alsatian teacher, well established in Jersey, who felt bound to improve the standard of local French, and complains in a thick Alsatian accent to a new French arrival that the Jersey Norman dialect is hard to follow: 'En entrant il s'écria: "J'ai pien te la beine à leur abrendre le vranzais. On barle ici badois."' ['Entering, he exclaimed: "I have great trouble teaching them French. People speak patois here"'].[13]

[10] Victor Hugo, *Les Travailleurs de la mer, précédé de l'Archipel de la Manche*, ed. D. Charles (Paris: Librairie Générale Française, 2002), 60.
[11] *L'Archipel de la Manche*, 60–1.
[12] *L'Archipel de la Manche*, 88.
[13] Ibid.

Hugo is quick to deny that Jersiais is merely a Norman patois: it is a real language. In fact he goes on to argue that it is original or 'primitive', and with an etymological sleight of hand, connects one of its characteristic syllables 'Hou' with words for questions about origins '*où*' and '*ou*' (Latin *unda* and *unde*), and thence with the sea.[14] In short, in this glancing aside, which clearly betrays a more poetic than philological impulse, he searches for a way to see Jersiais as an expression of ultimate origin: of a people born of the sea rather than bound to competing 'English' or 'French' claims over land.[15] In this, he bears yet another likeness to Wace, who spends much energy and linguistic pleasure on etymological speculation in his *Roman de Brut.*

The two directions in which Wace and Hugo face across the Channel, Wace looking animatedly towards the English coast, Hugo longingly back towards Normandy, represent the central desire of this book to offer a view of the literary relations between England and France in the later Middle Ages that does not emanate from only one side of the crossing. It may seem one-sided in that case to choose to begin with two writers who wrote in French, rather than one from each language. But perhaps the point is better made through this that the obvious differences between the two coastlines are not necessarily the most vital, and indeed, once we consider their relations more deeply, there is a constant sense of surprise that where we thought to locate difference we find similarity, and where we assume commonality we find divergence and misunderstanding. This is nowhere more true than in language. Wace is typical of many writers, at least up to the fourteenth century, who complicate a notion of Englishness by writing in French. Hugo, by contrast, seven hundred years later, expecting to find himself among French-speakers on the *îles normandes*, finds the language full of non-French idiosyncrasy as well as Anglicisms. A large part of my interest in this book has involved trying to understand what it means to write in French in England in the Middle Ages; conversely, this has also involved understanding that writing in English cannot be grasped independently of that equally fluent knowledge of French.[16] In the largely monolingual environment of modern literary criticism of the English Middle Ages, there is often an implicit assumption (against our better knowledge) that a medieval writer is also working and thinking monolingually. This study aims to redirect our attention to the subtleties and complexities of linguistic use in a period when language among the educated was a matter of choice and negotiation between overlapping linguistic worlds.

[14] *L'Archipel de la Manche*, 61.

[15] According to David Charles, Hugo is here (and elsewhere) drawing on Jules Michelet, *La Mer* (1861) and his exploration of the punning connections between la mer/la mère: see *L'Archipel de la Manche*, 60, n. 2; 392, n. 4 and 557, n. 2.

[16] Knowledge of Latin is, of course, also crucial to this story, but falls outside the immediate scope of this book.

'FATHER CHAUCER'

If this were a book about Englishness it would probably start with Chaucer. Or, to put it another way, since so many stories of Englishness start with Chaucer this one would have to too, if only to acknowledge the depth of narrative and cultural practice that lies behind it. Yet Wace and Hugo were deliberately chosen as a prologue to Chaucer in order to create a slight sense of displacement. We have been comfortable for so long with an idea of Chaucer as English that the question of whether Englishness was an idea that he was interested in or even conversant with has scarcely been raised. Indeed, rather than question his Englishness, the tide has turned even further towards an interest in the rise of English vernacularity, and to new ways of explaining its 'colossal rise . . . as a literary language after 1350'.[17] Much of the recent work on the Lollard movement and its immediate aftermath, on female spirituality, on legal practice, and on the new textual communities of the fifteenth and early sixteenth centuries has concentrated heavily on tracking the rise of the vernacular.[18] The attention to vernacularity has been further energized by the concurrent critical war on what has come to be seen (at least by medieval scholars) as 'the disabling logic of periodization'[19] that underlies the disciplinary distinctions between 'medieval' and 'Renaissance'. James Simpson's own bravura argument in his major work of literary history, *Reform and Cultural Revolution*, takes as his starting point the 'newly articulate vernacularity' evident from about 1350. An argument that looks so clearly and radically ahead to the sixteenth century is perhaps bound to focus on English; and indeed although Simpson is conscious of 'the lack of sustained reflection on other languages being used within England' in his book, it is justified, he briskly explains, by this 'powerful move to use English for literary writing'.[20]

For a variety of reasons, then, the old 'triumph of English' arguments are witnessing a widespread, if fundamentally reworked, revival. Chaucer's place in this is partly central, partly ignored because it is so central.[21] A good example of

[17] E. Steiner and C. Barrington, eds, *The Letter of the Law* (Ithaca and London: Cornell University Press, 2002), 9, n. 17. This turn has been remarked on by S. Stanbury, 'Vernacular Nostalgia and the *Cambridge History of Medieval English Literature*', *Texas Studies in Literature and Language*, 44/1 (2002), 92–107.

[18] For example, A. Hudson, *The Premature Reformation: Wycliffite Texts and Lollard History* (Oxford: Clarendon Press, 1998); *Idea of the Vernacular*; R. F. Green, *A Crisis of Truth: Literature and Law in Ricardian England* (Philadelphia: University of Pennsylvania Press, 1999); Steiner and Barrington, eds, *The Letter of the Law*.

[19] J. Simpson, *Reform and Cultural Revolution* (Oxford: Oxford University Press, 2002), 44.

[20] Simpson, *Reform and Cultural Revolution*, 6.

[21] This has long been a polemic of some Langland scholars; for a recent instance, see R. Hanna, *London Literature: 1300–1380* (Cambridge: Cambridge University Press, 2005).

how impossible it seems to be to distance oneself, however subtly, from the determinism of post-fourteenth century Chaucerian hagiography and its fundamental association with Englishness is Christopher Cannon's revisionist version of P. M. Kean's *Chaucer and the Making of English Poetry*.[22] For Cannon, as I have mentioned, Chaucer's English actually draws on older resources of English than the first editions of the *OED* had led us all to believe. Yet however much it draws attention to the myth over the fact, his book is sensitive to the paradox that it affirms Chaucer as the place where we look for new or apparently new English in the medieval period. The myth, he insists, is of '*vital* importance . . . to the history of English' (211, his emphasis). His argument cannot, and indeed does not, wish to refrain from crediting Chaucer with the status that it seeks to discredit.

The newer versions of the narrative of Englishness (as opposed to the older, Victorian and post-Victorian ones) position themselves, in an odd turn, as being somehow out of step with prevailing assumptions. D. Vance Smith, for instance, claims that 'to think about Chaucer as an English poet is, as strange as it may seem, an unusual idea'.[23] His point is that we can and should assert Chaucer's Englishness again because we have so thoroughly assimilated the notion that he is in fact a European writer. One of the ironies of this process, however, is illustrated once more by James Simpson, this time in his discussion, adjacent to Vance Smith's in the *Yale Companion to Chaucer*, precisely of 'Chaucer as a European writer'.[24] Simpson remarks, as many have before him, that 'writing in English had an especially low status in the cultural environment into which Chaucer was born'.[25] Yet this is a concession which turns out only to enhance the later, and deeply familiar, story of heroic triumph: the very lowliness of English's status as Chaucer is born demonstrates the scale of his achievement in its elevation after his death. Simpson's essay is really an effort to explain how Chaucer's Europeanness became English.

It must seem contrary, and perhaps even wilfully ignorant, to argue against the importance of Chaucer's role in the story of English. There *is* a determinism at work here which it is vital to acknowledge. Chaucer's decision to write largely (perhaps exclusively) in English evidently had major repercussions for him as a writer and for literary history. But it is also vital to acknowledge—as far as one

[22] P. M. Kean, *Chaucer and the Making of English Poetry*, 2 vols (London: Routledge & Kegan Paul, 1972); C. Cannon, *The Making of Chaucer's English* (Cambridge: Cambridge University Press, 1998).

[23] D. Vance Smith, 'Chaucer as an English Writer', in S. Lerer, ed., *The Yale Companion to Chaucer* (New Haven and London: Yale University Press, 2006), 87–121 (89).

[24] J. Simpson, 'Chaucer as a European Writer', in Lerer, ed., *Yale Companion*, 55–86.

[25] Simpson, 'Chaucer as a European Writer', 59.

can—the powerfulness, not only of the later perspective, but also of its retrospective force. Moreover, retrospectivism often permeates the very moments when due is apparently being granted to the wider linguistic environment of medieval England. The due is normally granted precisely in order to make the vernacular argument more convincingly self-limiting. Emily Steiner and Candace Barrington, for example, in their recent introduction to a collection of essays on the connections between legal and literary production in medieval England, point out that this concentration on what is geographically, historically, and linguistically English might seem to 'ignore the trilingual character of insular law—specifically, Anglo-Norman or "law French"'.[26] The next sentence, however, bounces back by arguing that 'it is precisely the failure of England's other vernacular to maintain a working relationship between the legal and the literary that illustrates what is finally at stake in the resurgence of English as a literary medium.' It is the phrase 'illustrates what is finally at stake', and especially the word 'finally' that is revealing of this retrospectivism: whatever the rightness or otherwise of the assertion about Anglo-Norman, it creates a chronological wrinkle between what can be illustrated now and a future event. A cause or an agenda or a motive may seem explanatory of people's behaviour (their writing, speech, or actions) and yet very often this identification anticipates rather than describes or analyses. It does not so much see through to the heart of the matter—what is at stake—as prophesy on the basis of the retrospective knowledge afforded by history.

It may be time to try out the opposite tactic, to argue that it is important not to think of Chaucer as English. Rather than present current acceptance of his 'Europeanness' as a reason for ignoring it, we need to revisit his 'Europeanness' all the more urgently. However counter-cultural it may feel, it may be necessary to start again with these ideas of Englishness and analyse 'our' desires for a foreshortened narrative. The counter-argument to this, that of course Chaucer *wrote* in English, is not in these terms a counter-argument. We have used it too long to prevent ourselves from meaning something quite alien by it. In short, to paraphrase, to think about Chaucer as a European poet is, as strange as it may seem, an unusual idea. We may all agree with the epithet, just as we all agree that Chaucer is English, but we have scarcely begun to examine or understand either. This book, then, does not begin with Chaucer because it is not about Englishness. One of its fundamental aims is rather to raise questions about Englishness, and to argue that a story of Englishness is retrospective to an extent that is surprisingly unacknowledged. Englishness may turn out to be better described as 'Europeanness', or as something else entirely, perhaps only a category of our own making. We still have not investigated fully enough what being 'English' meant in the fourteenth century, during Chaucer's lifetime rather than after it.

[26] Steiner and Barrington, eds, *The Letter of the Law*, 8.

ENGLAND'S VERNACULARS

Revisiting what Elizabeth Salter called the 'international' character of Chaucer's writings will not mean simply rehearsing the perhaps over-familiar evidence for his knowledge of and interest in French culture (although in fact it is considerably less familiar in detail than one might think).[27] It will involve thinking again about English as not the principal—and indeed to all intents and purposes the only—vernacular in England but as one of two vernaculars, both in use in a relationship lasting several hundred years. In this England was in a comparable (though not identical) situation to such other multilingual regions as the Savoie, La Suisse-Romande, Hainaut, Naples, and Sicily, and, thanks to the Crusades, as far as Syria, Cyprus, Constantinople, Jerusalem, and Antioch.[28] Ever since the early stages of nineteenth-century scholarship this relationship has been presented somewhat contortedly. On the one hand, French is recognized to have been the dominant vernacular for most of the medieval period, on the other, this dominance has always seemed retrospectively compromised by the eventual triumph of English. Scholars of English have never needed to give too much attention to insular French because of its eventual eclipse. Rolf Berndt's influential 1972 article speaks for this view in its title, 'The Period of the Final Decline of French in Medieval England': whatever arguments are made for the importance of French to English culture, there is a sense that they can only carry so far and that they are dealing with a dying topic.[29]

That England was a trilingual country right through the period is an often asserted but remarkably unacknowledged point in English literary history. Despite the existence of a substantial body of writing in French and Latin produced in England, and an important and growing body of work on the trilingual manuscript culture of late-thirteenth and early-fourteenth century England, the conventional literary history elides this in favour of writing in English.[30] Research on such manuscripts as London British Library MSS, Harley 913 and 2253, BL MS Addit. 46919, and Oxford, Bodleian Library MS Digby 86 continues apace, but writings in English in these manuscripts, and monolingual compilations such as

[27] E. Salter, *English and International: Studies in the Literature, Art and Patronage of Medieval England*, ed. D. Pearsall and N. Zeeman (Cambridge: Cambridge University Press, 1988).

[28] On 'the aristocratic diaspora' of the tenth to thirteenth centuries, see R. Bartlett, *The Making of Europe: Conquest, Colonization and Cultural Change, 950–1350* (Princeton: Princeton University Press, 1993), 24–59. On aspects of the linguistic diaspora of French, see S. Kinoshita, *Medieval Boundaries: Rethinking Difference in Old French Literature* (Philadelphia: University of Philadelphia Press, 2006).

[29] R. Berndt, 'The Period of the Final Decline of French in Medieval England (Fourteenth and Early Fifteenth Centuries)', *Zeitschrift für Anglistik und Amerikanistik*, 20 (1972), 341–69.

[30] See, for instance, S. Fein, ed., *Studies in the Harley Manuscript: The Scribes, Contents, and Social Contexts of British Library MS Harley 2253* (Kalamazoo: Western Michigan University, Medieval Institute Publications, 2000), and the discussion in Turville-Petre, *England and the Nation*, 181–221.

the Auchinleck MS, still tend to gain the lion's share of attention in discussions of Englishness. The fourteenth-century poet John Gower is a case in point. Although his output in English forms but a third of his whole oeuvre (the remaining two-thirds neatly dividing between French and Latin) he is defined as an English poet on the basis of his writings in English. What Gower wrote in French and Latin has in effect been taken to be a distraction from the larger purpose of Anglicization.[31] The grounds on which to discuss Gower's French writings thus remain uncertain and confused—what *are* the stakes involved in describing him as a 'French' poet?[32]

The case of Gower shows that our attempts to understand more about the use of language in England in the medieval period are freighted with national assumptions. It seems impossible to think about his French writings in 'neutral' terms: what would they be? For many modern scholars of Middle English, the use of French in England in the fourteenth century is already anachronistic; English writing is defined by writing in English, and anyone writing in French is doing something inherently marginal. The situation is complex because there are (at least) three points of view here: from those who work on English literature, those who work on French literature, and those who work on Anglo-Norman. Anglo-Norman is the ugly duckling in this family, despised by both sides, yet for different reasons. It is despised by the French for being 'une langue déformée' and by the English, as we have seen, for not being English. For the Anglo-Normanistes themselves, the only solution seems to have been to become even more fiercely 'English': Anglo-Norman is thus insistently described as separate, distinctive, and as possessing its own linguistic integrity.[33]

Yet (as all sides implicitly recognize) 'Anglo-Norman' is not a straightforward category, linguistically, socially, or culturally. Its relations to both 'Frenchness' and 'Englishness' are fraught with interpretive questions and burdened by a history of partisan scholarly assumptions. French scholars have tended to be dismissive of Anglo-Norman writings. In the case of fabliaux, for example, several works previously collected under this generic label were excluded from the most recent magisterial collected edition by Willem Noomen and Nico van

[31] This is not meant to imply that Gower's French and Latin works have not received attention, but that to date they have been perceived as playing a markedly less significant role in English literary history than his English *Confessio amantis*. See also Chapter 7 below.

[32] There are very few studies of Gower's French writings: see R. F. Yeager, 'John Gower's French', in S. Echard, ed., *A Companion to Gower* (Cambridge: D. S. Brewer, 2004), 137–51.

[33] For references to Anglo-Norman as 'déformée' see n. 35 below; Chapter 2, n. 45 and *passim*, Chapter 3, n. and also R. Ingham, 'Syntactic Change in Anglo-Norman and continental French chronicles: was there a 'middle' Anglo-Norman?', *French Language Studies*, 16 (2006), 25–49 (27). Such a description is now gaining a vigorous reassessment in the work of such linguists as David Trotter and Ingham, see D. A.Trotter, 'Not so eccentric as it looks: Anglo-French and French French', *Forum for Modern Language Studies*, 39 (2003), 427–38 and 'L'Anglo-Norman: variété insulaire, ou variété isolée?', *Médiévales*, 45 (2003), 43–54, and Ingham, 'Syntactic Change'.

den Boogaard, and as a group they have received at best faint praise.[34] Conversely, it is often hard to isolate texts as being Anglo-Norman: the term has been used variously to apply to texts of Anglo-Norman origin, texts which were copied in manuscripts that circulated in England as well as on the continent, and texts which have a continental counterpart but are sufficiently divergent from them 'to warrant their being considered as independent texts'.[35] Yet these are significantly different ways of thinking about Anglo-Norman literary culture and its identity. More extended discussion would be profitable amongst literary scholars on both sides of the Channel, of whether Anglo-Norman literature means an independent literary tradition, a tradition that works in partnership with or even as part of continental French writing, or one that exists as a poor relation to continental French writing, reduced to copying its elevated effusions in a degraded and often barely comprehensible dialect.[36]

Moreover, by the time Anglo-Norman reaches the fourteenth century the terms of discussion are different. If Anglo-Norman means anything as a linguistic description (and this is by no means agreed, as I will shortly discuss) then it would apply most closely to the twelfth and thirteenth centuries: by the fourteenth century, as recent work has shown, such factors influencing linguistic exchange as the sharp rise of legal and diplomatic French and more intense trade contacts mean that there is far more 'confusion' between insular and continental French. As David Trotter remarks, 'some later Anglo-Norman non-literary documents, destined for royalty or for the Papacy, are indistinguishable from central Continental French material.'[37] The narrative of decline is prematurely applied to fourteenth century French writing in England, and has been told without enough

[34] See the introduction to I. Short and R. Pearcy, eds, *Eighteen Anglo-Norman Fabliaux*, ANTS 14 (London: ANTS, 2000), 1–5 and, as an example of faint praise, N. van den Boogaard, 'Le Fabliau anglo-normand', in *Nico H. J. Boogaard autour du XIIIe siècle – études de philologie et de littérature médiévale*, ed S. Alexandrescu, F. Trijkoningen, and W. Noomen (Amsterdam: Rodopi, 1985), 179–89.

[35] Short and Percy, eds, *Eighteen Anglo-Norman Fabliaux*, 4.

[36] A classic expression of the latter position (evident in his title) is provided by J. Rychner, *Contribution à l'étude des fabliaux: variantes, remaniements, dégradations*, 2 vols, Université de Neuchâtel: Recueil de travaux publiés par la Faculté des lettres, 28 (Neuchâtel: Faculté des Lettres, 1960); for a specific refutation see R. J. Pearcy, 'Anglo-Norman Fabliaux and Chaucer's Merchant's Tale', *Medium Aevum*, 69 (2000), 227–60 (231), with references to further reaction provoked by Rychner in his n. 15. New linguistic research, by contrast, has started to come to very different conclusions about the 'supposed isolation of Anglo-Norman', in the words of Trotter, 'Not so eccentric as it looks', 427.

[37] D. A. Trotter, 'Anglo-Norman', in Glanville Price, ed., *Languages in Britain and Ireland* (Oxford: Blackwell, 2000), ch.17, 197–206 (202). See also his 'Not so eccentric as it looks' and 'Language Contact, Multilingualism, and the Evidence Problem', in U. Schaefer, ed., *The Beginnings of Standardization: Language and Culture in Fourteenth-century England* (Frankfurt: Peter Lang, 2006), 73–90. For the work of Brian Merrilees on the French of John Gower, see Chapter 7, n. 41. As M. Dominica Legge long ago remarked, Guillaume de Berneville 'wrote orthodox French, so orthodox that he has been accused of being a foreigner', *Anglo-Norman in the Cloisters* (Edinburgh: Edinburgh University Press, 1950), 131.

specific reference to the vast resources of that writing.[38] So much primary research and reading awaits that the re-telling must yet be incomplete, but it is possible even now to see further than the current, often repeated stereotypes of a French under threat from English and incompetently handled in its own right.[39]

One assumption about the French of England that is changing as a result of new research is that it is a single language. Work on dialect, code-switching, and multilingualism is in its infancy in relation to medieval language use, but the more it proceeds the more we are reminded that languages do not function autonomously in multilingual environments, but rather form a shifting set of relationships in which meanings are produced through a constant process of contrast, discrimination, overlap, and rivalry. In the case of Anglo-French, two relationships are at issue (to speak only of the vernacular): that between insular and continental French and between insular French and English. With regard to the latter, William Rothwell and David Trotter have done much to demonstrate how from the mid-fourteenth century the contact between English and Anglo-Norman administrative culture 'relexified English with a vast array of words . . . directly drawn from the Anglo-Norman language with which the scribes and authors of Middle English were in daily contact.' Trotter goes on to say:

> The importance of the emergence of written records can hardly be overstated: it brought into being a complete scribal class habitually accustomed to move between languages, to translate and transpose from one to the other, and to appropriate, misappropriate, or simply to merge vocabulary, structures and orthographic features from one language to the next.[40]

We have barely begun to recognize these features of scribal practice in Middle English copying: if we did, we would have a much clearer sense of how distinctive English writing really was, or to put it another way, how dependent on practices developed in copying French.

This lively movement between languages makes it harder to talk confidently about dialect. French historians of the language have been more ready to concede this than scholars of Anglo-Norman. For Ferdinand Brunot, founder in 1901 of the magisterial twenty-six-volume *Histoire de la langue française* (completed only in 2000):[41]

[38] Among many articles urging a similar case, see W. Rothwell, 'Henry of Lancaster and Geoffrey Chaucer: Anglo-French and Middle English in Fourteenth-Century England', *MLR*, 99 (2004), 313–27. Important writers of Anglo-French in the late thirteenth and fourteenth centuries who await proper inclusion in our assessments of these periods include Pierre Langtoft and Nicole Bozon.

[39] Legge rightly comments, for example, that a reference by Peter of Peckham to his difficulty in translating a work into French does not indicate 'as Vising thought, that "he was evidently an Englishman by birth and was not fully master of the French language"' [J. Vising, *Anglo-Norman Language and Literature* (London: Oxford University Press, 1923), 17], but that he was more familiar with writing Latin than English (*Anglo-Norman in the Cloisters*, 132).

[40] Trotter, 'Anglo-Norman', 202–3.

[41] F. Brunot, *Histoire de la langue française des origines à 1900, I: De l'époque latine à la Renaissance* (Paris: Armand Colin, 1905).

l'anglo-normand n'est pas un dialecte à proprement parler, même si on n'attache pas à ce mot une idée d'unité exagérée, c'est-à-dire que dans un même endroit on ne retrouveras pas une caractéristique constante, mais une manière d'écrire qui varie avec les individus, suivant leur culture, la société dans laquelle ils vivent, les relations qu'ils entretiennent avec le continent. (319)

[Anglo-Norman is not a dialect properly speaking even if one does not attach to this term an idea of exaggerated unity, that is, one would not find a constant characterisation in a single region but a way of writing that varies with individuals according to their culture, the society in which they lived, and the relations they held with the continent.]

He is speaking of the twelfth and thirteenth centuries. He attempts a dialect description, but it is remarkably non-committal: a base of 'normanno-picard' with a superimposed layer of strongly Angevin elements (319). 'Ce mélange, déjà composite, fut encore troublé sans cesse par l'influence de la langue littéraire, et l'imitation voulue du français du continent' (319) 'This mixture, already a composite one, was still constantly disturbed by the influence of literary language, and the desire to imitate continental French'. After some rather half-hearted listing of spelling characteristics, he quickly concludes: 'Toutefois, après ce que nous venons de dire, il semble superflu de faire une énumération spéciale des caractères de l'anglo-normand' 'However, after what I have just said, it seem superfluous to make a special list of Anglo-Norman characteristics'.[42] Brunot, notorious for seeking to introduce a centralized and simplified orthography into French schools in order to reflect a 'pure' form of Parisian French as free as possible from greco-latinisms and provincial pronunciation,[43] may seem now a dubious authority on Anglo-Norman. But there are several issues worthy of comment. One, certainly, is the disdain—one detects a hint of indifference—in a French scholar's view of Anglo-Norman. But another, for that very reason, is his dispassionate and convincing assessment of the difficulties in regarding this 'mélange' as a stable language. Brunot's pupil, Alexis François, writing in the late 1950s, adopted a noticeably more stridently nationalist tone in his description of French and hence has a less supple and questioning attitude towards dialect than his great master. As Brunot was prepared to admit, and as French linguists have begun to reassert, the very notion of dialect is much less clear-cut than the standard descriptions imply.[44] There is competition between a geographical and

[42] Introducing a note of disapprobation, he asserts that most Anglo-Norman texts have the following distinguishing feature: 'c'est l'abus de *u* to represent *u, o* and later *eu*: eg hume, tuner, flur, dolur, ure (heure)'. This 'confusion' hardly ever occurs on the continent except before nasals. Otherwise, apart from the addition of *u* in the nasal *an*: aunt (fr. ante), gauntelet (fr. gantelet) (but only after the twelfth century), differences are more a matter of vocabulary, and because the decline of declining happens quicker in Anglo-Norman than on the continent.

[43] *La réforme de l'orthographe: Lettre ouverte à Monsieur le Ministre de l'Instruction publique* (Paris: Armand Colin, 1905).

[44] See, for instance, B. Cerquiglini, *La naissance du français* (Paris: PUF, 1993), and P. Lusignan, *La langue des rois au Moyen âge: le français en France et en Angleterre* (Paris: PUF, 2004), and, in

a written basis for understanding language, and indeed between a written and oral one. Written evidence for dialect in the Middle Ages is rarely consistent, and hard to locate with precision. In short, not only is Anglo-Norman a term that covers a very changeable linguistic situation in England over a geographically wide area, a not wholly uniform social spectrum, and a chronologically extended period, but continental French is itself a variable and far from single category. Understanding 'Anglo-Norman' involves realizing its double affiliation with two fluid terms, English and continental French.[45]

I have cited Brunot to reiterate that one of the major arguments of this book is that perspective is crucial, and especially on language. The more one works with material in different languages, the more one comes to realize that the aspect and value of each is not broadly consensual but modulates according to the perspective being adopted. From the continent until very recently 'Anglo-Norman' was a species of debased French, with the same degree of remoteness from a centralized Parisian point of view as *breton* or *poitevin.* But by the same token, *lorrain* or *normand*, and certainly *gascon* were hardly straightforwardly equivalent to 'French'. The assimilation of 'French' with 'francien' is yet another story (which will be taken up in Chapter 2), and has powerful repercussions upon the way in which medieval texts from many regions of what is now France have been edited. Yet increasing recognition of this from within France as work develops on 'la francophonie' means that 'peripheral' French is gaining both respect and a new sense of its diversity. From England, by contrast, the insular characteristics of 'Anglo-Norman' have perhaps gained a disproportionate emphasis over the links with the continent, with the result that 'Anglo-Norman' has seemed sealed off from the new waves of fourteenth century writing on the continent. I will be arguing that, especially in the fourteenth century, taking

particular, the trenchant conclusions of A. Dees, 'Propositions for the Study of Old French and its dialects', in J. Fisiak, ed., *Historical Dialectology: Regional and Social*, Trends in Linguistics, Studies and Monographs, 37 (Berlin: Mouton de Gruyter, 1988), 139–48, summarizing his substantial research on dialect, notably *Atlas des formes linguistiques des textes littéraires de l'ancien français*, with M. Dekker, O. Huber and K. H. van Reenen-Stein, Beiheft zur Zeitschrift für romanische Philologie, 212 (Tübingen: Niemeyer, 1987), and his important article, 'Dialectes et scriptae à l'époque de l'ancien français', *Revue de linguistique romane*, 49 (1985), 87–117.

[45] This argument has been expressed, from the perspective of Anglo-Norman lexicography, by Trotter: see especially, 'Not as eccentric as it looks'; it also receives support from work on multilingual London documents by L. Wright, *Sources of London English: Medieval Thames Vocabulary* (Oxford: Clarendon Press, 1996) and 'The Records of Hanseatic Merchants: Ignorant, sleepy or degenerate?', *Multilingua*, 16 (1997), 339–50. However, the difference between their perspective and the literary concerns of this book is perhaps best indicated by Trotter's choice of example of language contact, the technical shipbuilding term 'bonnet', in his 'Language Contact, Multilingualism, and the Evidence Problem'. As I understand it, he wishes precisely to emphasize the importance of *non*-literary evidence for understanding medieval linguistic norms ('Not as eccentric as it looks', 431–3). My own work, while not seeking to demur from Trotter's choice of evidence, nonetheless hopes to argue that the literary material can also provide insight into such norms.

account of the creative tensions between insular and continental writers, in French as well as English, opens up new avenues for appreciating the inventiveness of the English vernaculars.

MULTILINGUALISM AND THE WAR

War and its histories

War is an overwhelmingly important context for investigating the relationship between 'English' and 'French' throughout the later Middle Ages. Written by a literary scholar rather than an historian, this book is not so much military or political as cultural in approach. Its interest is as much in the way that cultural identities are imagined and constructed as in investigating specific historical events. Its means of doing this are largely literary and linguistic, for despite the huge amount of modern historical commentary on the Hundred Years War there is still much to be done on its literary representation. Yet by the term literary representation a distinction again must be made. *The Familiar Enemy* is not looking simply to find a picture of the war in fiction or poetry. Instead, its broader concern is to think about how language is used to create notions of identity. In looking then at the relationship between France and England in the later Middle Ages, my particular interest is in the relationship between their two languages, and how this shapes and is expressed in the cross-channel traffic between writers of all kinds.

Specific instances of this traffic will be discussed in detail in forthcoming chapters. It may be useful to sketch out briefly here some of the main historical factors that inform and influence the choice of material. First, it is difficult to put precise limits on the chronology of war. People often point to the moment in 1337 when Philippe de Valois challenged Edward III for possession of Gascony as the start of full hostilities, but the intimate relationship of aggression and affiliation between the island and French-speaking continent extended back into the very earliest centuries of post-Roman habitation, and remains as a present (though rather differently expressed) element in our modern culture.[46] This book cannot, of course, attempt anything like a complete account of the Hundred Years War (so mis-called), even as a backdrop to its more literary and linguistic concerns, yet it does try to show through its selection of material that issues of importance in this relationship were not confined to the fourteenth and earlier fifteenth centuries, but were rooted in much earlier events.[47] In

[46] M. Vale, 'England, France and the Origins of the Hundred Years War', in M. Jones and M. Vale, eds, *England and her Neighbours 1066–1453: Essays in Honour of Pierre Chaplais* (London: Hambledon, 1989), 199–216 (199).

[47] B. Guenée makes a similar point about the importance of thirteenth-century evidence, *L'Occident aux XIVe et XVe siècles: Les Etats* (Paris: PUF, 1971), 301.

particular it will make some attempt to keep a close eye on the chronology of remarks about language use in the period: it seems an obvious point, but too often in the past the basic questions about when and where and to whom a remark was made have not been given enough attention.

A secondary narrative will also attend to a further chronological layer in the relationship: the differing chronologies assumed and described by modern commentators. Malcolm Vale has remarked that 'whether one dates the beginnings of that conflict [between the kingdoms of England and France] to 1066, 1152, or 1294, and its end to 1453, 1492, 1558 or even 1802, is probably immaterial.'[48] He may be right in one sense, but in another, each choice of date has wide implications for a modern understanding of nation. I will discuss this in more detail later, but want to emphasize here that one of my interests is to place the chronologies of war alongside the chronologies of philology. Language use and change have not been studied as closely as they might in relation to the fluctuating conditions of aggression and truce that characterize the period. Much research remains to be done, and many questions do not yet have precise answers, but the larger enquiry has the potential to tell us a great deal about how and why vernacular languages developed in both England and the French-speaking continent, and under what—sometimes very specific—pressures.

For an example of how choices of date can crucially shape historiography, we can consider the changing character of English possession of what is now modern France (see Maps 1 and 3). This begins and ends with two high water marks: the vast areas ruled by Henry II and his queen, Eleanor of Aquitaine, in the twelfth century and the similarly extensive holdings claimed as the Hundred Years War was drawing to an end by Henry VI who, in 1422 as a nine-month-old baby was proclaimed heir to the kingdom of France as well as of England. Just as Henry II controlled most of north-west France in his own right as an Angevin ruler, Maine and Anjou itself, Normandy (from his mother), Brittany (through the marriage of his brother), and the large area of Aquitaine through Eleanor, so with Henry VI once more the whole of northern France as well as the region of Bordeaux were under English rule. In the time between these two periods of English dominance, lands were extravagantly as well as obscurely ceded and reclaimed, and the English title of king over those lands asserted and refuted.

For some historians and many literary historians this period was 'marked by a rising tide of national sentiment'[49] so that by the time we reach the early decades of the fifteenth century two nations have been born. There is an implicit contrast here between the type of rule exercised by twelfth-century kings and nobles and that achieved by the early Tudors: as Philippe Wolff first argued in the 1950s,

[48] Vale, 'England, France and the Origins of the Hundred Years War', 199.

[49] T. F. Tout, *France and England in the Middle Ages: their relations in the Middle Ages and now* (Manchester: Manchester University Press, 1922), 78.

'the origins of the Hundred Years War lay in "the liquidation of the feudal world"'.[50] Yet the very symmetry of the English hold over French lands first in the twelfth and then in the fifteenth centuries is revealing. It reminds us that the situation in the fifteenth century was not merely the result of an evolutionary process. On the contrary, fifteenth-century English control over France was very much a reversion to former patterns of possession, and indeed it could be argued that all English attempts to claim French land up to the fifteenth century were ways of reclaiming history rather than moving on towards the goal of national self-definition. If we took instead the period between 1337, when Edward III began his military campaigns, and the late 1390s, when Richard II was looking instead for peace and retrenchment (and fighting for his own political life) we would have the very different sense that English ambition was in a state of decline.[51] This Anglo-French relationship was long and enduring, but also cyclical and fitful, peaks followed by abrupt lows, times of peaceful and amicable truce and rich cultural exchange as well as of sharp recrimination.

The context of war was hardly a stable one throughout the period. This can be demonstrated by considering the rather different historical perspectives on its causes that exist on both sides of the Channel.[52] The impetus to war clearly came from a complex of factors: in one version, as we have seen, there was specific dispute from the early thirteenth century. The 1259 treaty between Louis IX and Henry III made Henry a peer of France. Although this might have seemed a generous gesture, in fact it created a profound feudal awkwardness. Henry, and English kings after him, were required, as Dukes of Aquitaine, to pay liege homage to the French king. This subtly transferred power to the French kingdom over land that the English royalty regarded as theirs by right. Amidst growing tension, a problem of succession arose for both realms. Edward II was deposed, and with his mother Isabella's support, Edward III was crowned. Only a year later, Charles IV, Isabella's brother, died and left no heir. Edward III decided, through his mother's line, to secure Aquitaine once and for all by claiming the throne of France. The start of the war proper is usually described as the moment in 1337 when Philippe de Valois, a relation of Charles IV (though less close than Edward) chosen to succeed him by the French nobles, declared the duchy of Aquitaine as confiscated to the French crown.

We might ask why this moment is taken to be crucial when earlier conflict existed. One reason, from an English point of view, might be to do with the

50 Cited in Vale, 'England, France and the Origins of the Hundred Years War', 205.

51 For further discussion, see Chapter 9 below.

52 Among a vast bibliography, see in particular the classic accounts by C. Allmand, *The Hundred Years War: England and France at War c.1300–c.1450* (Cambridge: Cambridge University Press, 1988); J. Favier, *La Guerre de Cent Ans* (Paris: Fayard, 1980); and J. Sumption, *The Hundred Years War*, 2 vols (London: Faber, 1990 and 1999), alongside the earlier biographical studies by R. Delachenal, *Histoire de Charles V*, 5 vols (Paris: Picard, 1909–31) and F. Lehoux, *Jean de France, Duc de Berri: Sa Vie, son action politique (1340–1416)* (Paris: Picard, 1968).

figure of Edward III. He stands out as a king who had exceptional consistency of purpose throughout his reign; he also made a specific claim to kingship. However, it is interesting to consider how differently this narrative reads if we take a continental perspective. From here, the Hundred Years War is not so much about two countries warring over territory but something more like a civil war between two contrasting models of exercising power. For during this period French kingship began a centralizing process in which one ruler attempted to exert unifying power over rival lordships. The crucial problem in this effort was thus to renegotiate an essentially internal relationship between the king of France and the duc d'Aquitaine. Taking a broader view still, the struggle was between this new centralizing model of power and the older style of Angevin rule that encompassed traditions of insular independence gained from the period of English conquest. The assertion of right to the French throne by Edward III looks less, from this perspective, like a modern-style annexing of a rival state, and more like a family conflict, a means of seizing back control from a rival sibling. The enlarged family structure here sees England not as an independent state so much as a constituent and parallel area of aristocratic rule.[53]

The duchy of Aquitaine has a pivotal role in the story on several counts. It reminds us that 'France' was not a single entity. On the contrary, until the end of the fifteenth century the various regions of 'France' were ruled by a variety of more or less powerful lords, some of whom were 'English'. Depending on marital and sibling alliances, the shifting winds of papal interest, and economic pressures, these lords colluded, plotted, supported, fought and, occasionally murdered one another in ways that sometimes created new blocks of regional power, and sometimes isolated pockets of territory such as Aquitaine, and later, Calais. At the same time, the history of Aquitaine and in particular the longevity of its association with the 'English', shows us how broad a definition of Englishness we need to understand the political realities of this period. Being English for the Gascons did not mean acquiring alien stereotypes, customs, or language, but rather protecting their own character and customs. When they fought for the English they did so, paradoxically, to assert their own independence, to maintain that distance between their way of life and the centralizing desires of northern French kings that being 'English' had enabled for many generations.[54]

There is an irony, then, in the way that Aquitaine proved to be so fundamental to English interests in France. It further reminds us of our need for a double perspective: what seems 'English' or 'French' from one side of the sea may not look the same from the opposite shore. Just as 'English' is a broad category, so is

[53] J. Krynen, *Idéal du prince et pouvoir royal en France à la fin du Moyen Âge (1380–1440)* (Paris: Picard, 1981), 259–60.

[54] M. Vale, *English Gascony 1399–1453: A Study of War, Government and Politics during the later stages of the Hundred Years' War* (London: Oxford University Press, 1970).

'French'. The Gascons felt no more 'French' than they felt 'Norman' or 'Burgundian'.

If on the French side of nationhood we need to consider the fluidity of territorial acquisition and loss on the continent, on the English side we need to take account of the relations between England and the rest of the peoples of Britain, the Scots, Irish, and Welsh. Again, the two histories are connected: one of the most strongly defined features of Edward III's rule was his attempt to alternate campaigns against the Scots and campaigns within France throughout the active part of his reign. Several histories collide here: from the point of view of the Scots, the thirteenth and fourteenth centuries were an intense drive towards independence, marked by seemingly endless war. The complexity of Norman descent among the Scots, Irish, and Welsh worked in significantly different ways: whereas the Anglo-Irish and the Anglo-Welsh were subject to the English crown, the Anglo-Scots were subject to the Scottish crown. Their aristocratic descendants therefore became much more effective leaders in the cause of independence than the Welsh or Irish. Also, by the fourteenth century, they sought alliances with the French, and the French crown with them, in ways that greatly complicated and occasionally destabilized English campaigns in France.[55]

The issues of sovereignty in Britain meant that Edward III's sense of himself as a ruler was rather different from that of Jean II or Charles V of France. In other words, each ruler had a different sense of the limits and extent of his power, which in turn influenced any broader perceptions they had of their royal identity. In the case of Edward III, it was probably a moot point whether his efforts to subdue the Scots emboldened him in his quest for kingship on the continent, or whether the extraordinary, and in some ways, rather improbable, successes of Crécy and Poitiers gave him the impetus to see himself as a ruler of Britain and not just of England.[56]

Fourteenth-century relationships between England and the continent, though dominated by the Hundred Years War, thus involved more than the 'local' squabble between the English and French kings. In the 1380s war involving English troops took place in Flanders, Castile, and Portugal as well as Scotland. In this decade, one in which Chaucer was producing a succession of major works, the course of war faltered. Richard II (at the age of ten) had inherited the war from his grandfather, Edward III. He also inherited a carefully fashioned narrative image of war, which has been handed on almost intact to the present day

[55] It is an important, and pioneering strength of *The Cambridge History of Medieval English Literature* (Cambridge: Cambridge University Press, 1999), ed. D. Wallace, that it gives independence to literature in Welsh, Scottish, and Irish. On Froissart and Ireland, see C. Sponsler, 'The Captivity of Henry Chrystede: Froissart's Chroniques, Ireland, and Fourteenth-Century Nationalism', in K. Lavezzo, ed., *Imagining a Medieval English Nation* (Minneapolis: University of Minnesota Press, 2004), 304–39.

[56] For further discussion, see 'The British Isles', *The New Cambridge Medieval History, VI c.1300–c.1415*, ed. M. Jones (Cambridge: Cambridge University Press, 2000), ch.13, 273–387.

(and is gleefully resurrected by English sports feature writers at any French–English contest). In this narrative, the English faced huge French armies and through matchless bravery, regard for honour, and superior skill cut down the flower of French aristocracy, first at Crécy (26 August 1346), Calais (4 August 1347), and then Poitiers (19 September 1356). These were undoubtedly highly significant victories: Calais became a crucial English port for several centuries, and the most visible result of Poitiers was that the French king, Jean II, was taken prisoner and kept intermittently as a hostage over a period of some eight years in total as security for the payment of a huge ransom. It would be hard to find a more extravagant symbol of victory than that of a French king languishing in the Tower of London (poetically, if not actually) for so extended a period, humiliatingly required to forfeit most of the wealth of his kingdom and many of his claims to territorial power. (In fact, the ransom was only partially paid and Jean was permitted many luxuries and courtesies, able to return to France in 1360, his place taken by forty further hostages, including four royal princes.)

Yet by the time of Richard II's maturity, these glorious victories had lost some of their shine: a prolonged period of attrition, following the peace treaty of Brétigny in 1360, and complex domestic and economic troubles, partly caused by plague outbreaks, led to a profound change of atmosphere. Triumphalism, and the heady glamour of Arthurian mythology, was replaced by a fragile relationship between king and commons, and a desire, through a variety of initiatives, to broker negotiated peace. On the French side, the capture of Jean II had created a severe crisis, leaving large areas of land vulnerable to the attacks of rioters, looting mercenaries, and rival factions for the crown.

In trying to understand the wider (rather than merely domestic) political climate of the 1380s and 1390s, it seems important to be sensitive to the near memory of English hauteur that was so dominant in the 1350s. Yet clearly, for both sides there was also a sense that this time was past, and that the current climate was less about clinging to certainties and asserting claims and more about surviving confusing, and at times overwhelming bids for change. Whatever Edward III had achieved, it was not a continuing feeling of nationalism. In the treaty of Brétigny he renounced his claim to the French crown, in return for acknowledgement of his sovereignty over the lands originally ceded by Henry III. The negotiation was complex and parts left unresolved; nonetheless, the treaty does seem to have been about feudal power and its extent, and not about nationhood. It may be hard for us to grasp, but kingship does not appear to have been synonymous with nationhood for either Edward III or Jean II.

In this respect, Richard's efforts to finish the unresolved business seem to rest on the same assumptions. The same old problem of Aquitaine remained, and he tried to solve it in the same terms in which it had arisen several centuries earlier.[57]

[57] R. Studd, 'England and Gascony 1216–1337', in N. Saul, ed., *England in Europe 1066–1453* (London: Collins and Brown, 1994), 97–107.

In 1390, in what must have seemed like a brilliant escape from the dilemma, he devolved his own title of duc d'Aquitaine onto John of Gaunt. The idea was that Aquitaine would remain under the same conditions of English control, yet there would no longer be any need for an English king to do homage to the French crown. Ironically, it was not the French king who raised violent objections to this, but the Gascons. They were very wary of any arrangement that appeared to weaken English rights over the land: an absent English crown was far preferable to a present 'French' prince in the person of Gaunt.[58]

After Richard II was deposed in 1399, Henry IV's son, Henry V, showed a quite different ambition from his predecessors. Like Edward III he proclaimed himself King of France, but this time his sense of what was involved included not only making good ancient English rights, but also seizing land, and conquering it through settlement as well as force of arms. Once again, the glamour and enduring mythology of Henry V's actions are misleading, particularly as a context for the climate of Chaucer's lifetime. It is tempting to link, retrospectively, the aims of Henry V and those of Edward III. Yet as later chapters in this book will attempt to substantiate, the late fourteenth century was not a period of increasing, or even incipient, nationalism. It seems much closer to the truth to see the medieval history of English and French relations to be part of a fluctuating and broken sequence of events rather than points on a neatly defined upward curve towards modern views of nation. For Chaucer and his contemporaries, the French were still feudal cousins, bound by ancient family ties to the English, but also engaged in alliances and enmities with other relations: the Burgundians, the Flemish, Spanish, Castilians, Germans, Bohemians, Luxembourgeois, and Italians, to name but a few.

War and invective

Where literary scholars have considered war, it has often been through the rather under-studied texts of invective and propaganda produced by writers on both sides of the Channel, often in response to specific battles, such as Crécy, Poitiers, and Agincourt.[59] Such writings play a significant part in the linguistic relations between England and France and some will be discussed during the course of this book. The best known from the English side are fifteenth-century texts such as the 'Agincourt Carol' and *The Libelle of Englyshe Polycye*, a sizeable range of pieces by Lydgate, and also the collection of strident fourteenth-century battle poems by Laurence Minot. But there is a great deal more, from the thirteenth to the fifteenth centuries, ranging from chronicle material, many shorter verse narrative pieces, such as John Page's *Siege of Rouen*, and instances of flyting, such as the *Débat des hérauts d'armes de France et d'Angleterre*

[58] Allmand, *The Hundred Years War*, 23, 25–6.

[59] See, for a recent instance, C. Saunders, F. Le Saux, and N. Thomas, eds, *Writing War: Medieval Literary Responses to Warfare* (Woodbridge: D. S. Brewer, 2004).

(1453–61). On the French side, amongst a mass of material one might single out several acerbic ballades by Deschamps; *Le Songe du Vergier* (first written in Latin in 1376 and translated by order of Charles V into French in 1378);[60] Christine de Pizan's *Livres des fais et bonnes moeurs du sage roy Charles V, Livre de la Paix*, and *Dittié de Jehanne d'Arc*;[61] Chartier's *Le Quadrilogue Invectif* (1422) and *Prétensions des Anglois à la couronne de France* (1461–71). There is also a body of polemical treatises and pamphlets by diplomatic officials such as Jean de Montreuil, who wrote *Traité contre les Anglais* (1413–16), and the anonymous author working in the Chambre des Comptes who wrote (in the French version) *Réponse d'un bon et loyal François*.[62]

Clearly, much of this has a specific impetus, often describing a particular battle or political moment, yet, as recent historians have insisted, to call it propaganda may be misleading. If propaganda implies the carefully promulgated doctrine of a coherently organized ecclesiastical institution or government body, then it cannot be applied to these often seemingly spontaneous, fairly private (as Bernard Guénée puts it 'confidentiel') and, judging from the surviving copies, narrowly circulated writings.[63] We need to be sensitive to the exaggerations and manipulations of the language of abuse and splenetic assertion. A rhetoric of invective must not be equated too readily with nationalism, let alone taken as evidence for the state of the language. It is illuminating to compare such material with some less obvious or blatant examples of rivalry and linguistic horsetrading in the period. I will be looking partly at another type of writing, the so-called 'textes en jargon franco-anglais', and more broadly still, on how all these comparisons shed light on some of the more widely circulated writings of the period, by Chaucer in particular, and also Gower, Froissart, Machant, and Christine de Pizan. As I begin to discuss in the next chapter, the texts where invective is sharpest point us to the more subtle means used by a wide range of writers to perform rivalries and identifications across languages and across social and cultural groupings. We see evasions as well as many forms of self-assertion, attempts to create differences and alliances, not always successfully in either case, and recognition of the power of language to convey forms of victimhood as well as of domination.

[60] *Le Songe du Vergier, édité d'après le manuscrit royal 19 C IV de la British Library*, ed. M. Schnerb-Lièvre, 2 vols, Sources d'Histoire Médiévale publiées par l'Institut de Recherche et d'Histoire des Textes (Paris: CNRS, 1982), ix.

[61] Translated into English by William Caxton: *The Book of Fayttes of Armes and of Chyualry: Translated and Printed by William Caxton from the French Original by Christine de Pisan*, ed. A. T. P. Byles, EETS, OS 189 (London: Oxford University Press, 1937; 1st pub.1932).

[62] C. Taylor, 'War, Propaganda and Diplomacy in Fifteenth-Century France and England' in C. Allmand, ed., *War, Government and Power in Late Medieval France* (Liverpool: Liverpool University Press, 2000), 70–91 (71).

[63] B. Guénée, 'Les Tendences actuelles de l'histoire politique du moyen âge français', *Actes du 100e Congrès National des Sociétés Savantes, Paris, 1975*, 2 vols (Paris: Bibliothèque nationale, 1977), I, 45–70, (59); cited in Taylor, 'War, Propaganda and Diplomacy', 72, n. 7.

Informing this discussion will be an exploration of what Serge Lusignan has called the fundamentally 'diglossique' character of 'la conscience linguistique d'un intellectuel du XIIIe siècle'.[64] He is talking here of French and Latin and his point with this remark is to comment on the very different functions of these two languages in this period. Although the use of Latin is not properly part of the scope of this book, it may be worth remarking that texts such as the *Quinque incitamente ad Deum amandum ardenter* by Gérard de Liège, in which love refrains in French are thoroughly interwoven with Latin, and macaronic sermons more generally, perhaps indicate that the relationship between the two languages, even in the thirteenth century, could in certain contexts be far from rigidly distinct. The term diglossic begs the question it raises: how did, indeed, an intellectual trained to write and read in Latin make use of the vernacular that he certainly knew orally but could hardly help himself using in an educated, literate fashion? When we transfer this question to the situation in England and on behalf of the educated communities of people who lived as well as spoke and wrote on both sides of the water, then we see that the pressures on linguistic choice and use increase as people move between two main vernaculars as well as Latin.

NATION AND MODERNITY

To return for a moment to Victor Hugo: like many of his contemporaries, his sense of Frenchness was a matter of looking back into the past. He scatters his commentary with medieval references, and even cites Wace.[65] But of course, located offshore as he was, his perspective was inescapably coloured by Jersey's peculiar brand of Englishness.[66] For Hugo, in common with such French Anglophiles as Voltaire and Proust, being French is always to be already entangled with an 'English' as well as a 'French' past.[67] The last part of this introductory chapter will consider some of the intersections between the long-running Anglo-French relationship which is at the heart of this book, and ideas of nationhood and the past. Some of these intersections are perhaps better described as frictions. For example, many modern commentators regard the nation as a term that is simply irrelevant to the medieval period. A central question, then, for this book concerns the connection between the nation and

[64] *Parler vulgairement*, 91.

[65] For instance, in *L'Archipel de la Manche*, he refers to Tristan and Yseut (47), Abelard (56) and Wace (47, 113).

[66] Hugo writes ruefully of a mistake he made in the first edition of *Les travailleurs de la mer* (and for which he claims to have been excoriated for his poor English) where he misspelt the title of one of the chapters, 'bug-pipe' instead of 'bag-pipe', *L'Archipel de la Manche*, 74.

[67] Voltaire, *Letters Concerning the English Nation* (1733); D. Karlin, *Proust's English* (Oxford: Oxford University Press, 2005) offers an absorbing account of nineteenth- and early twentieth-century Anglo-French relations.

modernity, and (although this may sound contradictory) whether this is a connection that excludes or includes the medieval.

The concept of the nation seems particularly and newly unstable in these early years of the twenty-first century. In the face of a much more fluid and changeable set of relationships between, for example, different European peoples, some certainties about nationhood are in doubt. The notion of Europe itself has widened dramatically since the early 1990s (ten countries joined the European Union in 2004 and two more in 2007) and is set to widen yet further.[68] In the process, nation has become an oddly passé term: for every passionate and often violently angry articulation of nationhood, as in the emerging nations from the former Soviet bloc, there is an equally powerful resistance to the very idea of the nation. We are not only in a post-national era, but also in a 'transnational', 'supranational', or even 'post-multinational' one: the very proliferation of terms 'beyond' nation reveals how much nation itself seems inadequate as a means of comprehending, let alone resolving current large-scale struggles for self-determination. These struggles, in short, are not only about political boundaries, but also about creating a new meaning for nation.[69]

Ironically, perhaps, the business of creating new meanings relies heavily on the excavation of old ones. In asserting a right to an area of land or an ethnic identity, people are again harking back to history, to moments where they can claim an original form of possession of that place, name, or lineage. Yet as Patrick Geary has remarked in his account of 'The Medieval Origins of Europe', *The Myth of Nations*, these claims can be controversial and easily disputed. The former Serbian leader Slobodan Milošević arranged for a huge assembly to take place on the 'Kosovo polje' or 'Blackbird Field' on 28 June 1989. The event was to mark the 600th anniversary of the defeat of the Serbian army by the Ottoman Turks, and by this means to proclaim the tenacity of Serbian desire with respect to this territory. However, even the medieval past can be considered too recent: the longevity of purpose implied by this symbolic act is rivalled by Albanian claims to be traceable back to the ancient Illyrians.[70] This case shows how much the past is coveted by present nationalists: history is the new now, a commodity that is not merely relevant to the present but energetically re-enacted as the present to serve future imaginings.

[68] From a total of fifteen in 1995, the ten that joined in 2004 were Cyprus, Czech Republic, Estonia, Hungary, Latvia, Lithuania, Malta, Poland, Slovakia, Slovenia; Romania and Bulgaria joined in 2007, with Croatia, Macedonia and Turkey as official candidates to join.

[69] The classic account of the 'short twentieth century' is E. Hobsbawm, *The Age of Extremes: The Short Twentieth Century, 1914–1991* (London: Michael Joseph, 1994) ending (in Roger Brubaker's words) with Europe 'entering not a post-national but a *post-multinational* era'. Yet Brubaker argues that Europe, at the end of the twentieth century, 'far from moving *beyond* the nation-state'...was moving *back to* the nation-state', see R. Brubaker, *Nationalism Reframed: Nationhood and the national question in the New Europe* (Cambridge: Cambridge University Press, 1996), 2.

[70] P. J. Geary, *The Myth of Nations: The Medieval Origins of Europe* (Princeton: Princeton University Press, 2002), 7.

Given the significance and often irrepressibly bulky presence of the past, it becomes all the more important to analyse the uses we now make of it. This is Geary's larger point made with respect to the early medieval period. He writes in the context of what he sees to be a resurgence of nationalist, ethnocentrist, and racist claims in the wider Europe of the late twentieth and early twenty-first centuries. In particular, as a historian of the early Middle Ages 'who listens to the rhetoric of nationalist leaders, and who reads the scholarship produced by official or quasi-official historians', he 'is immediately struck by how central the interpretation of the period from circa 400–1000 is to this debate' (7). His 'period of history [is] suddenly pivotal in a contest for the past' (8–9). One might expect him to see this as a welcome attention to the Middle Ages as being a point of origin for later developments. On the contrary, it fills him with 'apprehension and disdain'. Geary argues forcefully that such searching of the past to provide evidence for the longevity of national characteristics and a rationale for current assertions of national identity can lead to an attempt to find a justification in the past for some highly dubious present claims. He is understandably anxious to disassociate the medieval—especially the early medieval—from some of the more unpleasant aspects of nationalism that can arise out of this type of retrospectivism. He sees it as the historian's duty to present as full and responsible a picture of the past as possible to avert the danger of 'pseudo-history' passing unrecognized.

Medievalism thus matters to current attempts to construct nationhood. It is equally, though more controversially, true to say in reverse that nation is central to medievalism. Perhaps the most important consideration concerns the conjunction of a marked surge in nationalism in the nineteenth century with the professional beginnings of medieval studies. As many have remarked, the rise of medievalism was characterized by an explicit desire on behalf of German, French, and English scholars to locate the intellectual and cultural origins of their respective national heritages. In short, despite a well-founded wariness about the dangers of current nationalist reclamations of the medieval period, medievalists cannot avoid the term 'nation' because the discipline of medieval studies has always been in its shadow. More particularly, in relation to English and French—the double focus of this book—modern medieval studies on the continent as well as on the island were founded precisely in a desire to find national meaning across the trilingual cultures that so dominated intellectual and political life in England throughout the medieval period.[71]

Nonetheless, the reaction of scholars of the medieval period, both historians and literary historians, to the topic of nation has been noticeably defensive. The

[71] See next chapter. Medievalism has rapidly become an important focus for modern Middle English scholars, stimulated recently by such studies as D. Matthews, *The Making of Middle English, 1765–1910* (Minneapolis: University of Minnesota Press, 1999), and S.Trigg, *Congenial Souls: Reading Chaucer from Medieval to Postmodern* (Minneapolis: University of Minesota Press, 2002).

field is still relatively small, though growing.[72] The history of medieval studies may be tied to nation, but that does not mean medievalists are allowed to possess the discourse of nation. Modernist discussion of nation has been keen to dismiss pre-enlightenment periods as irrelevant. The generally held view is that concepts of nation and nationhood share a fundamental origin with the huge historical turmoils of the French and American Revolutions of the late eighteenth century. Before that period, people may well have felt stirrings of what we would now call national sentiment, but since nation-states did not yet exist, those stirrings can hardly be described as feelings for a nation. Once we cast our imaginations as far back as the Middle Ages, concepts of nation must be especially anachronistic.[73]

Broadly speaking, recent historians of the Middle Ages have adopted two main positions against the modernist view that the medieval is simply an uninteresting or irrelevant period in which to talk of nation. The first is an argument about continuity; the second about discontinuity. The most influential 'opponent' here, Benedict Anderson, offers a lifeline as well as an attack in his arguments, first offered more than twenty years ago. For although Anderson is adamant that the term 'nation' is anachronistic in the context of the Middle Ages, the framework he uses to define nation—'imagined communities'—so often repeated now as to be almost hackneyed, seems precisely, and excitingly, to open up ways of understanding the past that are not necessarily confined to the eighteenth century or later.[74]

Various ironies surface here: the term 'imagined' is the main reason Anderson has been so influential. It frees the idea of nation from a strict sense of time and period and opens it up to much wider possibilities of interpretation, indeed makes it a matter of interpretation. The act of defining nationhood is also made

[72] It includes S. Reynolds, *Kingdoms and Communities in Western Europe 900–1300*, 2nd edn (Oxford: Oxford University Press, 1997); Bartlett, *The Making of Europe*; S. Forde, L. Johnson and A. V. Murray, eds, *Concepts of National Identity in the Middle Ages* (Leeds: School of English, University of Leeds, 1995); T. Turville-Petre, *England the Nation: Language, Literature and National Identity 1290–1340* (Oxford: Clarendon Press, 1996); A. Hastings, *The Construction of Nationhood: Ethnicity, Religion and Nationalism* (Cambridge: Cambridge University Press, 1997); J. Gillingham, *The English in the Twelfth Century: Imperialism, National Identity and Political Values* (Woodbridge: Boydell, 2000); Lavezzo, ed., *Imagining a Medieval English Nation*; D. Wallace, *Premodern Places: Calais to Surinam, Chaucer to Aphra Behn* (Oxford: Blackwell, 2004); K. Lavezzo, *Angels on the Edge of the World* (Ithaca and London: Cornell University Press, 2006).

[73] Important instances of this modernist position include E. Hobsbawm, 'Introduction: Inventing Traditions', in *The Invention of Tradition*, ed. Eric Hobsbawm and T. Ranger (Cambridge: Cambridge University Press, 1983), 1–14 and *Nations and Nationalism since 1780* (Cambridge: Cambridge University Press, 1990); E. Gellner, *Nations and Nationalism* (Oxford: Blackwell, 1983) and *Encounters with Nationalism* (Oxford: Blackwell, 1994); and J. Breuilly, *Nationalism and the State* (Manchester: Manchester University Press, 1982).

[74] Anderson, *Imagined Communities*. See also Larry Scanlon's comments on Anderson in 'King, Commons and Kind Wit: Langland's National Vision and the Rising of 1381', and P. A. Knapp, 'Chaucer Imagines England (in English)', both in Lavezzo, ed., *Imagining a Medieval English Nation*, 191–233 and 131–60; and Charles King's review of M. Mazower, *Salonica, City of Ghosts*, in *TLS*, November 19 (2004) 8–9.

to seem not a category of analysis so much as something creative: an act of imagination rather than of political philosophy. For this reason, Anderson opens up the topic to literary scholars and not just to historians: an 'imagined community' is more likely to include writers and artists and less likely to be limited by precise chronologies or specific events. What is ironic, however, is that Anderson himself combines this seemingly unrestrained gesture towards the imagination with a determined attempt to fix the idea of the nation to the modern. His book is full of originary moments; for him it is self-evident that what he is seeking to explain started in the late eighteenth and early nineteenth century in Spanish America. Anderson is very far from being a medievalist, or from claiming to be (though he does use the Middle Ages quite often as a point of comparison), so it is perhaps unfair to press him on points of detail. But one area of (interesting) confusion lies in the inconsistency between two of his main examples of the difference between pre-enlightenment and post-enlightenment imaginings. He isolates this difference as being a matter first, of religion and second, of political system. Before the Enlightenment the predominant community was 'the religious community': this had an 'unselfconscious coherence' made possible through the confidence it placed in sacred languages and their power to make links across the community.[75] In Western European terms, this was the power seen as invested in and by the use of Latin. The second principal difference was 'the dynastic realm'. In this system of 'older imaginings' where monarchical government held sway, 'states were defined by centres, borders were porous and indistinct and sovereignties faded imperceptibly into one another'.[76] Both ways of imagining, as Anderson sees it, declined because:

> a fundamental change was taking place in modes of apprehending the world, which, more than anything else, made it possible to 'think' the nation.[77]

It is not the singling out of these two instances—both undeniably central factors in any attempt to characterize the premodern—that one might query, but the language Anderson uses to describe them. For although they are each seen as fundamental, they appear to be constructed from opposite dynamic impulses. 'The dynastic realm' is plural, mobile, and energetically controlling, whereas 'the religious community' is single, static, and inert—a little later, in fact, he reduces its character further by talking of '*the* older imagining'.[78] It does seem unlikely

[75] Anderson, *Imagined Communities*, 16.
[76] Anderson, *Imagined Communities*, 19.
[77] Anderson, *Imagined Communities*, 22.
[78] Anderson, *Imagined Communities*, 19 (my emphasis). The locus classicus of medievalist objection to this kind of characterization of the Middle Ages, alluding especially to D. W. Robertson's phrase 'quiet hierarchies' is that by D. Aers, ed., 'A Whisper in the Ear of Early Modernists; or Reflections on Literary Critics Writing the "History of the Subject"', in *Culture and History 1350–1600: Essays on English Communities, Identities and Writing* (London and New York: Harvester Wheatsheaf, 1992), 177–202.

that if the dynastic realm is indeed plural, mobile, and dynamic, the means of imagining community in the Middle Ages would be so monolithic. As many scholars have remarked, it is one of the most persistent (modern) clichés about the period that it had a univocal, simple, and universal religious belief, and so it is perhaps not surprising that Anderson indulges in it. Nonetheless, the inconsistency is important. On the one hand, the medieval sense of community is not precise enough—too indistinct—to constitute 'nation'; on the other hand, it is too inflexible.

Such indecision at the heart of his argument might seem to justify almost any approach to the nation in the medieval period. In practice, the debate has hinged on the larger philosophical conundrum of the separateness of the past. To put it starkly, are we continuous with or cut off from the past? For Anderson, as we have seen, there is a radical break. Many historians of the medieval period prefer to think in terms of continuity. Or at least, without necessarily explicitly formulating it in such a way, they begin from the premise that the study of the past yields to present description and analysis not because it is impossibly remote, but because it makes sense, at a profound level, of our own contemporary concerns.

A significant number of historians have thus argued that nationhood actually 'starts' much earlier than the eighteenth century. Such scholars as Liah Greenfeld, who makes a case for the early sixteenth century, and Adrian Hastings and John Gillingham, who make it for the fourteenth century or earlier, see it as important to assert that nationhood is as central an issue within the 'premodern' as it is perceived as being for later periods.[79] Impatient with modern prejudices about periods that modernist scholars (by definition) know little about, an increasing number of medieval historians have been concerned to investigate freshly the evidence for 'national' opinion in these earlier centuries. Hastings puts it bluntly: 'the key issue at the heart of our schism [with modernists like Hobsbawm, Gellner, Kedourie, Breuilly, and Anderson] lies in the date of commencement'.[80] Hastings's concern is to push back the chronological boundaries of the term 'nation' to 'his' period, while keeping its intellectual boundaries—as they are broadly defined for later periods—largely intact. In a quite different vein, Susan Reynolds has put forward the alternative influential argument that the medieval period is a crucial one in which to discuss nation, precisely because its terminology is so redolent of its *differences* from modern understandings.[81]

[79] L. Greenfield, *Nationalism: Five Roads to Modernity* (Cambridge, Mass., and London: Harvard University Press, 1992); Hastings, *The Construction of Nationhood* and Gillingham, *The English in the Twelfth Century*.

[80] See Hastings, *The Construction of Nationhood*, 9; A. D. Smith, *Nationalism and Modernism: A Critical Survey of Recent Theories of Nations and Nationalism* (London and New York: Routledge, 1998), 176.

[81] Reynolds, *Kingdoms and Communities*.

Reynolds's position makes it clear that the medieval historian's relation to the past is no simpler than that of the modernist. In reacting to an attempt to dismiss the relevance of the past to present concerns, two contradictory kinds of argument have been offered. One seeks to assert the past's relevance by bringing it within the intellectual framework from which others have rejected it, while the other paradoxically asserts its relevance by insisting on the anachronism of such a framework. The two positions together show that to speak of an approach to the past that sees it as continuous with, rather than irreparably broken off from, the present is thus to simplify. In fact this distinction is neither necessarily one that divides modernists and medievalists, nor is it clear-cut.

There is perhaps no better way to illustrate this than by turning to a late seventeenth-century writer, and therefore someone who—in Anderson's terms—is on the cusp of modern and premodern apprehensions of nation. I am referring to Dryden's comments on Chaucer:

> [Chaucer] has taken into the compass of his Canterbury Tales the various manners and humours (as we now call them) of the whole English nation in his age. Not a single character has escaped him . . . 'Tis sufficient to say, according to the proverb, that here is God's plenty. We have our forefathers and great-grand-dames all before us, as they were in Chaucer's days: their general characters are still remaining in mankind, and even in England, though they are called by other names than those of Monks, and Friars, and Canons, and Lady Abbesses, and Nuns; for mankind is ever the same, and nothing lost out of nature, though every thing is altered.[82]

It is a rich remark, and encompasses many lines of thought. Stephanie Trigg, in her lucid setting of Dryden into the genealogies of modern criticism has well described the long influence of his projected relationship with Chaucer as that of a 'congenial soul' that nonetheless includes a sense of 'historical distance'.[83] Dryden was writing at a time when Chaucer was regarded as obscure and linguistically remote. (So much so, that his works were translated into Latin to make them more accessible.)[84] In order to explain his high regard for Chaucer, Dryden therefore stresses his modernity: the names may have changed but the characters of which he writes 'are still remaining in mankind'. At the same time, this is not a claim that seeks to gloss over any sense of what makes Chaucer's writings distinctively of 'his age'. In a remarkably subtle and perhaps equivocal formulation, Dryden insists that 'nothing' is 'lost out of nature' while conceding that 'every thing is altered'. The strength of the remark lies in the sense it gives that he is genuinely struck by the difference of the past. His desire to assert

[82] John Dryden, 'Preface to Fables Ancient and Modern', in G. Watson, ed., *Of Dramatic Poesy and Other Critical Essays*, 2 vols (London: Dent, 1962–8), II, 284–5.

[83] Trigg, *Congenial Souls*, 150.

[84] Sir Francis Kynaston's translation of the first two books of *Troilus and Criseyde* was published in 1635; see Item 1265 in J. C. Boswell and S. W. Holton, eds, *Chaucer's Fame in England: STC Chauceriana, 1475–1640* (New York: MLA, 2004), 322–35.

Chaucer's importance to modern readers does not involve sentimentalizing or falsifying that experience of strangeness. The vagueness of 'every thing' is countered by its idiomatic force and its position at the end of the sentence: where we might have expected special pleading, we are pulled up short with pungent, almost contradictory, honesty.

Dryden's more obvious trump card in this passage is his equating of Chaucer's qualities as a writer with his ability to represent 'the whole English nation'. Chaucer achieves this through his capaciousness—'not a single character has escaped him'—but also through his talent in conveying these characters as if they were members of the same family. Dryden's sense of nationhood is here expressed entirely through the figure of ancestry: Chaucer is a poet of the English nation because he provides us with a glimpse of 'our forefathers and great-grand-dames all before us'. Only after lingering with this comfortingly personal, generational view of history does Dryden briefly allow himself (and by extension, his readers) a more philosophically disquieting reflection on the problems of trying to understand the past by means of present perspectives.

Dryden was not the first to associate Chaucer and the English nation, but his work in promulgating his translations of the *Canterbury Tales* has been instrumental in promoting the view of Chaucer as the writer who most profoundly shaped and directed the course of English literary history. Clearly this role is also accorded to Shakespeare: the difference is that Chaucer, by virtue of his earlier date, more obviously fits the role of originator or father figure. Chaucer, in short, provides a central instance of the way in which the medieval past has been not only yoked to a notion of Englishness, but also consistently used historically to define and maintain it. But as Dryden's remarks reveal, this use of the past, and of Chaucer's role in promoting it, is caught between two contradictory views of Chaucer as at once modern and antique.

The argument that the past can speak directly to present experience turns out not to be diametrically opposed to the view that it cannot so speak. Rather, both are constructed positions and this is true even, or perhaps especially, of the position which is most attached to a rhetoric of scientific, historical validity. This has implications for Geary's attack on 'pseudo-history' which we discussed earlier. His attack is founded on his seeing 'the myth of nations' as—precisely—myth rather than a genuine attempt to understand the past on its own terms. He distinguishes sharply between the two. Yet his characterization of the myth-making processes of contemporary historical writing comes uncomfortably close to current scepticism about the capacity of any historical approach—especially on the topic of nation—however grounded in the traditional tasks of documentary and archival research, to be entirely free from these processes. As two social psychologists writing on nationhood in Scotland have commented, 'the idea that national pasts are constructed, that traditions are invented and that "time immemorial" refers mainly to the span of social memory, have all assumed the status of orthodoxies'.[85] What seems to be an understanding of history as continuous often turns out to be an attempt to present history as continuous, which is a rather different enterprise. The distinction between history and 'pseudo-history' is unfortunately not always self-evident.[86]

Geary raises subtle and searching questions about our contemporary 'contest for the past' that are of acute importance to scholars of the present as well as of the past. For medieval literary scholars, this contest has involved lively re-evaluation of periodization. Comparing the divide between 'medieval' and 'modern' to that between BC and AD, Margreta de Grazia has wittily commented:

> Whether you exist on one side or the other of the BC/ AD divide determines nothing less than salvation. Whether you work on one side or the other of the medieval/modern divide determines nothing less than relevance. Everything after that divide has relevance to the present; everything before it, is *ir*relevant. There is no denying the exceptional force of that secular divide: indeed it works less as an historical marker than a massive value judgment: determining what matters and what does not. It is no wonder that Renaissance studies should covet its inaugural title 'early modern', and that Medieval studies might wish to preempt it with a still earlier claim, 'premodern'.[87]

The perspective of nation bears on this preoccupation because of the coincidence of 'nation' and 'modern': the closer the medieval comes to defining itself as modern—or at least as early modern—the closer it comes to being allowed to debate nationhood.

It may be, however, that medievalist anxiety about nation, about periodization, and about the representation of the past, has lagged behind the current terms of the debate. More positively, it is possible to see the debate—at least on nation—to be part of a twentieth-century perspective that we have now post-dated. In the bitter context of contemporary worldwide conflicts, the modernist claim to exclusive and originary rights over the term nation appears to have lost its historical cachet. In some ways, indeed, under the influence of Eric Hobsbawm's powerfully sharp-sighted view of the 'short twentieth century', and a 1986 lecture by another eminent historian, William H. McNeill, a new consensus is emerging that sees the premodern as not irrelevantly distinct from more recent periods, but on the contrary as oddly parallel with contemporary experience. For McNeill, nations and nationalism belonged to a single short period of history—the age of Western modernity (*c.*1789–1945). Just as in premodern

[85] S. Reicher and N. Hopkins, *Self and Nation: Categorization, Contestation and Mobilization* (London: Sage, 2001), 19.

[86] See John Breuilly, 'Changes in the political uses of the nation: continuity or discontinuity?' in *Power and the Nation in European History*, ed. Len Scales and Oliver Zimmer (Cambridge: Cambridge University Press, 2005), 67–101.

[87] 'The Modern Divide: From Either Side', in J. Summit and D. Wallace, eds, *Re-Thinking Periodization*, Special Issue of *Journal of Medieval and Early Modern Studies* 37:3 (2007), 453–67 (453).

times nations and nationalism were unknown, so they will be unknown again.[88] He characterizes history in terms of three epochs: a period of what he calls polyethnicity, then one of nations and nationalism, and finally (because currently) a return to polyethnicity. By polyethnicity McNeill seems to mean a way of viewing identity as a complex and multiple attribute that is not bound by a concept of nation but composed of concentric (as opposed to competing) circles of loyalty.[89]

McNeill's work has had a marked effect on contemporary perceptions of ethnic conflict. Its potential importance to contemporary thinking about the premodern past is also worth considering. His chiasmic view of history makes a radical claim for the historical equivalence of the remote past and the immediate present that stands apart from other efforts by modern scholars of the medieval period to engage with nation and nationhood. It is very doubtful whether such historical equivalence is precisely locatable, and what that would or could mean. Yet this is perhaps of lesser significance to the present discussion than the disruption his model causes to an evolutionary approach to history. It opens up the possibility that nation no longer need be pressed into service as a point of origin, but rather help us to have a more open view of the past. Nation is a prime example, as we have seen, of a term that is used to create a distinction between past and present. The founding of a nation is assumed to be an event that can be located at a specific historic moment. This makes it an inherently modern act, since in the instant of being founded, it establishes a premodern past. Yet this also makes for confusion, since nation is usually placed as happening not just after the Middle Ages but well after the early modern. The premodern becomes a moveable point tied, by definition, to an equally variable notion of the modern, which is itself tied, quite loosely, to any number of assertions of nationhood. From this perspective, nation is an anachronistic term in many periods of history, including our own.[90]

The insight suggested by McNeill is that nation can be disconnected from this imprisoning historical narrative. Perhaps we are now ready to see ourselves as back in limbo, in a time 'between' ages, or even 'beyond' them. *The Familiar Enemy* argues, somewhat contrarily (considering its subtitle), against an idea of nation. It connects up the 'post-national' with the 'pre-national' in order to move away from thinking about nationhood as a defining moment or act and towards a grasp of periods where boundaries are less clearly defined, and allegiances are understood to be multiple, parallel, and sometimes competing or contradictory. Rather than seeking to claim nationhood for the Middle Ages, this study is

88 Smith, *Nationalism and Modernism*, 199.

89 W. H. McNeill, *Polyethnicity and National Unity in World History, The Donald G. Creighton Lectures, 1985* (Toronto: University of Toronto Press, 1986).

90 On anachronism, see the strikingly elegant formulations of De Grazia's 'The Modern Divide: From Either Side'.

interested in seeing how the Middle Ages helps the current quest to dismantle or at least re-evaluate ideas of nation. It will show something of the huge variety of articulations of identity; of the ways different contexts shape these articulations, of the importance of language, social status and cultural history, not in creating nationhood, but in expressing some of the ways in which human beings negotiate that obscure boundary between individual and collective desires.

2

Origins and Language

'ORIGINS' AND EMPIRE

According to Hippolyte Taine, advertising a Scottish publisher's translation of his *Histoire de la littérature anglaise* in 1871,

> une nation ressemble beaucoup à un homme. Car, dans une carrière si longue et presque indéfinie, elle a aussi son caractère propre, son esprit et son âme, qui, visibles dès l'enfance, se développent d'époque en époque et manifestent le même fonds primitif depuis les origines jusqu'au déclin.[1]

> A nation closely resembles a man. For, in so long and seemingly indefinite a career, it has its own character, mind, and soul which, visible from infancy, develop from era to era and show the same primitive basis from their origins to their decline.

This classic statement of a human metaphor for historical change may now seem self-parodying in its glorification of manly development, yet it spoke for many in its view of history as a moment of birth growing through infancy into the distinctive maturity of a man who looks back on his origins with undisguised superiority as well as pride. Taine, the subject of current historical interest in his own right, took up the history of English literature with a strong consciousness of what he, as a Frenchman, could bring to the task. He remarks that it might have been better to let a member of the same family ('gens de la maison') describe this national character. Yet although they know him ('it') better, they are too familiar. The virtue of a stranger ('un étranger') is that he is struck more directly by the man's characteristics.[2] Why then, did Taine choose to write about the literature of the English, rather than, say, the Italian, Germans, or Spanish, or for that matter of Latin writing? Here he is more evasive. Ostensibly it is because he 'had to find a people with a grand and complete literature'. But tellingly, he finds only Ancient Greece, France, and England in this category. Implicitly, he admits to a 'peculiarity' that sets France and England apart from all other modern Western nations; their histories have this in common, as well as 'a forced

[1] H. A. Taine, *History of English Literature*, trans. H. Van Laun, 2 vols (Edinburgh: Edmonston and Douglas, 1871), I, vii.
[2] Taine, *History of English Literature*, viii.

deviation' in the case of England, which once again makes that history inseparable from that of his own nation. Taine, in short, is caught somewhere between claiming a special objectivity and a partial involvement; he can see the distinctness of the English because he is French, yet he defines that distinctiveness as a product of the 'constraining force' that the French imposed upon them.[3]

Taine's *History* instances the highly influential role played by nineteenth-century men of letters in shaping attitudes towards the medieval past that remain an underlying element in much modern scholarship.[4] His history alone was reprinted seventeen times in two editions between its first appearance in 1863 and 1911, and also translated into the popular English edition cited above. Taine's work gives prominence to two themes that will occupy this chapter: the quest (undertaken repeatedly then and since) for a moment of origin (what Paul Strohm has called a 'usable past')[5] to explain and indeed justify a modern sense of nation, and the particular intricacies of how that quest has unfolded on both sides of the Channel. For although there has been much interest in the rise of medievalism on the continent, and likewise in England, the two stories have been kept largely separate. However, as Taine admits, they are stories that separately have a double aspect. It is not just that the history of the English cannot be told without reference to the history of the French, and the history of the French—if only for that very reason—cannot escape an English perspective. It is also that these imperatives are themselves part of the story, and have often been resisted.

Hengist and Horsa

I want to discuss and illustrate these contentions initially through two case studies, one from the English and one from the French past. The first is the story of Hengist and Horsa, repeatedly retold in continental and insular French, Latin and English over some eight centuries. Mentioned briefly, but with increasing elaboration by Gildas (*c.*540), Bede (731), and Nennius (820s), the role of these leaders as the 'original' invading Saxons was recounted in much more emotive terms by a succession of twelfth-century chroniclers, from Henry of Huntingdon in his *Historia Anglorum* (first completed *c.*1129) to Geoffrey of Monmouth (*c.*1138) and Wace (*c.*1150–5).[6] As a story of origins it could hardly

[3] Taine, *History of English Literature*, 21.

[4] In fact, as John Haines reminds us, eighteenth-century scholarship was equally influential: see *Eight Centuries of Troubadours and Trouvères: The Changing Identity of Medieval Music* (Cambridge: Cambridge University Press, 2004), especially ch. 3.

[5] P. Strohm, *Theory and the Premodern Text* (Minneapolis: University of Minnesota Press, 2000), 77.

[6] Bede, *Bede's Ecclesiastical History of the English People*, ed. B. Colgrave and R. A. B. Mynors (Oxford: Clarendon Press, 1979; 1st pub.1969), 50–1. Gildas is also emotive about the Anglo-Saxons, but does not mention Hengist and Horsa by name.

be more entangled with betrayal. Vortigern, himself a usurper, invited the two brothers between 449 and 455 to help him fight against the Picts.[7] As Bede puts it, they came 'quasi pro patria pugnatura, re autem uera hanc expugnatura suscepit' [ostensibly to fight on behalf of the country, but their real intention was to conquer it].[8] For the twelfth-century chroniclers there was one incident in particular that revealed the depths of their treachery. Hengist and Horsa brought a huge army from Germany and arranged to meet Vortigern and his Briton soldiers to discuss the terms of their aid. But each Saxon was instructed to carry a knife hidden under his cloak, and when told, in Saxon, to take up his weapon, he was to kill the Briton placed next to him. Large numbers of barons were duly massacred and Vortigern forced to flee.

What makes the incident particularly extraordinary is that it depends on the shock of linguistic incomprehension. The treachery is achieved, not by ordinary military ambush, but by the deliberate exploitation of the Britons' ignorance of Saxon. In the many versions of the story in French and Latin, including its earliest surviving appearance in Latin by Nennius,[9] Geoffrey of Monmouth's *Historia regum Britanniae*, and several more in Latin dating from the reign of Edward I (before 1307) to the fifteenth century,[10] the Saxon command is consistently rendered in English. But it is Wace, writing the first vernacular chronicle of British history, who first makes these linguistic abrasions crucial to that history.[11] His attention to linguistic detail appears from the moment the two brothers are described stepping ashore at Sandwich. They are 'de grant estature/ E d'une estrange parleüre', 6709–10 [of great height and foreign speech], he says. These are handsome, plausible men, not invaders but guests, able to persuade Vortigern, himself cast as a cunning deceiver ('Fals fu e fausement parla', 6640 [false at heart and speaking falsehood]), that they come only to support his cause. The word 'estrange', however, disturbs that initial impression of well-meaning friendship and Wace follows this up with several further allusions to their difference in speech. Hengist gives a name 'En language de sun païs' (6918) [in the language of his country] to the castle which he builds on land granted to

[7] See J. M. Wallace-Hadrill, *Bede's 'Ecclesiastical History of the English People': A Historical Commentary* (Oxford: Clarendon Press, 1988), 212–14.

[8] Bede, *Ecclesiastical History*, 51.

[9] In his *Historia Brittonum*, in *British History and the Welsh Annals*, ed. and trans. J. Morris, Arthurian Period Sources, 8 (London: Phillimore, 1980), 50–84.

[10] A. G. Rigg, ed., *A Book of British Kings* (Toronto: Pontifical Institute of Medieval Studies, 2000). Rigg edits a collection of five texts, in prose and verse: the prose *Harley Epitome*, a versification of the *Harley Epitome* known as the *Metrical History*, a marginal prose commentary on the *Metrical History*, a verse continuation of the *Metrical History*, and a prose commentary on that continuation.

[11] Much of the incidental detail in what follows is in Geoffrey of Monmouth's *Historia regum Britanniae/The History of the Kings of Britain*, ed. M. D. Reeve and trans. N. Wright (Woodbridge: Boydell, 2007), but it is Wace who develops it into an extended argument about language and identity. Compare his famous reference to the jongleur Taillefer as singing the *Chanson de Roland* at the Battle of Hastings, and to the Normans as saying the English 'barked' because they could not understand their speech: *Le Roman de Rou*, ed. A. J. Holden (Paris: Picard, 1970–3), lines 8013–18, 8063–9, and 8229–32.

him by Vortigern, and this apparently minor act of linguistic colonization is shown subtly by Wace to have long-term significance, in that this name turns out to be the one that has survived (Wancastre) in place of the name in French (Chastel de cureie) or in 'British' or 'bretanz' (Kaër Carreï).[12]

The link between a foreign language and deceit is brought out here because Hengist cheats Vortigern over the size of the land. Wace develops the next incident to reinforce a growing sense of unease about the brothers. A beautiful daughter arrives, but again the narrative is directed towards language before romance or even lust: she offers Vortigern a cup and greets him in Saxon: 'Laverd King, Wesseil!' (6953). Wace comments fulsomely on the linguistic impasse which follows:

> Le reis demanda e enquist,
> Ki le language ne saveit,
> Que la meschine li deseit.
>
> (6954–6)

[The king, not knowing the language in which the girl spoke to him, enquired what she meant.]

An interpreter steps forward, described by Wace as 'bons latimiers, / Ço fu li premiers des Bretuns/ Ki sout le language as Saissuns' (6957–60) [a good linguist, the first of the British to know the Saxon tongue].[13] He explains both the language and the custom of exchanging kisses as well as the cup as a mark of friendship, and so Vortigern himself tries out the Saxon response with a grinning leer:

> Li reis, si cum cil li aprist,
> Dist 'Drincheheil!' e si sorrist.
>
> (lines 6971–2)

[The king, as soon as he learnt this, said 'Drinchail!' and smiled at her.]

Wace remarks that this was the beginning of this custom 'en cel païs'. It seems an innocent display of authorial antiquarian interest, and yet as we read on, we find that Vortigern's embrace of foreign speech and practices was both ill advised and fatally superficial.

His third summons to Hengist proves his last: Hengist arrives with 'three hundred thousand men' and plots the 'Night of the Long Knives'. It was part of the plot to speak in such a way that their enemies would not understand them:

[12] Wace is very fond of etymologies, but, as in this case, often provides rather garbled or fanciful versions. See *Wace's Roman de Brut: A History of the British*, ed. and trans. J. Weiss, rev. edn (Exeter: University of Exeter Press, 2002), 174, n. 6.

[13] For comment on this reference to an interpreter, see C. Bullock-Davies, *Professional Interpreters and the Matter of Britain* (Cardiff: University of Wales Press, 1966), 20–2.

Quant il as Bretuns parlereient
E tuit entremellé serreient,
'Nim eure sexes!' criereit,
Que nuls des Bretuns n'entendreint . . .

(7237–8)

[When they were mingling with the Britons and talking to them, he would call out: 'Grab your knives!', which none of the Britons would understand.]

When the actual order is issued Wace makes a point of stressing both that the Britons were unarmed and defenceless, and that each Saxon turns to his neighbour to carry out the killing. Wace has prepared the narrative carefully to create a many-layered response to the Saxons' act of butchery. Although their behaviour is reprehensible, it is qualified partly by Vortigern's own cowardly and illegitimate manoeuvrings, and partly by the irrefutable retrospective evidence that the Saxons were ultimately successful. He articulates both kinds of complex check on the reader's sense of outrage through a sensitive portrayal of the hiccups of misunderstanding between peoples perceived as foreign to one another. Hengist and Horsa represent a cultural threat that is all the more insidious because it is welcomed: they are brought in as guests and efforts are made to comprehend their speech and customs. Yet Vortigern's utterance of Saxon in words of hospitable acceptance and his over-eager bedding of Hengist's daughter are wiped out, in more ways than one, by the violent retort and quasi-erotic thrust of the Saxon soldiers' knives, acting in contemptuous denial of the British grasp of Saxon ways.

Linguistically, the cultural negotiations implicit in the story and also in Wace's retelling of it are full of partly repressed tensions, not all of which are easy to read from this distance, but perhaps were never fully transparent. One indirect clue to these tensions can be found in the hugely variant spellings of the Saxon/English command, both in the MSS of Wace's *History* and in the long textual history of the anecdote itself, in Latin as well as French.[14] It reminds us that this is precisely not a moment of code switching, in the normal sense. This harsh Saxon cry is meant to break up its linguistic surround, not flow easily in and out from it, and it is remarkable to see how it continues to have the power to do this well after its contemporary moment. In a sense, indeed, we of course have no evidence that this is 'how it happened' in the fifth century, although it is plausible enough in

[14] For example, in approximate chronological order, 'Eu, nimet saxas! (Nennius, *Historia Brittonum*, in *British History and the Welsh Annals*, ed. and trans. J. Morris, Arthurian Period Sources, 8 (London: Phillimore, 1980, ch. 46, 73); 'nimet oure saxas' (Geoffrey of Monmouth, *Historia regum Britanniae*, Book VI, § 104, 134–5); 'Nim eure sexes' (Wace, *Roman de Brut*, 182, lines 7237 and 7245); 'Nimmes our saxes' (*Metrical History* (Text C) in Rigg, ed., *A Book of British Kings*, 45, line 279; Pierre Langtoft (writing in French) gives 'neme yhoure sexes', *The Chronicle of Pierre de Langtoft*, ed. T. Wright, 2 vols (London: Longmans, Green, Reader, and Dyer, 1866), I, 108). In each case, there is further variety in the spelling of the phrase among the manuscript copies.

broad terms; but what we do know, as I have implied, is that it seems to become a central means for Wace, and many others after him, to render British history. British history, in short, ends, and English history begins with linguistic rupture, and this is an experience of which writers in the multilingual environment of later medieval Britain were acutely conscious.

This has some important implications for our modern quests for nation and points of origin. As I remarked in the introductory chapter, hard questions continue to be asked about some of the standard period divisions assumed and taught by scholars.[15] These have largely concentrated on the relationship between medieval and Renaissance or early modern. But the arguments are not all focused on the later boundary of the medieval period. If not exactly a turf war yet, there are some signs that a scuffle would actually be welcome at the other frontier, that between the Anglo-Saxon and Early Medieval. Linda Georgianna, working on the volume prior to James Simpson's in the same Oxford series, has called for some wider rethinking about the status of the Norman Conquest as a historical watershed. In articles anticipating her volume (which is being co-written by an Old English specialist) she argues that the Conquest is as much an invented as a 'real' turning point in literary terms. The belief, created by certain overtly nationalist English nineteenth-century scholars, that the Conquest represents a beginning rather than an event in between a phase of literary history that stretches from the middle of the seventh century to the mid-fourteenth has tended to leave some of the centuries out in the cold, especially the twelfth.[16]

For anyone working on nation the importance of this early boundary can hardly be overstated. At issue here are profound questions about what is 'English', and how modern assumptions about Englishness have been formed. These assumptions have been (and presumably always will be) distorted by retrospective attitudes to the Norman Conquest. Pedagogically, since the 1990s the gulf between Old and Middle English has grown wide, which has further encouraged scholars of the later medieval period to regard the Norman Conquest as the natural point of origin for medieval English. Yet in some of the 'original' historiographies, this was not the case. To return to Hippolyte Taine, for example, the Conquest was an unfortunate (300-year) blip in the otherwise

[15] David Wallace has been urging a reassessment of such assumptions for a decade or more, along with such scholars as Paul Strohm and James Simpson. In a sense it has been the central intellectual question of modern medieval studies, including the foundation of the Chair of Medieval and Renaissance English at Cambridge: see C. S. Lewis's inaugural lecture, *De descriptione temporum* (Cambridge: Cambridge University Press, 1955), cited in Helen Cooper's inaugural lecture, *Shakespeare and the Middle Ages* (Cambridge: Cambridge University Press, 2005), 2. A forthcoming volume of essays, *Cultural Reformations: Medieval and Renaissance in Literary History*, ed. Brian Cummings and James Simpson (Oxford: Oxford University Press) is a major cross-field reassessment of this period boundary.

[16] L. Georgianna, 'Periodization and Politics: The Case of the Missing Twelfth Century in English Literary History', *MLQ*, 64 (2003), 153–68 (154). See also Claire Lees, 'Analytical Survey 7: Actually Existing Anglo-Saxon Studies', *NML*, 7 (2005), 223–52.

powerfully continuous Saxon spirit of the English poetic genius. What the Normans did was in vain:

At the end of three hundred years the conquerors themselves were conquered; their speech became English; and owing to frequent intermarriage, the English blood ended by gaining the predominance over the Norman blood in their veins. The race finally remains Saxon. If the old poetic genius disappears after the Conquest, it is as a river disappears, and flows for a while underground. In five centuries it will emerge once more.[17]

It is particularly interesting to find Taine's self-confessedly 'French' perspective romanticizing the Anglo-Saxons over the Normans as the birth of English literary history. Far from approving of the French influence over the nation, Taine talks of the French culture imported by the Normans as a varnish that soon 'fades away or scales off'. Norman literature, for him, was merely a 'long impotence' that eventually gave way to the new virility of Chaucer. Norman, we realize, in Taine's eyes is clearly *not* French.[18] One might compare Horstmann's equally scornful dismissal of the post-Conquest period, which he sees as redeemed by a group of northern writers, Duns Scotus, Richard Rolle, Walter Hilton, and John Wycliff:

when after centuries of darkness, of struggles between conflicting elements, the state of things after the Norman Conquest had been sufficiently consolidated to make room for a revival of learning and literature, it is the North that leads . . .[19]

To put it very crudely, then, does 'English' start with the Normans or the Saxons? Or again, just how far is 'French' (or 'Norman') and Latin admitted into definitions of English? The current conventional view of Early Medieval literature in England as sparse suggests that there continues to be a general modern scholarly and pedagogic problem with thinking of French and Latin writing in England as 'English'. The importance to twelfth-century chroniclers of the treachery of Hengist and Horsa reveals that this problem was itself perceived as having a long history. By casting it as a story of linguistic conflict through incomprehension, Wace, and later Pierre Langtoft, amongst others, dare to raise the spectre of their own period's linguistic insecurities. Wace presents the complex case of someone writing after the Conquest, in French, who is caught precisely in the fray of trying to decide where and how his own cultural position was formed. His answers are sombre, perhaps, but also profoundly perceptive about the fault lines of linguistic contact in that history. The Saxons won the battle of Amesbury (an abbey on the Salisbury plain) through the treacherous use

[17] Taine, *History of English Literature*, 57.

[18] Taine, *History of English Literature*, 85–6, 105. Compare also Walter Scott's efforts to promote 'early Scottish' as a true English uncontaminated by French, remarked on by D. Matthews, *The Making of Middle English, 1765–1910* (Minneapolis: University of Minnesota Press, 1999), 66; and his *Ivanhoe.*

[19] C. Horstmann, ed., *Yorkshire Writers*, vi.

of their foreign language. The horror of this British loss is however redeemed, as Wace goes on to narrate, when the Christian king Aurelius defeats both Hengist and his son Octa and, on Merlin's advice, reclaims the plain as a place of victory by bringing over from Ireland the great standing stones that are there to this day.

But of course this is not so much a victory as a concession, and in the long vistas of history the ultimate concession, since Stonehenge continues to this day to function as a national icon more powerfully than any other physical location on the island.[20] That the tangled mess of betrayal and incomprehension describing the relations between British and Saxon should be summed up by an Irish monument, brought to Ireland from Africa (as Wace claims, 8065), in a history told by a Norman Jersiais, is almost too full of irony to grasp, and Wace seems sometimes overwhelmed by it. His obsession with etymology is perhaps one way for him of trying to gain control, yet there are many moments when his own language emerges through these excursions as oddly poised on the edge of the issue, such as when he explains that 'sex' (as in 'Nim eure sexes!') was later disowned by the English as a word for what we now call 'knife'. In French, he says, there are many other words again:

Sexes, ço dient li Engleis,
Plusurs culteus sunt en Franceis,
Mais cil les nuns alques varient
Ki ne sevent que senefient.
Engleis le repruvier oïrent
De la traïson que cil firent,
La fin de la parole osterent,
Les nuns des cultels tresturnerent,
Pur oblier la desonur
Que fait orent lur anceisur.

(7299–308)

['Sexes' is the English word for knives; there are many kinds of knife amongst the French, but they have somewhat changed their names, so that they do not know what 'sexes' means. The English heard themselves reproached for the treachery they had done, removed the end of the word and completely changed the name for knives, to forget the dishonour committed by their ancestors.]

As a piece of etymology it is weirdly garbled; yet as a comment on language and signification it is philosophically intricate. Wace is taking ideas about translation into a different sphere. It is not so much that there are different words in different languages for 'knife' but that he is interested in the possibility that one can use language, and specifically, the palette of choice offered by several languages to create meaning and not simply express it. Just before this passage, he has

20 According to the Icons project, sponsored by the Department of Culture, Media and Sport to promote Englishness, <http://www.icons.org.uk/introduction>. Amesbury is not to be confused with Avebury. Wace presents Stonehenge as the memorial for the Amesbury battle (7993–8000).

explained that Vortigern bribed Hengist with the gift of the counties of 'Sussexe', 'Essexe', and 'Midelsexe': they were given these names to commemorate 'la traïson/ Des cultels', 7298 [the treachery of the knives]. The word 'sexe' becomes a name, yet one that the later English want to disassociate from the hostile weapon itself. The complication is that Wace is of course explaining it all in French. The word 'knife' does not appear in his text, only the word 'cultel'. Thus although 'knife' is the word selected by the modern translator, there is no direct evidence that Wace is referring to it. In further commenting on what 'sexe' is in French, he is interestingly slippery: there are many 'culteus' in French and 'les nuns alques varient/ Ki ne sevent que senefient'. Could it be that there is a wry suppressed joke here? The French do not wish to be associated with treachery, and the problem for the English is that the Saxon language betrays itself. 'Sexe' means both knife and Saxon. No wonder the English want to disown their Saxon ancestors. They are better off using French and this will enable them to start the process of meaning afresh:

> Les nuns des cultels tresturnerent,
> Pur oblier la desonur
> Que fait orent lur anceisur.
>
> (7306–8)

[(the English) removed the end of the word and completely changed the name for knives, to forget the dishonour committed by their ancestors.]

It is as though once a word has been used as a name it can be somehow treated as denuded of meaning, or at least, as if it now exists in a different relation to its signified. Around and between the words chosen by Wace to tell his history is a sense of the often dangerous fluidity of meaning in a social context where languages have to compete for validity. He is careful to imply, too, that validity is itself a worryingly unstable concept, available for betrayers as well as those who regard themselves as illegitimately wronged.

The Strasbourg Oaths

If we turn now to the origins of the French literary past we find that there are some close parallels between its foundation narratives and those of the British. Once again the central text revolves around linguistic difference. In this case, the story of the beginnings of the French coincides (in many fascinating ways) with the earliest written evidence of the Romance vernacular. The Strasbourg Oaths occur in a Latin chronicle written in the 840s by Nithard, a grandson of Charlemagne, who was commissioned to write a history of the Carolingian empire for his patron and cousin, Charles the Bald. Nithard's four books of Histories include a vivid contemporary account of a complex series of negotiations between the three sons of Louis the Pious, Lothair (the eldest), Charles the Bald himself, and Louis the

German. The two younger sons had quarrelled with Lothair over the area between Germany and France (modern-day Alsace and Lorraine); the oaths were taken by them and their respective armies in 842 as a public gesture to confirm and strengthen their alliance against Lothair. As Nithard describes it, the oaths were taken in a highly deliberate display of vernacular translation. Louis, king of the Germanic East Franks, took the oath in the Romance language ('romana lingua') of his brother's people. Charles, king of the West Franks, whose language was Romance, with chiasmic reciprocity took the oath in Germanic ('teudisca lingva'). The symmetrical pattern of events continues with the army from each side swearing a further oath each, uttered in their own respective languages. Remarkably, Nithard does not simply relate this, he provides transcriptions of the oaths in their vernacular forms. This can be seen in Fig. 1, where each speech is clearly signalled on the manuscript page with an enlarged initial:[21]

Ergo xvi kal. marcii Lodhuvicus et Karolus in civitate que olim Argentaria vocabatur, nunc autem Strazburg vulgo dicitur, convenerunt et sacramenta que subter notata sunt, Lodhuvicus romana, Karolus vero teudisca lingua, juraverunt. Ac sic, ante sacramentum, circumfusam plebem, alter teudisca, alter romana lingua, alloquuti sunt. Lodhuvicus autem, quia major natu, prior exorsus sic coepit . . .

Cumque Karolus haec eadem verba romana lingua perorasset, Lodhuvicus, quoniam major natu erat, prior haec deinde se servaturum testatus est:

'Pro Deo amur et pro christian poblo et nostro commun salvament, d'ist di in avant, in quant Deus savir et podir me dunat, si salvarai eo cist meon fradre Karlo et in aiudha et in cadhuna cosa, si cum om per dreit son fradra salvar dift, in o quid il mi altresi fazet, et ab Ludher nul plaid numquam prindrai, qui, meon vol, cist meon fradre Karle in damno sit.'

Quod cum Lodhuvicus explesset, Karolus teudisca lingua sic hec eadem verba testatus est:

'In godes minna ind in thes christianes folches ind unser bedhero gehaltnissi, fon thesemo dage frammordes, so fram so mir Got guuizci indi mahd furgibit, so haldih thesan mînan bruodher, soso man mit rehtu sinan bruher scal, in thiu thaz er mig so sama duo, indi mit Ludheren in nohheiniu thing ne gegango, the, minan uuillon, imo ce scadhen uuerdhen.'

So, Louis and Charles met on 16 February in the town that used to be called Argentaria but which is commonly now known as Strasbourg, and they swore the oaths given below, Louis in Romance and Charles in Teutonic. But before swearing the oaths, they made speeches in Teutonic and Romance. Being the elder, Louis began, as follows . . .

[21] Cited from *Nithard: Histoire des fils de Louis le pieux*, ed. and trans. Ph. Lauer, Les Classiques de l'Histoire de France au moyen âge, 7 (Paris: Les Belles Lettres, 1926), 100–7. See also the edition and commentary in W. Ayres-Bennett, *A History of the French Language through Texts* (London: Routledge, 1996), 16–30. I have cited her translation for the Romance oaths. The text she cites from C. W. Aspland, *A Medieval French Reader* (Oxford: Clarendon Press, 1979), 2, is the same as Lauer's except for one piece of modern punctuation. The work survives in Paris BnF MS. lat 9768, a single early copy usually dated to the tenth century but recently redated to the eleventh by R. Posner, *The Romance Languages* (Cambridge: Cambridge University Press, 1996), 177–8: see R. Wright, *A Sociophilological Study of Late Latin* (Turnhout: Brepols, 2002), 182.

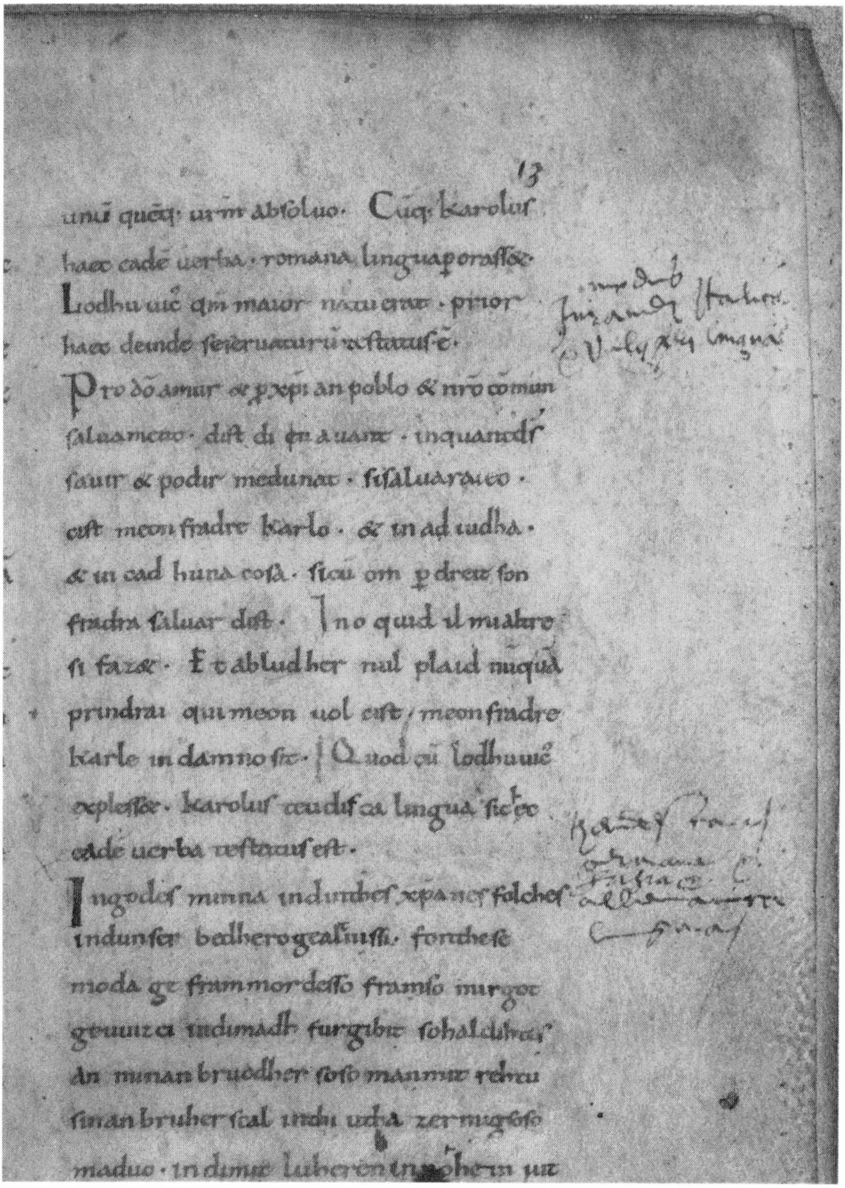

Figure 1. Strasbourg Oaths

Paris BnF lat.9768, fol.13r, col.2. Copyright Bibliothèque nationale de France: reproduced with permission.

Once Charles had finished off the speech with the same words in Romance, Louis, since he was the elder, then swore allegiance first:

'For the love of God and for the protection of the Christian people and our common salvation, from this day forward, in as much as God gives me wisdom and power, I shall help this my brother Charles both with aid and in all other things, as one should rightly help one's brother, provided that he does the same for me. And I shall never enter into an agreement with Lothair which, to my knowledge, will be detrimental to this my brother Charles.'

When Louis had finished, Charles swore with the very same words in the German vernacular:

'In God's love and for the protection of the Christian people and of us both, from this day forward, as far as God gives me wisdom and power, I will protect this my brother, as one rightly ought to, under the condition that he does the same towards me. I will not enter into any agreements with Lothar that might, through my will, redound to his harm.'[22]

These transcriptions have excited enormous interest and controversy for modern philologists, especially, in the case of the Romance oath, those working on the border between late Latin and early Romance. Put most simply, what exactly is Nithard recording? Is this Latin or vernacular? Is it how people spoke, or a written version of how people spoke, or indeed only a specific, that is local, form of writing? It is tempting, of course, to suppose that it actually represents the first time anyone tried to record a vernacular form of Romance speech in writing, but this makes assumptions about the differences between vernacular and Latin and the practices of recording language that are open to many further questions. In an important collection of essays edited by Roger Wright, a series of issues were broached that have far-reaching implications for the ways in which our understanding of later uses of vernacular languages, and the relation between oral and written forms of these vernaculars might be developed.[23] I will return shortly to

[22] The corresponding oath in the 'Romance' vernacular, sworn by Charles's followers, is as follows: 'Si Lodhuuigs sagrament, que son fradre Karlo jurat, conservat, et Karlus meos sendra de suo part non los tanit, si io returnar non l'int pois, ne io ne neuls, cui eo returnar int pois, in nulla aiudha contra Lodhuuuig nun li iu er' [If Louis keeps the oath which he swore to his brother Charles and Charles my lord for his part does not keep it (his oath), if I cannot prevent him from so doing, neither I nor anyone whom I can dissuade from it will give him any help against Louis], trans. Ayres-Bennett, *History of the French Language*, 18. For the German equivalent (that is, the oath sworn by Louis's followers), see C. Young, and T. Gloning, eds, *A History of the German Language through Texts*, (London and New York: Routledge, 2004), 61. I have used Young and Gloning's translation above for the Germanic oath. On the wider context for German in this early period, see D. Green, *Medieval Listening and Reading: The Primary Reception of German Literature 800–1300* (Cambridge: Cambridge University Press, 1994), 270–79. I am grateful to Mark Chinca for his help with these references.

[23] R. Wright, ed., *Latin and the Romance Languages in the Early Middle Ages* (London and New York: Routledge, 1991). See also the more recent collection of his essays in *A Sociophilological study of late Latin* and his translation of a revised version (first published in Spanish) of J. Herman, *Vulgar Latin* (1st pub. as *Le Latin Vulgaire*, 1967; rev. edn, 1997; trans. University Park: Pennsylvania State University Press, 2000). Rosamond McKitterick rightly cautions against

some of these matters in relation to dialect, language, and register, but first it may be worth commenting further on the account of the oaths itself.

In contrast to the story of Hengist and Horsa, these are two brothers who do not speak the same, foreign, language. Instead they each speak a different language. But the notion of foreignness is thereby differently calibrated. Implicitly the story disturbs the expected sense that language is part of the family, that as a mother tongue taught to children it is part of the very process of their being identified as siblings. Yet it does so in a curiously indirect way. They do in fact speak the same language, or at least each other's language, but it turns out ironically to be an act of speech that confirms them as foreign to one another. The stylized swapping of languages between them and their armies is hard to read as a reflection of a straightforward desire for communication or of actual linguistic practice.[24] As Rosamond McKitterick has argued, it seems rather that Nithard is using language difference to make a political point about the need for brothers to harmonize different peoples without riding roughshod over their distinctiveness.[25] Nithard's rhetorical purpose is subtly conciliatory, in contrast to Wace, who leaves the violence of miscomprehension all over his history.

Conciliation was not, however, the meaning of the story that most struck the nineteenth-century scholars who sought to understand in it the origins of the French language and nation. Renée Balibar and also Howard Bloch have commented on the way the linguistic uncertainties involved in deciphering this document struck at the heart of French efforts to define their language and themselves. Because it was (and still is) hard to decide precisely what language the oaths were written in, apparently straddling Germanic, Latin, or Gallo-Romance (or, as Wright would prefer, 'Pan-Romance'), they act as a literary figure for the twofold competition between France and Germany in the period between 1870 and 1914 (the Franco-Prussian war and the First World War) over national origins *and* over the rise of medieval studies.[26] In short, as Bloch puts it,

> the founding discourse of medieval studies allows no distinction between explanations of the genesis of France's earliest linguistic and literary monuments and the identity of the nation.[27]

making false analogies, but her point (as I understand it) is more to do with the way the later period has been used to make misleading assumptions about the earlier, rather than the other way round. Clearly, it is important in either case to proceed with care ('Latin and Romance: an historian's perspective', in Wright, ed., *Latin and the Romance Languages*, 130–45 (135)). My account does not, of course, attempt to intervene in the specialist debates on the nature of the languages involved, but seeks to respond to some of the wider literary historical as well as linguistic issues that the Oaths raise.

[24] The armies are represented as speaking in their own languages.

[25] McKitterick, 'Latin and Romance'.

[26] Wright, *A Sociophilological Study of Late Latin*, 183.

[27] H. Bloch, '842: The First Document and the Birth of Medieval Studies', in D. Hollier, ed., *A New History of French Literature*, (Cambridge, MA: Harvard University Press, 1989), 6–13 (13); R. Balibar, 'National language, education, literature', in F. Barker, P. Hulme, M. Iversen, and

The quest to identify the languages of these oaths was borne out of a French anxiety that the French were really German. In other words, if 'franc' means 'Frank' then French literature was from the start Frankish or at best a translation. 'France was really Germany in disguise' (p. 12). 'German spirit in a French form', 'this' wrote [Gaston] Paris, 'is exactly what the word '*français* expresses so precisely, with its German root and Latin suffix' (p. 12).

Nithard's clever overlaying of languages, each language formally substituting for the other, does imply that both forms of 'Frankish' are perceived as different by the two communities. At the same time, he is also implying that the two brothers, at least, are bilingual: the interchangeability of the oaths is mirrored in the interchangeability of the languages. Nineteenth-century sensitivities as to which vernacular is prior to the other might now seem over-developed, but they do alert a modern reader to the fact that seemingly 'scientific' linguistic description is much more embedded in national partiality than is usually recognized. Nithard, by contrast, seems to have it both ways. Franks are both Germanic and Gallo-Roman in equal measure. That both are ganging up against the elder brother of Latin is perhaps also slyly implied: it is very important to the public legalities of the story that Latin will not do, and there is even a suggestion that bad faith will be imputed to them unless they perform their oaths in this open and publicly comprehensible way:

> quoniam vos de nostra stabili fide ac firma fraternitate dubitare credimus, hoc sacramentum inter nos in conspectu vestro jurare decrevimus.[28]

> [since we believe that you doubt our firm faith and brotherhood, we shall swear this oath between us before all of you.]

Both foundational stories—of the English and the French—turn out to be stories of English and of French. Both also have German as a defining other, though German functions rather differently in each. Both raise questions of language and power. In neither is the structure and hierarchy of linguistic power simple or transparent. Wace's controlling language as a writer of his *Brut* is French, yet he is clearly highly conscious both of his decision to write in the vernacular rather than Latin, and of the other vernacular that has been a treacherous element in the history of the island's peoples but still persists in and through his own French. Nithard's controlling language is Latin; yet he also creates a space for two vernaculars that not only vie with each other but temporarily, at least, audaciously displace his Latin.

D. Loxley, eds, *Literature, Politics and Theory: Papers from the Essex Conference 1976–1984* (London: Routledge, 1986; new edn 2003), 126–47. Balibar elaborates (without, here, specific linguistic reference) on the notion that the 'languages became symbols of the territories inherited by Charlemagne's grandsons: to one went the lands where the people obeyed in Germanic, to the other the lands where the people obeyed in Roman French' (134).

[28] Nithard, *Histoire des fils de Louis le pieux*, 102–4.

LANGUAGE AND HISTORY

Nation is often assumed to break around language: differences in languages signal differences in national identity. Yet as a moment's reflection indicates, a modern map of language groups, for example in Europe, does not correspond to a map of nation-states. Some notorious flashpoints exist, but also some areas of bilingualism (Belgium), and even tri- or quadrilingualism (Switzerland and Cyprus) where—at least in the remarkable case of Switzerland—people experience a relatively peaceable coexistence of languages that does not threaten national identities. Medieval versions of founding histories similarly show a complex picture: in the case of the British, especially, as we have seen, linguistic allegiance was varied and shifting as well as overlapping.

Modern histories, by contrast, are often more misty-eyed and idealistic about the function of language in mapping a national literature than many of their medieval counterparts. Two instances are instructive: the 1988 *Columbia Literary History of the United States*, edited by Emory Elliott, and *A New History of French Literature*, edited by Denis Hollier and published by Harvard in 1989. Both histories are very conscious of their role as potentially nation-shaping constructs. The *Columbia History* claims in fact to be quite different from its 1948 predecessor in that it does not constitute 'a new consensus about the history of the literature of the United States'. 'There is today', it announces, 'no unifying vision of a national identity like that shared by many scholars at the closings of the two world wars.' Instead it describes its own project as 'modestly postmodern: it acknowledges diversity, complexity, and contradiction by making them structural principles, and it forgoes closure as well as consensus'.[29] But the general introduction goes on, in a series of increasingly passionate remarks, to assert a new vision of American national literature that encompasses this diversity. Not only should Asian American, Hispanic, and Jewish-American writers be regarded as having just as much a place in this history as the writers of New England, but that they 'are *and have always been* writers of the national literature and have contributed substantially to the literary heritage'.[30] Clearly it is difficult to have an inclusive approach to a literary history that does not in some way make a virtue of its inclusiveness; that is perhaps only proper. But what stands out here is that this ethic is expressed with ahistorical abandon. The present assertion (taking a different decision from Nithard) rides roughshod over the very distinctiveness of the traditions it is seeking to include. It cannot allow that such writers may not

[29] E. Elliott, ed., *Columbia Literary History of the United States*, (New York and Guildford: Columbia University Press, 1988), xi–xii.

[30] Elliott, *Columbia Literary History*, xxi–xxii; my emphasis.

have had any notion of, let alone a desire to participate in, a national literary heritage.[31]

Denis Hollier in the Harvard *History of French Literature* faces (with greater self-awareness) rather different issues. The main one for this US publication is precisely that it is a history of French literature that is not being written in France by the French. The editor and many of the contributors engage with this in very productive ways. For instance, there is no failure to comment on the way that an earlier French perspective would have seen their enterprise as impossible. Hollier quotes Châteaubriand, writing (like Taine) to justify his own history of English literature, 'What French person would not smile at the idea of a French literary history composed outside France's own frontiers?'[32] The exquisitely enjoyable irony of this citation is that Châteaubriand himself asks the question apparently without any irony: for him, as a Frenchman, quite different conditions apply to the writing of English literary history than they do to French. There are two reasons: one is that it could not of course be done adequately, but the other, more fundamentally, is that there is no other perspective than the French.

If an Anglophone reader is inclined to smile or raise an eyebrow at this, then that too is precisely the point. The French considered their language to be the voice of the universal. Antoine de Rivarol, author of *De l'universalité de la langue française*, writes in 1784: 'The time has come to call the world French.' It is salutary to be reminded that 'the word *nationalité* was still a neologism when Emile Littré included an article on it in his 1866 *Dictionnaire de la langue française*'. He claimed that although 'the principle of nationalities is transforming Germany', 'les Français n'ont point de nationalité'. Even Sartre in 1947, writing a short history of French literature called *Qu'est-ce que la littérature?*, implies there is no literature outside France.[33]

The Harvard *History* reacts to this sense of immediate post-war consensus evoked by Sartre in a different way from the Columbia historians of American literature. Bloch's founding entry on 842 polemically signals through the story of Nithard that the earliest perceptions of French as a vernacular language were not overriding and universal, but riven between Germanic and Latin. This then is the justification for a history of French outside France: its earliest historical representation showed it to be outside other languages. Hollier again: 'This *New History of French Literature* has been written from both sides of as many borders as possible.'[34]

31 B. Thomas, 'National Literary Histories: Imagined Communities or Imagined Societies?', in *MLQ: Special Issue: National Literary Histories*, ed. B. Thomas and M. Brown, 64 (2003), 137–52 (144–5).

32 Cited in Hollier, ed., *A New History of French Literature*, xxv.

33 For all these references, see Hollier, ed., *A New History of French Literature*, xxiii.

34 Hollier, ed., *A New History of French Literature*, xxv.

In discussing these modern histories alongside medieval foundational stories I am trying to show that medieval and modern are closely and not always transparently interwoven. We cannot read these six- or eight-hundred-year-old accounts except from within our current preoccupations which in turn have been formed by eighteenth- and nineteenth-century notions of the medieval. This may seem an obvious enough point, but what is also part of the history is that this process is incompletely acknowledged. National histories take shape through an attempt to control a narrative of the past; but this narrative is bound to be partial, in both senses of the word. The notion of control can always be dispelled by another's cultural perspective on the same narrative. What makes the history national, then, is a desire to tell it that wilfully ignores a genuinely inclusive point of view.[35] Moreover, even the secondary telling of a national history is subject to the same constraints; all national histories are secondary as well as primary in the sense that they are incorporating (whether they like it or not) an outsider's critique of that effort to narrate.

It is notable how the tremendous outpouring of histories in the post-Conquest period testifies to all of these kinds of partiality. The *Histories* of Henry of Huntingdon (first completed *c.*1129), William of Malmesbury (first completed c.1125), Geoffrey of Monmouth (completed *c.*1138), Gaimar's *Estoire des Engleis*, (after 1140), Wace (*c.*1150–5), and Layamon (late twelfth- to early thirteenth-century), and such anonymous writing as the Anglo-French *Description of England* (soon after 1139?) are all works that have been trawled by modern scholars for their incipient or actual nationalism, often in the quest for an understanding of the role of Arthur in notions of Britishness. Yet, as Lesley Johnson, Jocelyn Wogan-Browne, and Rosalind Field, amongst others, have done much to indicate, the linguistic explosion in twelfth-century writing, and the abrupt survival in the thirteenth of Layamon's massive epic in English testify to far more than nationalism.[36] To describe them as national histories risks falling into the colonizing retrospectivism of the Columbia *History*. We have writing that in its very diversity and multiplicity reveals powerful contradictions in linguistic choice and perspective among 'English' writers. Rather than provide yet another reading of these chronicles as (however complexly) nationalist, I want instead to turn in more detail to the background of their linguistic decisions. Much groundwork needs to be done on the linguistic context of twelfth- and thirteenth-century writing in England, not just of romances or chronicles, but of such other genres as hagiography, medical treatises, sermons and lyrics, and in the relations and differences between Latin, French, and English examples of any of these. I offer here a preliminary sketch of some aspects of the multiple linguistic worlds of 'English' in this

[35] I do not mean to imply complacently that a 'genuinely' inclusive point of view is easy, or even possible.

[36] See their respective essays, with further bibliography, in *Cambridge History*, ed. Wallace.

earlier part of the period. The aim is to look at instances of linguistic comment and self-description from within the period, to find out from the gossip, jokes, and implied snobberies of writers and their audiences something of what they saw in each other's languages. This will necessarily mean discussing the multiple linguistic worlds of 'French'.

DIALECT AND DIFFERENCE

The evidence for how people thought of one another's languages or forms of speech in the medieval period is surprisingly full. In the next chapter I consider in detail some short narratives, all written in French, in which ideas of Englishness or Frenchness come under (largely comic) scrutiny. They form part of a larger and rather neglected tradition of satiric writing (itself related to the works of invective mentioned earlier) from the thirteenth to the fifteenth centuries in which poets represent English being spoken by continental French speakers and French being spoken by the English. Usually called, in French, 'les textes en jargon franco-anglais', these writings offer a glimpse of how each side viewed the other through the language each uses and is represented as using. By way of introduction, it is important to assess what we might mean by linguistic difference and definition in the period.

The Strasbourg Oaths and the Battle of the Knives serve as ways of separately understanding the complexity of linguistic relationships more broadly on the continent, and more locally on the island(s) of Britain. To take the oaths first, among the many issues they raise is the difference the oral or written status of a language makes to any definition of it. The oaths mean so much to modern scholars because of their written character, but in a sense their very writtenness is misleading because they were, of course, quintessentially oral pronouncements. Ironically, Nithard's careful transcription of them misrepresents them to the extent that their contemporary significance (as he tells it) lies precisely in their being uttered in public, not written in private. However, it is the fact that he chose to *transcribe* them as different languages even when they were being *spoken* interchangeably that is so tantalizing. Nithard's account gives us more than a sense of linguistic diversity; it gives us a written *and* oral version of each vernacular.

In Nithard's period of late Latin, such doubleness is crucial because there remains so much scholarly uncertainty about the relationship between written and spoken Latin, and beyond that, between spoken Latin and the newly emerging romance vernaculars. Part of the issue concerns language naming. Before the ninth century no other language name was in use in Romance regions besides Latin. Yet as Tore Janson points out, language change is not the same as changes in language names: people may not have a name for the language they speak, or they may continue to call it Latin even though it has become quite distinct from Latin.[37] Then again, they may continue to call their language Latin because they continue to write in Latin, but their speech has diverged. The 'same' language, then, may have a quite distinct written and spoken form. When different names do appear from the ninth century on they seem to result from a new impetus to fix language in writing brought on initially by Alcuin's reforms of spelling and pronunciation. Cultural and political pressures evidently have a bearing on metalinguistic self-consciousness: if there is a desire, such as Charlemagne's, to make language use homogeneous for the sake of widespread intelligibility, then people will be encouraged to suppress any sense of difference or simply feel no need to articulate it. But once that political control falters, the experience of difference starts to count.[38]

Clearly, the case of England and France in the twelfth century and later does not make a straightforward comparison with ninth-century continental language use. Yet some connections are worth making. The case of Latin in the ninth century presents us with a picture of a master tongue gradually fragmenting linguistically, with new written forms emerging to rival its monoglot written status (though orally it must always have been somewhat diverse).[39] Broadly this is not a wholly inaccurate description of the status of French from the late thirteenth century onwards, just as it is of English from the nineteenth century on.[40] Latin and modern English have had a far more stable written existence than medieval French, but it is particularly important for our understanding of thirteenth- and fourteenth-century Anglo-French relationships to grasp the dominance of French, not just in England but across much of what we now call Europe. Various further factors must be taken into account: obviously, Latin itself continued to be a master tongue, so whatever status French had was one that it held in partnership with Latin. But although we tend to think of Latin in the later Middle Ages as the quintessentially learned, literate language, the ninth-century evidence reminds us of Latin's orality. It reminds us that however powerfully fixed a language appears to be, if it is widely used then it is in flux. And if this was true of Latin, it was all the more true of French, whose stability was earned in widely different contexts, and, like Latin, in some regions was more image than fact.

[37] Tore Janson, 'Language Change and Metalinguistic Change: Latin to Romance and Other Cases', in Wright, ed., *Latin and the Romance Languages*, 19–28.

[38] See Alberto Varvaro's eloquent metaphor for 'the linguistic universe of Latin' of a 'solid but elastic dome', 'Latin and Romance: fragmentation or restructuring?' in Wright, ed., *Latin and the Romance Languages*, 44–51 (48).

[39] Compare the masterly study by J. N. Adams, *Bilingualism and the Latin Language* (Cambridge: Cambridge University Press, 2003).

[40] The analogy breaks down if we try to push too hard the notion that French was already a master tongue: in reality it became culturally as well as linguistically dominant through the course of the thirteenth and fourteenth centuries, from a complex of bureaucratic, literary and crusading causes.

In turning back to the situation in England, many of these considerations apply. For one, although French is clearly the dominant vernacular in the earlier part of the post-Conquest period, the exact character of its dominance, and the length of its reign, are highly debated. The famous question asked first by Ferdinand Lot (1931) and then Dag Norberg (1966), 'A quelle époque a-t-on cessé de parler latin [en Gaulle]?' could equally be asked of French in England, with as great a sense of its subtle difficulty.[41] Scholars of Anglo-French have swung back and forth in their responses. But latterly, through the untiring efforts of William Rothwell and others, notably David Trotter, Tony Hunt, Brian Merrilees, Douglas Kibbee, Andreas Kristol, and Serge Lusignan, a more nuanced picture has begun to be drawn.

Among English scholars, research on the post-Conquest use of French in England has been carried out principally by linguists, especially those with more literary interests, and historians of law, contributing to the editing of texts, studies of lexis and syntax, and assessments of the function and influence of French in English culture.[42] The next decades saw substantial publication, both of editions supervised by Ian Short through the auspices of the Anglo-Norman Text Society, and the *Anglo-Norman Dictionary*, directed initially by William Rothwell, Louise W. Stone, and T. B. W. Reid, and subsequently in a comprehensive and still ongoing revision by David Trotter. Conclusions on the cultural impact of French in England have passed through striking vicissitudes. For earlier scholars, establishing a field, it was important to insist that Anglo-Norman had a wide and enduring influence in medieval English society. Many citations were assembled to argue that Anglo-Norman permeated even down to

[41] F. Lot, 'A quelle époque a-t-on cessé de parler latin?', *Archivum latinitas medii aevi*, 6 (1931), 97–159; D. Norberg, 'A quelle époque a-t-on cessé de parler latin en Gaule?', *Annales*, 21 (1966), 346–56.

[42] For a lucid account of the older literary research, see I. Short, 'On Bilingualism in Anglo-Norman England', *Romance Philology*, 33 (1979–80), 467–79. The earliest phase is characterized by a pioneering study by the Swedish scholar J. Vising, *Anglo-Norman Language and Literature* (London: Oxford University Press, 1923) and research by A. Ewert, *The French Language* (London: Faber and Faber, 1933), M. K. Pope, *From Latin to Modern French*, M. Dominica Legge, ed., *Anglo-Norman Letters and Petitions from All Souls ms. 182*, Anglo-Norman Texts 3 (Oxford: Blackwell, 1941) and M. Dominica Legge, *Anglo-Norman Literature and its Background.* Alongside, on law French, still valuable contributions include F. W. Maitland, 'Of the Anglo-French Language in the Early Year Books', Introduction to the *Year Books of Edward II*, Selden Society 17 (London: Quaritch, 1903); G. Woodbine, 'The Language of English Law', *Speculum*, 18 (1943); more recently, J. H. Baker's Introduction to *The Reports of John Spelman*, II, Selden Society 94 (London: Selden Society, 1978); P. Goodrich, 'Literacy and the Languages of the Early Common Law', *Journal of Law and Society*, 14 (1987) and, especially, the magisterial output of P. Brand, *The Making of the Common Law* (London: Hambledon, 1992), his editions of *The Earliest English law reports*, Selden Society 111–12, 122–3, 4 vols (London: The Seldon Society, 1996–2007), the *Curia Regis Rolls* (Woodbridge: Boydell Press, 1999) and the *Plea Rolls of the Exchequer of the Jews* (London: Jewish Historical Society of England, 2005), and *Kings, Barons and Justices: The Making and Enforcement of Legislation in Thirteenth-Century England* (Cambridge: Cambridge University Press, 2003).

lower social levels.[43] A 1943 article by R. M. Wilson, followed by Berndt's widely cited 1972 essay, took a counter view, arguing that the influence of French was always limited to the highest echelons of society and rapidly lost ground to English.[44] Notwithstanding the detailed studies by D. A. Kibbee and (for a later period) Kathleen Lambley, the narrative of Anglo-French's decline has largely taken hold in Middle English scholarship.[45] Yet the swathes of new research have changed, and are continuing to change, the terms of discussion.[46] The sheer scale of surviving material in Anglo-French is now more visible than ever before, and means that the field is no longer concerned with relatively small-scale shifts in debate about influence but rather of tackling the paradigm shifts that result from taking Anglo-French writing much more fully into account in our understanding of English as well as French medieval culture. It remains difficult, nonetheless, to assess the evidence, and this is partly because methodological approaches are caught between history, linguistics, and literature, as well as between Anglo-American and continental perspectives; Anglo-French and French philological approaches; English, Anglo-French, and French literary partialities.

Acutely aware that vast amounts of primary evidence have still to be found, read, and brought to bear, my own contribution will be limited to an attempt to suggest some ways in which insular and continental concerns can be fruitfully linked. The surveys of medieval linguistic comment on Anglo-French are still a little beset by a sense of endless tug of war between partisan arguments in favour of English knowledge of French, and those in favour of general English ignorance of French. We need, if we can, to escape that rather deadening atmosphere of

[43] See H. Suggett, 'The Use of French in England in the Later Middle Ages', *Transactions of the Royal Historical Society*, 28 (1946), 61–83.

[44] R. M. Wilson, 'English and French in England: 1100–1300', *History*, 28 (1943), 37–60; R. Berndt, 'The Period of the Final Decline of French in Medieval England (Fourteenth and Early Fifteenth Centuries)', *Zeitschrift für Anglistik und Amerikanistik*, 20 (1972), 341–69.

[45] D. A. Kibbee, *For to Speke Frenche Trewely: The French Language in England, 1000–1600: Its Status, Description and Instruction* (Amsterdam and Philadelphia: John Benjamins, 1991) and K. Lambley, *The Teaching and Cultivation of the French Language in England During Tudor and Stuart Times* (Manchester: Manchester University Press/London: Longmans, 1920).

[46] I refer to new work on the *AND* (with a profusion of articles by William Rothwell and more recently, David Trotter); on dialect (see references in Chapters 1 and 2 to Dees and others); work on multilingual material (by Wright); the gradual impact of the monumental specialist editions particularly by Tony Hunt and, recently, Daron Burrows, as well as important translations and contextual work especially of twelfth- and thirteenth-century female devotional texts (J. Wogan-Browne, *Saints' Lives and the Literary Culture of Women, c.1150–c.1300: Virginity and its Authorizations* (Oxford: Oxford University Press, 2001)); and the pioneering studies by Serge Lusignan on linguistic practices in royal administration in France and England. For instances of the new direction of literary focus, see R. M. Stein, 'Multilingualism', 23–37, and C. Baswell, 'Multilingualism on the Page', 38–50, both in P. Strohm, ed., *Middle English, Oxford Twenty-First century Approaches to Literature* (Oxford: Oxford University Press, 2007); Jocelyn Wogan-Browne with Carolyn Collette, Maryanne Kowaleski, Linne Mooney, Ad Putter, and David Trotter, eds., *Language and Culture in Medieval Britain: The French of England, c. 1100-c. 1500* (York: York Medieval Press, forthcoming); and a Worldwide Universities Network project called 'Multilingualism in the Middle Ages', led by Dr Ad Putter at the University of Bristol.

polarity and talk more about the situation 'on the ground'—the contexts and wider circumstances of individual writers, the enormous variety of situation and locality, the fluidity of bi- or trilingual competences, the different purposes of language choices and usages, the patterns of manuscript circulation. All of this will be more fully understood if we begin to consider the picture from the continent alongside the situation in England: the parallels, divergences, intersections, and rivalries are part of both the insular and continental stories. The increasing significance of English as a literary language will also enter the narrative, but in this book I want to stress the international context for these changes which normally gets left out of the story. Even those who emphasize the importance of Anglo-French to the story of English tend to take an insular approach. It is important to take a continental approach to Anglo-French as well as to English.

As a result, we will discover a more nuanced picture of 'French'. Anglo-French itself, usually treated like a single language, was actually much less fixed than the word 'single' implies. Slipping in and out of continental French over its centuries of use in England and—we must not forget—on the continent too, it was sometimes distinctive, sometimes renewed by a variety of linguistic processes including direct influx from continental French speakers and writers, or more indirectly, from Anglo-French speakers spending time on the continent, or again, from influences from English and Latin by means of those same Anglo-French and continental French speakers. We need more information on how varied Anglo-French was. To the extent that it was a spoken language, its use and practice would have varied from area to area; as a written language, and especially as a cultivated language, usage would have been more stable across the literate community, though rhetorically the demands of law, romance, devotional didacticism, hagiography, or medicine were disparate.

The vexed matter of the status of Anglo-French, as I have just implied, cannot be isolated from continental perspectives. Yet these continental perspectives are also more variable than they might appear from the English side of the Channel. In the light of Bédieriste editorial concerns about textual reconstruction it is astonishing to notice the degree to which the morphology, syntax, and grammar of medieval French texts were normalized in standard French editions throughout the late nineteenth and well into the twentieth centuries.[47] We gain some insight into the reasons for this from Brunot, once more. He is discussing *francien*, the so-called dialect of medieval French that is centred on Paris and its immediate environs. In the following passage, which he cites from Hermann

[47] On the normalizing tendencies of many studies of French grammar, see S. Fleischman, 'Methodologies and Ideologies in Historical Grammar: A Case Study from Old French', in R. H. Bloch and S. G. Nichols, eds, *Medievalism and the Modern Temper* (Baltimore, MD, and London: Johns Hopkins University Press, 1996), 402–38; and C. Clark, 'The Myth of "the Anglo-Norman scribe"', in M. Rissanen, O. Ihalainen, T. Nevalainen, and I. Taavitsainen, eds, *History of Englishes: New Methods and Interpretations in Historical Linguistics*, (Berlin: Mouton de Bruyter, 1992), 117–29.

Suchier, two points collide: the unquestioned assumption that *francien* is the original language of France and the hard fact that no written text in *francien* exists before the end of the twelfth century.

Suchier gets round this through a carefully worded and rather brilliant reclamation of *francien* as the 'langue des langues'. The first comment is a concession to the evidence:

Malgré des écarts, il est évident que la langue littéraire présente, chez les poètes continentaux et chez les poètes anglo-normands, les mêmes bases dialectales, et c'est là pour nous la forme la plus ancienne de français littéraire.

[Despite the gaps, it is evident that literary language presents, in the continental poets and the Anglo-Norman poets, the same dialectal bases, and for us that is the most ancient form of literary French.]

However, he soon moves on (my emphases):

Il est *vraisemblable* que le dialecte francien, sous sa forme *purement locale*, n'étant encore altéré par *aucune influence étrangère*, a été employé dans la littérature du XIIe s . . . toutefois il ne nous est parvenu aucun manuscrit de cette époque. C'est seulement peu de temps avant le milieu du XIIIe s qu'il se trouve des textes écrits à Paris ou aux environs, et présentant sous une forme à peu près *pure*, le dialecte qui s'y parlait, et que peu à peu la France entière adopta pour langue littéraire.[48]

[It is likely that the *francien* dialect, under its purely local form, not having been altered by any foreign influence, was employed in the literature of the twelfth century . . . however no manuscript of that period has come down to us. It is only a little before the middle of the thirteenth century that texts written in Paris or neighbouring areas appear, presenting in an almost pure form the dialect spoken there that little by little was adopted by the whole of France as its literary language.]

Nothing early survives in *francien*, but this must be an accident. What is likely ('vraisemblable'), owing to the regrettable lack of evidence, is that the thirteenth-century texts manifest a pure oral form of *francien*, untouched by foreign influence, that in due course became the literary language of the whole country.

The desire to create a linguistic history that is free from the foreign influence of England is palpable. This may also be the moment to recall that the term *francien* dates from 1889 when it was coined by the ever-inventive Gaston Paris.[49] Yet the evidence that does survive is more persistently indicative of the early importance of non-centralizing kinds of French than either Suchier or Brunot cared to

[48] H. Suchier, *Le français et le provençal*, trans. P. Monet (Paris: Émile Bouillon, 1891), 23–4, cited in F. Brunot, *Histoire de la langue française des origines* à *1900, I: De l'époque latine à la Renaissance* (Paris: Armand Colin, 1905), 326–7.

[49] He was translating *francisch*, a neologism invented by Suchier in 1888. See M.-R. Simoni-Aurembou, 'Le français et ses patois', in J. Chaurand, ed., *Nouvelle Histoire de la Langue Française* (Paris, Editions du Seuil, 1999), 547–80 (562). Again, it is revealing to note how this term for French, redolent of national sentiment, should be a translation from German.

emphasize.[50] First, it is certainly true that the earliest texts were copied in England. David Howlett registers this with pointed extravagance: 'For the first century of its existence most Old French literature was English.'[51] This is precisely the kind of claim that this book wants to scrutinize; the labels of 'Old French' and 'English' obfuscate rather than clarify here. Yet the larger point concerns the question of difference. The long, detailed textual introduction by Bartina Wind to her distinguished edition of *Les Fragments du Tristan de Thomas* reveals the entangled nature of modern efforts to identify Thomas's language and locality.[52] Much time and ink has been spent trying to determine whether a linguistic feature is continental or Anglo-Norman. As Wind remarks wryly from time to time, Bédier was convinced of the poet's Anglo-Norman identity ('Bédier fonde sur la décadence de la déclinaison sa conviction de l'anglo-normandicité de notre poète', 27 [Bédier founds his conviction of the Anglo-Norman character of our poet on the decayed nature of the declensions]),[53] yet she repeatedly points out that the evidence is mixed and does not point in a single direction. In the case of declension, for example, 'tel texte avec un nombre donné d'incorrections sera "français", tel autre qui en a davantage, sera anglo-normand' [one text with a certain number of errors would be "French"; another with more would be Anglo-Norman].[54] The difference between insular and continental practice here is hard to maintain, she concludes.

It is difficult to avoid the further conclusion that the earlier discussions she surveys often display a prior desire to find difference, rather than a balanced assessment of the often wildly conflicting linguistic clues.[55] Too often a poet is given an identity by means of his or her language by a modern scholar despite the more scrupulous admissions in the notes on language of the 'impurity' of the morphology or phonetics. Philip Bennett has pointed out that Old French is treated as if it were an already standardized language, tainted with dialectal usages.[56] The *Chanson de Roland*, perhaps most sensitively of all, is the prime

[50] For two sharply lucid commentaries on modern linguists' reluctance to acknowledge the difficulties with *francien*, and further references, see Simoni-Aurembou, 'Le français et ses patois', 562–3 and (in relation to Anglo-Norman) Trotter, 'Not so eccentric as it looks', 431–3. See also R. A. Lodge, *A Sociolinguistic History of Parisian French* (Cambridge and New York: Cambridge University Press, 2004), 54–7.

[51] D. Howlett, *The English Origins of Old French Literature* (Dublin: Four Courts, 1996), 165.

[52] Thomas, *Les fragments du Roman de Tristan: poème du XIIe siècle*, ed. B. H. Wind (Leiden: E. J. Brill, 1950).

[53] Thomas, *Les fragments*, ed. Wind, 27.

[54] Thomas, *Les fragments*, ed. Wind, 33.

[55] Compare Dees's comment that 'when a medieval text is nearly always an instance of dialect mixture... one may safely conclude that something could be seriously wrong with existing descriptions of Old French', 'Propositions for the Study of Old French and its dialects', in J. Fisiak, ed., *Historical Dialectology: Regional and Social*, Trends in Linguistics, Studies and Monographs, 37 (Berlin: Mouton de Gruyter, 1988), 140.

[56] P. Bennett, 'Le normand, le picard et les koïnés littéraires de l'épopée aux xiie et xiiie siècles', J. Landrecies and A. Petit, eds, *Picard d'hier et d'aujourd'hui, Bien Dire et Bien Aprandre: Revue de Médiévistique*, 21 (Lille: Université Charles-de-Gaule, 2003), 43–56 (44).

example of this tendency: the claims for the stirring and primal Frenchness of this work are rarely explicitly supported by dialectal observation.[57] Noting the importance of England as a source of manuscripts and texts from the earliest layer of French vernacular writing does not mean, however, that one may resort to claiming an 'Englishness' in their production. The cultural and personal exchange between England and the southern reaches of Henry II's Angevin empire indicates how extensively literary and linguistic assumptions travelled in the twelfth century. On the contrary, it is *picard* that turns out to be an early levelling factor in textual production, especially by the thirteenth century.[58] *Picard* is a literary koiné that begins to define the written character of continental French once its 'Norman' features became more markedly associated with insular copying. Given the importance of Arras as a literary centre from the early thirteenth century, as well as the political centrality (and geographical proximity) of the west and north French-speaking regions to England, this is well worth emphasizing.[59] One might add, though, that the designation '*picard*' should itself be taken broadly, since the linguistic (and cultural) borders between *picard, wallon, hainault,* and *artois* (not to mention Anglo-French) are notably fluid.[60] Two main points follow from this discussion. One is the sheer diversity and confusing mixture of linguistic characteristics that are evident across texts in French in the Middle Ages. There is not space here to comment on such other traits that scholars have identified as *breton, champenois, bourgignon, lorrain* and, further south, *gascon* and *catalan.* Yet the larger point is that dialectal variation, implied by these terms, is a treacherous means of identifying or locating either texts or people. Once texts are read in manuscript in an unregularized state, it is remarkable how often they either betray no distinctive dialectal traits at all, or a

[57] See F. Whitehead's airy and unsupported remarks in his edition (Oxford: Blackwell, 1946), xiii (also remarked on by Bennett, 'Le normand, le picard', 45).

[58] For a passage in *picard* from one of the oldest pieces of writing in French, a charter from the very end of the twelfth century composed near Arras, see S. Lusignan, 'Langue française et société du XIIIe au XIVe siècle', in Chaurand, ed., *Nouvelle histoire de la Langue Française*, 93–143 (103). He also gives examples of *wallon* (1236) and *lorrain* (1269).

[59] This view is strongly advocated by Lusignan; see 'Les Langues vernaculaires écrites dans le domaine roman', in M. Goyens and W. Verbeke, eds, *The Dawn of the Written Vernacular in Western Europe* (Leuven: Leuven University Press, 2003), 469–72: 'je retiens que cette région se distinguait du reste de la france par l'ancienneté et la puissance des pouvoirs municipaux. Le picard survécut dans l'aire où s'est affirmé avec le plus de vigueur le pouvoir communal' (472). I am grateful to him for some interesting discussion of this topic on which he is currently engaged in further research.

[60] On Arras, see (with further references) A. Butterfield, *Poetry and Music in Medieval France from Jean Renart to Guillaume de Machaut* (Cambridge: Cambridge University Press, 2002), 133–9 and 151–2; and on its political importance to Anglo-French affairs, Chapter 4 below. Note the complimentary proverb repeated by Machaut in his *La Prise d'Alixandre*: 'je croy quil fu la nez dartois/car il li fu dous et courtois', lines 177–8 (I believe that he had been born in Artois,/For he was kind and courteous to her), *La Prise d'Alixandre (The Taking of Alexandria)*, ed. and trans. R. Barton Palmer (London and New York: Routledge, 2002); J. W. Hassell, *Middle French Proverbs, Sentences and Proverbial Phrases* (Toronto: Pontifical Institute of Mediaeval Studies, 1982), A 196.

chaotic blend of many such traits.[61] There are usually too many variables to confirm whether a language is scribal or authorial. Anglo-French texts are no more or less exempt from these generalities than continental French writings, and the passage between island and continent of manuscripts and people requires us to be constantly vigilant of the possibilities of linguistic interchange.

The second main point concerns standardization. As we have seen, Old French has generally been taken to be far more stable, or to paraphrase Barthes, in a state of the *déjà fixé*, than the evidence permits.[62] Always already fixed, the Strasbourg Oaths, notwithstanding their isolated and hugely uncertain linguistic status, are often hailed as the fountainhead of modern French. To demonstrate this, Brunot helpfully provided six versions of them, five of which (brilliant linguist that he was) he naturally composed himself: in classical Latin, spoken Latin (seventh-century), the text itself, eleventh-century French, Middle French (fifteenth-century), and modern French.[63] But it is not so much that standardization is a chimera, as that we need to attend even more closely if we can to the ways in which writing inevitably has a fixing influence on speech. As a version of speech, writing may not be reliable, and may instead be creating its own independent rules of expression. We can never be sure, in other words, whether a scribe or author is inventing dialectal variation, rather than making a faithful transcription of the sounds people make.[64]

There is, however, a type of evidence that offers some hints of the relationship between dialect and writing. These are the 'textes en jargon franco-anglais' mentioned earlier. Before discussing some examples in the next chapter, it may be interesting to supplement them with a few contemporary comments on continental French dialect that may also serve as an instructive comparison with the comments on Anglo-French collected by Kibbee and others.

It is not hard to find instances of comic regional abuse. Perhaps the most celebrated is that by the Englishman Roger Bacon who wrote the following after a journey around the continent in 1260:

[61] Compare Dees, 'Propositions for the Study of Old French and its dialects', 140, who urges 'It is therefore essential that the text editor, for instance, should remain faithful to the forms found in his manuscript and that the dialectologist should respect scrupulously the absence of homogeneity observable in a certain dialect.'

[62] See I. Short, 'On Bilingualism in Anglo-Norman England', *Romance Philology*, 33 (1979–80), 467–79 (470).

[63] Brunot, *Histoire de la langue française*, 144.

[64] This is to cast the issue in rather different terms from those of such linguists as A. Dees, 'La reconstruction de l'ancien français parlé', in M. E. H. Schouten and P. T. van Reenen, eds, *New Methods in Dialectology* (Dordrecht: Foris, 1989), 125–33 or two interesting papers given respectively by Lodge, 'The sources of standardisation in medieval French: written or spoken?' and D. A. Trotter, 'Witnesses to Spoken Anglo-French? Evidential Problems and Documentary Transmission', paper presented at *Language Over Time: A Symposium On Anglo-Norman In The Context Of Medieval French Language Use*, Birmingham City University, 19 January 2008. However, there seems much potential for future cross-disciplinary discussion of the 'jargon' texts and their relationship to speech and its varied means of representation in the period.

Nam et idiomata ejusdem linguae variantur apud diversos, sicut patet de lingua Gallicana, quae apud Gallicos et Normannos et Picardos et Burgundos multiplici variatur idiomate. Et quod proprie dicitur in idiomate Picardorum horrescit apud Burgundos, immo apud Gallicos viciniores: quanto igitur magis accidet hoc apud linguas diversus?

(*Opus majus*, III, 44)[65]

[For the dialects of a single language vary according to the people, just as in the Gallic language which varies according to the different dialects of the Gallic people, the Normans, Picards, and Burgundians. And what is said properly in the *picard* dialect horrifies the Burgundians, and also even their closest Gallic neighbours: how much more does this risk happening between different languages?]

This has the amused detachment of an observer, and tells us much about the sense of multiple, jostling linguistic worlds that the French-speaking regions conveyed to an interested, and presumably fellow French-speaking, traveller. *Picard* is singled out for its ability to inspire horror in its Burgundian- and Gallican [*françois*]-speaking neighbours: whether this is because it was genuinely despised or a sign of its overweening and hence snubbable importance is perhaps a moot point. *Picard* snubs form a topos in their own right, however, as in the equally well-known chanson by the trouvère Conon de Béthune (*c.*1150–1219 or 1220), 'Mout me semont Amors ke je m'envoise'. Here he complains that:

. . . mon langaige ont blasmé li François
Et mes cançons, oiant les Champenois
Et la Contesse encoir, dont plus me poise.

La Roïne n'a pas fait ke cortoise
Ki me reprist, ele et ses fieus, li Rois
Encoir ne soit ma parole franchoise;
Si la puet on bien entendre en franchois,
Ne chil ne sont bien apris ne cortois,
S'il m'ont repris se j'ai dit mos d'Artois,
Car je ne fui pas norris a Pontoise.

(5–14)[66]

[In the presence of the *champenois*, the Français criticized my manner of speaking and my songs, and so did even the Countess, which pains me all the more. The Queen did not act in a courtly fashion when she rebuked me, neither did her son the King, 'Even if my speech may not be *françois*, it can still be understood in the Ile-de-France, and anybody

[65] *Opus majus*, ed. J. H. Bridges, 2 vols (Oxford, 1897), I, 66; cited in S. Lusignan, *Parler vulgairement : Les Intellectuels et la langue française aux XIIIe et XIVe siècles* (Paris; Montréal: Vrin; Les Presses de l'Université de Montréal, 1986), 68.

[66] This and the following references to Aymon de Varenne, Jean de Meun and Adenet le Roi are all cited in A. François, *Histoire de la langue française cultivée des origines à nos jours*, 3 vols (Geneva: Jullien, 1959), I, 93ff, from Brunot, *Histoire de la langue française*, 329. They form a standard group of examples in linguistic discussion. I cite Conon's lyric from Axel Wallensköld, ed., *Les Chansons de Conon de Béthune*, CFMA (Paris: Champion, 1921), 5.

who may have reproached me for using *artois* dialect is neither well-educated nor courtly, for I was not brought up in the Pontoise'.]

Again, the complaint is not quite what it seems: Conon uses the medium of the song not to be straightforwardly self-deprecating about his 'mos d'Artois' but to accuse the Countess Marie de Champagne, her stepmother queen Alix, second wife of the deceased Louis VII, and her son, Philippe-Auguste, of a lack of courtesy. Moreover, he adds, somewhat slyly, since they can evidently understand his '*franchois*', it is hard to see what the fuss is about. The strong atmosphere of a social in-joke, with the poet creating humour by exposing the snobbery and trumping it with his stubbornly artesian song, offers a glimpse of the regional rivalries that are familiar to any dialectically diverse linguistic community.

A further irony here—although it needs teasing out—is that the chanson genre, modelling itself on the troubadour *canso*, proclaims itself to be the epitome of high style. Conon seems to be playing with an impossibility topos: how could a chanson require reproof for its 'langage'? This too, moreover, is part of a favourite *canso* paradox, that its message is intelligible only to those worthy of its message. He has it both ways, in the end, since although this royal reproof seemed itself to prove the unworthiness of the audience, Conon reminds them that they could of course understand every word.

If this reading is accepted, then the song is evidence not so much of crude social contempt (though that does flicker in the background) but of the poet's subtle, playful interest in the issues of linguistic intelligibility and how they are affected by local variation. The play-off between *picard* and *françois* seems, at least partially, to be a matter of literary versus social cachet. In one of the earliest dated comments, Aymon de Varenne remarks in his romance *Florimont* (1188):

Chanson ne estoire ne plait
As Franceis se il ne l'ont fait.

[neither songs nor stories please those from the Ile-de-France, if they haven't made them themselves.]

Other thirteenth-century references include the ironically over-pitching provincial-turned-metropolitan academic Jean de Meun, in his translation of Boethius's *Consolatio*:

Si m'excuse de mon langage
Rude, malotru et sauvage,
Car nés ne suis pas de Paris

[and I apologise for my crude, maladroit and wild language since I wasn't born in Paris]

and Adenet le Roi (a Brabançon poet), who says, to compliment the French of his patron, Queen Berthe, that one would have thought her born on the 'bourc à Saint-Denis'.

All such incidental remarks remind us that continental French was not the monolith of correctness that it has often been claimed to be from both sides of the water. As soon as Bacon stepped ashore, he heard a clamour of tongues, each noisily asserting pre-eminence. One type of anecdote—the language miracle—is revealing of the attitudes on each side. Three Anglo-French examples, all of twelfth-century figures, are discussed by Ian Short, in which, according to their medieval biographers, the hermit St Godric, the anchorite Wulfric of Haselbury, and the Yorkshire saint John of Beverley, miraculously gain the ability to speak French.[67] Short deduces that Godric 'was incapable of speaking French' and 'it apparently needed nothing short of a miracle for this linguistic deficiency to be remedied.'[68] One might have some qualms about taking this story so directly as evidence of linguistic knowledge, especially since it seems unlikely that after sixteen years spent travelling as a merchant on the continent, including to Jerusalem and Rome as well as France and Spain, Godric would have got by with only English.[69] Short concedes that this kind of miracle story was popular, and indeed it may be compared to another dated 1270 from the continent in which Saint Louis restores speech to a deaf mute. The boy starts speaking not in his local *bourguignon*, but in 'proper' French, 'comme s'il fût né à Saint-Denis' ['as if he had been born in St-Denis'].[70] For Alexis François this story is corroborating proof of the early superiority and incipient centrality of *francien* in the history of the French language. Again, this seems an incautiously literal response. Looking at the two miracles together, it is clear that each sets up a hierarchy of linguistic power. Yet does not this tell us more about image than fact? In each, what strikes me as remarkable is the way a desire for eloquence, to speak beyond the barriers of human limitations of class, education, and physical skill is figured in the ability to speak another language. Language acquisition is itself seen as a source of special status.

As to what it reveals of the language 'on the ground', one might think that the reason why the deaf mute speaks the language of St-Denis is more to do with the royal miracle worker than because *bourguignon* was an incorrect form of French. In other words, he responds in the language that Louis himself speaks. One might also add that the central topos of the miracle is evidently applicable as much to the relationship between *bourguignon* and *françois* as it is to that between English and Anglo-French. The gulfs of understanding and misunderstanding

[67] Actually English as well, and in one case, Cornish and Latin: Short, 'On Bilingualism', 477, n. 40.

[68] Short, 'On Bilingualism', 475.

[69] Compare Allen J. Franzten's comments on the transcription of Caedmon's *Hymn* and the puzzle of why Bede does not provide it in Old English (*Desire for Origins: New Language, Old English, and Teaching the Tradition* (New Brunswick and London: Rutgers University Press, 1990), 137–44, 144–67). Whether or not one agrees with his suggestion that the existing OE version postdates, in fact translates Bede's Latin, it highlights the need to treat the genre of the miracle narrative with care.

[70] François, *Histoire de la langue française*, I, 94. St Louis's death in 1270 and consequent increased cultic status may be another factor in this story.

between one form of speech and another seem to be relative rather than absolute, less to do with modern divisions between language and dialect and more to do with specific circumstances of eloquence and intelligibility.

Looking back at Anglo-French from the continent, the issues of linguistic variation, of multiple and not always mutually comprehensible language use over several regions, have much more in common with the general state of French than is usually implied. Anglo-French does not provide a single story of isolated and gradually degenerating French, but rather follows a pattern of independent growth and fitful development that is very comparable to the numerous dialectal growth patterns of continental French. In the next chapter, we shall try to trace some of these patterns in detail in a selection of works that explicitly make the linguistic borderlands between Anglo-French, French, and English their subject.

3

A Common Language?

'LES TEXTES EN JARGON FRANCO-ANGLAIS'

The intimacy of Anglo-French with continental French, as I have been arguing, makes the description of it as a distinct dialect a delicate matter. There are many reasons for this. For one thing, the sense of geographic particularity, the sense that a language is being spoken in a specific region by people who identify with that region and with each other, is thrown off course by a language that is either mostly known to a ruling community that has newly expanded its control over local populations, or else has the status of a 'langue cultivée', a second language that has a different function from what might loosely be called a 'mother tongue'. For another, and as a consequence, Anglo-French has a special status, especially in the thirteenth and fourteenth centuries, as a language that does not function straightforwardly across the oral–literate divide. Alexis François's careful term 'cultivé' is an effort to signal that neither oral nor literate adequately represents the situation of a language whose powerful administrative function and literary presence compromise its orality yet do not negate it.[1] Although our evidence for the spoken character of Anglo-French is patchy and hard to assess, there are many indications that it was used orally in a variety of contexts throughout the period, by speakers with varying levels of competence and literacy.

My concern in this chapter is nonetheless to turn away from issues of description towards the question of how people interacted across language differences. This involves trying to gain a sense of how people thought about their own language use, what they understood by linguistic barriers, and what significance they attached to them. When they heard one another speak, what did they hear? How did an English speaker of French hear continental French, and how did a continental French speaker hear Anglo-French? As we have seen, this is not unrelated to how a Bourguignon heard a Picard or someone from St-Denis. I am particularly interested in the notion of 'sameness' across these various kinds of French: what did it mean to share the 'same' language? To put it another way, to what extent were people not only aware of differences but intrigued or even troubled by them? Moreover, in a period where fixity in writing and in language use are not necessarily correlated, we

[1] A. François, *Histoire de la langue française cultivée des origines à nos jours*, 3 vols (Geneva: Jullien, 1959), I, xiii.

need to ponder closely the form of what we are reading. How performative is the language of a written text in terms of its potential to express the sound of a language as well as its social and literary significance?

'Les textes en jargon franco-anglais' are of special interest here in being characterized by their citation either of French spoken by 'les Anglais' or (more rarely) English spoken by 'les Français'. A group of writings loosely associated by modern readers, they fall directly into a linguistic minefield located somewhere between Anglo-French, continental French, and English. Compared with other writings in Anglo-French, this is a body of writing which shows a particular self-consciousness about language. This is one reason why I have been drawn to them: we have a rare and explicit insight not just into how vernacular language in the period was viewed, but how people heard each other speak on both sides of the Anglo-French relationship, and how they reacted to what they heard. At the same time, they also raise acute problems of interpretation. I have described them as evidence, and they are probably the closest we are going to get to learning how the French heard the English and the English heard the French in their mutual use of the 'same' language. But they are literary constructs, not works designed to record speech for posterity: they show us what a poet has chosen to fashion as a result of his interest in language, what the vicissitudes of scribal transmission have fortuitously recorded, and what the passage of time has happened to leave undestroyed.

Moreover, they are writings whose aspect has been especially shadowed by modern disciplinary assumptions. Those working in English do not know them, those working in French have taken them as instances of a fairly straightforward continental derision of English French, and those in Anglo-Norman, conceding the derision, have tended to concentrate on other material. In general, then, all sides have tended to see them as evidence of the isolated, risible strangeness of Anglo-French to continental speakers. My effort in this chapter is to re-read some of them and look again at the attitudes towards language that they display. Let me briefly describe the texts. There is only one recent survey, as far as I am aware, by Elisabeth Lalou, apart from the older excellent but lone 1956 study by Peter Rickard.[2] Among the earliest material dating from the late twelfth or early thirteenth century is a fabliau, *Des Deus Anglois et de l'Anel*. Other thirteenth-century material includes a section from *Le Roman de Renart* where Renart disguises himself as a *jongleur*; some parodic charters between the English and the French (one in verse, two in prose);[3] Philippe de Remi's romance *Jehan et Blonde* (probably from the 1230s); Henri d'Andeli's comic *La Bataille des vins*,

[2] E. Lalou, 'Les textes en jargon franco-anglais du XIIe au XIVe siècle', in *La 'France Anglaise' au moyen âge: Actes du 111e Congrès national des sociétés savantes (Poitiers, 1986)* (Paris: Comité des Travaux Historiques et Scientifiques, 1988), 543–62; P. Rickard, *Britain in Medieval French Literature 1100–1500* (Cambridge: Cambridge University Press, 1956).

[3] One, *La Paix aux Anglais*, inspired by the Treaty of Paris in 1259; the others, Edmond Faral conjectures (*Mimes français du XIIIe siècle* [Paris: Champion, 1910]), dated 1264 (between Henry III and Louis IX) and 1299 (between Edward I and Philippe IV).

and some motet texts. From the fourteenth century, jargon occurs in *Pamphile et Galatée* and several *ballades* by Deschamps, followed in the fifteenth by various complaints and *ballades*, and drama: *Le Jeu Saint Loys, La Farce de maistre Pathelin*, not forgetting in due course Shakespeare's *Henry V.* Around and alongside these works is a much wider context of reference back and forth between English and French, and some between French and Scottish.[4] In this chapter I concentrate on some of the thirteenth-century material—three fabliau (or fabliau-like) texts, *Des Deus Anglois et de l'Anel, La Male Honte*, and *Le Roi d'Angleterre et le jongleur d'Ely*—together with a briefer look at *Jehan et Blonde, La Paix aux Anglais*, and a rather strange piece known as *Le Privilège aux Bretons.*

There is a further reason for concentrating on fabliaux. This rather loosely identified genre (there are very few 'fabliau manuscripts' as such) has had an early formative role in modern conceptions of a French literature.[5] Before an awkwardness arose in the nineteenth and twentieth century about the perceived obscenity of a significant minority of them, they were hailed as ambassadors for a national literature. They were edited in their original old French as early as 1756 by Étienne Barbazan; however, it was the popularizing work of Le Grand d'Aussy a few decades later that succeeded in giving fabliaux a role in representing French culture. Le Grand d'Aussy's paraphrases, collected in three volumes, were much more widely read than Barbazan's faithfully edited texts, and gave new impetus to the modern appreciation of medieval literature.[6] For Le Grand d'Aussy it was the very ordinariness of the fabliaux that gave them their representative power. As he said of them: 'ils montrent la Nation en déshabillé' [they show the Nation undressed].[7] The wit of the remark conveys a comic image of pomposity in its underclothing, yet also allows the nation to seem relaxed and at ease and not merely vulnerable or shamed. The connection between nationhood and social nakedness is an interesting one: it inverts a grandiose and abstract sense of nation and brings it face to face (as it were) with 'ordinary' physical experience. Unlike romances, which were bound by a narrow circle of subject-matter, fabliaux ranged more widely: 'ce ne sont point seulement des moeurs générales, ou celles des conditions les plus élevées, qu'ils nous représentent' [it was not only general behaviour that they represented, or that of the nobility]. Like comedy,

[4] See the *Testament du gentil Cossois* (*c.*1499), a mixture of 'franco-écossais' and picard, described by G. Ascoli, *La Grande-Bretagne devant l'opinion française depuis la guerre de cent ans jusqu'à la fin du XVI siècle*, 3 vols (Paris, 1927, 1930; repr. Geneva: Slatkine, 1971), I, 2.

[5] See n. 25 below.

[6] E. [de] Barbazan, *Fabliaux et contes des poëtes françois des xii, xiii, xiv, xves siècles, tirés des meilleurs auteurs*, 3 vols (Paris, Amsterdam 1756). Le Grand d'Aussy, *Fabliaux ou Contes du XIIe et du XIIIe siècle, fables et roman du XIIIe, traduits ou extraits d'après plusieurs Manuscrits...nouvelle édition, augmentée d'une dissertation sur les Troubadours*, 3 vols (Paris: Eugène Onfroy, 1781). See G. Wilson, *A Medievalist in the Eighteenth Century: Le Grand d'Aussy and the 'Fabliaux ou Contes'* (The Hague: Martinus Nijhoff, 1975).

[7] Le Grand d'Aussy, *Fabliaux*, I, lxxii.

their nature was instead to paint 'les actions ordinaires de la vie privée' (lxxii-lxxiii) [the ordinary actions of private (domestic) life].

Lurking in the gentility of this account, however, is a tacit admission that in fact many fabliaux go rather further than this. They do not merely show the ordinary side of life, they famously revel in bodily functions and fantasies. It might seem odd that a genre so renowned for its obscene language should be held up as an example of French national character. Le Grand d'Aussy is however unabashed. Seemingly intent on maintaining his admiration for them at all costs, he goes on to argue that the language is too obscene for it to have signified then in the way that it does now. With a certain historical condescension, he comments that the period was one when language was not yet fully formed, and indecency had not yet attained its modern subtlety. This manoeuvre enables him to recuperate the fabliau as a type of writing that achieves genuine, primordial openness. By a barely acknowledged pun, frankness in language is an illustration of frankness of spirit, and hence of a natural, French (Franc) national outlook.[8] Language in the fabliaux becomes a sign of original free expression. As Howard Bloch has well remarked, 'the fabliaux have offered historically the fantasy of a language of beginnings'.[9]

French editors no longer assert the logic that equates 'frank' and 'Frank'; however, it cannot be said that the desire to claim the fabliaux as French has also disappeared. The remaining embarrassment to this claim consists in the Anglo-Norman fabliau, the very existence of which has proved troubling to an equation of fabliau and Frenchness.[10] Reading the Anglo-Norman fabliau closely for its linguistic abrasions takes us closer to the naked processes of cultural assertion. I argue that these texts reveal that the raw exposure to language that we have come to recognize in the subtle uses of sexual and scatalogical euphemism in the fabliau is common to expressions of 'national' as well as physical identity. There may be a connection, in short, between the openness of fabliau to the tensions between naming and desiring and its capacity as a genre to articulate the visceral relationships between two speakers belonging to an apparently common linguistic heritage.

[8] Compare this memorable comment on their seductive qualities: he likes 'sur-tout cette sorte de bon-hommie d'un narrateur convaincu de ce qu'il vous raconte, & dont l'effet est de séduire, même au milieu des invraisemblances, parce qu'à son ton de franchise il vous paraît incapable de tromper...' (lxix–lxx) [above all this sort of genial character of a narrator convinced of what he is reporting, the effect of which is seductive, even in the midst of what is implausible, because in his frank tone he seems to be incapable of deception].

[9] R. H. Bloch, *The Scandal of the Fabliaux* (Chicago and London: University of Chicago Press, 1986), 8.

[10] See the collection by I. Short and R. Pearcy, eds, *Eighteen Anglo-Norman Fabliaux*, ANTS 14 (London: ANTS, 2000).

RENART JONGLEUR AND VULGAR INVENTION

Perhaps the most immediate characteristic of the jargon is comedy. In *Le Roman de Renart*, for example, the linguistic jokes are set within broad slapstick, trickery, and literary parody. Renart, having escaped being hanged for abduction and serial murder (amongst other misdemeanours) by promising fraudulently to go on a penitential pilgrimage, is now trying to outwit his sworn enemy, Ysengrin. Renart leaps into a vat of yellow dye and emerges with his clothes stained and a new identity as a foreign *jongleur*. In this guise he strikes up conversation with Ysengrin, putting on an exaggerated 'foreign' style of speech full of puns and double entendres.[11] His language has usually been described as 'English': Rickard, for instance, says he is pretending to be an English *jongleur*, and Mario Roques that his 'jargon franco-anglais, conventionnel sans doute, n'est pas arbitraire' since it is linked to the other texts mentioned above.[12] For Rickard and Roques, and especially Edmond Faral, editor of *La Paix aux Anglais* and *Le Privilège aux Bretons*, this is a language marked by its confusion and deformity. John E. Matzke and others of his scholarly generation summarized it as characterized by such features as aphaeresis or loss of the first syllable ('pelez' for 'appelé');[13] vowel differences, principally passage of /y/ to /u/, as suggested by spellings such as *fout* for *fut*;[14] flexibility of gender ('un viel' 2420, 2513, 'bon chançon' 2859, 2911), and some occasional semantic infiltrations from English (such as 'godistonnet', 2440).[15] While this sounds straightforward, as we have seen, Anglo-French and French are not as clearly or consistently distinguished as one might expect. It may be that these dialectal expectations have ridden over some of the complexities of this text and its dramatic representation.

Faral lists the linguistic features of this jargon in terms of their being 'formes barbares . . . impropres and lâches' ['barbarous forms . . . improper and slack']. Generalizing from these details, the very constancy, as he saw it, of the 'principes de déformation' [principles of deformation] in this language are proof that these are not 'bouffonneries tout à fait fantaisistes, conçues par chaque auteur à son gré, mais bien des imitations, dont les procédés sont

[11] *Le Roman de Renart*, ed. Mario Roques, CFMA, 78 (Paris: Champion, 1948), Première branche, lines 2403–612, 2858–3034.

[12] Rickard, *Britain in Medieval French Literature*, 171; *Renart*, ed. Roques, xx.

[13] *Renart*, ed. Roques, 2429, 2468, 2475; *chatera* for 'achatera' *Des deus anglois*, lines 41, 85.

[14] *Renart*, ed. Roques, 2424, 2429, 2468, 2475, 2565; foustes, *Des deus anglois*, line 16.

[15] 'mi'haue / mi'aue', *Des deus anglois*, lines 19, 20. For a fuller list see T. B. W. Reid, ed., *Twelve Fabliaux from MS f.fr.19152 of the Bibliothèque Nationale* (Manchester: Manchester University Press, 1958), 102f., and two older studies: J. E. Matzke, 'Some Examples of French as Spoken by Englishmen in Old French Literature', in *Modern Philology*, 3 (1905–6), 47–60 (53–60), and H. Albert, *Mittelalterlicher englisch-französischer Jargon*, Studien zur englischen Philologie, 63 (Halle: M. Niemeyer, 1922). All these should be considered in need of fundamental revision, a task not claimed by Ian Short's recent *Manual of Anglo-Norman* (London: ANTS, 2007).

constants . . . elles exprimaient . . . la réalité, et reproduisaient avec exactitude les particularités du français parlé en Angleterre' [fantastic farces, conceived by each author to his own liking, but in fact imitations, which follow consistent procedures . . . they express . . . reality, and reproduce exactly the particular characteristics of the French spoken in England].[16]

There are several issues here. One is whether this is 'English' as such. When asked by Ysengrin where he comes from, Renart is characteristically slippery:

dom estes vos? de quel païs?
vos ne futes pas nez de France
ne de la nostre connoissance.
– Naie, seignor, mes de Bretaing,
s'avra tot perdu mon gaaing
et fot cerchié par men conpaing,
ne trover neant que m'ansaing.
Toute France et tote Angleter
Fout cerchié por mon conpaing quer;
si voil Paris torner ainçois,
tant avrai mout bien pris françois.

(V.2406–16)

[Where are you from? From which region?
You weren't born in the Île de France
Nor from any other place I know.
'No, Sir,' but from Bretagne,
And was being sought by my friend,
And he will soon have lost everything gained by me,
Nor to find anything which might inform me.
All of France and all of England was sought
In order to find my friend.
But I am now going to turn towards Paris as
I will have learnt French very well there.][17]

He does not in fact claim to be from England but from Bretagne, and follows this up with a snarl of 'aaing' rhymes. English words (as I have just noted) are certainly sprinkled here and there: his first word in his new yellow garb is: 'Godehere' (2403) and a little later he says 'godistonnet' (2440) and 'iai' (2418, 2440, 2577). But the 'aaing' rhymes find an exact counterpart in a text satirising Bretons, called *Le Privilège aux Bretons*:[18]

[16] *La Paix aux Anglais*, in *Mimes*, ed. Faral, 39.

[17] In this and the following translations of the *jargon* texts, it should be pointed out that the complex linguistic play with sense and nonsense, dialect, and pronunciation makes these texts not only hard, but at times impossible to translate into 'correct' English. For example the 'aing' rhymes only work through substituting nominative for oblique in 'men conpaing', and aphaetic 'pris' for 'appris' could be taken (perhaps wrongly) as an erroneous use of 'prendre'. I am very grateful to Daron Burrows for generously offered advice; he is not responsible, however, for any errors or other shortcomings.

[18] *Mimes*, ed. Faral, 13–28.

Soiez en pais au mal eür,
Que vous aurez mal aventur
Comment qu'il praing!
Par saint Lagado de Bretaing,
Vous serez mis en .I. longaing,
Se plus fet meslé la compaing.

(101–4)

Be in peace, curses on you
that you will have misfortune
Whatever takes place!
By Saint Lagado of Bretagne
You will be put in a latrine,
If the crowd keeps making a riot

The joke in both cases seems to me to be caught up in the sense of an auto-rhyme: the identifying name of a people or a form of speech generates their very distinctiveness. A 'Bretaing' sounds 'bretaing': just to utter the name is to take on that identity. Yet the placing of this sound as a rhyme also displays the ease and versatility of poetry as a medium for expressing identity: we can rhyme our way in and out of identities just by performing the poem.

But to describe Renart as a Breton *jongleur* would be as misleading as to call him English. The association of Breton with English is full of intriguing implications: historically the Celtic links between the two give them important family ties. Perhaps the point is rather that Renart, in trying out a foreign persona, chooses to employ the half-concealing, half-revealing disguise of a French that is not quite French, but is not quite anything else either. Anglo-French functions not as a straightforward target for linguistic contempt, but as a type of language that has the potential to stand apart from *and* within French. One of the hilarious aspects of his speech is the play on the word 'foutre': drily described by Roques as 'l'extension de l'auxiliare *être*, sous la forme *fout*, à l'actif comme au passif' [the extension of the auxiliary *être* under the form *fout*, in the active as well as passive], Renart is speaking something more like the Skinhead Hamlet:

ACT I SCENE I
The battlements of Elsinore Castle.
Enter HAMLET, followed by GHOST.

GHOST : Oi! Mush!
HAMLET: Yer?
GHOST : I was fucked!
(Exit GHOST.)
HAMLET: O Fuck
(Exit HAMLET.)[19]

[19] R. Curtis, 'The Skinhead Hamlet', in S. Brett, ed., *The Faber Book of Parodies* (London: Faber, 1984), 316–20.

The parallel is not quite exact since all the characters in the Skinhead Hamlet speak the same (concisely honed) language: the humour and cleverness of the twelfth-century French dialogue depend on the slipperiness of the intra-lingual puns, on the way the vulgarisms sound through the faux Anglo-Breton pronunciation, and only to those willing or able to hear them.

The remarkable literal mindedness on the part of the great French editor seems to miss some tricks. A comic performance in dialect or one that satirizes an accent or social class depicts not so much how people speak, but how they are heard to speak. It deals, in short, with stereotypes and the fine line between parody and mimicry. That the jargon in *Renart* is produced by a *jongleur* gives further pause. Renart the fox's invented language is the by-product of his invention of himself as a *jongleur*: the implication is that poetry involves inventing language, and that this may not always be distinguishable from parodying or mimicking someone else's. Perhaps also, since he is a fake *jongleur*, we are meant to realize that he is also speaking a fake language: the situation suggests not that Renart is trying faithfully to reproduce a form of speech, but that he is trying to confuse the wolf by bombarding him with an unstable, elusive language, full of traps of meaning and pits of incomprehension.

The jargon spoken by *Renart jongleur* draws attention to the paradox of the French being parodied: what one might call the Anglo-French condition. In other words, these texts set up/ present the paradox of a language that is both the same and different. The texts appear to work across a clear cultural boundary—between English and French—yet when they are considered in more detail, the sense of cultural difference that they present is much more shifting and complex. That means not that *Renart jongleur* speaks Anglo-French, but that the language he speaks shows that Anglo-French is French and is not French. It is French in the sense that it is not English or Latin, but it is not French because as yet there is no such thing as French. The normative concept of French—as Derrida puts it 'tout ce lexique de l'avoir, de l'habitude, de la possession d'une langue' [this entire vocabulary of having, habit, and possession of a language] is not already there, but is in the process of being created, in part by the texts themselves.[20]

[20] J. Derrida, *Le monolinguisme de l'autre ou la prothèse d'origine* (Paris: Galilée, 1996), 44. I cite from the translation by P. Mensah, *Monolingualism of the Other; or, The Prosthesis of Origin* (Stanford: Stanford University Press, 1996), 22.

JEHAN ET BLONDE: POSSESSING LANGUAGE

Philippe de Remi's romance *Jehan et Blonde*, as well known as *Le Roman de Renart* for its use of jargon, has similarly been held up as a 'textbook' example of French mockery of Anglo-French. In brief, Jehan seeks honour in England, meets the French-speaking Earl of Oxford and his retinue, and so impresses him that he is invited to become a squire in the Earl's household. He falls in love with the Earl's daughter Blonde, and improves her French and that of her ladies, until he is called back to France to deal with his patrimony. In the meantime, the Countess of Oxford dies and Blonde is betrothed to the rich Earl of Gloucester. In an encounter which parallels his first meeting with the Earl of Oxford, Jehan, now back in England, runs into Gloucester. The Earl speaks in fractured French; Jehan replies in riddles. An armed struggle over Blonde is won, naturally, by Jehan. He now takes her to France, to the distress of her father. Yet, hearing that he has been ennobled by the French king, the Earl of Oxford is reconciled, and decides to come to live with them in France. Jehan and Blonde have four children; after two years they visit their lands in Oxford. The Earl lives on for ten years; Jehan then becomes Earl of Oxford for thirty years.

Even from this quick summary, it is clear that this story passes back and forth across the Channel in interesting and rather convoluted ways. The two male protagonists end by swapping places: the Earl of Oxford removes to France, Jehan becomes 'English'. Most commentators have focused on the sections where the Earl of Gloucester speaks garbled French:[21]

> Jehans premiers le salua
> Et Jehan tost respondu a:
> 'Amis, bien fustes vous vené,
> Coment fu vostre non pelé?'
> – Sire, dist il, j'ai non Gautier,
> Je sui nes devers Mondidier.
> – Gautier? Diable, ce fu non sot!
> Et ou vole vous aler tot?
> Cil varlet fou il vostre gent,
> Cui fu monté seul cheval gent?
> – Oïl voir, sire, il est à moi,
> Il me garde ce palefroy.
> – Voel le vous vendre? Je cater,
> Si vos vol à raison donner.
> Il fout mout bel prende deniers.
> – Sire, jel vendrai volentiers,

[21] For discussion of these features, see H. Suchier, ed., *Oeuvres poétiques de Philippe de Remi, sire de Beaumanoir*, 2 vols, SATF (Paris: Didot, 1884–5), II, 415–20. I have reservations, however, about his notion of error.

Fait Jehans, car marcheans sui.
Se vous volés avoir cestui,
Prendre volrai de vostre avoir
Itant com j'en vaurrai avoir.
Autrement point n'en venderai.
– Nai! par la goisse Biu, nai, nai!
Quo deble, ce sera trop chere,
En vous a bone sote entere!
N'en voelle plus, tiene vous pes.
– Sire, dist il, je n'en puis mais.
(2637–62)

[John greets him first,
And he has quickly answered John:
'Friend, well be you come!
How was your name call?
'Sir,' he said, 'my name is Walter;
I was born near Montdidier.'
'Walter! Devil! That was foolish name.
And where you want to go soon?
The lad was he your people,
Who was mounted on good horse?'
'Yes, sir, he is in my service.
He keeps that palfrey for me.'
'Want it you to sell? I buy,
If you want to give reasonable.
It be very good take money.'
'Sir, I shall sell it gladly,'
Says John, 'for I am a merchant.
If you wish to have this one,
I shall wish to take of your possessions
As much as I want.
Otherwise, I shall not sell a bit of it.'
'Nay, by crown of God, nay, nay!
What the Devil! This will be too dear.
In you is good, complete fool.
I no want it more, you keep quiet.'
'Sir,' said John, 'I can no more.'[22]

The important thing about this characterization is that it is not of the English in general, but of the villain of the piece (like baddies with cut-glass English accents

[22] I cite the text from the edn by S. Lécuyer, CFMA, 107 (Paris: Champion,1999) and translation (with different lineation) from P. de Remi, *Jehan et Blonde, Poems, and Songs, edited from Paris BnF fr. 1588, Paris BnF fr. 24006, and Paris BnF fr. 837 by B. N. Sargent-Baur,* Faux Titre, Etudes de langue et littérature françaises publiées, no. 201 (Amsterdam and Atlanta: Rodopi, 2001), lines 2631–62.

in American films). And again it seems to me that the directions of the satire are a more subtle and volatile matter than linguistic rivalry. Jehan and Gloucester no sooner see each other than they immediately enter into the language of commercial exchange; Gloucester wants to buy Jehan's palfrey. With an easy and mocking irony available to the audience though not to Gloucester Jehan sets the terms of a deal impossibly high, implicitly Blonde herself. In short, the poet swiftly uses the encounter to mark the central act of cultural exchange conveyed by the plot: Jehan's successful winning of Gloucester's fiancée. Philippe de Remi underlines the cultural struggle with the following couplet:

> Si vaut à lui parler françois,
> Mais sa langue torne en Englois.
>
> (2623–4)
>
> [And so he wanted to speak French to him
> But his language turns into English.][23]

The jargon is representational: it expresses the kind of bartering that was a measure of cross-channel self-esteem, in this text a kind of tug of war over a female prize in which both sides turn out to be evenly matched. *Jehan et Blonde* does not merely convey an image of Anglo-French, it is inventing a language that functions as a third language that is neither Anglo-French nor continental French. This language is almost incomprehensible; it verges on the opaque. There are not just the fairly common features of spelling and apocope—Gloucester's syntax is also truncated and simplistic to the point of stupidity.[24]

In turning now to the shorter narratives *Des Deus Anglois et de l'Anel, La Male Honte,* and *Le Roi d'Angleterre et le jongleur d'Ely,* we find that they offer further tantalizing 'evidence' of the variable cultural assumptions about what is 'English' and 'French' in the thirteenth century. We can see this partly by studying their manuscript forms, and how carefully matters of pronunciation are conveyed through spelling as well as thematic humour. I argue, in the case of *Des Deus Anglois,* that it does seem interested in a notion of phonetic accuracy as reflected by continental French orthography, but that the author makes play with this to disrupt his audience's sense of linguistic identity.

The complexity of the notion of possession is well illustrated first of all by considering matters of provenance and audience: can we tell for whom a franco-anglais text was written? *Des Deus Anglois et de l'Anel, La Male Honte,* and *Le Roi d'Angleterre et le jongleur d'Ely,* texts that range in date from the twelfth or

[23] 'Vaut' here is pret.3 of 'voloir', and not ind.pr.3 of 'valoir'. 'Torne' is ambiguous: it could also mean 'he turns it into English'.

[24] The translation by Barbara Sargent-Baur (though it sometimes paraphrases and avoids the more obscene jokes and puns) is a brave and lively attempt to convey in exaggerated Pidgin English the flavour of the Earl's speech. The linguistic jokes in this *roman* are well worth an extended study, which I cannot give here.

thirteenth centuries to the early fourteenth century, all have plots which concern the English and the French, yet each is a separate illustration of the complexity of deciding the nature and extent of the cultural boundary implied by these categories.[25] They also present different vantage points from which these cultural differences were viewed. One kind of evidence is that provided by the manuscripts. *Des Deus Anglois et de l'Anel* survives in a single continental copy, the collection in Paris BnF fr.19152.[26] We can reasonably conclude (in the absence of any other external evidence) that its description of two Englishmen whose pronunciation of the word 'agnel' creates comic confusion is made from a continental point of view. The case of *La Male Honte*, however, is less clear-cut. This narrative exists in two versions; one attributed to 'Guillaume', which survives in three copies, the other to Hues de Cambrai, which survives in a further three.[27] All six manuscripts are continental in provenance; however, the differences between the copies, in particular the varying endings, alongside the two attributions make the specific satiric directions of the text hard to unravel. Finally, *Le Roi d'Angleterre et le jongleur d'Ely* occurs uniquely in the English manuscript London British Library MS Harley 2253 yet derives from a work called *Le Riote du Monde* that has a long history in both continental French and Anglo-Norman, of versions written in prose as well as verse.[28]

[25] The history of the modern editing of fabliaux reveals much uncertainty over the definition of the genre. The latest ten-volume monumental edition, by Willem Noomen and the late Nico van den Boogaard, of which the last volume appeared in 1998 [*Nouveau Recueil complet des fabliaux* (hereafter *NRCF*), 10 vols (Assen: Van Gorcum, 1983–98)], reduces the corpus of 160 listed by P. Nykrog [*Les fabliaux* (Geneva: Droz, 1973), index, 311–24] down to 127. For a concise survey of the extensive scholarship on these problematic questions of genre, see D. Burrows, *The Stereotype of the Priest in the Old French Fabliaux: Anticlerical Satire and Lay Identity* (Bern: Peter Lang, 2005), 31–40. No single manuscript contains only fabliaux: there are five compilations in which twenty or more of these short narratives occur amongst other material (Paris, BnF fr.837; Bern, Burgerbibliothek 354; Berlin, Staatsbibliothek-Preußischer Kulturbesitz (Haus 1), Hamilton 257; BnF fr.19152; and BnF fr.1593). For further discussion, see K. Busby, *Codex and Context: Reading Old French Verse Narrative in Manuscript*, 2 vols (Amsterdam and New York: Rodopi, 2002), I, 437–63; and A. Butterfield, 'English, French and Anglo-French: Language and Nation in the fabliau', Special Issue of *Zeitschrift für deutsche Philologie*: '*Mittelalterliche Novellistik im europaïschen Kontext*' ed. M. Chinca, T. Reuvekamp-Felber, and C. Young (Berlin: Erich Schmidt, 2006), 238–59.

[26] For a convenient inventory of fabliaux and their manuscript sources, see Nykrog, *Les fabliaux*, index, as above; and more recently *NRCF*, X, xvii–xxii. BnF fr. 19152 is presented in facsimile by E. Faral, *Le Manuscrit 19152 du fonds français de la bibliothèque nationale. Reproduction phototypique publiée avec une introduction* (Paris: Droz, 1934). For discussion of the manuscript in the context of the other main fabliau compilations, see Busby, *Codex and Context*, I, 451–5.

[27] There has been some debate about the identity of the two authors: see *NRCF*, V, 87f. The six manuscripts, in their two groups, are: version I (Guillaume): D (BnF fr. 19152), K (BnF fr. 2173), and l (Cologny-Genève, Bodmer 113); version II (Hues de Cambrai): A (BnF fr. 837), B (Bern 354) and F (BnF fr. 12603).

[28] See J. Ulrich ed., '*La Riote du monde*', *Zeitschrift für romanische Philologie*, 8 (1884), 275–89; and B. Nolan, 'Anthologizing Ribaldry: Five Anglo-Norman Fabliaux', in S. Fein, ed., *Studies in the Harley Manuscript: The Scribes, Contents, and Social Contexts of British Library MS Harley 2253*, (Kalamazoo: Western Michigan University, Medieval Institute Publications, 2000), 289–327 (298, n. 19).

Thus although we might expect the manuscript provenance of these texts to help clarify their cultural geography, we find that it is but a starting point. Even if we know a manuscript has been copied on the continent, that knowledge takes us only a small way towards deducing the cultural attitude of its author or audience. These three texts turn out to have a particularly interesting bearing on the kinds of signals modern readers conventionally look for, or expect to find, in writings on nation. The different stories of (surviving) manuscript provenance in each remind us that a work can be Anglo-French in setting, yet continental French in audience (*La Male Honte*); or continental French in the telling, yet Anglo-French as well as continental French in audience (*La Male Honte*); continental French in the telling and hearing, yet Anglo-French in the plot (*Des Deus Anglois*); or again a work in which a memory of Anglo-French meanings might be refracted through a revised continental text aimed at an Anglo-French audience (*Le Roi d'Angleterre*). Rather than present clearly contrasting 'national' perspectives, these particular texts show the identity of Anglo-French to have a varied and entangled relationship with continental authors, copyists, and audiences, to the extent that the boundary between the two cultures becomes less certain.

DES DEUS ANGLOIS ET DE L'ANEL: 'LA LANGUE TORNE A ENGLOIS'

The little fabliau *Des Deus Anglois et de l'Anel* is a case in point. Apparently a fairly simple tale of a tourist phrase-book howler, it tells of two Englishmen, presumed to be travelling abroad in France. One falls ill; as he starts to recover his appetite he begs his friend Alein to buy him '.i. anel cras' (line 26) [a fat lamb/ass].[29] Alein tries to oblige, and asks for one in a nearby town 'au' mielz qu'il onques pot parler' (line 35) [as well as he ever was able to speak]. The 'preudons' gives him an 'anel', and Alein duly roasts it for his friend. Having eaten a leg with relish, the friend notices that it is much larger than he expected. Suspecting the mistake, he makes Alein show him the skin, hooves, and head of the beast: the ears and the muzzle clinch his realization that he has just eaten an ass rather than a lamb. They laugh, and, suddenly distancing himself from the author, the narrator comments that according to the person who composed the fabliau it did not seem to have done the 'Anglois' any lasting harm.[30]

[29] The text is cited from the *Texte diplomatique* in *NCRF*, VIII, no. 90, 176–77, lines 1–2. Editorial expansion of the scribal abbreviations is indicated by underlining.

[30] Daniel Karlin cites the wonderful example in the reverse direction of Hippolyte Taine who, when he asked for potatoes in England, got buttered toast (*Proust's English* (Oxford: Oxford University Press, 2005), 131, n. 22).

Ostensibly, then, it is a story of mispronunciation: the English have trouble with the gn sound (palatal *n*) in 'agnel'. Yet through rhyme and spelling, the poet makes clever play with the expectations of the audience: we are not sure until the end how to understand the joke, since it depends both on how the word 'anel' is pronounced by the narrator, and on how we hear it and read it. The first two lines go as follows:

> Un fableau uos uueil aconter
> De .ii. anglois sanz mesconter.
>
> (1–2)
>
> [I want to narrate to you without misnarrating it a fabliau
> Of two Englishmen.]

Des Deus Anglois has not received very much notice, and the few references that exist are somewhat dismissive.[31] However, a closer reading suggests it may have unremarked subtleties. Like the *Renart jongleur* and *Jehan et Blonde* passages, it seems a straightforward satire of English pronunciation of French; yet the process of reading the story soon reveals subtleties in its linguistic banter. The wit of the opening coupling ('aconter-mesconter'), as the audience grasps on a second hearing, comprises more than a narrowly chauvinistic joke. The plot is going to turn on a linguistic mistake caused by the deceptive similarity between two French words: 'agnel' (lamb) and 'asnel' (ass). The point about this latter pair of words, however, is that they do not fully rhyme in northern continental French (except by mistake): by starting his text with a pair of words ('aconter-mesconter') that make a mistake in a good rhyme the author is thus drawing attention, in homophonic French, to the clash of sounds, and of meanings, to come. In doing so, he shows that the game of telling, through language, is double-edged. He himself wants 'aconter' [to recount] not 'mesconter' [to mistell, miscalculate, deceive]: however, in order to render the mistakes to come, he will have to mistell. Telling this tale properly will necessarily involve telling it improperly. The author, in short, is implicated in the process of linguistic error: the rhyme 'aconter-mesconter' cleverly encapsulates this by articulating the art of mistelling so correctly.

As the tale proceeds, it becomes clear that mistelling also involves misspelling. Yet in its form as a medieval text, that is, a text produced in conditions of textual instability, the work becomes entangled in certain ironies of representation. The notion of a 'correct' spelling for a medieval text is often more vivid for a modern than it is for a medieval editor. This text invites the reader to wonder, during the

[31] For example, Anne E. Cobby sees it—in contrast to *La Male Honte*—as 'presenting no more than a joke which is neither subtle nor particularly funny' ('Understanding and Misunderstanding in *La Male Honte*', in G. Jondorf and D. N. Dumville, eds, *France and the British Isles in the Middle Ages and Renaissance: Essays in Memory of Ruth Morgan* (Woodbridge: Boydell, 1991), 155–72 (156). See also Rickard, *Britain in Medieval French Literature*, 172–3.

course of reading, whether its misspellings have been spelled correctly. This comes particularly—and ironically—to the fore in a story that concerns the relationship between spelling and pronouncing. Ostensibly, one reason why the 'anglois' is given an ass rather than a lamb by the butcher is that (from the butcher's perspective) he mispronounces the sound represented by *gn* (an *n mouillé*): we might think then that one way for the author to show this would be to make a consistent difference in the spelling of his use of the word compared to that of the continental French speakers in the poem (including, presumably, the narrator). In fact, it turns out that the distinction between 'agnel' and 'anel' seems to be a much less clear-cut (but no less intriguing) matter in the orthography of the narrative.[32]

It is worth following this through the poem as a whole (this very short story is only 116 lines long). We find that 'anel / 'asnel' / 'ainel' becomes a leitmotif: altogether there are thirteen occurrences, along with single instances of 'ainelet' (101), 'anesse' (109), and 'asnon' (110). The author builds up gradually: the word first appears in line 26, with only three more in the next sixty lines, but then there is a flurry of seven utterances in ten lines (82–92), and the piece finishes with another few, including one in the penultimate couplet. Nine out of the thirteen are spelled 'anel';[33] it is spelled 'asnel' and 'ainel' just twice in each case. Not once is 'anel' spelled with a *gn*.[34] The heart of the piece, and its comic linguistic nexus, is marked by this rapid exchange between the two 'anglois':

Quel beste m'as tu ci' porté?'
Anel fait il en charité
Anel fait il por seint almon
Cestui n'est mie filz moton
Si'est por ané ge chatai
Tot de plus grant que'ge gardai
Anel deable uoirement
Jl sanble char de uiel jument
Se fu asnel que ge uoi'ci
Ainz fu anel uostre merci
Se tu ne croiz que fout anel
Mi uos ira mostrer de pel.[35]

[32] Since only one manuscript survives of this text it is (a perhaps deceptively) easy matter to check its orthography. My comments are based on the manuscript facsimile, checked against the diplomatic edition in *NCRF*, and predicated on the assumption that it represents a choice, at least in terms of this particular version of the text, on the part of either the scribe or the author.

[33] 'Anel' occurs in lines 26, 40, 64, 82, 83, 87, 90, 91; 'asnel' in lines 89 and 114; and 'ainel' in 59 and 100. In one case, in line 85, the scribe gives *ané*.

[34] Although it is perhaps possible that the use of *i* in *ainel* (lines 59, 100) and *ainelet* (line 101) could be regarded as equivalent to *gn* in terms of being an indication of palatization, this would be very unusual. I am grateful to Olivier Collet for his discussion of this point.

[35] *NCRF*, VIII, no. 90, *Texte diplomatique*, 177, lines 81–92.

[What animal have you brought me here?
- 'An anel, he said, 'for goodness sake.'
- 'A anel?', he said by saint Almon,
- 'This isn't the son of a sheep!'
'Yes it is! I bought the
biggest anel that I ever saw'.
'An anel! By the Devil, truthfully
It seems to be the flesh of a young horse.
This is an ass that I see here.'
'But it was a lamb by your mercy.
If you don't believe it [fucking] was a lamb
I will show you the skin.]

To appreciate this passage we need to go back a little. The language of the two 'Anglois' is given in a different form from the narrator's 'français'.[36] Willem Noomen and Nico van den Boogard take the view that there is a clear difference and hierarchy between the two kinds of French. They describe Alain's Anglo-French with traditional contempt as 'un français défectueux et déformé par son accent anglais' [a defective French deformed by his English accent].[37] Yet the text is not so categoric. The various spellings of 'anel' / 'asnel' / 'ainel' are a case in point. According to Reid, the spelling 'anel' is a representation of an English pronunciation of 'agnel'.[38] However, Reid also gives 'anel' as an alternative spelling for 'asnel'.[39] Moreover, when the narrator describes the butcher handing over the meat, he uses the spelling 'anel' once more: 'Deuant l'anglois a mis l'anel' [he put the lamb/ass in front of the Englishman].[40] This is followed by 'normal' *françois* spellings such as 'acheter': 'Si le'uendi cil l'achata' (line 65). It seems possible that in fact the word is largely being presented in a studiedly neutral way, where it could be reasonably understood either as 'asnel' or as 'agnel'. Only at the end, where the joke is brought to the surface in the above passage of dialogue, does the spelling 'asnel' come into play to make it clear to

[36] The language of the main part of the text has hardly any distinguishing dialectal features (which is interesting in itself). Reid, for instance, describes it simply as 'Northern' (*Twelve Fabliaux*, 102). Fr. 19152 in general has very variable spelling, and Faral comments that determining the language of the scribe from the texts would be a delicate and deceptive task, *Le Manuscrit 19152*, 12.

[37] *NRCF*, VIII, 174.

[38] Reid, ed., *Twelve Fabliaux* Glossary, 125–6.

[39] Orthographical practice, and how it relates to dialect, is difficult to disentangle here. The spelling 'anel' is not once instanced for 'asnel' in the standard Old French dictionaries (TL; F. Godefroy, *Dictionnaire de l'ancienne langue française, et de tous ses dialectes du IXe au XVe siècle*, 10 vols, (Paris: F. Vieweg, 1881–1902 [1826–97]); and E. Littré, *Dictionnaire de la langue française*, 7 vols (Paris: J. J. Pauvert, 1956–8). In *AND*[2], however, *ane*, *anne*, and *aune* are attested for *asne*; extension of this to the diminutive is feasible. Reid's suggestion that *anel* is a variant of 'asnel' makes sense of the desire of this poet to use orthography creatively to convey cultural difference. See also B. Cerquiglini, *Le Roman de l'orthographe: au paradis des mots, avant la faute 1150–1694* (Paris: Hatier, 1996), 40, who happens to choose the example of *asinum* > *ane* to discuss orthographic change.

[40] *NCRF*, VIII, no. 90, *Texte diplomatique*, 176, line 64.

Alein that the animal he had been given was indeed an ass. Rather than merely chauvinistically mocking the French of the English, the author takes the more sophisticated route of showing language (and not only the 'Anglois') as open to such confusions. To enjoy the confusion, the reader, too, needs to be fooled by the spelling: when the joke is spelled out it is for the benefit of the external as well as the internal audience.

The joke has further layers. For the above passage to work orally as well as literally, the 'anglais' must try to say 'asnel' as well as 'anel', that is, in a way that sounds different. The author enjoys playing with this doubtful boundary.[41] The passage starts with a mock repetition: 'Anel fait il en charité / Anel fait il por seint almon'.[42] Are these two parallel phrases from two separate speakers pronounced the same or differently? The next time the word comes at the start of a line: 'Anel deable uoirement' (line 87) it is followed up with 'asnel' but this time the same speaker utters both:

Anel deable uoirement
Jl sanble char de uiel jument
Se fu asnel que ge uoi'ci
(lines 87–9).

But even this is not enough to make the distinction crystal clear. Although 'anel' is repeated almost to the point of meaninglessness in this short piece of dialogue, Alein does not fully grasp the point until the exchange of sounds has become truly meaningless:

Cestui n'est mie filz behé
Quoi dites uos alein que est
Ce ne fu mie fielz brebis
Tu'dites uoir par seint felix
Foi que ge doi a'seint iohan
Cestui fu filz ihan ihan
Encor fu d'anesse en maison
Et ge uos porté ci d'asnon
(lines 103–10).

['This thing isn't the son of a baa-baa.
What do you say, Alain? What is it?

[41] The question of whether this preconsonantal *s* would have been pronounced is tricky since the date of this poem is not known, but on the assumption that it is late twelfth or thirteenth century then it would not. Cf. Gaston Zink, *Phonétique historique du français* (Paris: PUF, 1986), 122–3, and Cerquiglini, *Le Roman de l'orthographe*, 36–41. The specific use of 'asnel' twice in the poem appears to be a matter of the scribe (or poet) choosing to use a conservative orthography to make a literal point.

[42] *NCRF*, VIII, no. 90, *Texte diplomatique*, 177, lines 82–3. This couplet is further paralleled in the rest of the poem by two separate lines beginning *Alein fait il* (lines 16, 98). For the argument that the author is playing on the similarity in sound between *Anel* and *Alein*, see below.

This was not the son of a ewe.'
"You are right, by saint Felix,
By the faith I owe to saint John
This was the son of a hee-haw
There was still a female ass in the house
And I brought an ass to you here]

Of course, the most obvious source of comedy here is that the two Englishmen have been reduced to making animal noises in order to understand each other. But the simple comedy runs alongside a larger, more intricate kind of humour about language, difference, and nation. Rather than show linguistic confusion as applying only in one direction, the author explores it along several fronts. Thus although considerable capital is made out of the scoffing reaction of the butcher to Alein's gibbering request ('Que uas tu fait il fastroillant / Ge'ne sai quel malfez tu diz', 176, lines 48f. [what are you doing, he said, garbling/ I don't know what rubbish you are talking]), the fact that the two Englishmen also seem to have trouble understanding each other shows how even within the same linguistic context language is not fully transparent. The reduction of the exchange between them to 'pure' sound, moreover, alerts us to the arbitrary character of signification. This is not just a matter of how the English speak, but of how people register the differences between languages. What makes this little fabliau anecdote so remarkable is that it plays with the process of recording speech in writing in such a way as to render both the subtle differences of pronunciation themselves and more than one perception of those differences.[43]

The fine line between these ways of speaking is most strikingly exhibited in the butcher's subsequent comment: 'Es'tu auuergnaz ou'tiois' (line 51) [are you from the Auvergne or a *tiois*?]. His prejudice, on hearing Alein speak, is not that he is English but rather from the Auvergne or else a German speaker.[44] This is interesting both because it seems to indicate that the category 'Anglois' was not as immediately characterizable as the fabliau likes to pretend, and because the first assumption of foreignness for this northern 'French' butcher is an area under the suzerainty of his own king.[45] We are also reminded of Victor Hugo's silent

[43] One loose thread, perhaps, concerns the misunderstandings between the two Englishmen. It is possible, for example, to interpret Alein as originally understanding his friend to ask him to buy an 'ass' rather than a 'lamb': in this case the mistake would be the friend's rather than the butcher's. In my view, the joke makes better sense if the butcher misunderstands Alein's pronunciation. But the very fact that alternative interpretations are possible bears out the playful socio-linguistic confusions of the tale.

[44] *Tiois*, 'German', can contrast with *Alemans* to mean 'North German', and in the North East it can refer specifically to 'Low German' (a broad category which includes Low Frankish and Dutch or Flemish). I am grateful to Mark Chinca, Christopher Young, and Janet van der Meulen for advice on this point.

[45] The issue of what *Anglois* means in relation to *Auvergnat* is however not easy to resolve in the twelfth and thirteenth centuries since Auvergne changed hands several times between English/ Angevin and French rulers. It was ceded to Philippe II in 1189 on the death of Henry II (who had

humour about the old Alsatian teacher who thought himself more French than the Jersiais he was trying to teach, but whose thick accent made him hard to understand.

There is a remarkable visual parallel to the linguistic comedy of confusion in this little fabliau. It occurs much later in illustrations of the story of Polycrates (Book 4, chapter 7) in some fifteenth-century manuscripts of Laurent de Premierfait's translation of Boccaccio's *De casibus*. Polycrates throws his ring into the water as a way of appeasing Fortune. The ring is swallowed by a fish which is then caught and the ring returned to king. In two manuscripts the fish and the ring are unambiguously depicted;[46] but in a copy owned by Girard Blanchet, the fish is shown on the riverbank with a lamb clambering out of its mouth.[47] The hilarious incongruity of this image raises many questions. Presumably, as Meiss first suggested, the illuminator misread *anel/asnel* for *annel* in the directions he was given for the pictures, or else perhaps the wrong word was copied down in the first place. Mistakes of course do happen; nonetheless it seems an astonishing example of blindly followed instructions, and it is tempting instead to credit the artist with a sense of humour. The extravagant visual difference between a lamb and a ring comically overwhelms the tiny aural and orthographic distinction between the two words: one wonders whether the artist enjoyed demonstrating the disjunctive borders between image and sound in this way.

I cannot leave this text without one final comment about its own remarks about language. There are two concise couplets that appose 'anglois' and 'françois'. The first describes Alein's friend's way of speaking (he is not himself named): 'Son bon li velt dire en françois, / Mais la langue torne a englois' (lines 11–12.), a remark which we have already seen is also present in *Jehan et Blonde*. At least two readings are possible in this context. Perhaps the one that strikes a modern (English) reader first (especially if she or he has ever travelled in France) is that the friend appears to suffer from a kind of linguistic helplessness: the more he tries to speak French, the more the language turns into English. If however, we understand 'langue' punningly as tongue, then it can also be read as a remark about pronunciation: the language is French, but the tongue turns it in English ways. The second couplet expands on this by commenting more specifically on

himself gained the territory by marriage to Eleanor of Aquitaine in 1152). Louis IX then conferred the comté of Auvergne on his brother Alphonse in 1241 (see C. W. Previté-Orton, *The Shorter Cambridge Medieval History*, 2 vols (Cambridge: Cambridge University Press, 1952), II, 706, 712). The butcher's prejudice against the *Auvergnat* and *Tiois* also appears to involve regional snobbery, perhaps including a sense of urban versus rural superiority.

[46] Vienna Osterreichische Nationalbibliothek, HS S.n.12766, fol.122 and Paris Bibliothèque de l'Arsenal, MS 5193, fo.144.

[47] Getty MS 63, fol.106. I am grateful to Anne D. Hedeman for alerting me to these wonderful pictures. She discusses them (and includes plates) in *Translating the Past: Laurent de Premierfait and Boccaccio's De casibus* (Los Angeles: J. Paul Getty Museum, 2008), 143–6.

the process involved. With the brilliantly simple manoeuvre of using the same rhyme in reverse, the poet shows 'anglois' confused with 'françois' and 'françois' confused with 'anglois'. Alein tries to speak as well as he can, but he could not prevent himself from mixing the two languages together:

Mais onc tant ne s'i sot garder
Que n'i entrelardast l'anglois:
Ainsi farsisoit le françois.
(lines 37–9)

[But he never could prevent himself from seasoning the English with lardons [bacon]: in this way he stuffed the French]

Both these verbs are telling in more than one sense: the culinary metaphor of inserting or stuffing draws attention to a further property of the word 'anglois', that it is itself close in spelling and sound to both 'agnel' and 'asnel'.[48] The line: 'Devant l'Anglois a mis l'anel' (line 64) ['In front of him the Englishman put a lamb/ass'] says it all. 'Anglois' and 'asnels/agnels' are interlarded, the one is punningly and anagrammatically included in the others. Perhaps this is the reason why the only 'anglois' who is given a name, the sonically reminiscent 'Alein', is the one who brays: *ihan, ihan*. It was not so inappropriate then, that the 'anglois' ate the 'asnel', and that it did not do him any lasting harm:

Onques l'asnel que il menja
Ne li fist mal, si con cil dist
Qui le flabel des Anglois fist.
(177, lines 114–16)

[The ass that he ate did not do him any harm at all, so said the one who made the fabliau of the Englishmen.]

The humour is subtle since the relentlessly turning linguistic ploys seem to point in both directions. If the English asses are crudely stuffed by their French then the French find their language seasoned by this English joke; more positively, both, perhaps, give extra savour to each other. We can see how the last line also pivots in more than one direction: 'le flabel des Anglois' turns 'en anglois' since it means both the fabliau about the English and, in the speaking, the Englishmen's fabliau. We are left to wonder whether only the 'deus anglois' can pronounce the word that describes them, or whether they are best described by

[48] Both *farsir* and *entrelarder* are culinary terms, though the evidence for the date of this meaning is not completely clear. *Farsir*, 'to stuff', and *farsure*, 'stuffing', occur in Anglo-French: see *AND*; TL has the following reference for *entrelarder*: '*trans. dazwischen spicken*: La langue ai moult amee / De cerf entrelardee, *Méon* I 304, 101 (*La Devise aus lechëors*)'. *Le Nouveau Littré*: *Le dictionnaire* de *référence de la langue française*, gen. ed. Claude Blum (Paris: Garnier, 2005) makes reference to some thirteenth-century examples of *entrelarder* being used figuratively of the practice of Latin citation, and, in *Jehan et Blonde*, line 3560, of a meal being interrupted by kisses.

the French.[49] Finally, the narrator's sudden last-minute deflection away from authorship ('si con cil dist') points up the wider linguistic theme that has been persistently uttered throughout the story: that the writing up of this play on language has taken the audience into a much fuller excursus on the connections between meaning and sound than one might expect from any mere piece of writing.

The repeated citation of this couplet across fabliau and romance reinforces a sense that these texts are indeed in the process of turning, creating language. It seems to be evidence not that the English all spoke French badly but of a literary topos provoked by the very issue of shared language and its tensions and jokes. This language is indeed a jargon; a form of language that Alice Becker-Ho in her book on gypsies (*les Gitans*), *L'Essence du Jargon*, describes in the following way:

L'*essence du jargon* n'est rien d'autre que l'esprit même de ces classes dangereuses . . .

[The essence of jargon is nothing other than the very mindset of these dangerous social groups . . .]

She sees the speaking of jargon as a matter of articulating (and managing to live safely on) a borderline between the salaried and the non-salaried classes:

l'esprit des classes dangereuses, c'est savoir distinguer à tout moment qui est de ce côté de la frontière, ou de l'autre, et comment il faut se comporter dans chaque cas.[50]

[the mindset of these dangerous groups is to know how to distinguish at any moment what is on this side of the border, or on the other side, and how to behave in each case.]

This hint of social friction is a feature of the next work under discussion.

MISSPEAKING *LA MALE HONTE*

La Male Honte has a quite different relation to its cultural setting from that of *Des Deus Anglois*. Whereas *Des Deus Anglois* is plainly a story about the Englishman abroad, the action of *La Male Honte* is based firmly in England, though the endings offered by the five surviving manuscripts vary the final focus somewhat

[49] It is interesting to note that *anglois* is spelt *aglois* (without the /n/) when Alein describes himself to the butcher: *Nai nai fait il mi'fout aglois* (line 52). The editors draw attention to, and preserve, this spelling on the grounds that it may be an intentional representation of an English accent (see *NCRF*, VIII, p. 367). However, scribal omission of a nasal bar is extremely commonplace and therefore, in this case, likely to be a 'simple' mistake).

[50] A. Becker-Ho, *L'Essence du Jargon* (Paris: Gallimard, 1994), 52. See also P. Burke and R. Porter, eds, *Languages and Jargons: Contributions to a Social History of Language* (Cambridge: Polity Press and Blackwells, 1995).

confusingly. Perhaps one of the first points to remark upon is that there is less sense that the French spoken by the protagonists is a foreign language, either to them or to the narrator. To have this perspective juxtaposed with that of *Des Deus Anglois* is full of interest: it is important to recognize that the mockery of English speakers of French by the French could coexist alongside an assumption that they shared the same language. The term foreign begs the question of course: there is one reference in Guillaume's version of the fabliau which, as I shall shortly discuss, raises the possibility that a language may have degrees of strangeness.

The plot that is common to all the versions concerns the property of a man called Honte. On his deathbed, required by law to pay a form of inheritance tax to the king, he commissions a friend to take his money in a coffer ('une male') to the king in person. The friend duly seeks out the king, and tries to tell him that he has 'la male honte' to give him: the king, however, understanding the phrase in its more obvious meaning of 'foul shame' orders him angrily out of his presence. Only after 'li vilains' has received several humiliations does a courtier succeed in bridging the gap of misunderstanding. Each version introduces slight differences to this outline. Of the three non-Guillaume copies, one of which is attributed in the text to Hues and the other two (by modern scholars) to scribes working closely with that version, all are thirteenth-century (BnF fr.837 [A] and BnF fr.12603 [F]) and one is *bourguignon* [Bern, Burgerbibliothek MS 354 (B), *c.*1225–50]). B is the fullest text but this does not necessarily mean it has compositional priority. Scholars have in fact come to opposing conclusions about the relationship between the texts. For Långfors, Hues's version came first, and Guillaume's was probably based most closely on the F text; Rychner, however, thought that Hues's version was probably later than Guillaume's, which was closer on the whole to the B text.[51] Anne Cobby, more recently, has argued persuasively on critical grounds that Guillaume's version is indeed the earlier.[52] In discussing some of the differences between the texts, my concern is less to do with chronology than with certain of the social and cultural assumptions that appear to distinguish them.[53]

Perhaps one of the first points to note is that the cultural signals are thoroughly and intriguingly mixed between the 'national' and the social. On the face of it, at the beginnings and especially the endings of the various texts, one can detect a degree of anti-English sentiment. All the texts begin by locating the story in England, Hues's version a little more emphatically than Guillaume's. Guillaume

[51] For discussion and references, see *NCRF*, V, 85–8.

[52] Cobby, 'Understanding and misunderstanding'.

[53] I refer to 'Hues' and 'Guillaume' as convenient labels for the different versions rather than hard and fast authorial attributions: it is of course possible that the copies we have are at some remove from what either author 'originally' composed, or conversely that the ascriptions apply only to these individual recensions and not to some putative original. I quote from *NCRF*'s diplomatic texts of the Hues version (since there is greater variation between them), but from their edited text of Guillaume's.

begins in a fairly matter-of-fact way, announcing that the fabliau is about the king of England and explaining the property law that was current at that time. In the Hues texts, it is Honte with whom the story begins, specifically characterized in two of the texts as a rich and powerful Englishman ('.J. englois riches et puissanz' [Hues, B, line 4]). In addition, his name is given with a small but marked cultural rider 'ou pais': 'Del vilain dont ie'di le conte / On'l'apeloit v pais honte.' (Hues, F) [of the peasant about whom I am telling the story/ they call him in the region 'Honte'].[54] Both versions possess a slight distancing effect: this story is not happening locally, but in another country, where there are different customs and names. Cobby has made the interesting suggestion that the name Honte and the punning anecdote that is spun around it could have arisen from the poet's awareness that 'in the French spoken in England the Francien [ō] was pronounced [u]'.[55] Hearing *Hunt* pronounced as *Honte* could have given him the idea for the story and the comment 'ou pais' appears to support this: its placing just before *Honte* as a rhyme word (as it is in all three texts) means that in an oral delivery of the line the pronunciation of *Honte* is carefully anticipated.[56]

When we arrive at the main exchanges between the king and the 'vilain', however, the nature of the misunderstanding between them is quite different from that in *Des Deus Anglois*. It is not that the king speaks better French than the 'vilain', or that either speaks an Anglo-French that is treated with comic contempt. For both Guillaume and Hues, the comic confusion is all in the inability of each man to hear the other's meaning even when they are speaking the same language. Both meanings are available to either speaker, but each is caught up in a linguistically solipsistic world where the possibility of other meanings is (at least temporarily) not even imagined.

Guillaume, more than Hues, creates some ambiguity over the nature of this linguistic impasse. When the 'vilain' first addresses the king, Guillaume slips in a unique comment about his language. All the other texts start straight with his speech: 'Sire dist il oiez mon conte' (Hues, A, 96, line 31) [Sir, he said, listen to my story]; Guillaume, however, remarks: 'Sire, fait il en son language' (125, line 33) [Sir, he said in his [own] language]. The pronoun is strikingly double-

[54] *NCRF*, V, 94, lines 9–10. Variants:

> Li vilains dont ie di le conte
> Auoit a non ou pais honte (Hues, A, lines 11–12.);
> Li uilains don'ie di lo conte
> L'en l'apeloit o'pais honte (Hues, B, lines 11–12.).

[55] Cobby, 'Understanding and Misunderstanding', 171, who does not, however, go into detail on this point.

[56] Note the very public, oral nature of his addresses to the king, which would provide plenty of opportunity for comic exploitation of pronunciation in performance.

tongued: it could imply that the 'vilain' is speaking his own language and not the king's, but it can also mean the exact opposite, that he is speaking not his own language but the king's. It prefaces the first punning statement of his mission to give the king 'la male Honte', a concise five-line declaration that puts the king in a rage:

Quant li rois l'ot, si ot grant honte.
'Vilain, dist il, tu me mesdiz:
Mais tu aies honte touz diz!
De honte me puist Deus desfendre!
Prez va que ge ne te fas pendre!'

(lines 39–43).

[When the king heard it, he felt great shame.
'Peasant', he said, you misspeak me:
may you feel shame ever more!
May God defend me from shame!
I am very close to having you hanged!]

In context, especially when we note the king's sneering use of 'vilain' combined with 'tu' (contrasting with the 'vilain''s addressing him as 'vous') it is the social difference between them that causes this failure of comprehension. Yet the poet cunningly shows the king falling into the same, albeit inverse linguistic trap. Using the word 'honte' as a rhyme word to describe the king, Guillaume shows the king feeling shamed through his very insistence on understanding *Honte* as meaning 'shame'. Despite what the king says, the 'vilain' has not misspoken; the king has misunderstood. The ambiguous pronoun 'son' shows that language can be simultaneously possessed by two speakers, yet grasped by neither.[57]

In this reading of the internal dynamics of the story there is only one language being exchanged across two registers: however, from the point of view of Guillaume and the implied audience, another skein of comprehension is being unwound. The hints are slight, and the tone glancing, but the story has occasional moments when a larger national perspective surfaces. One example occurs near the start, reinforcing the slightly dry anthropological note struck in Guillaume's explanation of English inheritance law. A little later he comments that Honte's friend wandered up and down the country trying to find the king:

[57] Although it may be argued that this is to place too specific a play of meaning on 'en son language', a phrase which could have the vaguer sense of 'in these terms', my response would be that in this range of *franco-anglais* texts in which a greater self-consciousness about language is evident, authors seem to allow such phrases to acquire extra weight. See also Chapter 5 below and the examples discussed there from Froissart.

Maintenant prent la male Honte,
De la ville ist, le chemin monte.
Tant va, tant quiert et tant demande,
Tant a erré par Inguelande
Qu'il a trové le roi a Londre,
Aval desouz un pin en l'onbre

(124–25., lines 27–31).[58]

[Now he takes Honte's coffer;
He goes out of the town and climbs the path.
He went so far, asked and sought help from so many,
he wandered so much through England,
that he found the king in London,
down below a pine tree in the shade.]

This reads oddly: on the one hand it sounds like an observation made by a foreigner, because from an English point of view the king would surely not be very hard to find, especially if he was in London. On the other it may be an attempt to characterize the 'vilain' as an ignorant country bumpkin, for whom London—and the king within it—is unimaginably distant, and indeed 'foreign'. The latter is supported by the location of the king in the shade of a pine tree: this is a classic *chanson de geste* and also romance motif marking the entrance to the Christic or supernatural world and comically underlines the notion of the king as belonging to a world remote from the 'vilain', who is fleetingly cast as the romance hero in search of a 'merveille'. Again, it seems that both perspectives are present and in play: the distance of the continental French author/narrator gives him special insight into the perceptions of strangeness felt within as well as of the multiple linguistic worlds of the English.

As the action reaches its climax, Guillaume's version includes another unique remark that looks outwards to a wider national polemic. Desperate to save himself from being hanged, the vilain makes his speech for a third time, ending like this: 'Car vos d'Engleterre estes rois: / La male Honte aiés, c'est drois!' (127, lines 112–13.). This ostensibly innocent assertion nationalizes the implicit offence (you deserve shame because you are the king of England) in a way that anticipates the rather clumsy chauvinist humour of the ending:

[. . .] li vilains en a portee
La male Honte en sa contree,
Si l'a aus Englés departie.
Encore en ont il grant partie:
Sans la male ont il asez honte,
Et chascun jor lor croist et monte

(Guillaume, 128, lines 150–5).

[58] *NCRF* changes the line numbering because some of the lines are inserted from D.

[. . . The peasant carried away the evil shame/Hunt's coffer into his country
And shared it out amongst the English.
They still have a large amount of it:
Even without the bag they have enough shame
And each day it grows and increases for them.]

The other versions of the story end more neutrally or perhaps, inwardly: the A and F texts of Hues wish shame on the king, B on the 'vilain', indeed on all 'vilains: Que uilain aient male'honte' (Hues, B, 123, line 206) [may peasants have foul shame]. If Cobby is right, and there is much to support her case, then not only is Guillaume's version the earliest, but the later *remaniements* show some weakening of the original idea. Yet, as she argues, even in Guillaume's, the satiric moral seems a confused addition to the main fabliau plot. Moreover, the very plurality of the endings confirms this suggestion: the pun is the heart of the work and the satire 'no more than an overlay'.[59] Reading the versions from the point of view of their cultural location we find that there is a corresponding weakening in the 'nationalist' perspective: Guillaume's interest in characterizing the English dwindles in the Hues texts into a less angled account. For Hues and his copyists, it is less important that the protagonists are English than that they face each other across a social gulf. The early attention they give to the name *Honte* turns out to be a way not so much of making a snide Anglo-French jibe but of commenting proleptically on the punning potential of the name.

Anglo-French satire has a complex role in this fabliau. In many ways, it is understated: the continental author(s)—especially Guillaume—cannot resist making the odd supercilious gesture towards the English, yet their larger interest in language goes deeper than this kind of assertion of difference. By concentrating on the social barriers between king and 'vilain', they offer a critique of 'English' from inside, that is, in the language which not only the king and 'vilain' but also the continental and the insular French-speakers share. Misunderstanding is a concept that is certainly firmly yoked to the English, yet by rendering it in French the continental author(s) reveal themselves to be on the same side as their cousins. Moreover, unlike *Des Deus Anglois*, the linguistic misunderstanding here is not peculiarly English: the syntactical constructions used for the pun are common in continental French. The only singularly 'English' feature of the story concerns the onomastic issue that no Frenchman would be called 'Honte'.

Of course, the choice of language could be seen as symptomatic of a kind of imperialism: the unthinking use of French from this point of view is not necessarily a reflection of language use in England (particularly among peasants) but rather of the automatic priority of French as a vernacular. Yet even in this scenario, the very ease with which *La Male Honte* is expressed in French has significance for our

[59] Cobby, 'Understanding and Misunderstanding', 171.

understanding of 'English'. That the dilemma of English can be expressed so naturally in French and by the French is itself part of the history of English.

AN 'ENGLISH' DIALOGUE: *LE ROI D'ANGLETERRE ET LE JONGLEUR D'ELY*

Le Roi d'Angleterre et le jongleur d'Ely was rejected from inclusion in the corpus of fabliaux by Noomen and van den Boogaard.[60] One can see their point that it lies on the edge of the genre: indeed, one of the main sensations of reading it is of being taken through several genres simultaneously, the *dit* (the generic title given in the manuscript), exemplum, *sotte chanson*, even the *pastourelle*. In a sense it is a work about fabliaux and how they come to be written more than a fabliau itself. But in the process, one could argue, it mimes being a fabliau so successfully that it might as well be allowed to pass as one. By lurking on the edge, it also provides a prime example of the uncategorizable aspects of Anglo-French as well as of the fabliau genre. For clearly one element in its dubious reception among modern French scholars of fabliaux concerns its unique survival (in this form) in an English manuscript.

Just how English is it? Again, it wears its national status lightly. Like *La Male Honte*—and it is also a story about a king and a fool—it has a history of rewriting that complicates any sense of its natural cultural allegiances.[61] Several thirteenth-century manuscripts contain closely related material: there are three pieces in prose, surviving respectively in Paris BnF fr.1553 (a late thirteenth-century anthology), in Bern, Burgerbibliothek, MS 113 (from north-eastern France, second quarter of the thirteenth century, containing a wide range of narrative genres including romances, chansons de geste, and didactic and historical pieces) and Trinity College Cambridge, MS O.2.45 (a varied trilingual insular anthology, *c.*1240); and two in verse, one in BL MS Arundel 220 and the other on the flyleaf of Paris BnF fr.1588.[62] This

[60] The principal modern editions of the text are therefore in A. de Montaiglon and G. Raynaud, eds, *Recueil général et complet des fabliaux des XIIIe et XIVe siècles*, 6 vols (Paris: Librairie des bibliophiles, 1872–90), II, 242, and J. G. Raynaud, 6 vols (Paris: Librairie des bibliophiles, 1872–90), II, 242 and J. Ulrich, '*La Riote du monde*', *Zeitschrift für romanische Philologie*, 8 (1884), 275–89. My citations are from Montaiglon and Raynaud. The poem caught the eye, however, of the Baron Kervyn Lettenhove who copies a few lines from it in his charming account of a two-week visit to England to look through manuscripts, 'Notes sur quelques manuscrits des bibliothèques d'Angleterre, part 1', *Extraits des Bulletins de l'Académie royale de Belgique*, 2nd series, no. 12, vol. 20 (1868), 3–22 (17).

[61] As Barbara Nolan has pointed out, this process of rewriting continued into the nineteenth century with a pseudo-Anglo-Norman prologue added by Palgrave, mistakenly treated as part of the original text by subsequent editors, including Montaiglon and Raynaud ('Anthologizing Ribaldry', 292, n. 9).

[62] There might also have been a version in Latin verse: the table of contents for BL MS Arundel 292 refers to a text called *De rege et joculatore*. See Nolan, 'Anthologizing Ribaldry', 298, n. 19.

mixture of continental and insular manuscripts indicates that the material evidently appealed to and circulated between both audiences. In 1884 Jacob Ulrich published the three prose works and the Harley fabliau together under the collective title of 'Le Riote du Monde' signalling his sense of their close connection.[63] They share a neat and orderly structure: a long opening section of misfiring dialogue between the *jongleur* and the king which is followed by an even longer amplification of the whole topic of misunderstanding by the *jongleur*'s depiction of people's social prejudices.

Comparing the versions in a little more detail, we find that in the prose, which is written in the first person, the *jongleur* is riding between Amiens and Corbie when he meets the king and strikes up conversation. The Harley 2253 fabliau, written in the third person, is set in a meadow just outside London. The embryonic pastoral allusion in each (the motif 'jeo chevauchoie l'autrer si encontrai . . . ' ['I went out riding the other day and I met . . . '] in the prose is the standard opening formula of the *pastourelle*) is concisely evoked to set the scene for the kind of encounter that is central to the *pastourelle*, a dialogue between two people of widely different social backgrounds whose terms of linguistic and sexual exchange prove to be mutually incompatible.[64] Rather than rush baldly (in the manner of the prose) into the dislocated exchange, the fabliau author takes time to sketch out the brief pastoral setting for the encounter and describe the richly painted drum that hangs around the *jongleur*'s neck. In this way the props for the story's main dramatic encounter are remarkably similar to those of *La Male Honte*: an English king surrounded by his courtiers and a fool with a striking object (silk bag, gold-painted drum) dangling from his neck. In both, the English setting is prominent and, especially in the case of *Le Roi d'Angleterre*, evidently selected in preference to a northern French setting.

Yet the Englishness of its location remains skin deep in terms of the 'plot': there is no attempt to characterize the language as specifically 'English' and the work is free of anti-English (or anti-French) edginess. The fabliau author appears, once more, to be much more interested in the larger linguistic issues raised by the dialogue. These take a different form from *La Male Honte* and *Des Deus Anglois* in the sense that they do not turn on a single pun or punning phrase. Instead, in the tradition of the wise fool (one might compare the Solomon and Marcolf dialogues), he creates a form of language which is all pun, or all irony. The king asks him: 'Ou qy este vus, sire Joglour' ['to whom do you belong, sir *jongleur*?']. He replies, 'Sire, je su ou mon seignour' ['Sir, I belong to my lord']. Following this up, the king asks:

[63] See n. 60 above.

[64] Compare, to take just one representative example, J.-C. Rivière, ed., *Pastourelles: Introduction à l'étude formelle des pastourelles anonymes françaises des XIIe et XIIIe siècles*, 3 vols, TLF, 213, 220, 232 (Geneva: Droz, 1974–6), I, no. 1, 75 ('L'autre jour je chevachoie'). For further discussion of pastoral and pastourelle motifs, see Butterfield, *Poetry and Music in Medieval France from Jean Renart to Guillaume de Machaut* (Cambridge: Cambridge University Press, 2002), 160–2.

Quy est toun seignour? Fet le Roy.
'Le baroun ma dame, par ma foy.
Quy est ta dame par amour?
Sire, la femme mon seignour.
Coment estes vus apellee?
Sire, come cely qe m'ad levee.
Cesti qe te leva quel noun aveit?
Itel come je, sire, tot dreit.[65]

[Who is your lord? asked the king. By my faith, my lady's husband, the baron. Who is your lady, for love's sake? Sir, the wife of my lord. What are you called? Sir, after the one who raised me. The one who raised you: what name did he have? Just the same as mine, sir.].

The double meanings turn not on a single, unusual word or phrase but, more radically, on the fundamental verbs, pronouns, locatives, and interrogatives of human existence: 'who(se) are you? [. . .] where do you come from? [. . .] why are you speaking like this?' The replies keep shifting the questions around a sequence of semantic loops, moving ever further sideways until the questioner finds himself confronted by the same question with which he began: 'What are you called?—By the same name as the one who brought me up.—What is the name of the one who brought you up?—The same as mine' (lines 37–40). No question is permitted to settle: each reply enacts a process of refusal and deferral that is insistently destabilizing. Both exact and exacting, the *jongleur*'s childishly pedantic replies are nonetheless not merely redundant: the circles of associated meanings that they force the king to inhabit involve a series of profound definitions. The *jongleur*'s identity is indeed shaped by his relation to his lord, and by that of his lord to his lady; his name is not his to give, but determined by his parentage, as indeed his parents are further defined by him.

In the second half of the piece, the *jongleur* shifts gear again, but this time into a more consistently satiric mode. Like *Renart jongleur*, but with a little less drag and slapstick, he finally describes himself to the king, confirming his role as a speaker *à rebours* who lies, tricks, and undermines other people's professional self-descriptions, but then follows this with a fuller commentary on the way that in fact what passes as normal observation within society is corrupted by prejudice. His own profession turns out to be truthful rather than scheming since he is uncovering the falsities that people parade as truths. Humbled, the king who has at first been irritated and angry with the *jongleur* asks him for advice on how to conduct himself in a world where there is so much misspeaking (*mesparler*).

Le Roi d'Angleterre thus engages with the topos of *mesparler* with more philosophical and homiletic solemnity than either *La Male Honte* with *mesdire*

[65] Montaiglon and Raynaud, eds, *Recueil général*, II, 243, lines 29–50 (the numbering includes the false start, see n. 61 above).

or *Des Deus Anglois* with *mesconter*. It seems as if the one work that is unequivocally English in terms of its manuscript provenance has least to characterize it according to some visible token of 'national' sentiment. Yet since we can see that earlier versions of the material had a specifically continental setting, it seems equally clear that the decision to make the king English, and (however fleetingly) to attach the *jongleur* to Ely, was actively rather than passively made. A closer consideration of the context provided by Harley 2253 may help to illuminate this decision. *Le Roi d'Angleterre* is the first of a group of five fabliaux contained by the manuscript. As Barbara Nolan has recently argued, these works can be seen to have many thematic links with other English, French, and Latin material in adjacent pages in the manuscript. She gives eloquent prominence to *Le Roi d'Angleterre*, seeing its didactic (and only semi-humorous) assertion of the wisdom of the *jongleur* as a possible reason for the compiler to set it in the lead position among the other fabliaux in the manuscript.[66]

There may be further reasons for its location here. The other four fabliaux, *Les Trois dames qui troverent un vit, Le chevalier et la corbaille, Le Dit de la gageure*, and *Le Chevalier qui fist les cons parler*, all concern issues of linguistic misunderstanding.[67] In contrast to *Le Roi d'Angleterre* these contain some of the most blatantly obscene and violent plots among the whole fabliau repertory: what they share is a characteristic attention to language as it operates in the field of euphemism, its propensity to work metonymically even or especially as it struggles to represent the most bodily aspects of human fantasy. Why should these particular works have found their way into this manuscript? There is evidently no single answer to this question, yet it may be worth noting the extent to which this group follows through the preoccupations of the other Anglo-French fabliaux that we have been discussing. For most modern commentators, these four have been considered on their own terms (if at all): their appearance as a group in an English context has barely been remarked upon. Yet perhaps we see here a sensitivity to the ways in which language can be misappropriated, misspoken, and misunderstood that is explicable within a complexly coordinated trilingual collection.

FRENCH AND ANGLO-FRENCH: PRONOUNCING THE DIFFERENCE

We are used to seeing fabliaux as sophisticated sources of linguistic display, as often shocking mediators between the physical experiences of sex and excretion

[66] Nolan, 'Anthologizing Ribaldry', 304.

[67] Of these four works, the copies of *Le chevalier et la corbaille* and *Le Dit de la gageure* are unique to Harley 2253; *Les Trois dames* occurs also in Bnf fr. 1593 and *Le Chevalier qui fist les cons parler* in six further copies.

and the equally compulsive human instinct to verbalize. What this collection of fabliaux in Harley 2253 suggests is that there might be a connection between this extreme search for a natural language and the recognition that languages may have more than one form of natural expression. Reading *Des Deus Anglois, La Male Honte*, and *Le Roi d'Angleterre* together shows that misunderstanding is very broadly induced. Their particular contribution to the widespread medieval debate about language is their interest in the foreignness of language. They explore this through the subtle and complex boundary between two separate cultural contexts for the 'same' language. Sameness in language is shown up to be both more reliable and more illusory than people often admit. The public exposure of a total failure of communication between king and vilain in *La Male Honte* is prefaced by an assumption of total comprehension on the part of each: this has the potentially comic but also disturbing implication that we may not know where the boundary lies between our own understanding of the language we are speaking and someone else's. Superficially, the effort of *Des Deus Anglois* is to make this boundary visible: the 'deus anglois' are given a French that is represented as being different from the French of the narrator. Yet the work also cleverly masks that representation, weaving between an oral and a literate perception of both languages in such a way that the reader is forced to recognize the artificiality (and relative character) of the distinction between them.

The issues in this fabliau have an interesting resonance with contemporary French efforts to deal with the increasingly large infiltration of English words into French. As L'Académie française remarks on its website, 'Jugeant que la concurrence de l'anglais, même dans la vie courante, représentait une réelle menace pour le français et que les importations anglo-américaines dans notre lexique devenaient trop massives, les autorités gouvernementales ont été amenées, depuis une trentaine d'années, à compléter le dispositif traditionnel de régulation de la langue' [judging that the competition of English, even in everyday life, represented a real threat for French and that the Anglo-American imports into our lexis were becoming too numerous, the government authorities have been led, in the past thirty years, to fulfil their traditional aim of regulating the language].[68] In a recent essay in the *Journal of the British Institute in Paris*, Lorella Sini writes about some of the ways modern French speakers pronounce these English imports.[69] She points out that contrary to popular English belief, the French do not chauvinistically translate all Anglicisms into 'correct' Academy French. On the contrary, unaffected (and unremarked) use of such constructions as 'j'ai booké ma copine pour samedi soir' is commonplace. However, certain interesting issues of pronunciation arise—should one pronounce words of an English origin with an English accent? This causes a problem because one does

[68] <http://www.academie-francaise.fr/langue/index.html>.

[69] Lorella Sini, 'Ces mots franglais qui fâchent les Français', *Franco-British Studies: Journal of The British Institute in Paris*, 32 (Spring 2003), 17–31.

not want to sound too authentic: that would be a case of 'malsonnant' and would be regarded as a lapse of taste. The French, in other words, prefer to pronounce a word of English origin 'à l'anglaise', that is, not with an attempt to sound genuinely English, but marked out in a kind of special hybrid pronunciation:

free lance
rewriting
week-end
hand ball

This pronunciation oscillates between being 'naturalized' or more 'exotic' depending on how recent the absorption of the English is within the language.[70]

In talking about 'cette insécurité énonciative, souvent inconsciente' ['this often unconscious insecurity about pronunciation'], Sini alerts us to some of the intricacies of cross-linguistic exchange: people can share a language, but still wish to disassociate themselves from the way other people speak it. This is not necessarily a one-way form of snobbery; it is a more complicated process of asserting—even in the same language—one linguistic identity against another. From a modern perspective, especially the largely monolingual environment of literary criticism of the English Middle Ages, it may seem unnerving to have conducted a discussion of Englishness entirely on the basis of works written in French. But a further modern commentary on monolingualism and its hidden affinities to linguistic pluralism offers a means to grasp the unsettling imperatives of cross-lingual analysis.

Jacques Derrida's *Le Monolinguisme de l'autre ou la prothèse d'origine* (1996) is a partly autobiographical exploration of language and personal identity. His own condition as an Algerian Jew, a *franco-maghrébin*, born near Algiers and subject to the anti-semitic Vichy laws introduced in 1940, shapes his whole argument. For these Jews, French was the only language they were permitted to learn, yet it was not their language. Their experience of language was as something doubly forbidden: they were not allowed to speak either Arabic or Berber, but French was also forbidden territory, in the sense that their access to it was at times refused as well as forced upon them. In 1942, after only a year in the nearby lycée, he was expelled as a Jew and was not able to resume regular schooling until 1944. Yet although he writes very movingly of the pain and terror of this prohibition, his argument is more than merely personal. He describes himself as a case that is at once unique yet exemplary: 'à la fois *exceptionnel* et *fondamental*'.[71] He is a witness—in the sense of both martyr and example[72]—of the exceptional *and* fundamental alienation of human beings from language.

[70] I am grateful to my younger son for providing me with the further example of 'Lucky Luke'.
[71] Derrida, *Le monolinguisme de l'autre*, 58.
[72] Ibid., 50.

He puts forward two famously contradictory propositions:

On ne parle jamais qu'une seule langue.
On ne parle jamais une seule langue.

[We only ever speak one language
We never speak only one language][73]

To which he adds a third:

'*Oui, je n'ai qu'une langue, or ce n'est pas la mienne.*'[74]

['Yes, I only have one language, yet it is not mine.]

The ironies of being self-professedly monolingual yet in a language which is not his, push Derrida in characteristically freewheeling directions. Of particular relevance to the present discussion, monolingualism for him is both strangely plural and less than nothing. He does not like the notion of possession: you cannot really 'own' a language; you can only adopt an attitude of possession towards it. This is because there is no such thing as a metalanguage: you cannot speak outside your language (although you can in another sense do nothing else *but* speak outside it): possessive pronouns (this is my or your language) are proscribed—emptied of meaning—by the language in which they are uttered.

une langue ne peut que parler elle-même d'elle-même. On ne peut parler d'une langue que dans cette langue.[75]

[a language can only speak itself of itself. One cannot speak of a language except in that language.]

—Ce que j'ai du mal à entendre, c'est tout ce lexique de l'avoir, de l'habitude, de la possession d'une langue qui serait ou ne serait pas la sienne, la tienne, par exemple. Comme si le pronom et l'adjectif possessifs étaient ici, quant à la langue, proscrits par la langue.[76]

[What I am having some difficulty understanding is this entire vocabulary of having, habit, and possession of a language that would or would not be one's own - yours, for example. As if the possessive pronoun and adjective were, as far as language goes, proscribed here by language.]

He is impatient with the idea that a language can be colonized. The colonial masters may think they own the language that they impose on their subjects but they are just as powerless as anyone else to force complete control over language.

[73] Derrida, *Le monolinguisme de l'autre*, 21; *Monolingualism*, 7.
[74] Derrida, *Le monolinguisme de l'autre*, 15; *Monolingualism*, 2.
[75] Derrida, *Le monolinguisme de l'autre*, 43; *Monolingualism*, 22.
[76] Derrida, *Le monolinguisme de l'autre*, 44.

After all, any process of education is a colonization: it involves naming things in order to acquire cultural and scientific power. Not unrelatedly, he goes on to admit with engaging honesty his own desire to speak a pure language. He never stops striving for a certain sort of pronunciation, especially while teaching. It is like a disease he contracted at school, this extravagant taste for purity of language:[77]

J'avoue donc une pureté qui n'est pas très pure. Tout sauf un purisme. Du moins est-ce la seule impure 'pureté' dont j'ose confesser le goût. C'est un goût prononcé pour une certaine prononciation. (80)

. . . J'ai été le premier à avoir peur de ma voix, comme si elle n'était pas la mienne, et à la contester, voire à la détester. (80–81)

. . . je l'ai aussi contracté à l'école, ce goût hyperbolique pour la pureté de la langue . . . Une hyperbolite incurable. Une hyperbolite généralisée. Enfin, j'éxagère. J'éxagère toujours. (81)

[I therefore admit to a purity which is not very pure. Anything but purism. It is, at least, the only impure 'purity' for which I dare confess a taste. It is a pronounced taste for a certain pronunciation . . . . (47)

I was the first to be afraid of my own voice, as if it were not mine, and to contest it, even to detest it. . . . (48)

. . . this hyperbolic taste for the purity of language is something I also contracted at school . . . An incorrigible hyperbolite. A generalized hyperbolite. In short, I exaggerate. I always exaggerate.] (48)

If we turn back to the medieval 'franco-anglais' texts, there is much that strikes a chord. What I have been fascinated by is the condition of the French in which they are written: 'this French which is not one'. It is clear that there are issues of ownership in these texts. Someone, either producing or receiving the text, thinks of himself as being in a possession of power and this manifests itself in certain aspects of plot, theme and especially linguistic form and orthography. At this relatively early date in the history of Middle English, it is interesting to find this discussion of cultural rivalry taking place entirely in French. It suggests that giving due weight to the practice of French in England in the thirteenth and first half of the fourteenth centuries means more than merely acknowledging the existence of French texts circulating in England; it means more than identifying a separate 'Anglo-Norman' culture; it means grasping that 'English' could be defined precisely as a form of French. For writers and readers of both languages (who were likely to know Latin as well) 'English' is not therefore a single concept that works merely in polarity with French; it contains and is contained by French in a subtle, constantly changing, and occasionally antagonistic process of accommodation.

[77] Known in his earlier years as Jackie, Derrida later adopted a more 'correct' French version of his first name.

And yet these texts also show us that Anglo-French creates—or perhaps simply makes explicit—an uncertainty and instability in the notion of French. Before we leap too quickly ahead in thinking of French as the master vernacular tongue of the medieval West, the jargon texts provide a brake. The context for Derrida's comments on the powerful status of modern French is a world away from these medieval writings but even he, in a situation of manifold colonial vulnerability, insists that to talk of linguistic power as a matter of linguistic colonization is simplistic. Anglo-French changed French; it unsettled French and in giving it an insular aspect acted as a reminder that French was a construct rather than a solid structure. The language of possession, 'tout ce lexique de l'avoir, de l'habitude' develops as a means of articulating control, not necessarily of obtaining, let alone wielding it.

What is interesting about *Des Deus Anglois* is that in asserting linguistic power, the poem reveals its inability to wield it. It plays on the different forms taken by a language in terms of writing and performance as well as geographical context. We are not just hearing about the joke, the joke takes shape in the telling, and on paper, through pronunciation and spelling. We could say that the poem (and other franco-anglais texts) is setting up its own language as a metalanguage: this is how 'other' French is spoken, and the poet shows it through a kind of master colonial tongue. Yet, as Derrida warns, it is also important to observe the transparency of this sense of control.[78] How *should* one pronounce 'agnel' and, even more so, how should one spell it? In fact, as Faral and others have pointed out, once again the dialect of the whole manuscript (BnF fr.19152) lacks dominant traits—it is not possible to locate geographically any one of the texts it contains—and certainly not the manuscript as a whole—from the way they are written. The 'impure' pronunciation of these Anglais is a matter of perception, but one that cannot be rendered visually with any confidence.

In the same way, with *Jehan et Blonde* or *Le Privilège aux Bretons* and taking a hint again from Derrida, this wilfully and often comically opaque Anglo-French jargon disrupts the poet's metalanguage: in a sense it is part of his controlling ploy to create linguistic difference, yet the ploy's very success testifies to Derrida's insistence that one cannot speak outside one's own language, just as one cannot speak anything but one's own language. Again, in *La Male Honte*, the king's use of metalanguage is shown up as vulnerable: the activity of naming can go just as wrong in the 'master' language as it can in the language of the colonized speaker. French, then, is open to parody, mimicry, 'foreign' appropriation, even by the

[78] Derrida is typically complex on accent and especially his own 'français d'Algérie' which he says he fiercely seeks to repress in favour of 'le français pur': 'l'accent, quelque accent français que ce soit, et avant tout le fort accent méridional, me paraît incompatible avec la dignité intellectuelle d'une parole publique. (Inadmissible, n'est-ce pas? Je l'advoue.)', 77–82 (78).

'French'. Conversely, and just as significantly, to read writing produced in England that is not written in English is precisely to find that 'Englishness' becomes strangely elusive: we find ourselves in a verbal world that is both fragmented and plural, where audiences are not merely 'English', but multilingual (in varying degrees), partly local, partly international, and from more than one social, cultural, and intellectual background.[79] In this period, on both sides of the Channel, poets seem fascinated by the brilliant failures as well as the limited successes of both kinds of linguistic assertion.

[79] This is most clearly evidenced in the two trilingual collections British Library MS Harley 2253 and Oxford, Bodleian Library MS Digby 86. For recent discussion, see T. Turville-Petre, *England the Nation: Language, Literature and National Identity 1290–1340* (Oxford: Clarendon Press, 1996), 181–221; T. Hunt, 'Insular Trilingual Compilations', in *Codices Miscellaneaum, Brussels Van Hulthem Colloquium 1999*, ed. R. Jansen-Sieben and H. Van Dijk (Brussels: Archives et Bibliothèques de Belgique, 1999), 51–67; and *Studies in the Harley Manuscript*, ed. Fein.

Map 2. France in 1360

PART II
EXCHANGING TERMS: WAR AND PEACE

As we enter the fourteenth century, the evidence of cross-channel exchange shows an unmistakeable hardening of tone. Between the last chapter and this section occurs a declaration of war. In itself, as I remarked in Chapter 1, the event usually described as the beginning of the Hundred Years War, Philippe de Valois's 1337 challenge to Edward III's possession of Gascony, was but one of a long series of challenges and counter-challenges between the English and French aristocracy that could be dated back to before the Norman Conquest and forward as late as 1802. One purpose of Part I of this book was to show that the linguistic frictions of earlier centuries are very much part of the thickening texture of war in the fourteenth. To think of the Hundred Years War as beginning only in 1337 is to understand it as dominated by fourteenth-century military and diplomatic pressure points. However, it also makes sense of the war to realize that these moments of military and diplomatic strain are precipitated from much larger and longer cultural engagements (in both senses of the word). Part II continues to investigate how linguistic practices interlink with territorial, political, and mercantile structures. It addresses the larger context of war by discussing examples of writing provoked by conditions of war such as siege, truce, imprisonment, and exile. In this slightly more extended preliminary, as well as outline each chapter I offer further context to the issues and instances selected for discussion. They cover four areas: invective, diplomacy, trade, and the language of love.

An underlying question that surfaces many times in the book as a whole concerns the relationship between war and nation. There are two issues: whether in view of the quickening pace of conflict we are right to suspect, as many have, that the mid-fourteenth century was a crucial stage in a process of creeping nationalism between England and France; and second, from the literary perspective followed in this study, whether the writings associated with the major battles and treaties of the fourteenth century give us evidence of this. In a sense I try to turn both questions round. On the grounds for which I have argued in previous chapters, rather than assume from the start that nationalism is necessarily on the increase, I select some key examples of cross-channel writing and work outwards from what they seem to reveal. Those that recount the symbolic encounter between Edward III and Philippe VI are particularly allusive. The evidence we have already seen of the rich and subtle linguistic awareness of the complexity of defining differences between peoples who share so much—in genealogy, goods, and language—suggests that we should continue to take a broad view of the means and materials of nation. The larger claim is that literary texts do not simply *illustrate* processes of nation-building that must first be learned or inferred from historical and economic analyses, they actually participate—in every interlinguistic encounter—in fabricating identity. Implied in this claim is that we must always also be asking through these same texts what nation-building could possibly mean in this period.

Chapter 4, 'Fighting Talk', uses the vituperative mid-century ballade exchange between Philippe de Vitry and Jehan de le Mote, in which Philippe accuses Jean, a Hainuyer working for Edward III, of being an English traitor, as a focus for a broader consideration of the language of invective in the period. I argue that Deshamps's famous ballade extolling Chaucer as a 'grant translateur' is part of this larger cross-channel dialogue, and that it is a subtle articulation of praise and insult, playing on the witty, mutually condemning admiration (or mutually congratulatory contempt) of the Vitry–Mote exchange. Invective initiates and underlies this section. Its roots are deep and far more subtly pervasive than we might at first think. My effort is on the one hand to show how a condition of warlike opposition affects writing on a broad scale, and on the other, that writers are deploying long-standing literary genres to mediate and articulate the Anglo-French relationship in ways that go far beyond mere opposition. The process of exchanging terms is at once richly controversial and creative. It rises from shared sources but in the course of exchange, new springs of difference cause new terms to proliferate.

Although the fifteenth century marks the apogee of 'fighting talk', the fourteenth first sees a noticeable increase in writing that, on the one hand, explicitly indulges in a rhetoric of invective and antagonism and, on the other, more benignly, begins to use and ponder a language of 'nation' (*natio, nacioun, nascion*). Selecting material itself prompts various questions of interpretation that impinge on the notions of cultural difference that are at issue. It is noticeable, for instance, how much of the explicitly rebarbative writings, or else those that arise directly out of specific military events, are 'French'. Two instances of literary 'by-products' of war include a poem by Colin, 'fils de Renault', one of the servants of Jean de Hainaut, who laments the fall of French knighthood at Crécy (1346); and the anonymous, equally plangent *Complainte sur la bataille de Poitiers* (1356). Also on the French side, but evidently aiming to ruffle an English auditor is the *Songe du vergier*, a work completed in Latin (*Somnium Viridarii*) on 16 May 1376 that was translated into French in 1387 by order of Charles V, and takes the form of a long debate about the relation between ecclesiastical and secular power that touches on central sensitive issues of Anglo-French political argument.[1] The question of whether a work was English or French gains complexity, however, with, for instance, the partly versified narrative on the deposition of Richard II that was written right at the end of the century by Jean Creton, a visiting French member of Richard's household. The very existence of Creton shows how thoroughly a 'French' perspective complicates the notion of what an English royal household might be. There were also works written by French poets in England, such as *Le Roman des deduis* by Gace de la Buigne, which one might describe as forcedly 'English' since, in the case of Gace, his presence in England was caused by the imprisonment of Jean II after Poitiers.[2] Other writers of French poetry in England were, on the other hand, not 'French' but francophone such as the Savoyard Othon de Grandson and the Hainuyers Jehan de le Mote and, most famously, Froissart, both of whom worked under the patronage of Philippa of Hainault, Edward III's queen.

Le Roman des deduis is not polemical except in the context of its author's situation, and Froissart's early *dits amoureux* (written some time between 1365 and 1371), from *Le Paradys d'amour* perhaps as far as *L'Espinette amoureuse*, are the result of the kind of deep-seated familial connection between England and the continent that existed as the reverse coin of antagonism.[3] It seems important to stress that much other writing—in English as well as French—not normally regarded as having a significant connection with war comes under this purview. The allusion in Guillaume de Machaut's *La Fontaine amoureuse* to the exile of Jean de Berri (forced to come to England after Poitiers with his father, Jean II) reminds us that Machaut lived through the humiliations of English attack on France (his *Livre du Voir Dit* makes several direct references to the brigands who menaced routes between Reims and Paris in the 1360s)[4] and that this might inform our sense of his poetic relation to Chaucer more than it often does. Those cross-channel literary relationships, in other words, which seem to show nothing but close and easy familiarity, are also breathing the uneasy atmosphere of a fluctuating and fitful war. It is within this observation that I want to situate Chaucer, along with other writers and works such as Gower, Langland, and (though there's no space to consider them directly) the *Gawain*-manuscript

[1] *Le Songe du vergier, édité d'après le manuscrit royal 19 C IV de la British Library*, ed. M. Schnerb-Lièvre, 2 vols, Sources d'Histoire Médiévale publiées par l'Institut de Recherche et d'Histoire des Textes (Paris: Editions du CNRS, 1982).

[2] Gace de la Buigne, *Le Roman des deduis*, ed. A. Blomqvist (Karlshamm: E. G. Johansson, 1951).

[3] As Anthime Fourrier indicates, the order of works in BnF fr. 830 is probably chronological, and before *L'Espinette* includes *Le Temple d'Onnour, Le Joli Mois de May, L'Orloge amoureus, Le Dittié de la Flour de la Margherite, Le Dit du Bleu Chevalier*, and *Le Débat du Cheval et du Levrier* (Fourrier, ed., *Jean Froissart, L'Espinette amoureuse*, 2nd rev. edn (Paris: Klincksieck, 1972), 33.

[4] See Letters X and XXI, Guillaume de Machaut, *Le Livre du Voir Dit*, ed. P. Imbs and J. Cerquiglini-Toulet (Paris: Librairie Générale Française, 1999), 186, 402. For further references and discussion, see D. Leech-Wilkinson, '*Le Voir Dit*: A Reconstruction and a Guide for Musicians', *Plainsong and Medieval Music*, 2 (1993), 103–40.

poems. My argument is that attention to the context of war stimulates a perspective on these writers as more than merely, that is insularly, 'English'. Being 'English', if it meant anything in the fourteenth century, had meaning in the context of an overarching continental argument conducted by English royalty (Edward in the Low Countries and northern France, the Black Prince in Gascony, and Gaunt in Spain).[5] The penetration of French personnel and French writing into England gave writers of English with court connections a constant apprehension of this wider argument.

It is the work of Deschamps that perhaps provides the best means of deducing latent pugnacities in the civilized air of Anglo-French courtly pleasure-making. Deschamps is a significant presence in Part II for several reasons. First, as an exact contemporary of Chaucer, he forms a striking cultural parallel to him. Second, he happens to be perhaps the most outspoken, vociferous, and eloquent poetic commentator of the time on nation. In the context of Chapter 4, with its emphasis on 'fighting talk', Deschamps provides a key means of observing how the growing military tensions were displayed linguistically. Close attention to the way he expresses his often strident attacks on the Flemings and the English will help us build up a sense of his aggressive-defensive postures and their consequences for his vocabulary of 'nation'. It will also provide a necessary context for his poetic comments on Chaucer.

A third reason for the presence of Deschamps will take more time to articulate. It concerns the lyric form of his compliment. The two chapters that frame this section, Chapters 4 and 7, give special due to lyric. It is traditional in current English literary criticism to emphasize the importance of narrative as a central mode in medieval English writing.[6] John Burrow's pioneering account of a Ricardian poetry marked by its narrative character, has spoken for many modern readers for whom the 'short poems' in Chaucer's oeuvre are of minor interest. Yet, from a continental perspective, lyric was a powerful and ubiquitous choice of poetic medium for the most significant poets and poet-composers of the period. For Dante, Petrarch, and Machaut, lyric was the means of articulating the highest hopes of vernacularity expressed in the hyperbolic and brilliantly manipulative language of erotic desire. Deschamps's *L'Art de Dictier* (1392), the first *ars poetica* in the langue d'oil, concentrates exclusively on lyric composition. The meteoric rise of the *formes fixes* in the fourteenth and fifteenth centuries, in the hands of

[5] Scotland, of course, Wales, and Ireland (especially in Richard II's reign) provided different (though involved) kinds of counter-identity to 'English'. See in particular, the fine account by R. R. Davies, *The First English Empire: Power and Identities in the British Isles, 1093–1343* (Oxford: Oxford University Press, 2000), ch. 7, 172–90, who stresses 'the shifting, multilayered, and complex cultural worlds of the British Isles in the fourteenth century' and makes the further important point that in Wales and Ireland 'the linguistic tide turned during the course of the century' and 'indigenous languages were making substantial gains at the expense of, or at least alongside, English' (182).

[6] 'Perhaps no subsequent period is so dominated by the narrative voice', J. A. Burrow, *Ricardian Poetry: Chaucer, Gower, Langland and the 'Gawain' Poet* (London: Routledge and Kegan Paul, 1971), 47.

Machaut, Froissart, Gower, Grandson, Deschamps, Christine de Pizan, Charles d'Orléans, the writers of the *Les Cent Ballades*, and many others, has tended to suffer (for readers of Chaucer) by being cast as mere love poetry.[7] The perception of an older generation (Johan Huizinga, Daniel Poirion, and Charles Muscatine, for example) that lyric starts off on a high with the troubadours and then declines into mere prettiness (or worse) has been so influential that Deschamps's huge oeuvre of short poetry (approaching 1,500 poems) has been notably understudied by modern readers.[8]

The chapters on lyric aim to draw attention to the use made of short fixed structures, for example of envoys as both political go-betweens and poetic devices of closure and transmission, to articulate many types of cross-channel literary and political argument, often in the heat of battle or the frustrations of imprisonment. The emphasis on lyric will also serve as a way of scripting another cross-channel exchange, of genre. To what extent did generic interests coincide on either side of the Channel? Or to put it another way, how deep is the apparent division between insular interest in narrative and continental obsession with lyric?[9] This has importance for our larger enquiry since it touches on one of the ways in which modern readers have expressed a sense of difference between English and French medieval writing. Chaucer is usually credited with this sense of difference, and the argument runs that he begins his work as a poet by absorbing and reacting to French love poetry and its emphasis on lyric, but then moves on through an Italian phase into ever more narrative—and English—preoccupations. This discussion will be given more space in Part III, Chapter 8, where Chaucer's role in creating Englishness will be more fully reassessed. My purpose here is to create a context for the discussion by focusing on the international attachment to lyric. It strikes me that one reason why Deschamps's famous description of Chaucer as a 'grant translateur' has troubled modern admirers of

[7] To Robinson, and many others, the *Book of the Duchess* belonged to an 'artificial tradition' from which it made a narrow and fortunate escape into 'real feeling' (267). See, for instance, G. Reaney, 'Guillaume de Machaut: Lyric Poet', *Music and Letters*, 39 (1958), 38–51 who writes: 'It may well be asked what is to be gained from reading poetry of this artificial kind, in which an unreal code of love provides the majority of themes and where emotion seems at a discount' (39).

[8] K. Becker, *Eustache Deschamps: L'État actuel de la recherche* (Orléans: Paradigme, 1996), for instance, calls her first chapter 'la redécouverte d'un poète injustement oublié'. Attention to Deschamps (with the important exceptions of D. M. Sinnreich-Levi and L. Kendrick) has lagged well behind that given to Machaut in the past two decades. However, see D. Buschinger, ed., *Autour d'Eustache Deschamps: Actes du Colloque du Centre d'Études Médiévales de l'Université de Picardie-Jules Verne Amiens, 5-8 Novembre 1998*) (Amiens: Presses du Centre d'études médiévales, Université de Picardie-Jules Verne, 1999); J.-P. Boudet and H. Millet, eds, *Eustache Deschamps en son temps* (Paris: Publications de la Sorbonne, 1997); and, more recently, *Eustache Deschamps: Selected Poems*, ed. I. S. Laurie and D. M. Sinnreich-Levi, trans. D. Curzon and J. Fiskin (New York and London: Routledge 2003).

[9] I allude here to Elisabeth Salter's projected title *An Obsession with the Continent* for her unfinished study on literature in England and its cultural contexts (see D. Pearsall and N. Zeeman, eds, *English and International: Studies in the Literature, Art and Patronage of Medieval England* (Cambridge: Cambridge University Press, 1988), xii.

Chaucer is that he utters it in a lyric—a *ballade*—a form which we do not associate with Chaucer's best work. It is as if the mismatch between the genre of the praise and what is seen as the characteristic genre of the recipient of the praise renders it slightly suspect. Deschamps's further association of Chaucer with the *Rose* adds to the confusion. Only three fragments of an English verse translation of the *Rose* exist,[10] and the one that is usually (though only tentatively) ascribed to Chaucer is not what would now be singled out as his masterpiece. We cannot quite apply the term 'grant translateur' (as Deschamps seems to have meant it) in a way that makes sense of the (narrative) works by Chaucer we most admire. It is *Troilus and Criseyde* that best fits the description of a long narrative work of translation, yet it would seem odd for Deschamps to be drawing attention to Chaucer's skills as a translator of Italian. Putting Deschamps centre stage, a poet who not only writes on love but also revolutionizes the range of topic and tone of the first-person lyric, from light comedy to bitter satire, invective, and sharp propaganda, may help us grasp more fully a continental sense of Chaucer as a lyric poet that allows a broader perspective on French *and* Italian.

Chapter 5, 'Exchanging Terms'. This chapter will turn to *Troilus* in the light of this. First, however, it aims to outline a more detailed picture of the diplomatic arena in which terms between the English and the French, especially between Edward III and Jean II, were exchanged through the fourteenth century. We see from a broad range of writing how potential linguistic misunderstandings are used as a subtle means of exerting diplomatic leverage on both sides of the Channel. This chapter investigates the language of diplomacy in more detail, looking at evidence from Froissart's *Chroniques* of his views on language and language use, and at the role language played in the battles for supremacy between English and French diplomats, lords and kings. The language of the negotiators and Froissart's comments on language teach us much about the fraught circumstances in which vocabularies across English and French were both shared and contested. I hope to develop through this a sense of a lexis of nation, not in the sense of a defining set of terms, but rather a cluster of words that gives us insight into how certain relationships were conceived and articulated across those difficult family ties of brotherhood or cousinship. With specific reference to Jean's captivity in England after Poitiers, Chapter 5 argues that two of Chaucer's major narratives, the *Knight's Tale* and *Troilus and Criseyde*, are saturated with this language of negotiation and represent subtle accounts of the tensions involved in fraternal relationships caught up in war.

Chapter 6, 'Trading Languages', then takes us into the urban culture of London. It situates Chaucer's accounts of mercantile behaviour and speech—notably the *Shipman's Tale* and the portrait of the Merchant in his *General*

[10] Simon Horobin has recently announced the discovery of a new leaf from fragment B in the National Library of Scotland in Edinburgh, now Glasgow University Library Hunter 409 (V.3.7), 'A New Fragment of the *Romaunt of the Rose*', *SAC*, 28 (2006), 205–15.

Prologue—within the busily multilingual world of city trade. London English, as evidence in the guild and other official records indicates, fought for recognition amongst other linguistic communities seeking power and influence in the city. Through tracing puns and other examples of cross-linguistic influence, Chaucer's English is placed within the sometimes violently competitive multilingualisms of a fractured, intermittently cohesive urban community in which many forms of alliance between family, friend, mercenary, stranger, and foreigner were under pressure. To match the ebb and flow of conflict that so marked the fourteenth century, Chapter 6 provides various kinds of contrast. It concentrates, firstly, on an urban and specifically mercantile context for language exchange rather than the courtly discourse examined in the other chapters.[11] It refers more to narrative than lyric, to prose as well as verse, non-fiction as well as fiction. Thirdly, it includes (though not exclusively) material produced by and in response to conditions of truce when trading was able to flourish and lines of communication reopened. In this sense it is looking at an urban and mercantile context for 'nation'. It is also beginning to raise the issue of the status of English as a public language.

Chapter 7, '*Lingua franca*: The International Language of Love', turns back to courtly discourse, but this time by concentrating on the language of love—its themes, images, mythologies, and vocabularies—and how it is shared across languages and poets. The object of attention in Chapter 7 is deliberately set to follow the more stringent antagonisms of the previous chapters. This is to remind us that love poetry of the period had this sharp backdrop, and must not be read naively, or as an expression of naive sentimentality. My particular interest is to develop the argument of Chapter 5 by comparing groups of *ballades*, written in both English, French, and Anglo-French, on the continent and on the island, specifically composed in the 'international' language of love. Reading across and between Machaut, Froissart, Chaucer, Gower, and Grandson, teaches us to move on from the notion of source and 'original', towards a much more flexible sense of love poetry as a deeply layered linguistic process, that passes from a large area of mutual self-reference up through to examples of individual retorts and ripostes. Such a process cannot be easily characterized as 'English' or 'French': instead, poets are working with a much less rigid notion of linguistic difference. The chapter aims to discuss the implications of this international language for a contemporary sense of poetic identity. Together, the four chapters of this section sketch a variety of ways—invective, diplomacy, urban networks, and the language of love—in which language was traded across the Channel. Such contexts reveal rich insights into perceptions of cultural difference in the period, and have broad implications for our sense of Chaucer's Englishness.

[11] Though see the comments on the puy in Chapter 7 below.

4

Fighting Talk

INVECTIVE

Invective is probably where most people would first register a visceral sense of how national feeling is articulated. It is the kind of language where ideas of identity, especially the identity of *others*, are at their most gratingly audible. Usually taken 'straight' as easy instances of nationalistic abuse, there are certainly plenty of examples in which the language is colourful, sometimes painfully, sometimes humorously offensive, the latter register being particularly marked in Latin, as we shall shortly see.[1]

In the fourteenth century, as I briefly indicated in Chapter 1, the material is more sparse than in the fifteenth. On the English side, apart from such relatively well-known poems as the 'Agincourt Carol', *The Libelle of Englyshe Polycye*, pieces by Lydgate and the fourteenth-century battle poems by Laurence Minot, there is a great deal more which is rather less known from the thirteenth to the fifteenth centuries, ranging from chronicle material,[2] many shorter verse narrative pieces, such as John Page's *Siege of Rouen*, and dialogues and debates, such as Honoré Bonet, *Arbre de batailles* (1387) and the *Débat des hérauts d'armes de France et d'Angleterre* (1453–61).[3] The term invective is of course rather unspecific. Many of these poems, especially the earlier ones, tended to come under that older editorial category of 'political', as in Wright's 1859 *Political Poems and Songs* and Isabel Aspin's 1953 edition of *Anglo-Norman Political Songs*. As these editions, particularly Wright's, suggest, works of invective fall within the compass of

[1] T. Wright, ed., *Political Poems and Songs Relating to English History*, Rolls Series, 2 vols (London: Longman, Green, Longman, and Roberts, 1859–61) gives several examples, such as the poem he entitles *The Dispute Between the Englishman and the Frenchman*, I, 91–3 (*Anglia, faex hominum, pudor orbis*), and *Francia, foeminea, pharisaea, vigoris idea*, I, 26–40, which appears to have been composed soon after Crécy.

[2] See T. Summerfield, 'The Political Songs in the *Chronicles* of Pierre de Langtoft and Robert Mannyng', in E. Mullally and J. Thompson, eds, *The Court and Cultural Diversity*. (Woodbridge: D. S. Brewer, 1997), 139–48; and J. Boffey and A. S. G. Edwards, 'Middle English Verse in Chronicles', in S. Powell and J. J. Smith, eds, *New Perspectives on Middle English Texts. A Festschrift for R. A. Waldron* (Cambridge: D. S. Brewer, 2000), 119–28.

[3] H. Bonet, *The Tree of Battles*, trans. G. W. Coopland (Liverpool: Liverpool University Press, 1949) and L. Pannier, ed., *Le Débat des hérauts d'armes de France et d'Angleterre suivi de The Debate between the Heralds of England and France by John Coke*, SATF (Paris: Firmin-Didot, 1877).

several other traditions as well: namely flyting (ranging from Norse-Germanic cultures, Scottish fifteenth- and sixteenth-century to modern African American rap); and lyric exchange, such as those stimulated by the *puy* and *confrèrie* contests (the *jeux-partis* and later chansons and *ballades*). In all these arenas, the sense of public performance is central and tends to involve a rhetorical sharpening of the knives, a kind of witty intellectual jousting.

Although discussion of war texts is relatively rare among literary scholars, Christine de Pizan has often been the stimulus—namely her *Livres des fais et bonnes moeurs du sage roy Charles V*, *Livre de la Paix*, and *Dittié de Jehanne d'Arc*. Also on the French side, as well as Chartier's *Le Quadrilogue Invectif* (1422) and *Prétensions des Anglois à la couronne de France* (1461–71),[4] diplomatic officials such as Jean de Montreuil wrote polemical treatises. Two works by Montreuil *Regali ex progenie* (1406–13) and *Traité contre les Anglais* (1413–16)[5] served as models for a rash of others: Jean Juvénal des Ursins, *Audite celi* (1435) and *Tres crestien, tres hault, tres puissant roy* (1446), Noël de Fribois, *Mirouer historial* (1451) and *Abregé des chroniques* (1453–61) and Louis Le Blanc, *Pour vraye congnoissance avoir* (1471). By far the most successful and widely circulated of these was the tract *Pour ce que plusieurs*, recently edited by Craig Taylor, who argues that it is probably datable to 1464 and composed by the diplomat Guillaume Cousinot de Montreuil (*c.*1400–84).[6]

I mention so many works (and this is only a selective survey) not because there will be room to discuss many of them during the course of this book, but in order to indicate the very wide generic range of writing stimulated by the Anglo-French war. One interesting characteristic of the material is the way it alternates across the Channel. Overall it takes the form of a verbal tug of war, with response and counter-response, like a *jeu-parti* writ large, stimulated at first by specific events and then increasingly by diplomatic battles, where the French respond to English supremacy in the fifteenth century by attempting to provide more and more 'proof' of French claims, especially by means of Salic law. The English response is to provide taunts, of an often rather crude kind. We can see this in a Tudor 'translation' of *Pour ce que plusieurs*, which blatantly switches its arguments for the French to the English and ascribes its attacks on the English to the French. Much of this writing has been unexplored by literary scholars; it does after all seem far from the literary sophistication of the *Voir Dit* or the *Canterbury Tales*.

[4] Two fifteenth-century English translations of *Le Quadrilogue* are extant, edited by M. S. Blayney, *Fifteenth-century English Translations of Alain Chartier's 'Le Traité de l'Esperance' and 'Le Quadrilogue Invectif'*, EETS 270, 2 vols (London: Oxford University Press, 1974–80).

[5] C. Taylor, 'War, Propaganda and Diplomacy in Fifteenth-Century France and England', in C. Allmand, ed., *War, Government and Power in Late Medieval France* (Liverpool: Liverpool University Press, 2000), 71.

[6] C. Taylor, ed., *Debating the Hundred Years War: Pour ce que plusieurs (la loy salique) and a declaracion of the trew and dewe title of Henry VIII*, Camden Fifth Series, 29, Royal Historical Society, UCL (Cambridge: Cambridge University Press, 2006). A Tudor translation survives, written between 1509 and 1547, probably by 1513.

Yet as a result it has too often been treated as the proof it claims to be, as evidence of raw nationalist feeling. But that is to be taken in by the rhetorical ploy. It seems to make better sense of this multifarious tradition to think of it alongside the Anglo-French jargon texts that were considered in the last chapter. There is much more at work than simple abuse, even in the cases of simple abuse. The rising tide of verbal bellicosity is part of a larger desire during the intermittent war between England and France to establish grounds of difference and similarity, to understand the deep structure of exchange between the two cultures—after all a very complex business—and all through the often disorienting fact that they share the 'same' language. Moreover, we might argue in the other direction that the texts that are much more familiarly literary to us are also part of this cross-channel argufying. Exchanges between the English and the French are about establishing grounds *for* arguing, creating not just defending terms of discourse, finding—inventing—a cross-channel language in the process of hurling talk back and forth.

This chapter will illustrate this by apposing two instances of intellectual duelling: the first, a mid-century *ballade* exchange in which Philippe de Vitry, a Parisian-based bishop and statesman, angrily denounced the treachery of Jehan de le Mote, a poet who worked for the courts of Hainaut and England, and the second, between Deschamps and Chaucer, probably in the 1380s. In between there will be an attempt to look through Deschamps's eyes at 'Frenchness' and 'Englishness' and various issues of identity such as that provoked by his relationship with Othon de Grandson. Deschamps's articulation of 'nation' will be set in the context of three, disparate environments in which 'nations' had a specific social and structural meaning in the medieval period: trade networks, the universities, and the ecclesiastical factions that later found themselves in fractious debate at the Council of Constance of 1414–18. All provide a pattern of complicated, interweaving allegiances and rivalries that offer insight into the diverse intellectual, cultural, and personal frameworks for identity that lie behind the world of invective and argument on display in these poetic contests.

These two main literary contests will act as structural pins: around them a broader culture of linguistic debate, at times dissension will be evoked.[7] Certainly in modern Chaucerian circles, the Deschamps *versus* Chaucer exchange is very well known, Le Mote *versus* Vitry less so. That in itself is part of my topic, because it is part of the larger story about Anglo-French exchange. Until very recently, the 'grant translateur' *ballade* was the only lyric among his 1,500 or so to attract much attention from modern Chaucerian scholars.[8] This is partly a

[7] Compare the formal quasi-legal response structures created by Machaut in his *Jugement dou Roy de Behaigne* and *Jugement dou Roy de Navarre,* imitated by Chaucer in his *Troilus and Criseyde* and *Legend of Good Women.*

[8] James Wimsatt devotes a whole, very informative chapter to Deschamps but argues that the evidence for their poetic relationship, in either direction, is 'disappointingly small' and has been overplayed by previous scholars (J. Wimsatt, *Chaucer and His French Contemporaries: Natural Music*

consequence of its seemingly unique, explicit attestation to Chaucer as a poet read on the continent; contemporary vernacular poets, especially perhaps those who write in English, are notoriously shy of mentioning one another by name.[9] It functions, then, as precious evidence of 'Englishness' as defined from without in the fourteenth century, rather than within. Yet it seems all the more important in that case to avoid taking a singular approach to it. A 'Chaucerian' view of Chaucer and Englishness has meant that Le Mote, accused of being too English by Vitry, does not come into consideration; he writes in French after all and comes from Hainaut. This chapter will be urging a corrective emphasis that these two moments of cross-channel exchange are indeed parallel in ways that, despite the important work of James Wimsatt, have tended to escape notice.[10] And the very omission tells us something, perhaps, about the character of that (still continuing) Anglo-French relationship.[11]

Partly in the light of that comment, I will be presenting the medieval material with continuing reference to that rather different kind of commentary on linguistic identity by Jacques Derrida in his *Le monolinguisme de l'autre ou la prothèse d'origine* (1996) and also, later on, *La Carte Postale.*

JEHAN DE LE MOTE AND PHILIPPE DE VITRY

An account of the Jehan de le Mote and Philippe de Vitry duel must look back to a slightly earlier cluster of romance texts, beginning with Jacques de Longuyon's *Les Voeux du paon, c.*1310. Itself part of the tradition of Alexander romances, *Les Voeux du paon* creates a diversion in the tradition by containing an elaborate ceremonial vowing or boasting scene and also a set-piece description of the Nine Worthies. Both these new elements—the former is of particular interest here—

in the Fourteenth Century (Toronto: University of Toronto Press, 1991, 271). The Calais ballade has also received some attention: see n. 85 below.

[9] Deschamps is an important exception: see, for instance, his references to Machaut (Ballades 127, 447, 493, 872, 1474) including the famous elegies (Ballades 123, 124) and to Christine de Pizan (Ballade 1242), among others (*Oeuvres Complètes de Eustache Deschamps*, ed. le Marquis de Queux de Saint-Hilaire and G. Raynaud, SATF, 11 vols (Paris: Firmin Didot, 1878–1903), XI, 266–8). There are earlier examples too, such as the admiring references to Adam de la Halle by Nicole de Margival in his *Le Dit de la panthère*, ed. Bernard Ribémont, CFMA, 136 (Paris: Champion, 2000), 1516–1628, itself part of a long-established tradition in which romance authors cite lyric poets, sometimes by name (see A. Butterfield, *Poetry and Music in Medieval France from Jean Renart to Guillaume de Machaut* (Cambridge: Cambridge University Press, 2002), 259–61 and *passim*).

[10] See also the brief remarks by D. Pearsall, *The Life of Geoffrey Chaucer: A Critical Biography* (Oxford: Blackwell, 1992), 70.

[11] Deschamps's own awareness of Vitry is attested by his famous ballade, *Oeuvres*, no. 1474 'Veulz tu la congnoissance avoir' VIII, 178, and also, no. 872 'He! Gentils rois, dus de Poligieras' V, 53.

seem to capture the imagination of the next generation of writers.[12] The vows are made to a peacock—or in one case a heron—and are the occasion for curious rhetorical displays. Jean le Court (dit Brisebarre) produced a follow-up version in his *Restor du paon* (before 1338); this was then in turn imitated in two further works: the anonymous *Les Voeux du héron* (*c.*1340), and *Le Parfait du paon* (1340) by Jehan de le Mote.[13] All these works have relevance to the present chapter because they represent a confluence of three things: a verbal competition, a set of lyric set pieces, and a coincident political situation where the verbal contest has a sudden much wider resonance and potential political meaning.[14]

The anonymous *Les Voeux du héron* makes this triple connection most overtly. In many ways, indeed, it could be regarded as the first literary blow in the Hundred Years War. It claims to tell how it all began, how Edward III, seemingly uninterested in pursuing his claim to the French crown, was spurred into the war by a courtly challenge. Its bizarre story is that Robert d'Artois, who had been banished from France, pointedly presented Edward at a London banquet with a roast heron. Reputedly the most timid of birds, the heron was a public symbol of Edward's cowardice in failing to take up his French inheritance. To counter the shame of this slur, Edward immediately resolved to take up his claim, and several English lords (and even Philippa herself, pregnant as it happened) made vows to support his action.

It is tempting to wonder whether the heron alludes to that famous Artois-Neapolitan production *Le Jeu de Robin et Marion*. The 'hairon' is one of the marauding knight's 'courtly' terms that Marion claims not to know;[15] and it would be a fitting extra twist to the insult to imply that Edward was in the same category for humiliation as the feckless, but also rather pathetic over-sexed stock

[12] G. de Machaut in *La Prise d'Alexandrie (The Taking of Alexandria)*, ed. and trans. R. Barton Palmer (London and New York: Routledge, 2002), makes Pierre de Lusignan the tenth; Deschamps also refers to ten worthies in a ballade about Bertrand du Guesclin II, no. 207. A female version of Les Neuf Preuses also existed, perhaps inaugurated by Le Mote, as Wimsatt argues, and was taken up by Chaucer in his *Legend of Good Women*: see Wimsatt, *Chaucer and His French Contemporaries*, 67 and 310, nn. 76 and 77.

[13] The date of 1340 for *Le Parfait du paon* was proposed by Richard Rouse and Mary Rouse who connect it with a jewelled peacock made for Philippe VI by his goldsmith Simon de Lille in 1340; see 'The Goldsmith and the Peacocks: Jean de la Mote in the Household of Simon de Lille, 1340', *Viator*, 28 (1997), 281–303.

[14] Jacques de Longuyon, *Les Voeux du paon* is edited by R. L. Graeme Ritchie, *Buik of Alexander*, Scottish Text Society, New Series 17, 12, 21, 25, 4 vols (Edinburgh: Blackwood, 1921–9), II–IV. It was followed by two further vowing poems: *Le Restor du paon* by Jehan le Court, dit Brisebare, ed. R. J. Carey (Geneva: Droz, 1966) and E. Donkin (London: MHRA, 1980); and *Le Parfait du Paon* by Jehan de le Mote, ed. Richard J. Carey (Chapel Hill: University of North Carolina Press, 1972). For further discussion of the vowing tradition, see B. J. Whiting, 'The Vows of the heron', *Speculum*, 20 (1945), 261–78; R. S. Loomis, 'Edward I, Arthurian Enthusiast', *Speculum*, 28 (1953), 114–27; *Les Voeux du héron* is edited by Wright, *Political Poems and Songs*, I, 1–25.

[15] Rosanna Brusegan, 'Le *Jeu de Robin et Marion* et l'ambiguïté du symbolisme champêtre', in H. Braet, J. Nowé, and G. Tournoy, eds, *The Theatre in the Middle Ages*, (Leuven: Leuven University Press, 1985), 119–29.

chevalier of the Artois pastourelle. This pastourelle context for the heron also serves as a reminder of the other major genre of debate poetry from Arras (in which English kings sometimes figure): the *jeu-parti.* There is a large hinterland of social and cultural aggression that forms part of the generic landscape of Anglo-French interaction throughout the Middle Ages, and we need to be alert to its many and varied genealogies.[16]

What we also learn from these particular posturing narratives is that the lines of alliance and insult are subtle and shifting. The big face-off here between Edward and Philippe VI, both nephews of Charles IV, was negotiated, provoked, and muddied by the relationship between both kings and the variable fortunes and loyalties of Hainaut, Artois, and Picardie. Robert d'Artois had been a thorn in the flesh of his brother-in-law Philippe for some years.[17] In a vain attempt to recover his rights to the county of Artois which he lost through a legal nicety at the end of the thirteenth century, he had attempted to work his way into the king's favour. But his schemings failed, and he was banished in April 1332.[18] He took up with Edward in 1334, and began to work actively with him from 1336 onwards. This was one of many stories of cross-channel, and cross-lingual, relationships in which the directions of interest turn out to be far from straightforwardly 'English' or 'French'.[19] Something of the flavour of uncertainty about Robert's role in inflaming larger acts of aggression is captured in the Peacock romances. Written by Picard, Lorrain, and Hainuyer writers, their tone is odd and slides uneasily between burlesque, satire, and indulgent court fantasy. The way in which Robert's transparently self-interested support for Edward manifests itself in *Les Voeux du héron* in a publicly staged insult seems an ambiguous, to say the least, account of how Edward was propelled into war. It would be naive to believe that *Les Voeux du héron* reports an actual occasion, but the very strangeness of the atmosphere of confused praise and insult that suffuses it may well represent the blend of ideologies and prejudices that were at issue as the first battles of the war were planned and executed.[20]

[16] This book attempts to include instances from *jeu-parti*, debate and dialogue, fabliaux, romance, chronicle, lyric exchange: clearly in each of these areas there is much scope for further study.

[17] J. Sumption, *The Hundred Years War*, 2 vols (London: Faber, 1990 and 1999), I, 170–3.

[18] See S. H. Cuttler on his criminal trial, *The Law of Treason and Treason Trials in Later Medieval France*, (Cambridge: Cambridge University Press, 1981), 96–7.

[19] Enguerrand de Coucy was a famous instance: a hostage at Brétigny he married Edward III's daughter Isabelle, but maintained his allegiance to France, resigned his English titles on the accession of Richard II and was later in the pay of Charles VII (J. Favier, *La Guerre de Cent Ans* (Paris: Fayard, 1980), 483). See also Chapter 10.

[20] M. Vale, *The Princely Court: Medieval Courts and Culture in North-West Europe* (Oxford: Oxford University Press, 2001), 207–20. N. J. Lacy, 'Warmongering in Verse: *Les Voeux du Héron*', in D. N. Baker, ed., *Inscribing the Hundred Years War in French and English Cultures*, SUNY series in Medieval Studies (Albany: State University of New York Press, 2000), 17–26, and P. DeMarco, 'Inscribing the Body with Meaning: Chivalric Culture and the Norms of Violence in *The Vows of the Heron*', in Baker, ed., *Inscribing the Hundred Years War*, 27–54.

The Le Mote and Vitry exchange thus comes at a sensitive moment in the newly developing war. To understand its context further we need to take cognizance of the importance of this larger north-western francophone and Dutch region for English polity and culture during the fourteenth century. Major studies on the court cultures of the Low Countries and their metamorphosis under Burgundian rule after Philippe le Hardi's accession to his wife Margaret de Male's lands in and around the County of Flanders in 1369 have sketched very full portraits of the independent vitality and cultural power of the major Flanders cities of Ypres, Bruges, and Ghent, and the courts of Guelders, Hainaut, and Brabant.[21] David Wallace's pioneering attempt to draw Chaucerians' attention to 'Flaundres' indicates how important it is to absorb what these wider studies mean for contemporary English historical and literary interests.[22] The area pertinent to English political manoeuvrings stretched from the county of Flanders in the centre, to the counties of Holland, Zeeland, and Guelders to the north-east, the duchy of Brabant (containing Antwerp) and below it the county of Hainaut to the East, and Artois and Picardie to the west and south-west, with Calais poised at the sea edge between Flanders and Artois. From the thirteenth century the economic interests of England and Flanders were closely interdependent. The great Flemish weaving towns of Ypres, Ghent, and Bruges, reliant on English wool, formed an alliance with the English in the wake of the rebellion organized by Jacob van Arteveldt against the count of Flanders. Edward III married Philippa of Hainaut in 1328 and worked to secure the support of Brabant and (less successfully) Flanders as well. Philippa's connections were of key strategic importance to Edward, first as he consolidated his own position on the throne with the help of his French mother, Edward II's queen Isabella, and then as he used Flemish backing to defeat the Scots and bolster his claims against France. When he claimed the French crown in January 1340 it was Ghent that recognized him as King of France. Victory at Sluys in June 1340 was further confirmation of Edward's dominance in the region, and even once his military advantages became more tenuous he continued to use Philippa's continental affiliations through marriage to apply diplomatic pressure on French royal polity.

[21] Note in particular, W. Blockmans and W. Prevenier, *The Promised Lands: The Low Countries Under Burgundian Rule, 1369–1530*, trans. E. Fackelman, rev. and ed. E. Peters (Philadelphia: University of Pennsylvania Press, 1999); G. Nijsten, *In the Shadow of Burgundy: The Court of Guelders in the Late Middle Ages* (Cambridge: Cambridge University Press, 2004); C. Wright, *Music at the Court of Burgundy 1364–1419: A Documentary History* (Henryville: Institute of Mediaeval Music, 1979); R. Strohm, *Music in Late Medieval Bruges*, rev. edn (Oxford: Clarendon Press, 1990); Vale, *The Princely Court*; and by D. Nicholas, *The Van Arteveldes of Ghent: The Varieties of Vendetta and the Hero in History* (Ithaca: Cornell University Press, 1988) and *Medieval Flanders* (London: Longman, 1992).

[22] 'In Flaundres', D. Wallace, *Premodern Places: Calais to Surinam, Chaucer to Aphra Behn* (Oxford: Blackwell, 2004), 91–138.

As Wallace has argued, there is a discourse of Flanders which makes itself known in Chaucer and more broadly in English cultural and social life.[23] I will return to this in the next chapter, but in the meantime I want to stress the complex triangulations of the Anglo-French-Low Countries relationship. These took an economic and cultural form. Both England and France had strong reasons for wanting to trade with and, if necessary, annex these lucrative Flemish sources of capital and financial acumen; conversely, the Flemish courts and cities needed grain from France as well as wool from England, and could not afford to allow either side to deny them access to the other. Alongside these economic factors, the triangulation of languages between Dutch, French, and English points up various intersecting issues of power and influence. For just as English had a competing relationship with Anglo-French and continental French, so Dutch on the continent had a competing relationship with Walloon French (the French used in the southern areas of the Low Countries). Dutch was an important model of vernacular diglossia for English writers (that is, writers in England of French and Latin as well as those who wrote in English): overshadowed, like English, by French, it nonetheless possessed greater historical autonomy than English both as a spoken and as a written language.[24] For both Dutch and English writers, though perhaps more for English, vernacular communication was always a matter of working with and between French. And given the political tensions between Flemish burghers and French and English overlords in the region, French was a language that divided and exposed allegiances as well as one that was widely used as a lingua franca. The chronicler Lodewijk van Velthem reports that the Brabantine knights in the French army at the battle of Courtrai (1302), realizing that the Flemish forces were winning, suddenly swapped their French battle cries for Dutch ones in a desperate attempt to save their lives.[25]

[23] For a reference in John Trevisa's translation of Higden to 'Flemmyngs' in Wales, see R. Higden, *Polychronicon Ranulphi Higden monachi Cestrensis*, ed. C. Babington and J. R. Lumby, Rolls Series 41, 9 vols (London: Longman, Green, Longman, Roberts, and Green, 1865–86), II, 158–89.

[24] Linguistic research on Middle Dutch has been given new impetus by the new Corpus Gysseling of thirteenth-century Dutch material: see J. Van Keymeulen, 'Geographical Differentiation in the Dutch Language Area during the Middle Ages', in M. Goyens and W. Verbeke, eds, *The Dawn of the Written Vernacular in Western Europe* (Leuven: Leuven University Press, 2003), 391–404. Dutch was used in administrative and chancery records far earlier and more widely than any other Germanic language (the earliest surviving charter comes from county of Flanders, dated 1249). The strength of vernacular usage is also indicated by precociously early adoption of French (over Latin) for written charters in Hainaut and Flanders at the end of the twelfth century. See G. Croenen, 'Latin and the Vernaculars in the Charters of the Low Countries: The Case of Brabant', in Goyens and Verbeke, eds, *The Dawn of the Written Vernacular*, 107–25.

[25] Croenen, 'Latin and the Vernaculars', 115, who cites W. Waterschoot, *Lodewijk van Velthem, De Guldensporenslag. Een fragment uit de voortzetting van de Spiegel Historiael* (The Hague: Martinus Nijhoff, 1979), 100–1.

Bearing in mind that Philippa and Edward spent much time in Ghent and the neighbouring area in the 1330s and 1340s the language contact between 'English' and 'French' would have included these fine-grained alliances and distinctions between kinds of French and kinds of Germanic vernacular. Some of the cross-channel cultural mixing that resulted from their union is implied by the manuscript of secular French writings exchanged between them on their wedding, now BnF, fr.571.[26] English illuminators appear to have worked on the decoration using Franco-Flemish materials; some scribes are English and one is from Valenciennes. Moreover, back in England Philippa's presence, and the evidence of considerable Flemish immigration based in London but also in other towns such as York, Norwich, and Winchester, subtly complemented the dominance of Parisian French in the fields of law, bureaucracy, and literature.[27] There is some interesting, though as yet inconclusive, evidence that Philippa, whose primary language was most likely French through her French-speaking mother, Jeanne de Valois, had a personal motto *Ich wrude muche.* According to one source, the motto was embroidered on a corselet given to her by Edward in 1364.[28] Trying to establish the meaning of the motto is teasingly difficult: it appears to have Dutch, English, and perhaps German elements, but not straightforwardly.[29] If this motto was indeed hers, then it would raise interesting questions about her linguistic choice, perhaps implying that she wished to reach out to her English-speaking subjects and did so by means of Dutch, a vernacular that she must have been very familiar with, at least passively. Jean Froissart, by contrast, born like Philippa in Valenciennes, perhaps for reasons of international patronage and

[26] See A. Wathey, 'The Marriage of Edward III and the Transmission of French Motets to England', *Journal of the American Musicological Society*, 45 (1992), 1–29, and A. Butterfield, 'French Culture and the Ricardian Court', in *Essays on Ricardian Literature in Honour of J. A. Burrow*, ed. A. Minnis, C. C. Morse, and T. Turville-Petre (Oxford: Clarendon Press, 1997), 82–121 (89–91).

[27] C. Barron, 'Introduction: England and the Low Countries, 1327–1477', in C. Barron and N. Saul, eds, *England and the Low Countries in the Late Middle Ages*, (Stroud: Alan Sutton, 1995), 1–28 (13).

[28] The motto is mentioned by B. C. Hardy, *Philippa of Hainault and her Times* (London: Long, 1910), 136, 279 and by Sir Nicholas Harris Nicolas, *History of the Orders of Knighthood of the British Empire* (London: John Hunter, 1842), 4 vols, II, 485, n. 7. Neither however, gives a source. Nicolas also mentions a second corset with the motto *Myn Biddenye.*

[29] This tiny phrase is full of oddities. 'Ich' is not obviously Flemish (which is 'Ik'), though it does occur in eastern Dutch dialects. It could be 'English' or 'German'. 'Wrude' is not attested in the *MED*, nor does it appear to be a Middle Dutch word as it stands: possible words to which it might relate are 'wrocht' (wrought), 'wruedt' (toil), or 'vroede' (understand). 'Muche' is certainly Middle English. The other motto '*Myn Biddenye*' could be an Anglicized (or simply confused) rendering of Mijn biddinge: 'my prayer'. (I am very grateful to Sjoerd Levelt, Janet van der Meulen, and Ad Putter for their help with these suggestions.) It could be the product of a Flemish speaker attempting to produce an English motto, or an English embroiderer trying to transliterate a Flemish motto. The German colouring is also interesting: it may give a clue to the region of the Flemish speaker, or else simply bear witness (in a pre-dictionary culture) to the porous character of low Germanic and its contacts with English.

reputation, gives no clue (at least in his writings) that he ever used anything but 'franchois'.[30]

Le Mote was part of a generation of Walloon writers and courtiers who came over from Hainaut with Philippa on her marriage to Edward III in 1328. Like Gervès du Bus, author of the greatly embellished fr.146 version of the satiric narrative *Le Roman de Fauvel*, and Philippe de Vitry, Le Mote was a chancellery clerk: there is a record that he was working in this capacity in Hainaut in 1327.[31] His connection with Philippa was confirmed and maintained by Edward, who, in 1338, appears to have given the poet an annuity of twenty pounds. Perhaps best known for his *Regret Guillaume*, an elegy commissioned by Philippa in 1339 for her father, Guillaume I, comte de Hainaut (III of Holland and Zeeland), there are records of his established presence in English royal circles until at least 1343, when he entertained the king as a minstrel at Eltham.[32] This anticipates Froissart's composition of a pastourelle to record a visit paid by Jean II to Eltham in 1364 during his time as hostage.[33] Jehan le Bel, who fought in Edward's service in Scotland in 1327 with Philippa's uncle Jean de Hainaut (Jean de Beaumont), was another poet-predecessor of Froissart who found patronage in the English court.[34]

If we look back to the last quarter of the thirteenth century, then the network of poets, composers, and diplomats in which Le Mote was placed maps an even broader history of exchange between England, Wallonie, and the north-west region of France. In his autobiographical *L'Espinette Amoureuse* Froissart mentions reading in his youth Adenet le Roi's *Cleomadés* (1285) and *Le Court d'Amours*.[35] Adenet (*c.*1240–1300) started his career as court poet with Henri III, duc de Brabant (himself a trouvère), moving later to Flanders and the patronage of Gui de Dampierre and then to Paris and further south. The anonymous author of *Le Court d'Amours* was attached to the court of Guillaume

[30] In 1405 Jean sans Peur agreed that as count of Flanders, he might be addressed in Flemish; he had a Flemish motto ('Ik houd' – I maintain), J. G. Russell, *Diplomats at Work: Three Renaissance Studies* (Stroud: Alan Sutton, 1992), 35. For further discussion of the term 'franchois' see Chapter 5.

[31] N. Wilkins, 'Music and Poetry at Court: England and France in the late Middle Ages', in V. J. Scattergood and J. W. Sherborne, eds, *English Court Culture in the Later Middle Ages*, (London: Duckworth, 1983), 183–204 (192).

[32] Wilkins, 'Music and Poetry at Court', 192.

[33] Froissart, *Oeuvres: Poésies*, ed. Scheler, II, 308–10; cited with translation by K. M. Figg, *The Short Lyric Poems of Jean Froissart: Fixed Forms and the Expression of the Courtly Ideal* (New York and London: Garland, 1994), no.2, 213–16.

[34] Froissart drew heavily on Jehan le Bel's *Vrayes Chroniques* for the first stages of his own *Chroniques* while in Philippa's service: J. Le Bel, *Chronique de Jean le Bel*, ed. J. Viard and E. Déprez, SHF, 2 vols (Paris: Renouard, 1904–5). Le Bel also composed songs and virelais, but none has survived. On his fervent support for Edward III over Philippe VI, see J. J. N. Palmer, 'Book I (1323–78) and Its Sources', in J. J. N. Palmer, ed., *Froissart: Historian*, (Woodbridge: Boydell, 1981), 7–24 (17).

[35] Ed. A. Fourrier, 2nd rev. edn (Paris: Klincksieck, 1974), lines 705 and 871 respectively.

I, Count of Hainaut, and would have been a contemporary of Jean de Condé, who also worked for Guillaume I. Jean de Condé was born between 1275 and 1280 and died in 1345: his *Messe des Oisiaus* bears interesting comparison with Chaucer's *Parliament of Fowls*. Jean de Condé knew two important works from the Arras–Lille region: *Renart le Nouvel* and *Le Tournoi de Chauvency*.[36] In fact, he declares in his *Dit d'Entendement* that he had heard *Renart le Nouvel* ('J'ai oï de Renart les vers . . . ').[37] Ribard declares that *Renart le Nouvel* inspired Jean 'avant tout'; the influence of *Le Tournoi* can also be detected in more than one of his compositions. Like Froissart, Jean seemed to know *Cleomadés*; he also knew *Le Castelain de Couci*, itself written by a fellow Hainuyer, Jakemés.[38] Another of Jean's contemporaries was Watriquet de Couvin (fl.1319–29) from a village in Hainaut, two of whose works experiment with lyric grafting, a trait of narratives from this wider region: the comical *Trois Dames de Paris*, and the *Fatrasie*. Watriquet himself worked further south as a court minstrel attached to Blois and Châtillon, and there are links between his work and that of Le Mote and Machaut.[39]

Hainuyer and Picard writers voiced the vernacular literary interests of the English aristocracy for several decades of the fourteenth century. They were supported by a significant poetic community that traded contacts across north-western France and the Low Countries which, in addition to those I have mentioned thus far, included Jehan Acart de Hesdin, and, from Tournai, Gilles li Muisis and Jean Campion.[40] Such personal and literary traffic indicates the different contexts there were for the use of French on each side of the Channel,

[36] Butterfield, *Poetry and Music*, and 'The Musical Contexts of *Le Tournoi de Chauvency*', in *Autour du Tournoi de Chauvency*, ed. M. Chazan and N. Regalado, Publications romanes et françaises (Geneva: Droz, forthcoming).

[37] J. Ribard, *Un Ménestrel du XIVe siècle: Jean de Condé* (Geneva: Droz, 1969), 384–5. For further information on the life of Jean and Baudouin de Condé, see Baudouin de Condé and Jean de Condé, *Dits et contes de Baudouin de Condé et de son fils Jean de Condé*, ed. A. Scheler, 3 vols (Brussels: Devaux, 1866–7), I, xiii. Wimsatt points out that Scheler's surmise for the date when Baudouin began writing (1240) seems early 'since Jean was still writing in 1337, ninety-seven years later': *Chaucer and the French Love Poets: The Literary Background of 'The Book of the Duchess'* (Chapel Hill: University of North Carolina Press, 1968), 166, n. 1.

[38] Ribard, *Jean de Condé*, 373–6.

[39] For a recent collection of essays on poets of this region, see J.-C. Herbin, ed., *Richesses médiévales du Nord et du Hainaut* (Valenciennes: Presses universitaires de Valenciennes, 2002), and the synthesis in J. Devaux, 'From the Court of Hainaut to the Court of England: The Example of Jean Froissart', in Allmand, ed., *War, Government and Power*, 1–20.

[40] Gilles li Muisis (1272–1353) was abbot of the monastery of St-Martin of Tournai and a chronicler and poet. Campion, mentioned by Gilles, was a cleric of Tournai and later of Bruges (Wimsatt, *Chaucer and the French Love Poets*, 66 and n. 72; who cites E. Pognon, 'Ballades mythologiques de Jehan de le Mote, Philippe de Vitry, Jean Campion', *Humanisme et Renaissance*, 5 (1938), 385–417 (407–17), and Gilles li Muisis, *Poésies*, ed. K. de Lettenhove, 2 vols (Louvain: Lefever, 1882), I, xxxi–xxxii; II, 259–79.

and its varying political meaning and significance as a language for writers of sometimes conflicting sympathies.

All of this is by way of introducing the confusing, comic yet vituperative lyric exchange between Jehan de le Mote and Philippe de Vitry. In its full extent the sequence comprises six *ballades* copied into the fifteenth-century manuscript BnF lat. 3343, fols 109r–111v. There are two by Le Mote, one by Vitry, a response from Le Mote, then a final pair by Jean Campion and Le Mote again.[41] The third and fourth *ballades*, by Vitry and Le Mote, occur as a separate pairing in the lyric compilation now in the University of Pennsylvania Library, MS Codex 902 (formerly MS French 15). Fig. 2 shows the last stanza of de Vitry's followed by the response from Le Mote. Clearly, then as now, this pair was seen (given the rubrics 'Balade' and 'La Response') as containing the heart of the exchange, its (as it were) vitriolic core. Philippe de Vitry accuses Jehan of being a traitor and of seeking to support a country cursed by God (*Albion de Dieu maldite*). Jehan replies mildly and respectfully, insisting that although the land of Gaul is, by contrast, loved by God (*Gaulle de Dieu amee*) he does not belong to it.[42]

Balade [Maistre Philippe de Vitry]	
De terre en Grec Gaule appellee,	Out of the land called Gaul in Greek,
Castor[fuitis, fuyans] comme serfs,	Runaway beaver, fleeing like a deer
En Albion de flun nommee,	To Albion named after the river,
Roys Antheus devenus serfs.	Rude Actaeon, turned into a stag;
Nicement sers	You serve foolishly
Quant sous fais d'anfent fains amer	When childishly you pretend to love
D'amour qu'Orpheus ot despite.	With a love that Orpheus despised.
[Lou], tu n'as d'amour fors l'amer,	Wolf, you have no love except bitterness
En Albion de Dieu maldicte.	In Albion cursed by God.

[41] These six ballades were first described by Pognon, 'Ballades mythologiques'; four of them (the Vitry/Le Mote and the Campion/Le Mote pairings) were discussed, edited and translated by James I. Wimsatt in his study of poems from the Pennsylvania MS, *Chaucer and the Poems of 'Ch' in University of Pennsylvania MS French 15* (Cambridge: D. S. Brewer, 1982), 51–60 and 75–7. F. N. M. Diekstra then presented a new edition and translation of the Vitry/Le Mote pair that placed greater weight on readings from the Paris MS, and suggested several changes and corrections to Wimsatt's edition: 'The Poetic Exchange between Philippe de Vitry and Jean de le Mote: a New Edition', *Neophilologus*, 70 (1986), 504–19. Wimsatt returned to the ballades—now including all six—in his *Chaucer and His French Contemporaries*, 63–7, 71–5. For further details of Vitry and his associates, see M. Bent and A. Wathey, 'Vitry, Philippe de', *Grove Music Online*, ed. L. Macy <p://www.grovemusic.com> (accessed 30 January 2008). I am grateful to Yolanda Plumley for her comments on a draft of this chapter, and for kindly allowing me to read her unpublished paper The 'Mythological' Ballades by Philippe de Vitry, Jehan de Le Mote, and Jehan Campion Revisited', read at the *Leeds International Medieval Congress*, July 2008, which considers all six of the ballades.

[42] For further comment on the classical references in some of these pieces, see N. McDonald, 'Doubts about Medea, Briseyda and Helen: interpreting classical allusion in the fourteenth-century French ballade *Medee fu en amer veritable*', in *Studies in English Language and Literature: 'Doubt wisely' Papers in Honour of E. G. Stanley*, ed. M. J. Toswell and E. M. Tyler (London and New York: Routledge, 1996), 252–66.

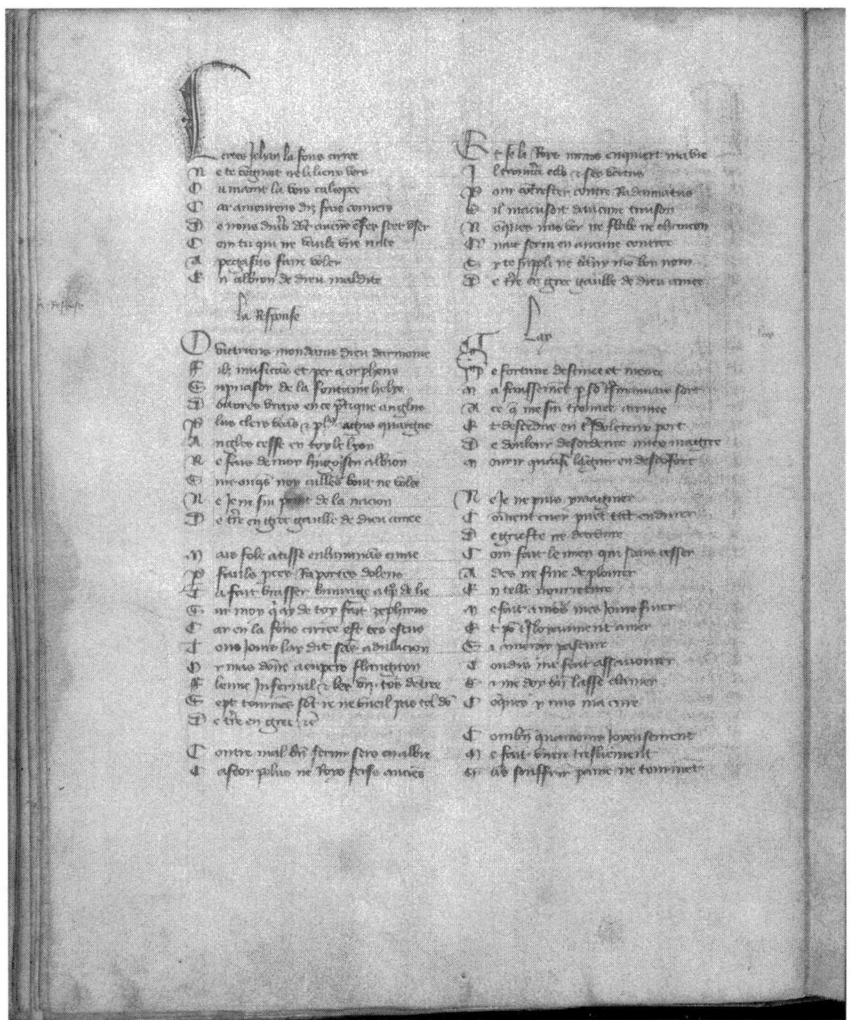

Figure 2. Jehan de le Mote/Philippe de Vitry exchange of *ballades*

University of Pennsylvania Library, MS Codex 902, f.23rb.

T'umbre de fuite yert accusee	Your shade in flight will be accused
Par Radamancus le pervers	By the malevolent Rhadamanthus
Et de Roy Minnos condempnee	And condemned by King Minos
A vij tours de queue a revers.	With seven turns of his tail backwards.
[Eacus pers]	The pale Aeacus
Contraindra ta langue a laper,	Will constrain your tongue to lap,

Comme de renoié traïte,
De Flagiton, l'amere mer,
En Albion de Dieu maldicte./

Like that of a renegade traitor,
From Phlegethon, the bitter sea,
In Albion cursed by God.

Certes, Jehan, la fons Cirree
Ne te congnoit, ne li lieux vers
Ou maint la vois Caliopee.
Car amoureus diz fais couvers
De nons divers,
Dont aucuns enfés scet user
Com tu, qui ne vaulz une mite
A Pegasus faire voler
En Albion de Dieu maldicte.

Indeed, John, the fountain of Cirrha
Does not know you, nor the green place
Where the voice of Calliope stays.
For you make amorous poems filled
With divers names.
Which any child knows how to use
Like you, who are not able one whit
To make Pegasus fly
In Albion cursed by God.

La Response [Jehan de la Mote respond a ladite balade Maistre Philippe de Victry]

O Victriens, mondains Dieu d'armonie,
Filz Musicans et per a Orpheus,
Supernasor de la fontaine Helye,
Doctores vrays, en ce pratique Auglus,
Plus clerc veans et plus agus qu'Argus,
Angles [en chant], cesse en toy le lyon;
Ne fais de moy Hugo s'en Albion
Suis. Onques n'oÿ ailleurs bont ne volee;
Ne je ne sui point de la nacion
De terre en Grec Gaulle de Dieu amee.

O man of Vitry, worldly god of harmony,
Son of Musicians and peer of Orpheus,
Superlative Naso of the fountain of Helicon,
True doctor, Aulus Gellius in the world of affairs,
More clearsighted and more acute than Argus,
Angel in song, restrain the lion in you;
Do not make Hugo of me because I am in Albion.
I have never heard that anywhere else anyway;
And I in no way belong to the nation
Of the land in Greek called Gaul, loved by God.

Mais [foleanse] enluminans envie
Par fauls procés, raportés d'Oleus.
T'a fait brasser buvrage a trop de lie
Sur moy, qui ay de toy fait Zephirus;
Car en la fons Cirree est tes escus;
Tous jours l'ay dit sans adulacion.
Or m'as donné Acu pers Flangiton,
Fleuve infernal, et les vij tours d'entree

But folly which incites envy
Through false information reported by Aeolus
Has made you brew a drink with too many dregs
For me, who have made of you Zephirus;
For your escutcheon is in the fountain of Cirrha;
I have always said it without flattery.
Now you have given me the pale Aeacus of Phlegethon,
The infernal river, and the seven turns upon entering

Sept tourmens sont. Je nene vueil pas tel don	Are seven torments. I do not wish such a gift
De terre en Grec [Gaulle de Dieu amee].	From the land in Greek called Gaul, loved by God.
Contre mal bien [ferme] sers en Albie,	Firm against evil I serve in Albion;
Castor, [ne leus], ne roys serfs [Antheus]./	I am neither beaver nor wolf nor rude stag Actaeon.
Et si li Roys Minos enquiert ma vie,	And if King Minos investigates my life,
Il trouvera Eclo et ses vertus	He will find Echo and her powers
Pour contrester contre Radannatus,	To refute Rhadamanthus,
S'il m'acusoit d'aucune traïson.	If he accused me of any treason.
[N'ains noms ne mis en fable n'en] chançon	Nor have I ever put any name in fiction or in song
Qui n'ait servi en aucune contree.	Which has not served in any country.
Sy te suppli, ne banny mon bon nom	So I entreat you, do not banish my good name
De terre en Grec Gaulle de Dieu amee.[43]	From the land in Greek called Gaul, loved by God.

Both poems, and Philippe's especially, are opaque and allusive.[44] Philippe's stanza pattern is quite compressed: two sections of four octosyllabic lines connected by a short four-syllable line. His central metaphors are of flight and failed eloquence: Jehan is accused of fleeing, a traitor (traïte), into a cursed land.[45] From Gaul, a land blessed with classical learning, Jehan has retreated to Albion where the muse Calliope does not know him. The second stanza is remarkable for containing seemingly the earliest literary reference to Dante in French—his *Inferno*, Canto V.[46] Here Philippe develops a multiple, layered set of insults. Jehan is presented as being one of the damned, condemned by Radamanthus and Minos, judges of the underworld in Virgil and Dante respectively. Minos makes seven reverse turns of his tail and forces Jehan's tongue to lap the bitter water. This curious reference has previously been linked to the third stanza where Philippe appears to sneer at Jehan's rather random use of poetic name-dropping ('Car amoureus diz fais couvers/De nons divers') [For you make amorous poems filled with divers names]. But there may be another, less elevated, point to the description. The English had been branded with tails (and by extension with

[43] Diekstra, 'The Poetic Exchange'. I have regularised the abbreviations. Text in square brackets is added from the Paris MS.

[44] Although Diekstra resolved many of the points found obscure by Wimsatt (see n. 38 above).

[45] It is interesting to compare a passage in Du Bellay's *La Deffence et Illustration* where he says bad translators, and especially those who attempt to translate poetry, deserve to be called traitors (J. Du Bellay, *The Regrets: A Bilingual Edition*, ed. and trans. R. Helgerson (Philadelphia: University of Pennsylvania Press, 2006), 335).

[46] According to Wimsatt, *Chaucer and the Poems of 'Ch'*, 56.

cowardice) by the French ever since the twelfth century. The story occurs in Wace, with other early references in Latin (1163) to a *caudatus Anglicus* and in Occitan (Peire d'Auvergne).[47] As Wace tells it, some people near Dorchester would not listen to the preaching of St Augustine and hung skate-tails on the back of his clothing. He retaliated by praying that their children be born with tails, a punishment that Wace reports with a thudding repetitiveness fit for such a playground activity:

Kar trestuit cil ki l'escharnirent
E ki les cues li pendirent
Furent cué e cues orent
E unkes puis perdre nes porent;
Tuit cil unt puis esté cué
Ki vindrent d'icel parenté,
Cué furent e cué sunt,
Cues orent e cues unt,
Cues unt detriés en la char . . .

[For all those who mocked him and hung tails on him got tails and were tailed and could never lose them thereafter. Everyone from this family has been tailed ever since; they were and are tailed, they had and have tails, tails are behind them . . .][48]

I have quoted this for two reasons. First, it shows the irresistible potential (seized by Wace) for wordplay in this miniature exemplum—it gives the English not a generalized character description such as drunkenness or lechery but a resonant verbal tag. Second, Wace emphasizes the idea of family: rather like Marie de France's *Bisclavret* where the wicked noblewoman whose nose is bitten off by her werewolf husband has children without noses, these local hooligans have children with tails, a story with a surplus instead of a lacuna. That the English as a whole should be called 'coué' characterizes them as being all somehow related.

'L'Anglois coué' became a widely repeated taunt that (as we shall see) continued into the fifteenth century, in Machaut and Deschamps as well as in exultant war poems such as this dauphinois poem:

Arière, Englois couez, arière,
Aiés la goutte et la gravelle,
Et le coul taillé rasibus![49]

[47] P. Rickard, 'Anglois coué and l'Anglois qui couve', *French Studies*, 7 (1953), 48–55; and his *Britain in Medieval French Literature 1100–1500* (Cambridge: Cambridge University Press, 1956), 165–6.

[48] Wace, *Wace's Roman de Brut: A History of the British*, ed. and trans. J. Weiss, rev. edn (Exeter: University of Exeter Press, 2002), 345, lines 13711–44.

[49] Cited by Charles Petit-Dutaillis in E. Lavisse, *Histoire de France*, 9 vols (Paris: Hachette, 1900–11), IV.2, 54. For other references, see also Machaut, *La Prise d'Alixandre*, ed. and trans. B. Palmer, lines 8124–31; a *sotte* chanson by the trouvère Jehan de Baillehaut discussed by M.-G.

Get back, tailed English, get back,
May you get gout and stones in your urine
And a tailed arse alongside both!

It is hard to resist the thought that Vitry is likewise gleefully putting that old slur to work in this somewhat gloomy reference. Even more slyly, with a pair of contrary rhymes ('pervers', 'revers') he implies that Jehan's retreat is linguistic as well as geographical: his tongue as he passes over the fiery channel between Gaul and Albion has been condemned for speaking disreputable, unlearned, indeed childish babble.

Jehan's reply, in a more expansive ten-syllable, ten-line stanza form, disarms blame with praise. It is a cunning riposte, since if his tongue has indeed learnt another, lower mode of speech, then it is expressing it only as a string of compliments to Vitry. Each point is returned: Vitry's refrain ('En Albion de Dieu maldicte') is cleverly combined with the first line ('De terre en Grec Gaule appellee') to produce a new refrain: ('De terre en Grec Gaulle de Dieu amee'). If Jehan is ignorant of the 'fountain of Cirrha' then for Vitry it is his shield ('en la fons Cirree est tes escus'); he notes the sevenfold taunt about Minos's tail, and turns it back, saying that it is a gift he does not wish to receive. In the third stanza his rhetorical strategy is made even more explicit: Minos will find only Echo when he seeks the so-called traitor. Jehan may not be of the nation called Gaul ('. . . je ne sui point de la nacion/ De terre en Grec Gaulle de Dieu amee') but (if I read him right) that is because his poetry does not speak narrowly from within one context:

[N'ains noms ne mis en fable n'en] chançon
Q*ui* n'ait *ser*vi en aucune contree.

Nor have I ever put any name in fiction or in song
Which has not served in any country.

The whole *ballade*, in short, functions as a returned gift, a blow-by-blow denial that not only refuses to be cowed, but even manages to flatter as it repudiates.

So what is the real issue in this poetic quarrel? Philippe de Vitry, a bishop and statesman, music scholar and composer, played an important role in Anglo-French diplomatic relations in the first decades of the fourteenth century. He had close connections over many years with Louis de Clermont, comte and later duc

Grossel, 'Trouvères du Hainaut', in *Image et Mémoire de Hainaut Médiéval*, ed. J.-C. Herbin (Valenciennes: Presses Universitaires de Valenciennes, 2004), 85–98 (97–8); the 11th fatrasie d'Arras, lines 8–9 in L. C. Porter, ed., *La Fatrasie et le fatras, essai sur la poésie irrationnelle en France au Moyen Age* (Geneva: Droz, 1960), 124. The relationship between this taunt and the widespread use of *rime couwee* in Anglo-Norman verse deserves further investigation though it cannot have been an exclusive one. As D. L. Jeffrey and B. J. Levy, eds, *The Anglo-Norman Lyric: An Anthology* (Toronto: Pontifical Institute of Mediaeval Studies, 1990; 2006), 20–23 point out, continental poets also used *rime couwee*, such as Rutebeuf in his *Complainte de Saint Amour*. Compare also Robert Mannyng's reference to *rime couwee* in his *Chronicle* (lines 47 and 51).

de Bourbon: from 1340 he worked in several capacities as a senior member of the royal administration, and represented Jean II shortly after his coronation in 1350 in the papal court at Avignon. Present at the contentious event of Edward III's homage to Philippe VI for Gascony and Ponthieu in April 1331, he may have accompanied the duc de Bourbon to London in the previous month.[50] Petrarch, who particularly admired him, described him as 'the only true poet among the French', and personified him as 'Gallus' in a debate between music and poetry in the fourth eclogue of the *Bucolicum carmen* (?1344).[51] This suggests that Vitry had something of a reputation as a spokesman for French interests, and this can also be gleaned from notes he wrote into his own copy of Guillaume de Nangis's *Chronicon* about the treachery of Edward I in 1301 and, later in the manuscript, on the danger posed to Paris by the English in 1346.[52] Was he really furious with Jehan de le Mote for going over to the English side? It is hard to tell whether there is a specific political grievance here, largely because the dispute is cast in such literary terms. Philippe de Vitry was certainly capable of far stronger invective, as we can see from the Latin text of his motet *Phi millies/ O Creator/ Iacet granum/ Quam sufflabit*, which occurs in the same manuscript as the *ballades*:

Phi millies ad te, triste pecus,
cauda monstrum, quod in Francum decus
linguam scribis quam nescis promere!
Quid? Mugitum pro melo vomere
quod musicus horret ebmelicum!
Non puduit carmen chimericum
palam dare quod Flaccus versibus
primis dampnat. Ve! qui tot fecibus
Danos pascis, olei venditor,
mendacii publici conditor . . .

(Triplum, 1–10)

[Fie! a thousand times on you, sad brute, monsters' tail, for your writing in the tongue of the Franks, their glory, what you don't know how to express! What! To vomit unmelodious bellowing instead of song, which makes Music shudder! He has not blushed to present openly what Horace damns in his first verses. Woe! You who feed the English [Danos] with so many feces, vendor of oil [flatterer], maker of public lies . . .][53]

[50] Bent and Wathey, 'Vitry, Philippe de'. A. Wathey, 'European Politics and Musical Culture at the Court of Cyprus', in *The Cypriot-French Repertory of the Manuscript Torino J.II.9* (Stuttgart: Hänssler, 1995), 33–53.

[51] Two letters from Petrarch to Vitry survive, from 1350 and 1351; Petrarch called him 'litteratissimus homo': A. Wathey, 'Myth and Mythography in the Motets of Philippe de Vitry', *Musica e storia*, 6 (1998), 81, 106 (81).

[52] Wathey, 'Myth and Mythography', 98; A. Wathey, 'Philippe de Vitry's Books', in *Books and Collectors 1200–1700: Essays Presented to A. G. Watson*, ed. J. P. Carley and C. G. C. Tite (London: British Library, 1997), 145–52.

[53] Wimsatt, *Chaucer and His French Contemporaries*, 73–4 ('puplici' has been corrected to 'publici'). I have used his translation, except for 'member' which I have changed to 'tail' (see below).

This outburst takes the insulting language further into the realm of bestiality (already present in the *ballade*): his addressee is given a tail and a tongue that bellows rather sings in terms that are close to a passage in Gace de la Buigne's *Roman des Deduis* (1359–77), where the sound of dogs barking is compared to hocketed polyphonic singing. Gace particularly mentions the unsavoury habit dogs have of eating their own vomit, and his reference to Vitry elsewhere in the roman could imply that he knows this motet.[54] Although James Wimsatt translates *cauda monstrum* as 'monsters' member' it seems more likely to refer to the *caudatus Anglicus*.[55] This was often associated with dogs, and the English often cast the insult back on to the French. As we will see later in the chapter, Deschamps claims to have the phrase 'dogue' turned on him as a Frenchman, and in 1477–9 Charles Martigny, Bishop of Elne and Louis XI's visiting ambassador, heard cries in the London streets of 'Franche dogues'.[56] Vitry falls short of making a specific animal allusion here (although he calls Le Mote a beaver, deer and wolf in the *ballade*), but amplifies grotesquely the inappropriate sounds produced by le Mote's inarticulate bestial attempts to 'write in the tongue of the Franks' (*in Francum decus linguam scribes*).[57]

Philippe's *ballade* seems to me a subtler, perhaps more delicate matter. Using the tried and tested competitive arena of lyric riposte, Vitry raises the question of poetic, as opposed to political, allegiance. Precisely by casting his aspersions in terms of classical allusion, Vitry makes the debate a broad matter of poetic authority, and not a narrow one of mere chauvinism. In a sense the question becomes: what happens to a poet who crosses the Channel? Does he find himself still speaking the same language? What happens to his French? For whom does he now speak? These questions are all the more pressing when the language remains ostensibly the same. Has anything in fact changed?

As Derrida reminds us, the language of colonization—of naming names—gives power as much as it wields it. Vitry sets up this language in a paradoxical and partial way. His fury at Le Mote seems oddly misplaced, since it is side-tracked into a matter of how a vernacular French poet should refer to his classical

[54] E. E. Leach, *Sung Birds: Music, Nature and Poetry in the Later Middle Ages* (Ithaca: Cornell University Press, 2007), 209–37. See especially 212 (on vomit) and 229–32 (on Vitry).

[55] R. E. Latham, *Revised Medieval Latin Word-List from British and Irish Sources* (London: Oxford University Press, 1965) has several references to English tails under *caud/a*. The first continental version of *Boeve de Hantoun* contains the claim that 'L'Anglois coué' was descended from a hideously deformed giant (Rickard, *Britain in Medieval French Literature*, 165–6). If this interpretation is accepted it strengthens Wimsatt's case that the unnamed addressee of this motet is again Le Mote (*Chaucer and the Poems of 'Ch'*, 57 and *Chaucer and His French Contemporaries*, 73).

[56] Russell, *Diplomats at Work*, 38–9. The continuing life of the insult is shown in the complaint by Etienne Perlin, a French priest and physician of the university in Paris, of being called a 'French dogue' in London in the last two years of Edward VI's reign (1551–3), (K. Lambley, *The Teaching and Cultivation of the French Language in England During Tudor and Stuart Times* (Manchester: Manchester University Press/London: Longmans, 1920), 117–19). Cp Wace on the 'barking' and 'howling' English, Chapter 2, n. 11 above.

[57] Cf. Deschamps's references to animals in Ballade no. 192, II: the lion (Jean le Bon), boar (English king); 'l'asne blanc' (Charles V); 'le cerf volant' (Charles VI).

masters. Both Vitry and Le Mote, in that sense, are equally subject to a master tongue, as Le Mote insists, yet Vitry is rightly sensitive to the difference that context makes. Speaking from 'over there' puts Le Mote on a different cultural footing from Vitry. Both poets, however they express themselves, are aware that something is different about their French, even if it cannot easily be expressed. Their language is both the same and different. Neither is in a position to speak outside it, yet each seems to feel the other has impugned his right to speak from within it.

DESCHAMPS AND THE *ESTRANGE NASCION*

As I remarked earlier, Deschamps is often credited with a 'rather modern-sounding partisanship for France'.[58] Yet as is also remarked, he uses the word 'nacion' rarely and such commentators as Gaston Duchet-Suchaux and Liliane Dulac have rightly warned against modern misunderstandings of his usage.[59] In what follows here and in the next chapters my aim is to work with and through some of the words that he and other authors offer us in contexts of cross-channel or continental tension: a mixed and eclectic, but also, I hope, profitably cumulative strategy.

Born in about 1340, as was Chaucer, Eustace Morel Deschamps was from Vertus in Champagne. Of modest lineage in the minor nobility, with the title of *écuyer*, he went to the university of Orléans, was married during 1366–73 and had three children. Like Chaucer he had a career of aristocratic and in due course royal service, first to les comtes de Vertus as a *huissier d'armes* (sergeant-at-arms); then as a member of the royal household. From 1375 to 1380 he was *bailli de Valois* in service to Philippe d'Orléans, brother of Jean le Bon; from 1389 *bailli de Senlis* until his death in 1405. He was more directly and consistently involved in a military career than Chaucer, whose own efforts seem to have come to a vaguely recorded and not particularly distinguished end with his ransom in 1361.[60] Deschamps's vast lyric output contains some bitterly abusive language directed especially against the Flemish as well as the English, and some vivid

[58] Wimsatt, *Chaucer and His French Contemporaries*, 244.

[59] G. Duchet-Suchaux, 'Emergence d'un sentiment national chez Eustache Deschamps', in D. Buschinger, ed., *Autour d'Eustache Deschamps: Actes du Colloque du Centre d'Études Médiévales de l'Université de Picardie-Jules Verne Amiens, 5–8 Novembre 1998* (Amiens: Presses du Centre d'études médiévales, Université de Picardie-Jules Verne, 1999), 73–7; L. Dulac, 'La representation de la France: Eustache Deschamps et Christine de Pizan', in Buschinger, ed., *Autour d'Eustache Deschamps*, 79–92.

[60] *Chaucer Life-Records*, ed. M. M. Crow and C. C. Olson (Oxford: Clarendon Press, 1966), 23–8.

depictions of the grubby and lice-ridden privations of military journeys across the continent.[61]

Three areas will be briefly considered here: his sense of his own locale and people, his sharp comments about other peoples, and finally the portrait he offers of the linguistic and cultural relations between the French and the English. Interleaved will be some remarks on the wider cultural meanings of the term nation in the medieval period.

The principal gloss of *natio* in Latin, *nation/nascion* in French, *nacioun* in Chaucer (where it occurs eight times), is not the modern 'state' but birth, family, or lineage. The word 'nativitez' is indeed often used as a synonym, as in this *ballade* by Deschamps:

> . . . François ou Allemans
> Anglès, autres nativitez,
> Bourgoingnons, Bretons et Normans . . .
> (Balade no.1472, VIII, pp. 174–5, lines 21–3)

[French or German, English or other 'nations', Burgundians, Bretons and Normans . . .]

The perception of self and the community radiates outward from the condition of one's birth and family, and involves a fluid idea of the public domain in which one might see oneself. Language is crucial: it is not just that a word might have a different meaning in one language than in another, but that one language might depend on another for its meaning. We are not observing a static concept, but a fluid set of terminologies which include (among many others) *pays, royaume, région, contrée* in French and *folk, contree, kynde, comonalte* in English. Careful attention to the wider practice of translation finds a desire not so much to create simple equivalence as alternative inventions, meanings which arise out of efforts to articulate difference.

What may seem surprising, at least initially, is that 'nativitez' in the above quotation clearly refers to regional francophone peoples and not simply to the French, Germans, and English. This requires some disentangling in relation to two other broad cultural uses of 'nation' in the context of universities and of merchants. Both in universities and in trade we find a use of 'nation' that connects the personal and local with broader institutional practices. The earliest vernacular use of the word *nascïon* to apply to university groupings occurs in a

[61] All references to Deschamps's works are to the *Oeuvres complètes*, ed. de Saint-Hilaire and Raynaud. See also two recent anthologies with extensive commentary: J.-P. Boudet and H. Millet, eds, *Eustache Deschamps en son temps*, (Paris: Publications de la Sorbonne, 1997) and *Eustache Deschamps: Selected Poems*, ed. I. S. Laurie and D. M. Sinnreich-Levi, trans. D. Curzon and J. Fiskin (New York and London: Routledge, 2003). For details of his biography, see vol. 11 of the *Oeuvres complètes*, 'Vie de Deschamps', 9–99, and more recently, I. S. Laurie, 'Eustache Deschamps: 1340?–1404', in D. M. Sinnreich-Levi, ed., *Eustache Deschamps, French Courtier-Poet: His Work and his World* (New York: AMS Press, 1998), 1–72. See further K. Becker, *Eustache Deschamps: L'État actuel de la recherche* (Orléans: Paradigme, 1996), 24–6.

thirteenth-century stanzaic poem, *Le Chastiement des clers*.[62] University nations arose as a form of student organization or guild.[63] Initiated as a system in Bologna in the late twelfth century, the 'nations' in Paris consisted of the French, English, Norman, and Picard, loose groupings to enable students to congregate with others from certain birthplaces, where for instance, the French nation included Spaniards, Italians, and Levantines; and English meant also Flemings, Scandinavians, Finns, Hungarians, Dutch, and Slavs. In the early history of the university at Bologna, the fluidity of these groupings is underlined by the evidence that one daughter university in the region had as many as fourteen nations (France, Picards, Burgundians, Poitevins, natives of Touraine and Maine, Normans, Catalans, Hungarians, Poles, Germans, Spanish, Occitan, English, and Gascons), although the most enduring structure was between Lombards, Ultramontanes, Tuscans, and Romans.[64] The Parisian division seems to have been more arbitrary than the Bolognese: the latter grew directly out of groups of foreign students seeking protection and conviviality, the former was more of an abstract system in imitation of the Italian model, which gradually took on more complex bureaucratic forms.[65]

Although it is tempting to see a modern sense of national distinction operating in these structures, other elements override. These—presumably very roughly linguistic—categories (which recall Bede's characterization of England as being made up of five languages) were evidently able to be redrawn or subsumed under broader headings according to context and need. What is especially striking is that universities were such multilingual institutions, whose function created an intellectual environment where (at least in principle) great diversity was tamed under a single pedagogic impulse. In terms of what 'French' and 'France' signified, France meant 'île de France' and the other 'French' regions were as distinct from that and from one another as Catalan, Tuscan, or Spanish, which is to say that they were not necessarily entirely distinct. To put it another way, like the butcher in *Des Deus Anglois et de l'Anel* who wonders whether the Englishmen are 'auuergnaz ou tiois', linguistic differences are perceived as such in far from uniform ways. Thus although the justly famous account of the nations in the thirteenth century by Jacques de Vitry, a student and master at Paris and an Austin canon, exuberantly badmouths everyone in the comic invective of student journalism, it also shows, in its very excessiveness, that these alleged caricatures were hardly intellectually serious even if they led to violence. The English were supposed to be drunkards and had tails ['anglicos potatores et caudatos affirmantes']; the French full of pride and like women in their appearance ['molles et

[62] D. Burrows, '*Le Chastiement des clers*: a *dit* concerning the Nations of the University of Paris, edited from Paris, Bibliothèque Nationale, MS fr.837', *Medium Aevum*, 69 (2000), 211–26.

[63] H. Rashdall, *The Universities of Europe in the Middle Ages*, rev. and ed. F. M. Powicke and A. B. Emden, 3 vols (Oxford: Oxford University Press, 1936), I, 151.

[64] Rashdall, *The Universities*, I, 155–6.

[65] Rashdall, *The Universities*, I, 161, 319.

muliebriter compositos asserentes']; the Germans were full of rage and bad language at their feasts ['teutonicos furibundos et in conuiuiis suis obscenos dicebant']; the Normans, vain and boastful ['inanes et gloriosos']; the Poitevins, traitors and friends of fortune ['proditores et fortune amicos']. The Burgundians had a reputation for being vulgar and stupid ['brutos et stultos']. The Bretons were often blamed for the death of Arthur. Lombards were avaricious, evil, and cowardly; the Romans, full of trouble and violence; the Sicilians, tyrannical and cruel; the Brabantines, men of blood, incendiaries, robbers, and rapists; the Flemish, in a final glut of adjectives, fickle, spendthrift, dedicated to feasting, soft, and slippery as butter, and unreliable ['flandrenses superfluos, prodigos, comessationibus deditos, et more butyri molles et remissos, appellabant'].[66] The university nations provide fascinating material for observing how social, pragmatic, and political needs worked across and through a hugely diverse linguistic population to create factions and communities.

The parallel world of trade also organized itself as a conglomeration of nations. Here the epicentre was Bruges, where merchant guilds and companies from all over Europe were based. Each 'nation' had its own hostel and many had streets named after them: thus the English Merchant Adventurers (of whom Caxton was later Governor) had a *domus Anglorum* on English Street and their own chapel in the Carmelite convent. Other hostels are listed for 'the Austrians, Biscayans, Castillians, Florentines, French, Genoese, Germans, Irish, Luccans, Portuguese, Scots, men of Smyrna, Spaniards, Turks, and Venetians, and streets named after the merchants of Lübeck, Bayonne, Scotland, Ireland, Florence, Gascony, Bordeaux, Denmark, Hamburg, Norway, Portugal, Venice, and Bilbao'.[67] Again, it is striking not just to note the sheer number of companies, but how their character indicates that trading interests were as much urban and regional as 'national'. The apparent proliferation of and desire for difference is mitigated when we realize how small Bruges was and hence how deeply interlinked individuals were, and also how specific institutions acted as centres for many trading nations at once. The Carmelite convent, for instance, hosted not only the English, but also the Hanseatic merchants from Lübeck, Hamburg, and Danzig, the Scots, Flemish, and Aragonese.[68] Like the universities, there was an intense intermixing of linguistic and cultural identities in a small space, in which larger trading interests were constantly cutting across the grain of what we would now call national differences. An individual like Anselmo Adornes, a Flemish nobleman of Genoese descent who had strong personal links with James III of

[66] J. de Vitry, *The Historia Occidentalis of Jacques de Vitry: A Critical Edition*, ed. J. Frederick Hinnesbusch, Spicilegium Friburgense, 17 (Fribourg: The University Press, 1972), 92.

[67] G. D. Painter, *William Caxton: A Quincentenary Biography of England's First Printer* (London: Chatto & Windus, 1976), 23, n. 1.

[68] R. Strohm, *Music in Late Medieval Bruges*, 64–5.

Scotland and owned a Scottish castle, testifies to the potential for cross-cultural mixing in the merchant communities.[69]

The question of how concepts of community and identity met across and were formed by these university and financial structures is intriguing. Notions of identity were evidently rich and overlapping: even within the merchant companies there was an international as well as local network of allegiances (for instance the silk merchants from Lucca had nations in Genoa, Rome, Paris, Bruges, and London), but such networks of professional loyalties also intersected with feudal, legal, or ecclesiastical obligations in complex and sometimes awkward ways.[70] One clue to the importance of the universities in shaping wider assumptions can be found in the disputes of the Council of Constance of 1414–18. University personnel were instrumental in bringing about General Councils as a response to the Great Schism: Constance, called by the Emperor Sigismund, took place in volatile and highly contentious political circumstances, bisected by the devastation of Agincourt. Unsurprisingly, matters of representation became extremely sensitive between the English and the French. There were four 'nations' at the outset—Italians, Germans, French, and English—a structure inherited from the 1409 Council of Pisa. It was a measure of English political clout that they held this place with only fifteen delegates out of the total of five hundred. By Constance, complications were caused by Sigismund's (unsuccessful) desire to make Hungary a fifth nation, and the late arrival of the Spanish. But the most explosive intervention was that of the French cardinal Pierre d'Ailly, who, already embroiled in efforts to denounce the Burgundians, turned on the English and argued that they should not be considered a separate nation but merely part of Germany. Since England was only one thirty-sixth of the Roman obedience, how could it have the status of a single nation?

The angry response of the English included such arguments as that they were not one nation but eight ('England, Scotland, and Wales—the three that together compose Great Britain—the kingdom of the Sea—and in Ireland, near to England, four large and notable kingdoms—Connaught, Galway, Munster, and Meath . . . also . . . the Orkneys', with five languages (English, Welsh, Irish, Gascon, and Cornish).[71] The famous definition of nation which emerges is interestingly capacious: England is just as much a nation as the Gallic nation 'whether nation be understood as a people marked off from others by blood relationship and habit of unity or by peculiarities of language, the most sure and positive sign and essence of a nation in divine and human law . . . or whether nation be

[69] R. Strohm, *Music in Late Medieval Bruges*, 65.

[70] L. R. Loomis, 'Nationality at the Council of Constance: An Anglo-French Dispute', *The American Historical Review*, 44:3 (1939), 508–27 (510). This article remains a very useful commentary on the Council.

[71] Loomis, 'Nationality at the Council of Constance', 524. It is interesting that in contrast to Bede's list, Latin is not included and Gascon is.

understood, as it should be, as a territory equal to that of the French nation'.[72] That language should be so important to the definition is as notable as the sheer flexibility of the claims. No one ground for claiming international importance is sufficient; England's status must depend on many factors, some of them contradictory. Altogether, the document is a revealing admission of the inconsistencies of 'national' claims, a recognition that territory, language, blood, and habit pull in different directions and are fiercely and confusingly at issue between 'English' and 'French' (where Gascon is English and Burgundian French).

Although the university had a powerful role in shaping the character of ecclesiastical debate in the Councils, the ideas of nation did not overlap: the four Paris 'nations' were not identical to the four Council nations and the composition of the Council nations, as we have seen, were subject to much wrangling. The Council of Constance has its points of connection with the modern European Union, but we must recognize the fluidity of its conceptual categories and the tensions between ecclesiastical, political, and financial interests that forced discussions of identity out into public debate. In inventing arguments about international status the English were having to pretend to a size and weight that belonged to them only through conquest and alliance; similarly, the French were forced to admit that 'France' was a much smaller entity than seemed right or plausible. Nation, in short, is obscurely as well as insistently claimed.[73]

Deschamps, likewise, though a little earlier, seems to have a variety of ways of imagining a relationship between an individual and his larger social context. He goes from the very local to the nebulously large: from *cité, bonne ville*, and *lieu* to *royaume, région, contrée, pays, terre*:

> O doulz pais, terre treshonourable,
> Ou chascuns a ce qu'il veult demander
> Pour son argent, et a pris raisonnable,
> Char, pain et vin, poisson d'yaue et de mer,
> Chambre a par soy, feu, dormir, reposer,
> Liz, orilliers, blans draps flairans la graine,
> Et pour chevaulz foing, litiere et avoine,
> Estre servis, et par bonne ordonnance,

[72] 'sive sumatur natio ut gens secundum cognationem et collectionem ab alia distincta, sive secundum diversitatem linguarum, quae maximam et verissimam probant nationem et ipsius essentiam, jure divino pariter et humano, ut infra dicetur; sive etiam sumatur natio pro provincia aequali etiam nationi Gallicanae, sicut sumi deberet.' (H. von der Hardt, *Magnum oecumenicum Constantiense Concilium*, 6 vols in 4 (Frankfurt, 1700), V, 92; cited in Loomis, 'Nationality at the Council of Constance', 524–5).

[73] For detailed discussion, see Loomis's classic account; Rashdall, *The Universities*, reflects on the wider role of the universities on 572–84.

Et en seurté de ce qu'om porte et maine:
Tel pais n'est qu'en royaume de France!
(Balade no.1317, VII, pp. 79–80, lines 1–10)

[O sweet country, very honourable land, where everyone has what he wants to ask for his money, and at a reasonable price: meat, bread and wine, fish from the river and sea, a room to oneself, a fire, sleep, rest, a bed, pillows, white oak-scented sheets, and hay, stable-fodder and oats for the horses; to be served properly and secure in what one carries and transports; such a country does not exist except in the realm of France!]

This *ballade*, an instance of *laudatio loci*, makes an effort to associate stability with the notion of France, calling on and affirming ideas of peace, justice, and plenty.[74] The characterization is comically close to the positive features of the current national stereotype, and reads a little like a tourist brochure: come to a place of good food and wine, with the latest in luxury bedlinen, the best service and reasonable prices. That element of marketing hype is a softer version of Chaucer's rather more hard-hitting 'The Former Age', where 'a blysful lyf, a paisible and a swete' (1) describes not the present but the irretrievable past. The 'doun of fetheres' and 'bleched shete' (45) are a sign not of present comfort but the indulgent habits of those 'forpampred with outrage' (5); 'seurtee' in the English poem is precisely what cannot be found except in the golden world of the pre-civilized. The effect of the comparison is to highlight the hint of special pleading, even perhaps comic irony in Deschamps's poem: the results of English chevauchées and the pillaging local *routiers* left France miserably ravaged rather than brimming with rosy-cheeked *hosteliers*. But Deschamps characteristically plays the positive spin for all it is worth, and ensures the hollowness of the claims works to promote rather than denigrate his *pays*. This is a landscape for a merchant to feel at ease in, he goes on, unlike Germany, Moravia, Luxembourg, and Bohemia. France is all firmness, justice, and stability ('ferme et estable'); the mental construct is purposely strong and comfortable, one created in opposition to doubt, vulnerability, uncertainty, and fluidity.

Deschamps performs a very similar act in other *ballades* with Paris and Champagne. What we see is an effort to create a stable idea that is not necessarily itself stable and that can be applied to a local as much as a 'national' community. His famous poem on his own hometown, Vertus, which he connects through paranomasia with his own name ('Je fu jadiz de terre vertueuse,/ Nez de Vertus' [I was formerly from a virtuous land, /Born at Vertu] takes a more Chaucerian descent towards sharply expressed pessimism. Having been called 'Eustace' from early childhood he is now burned; from now on his name has changed to 'Burned of the Fields':

[74] For similar sentiments, see Gilles li Muisis, *Des estas de tous gens séculers*, in *Poésies*, II, 18.

Eustace fu appellé dès enfans;
Or sui tous ars, s'est mon nom remué:
J'aray desor a nom Brulé des Champs....

Las! ma terre est destruitte et ruyneuse,
Je suis desert, destruit et desolé...

[Eustace is what I have been called since my childhood;
Now I am completely burned, my name is changed;
I will have from now on the name Burned of the Fields.

Alas! My land is destroyed and ruined,
I am ravaged, destroyed and desolate...

(Balade no. 835, V, pp. 5–6, lines 6–8, 17–18)

The subtlety of this poem's identification of the first-person speaker with the ruined landscape of his own sense of self is all contained within the way 'ma terre est destruitte et ruyneuse' passes with painful continuity into 'Je suis desert, destruit et desolé'. Deschamps's passionate evocation of his profound attachment to his 'terre' is matched only by his denunciation of the English violence that burned it to the ground. But in this complex complaint Deschamps uses English military action as a stimulus not merely to express outrage against the enemy but to create a new kind of poetic self, one that is grounded, if we can forgive the pun, in a vehemently local sense of possession. This new self is also perhaps playing on the name of the great trouvère Gace Brulé: Eustace rises from the ashes of English devastation to become a latter-day poetic master.[75]

If this kind of moment in Deschamps's writing reminds us of modern-day wine producers who attach great importance to the old-fashioned values of 'terroir', then at other times he is more interested in creating a much larger image of the land through personification. In *Ballade* No. 164, Deschamps turns France into a figure of pathos and dignity, appealing to her subjects and engaged in sentimental debate.[76] France is not named directly: she is 'la douce flour' (fleur-de-lys), the abandoned and wretched widow, the orphan. One might compare the angry and 'woofull lady' with streams of tears running down her face described by Chartier in his *Quadrilogue.*[77] Once again this is a powerful

[75] The house that the English burned was not his childhood home, but a more recently acquired property (see I. S. Laurie's introduction to *Eustache Deschamps: Selected Poems*, ed. I. S. Laurie and D. M. Sinnreich-Levi, trans. D. Curzon and J. Fiskin [New York and London: Routledge, 2003], 2). His name, 'Deschamps', may have been invented by him in the course of creating wordplay in this and another poem. This would support a reading of this poem as not merely elegiac but representing a desire to create a new poetic and personal identity.

[76] I, pp. 294–5; Compare also 'Je plain et plour le temps que j'ay perdu', II, no.155, pp. 93–4.

[77] A. Chartier, *Le Quadrilogue Invectif*, ed., E. Droz (Paris: Champion, 1950); see also the French translation and annotated edition by F. Bouchet (Paris: Champion, 2002). I quote here from the anonymous English translation, *Fifteenth-Century English Translations of Alain Chartier's Le Traité de l'esperance and 'Le Quadrilogue invectif'*, ed. M. S. Blayney, EETS 270, 2 vols (London: Oxford University Press, 1974–80), I, 164–6.

imaginative act that draws deeply on wellsprings of sentiment by means of the long-established language of complaint and redirects it to a new and arresting topic. Here it is the device of personification that works to create conceptual unity, like Chaucer's *The Complaint unto Pity*. Colette Beaune remarks how slowly France was personified: and it is important not to treat this instance as necessarily representative either of Deschamps or of a prescient unifying sense of France as a nation-state. As the very variety of these examples indicates, Deschamps is trying out more than one emotional framework. Consistency does not seem to be the object so much as the drive to create plausible sentimental links between speaker and concept.[78]

Distinct from this in Deschamps is the creation of a concept of identity through systematic opposition and invective. Where Chaucer makes discreet reference, for instance in *Lenvoy a Bukton* to being taken prisoner 'in Frise' (23), a fate reputed to involve certain death, *Ballade* no. 16 (I, pp. 92–3) has the wild claim in its refrain that the Flemings are the most evil people of any country:

De tous pais le plus mauvais pueple a.

And there is more in the same vein in *Ballade* no. 812 (Contre le froid pays de Flandres), where in the envoy, he urges violent attack on them:[79]

L'ENVOY
Prince, aux Françoiz, Picards et Bourguignons,
Bar, Bourbonnoiz et Bretons bretonnans,
Devez prier et a tous vos barons:
Lances, courez, ferez sur ces Flamens.

(31–4)

[Prince, you must beg the French, the Picards and Burgundians, those from Bar, the Bourbonnais and the Bretons, and all your lords, to attack and strike at these Flemings with lances.]

It is notable how, in the interests of singling out the Flamands, he presents their opponents as very far from forming a unified 'France', but as emphatically separate peoples.[80] The impulse here is not to create a single concept of France but the opposite, to fragment France into multiple enemies.

[78] C. Beaune, *Naissance de la nation France* (Paris: Gallimard, 1985); I cite from *The Birth of an Ideology: Myths and Symbols of Nation in Late-Medieval France*, trans. S. R. Huston and ed. F. L. Cheyette (Berkeley: University of California Press, 1991), 288. Although Beaune's influential study presents a more nuanced argument about nation than her (French) title implies, her largest framework is retrospective in a way which differs from mine (see Chapter 10).

[79] IV, pp. 329–30.

[80] For more complaints about Flemish, see Beaune, *The Birth of an Ideology*, 274 and notes.

'FRANCHE DOGUE, DIST UN ANGLOIS'

His remarks about the English are more involved. Deschamps partly indulges in the coarse humour of the classic stereotypes: the English love of heavy drinking (Henri d'Andeli, *Bataille des vins*) and violence (particularly wrestling), and their tails.[81] Deschamps has five poems that refer to the 'queue' of the Anglais.[82] There is outright anger:

> Angleterre, sur toutes nascions
> Et au jour d'ui haie pour tes maulx
> (Balades, no.1200, VI, pp. 184–5, lines 11–12)

[England, hated today above all nations for your evil]

And yet, there is more to his response than straightforward denigration, or rivalry.[83]

'Nascion' itself seemingly occurs only once in Deschamps with respect to France:

> France, tu es Jherusalem: se sente
> Et puet sentir estrange nascion,
> Qui tant as eu de paine et de tourmente
> Par les gens Bruth . . .
> (Balade no.1139, IV, pp. 65–6, lines 17–20)

[France, you are Jerusalem; a nation can and does feel itself to be strange who has experienced so much pain and torment from the people of Brut . . .]

It occurs in the context of his talking about the English invasion. Like the Jews who were renewed through their experience of captivity in Babylon, so the French people have become a 'strange nation' through the invasion of the English ('les gens Bruth'). This very powerful simile gives expression to some of the extraordinary and conflicting pressures of this period of prolonged war. France is not merely a 'nascion' but one that is 'estrange', an alien nation: the assertion of unity in the face of the enemy is also an experience of estrangement. Like the Jews, the French are forced into cohesiveness not through a comfortable feeling of homeliness but through being captive, *heimlich*, with its turn on *unheimlich*.[84]

[81] Rickard, *Britain in Medieval French Literature*, ch. 7, 'The English Character', 163–89.

[82] No. 159, I, p. 259; no. 671 (rondel), IV, p. 130; no. 847, V, pp. 20–1; no. 868, V, pp. 48-9; no. 893, V, pp. 79–80.

[83] See also E. J. Richards, 'The Uncertainty in Defining France as a Nation in the Works of Eustache Deschamps', in Baker, ed., *Inscribing the Hundred Years' War*, 159–75 (170).

[84] Compare the interesting comment by Michel Pintoin, chronicler, monk of Saint-Denis, *Chronique de Charles VI* (I have translated his 'pays' here as homeland): 'Il y a la France qui est un royaume et ne saurait être un pays. Et il y a dans le royaume des pays, dont aucun ne doit être appelé la "France"' [there is France which is a kingdom and would not know how to be a homeland. And there are homelands in this kingdom, none of which ought to be called France]. Cited in Boudet

Yet what makes this go beyond the simile is that Deschamps says this of people who are not actually driven out of their land but rather remain estranged within it. Whatever notion emerges of France it is oddly—contrarily—connected with the *pays*: it is also deeply entangled with English assertions and prerogatives. Deschamps strongly registers the experience of an invaded people, one which was naturally not shared (though at certain times fearfully anticipated, as in 1386–7 when the French made preparations to invade England) by the invading English.

Such complexities form the very tissue of the famous Calais poem, written probably in 1384, involving two English soldiers, Deschamps himself and his friend, the Swiss-Savoyard in English service, Othon de Grandson. The poem comments acerbically yet also comically on the convoluted relations between English and French, between French poet and francophone poet in English service.[85] Its context is Calais, probably in August or September 1384 when Deschamps was inspecting the fortresses and defences in Picardie at the request of Charles VI. It was also a time (May–August) when a permanent peace treaty was being negotiated in Boulogne.[86] Deschamps is with Grandson, but has come without an official permit ('san congié'). Two Englishmen challenge him; when Deschamps replies rudely, they threaten him ('Prinsonnier, vous estes forfais'). Instead of helping him out, Grandson pretends to abandon him, laughing loudly, and says in English that he disclaims him:

Mais Granson s'en aloit adès
Qui en riant faisoit la vuide:
A eulx m'avoit trahi, ce cuide;
En anglois dist: 'Pas ne l'adveue.'

[But Grandson went straight on, and laughing cleared off: he has betrayed me to them, I think. In English he said, 'I do not vouch for him.']

Getting desperate, Deschamps appeals to his friend, who at the last minute vouches for him after all:

and Millet, 158. B. Guenée, 'Un royaume et des pays: la France de Michel Pintoin', *Un roi et son historien: Vingt études sur le règne de Charles VI et la Chronique du Religieux de Saint-Denis*, Mémoires de l'Académie des Inscriptions et Belles-Lettres, nouvelle série, vol. 18 (Paris: Boccard, 1999), ch. 17, 395–406 argues that Pintoin sees a basic distinction between unity and diversity: the love of the realm (*royaume*) and the love of the country (*pays*).

[85] Deschamps, *Oeuvres*, no. 893, V, pp. 79–80. The poem is discussed by A. Piaget, *Oton de Grandson: sa vie et ses poésies* (Lausanne: Payot, 1941), 167–8; H. Braddy, *Chaucer and the French Poet Graunson* (Baton Rouge, La.: Louisiana State University Press, 1947), 8–9; Wimsatt, *Chaucer and His French Contemporaries*, 239–40, who quotes and translates the poem in full; Butterfield, 'French Culture and the Ricardian Court' (96–7); Wallace, *Premodern Places*, 54–6. Compare his reference to the siege of Reims, *Miroir de Mariage*, IX, 11660–98; and that of Machaut 'A toi, Hanri'; Wimsatt, *Chaucer and His French Contemporaries*, 79–82.

[86] *Selected Poems*, ed. Laurie and Sinnreich-Levi, 'Introduction', 11.

Delez Graunson fut mes retrais.
La ne me vault treves ne pais,
De paour la face me ride,
De tel amour ma mort me cuide;
Au derrain leur dist: 'Je l'adveue.' (24–8)

[I retreated over by Grandson. There neither truce nor peace is worth anything; my face creases with terror. With that kind of friendship I think I'll die. At last he said to them, 'I vouch for him.']

The poem plays wittily on the notion of friendship and betrayal and the negotiations involved in turning one into the other by showing the larger political situation between France and England through a small personal incident. Deschamps presents himself as darting back and forth between attack and defence; one moment he is cowering with fear, the next he is insistently repeating (by means of the refrain) the same old insults against the English:

L'un me dist: 'dogue', l'autre: 'ride';
Lors me devint la coulour bleue:[87]
'Goday', fait l'un, l'autre: 'commidre'.
'Lors dis: 'Oil, je voy vo queue.' (7–10)

[One said to me, 'Dog!', the other, 'Ride!' Then I went blue: 'Good day', said one, the other: 'Come here!'. Then I say, 'Yes, I see your tail.']

The situation is depicted as turning nasty when Grandson speaks betrayal in the very language of the enemy. Yet unlike the speech of the English, which Deschamps renders in a kind of French accent ('dogue . . . commidre'), Grandson's English is actually rendered as French: 'En anglois dist: Pas ne l'adveue.' Deschamps keeps up the sense of linguistic and cultural ambiguity through the timing of the refrain, which sounds increasingly as if it is being aimed at Grandson rather than the English:

'Chien,' faisoit l'un, 'vez vous vo guide?'
Lors dis: 'Oil, je voy vo queue.' (29–30)

['Dog', said one, Do you see your guide? Then I say, 'Yes, I see your tail.']

The joke here seems to be an allusion to the fact that Deschamps is riding behind Grandson, as he tells us in the first stanza: Grandson has turned tail on Deschamps in more ways than one. This is Anglo-French writing with a vengeance.[88]

[87] Deschamps seems to be playing on the traditional notion of blue as the colour of loyalty (cf. Machaut's ballade: 'Qui de couleurs saroit à droit jugier' which has the refrain 'Que fin azur loyauté signefie', *Poésies lyriques*, ed. V. Chichmaref, 2 vols (Paris: Champion, 1909; repr. Geneva, 1973), CCLXXII, 235 and 'Se pour ce muir, qu'Amours ay bien servi', with the refrain: 'Qu'en lieu de bleu, dame, vous restez vert', Chichmaref, CCXLVIII, 218).

[88] Deschamps's vignette of the tense niceties of Anglo-French relations during periods of truce has much in common with Froissart's retrospective account of a duel probably in 1383 between the

This remarkable *ballade* performs all three of the 'nationalist' manoeuvres I have been outlining. It indulges in invective—the old tail joke—yet it also reveals a profound vulnerability: Deschamps, as he does in several other poems, mythologizes the English, giving them a proverbial dominance that reinforces their status. Mixed in with this is a third, contradictory impulse that finds expression through the topos of cross-linguistic misunderstanding. Deschamps claims not to understand English, but his own slippery, double-jointed French delights in using English against itself: 'Franche dogue, dist un Anglois'.[89] Here he participates in what we have seen to be a much older thirteenth-century practice and was indeed observed by Wace in his comments on Hengist and Horsa as speaking 'd'une estrange parleüre' [of foreign speech]. That noticing and identifying of language as *estrange* or 'foreign' seems to be a crucial element in these medieval explorations of cultural difference. The situation in Deschamps's *ballade* also recalls the complex negotiations around linguistic difference that we noted in Chapter 2 between the sons of Louis the Pious, with Charles the Bald speaking in Teutonic and Louis the German speaking Romance. In the Strasbourg Oaths—and in many other Anglo/Germanic/Flemish-French linguistic encounters—a further tension exists when foreignness is experienced of a language that should be homely. In the same way that Charles and Louis found themselves—as brothers—creating an act of speech that confirmed them as foreign to one another, so the close, semi-fraternal francophone relationship between Deschamps and Grandson disintegrates when Grandson speaks 'anglois'.

And yet this moment, under still further scrutiny, seems oddly rendered. Why should Deschamps give the 'anglois' as spoken by the English soldiers a French accent, and write Grandson's 'anglois' as French? It might seem enough to say that he wants to render the uncomfortableness of the situation with bluff military comedy. But the comic tension—at least potentially—stretches in many more directions. One is the playoff between speech and writing. 'Franche dogue', 'commidre', and 'ride' are not exactly 'English' words. They read to a modern ear not just like someone speaking English with a French accent, but someone trying to speak in an exaggeratedly 'French' way. Is this a misinterpretation? How can we tell? They include phrases and words which come up regularly in the franco-anglais texts and seem to function as shorthand for 'English'. It is thus possible to interpret them as an attempt by a French speaker to write down English: the

English knight Pierre de Courtenay and the French seigneur de Clary carried out in the pale of Calais, and for which Clary received much condemnation from Charles V. For a subtle reading of Froissart's narrative, see A. Varvaro, 'La condamnation du sire de Clary: Froissart entre code chevaleresque et loi du roi', *Actes du colloque international 'Jehan Froissart' (Lille 3 – Valenciennes, 30 sept.–1er oct. 2004)*, ed. M.-M. Castellani and J.-C. Herbin, *Perspectives Médiévales*, Supplément au n°30, mars 2006 (Paris: Société de Langues et Littératures Médiévales d'Oc et d'Oïl, 2006), 277–87. Advice on legal and practical conduct during truce forms the subject of several chapters of H. Bonet's *Arbre de Batailles* (chs 100–107). One should add that, from Oton's Savoyard perspective, his characterisation on either 'English' or 'French' may be an equally moot point.

[89] Balade No. 868, V, pp. 48–9.

Frenchness of the accent could then belong to the ear of the writer rather than the ear of the speaker. I am labouring the point because, as in *Des Deus Anglois*, a crucial instance of spelling reminds us that the sound of an accent depends entirely on the listener. These words *could* be written as a Frenchman might sound to an English listener. They could also function quite distinctly as something else again. The gap between writing and speech allows us to wonder whether Deschamps is actually registering that the English soldiers spoke in 'funny' French accents to mock their French prisoner. The fact that 'ride' occurs twice as a rhyme word, once as 'French' and once as 'English' suggests that, like the author of *Des Deus Anglois*, he is enjoying the way the two languages chime as they differ, or differ as they rhyme. Finally, it is even possible that all the dialogue is really imagined as taking place in French, but that Deschamps wants to represent it in three different ways, as his own French, as Anglo-French (under the guise of Grandson's Savoyard Anglophilia), and as 'anglois'. The polemic here would be that all sides are indeed speaking the same language in the same place but in different territories, and that the resident tongue has been usurped in its own guise on its own soil.

As we have seen, Deschamps's vehement assertiveness as a writer is partnered by a multiplicity of imaginative constructions. They form not a single concept but several, in several types of formulation, each with different histories. This well illustrates the interlaced, sometimes entangled or conflicting nature of allegiances in the period, on the continent and across the Channel. More than this, we find that the aggressive presence of the English acts as a spur—a painful impulse—to ideas of unity. For Deschamps, this was a matter for anger, humour, and sharp cross-linguistic exchange provoked by the deep ironies of a long-standing, close and yet often antagonistic relationship. As *Ballade* No. 893 brilliantly shows, even between friends, in one context there is no need for translation, in another, not just comprehension, but any kind of connection, may be painfully denied.

DESCHAMPS AND CHAUCER: 'GRANT TRANSLATEUR'

In coming finally to *that* poem by Deschamps, with the refrain: 'Grant translateur, noble Geffroy Chaucier!' it is worth remarking that this *ballade* is not usually discussed as an instance of invective. Reactions to it have occasionally been sceptical, but the usual assumption has been that it captures Deschamps not in angry or caustic mode, but speaking praise of his English contemporary.[90] A further reason for wondering whether it belongs in the same camp as the

[90] William Calin is an instance of such scepticism: Deschamp's 'Ballade to Chaucer' Again, or, The Dangers of Intertextual Medieval Comparatism', in Sinnreich-Levi, ed., *Eustache Deschamps, French Courtier-Poet*, 73–8.

Le Mote/Vitry exchange is that it does not comprise an exact formal parallel. This is not two poems but one, or at least a single poem that implies another poem rather than confronts it in any kind of written context. Moreover, the implied poem is in another language—English. No doubt this changes the terms of debate, but how far? One of the intriguing comparisons between the Graunson–Calais *ballade* and this *ballade* concerns the presence of English: in the one pronounced strangely, and in the other heard only in the background. I will address both issues—whether the poem insults or compliments, and its sense of English and Englishness—by means of a word that up to now (even in this overfamiliar poem) has proved difficult for modern (Chaucerian and English) readers to translate. My reading of the word and of the poem continues to be inspired by Derrida, in particular *La Carte Postale* and *Otobiographies*. It remains a preliminary reading, since the poem will surface again in subsequent chapters.[91]

Before turning to the word itself, a few comments on meaning should be aired. The problem is that this tricky word has been treated as primarily a matter of translation, in the sense of the need for modern English readers to find a modern English equivalent for it. However sophisticated such readers may be, the humbly pragmatic needs of translation—what *does* this word mean?—cannot entirely avoid starting with a simple form of that question. And yet, my broader argument through this one word is that the kind of attention it demands tells us something about the possible social and political significance of vernacular writing in England that goes beyond and behind the monolinguistic assumptions of much modern criticism. This is partly a metacritical point: as such readers we may talk as if we expect meaning to be rich and open-ended, but this usually assumes that we are reading in our own tongue. In practice, working across languages means that far more fundamental simplifications are also in play. These may turn out to be just as complex.

So what is the word? *pandras*:

O Socrates plains de philosophie,	O Socrates, full of philosophy,
Seneque en meurs et Anglux en pratique,	Seneca in morality, Aulus in the world,
Ovides grans en ta poeterie,	great Ovid in your poetry,
Bries en parler, saiges en rethorique,	concise in speech, and wise in rhetoric,
Aigles treshaulz, qui par ta theorique	an eagle on high, who, by your knowledge
Enlumines le regne d'Eneas,	illuminates the kingdom of Aeneas –

[91] No. 285, II, pp. 138–40. I am glad to acknowledge Wimsatt's pioneering discussion of this poem and its multiple allusions, *Chaucer and His French Contemporaries*, 248–54. This translation is mine. On the reading 'd'escuiye' / 'd'escuirie' in line 31, see T. Atkinson Jenkins, 'Deschamps' Ballade to Chaucier', *Modern Language Notes*, 33 (1918), 268–78 (277). For a concise survey of the range of datings proposed for the poem, see J. Coleman, 'The Flower, the Leaf, and Philippa of Lancaster', in C. P. Collette, ed., *The Legend of Good Women: Context and Reception* (Woodbridge: D. S. Brewer, 2006), 33–58 (53, n. 87).

L'Isle aux Geans, ceuls de Bruth, et qui as	The island of the Giants, those of Brutus –
Semé les fleurs et planté le rosier,	and who has sown flowers and planted the rosebush,
Aux ignorans de la langue pandras,	you will take the language to those who don't know it:
Grant translateur, noble Geffroy Chaucier.	Great translator, noble Geoffrey Chaucer.
Tu es d'amours mondains Dieux en Albie:	You are the earthly God of love in Albion,
Et de la Rose, en la terre Angelique,	and of the Rose, in the [angelic] land of Angles,
Qui d'Angela saxonne, et puis flourie	which from the Saxon Angela, then flowered
Angleterre, d'elle ce nom s'applique	into the name of Angleterre, the last name
Le derrenier en l'ethimologique;	in the etymological series;
En bon anglès le livre translatas;	and you translated the Rose into good English;
Et un vergier ou du plant demandas	and for a long time you have been constructing an orchard
De ceuls qui font pour eulx auctorisier,	for which you asked for plants from those
A ja longtemps que tu edifias	who create authority for themselves.
Grant translateur, noble Geffroy Chaucier.	Great translator, noble Geoffrey Chaucer.
A toy pour ce de la fontaine Helye	And for this reason, from the fountain of Helicon
Requier avoir un buvraige autentique,	I ask to have from you a genuine draught
Dont la doys est du tout en ta baillie,	of which the source is entirely under your jurisdiction
Pour rafrener d'elle ma soif ethique,	with which to quench my feverish thirst,
Qui en Gaule seray paralitique,	and I'll remain in Gaul paralysed
Jusques a ce que tu m'abuveras.	Until the time you let me drink it.
Eustaces sui, qui de mon plant aras:	I am Eustache; whose plants you will have;
Mais pran en gré les euvres d'escolier	But take them in good spirit, these school-boyish writings,
Que par Clifford de moy avoir pourras,	That you will receive from me by Sir Lewis Clifford.
Grant translateur, noble Gieffroy Chaucier.	Great translator, noble Geoffrey Chaucer.

L'Envoy	Envoy
Poete hault, loenge destruye [d'escuiye/d'escuirie],	Elevated poet, famed among squires,
En ton jardin ne seroye qu'ortie:	I would be a mere nettle in your garden
Considere ce que j'ai dit premier,	if you consider what I said at the beginning
Ton noble plant, ta douce mélodie.	about your noble plant, and your sweet melody.
Mais pour sçavoir, de rescripre te prie,	But I beg you to provide me with an official response, so that I can confirm it:
Grant translateur, noble Geffroy Chaucier.	Great translator, noble Geoffrey Chaucer.

Pandras comes in the penultimate line of the first stanza of this three-stanza *ballade* and envoy (9). We can immediately see the debts owed by Deschamps to Jehan de le Mote: he is praising Chaucer through comparing him with Socrates, 'Anglux' (probably Aulus Gellius), and Ovid.

Mote: *O Victriens, mondains Dieu d'armonie* (1)
Deschamps: *O Socrates* plains de philosophie (1)
Tu es *d'amours mondains Dieux* en Albie (9)

Mote: *Supernasor de la fontaine Helye* (3)
Deschamps: *Ovides grans* en ta poeterie (3)
A toy pour ce *de la fontaine Helye* (21)

Mote: T'a fait brasser *buvrage* a trop de lie (13)
Deschamps: Requier avoir un *buvraige* autentique (22)

Mote: Doctores vrays, *en ce pratique Auglus* (4)
Deschamps: Seneque en meurs et *Anglux en pratique* (2)

Like all these great poets, like a lofty eagle, Chaucer has illuminated the land of Brutus. Chaucer is the earthly God of love in Albion, and the God of the *Rose* which he translates into 'bon anglès' (good English). For all these reasons, Deschamps wants to drink from Chaucer's fountain of poetic inspiration, but will also send him some of his own scribblings. Deschamps uses similar terminology in *ballades* to two of his contemporary French writers: Guillaume de Machaut and Christine de Pizan.[92] The envoy finishes by urging 'de rescripre te prie' [do write back!][93]

So what does *pandras* mean? It is a notorious crux. No help is provided by comparing manuscript readings since the poem survives in a unique source (see Fig. 3).[94] The most recent editor and translator work through the problems

[92] Nos 123, 124 in *Oeuvres*, I, pp. 243–6; no. 403, III, pp. 318–19, and no.1242, VI, pp. 251–2.

[93] Jenkins plausibly suggests that Deschamps is alluding here to a *rescript*, an official decision in writing from a pope or emperor (278).

[94] For a list of mss containing Deschamps's poems, see T. Lassabatère, 'La Cité des Hommes. La vision politique d'Eustache Deschamps' (unpublished doctoral dissertation, Paris IV – Sorbonne,

and suggestions inconclusively, though they tentatively suggest it might be a verb: *pander*, 'which perhaps means to open'.[95] James Wimsatt also argues for its being a verb, but a different one from theirs: *pandre*, 'to disseminate or illuminate'.[96] Chaucerian scholars have not been able to resist thinking it must have something to do with Pandarus, and pandering.[97]

The view that *pandras* is a verb form seems convincing though not (in the first instance at least) one to do with pandering. It seems quite likely (following on from Wimsatt) that it could be an aphaetic form of *espandre* (*épandre*), meaning to spread out or spill, be diffused, to scatter or spread abroad.[98] Could it alternatively be from the verb *prendre*? In that case it would mean, as I have translated it, 'you will take the language to those who don't know it'. It would continue to mean that Chaucer is the mediator of continental French to the English. But this is not perhaps as complimentary as it first seems. We have seen that Deschamps participates vigorously in the 'franco-anglais' tradition, not just by repeating insults but also more specifically in his use of jargon. One of the standard features of *le jargon franco-anglais* is a rewriting of vocabulary with inversions of spelling and syllabic placing. A standard instance is the word *pandras* for *prendras* (*pandre* for *prendre*). In the thirteenth-century *La Paix aux Anglais*, Henry III is shown as boasting:

> 'Je pandra bien Parris, je suis toute certaine;'[99]
>
> ['I will take Paris, I am completely certain of it']

Neither the *DMF* nor the *AND* give 'pandre', either in its own right or as a version of 'prendre'. Yet in both cases it seems to be an omission, since this spelling is fairly commonly attested.[100]

2002), appendix. For recent discussion of the huge volume of his collected works, BnF fr. 840, and its scribe Raoul Tainguy, see J. Taylor, *The Making of Poetry: Late-Medieval French Poetic Anthologies* (Turnhout: Brepols, 2007), 61–7.

95 *Selected Poems*, ed. Laurie and Sinnreich-Levi, 70–71 and 219, n. 9.

96 Wimsatt, *Chaucer and His French Contemporaries*, 251 and 340, n. 32.

97 See *Selected Poems*, ed. Laurie and Sinnreich-Levi, 219; Wimsatt, *Chaucer and His French Contemporaries*, 251 and 340, n. 31. The most detailed (though occasionally eccentric) line-by-line commentary on the poem remains that of Jenkins, 'Deschamps' Ballade to Chaucer'. There are two men named Pandras in Wace, one is king of Greece (252, 307), the other king of Egypt (11097): both have been claimed as sources for Deschamps.

98 *DMF* épandre; *AND* espandre. However, in neither case is the aphaetic form recorded. The form is, however, given in W. Rothwell, Of Kings and Queens, or Nets and Frogs: Anglo-French Homonymics, *French Studies*, 48 (1994), 257–73, who is discussing Bibbesworth's references to the following collection of homonyms: espandre, espaundre, espendre, pandre, and espandere. I am grateful to David Trotter for his discussion of this, but as he will no doubt be relieved to know, I exonerate him of any responsibility for my lexical speculations here.

99 E. Faral, ed., *Mimes français du XIIIe siècle* (Paris: Champion, 1910), line 69.

100 See also line 28 of the ballade, and Rickard, *Britain in Medieval French Literature*, 177. Another example from Deschamps (where he plays *prandre* against *pendre*) occurs in the Envoy of his Langland-reminiscent ballade 'Je treuve qu'entre les souris' (no.58):

> Prince, on conseille bien souvent
> Mais on puet dire, com le rat,

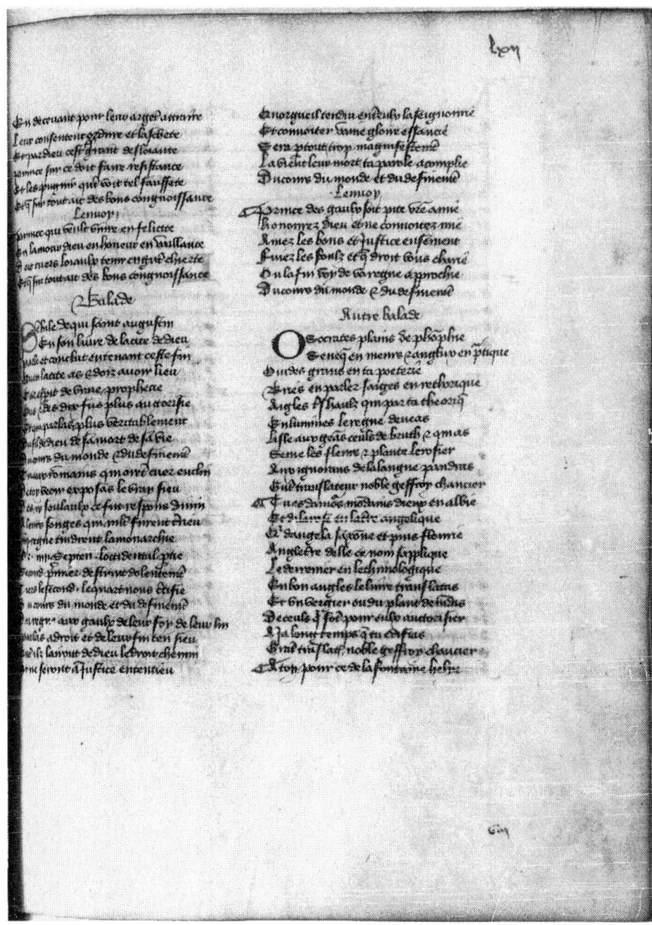

Figure 3. Eustache Deschamps: *ballade* to Chaucer (No.893) V, 79–80

Paris BnF fr.840, fol.62r-v b-c. Copyright Bibliothèque nationale de France: reproduced with permission.

Deschamps is a master of *le jargon franco-anglais.* As we have seen, he wears the old tail joke out through a whole series of *ballades* and frequently uses 'French

Du conseil qui sa fin ne prant:
Qui pendra la sonnette au chat?

See also *La Passion d'Autun,* ed. Grace Frank (Paris: SATF, 1934), *c.*1400–71:

Or prions tuis le chier sire
Que aut jour d'uy pandra martire
Que de nous aye misericorde. (lines 594–5; 198)
Pres de Jhesucrist les pandrons. (line 1252; 115).

It is also possible that *pandre* could be an aphaetic form of *apprendre* (cf the elaborate joke in Renart jongleur, discussed in Chapter 3, n. 17 above), though the syntax would be more awkward to construe.

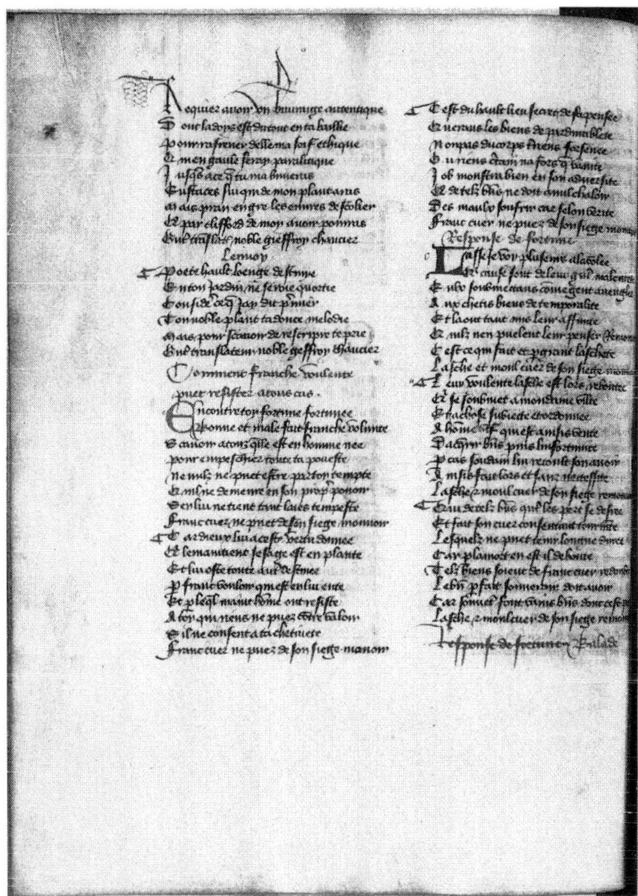

Figure 3. (Continued)

English' and 'English French'. This *ballade* seems to me to be perhaps his supreme example. It is full of puns and inversions, sly jokes that stretch out the representations of 'English' from Anglux (Latin) to Angela (Saxon) and Angleterre (Anglo-French). The notion that 'Angela' was the daughter of a Saxon and produced the Angles seemed to appeal to Deschamps: he refers to it in *Le Miroir de mariage*, 'Et d'Angela sont maint Anglès', 270 and in No.1154 (*Oeuvres*, VI, pp. 87–8):

> D'Angela ont Anglès la renommee:
> C'est de ce mot l'interpretacion . . .
>
> (23–4)

In the Chaucer *ballade*, this enables Deschamps to spin an etymological narrative that shows the English turning through different languages into their present aggressively hybrid condition.[101] Deschamps constantly insists, right through his praise of Chaucer, that the terms are two-edged: Chaucer's poetic talents are drawn from a source 'en ta baillie', a choice of word which pointedly underlines the uncomfortable fact of English military control while it pretends merely to laud Chaucer's poetic mastery. His use of *pandre* for *prendre* could similarly be alluding to a boastful taking, a form of reverse conquest that Deschamps praises with the hint of a sneer and through gritted teeth using the conqueror's own language. One might add that the spirit of contest is generally uppermost in a request for a poem in late medieval French poetry: the request functions as an aggressive challenge. A further hint as to Deschamps's competitive tone occurs in the image of the garden in Stanza 2: he grows the plants, Chaucer merely picks them.[102]

In short, this is a very complex compliment to Chaucer. Some more can be teased out via *La Carte postale*.[103] Derrida's extravagant freewheeling meditation on a thirteenth-century drawing of Plato prodding Socrates in the back ponders the status of an open, unaddressed letter. Taking his cue from Edgar Allen Poe's *The Purloined Letter*, Freud and Lacan, Derrida discusses some of his central preoccupations with meaning, such as the reader's role in counter-signing a piece of writing to guarantee its intelligibility, and the already-thereness of the text for both reader and author, since the author is *already* an addressee at the moment when he or she writes. In a long section entitled 'Envois', he moves in and out of the possibilities of comprehension between the writer of the postcard and its imagined recipient.[104]

We may single out first, the structural connection between Derrida's postcard and the Deschamps *ballade* (itself a letter, with envoy). In both, as Derrida insists, meaning does not reside in the letter but in the giving and returning—and the already having given and returned—of meaning between sender and receiver. Second, just as Deschamps plays with sending and resending a distorting language, a jargon, so Derrida constantly puns and slides between words, across meanings, and across meanings in more than one language. *La Carte postale* is a translator's nightmare. *Envoyer* is a very full example; '*legs*' is a more comic one, a bilingual pun on 'legacy' and lai or narrative poem and the English 'legs' or 'jambes'; '*Dos*' another.

My reading, then, is that Deschamps is engaged in an act of translation that will not allow meaning to rest in one language. Geoffrey is taking French into

[101] See Wace, 1175–200.

[102] I am grateful to Adrian Armstrong for discussing the poem with me, especially in relation to later French poetic exchanges. Deschamps' references to the English are generally aggressive: see no. 26, I, pp. 106–07; no. 211, II, pp. 33–4; no. 222, II, pp. 48–9, and no. 845, V, pp. 17–18.

[103] Cf. M. Camille, 'The Dissenting Image: a Postcard from Matthew Paris', in *Criticism and Dissent in the Middle Ages*, ed. R. Copeland (Cambridge: Cambridge University Press, 1996), 115–50.

[104] J. Derrida, *La carte postale: de Socrate à Freud et au-delà* (Paris: Flammarion, 1985); *The Post Card from Socrates to Freud and Beyond*, trans. A. Bass (Chicago and London: University of Chicago Press, 1987), ch. 1 Envois.

English, an act for which Deschamps cannot help but praise him. But he couches his praise in the old language of internecine warfare: a half language, an English that is 'bon' but unfixed, somewhere between Latin, Saxon, and French, somewhere in the crossing between island and continent. It is a language of comic abuse, but one that is constantly turning on itself. Write back, he asks, translate me back, abuse me while you cultivate me.

We have learnt through the work of Rita Copeland, amongst many others, that translation is not a secondary exercise.[105] This *ballade*, however, encourages us to take the idea of *translatio studii* back into the intimacy of lexical exchange. For Derrida's constant polemic is that translation is not something we do only from one language into another. It is an activity that accompanies every act of understanding language. The foreign and untranslateable is part of our own language, to whatever extent we have our own language. It is therefore a continuous process; one that cannot easily be halted.

> 'Je n'ai qu'une langue, ce n'est pas la mienne.' (*Monolinguisme*, 13)
>
> ['I only have one language, it is not mine.'] (2)

To return to Jehan de le Mote: in what sense can he be accused of being a traitor purely by being francophone? Simply by working for Edward III, does he speak any less 'Frenchly'? Deschamps seems to level the opposite accusation at Chaucer. He cannot ever be francophone; he is a 'translateur' at best. However much of a French speaker and writer Chaucer may think he is, Deschamps wants to keep him firmly on the other side of a linguistic boundary. Yet in terms of the larger political and linguistic situation, Edward III's claim is precisely that he is indeed entitled to francophone control, as 'English' kings have been in the past and will be again through Edward himself, the Lancastrians, and early Tudors. It is not as if Chaucer is any less French in that case than Le Mote, a Hainuyer. Vitry is appealing to a notion of treachery which cannot possibly be based on an idea of a nation-state. It makes no sense of Hainaut's separateness from Parisian royal power. But this, too, seems to be the point: perhaps Vitry's exasperation is directed at a sense that using French is a far from unifying activity.[106] It turns out to be a language that is devolving into rival poetic vernaculars even as people continue to write it in ostensibly the same way.

[105] R. Copeland, *Rhetoric, Hermeneutics and Translation in the Middle Ages: Academic Traditions and Vernacular Texts* (Cambridge: Cambridge University Press, 1991), and on *translatio studii*, the earlier work of Douglas Kelly, '*Translatio Studii*: Translation, Adaptation, and Allegory in Medieval French Literature', *Philological Quarterly*, 57 (1978), 287–310 and M. A. Freeman, *The Poetics of 'Translatio Studii' and 'Conjointure': Chrétien de Troyes's 'Cligés'* (Lexington, KY: French Forum, 1979).

[106] As an instance of such dissension, Petrarch, a friend and admirer of de Vitry, made attacks on French scholars in the humanism debate between France and Italy in the 1360s and 1370s (Olson, 'Geoffrey Chaucer', 578–9).

5

Exchanging Terms

Aggressive assertion in the fourteenth century was quickly supplemented, and for some periods replaced, by diplomatic negotiation. These negotiations rarely lapsed altogether but intensified around certain key moments of truce or treaty: Guines, repeatedly in the late 1340s and early 1350s, Brétigny in 1360, Bruges in 1375, the Truce of Leulinghen in 1389, Paris in 1395–6. This chapter will consider some of the moments when language itself becomes an issue in the debates. It has several purposes. One is to continue the discussions begun in earlier chapters about how people thought of each other's languages across the Channel. What difference did the circumstances of war make to their sense of French or for that matter of English? Did French still function as a shared language, and if so what were the perils or advantages of that point of connection? What role did English now have? The last chapter suggested that the quarrel between Vitry and Le Mote is indicative of deep-seated sensitivities about the role of French as an international language in a period of international aggression. Deschamps's *ballade* to Chaucer in this light revealed that he too saw Chaucer as both a laughably divergent and threateningly rival source of eloquence.

For this reason, it does look from the continent as if Deschamps's sense of poetic exchange, especially where it involved England, always had an edge. Chaucer's English for him was a kind of French, or, to put it another way, a taking from French into English. Under his language of gift exchange lurks the accusation of theft. Having heard Chaucer's voice only in its absence through Deschamps's *ballade*, this and subsequent chapters will now turn to the body of Chaucer's writings as a means of trying to recover what Deschamps was hearing. Ironically, there is no consensus about precisely what Deschamps knew of Chaucer's poetry despite the certain—and tantalizing—evidence of the *ballade* that he did indeed know him as an author.[1] This chapter does not concern itself so much over whether we can prove borrowings or specific points of influence in one direction or the other, but seeks to look outwards from that pair of *ballade* exchanges towards the broader story of the language of exchange as it was practised, observed, and figured in the negotiations of war. Some more specific

[1] Wimsatt was keen to downplay the links earlier asserted by older generation of scholars, see J. I. Wimsatt, *Chaucer and His French Contemporaries: Natural Music in the Fourteenth Century* (Toronto: University of Toronto Press, 1992), ch. 4, n. 10, but the question is far from closed.

questions may first be asked: what languages did people know across the continent, and how did they use them? In what way does this shed light on the role of language in the Anglo-French diplomatic negotiations? These contexts for exchanging English and French, rich in political, cultural, and linguistic implications, are important to our understanding of language in the literature of the later fourteenth century, both English and French.[2]

The pragmatics of debate between two sides sharing and yet competing over language require and repay close analysis. The new mood of conflict pursued so vigorously by Edward III had many consequences for the use of language on both sides of the Channel. First, there was a huge increase in the volume of official—legal and diplomatic—writing generated by the proliferation of treaties and the efforts on both sides to record and justify the progress of war. As Serge Lusignan has so thoroughly demonstrated, the French royal administration had been developing its use of the vernacular for the promulgation of laws throughout the thirteenth century.[3] A similar, though slower, process is evident in England, with French again as the central vernacular tool.[4] During Edward's reign the need for a sophisticated use of French in diplomatic and legal negotiation with the continent had never been greater. This diplomatic writing is a rich resource for the study of nation, regretfully too large to tap fully here; yet even a preliminary awareness of its role as a public arena in which issues of possession and identity were articulated and disputed can be of great value in opening up our sense of how literary languages of debate were reconceived in this period. The *Songe du vergier* is a prime literary example; alongside it can be placed the substantial evidence from chronicles, especially Froissart's, of the way in which language itself became a bargaining tool in the negotiations. A self-consciousness about language, a need to reflect on the limitations of language at the hard edge of violent disagreements over what had been or was going to be promised or refused, occurs dotted throughout Froissart's reports of diplomatic meetings and other Anglo-French contretemps. Here remarkable evidence can be found of lawyers and other officials attempting to draw lines by means of language, to insist on incomprehension where that seemed the only way to avoid an unsought-for outcome.

One of the principal strategies employed by Deschamps in his *Ballade* No. 285 is to counterbalance carefully worded praise with equally careful

[2] For two complementary contextual studies, see E. Schulze-Busacker, 'French Conceptions of Foreigners and Foreign Languages in the Twelfth and Thirteenth Centuries', *Romance Philology*, 41 (1987), 24–47 whose references are mainly to material in French (but not including Anglo-Norman) and Occitan and contiguous linguistic regions, and the very wide-ranging B. Bischoff, 'The Study of Foreign Languages in the Middle Ages', *Speculum*, 36 (1961), 209–24.

[3] S. Lusignan, *La Langue des rois au Moyen âge: le français en France et en Angleterre* (Paris: PUF, 2004), 68–94.

[4] P. Brand, *The Making of the Common Law* (London: Hambledon, 1992) and 'The Languages of the Law in Later Medieval England', in *Multilingualism in Later Medieval Britain*, ed. D. A. Trotter (Cambridge: D. S. Brewer, 2000), 63–76.

self-deprecation. The effect is disconcerting since the comic depiction of himself as a nettle[5] and of his desperate, quasi-invalid's desire to drink from Chaucer's 'buvraige autentique' slightly undermines the terms he lavishes on Chaucer by implying that they are equally exaggerated. Caught up in this effect is the word 'ignorans'. This leaves a faint whiff of insult, especially when combined with the traditional description of England as an island of giants, creatures not famed for their cleverness or learning. We hesitate over this word, unsure of its wider resonance, not least, as we discussed in the previous chapter, because of the puzzling and puzzlingly adjacent *pandras*.

The peculiarities of this extraordinary *ballade* pose central questions about Anglo-French relations in the fourteenth century. Although Chaucer scholars from an earlier generation were happy to see it as an expression of high praise for Chaucer, I have argued that this cannot stand without qualification. The *ballade* encapsulates, indeed figures a crucial dilemma for modern readers about knowledge and perspective. It partly figures our own ignorance about nuances of meaning, linguistic, social, and cultural. How *did* Deschamps, or other continental French poets, view Chaucer? Writing in English obviously counted for something, as we read this poem, but for how much and to whom? The *ballade* makes us see that this question is inseparable from questions about literary merit or repute: Deschamps precisely cannot disentangle his sense of Chaucer as a writer from his tense awareness of the aggressive political meaning of English for him as a continental French writer. But it also figures his own bafflement, which was also evident in the Vitry and Le Mote exchange. It seems to figure a realization that each side is newly unknowable to the other, and that this is caused by changes in the linguistic relationship between their various kinds of French, and—even more disconcertingly—Chaucer's kind of *franco-anglais*.

In investigating ignorance for its wider cultural resonance, we find that it was a charge occasionally put up against English negotiators by their French counterparts and commentators. Perhaps the most frequently cited 'evidence' in support of this is a remark made by Froissart:

> Car en parlure françoise a mots soubtils et couvers et sur double entendements, et les tournent les François, là où ils veulent, à leur prouffit et avantage: ce que les Anglois ne sçauroient trouver, ne faire, car euls ne le veulent entendre que plainement.[6]

[5] Compare Gower's use of the same metaphor in 'El mois de mai la plus joiouse chose', *The Complete Works of John Gower*, ed. G. C. Macaulay, 4 vols (Oxford: Clarendon Press, 1899-1902), I: *The French Works*, XXXVII, 367, discussed in A. Butterfield, 'French Culture and the Ricardian Court', A. Minnis, C. C. Morse, and T. Turville-Petre, eds, *Essays on Ricardian Literature in Honour of J. A. Burrow* (Oxford: Clarendon Press, 1997), 109–12.

[6] References to Froissart's *Chroniques* will be to the following editions: J. Froissart, *Chroniques. Livre I. Le manuscrit d'Amiens*, ed. G. T. Diller, 5 vols (Geneva: Droz, 1991–8) [Amiens]; J. Froissart, *Oeuvres de Froissart: Chroniques*, ed. J. B. M. C. Kervyn de Lettenhove, 25 vols in 28 (Brussels: V. Devaux, 1867–77) [KL]; J. Froissart, *Chroniques, début du premier livre. Edition du manuscript de Rome Reg.lat.869*, ed., G. T. Diller TLF, 194 (Geneva: Droz, 1972) [*Livre I Rome*

[For in French speech there are subtle and hidden words, based on double meanings, and the French turn them where they wish to, to their profit and advantage: this is what the English would not know how to find, or engineer, for they only want to understand plain meanings.]

This remark, like Deschamps's *ballade*, also has wider significance for our approach to the period, though in an opposite direction. It is normally taken to mean that English competence in French was not sufficient to follow the subtle twists and turns of phrase put in by the French and thus left them open to be manipulated into situations that were to their disadvantage. Many modern readers take this as proof of the dwindling knowledge of French on the part of the English diplomats and therefore as an explanation both of their cumulative failure to create long-lasting treaties, and of the triumph of English. To put it crudely, there is such modern pressure to explain and chart the rise of English through the fourteenth century that it produces a corresponding pressure to interpret such remarks as proving increasing English ignorance of French. In a sense it becomes part of a larger invective about English insufficiency in French that, as we have seen, was promulgated through the period itself. However, looked at more carefully, and in the light of a broader sense of the linguistic competence and awareness among these personnel on both sides of the treaty tables and battlefields, such comments suggest other conclusions.

FROISSART ON LANGUAGE

Froissart gives us a great deal of information about language.[7] It is never wise to take him at face value especially on matters of date, name, or chronology, but on the other hand, read with due care the asides and more unguarded observations can offer acute kinds of commentary on a wide range of issues. As one reads through the *Chroniques*, Froissart's habit of commending the people he meets for their 'bon francois' or 'bel langaige' is perhaps initially rather puzzling, given that he himself came from Hainault. He praises the comte de Foix, for example, for greeting him 'en bon françois' and for talking to him always in French rather than Gascon:

MS]; J. Froissart, *Chroniques, Livre I*, ed., S. Luce, I–VII (Paris: Mme Ve. J. Renouard, 1869–88), *Livre II*, ed. G. Raynaud, VIII-XI (Paris: Mme Ve. J. Renouard, 1894–9), *Livre III*, ed. L. and A. Mirot, XII–XV (Paris: Champion, 1931–75) [SHF]. KL, *Livre IV (1392–1396)*, 15, p. 114. This passage has been much discussed. See, in particular, Lusignan, *La Langue des rois*, 242; G. T. Diller, '"Pour la cause de ce que j'estoie François." Langue(s) et loyauté(s) dans les *Chroniques* de Froissart', *Le Moyen Age*, 104 (1998), 461–71 (464).

[7] I must record my thanks to Godfried Croenen who generously provided me with abundant references and the benefit of much expert advice. Naturally, he is not responsible for the argument put forward here or for any errors it contains. For specific published discussion on some of these passages, see Diller, '"Pour la cause de ce que j'estoie François."'

trop volontiers en parloit à moy, non pas en son gascon, mais en bon et bel françois.
(SHF, *Livre III (1356-88)*, 12, p. 76)

[he spoke very willingly to me, not in his own *gascon*, but in good and fine French]

Froissart is careful to mention the comte's flattery of him, that although he had never met him he had heard good things about him and knew of him well. It clearly improves the portrait of the comte even further that he had such good French, and Froissart emphasizes this by remarking later on the comte's use of Gascon to speak angrily to his son: 'le premier mot que le conte dit, ce fut en son gascon: "Zo, Gaston, traitre"' ['the first word that the spoke was in his own *gascon*: 'Zo, Gaston, you traitor'].[8] We have a hint here of the different registers of language choice: French for court visitors and Gascon for the family and especially for moments of informal spleen. The extract tells us, in reverse, how keen Froissart was himself to be treated as such a visitor, and once again the badge of that social categorization was *his* ability not only to speak 'bon et bel françois' but to recognize it and, precisely, esteem it.

What is more difficult to tease out is Froissart's own sense of linguistic identity. How far did he seek to claim to be *franchois*? It may have been his Hainault extraction that provoked his sensitivity to fine registers of French: but this is not the same as saying that he aspired to be *franchois*, nor should we assume too quickly that we know what *franchois* meant for him. Two further comments are pertinent here, though in some respects they pull in opposite directions. On arrival at Orthez, he was taken to the household of a local dignitary, Ernauton du Puy, who received him so graciously, he says, *because he was French*:[9]

lequel me receupt moult liement, pour la cause de ce que j'estoie Franchois.
(SHF, *Livre III (1356-88)*, 12, p. 75)

[who received me very graciously because I was *franchois* [French]]

The politics of recognition are potentially intricate here: in these southern regions, allegiance to French royalty was either non-existent or mixed and volatile. Gaston III Fébus of Foix-Béarn was one of the most politically slippery operators of the region who managed his relationships with both English and French royal houses with skill and cunning.[10] His warm reception of Froissart and the reaction of more minor local seigneurs strikes one as like the way a modern celebrity might welcome a visiting documentary crew: keen for the publicity and therefore careful

[8] SHF, *Livre III (1356–88)*, 12, p. 85.

[9] Diller, whose article title cites part of this remark, argues that such a comment forms part of Froissart's larger celebratory attitude towards French, the language in which he seeks international fame as a writer. This interesting and convincing case complements the one I seek to make here.

[10] P. Tucoo-Chala, 'Froissart dans le Midi Pyrénéen', in J. J. N. Palmer, ed., *Froissart: Historian* (Woodbridge: Boydell, 1981), 118–31.

to be ingratiating. How far, and in what way *franchois* came into the equation is hard to judge, although Gaston at least must have been well aware that Froissart was no mere mouthpiece for French interests.[11]

The other comment, from Book IV of the *Chroniques*, is complex in a different way as it raises issues about English perceptions of *franchois*. One Guillemme de Lisle, a 'ung très-gentil chevalier' from England, on meeting him:

me vey estrangier et des marches[12] de France (car toutes gens de la langue galicque, de quelle contrée et nation que ils soient, ils les tienent et réputent pour Franchois.)

(KL, *Livre IV (1392–1396)*, 15, p. 144)

[saw me as a foreigner and from the marches of France (for everyone whatever country and people they come from, when they hear someone speaking northern French always assume and take him to be a *franchois* [Frenchman]).]

This is classic Froissart, always quick to offer social observation on the cultural meaning of his own encounters. Again, though, it is a hard comment to understand (and translate). Out of context, it might sound like an instance of parochial Englishness, perhaps indicating a non-French speaker, who on hearing any kind of French assumes the French speaker to be *franchois*. But this does not make sense in the passage, since the comment introduces a long, very amicable conversation held between Guillemme and Froissart. Could Froissart be speaking English to Guillemme? As we shall shortly see, he was certainly happy to report another Hainuyer, Walter de Manny, as speaking English.[13] This passage is inscrutable, but Froissart is so free with his comments on language that one would have thought he would remark somewhere if he were making bilingual choices on his travels around England.[14] Moreover, Guillemme's name is strongly Anglo-French. In that case, there must be different implications. The remark is actually set within a causative clause: 'Pour tant que le gentil

[11] For a subtle discussion of this part of the *Voyage*, see P. F. Ainsworth, *Jean Froissart and the Fabric of History* (Oxford: Clarendon Press, 1990), 151–6, and, on Froissart's wider narrative tactics, M. Zink, *Froissart et le temps* (Paris: PUF, 1998), ch. 5: 'Le temps d'un voyage', 63–87.

[12] A. Tobler and E. Lommatzsch, *Altfranzösisches Wörterbuch*, 10 vols (Berlin: Weidmannsche Buchhandlung, 1925–76), gives a military meaning as its first definition of 'marche' ('Frontière militaire d'un État; région frontalière', with a fifteenth-century citation), and see P. Contamine, *War in the Middle Ages*, trans. M. Jones (Oxford: Blackwell, 1984; repr. Barnes & Noble, 1998; 1st pub. *La Guerre au moyen âge*, 1980), 219–20 and n. 48; but the word also means more broadly country, region, land, also border country. On *la marche* as a border zone, see B. Guenée, 'Des limites féodales aux frontières politiques', in P. Nora, ed., *Les Lieux de mémoire*, 7 vols (Paris: Gallimard, 1984–92), II: *La Nation*, ii, 'Le Territoire', 11–33 (15). The zones were often a site of conflict but also crossroads and places for meetings, tournaments, places where homage was received, judicial hearings, even hangings and toll payments.

[13] Pierre Chaplais mentions a letter of 1438 in which the writer, Aeneas Silvius Piccolomini, the future Pope Pius II, opined that a Fleming had no difficulty in understanding English: P. Chaplais, *English Diplomatic Practice in the Middle Ages* (London and New York: Hambledon and London, 2003), 131, n. 355.

[14] I agree with Diller who argues that Froissart gives every impression of being a monolingual: Diller, '"Pour la cause de ce que j'estoie François."', 469.

chevalier . . . me vey estrangier' (Because the noble chevalier thought me a stranger . . .) and finishes with 'si se accointa de moy et je de luy' (he greeted me and I him) for the English are so courteous, affable, and welcoming. Is it reading too much to find lurking here a war moment, a well-concealed stutter caused by the Englishman's temporary assumption that he is talking to the enemy? But this still leaves us wondering what exactly he was hearing and thinking about Froissart's French, and what Froissart means by his remark. Froissart could be bridling ever so slightly at the assumption that he is *franchois* not merely because he is from Hainault, but perhaps also because he does not think of himself as foreign (estrangier).

From these two examples together some distinctions can be made. As we discussed in the last chapter, France and hence *franchois* have the specific meaning of someone born in the Île de France. France also overlaps with a reference to the kingdom or realm of France, though it is important to recognize that these two meanings are not synonymous, and that the latter is very variable territorially throughout the medieval period. Here, when applied to language, we learn implicitly that *franchois* can be a general, loosely used term, available for many purposes, political and cultural. The enquiry of Chapters 2 and 3, continued here, was in part to ask how far language could itself function as a geographical, or territorial marker. From Froissart perhaps we learn even more how instant impressions can be sweeping and little related to social truths.

There is an instance where the phrase 'la langue françoise' is taken metonymically for 'French-speaking peoples'. It is a view reported of the exotically described Turkish commander L'Amourat Bakin, engaged in the defeat of the Serbians commemorated by Slobodan Milošević in 1989:

> et aime L'Amourat Bakin grandement la langue françoise et ceulx qui en viennent . . .
>
> (SHF, *Livre III (1356–88)*, 12, p. 212)
>
> [and L'Amourat Bakin was greatly enamoured of the French-tongue and of those who belonged to it . . .]

Here the perspective is more 'other' than that of an English knight, and the broad sweep of the comment makes more sense.[15]

Other moments where Froissart praises someone for his 'bel français' tend to involve bi- or even trilingualism. Certain individuals are singled out for their professional skill as linguists, such as:

> uns clers d'Engleterre licensiiés en drois et en lois, et moult bien pourveus de trois langages, de latin, de françois et dou langage englés; et conmenç[a] a parler moult sagement.
>
> (*Livre I Rome MS*, 232)

[15] Ottoman sultan (1359–89), Mourad I, who crushed the Serbians and their allies at Kosovo in 1389. See Chapter 1, p. 26.

[a clerk from England, with a degree in canon and Roman law, and extremely well equipped in three languages, Latin, French and the English language; [then got up] and began to speak very advisedly.]

The Bishop of Cambray, Pierre d'Ailly, is another: 'comme sur tous bien enlangagié en latin et en franchois' [more than any of them well versed in Latin and French][16] and who 'en latin remonstrat tout au long son message' ['elaborated at length in Latin on his message'].[17] Froissart was also struck by:

ung Breton bretonnant qui estoit de nacion de Vennes . . . et lequel savoit bien troix, voires IIII. langaiges, le breton bretonnant, le franchois, l'anglois et l'espaingnol . . .

(SHF, *Livre III (1387–1389)*, 15, p. 64)[18]

[a Breton-speaking Breton who was born in Vennes . . . and knew three, in fact four languages: breton, franchois, English and Spanish . . .]

The other group who are included here are the interpreters: these range from Saracen 'drugemans' or 'trucemans' to court interpreters.[19] In one fascinating case, at a French siege of the African town Mahdia (or al-Mahdiyya) described in Book IV, the efforts to communicate between the two sides involved finding first a 'drugeman' who could speak Genoese ('ils prindrent ung drugeman qui moult bien et bel le langaige jennevois parler sçavoit . . . ' [they took an interpreter who knew how to speak Genoese very well and elegantly . . .] (KL, *Livre IV (1389–1392)*, 14, p. 232)) and then a Genoese centurion (clearly skilled rhetorically) who was able to take the Saracen message to the duc de Bourbon and the seigneur de Couchy:

lesquels le veirent et oyrent moult voulentiers parler; et les paroles que les seigneurs ne sçavoient entendre, le centurion leur exposoit et refourmoit en bon françois, car bien l'entendoit.

(KL, *Livre IV (1389–1392)*, 14, p. 233)[20]

[16] KL, *Livre IV (1397–1400)*, 16, p. 121.

[17] KL, *Livre IV (1397–1400)*, 16, p. 123.

[18] The phrase 'breton bretonnant' is cited six times in *DMF*, largely in chronicles. It means simply a Breton-speaking Breton (from the east of Brittany) as distinct from a French-speaking Breton (from the western part) (TL: bretoner; *Godefroy Complément:* bretonnant; *Trésor de la langue française* IV, 942b: bretonnant, [D'un lieu] 'Où l'on parle breton'/'Qui parle celtique; où l'on parle celtique').

[19] A pioneering lecture by Bullock-Davies, *Professional Interpreters*, discusses the evidence for interpreters or latimers in Britain in the eleventh and twelfth centuries.

[20] For another reference to a Saracen 'trucemans', see 'telles paroles et plus grandes assés avoit-il oy dire les latiniers et trucemans qui portent les langaiges de l'un à l'autre' (KL, *Livre IV (1397–1400)*, 16, p. 67).

[who saw and heard him speak very willingly, and the words that the lords did not understand the centurion explained and rephrased into good French, for he understood it well.]

Such a story hints at the importance of Genoa, not merely for its role in trading networks per se, evident from the career of Geoffrey Chaucer who travelled there, but as a location for multiple linguistic contacts, and ones that forged links between East and West.[21]

The continental courts also needed interpreters. Froissart mentions one who mediated between the king and Jean sans Peur, the conte de Nevers, later duc de Bourgogne:

parloit tous les jours le roy au conte de Nevers bien et largement, voire par le moyen d'un latinier, qui les paroles de l'un et de l'autre remonstroit.

(KL, *Livre IV (1397-1400)*, 16, p. 43)[22]

[and the king spoke every day to the count of Nevers well and freely, by means of an interpreter, who revealed the words of each to the other.]

The machinery that enabled a message to be sent from the count of Navarre to England was elaborate, in Froissart's description at any rate. A squire called Laurentien Fougasse, described as 'ung moult saige et discret escuier, et qui bien et bel savoit parler françois' [a very wise and discreet squire who knew how to speak French well and elegantly] was sent because, in the opinion of the advisors of the King of Portugal,

on n'y povoit envoier pour le present gens qui point mieulx saroient faire la besongne. Si furent lettres escriptes et bien dictées et discrectement[23] en bon françois et aussi en latin, lesqueles se devoient adrecier au roy d'Engleterre et au duc de Lancastre, et à ses freres . . .

[one could not send anyone at that time who knew better how to carry out the business. Thus letters were written that had been well and discerningly dictated in good French and also in Latin, which were to be addressed to the king of England and the duke of Lancaster, and to his brothers . . .]

(SHF, *Livre III (1356–88)*, 12, p. 241)

[21] On Genoa as the 'premodern id' and centre for trading, including slaves, see D. Wallace, *Premodern Places: Calais to Surinam, Chaucer to Aphra Behn* (Oxford: Blackwell, 2004), 6 and ch. 4, 'Genoa'. On Chaucer's mission to Genoa in 1372–3, see also D. Pearsall, *The Life of Geoffrey Chaucer: A Critical Biography* (Oxford: Blackwell, 1992), 102–5; M. M. Crow and C. C. Olson, eds, *Chaucer Life-Records* (Oxford: Clarendon Press, 1966), 32–40.

[22] For a further reference to a *latinier*, see: 'Le dit Amourath parla au conte de Nevers, voire par la bouche d'un latinier qui transportoit la parole' ['The aforementioned Amourath spoke to the Count of Nevers, at least through the mouth of a translater who conveyed their words'] (KL, *Livre IV (1397–1400)*, 16, p. 47).

[23] Although de Lettenhove gives 'distrectement', it is likely that the correct reading is 'discrectement', which is the one I adopt here. I am grateful to Godfreid Croenen for his advice on this point.

Froissart keeps the linguistic narrative going right into the chamber of the duke and duchess of Lancaster, where Laurentien is first in order of speech because he knows how to speak French:

et pour ce que Laurentien savoit bien parler françois il parla tout premierement . . .

(SHF, *Livre III (1356–88)*, 12, p. 243)

[and because Laurentien knew how to speak French well he spoke first . . .]

Both duke and duchess read the letters, and the duke addresses him a little later, again because 'Laurentien Fougasse savoit parler très bel francoys' [Laurentien Fougasse knew how to speak extremely good French] (p. 247). The slightly fussy way in which this is told gives the impression that degrees of linguistic competence were not only noted but formed part of the social display of diplomacy: it was an implied compliment to the addressee that the message was in an appropriate language and in an appropriately polished style.[24]

The English, too, were often either able to draw on their own knowledge of other languages, or find ready sources of knowledge near at hand. In recounting the Galician campaign of 1386, Froissart describes a linguistic impasse where men come before the mareschal on their knees for a parley and speak 'en leur langaige espaignol' ['in their Spanish language'] (SHF, *Livre III (1386–87)*, 13, p. 58). Luckily:

le mareschal avoit dalez lui ung Englois qui bien savoit entendre le galicien; si lui disoit en englois toutes les paroles si comme ceulx les disoient.[25]

[The marshall had with him an Englishman who could understand Galician well; he thus told him in English all the words just as they said them.]

Even a duchess could also interpret, if the need arose. A little further on in the campaign, the duke of Lancaster is silent but his wife, Constance of Castile, speaks up:

A ces parolles ne respondy point le duc à eulx, mais laissa la duchesse parler qui très bien avoit entendu leur langaige, car elle estoit du pays . . .

(SHF, *Livre III (1386–87)*, 13, p. 166)

[At these words the duke did not respond to them, but let his wife speak who had understood their language extremely well since she was from that region . . .]

[24] See Chaplais, *English Diplomatic Practice*, 130. As he comments, Latin was used for formal and the vernacular for informal diplomatic letters (131): however, anecdotes like these imply that the vernacular had a much bigger role in oral diplomacy.

[25] SHF, *Livre III (1386–87)*, 13, p. 58. Compare, a little later, a herald sent from the English captain to talk to a great crowd of 'vilains'. He was able to convey his message 'car bien savoit leur langaige' (p. 64). He was from Portugal and spoke 'en bon galicien' (SHF, *Livre III (1386–87)*, 13, p. 64).

Froissart follows this up later to give her an important functional role in peace discussions:

Premierement ilz parlerent de traitier de paix, et luy prescha le frere confesseur en la chambre du duc, present la duchesse, qui depuis relata au duc touttes les paroles ou en parties, car le duc ne les avoit pas touttes bien entendues, mais la dame les entendy bien, car elle y avoit de sa jonesse esté nourrie.[26]

[Firstly they spoke about a peace treaty, and the friar confessor preached to him in the duke's chamber, in front of the duchess, who afterwards relayed to the duke all or most of the words, for the duke had not entirely followed everything, but the lady understood them very well for she had been brought up there from her youth.]

All these examples, varied and opaque, and no doubt gilded with invented circumstantial detail as they are, reveal an enormous amount of linguistic activity across the continent and England (and Scotland, Ireland, and Wales). Stimulated by the circumstances of war, peoples from diverse regions found themselves in close proximity, sometimes fighting on the same side, sometimes on the opposite, but in both cases needing to communicate. As Jonathan Sumption vividly describes, the Black Prince's army that he assembled to invade Castile on behalf of Don Pedro in 1366 had a huge assortment of soldiers from Anglo-Breton companies, groups of Bretons and Hainuyers, Castilian and Aragonese exiles, Navarrese, large numbers of Gascons, and a contingent of English troops led by Gaunt.[27] Naturally there were different levels of competence, and different social contexts for language use, but the overwhelming impression (as one might expect) is that where a language barrier existed, efforts were made to overcome it.

This needs to be stressed if we are to interpret other kinds of passage where linguistic ignorance rather than linguistic competence is the issue. I want to group together several anecdotes that have a similar pattern and that will in due course take us back to Froissart's comments about English abilities to handle the devious subtlety of French diplomats. The first occurs in the 1386 Galician campaign. Seeing that they are in trouble, some Galicians cry loudly 'Nous nous rendons, nous nous rendons!' ['We give ourselves up, we give ourselves up!'] But the English are not in the mood to be conciliatory. Instead they taunt their victims:

mais nul ne les respondoit, et avoient les Anglois bon ris de ce qu'ilz veoient, et disoient: 'Ces villains nous ont batu et tant fait de paine et encoires se mocquent-ilz de nous, quant ilz vueillent que nous les recueillons à merchy, et s'est la ville nostre.'—'Nennil, nennil', respondirent aulcuns des Anglois, 'nous ne savons que vous dictes; nous ne savons parler l'Espaignol; parlez bon Franchois ou Anglois, se vous voulez que nous vous entendons.'

SHF, *Livre III (1386–87)*, 13, pp. 154–5)

[26] SHF, *Livre III (1387–89)*, 15, p. 49.
[27] J. Sumption, *The Hundred Years War*, 2 vols (London: Faber, 1990 and 1999), II, 546–7.

[but no one replied to them, and the English laughed greatly at what they saw and said: 'We have beaten these peasants and given them much grief and still they mock us, when they want us to take them with mercy, and when the town is ours.' 'Not at all, not at all', replied others among the English, 'we do not know what you are saying; we don't know how to speak Spanish; speak good French or English if you want us to understand you.']

This story is remarkable for its attention to blank incomprehension, silence, and resistance. Instead of replying to the plea the English at first say nothing. Amongst themselves, however, they laugh and scorn the attempt by their victims to turn their weak situation around. The method of retaliation they choose is through language: claiming not to understand them, they order them to speak only in 'bon Franchois ou Anglois'. A claim of ignorance conceals subtle military tactics: by asserting that they cannot understand 'l'Espaignol', the English—in this story—insist on 'their' languages from a position of power.

Froissart's famous description of the siege of Calais offers another example. Perhaps the most retrospectively gazed upon event of the whole Hundred Years War, its narrative ingredients in the master chronicler's hands of harsh military violence, rough justice, bare-footed symbolic gestures of humiliation, a desperate but dignified plea for mercy and a heavily pregnant queen, have given it irresistible potency as a representation of regal power in action.[28] Here just one detail may be singled out. For some reason it is important to Froissart to comment that Edward III and his trusted advisor, the Hainuyer Walter de Manny (Gautier de Mauny), spoke *in English*:

Gautier de Manni . . . s'en vint devant le roi et li dist en langage englois: 'Tres chiers sires, vechi la representation de la ville de Calais a vostre ordenance.'

(*Livre I Rome MS*, p. 846)[29]

[Walter Manny . . . went in front of the king and said to him in the English language: 'Very dear lord, here is a representation from the town of Calais awaiting your instruction.']

The King, says Froissart, looked at them very cruelly, and could barely speak with anger. But again, when he does speak, the order is given 'en langage englois':

qant il parla, il conmanda en langage englois que on lor copast les teste tantos.

(*Livre I Rome MS*, p. 847)

[28] Among the vast bibliography on this siege may be singled out the major recent study by J.-M. Moeglin, *Les Bourgeois de Calais: Essai sur un mythe historique* (Paris: Albin Michel, 2002). On Froissart's (via Le Bel's) representation of the 'presuppositions of intercessionary queenship', see P. Strohm, *Hochon's Arrow: The Social Imagination of Fourteenth-Century Texts* (Princeton: Princeton University Press, 1992), 99–105.

[29] Froissart draws heavily on Le Bel for this episode (see L. Chalon, 'La scène des bourgeois de Calais chez Froissart et Jean le Bel', *Cahiers d'analyse textuelle*, 10 (1968), 68–84, and Moeglin, *Les Bourgeois de Calais*, ch. 1, 33–48) but Le Bel makes no mention of language: *Chronique de Jean de Bel*, ed. J. Viard and E. Déprez, 2 vols, SHF (Paris: Librairie Renouard, H. Laurens, 1904–5), II, 162–7; SHF, *Livre I*, 4, 56–62; KL, 5, p. 198; *Livre I Rome MS*, 835–49.

[when he spoke, he ordered in the English language that their heads should be cut off immediately.]

There may be many practical reasons why the king should choose to speak in English, and of course we have no 'proof' that he really did. But Froissart seems keen to give it public significance. Just before Manny speaks, Froissart writes that 'En la place toutes gens se ouvrirent a l'encontre de li' [in the place the crowd opened up for him]. And just after he creates a narrative hiatus of terrifying kingly silence: 'Li rois se taisi tous quois et regarda moult fellement sus euls' [The king held himself completely silent and looked at them with great fury]. The six bourgeois then interrupt that silence, presumably in French, with their speech for clemency. Once again, the king's response is furiously mute:

> Li rois regarda sus euls tres crueusement, car il avoit le coer si dur et si enfellonniet de grans courous, que il ne pot parler.
>
> (*Livre I Rome MS*, p. 847)

[The king looked at them very cruelly, for he had a heart so hard and terrible with great anger that he could not speak.]

When the royal voice is finally heard it shocks twice over: mercy is denied, and in English. Language becomes a defining element in the dynamics of the scene: Froissart brilliantly frames the central moment of political exchange, symbolized in the keys to the city, within two English utterances. This creates two linguistic clashes signifying Edward's display of separate, superior power, in which he and Manny (the latter caught up in speaking English despite being a French-speaking Hainuyer) are presented as being in a distinct linguistic world that cuts violently across the French identity of the city they want to seize.

In this story English is proclaimed with very public deliberation outside its own shores as a means of asserting power on the continent. Froissart depicts a moment when Edward asserts his francophone control through English. The story shares this to a certain extent with the previous story from Galicia. But in the former there is much more interest in the political capital to be gained from claiming linguistic ignorance. Edward rides roughshod through any question of whether the burghers understand his order: the important thing is that his executioners should. But in Galicia the soldiers taunt their opponents both with their own (claimed) ignorance of Spanish, and implicitly with the (very likely) Galician ignorance of English. The threat has its point if we assume that they are asking the impossible ('Goe and catch a falling star'). Linguistic ignorance, in short, has the potential to be a powerful weapon of its own in English dealings with the continent.

NEGOTIATING LANGUAGES

To turn back to Froissart's description of the 1393 Leulinghem negotiations, there are grounds for seeing it as belonging to a wider perception on Froissart's part of the role performed by language and language choice in the unrolling sensitivities of the Hundred Years War.

As Lusignan has recently discussed, these talks were conducted at the highest level, with France represented by Philippe le Hardi, duc de Bourgogne and Jean, duc de Berri, both uncles of Charles VI, and England represented by John of Gaunt, duke of Lancaster, and Thomas Woodstock, duke of Gloucester, both uncles of Richard II.[30] Deschamps was also present.[31] The negotiations concerned the very delicate matter of Richard's appointment of Gaunt as duc d'Aquitaine, first conferred in 1390. This was the old dispute at the heart of the war over English rights in Aquitaine and the allegiance required by France from the English ruler in his role as a duc of the French crown. In devolving his title as duc d'Aquitaine to Gaunt, Richard displaced the matter of allegiance from his role as sovereign to Gaunt's role as duc. Acutely aware of the potential awkwardness of these talks, Gaunt took a leading position in the negotiations over the period from 1389 to 1394.[32] The first round at Amiens seemed to go amicably;[33] subsequent discussions, however, grew more tense and, in the event, although the existing truce was extended for four years, the peace treaty itself, urged by Richard and several of his advisors from the autumn of 1391, was not ratified.

It is not surprising that the negotiations were prolonged and began to be full of charges and counter-charges. Froissart's version of some of the points of impasse is remarkable, once more, for his emphasis on matters of language; but it is also remarkable how often his comments have been discussed out of context in his own narrative. Two nuggets are usually extracted, the passage cited above and repeated below, and a statement that the French learned by the English was not of the same order as that spoken in France and used by the French clerks:

> Car en parlure françoise a mots soubtils et couvers et sur double entendement, et les tournent les François, là où ils veulent, à leur prouffit et avantage: ce que les Anglois ne sçauroient trouver, ne faire, car euls ne le veulent entendre que plainement.
>
> (KL, *Livre IV (1392–1396)*, 15, p. 114)

[30] Lusignan, *La langue des rois*, 242.

[31] R. F. Yeager, 'John Gower's Audience: The Ballades', *Chaucer Review*, 40 (2005), 81–105 (85).

[32] On the internal domestic problems surrounding the appointment, see A. Goodman, *John of Gaunt: The Exercise of Princely Power in Fourteenth-century Europe* (Harlow: Longman, 1992), 150–4.

[33] Goodman, *John of Gaunt*, 150–1.

[For in French speech there are subtle and hidden words, based on double meanings, and the French turn them where they wish to, to their profit and advantage : this is what the English would not know how to find, or engineer, for they only want to understand plain meanings.]

le françois que ils avoient apris chiés eulx d'enfance, n'éstoit pas de telle nature et condition que celluy de France estoit et du quel les clercs de droit en leurs traittiés et parlers usoient.

(KL, *Livre IV (1392–1396)*, 15, p. 115)

[the French which they had learnt from their childhood at home [in England] was not of the same nature and type as the French of France, and which was used by the legal clerks in their treaties and speeches.]

Cited in this form by several generations of scholars, these passages read rather differently once the larger narrative is considered.[34] The first comes after the four dukes have become weary from the sheer repetition of the proposals from the French side:

les corps des quatre ducs avoient trop grant charge pour oyr lire et répéter tant de paroles qui là estoient répétées et proposées de la partie des François . . .

(KL, *Livre IV (1392–1396)*, 15, p. 114)

[the four dukes were too exhausted to hear read out and repeated the great quantity of words which had been rehearsed and proposed on the part of the French . . .]

Froissart then puts in the opinion that:

aussi ils n'estoient pas si enclins, ne usés de l'entendre et concepvoir sur la fourme et manière que les François les bailloient comme les François estoient . . .

(KL, *Livre IV (1392–1396)*, 15, p. 114)

[also they were not so inclined as the French were, nor as accustomed to follow and understand the matter in the particular form and style in which it was conveyed to them by the French . . .]

The picture this might at first sight present of a side who were simply not used to French diplomatic ways is highly misleading. The English placed enormous importance on these negotiations and were using their most socially elevated and also experienced personnel who themselves had men of great diplomatic experience to advise them.[35] The key word here is 'enclins' and is explained by

[34] For an early twentieth-century account of Anglo-French relations during the Hundred Years War whose attitudes and citations have been much repeated, see G. Ascoli, *La Grande-Bretagne devant l'opinion française depuis la guerre de cent ans jusqu'à la fin du XVI siècle*, 3 vols (Paris, 1927, 1930; repr. Geneva: Slatkine, 1971), I.

[35] From 1364 to 1398 Gaunt alone was involved in fifteen separate diplomatic missions as part of the Anglo-French negotiations (S. Walker, *The Lancastrian Affinity, 1361–1399* (Oxford: Clarendon Press, 1990), 39).

the passage that follows, in which Froissart points out that, in the past, the English had been caught out by French attempts to insert extremely obscure clauses into the drafts of peace articles which they then claimed gave them reason to refuse to carry them out.[36] The English response, says Froissart, is to realize that they must be all the more diligent in scrutinizing the material ('en estoient les Anglois plus diligens de l'entendre' [the English were all the more diligent in following it]). At the first sign of obscurantist small print, they set themselves and their lawyers the task of examining every detail and insisting on clarity and transparency:

> . . . quant ils veoient escript, ens ès traittiés et articles qui là estoient proposés de par les François, aucune parlure obscure et dure ou pesant pour euls à entendre, ils s'arrestoient sus, et par très-grant loisir le examinoient, et excrutinoient, et demandoient ou faisoient demander par leurs clers de drois et de loix aux prélats de France ou au duc de Berri ou au duc de Bourgoingne comment ils l'entendoient, ne nulle chose, ne parlure obscure à entendre ne vouloient passer oultre les ducs d'Angleterre qui là estoient, qu'elle ne fuist justement examinée et visitée et mise au cler; et, se riens y avoit de different ou de contraire à leur entendement, ils le faisoient en leur présence canceller et amender, et disoient bien que ils ne vouloient riens mettre, ne laissier en tourble; et pour euls raissonnablement excuser, ils disoient bien que le françois que ils avoient apris chiés eulx d'enfance, n'éstoit pas de telle nature et condition que celluy de France estoit et du quel les clercs de droit en leurs traittiés et parlers usoient.
>
> ((KL, *Livre IV (1392–1396)*, 15, pp. 114–15)

[When they saw written down, in the treaties and articles which had been proposed by the French, any speech that they found obscure, difficult or obfuscating, they stopped at that point, and with tremendous care examined and scrutinised it and asked or required their experts in canon and Roman law to ask the prelates of France or the duc de Berri or the duc de Bourgogne how it was intended, nor did they want anything at all, any speech that was unclear to follow to pass beyond the dukes of England that were there, without being properly examined, attended to and clarified; and, if anything was different or contrary to their own intentions, they made them cancel and amend them in their presence, and said that they did not want to put that nor leave it in confusion; and in order to make reasonable excuses for this they asserted that the French which they had learnt in England since childhood was not of the same nature and character as that of France and which the canon law lawyers were using in their treaties and their speeches.]

Far from being trapped in a situation in which they were simply losing out through their linguistic ignorance to French subtlety, the English were reacting with hard-nosed caution to French tactics and exposing them for what they were.

[36] Only Froissart characteristically passes comment on linguistic matters: other evidence from the time, such as the journal of one of the French negotiators, Nicolas du Bosc, bishop of Bayeux, does not mention this. See S. Lusignan, 'Parler français: les enjeux linguistiques des négociations entre Français et Anglais à la fin du Moyen Âge', to be published in the proceedings of the colloquium *Zwischen Babel und Pfingsten: Sprachdifferenzen und Gesprächsverständigung in der Vormoderne*, ed. P. von Moss (forthcoming). I am grateful to him for generously sharing a copy of this with me before publication.

Froissart allows a hint of scorn to enter his threefold 'obscure et dure ou pesant': obscurity is not cast as threatening but tiresome and tedious, requiring an opposing three-pronged approach of being 'examinée et visitée et mise au cler'. This is very much a picture of lawyers at work on behalf of large corporations, each trying to outwit the other, each occasionally being caught out and then working all the harder to regain the upper hand. The famous explanation that the French of the English was not as good as that of their opponents is, firstly, their explanation not Froissart's, and, secondly, turns out to be a carefully plotted reverse strategy to excuse their desire to work over the French documents with a toothcomb: 'pour euls raissonnablement excuser, ils disoient bien que . . . '.[37]

An important additional factor in the politics of negotiation concerned the relation between oral and written discussion. Building on research by Paul Brand, in particular, and his own detailed archival studies, Lusignan has demonstrated that the English developed a clear policy around the turn of the fifteenth century against conducting business orally rather than in writing.[38] The case was more complex than a simple matter of desiring to keep adequate records, since it concerned cross-channel legal practices. In essence, law French was one of the liveliest areas of Anglo-French which, far from declining through the fourteenth century, continuously evolved and became more refined and precisely focused, even to the extent of rivalling the function of Latin. To that extent law French in England was similar to the language of law in France, but it had nonetheless developed its own character and history. Lusignan's argument is that the difficulty between the English and French negotiators was caused by the relatively fixed status of Anglo-French compared with continental French. The very precision which made Anglo-French law distinctive and functional within England worked to the disadvantage of the English lawyers abroad who had to deal orally on very different terms with their French counterparts, for whom French was naturally more widely but therefore also more loosely used. The great lawyer John Fortescue remarked at the end of the fifteenth century that pleading in French could not be 'whollye abolished', because 'of certein termes, whiche pleaders do more properly expresse in Frenche, then in Englishe'.[39] Perhaps

[37] Compare further remarks, such as 'les cavillations et deceptions des paroles couloureés et entouillies des François (120) [the cavilling and deceits of words tainted and entangled by the French]; and 'Li conssaux de Franche y missent ung point par maniere de langage, que li Englès au lire n'entendirent mies bien, ne n'examinerent, mes le laissierent legierement passer' [the counsellors of the French king put a point there through a turn of phrase that the English did not follow well as they read it, nor did they examine it but casually let it pass], KL, 6, pp.276–7. D. Angers, 'La guerre et le pluralisme linguistique: aspects de la guerre de Cent Ans, *Annales de Normandie*, 43 (1993), 125–39.

[38] I am grateful to him for indicating in a personal communication (February 2008) that further research in Lille confirms this.

[39] 'Propter terminos quosdam quos plus proprie placitantes in Gallico quam in Anglico exprimunt', J. Fortescue, *De Laudibus Legum Anglie*, ed. S. B.Chrimes, (Cambridge: Cambridge University Press, 1942),114. I cite from Mulcaster's translation, *A learned commendation of the*

most interestingly, for our purposes, he declared continental French to be inferior on the grounds that it was *vulgariter quadam ruditate corrupta*, which Robert Mulcaster translated as 'by a certeine rudenes of the common people corrupte'.[40] The fluidity of French on the continent made it less admirable an instrument of the law than Anglo-French.

Lusignan's is a powerful argument, and neatly shows that the arguments about linguistic competence were capable of being turned round by English lawyers to prove their superiority rather than the reverse. But perhaps it is also worth noting that in the century before Fortescue the position of Anglo-French was less clearly demarcated from continental French, and that this applied to oral as well as literate communication. English lawyers were trained to conduct their business with formality and verbal exactitude in the public speeches of the courtroom, not just to write French. The long processes over decades of diplomatic communication, both oral and written, as Pierre Chaplais has outlined in detail, had their own history and effect upon the French used by both sides.[41] It seems inherently unlikely that there was very much practical and functional difference between the two sides linguistically in the fourteenth century. The real tensions in 1393 were to do with the battle of wills over territory and seigneurial authority, and were expressed in a self-consciousness over the shared language. As seen through Froissart's perceptive eyes, these issues went so deep that they were articulated as issues *of* language. The jurisdiction of English and French, of Anglo-French and Parisian French was inextricably entangled with this long-running contention over land and power.

A detail from the many documents of and leading up to the Brétigny treaty of 1360, also brought to our attention by Lusignan, illustrates this entanglement with astonishing particularity. It also reminds us of the culpability of the shorthand reference to 'continental French': just as English law French operated in a parallel, and to some extent separate, linguistic sphere from court Anglo-French (and English), so on the French side, although law French was becoming coterminous with Parisian French, the latter was very far from being a universal French that was widely used in France. Paris itself, as Anthony Lodge has shown, as a result of high and frequent immigration was a babble of different varieties of French: *picard, normand, breton, bourguignon, champenois.*[42] But the negotiators' French, *françois*, although subject to all these linguistic influences, was different again, and heavily influenced by university as well as royal

politique lawes of Englande newly translated into Englishe by Robert Mulcaster (London: Richard Tottell, 1567), Sig. O8r; f. 111r.

40 *A learned commendation*, Sig. O8r; f. 111v.

41 See Chaplais, *English Diplomatic Practice*, ch. 3, 'Letters of credence', 175–251.

42 R. A. Lodge, *A Sociolinguistic History of Parisian French* (Cambridge and New York: Cambridge University Press, 2004).

administrative practice.[43] The English victory at Poitiers on 19 September 1356, described plangently by Ernest Petit in 1896 as 'date mémorable et funeste de l'une des plus désastreuses journées de nostre histoire',[44] may have been devastating, but, even in these circumstances of overwhelming English advantage, the production of an agreed and workable set of written agreements between Edward and Jean II proved tortuous and, in the end, was not properly achieved. Brétigny was preceded by the Treaty of London in 1359; this was subject to much rewriting and secrecy, and only two months after it had been sealed was flatly rejected by the Etats-Généraux in Paris.[45] The new treaty made heavily revised demands of the French, greatly reducing the territory originally claimed by Edward and the amount of the ransom, and was finally ratified, with further revisions and corrections, on 24 October 1360.

The processes of revision turn up some interesting linguistic matters. The Treaty of London was written in Anglo-French; the final sealed treaty of Brétigny, like all the surviving copies of sealed treaties, was in Parisian French.[46] Several paragraphs from the London treaty were reused in its final version, and recast in Parisian French. Just one word survives in its Anglo-French meaning: the word 'bonde', which occurs repeatedly as 'bounde' in the Anglo-French draft (my italics):

et aussi le dit seigneur le Roi aura et tendra pur lui et pur toutz ses heirs rois d'Engleterre, perpetuelment, la ville et le chastel de Caleys, et toute la terre et le pais environ dedans les *boundes* desoutz escriptes . . . avec toutes autres terres, villes, chasteaulx, forteresces, honurs, seignuries, fées, jurisdictions, soverainetez, patronages et avoesons des eglises, hommages, services, rentes, profitz, forestes, boys, marrez, rivieres, layes et eaues, et lieux entregisauntz, et toutes appartenances et appendances d'icelles dedans meismes les *boundes* . . .[47]

[and also the aforementioned lord the King will have and will hold for himself and all his heirs as Kings of England, in perpetuity, the town and castle of Calais, and all the land and surrounding countryside within the bounds described below . . . with all other lands, towns, castles, fortresses, honours, lordships, fiefs, jurisdictions, sovereignties, patronages

[43] The relations between *picard* and *françois* are puzzling and the subject of ongoing research, as Serge Lusignan and Stéphanie Brazeau outlined in a joint paper 'Étude diachronique d'un exemple de la graphie picarde: les chirographes de l'échevinage de Douai (1223–1500)', paper presented at *Language Across Time: A Symposium on Anglo-Norman in the Context of Medieval French Language Use*, organized by Richard Ingham at Birmingham City University on 19 January 2008.

[44] E. Petit, *Séjour du Jean II (1350–1356)* (Paris: Imprimerie Nationale, 1896) [Extrait du Bulletin historique et philologique, 1896], 3.

[45] E. Cosneau, *Les grands traités de la guerre de cent ans* (Paris: Picard, 1889), 33–9.

[46] Lusignan reports that he has not found a single signed treaty written in Anglo-French, 'Parler français'. Why this should be the case requires further investigation. On the whole phenomenon of what he calls 'la pratique d' "anglo-franciser" ', see *La langue des rois*, 236–42.

[47] For this text of the preliminary version in Anglo-French (MS BL Cotton Caligula D.III, nos 84–8), see R. Delachenal, *Histoire de Charles V*, 5 vols (Paris: Picard, 1909–31), II, 402–11 (404); for the final version in Parisian French, see Cosneau, *Les grands traités*, 6. The passage is discussed by Lusignan, *La langue des rois*, 241.

and rights of churches, fealties, services, rents, profits, forests, woods, marshlands, rivers, streams and watercourses, and all the land lying between them, and all appurtenances and appendages of these within the same bounds]

In the Parisian French, the word 'bonde' is used several times on its own and also as a doublet with the Parisian French term 'mete' (boundary, limit, or frontier, from Latin *meta*).[48] It is tempting to speculate that so sensitive a word could not have been left in its Anglo-French meaning by accident: it seems a tiny sign of French recognition that the very term 'bounde' was necessary to express the territorial demands of the English. It circles the English demands for the land surrounding Calais in the above sentence with mimetic insistence, each item of land, property, or act of homage forming an extended space in the sentence that is literally circumscribed by 'bounde', the English boundary.

This example of an Anglo-French 'neologism' (the word occurs from the thirteenth century) forcing itself onto Parisian French is symbolically revealing of the larger linguistic relationships we have been exploring. It is evidence 'on the ground' of the almost imperceptible ways in which the English and the French were shaping their linguistic identity under the constant pressure of war. While all the words were being exchanged by diplomats and officials, Edward's armies were crashing (and at times limping) through the French *pays*, violently but not very successfully trying to force through the verbal aggression with displays of physical power.[49] More broadly, this language of negotiation shows how tensions developed in and through a growing awareness that a difference was being forced between the two cultures. Such differences forced close attention to the relationship between oral and written language, a consciousness which I have argued can also be detected in thirteenth-century texts. English diplomats, in learning to refuse to deal orally with their French counterparts, indicate a profound sense not only of the differences between the fixity of oral claims as against written ones but also of the influence of those perceptions of difference on the relative status of English and French languages.[50]

Yet this was not a simple matter of acknowledging English inferiority in French. On the contrary, the balance of power was extremely delicate, both practically and linguistically. The military and political strength of the English in France in the fourteenth century was never unequivocal, even after the triumphs of Sluys, Crécy, and Poitiers. The inequality of size and the sheer dispersal of

[48] The doublet also occurs in Anglo-French material, see *AND* bounde[1]. On *la marche* as a border zone, see Guenée, 'Des limites féodales aux frontières politiques', in n. 12 above. *Faire frontière* is the phrase used to mark a boundary. Guenée reports that the first use known to him of the word *frontière* in its current sense of border is in *c.*1312, a text called *In frontariam Aragonie* (under Philippe le Bel). See also the word *frontieres* in J. le Seneschal, *Les Cent Ballades*, ed. G. Raynaud, SATF (Paris: Firmin-Didot, 1905), no. 10.

[49] See Sumption, *The Hundred Years War*, II, ch. 9.

[50] Chaplais reports the wonderful remark by the seneschal and council of Gascony in 1317 that 'the French think too much', *English Diplomatic Practice*, 80. Compare Deschamps, roundel no. 673, IV, p.132, line 8: 'les françoiz ont longue oppinion'.

French interests across different regions and rulers, some very weakly affiliated to the royal prerogative, combined with long-standing English possession especially in Aquitaine and Brittany, made the French position highly vulnerable. Yet Edward's exploitation of that vulnerability, though at times brilliantly speculative, was also patchy, often poorly planned and executed, and disrupted by his dealings with the Scots, Irish, and Welsh. The moments of utter French humiliation were never as complete or long lasting as one might have expected, and the deep familial and cultural affinities between both sides no doubt played a part in this. Linguistically, by contrast, French cultural power was immense: but again, it would be misleading to think that, before the fifteenth century, the English necessarily saw that cultural capital as distinct from their own. French literature only became more closely identified with the French of Paris under Charles V. Until then, *picard* was the dominant language of French writing, and the English had a great deal invested in it and the related *wallon.* French literature did not have a single sense of itself as 'French', but rather a multiple one, in which Anglo-French was a part. What we see in the *ballades* of Vitry, Le Mote, and Deschamps are poets painfully declaring a French realization that the cultural meaning of French is becoming more elusive and out of their control. The English 'ignorans' were learning to flaunt French perception of their ignorance politically as a means of asserting political power. But they did so by demonstrating that their old, ancestral definition of 'French' was now asserting something new, a definition of French that included English. For Deschamps, the realization included seeing that French meant English as well as Anglo-French.

THE KING'S TALE AND *THE KNIGHT'S TALE*: JEAN II IN ENGLAND

Chaucer is the third figure in a triad of writers (Deschamps, Froissart, Chaucer) who each represent one corner of the triangulation discussed in the last chapter and which constantly influences the cross-channel writing that forms the subject of this book. If Chaucer has not yet been described as 'English' thus far, then one reason is that none of these writers easily fits such broad labels as 'English', 'French', or 'Hainuyer'. It is arguable that no one, perhaps even including the sovereigns themselves, was sure of his or her identity in this period, in the sense that the old meanings of territorial possession and feudal loyalty were being stretched, cut back, and refashioned in disturbingly volatile ways. The instances of side-changing, of the character of the 'transfuge' are so numerous that they can scarcely be reckoned: from Robert d'Artois and Enguerrand de Coucy, to the humblest terrified or quick-witted soldier mentioned in so many of Froissart's war stories, people were crossing camps on a seemingly daily basis, sometimes more than once.[51] Froissart's extraordinary tale of the capture of Jean II at Poitiers (which I translate using Berners's stirring (if shortened) rendition) itself captures this insecurity of identity at the heart of the theatre of war. In the confusion after Geoffroi de Charny the bearer of the *oriflamme* (the royal banner), had been killed, 'La eut adonc trop grant presse et trop grant bouteis sus le roy Jehan, pour le convoitise de li prendre [there was a great press to take the king]. Froissart goes on: 'it happened so well' that the person who was next to the king when he was about to be seized was 'un chevalier de le nation de Saint Omer, que on clamoit monsigneur Denis de Morbeke; et avoit depuis cinq ans ou environ servi les Englés' [a knight of Saint-Omer's, retained in wages with the king of England]. He beat off the press and asked the king 'en bon françois' [in good French] to yield. On being asked by the king to identify himself, he replied:

Sire je sui Denis de Morbeke, uns chevaliers d'Artois; més je siers le roy d'Engleterre, pour tant que je ne puis ou royaume de France et que je y ay fourfait tout le mien . . .

['Sir', quoth he, 'I am Denis of Morbeke, a knight of Artois; but I serve the king of England because I am banished from the realm of France and I have forfeited all that I had there . . .']

(Berners, 128).

There is a supreme irony (presumably not lost on Froissart) in the French king being taken prisoner by one of his own renegades from the border of the Low Countries; but at least the dialogue was able to take place 'en bon françois'.[52]

Froissart, himself, as we have discussed, was too cosmopolitan a traveller and writer to be described merely as Hainuyer: the epithet '*franchois*' and his own service to Philippa of England each qualify that in opposing directions. Deschamps of the three seems most categorizable, in his case firmly '*franchois*', but he combines this with the capacity to make close friends with various kinds of enemy, Savoyard and English among them.[53] Chaucer, in the early 1360s, was just beginning his career, as a household emissary if not yet as a writer: he did this in a period of busy cross-channel travel that included direct involvement in the war, both in the fighting and the exchanging of terms. His life records indicate that he went to France in September 1359, probably as a member of the company of Prince Lionel, earl of Ulster.[54] Lionel's route went from Calais to Reims via the town of Rethel. Chaucer explains in a court testimony several years later in 1386 that, as a young man, he had seen the arms of Sir Richard Scrope outside the town of

[51] Out of many instances, the Welsh captain to whom Gaunt leased his holdings of Beaufort and Nogent-sur-marne changed sides in 1369: Walker, *The Lancastrian Affinity*, 53. See also Chapter 10.

[52] SHF *Livre I*, 5, pp. 54–5. These details are not in Le Bel, whose account is considerably more terse (*Chronique*, 234–6).

[53] Othon de Grandson (Savoyard), and the English Lewis Clifford, Richard Stury, and Philippa of Lancaster, among others.

[54] Crow and Olson, eds, *Life-Records*, 26–7.

Retters (Rethel), and throughout the whole journey until Chaucer himself was captured (in his own words, relayed in law French):

Demandez si lez armeez dazure ove un bende dor apparteignent ou deyvent apparteigner au dit Monsieur Richard du droit et de heritage dist qe oil qar il lez ad veu estre armeez en Fraunce devaunt la ville de Retters et Monsieur Henry Lescrop armez en mesmes les armeez ove un label blanc et a baner et le dit Monsieur Richard armeez en lez entiers armez dazure ove un bende dor et issint il lez vist armer par tout le dit viage tanqe le dit Geffrey estoit pris. (370).[55]

[Asked if the arms of azure with a *bende dor* belonged or ought to have belonged to the aforesaid Monsieur Richard by right and heritage. He said yes, for he had seen them bearing arms in France in front of the town of Retters [Rethel] and Monsieur Henry Lescrop bearing the same arms, his arms having a white label and banner and the aforesaid Monsieur Richard armed in the full arms of azure with a *bende dor* and having proceeded forth he saw them in arms during the whole campaign until the aforesaid Geffrey was captured.]

It is not clear precisely where Chaucer was taken prisoner, but he must have seen some action, however slight, for that to have taken place. Edward's army began the siege of Reims in December 1359, but, after spirited resistance from the city and supply problems outside, was forced to withdraw on 11 January 1360.[56] Chaucer's ransom was paid on 1 March 1360; a truce on 10 March followed soon after his release, and he was back in England by the end of May. A few months later in the autumn he travelled to Calais for the formal ceremonies on 24 October when the Treaty of Brétigny was ratified, Jean II was (temporarily) released back into France to raise the ransom and two of his sons (Anjou and Berri), his brother the duc d' Orléans, and the duc de Bourbon) were taken to England as hostages in his place.[57] One record survives of payment to Chaucer by the Earl of Ulster for carrying letters from Calais to England at about that time.

All three writers were entangled as writers and as actors or observers of war, with many connections outwards to other writers. Perhaps the most famous brief encounter—and hardly imaginable in practice—was that between Chaucer, Machaut, and Deschamps during the siege of Reims. In his poem 'A toi, Hanri' Machaut complains that he has been forced to stand at the gates of Reims with a coat of iron on his back; Deschamps (who was born in Reims) also claims to

[55] *Life-Records*, ed. Crow and Olson, 370–1. Crow and Olson mistakenly give 'Rethel' as 'Réthel'. The Ardennes city is spelled Retheis, Rethel, and Rethers in the manuscripts of Froissart's *Chronicle*: since the last spelling is closest to what Froissart could have written, it seems appropriate to give 'Rethel' here for Chaucer's reference. I am grateful to Godfried Croenen for information and advice on this point.

[56] Sumption, *The Hundred Years War*, II, 427–32.

[57] Cosneau, *Les grands traités*, 48–52.

remember the siege.[58] As Wimsatt remarks, a more likely chance of a meeting between Chaucer and Machaut was in Calais a few months later: Machaut implies in his *La Fontaine amoureuse* that he travelled to Calais with the duc de Berri to see him off as he left for exile in England. In later decades, Deschamps certainly shared friends in common with Chaucer as well as knowing of him first hand: he speaks admiringly of Guichard d'Angle (who was imprisoned in Spain with Grandson), and knew Richard Stury: Guichard, Stury and Chaucer are all listed by Froissart as English envoys to Montreuil in spring 1377.[59] The so-called Lollard or Chamber knights closely associated with Chaucer (of whom Stury was one, and Sir John Clanvowe) were nearly all seasoned military campaigners and diplomats with strong connections in France.[60] Froissart, of course, was in England from 1362 to 1367 with ample opportunity to meet not just Chaucer but several other francophone poets, musicians, sculptors, and artists, such as the older Jehan de le Mote and other figures such as Chandos Herald and André Beauneveu (a sculptor from Valenciennes).[61] The hostage community was an important stimulus to further cross-channel contact and patronage, including Gui de Blois (who later retained Froissart in Beaumont), Jean II's chaplain, Gace de le Buigne, and the retinue of the comte d'Eu.[62]

These links, associations, contacts, and friendships, some often rehearsed as part of Chaucer's 'French phase', some less well known, are not being gathered here simply to bolster a sense of Chaucer as 'French'. It is rather the reverse, to show how the centre of gravity in these years was precisely the space of exchange between the continent and the island, and hence that a notion of Chaucer as English is harder to find. The English and the French were in ceaseless travel back and forth across the channel in the fourteenth century and all these writers were caught up in that flux. The large numbers of safe conducts, letters, sea voyages, road journeys, and massed military and political progresses of battle, marriage or

[58] On Machaut, see Wimsatt, *Chaucer and His French Contemporaries*, 78–82; on Deschamps, see *Oeuvres*, IX, p. 375, *Miroir* 11666; Wimsatt, *Chaucer and His French Contemporaries*, 245, nn. 14 and 15.

[59] A. Crépin, 'Chaucer et Deschamps', in *Autour d'Eustache Deschamps*, ed. Buschinger, 37–43 and n. 4. Richard Stury was one of the contacts whom Froissart called to mind in Dover as he sought an audience with Richard II in 1395 to give him a copy of his love poems (although, since Stury was in London, Froissart turned to Percy instead).

[60] See K. B. McFarlane, *Lancastrian Kings and Lollard Knights* (Oxford: Clarendon Press, 1972), 177–81.

[61] For the case that he arrived in 1362, see *'Dits' et 'débats'*, ed. A. Fourrier (Geneva: Droz, 1979), 7–9, supported by Ainsworth, *Jean Froissart*, 44 and J. Devaux, 'From the Court of Hainault to the Court of England: The Example of Jean Froissart', in C. Allmand, ed., *War, Government and Power in Late Medieval France* (Liverpool: Liverpool University Press, 2000), 13–14. It is usually assumed that Froissart stayed in England until Philippa's death in 1369, but, as Derek Pearsall points out, he was actually on the continent from 1367, went to Milan in 1368 for the wedding of Lionel and heard of her death in Brussels (*Life of Geoffrey Chaucer*, 68).

[62] N. Wilkins, 'Music and Poetry at Court: England and France in the late Middle Ages', in V. J. Scattergood and J. W. Sherborne, eds, *English Court Culture in the Later Middle Ages* (London: Duckworth, 1983), 194–7.

crusading council, radically shook up the processes of contact throughout the continent. At any town or siege or court one might find travellers, mercenaries, and exiles from north, south, east, and west. Froissart's remarkable pastourelles imaginatively recreate such scenes through the startled and sometimes world-weary eyes of contrastingly static local peasants, as we see in this one written to mark the return of Jean II to England in 1364:

> Dist une bregiers qui la estoit:
> 'Efforçons nous, pour Saint Denis,
> Car errant par chi passer doit
> *Chils qui porte les fleurs de lis.*'[63]
>
> [Said one of the shepherds who was there:
> 'Let's do our best, by Saint Denis,
> For passing by here will be
> *The one who bears the fleurs de lis.*']

The latter reminds us that part of this traffic created the cultural disturbance caused by the presence of large numbers of hostages in England over several years. A great number came over after Poitiers, with Jean II at their head, but there had also been years of hostage-taking on a smaller scale and certain individuals on both sides found themselves displaced for long periods.[64] The presence of Jean II was of particular weight because he created a secondary court. Details of his domestic circumstances in England are fairly full: there is a journal kept by the official who was in charge of Jean's finances while he was in England, the chaplain Denys de Collors, which includes lists of Jean's expenses, and a letter and inventory of his queen's Jehanne de Bouloigne's possessions and of his own silver plate.[65] From this we learn that he was surrounded by several key figures: some of state such as Pierre de la Forest, Cardinal Archbishop of Rouen and Chancellor of France and Jean de Melun, comte de Tancarville, grand chamberlain de France; and other more humble servants such as a squire from the Artois, Jean de Damville (or Dainville), maître d'hôtel du Roi, who seems to have been in charge of all the details of the king's household, Messire Arnoul de Grantpont ('aumônier'), Yves Derian and Jean le Royer ('secrétaires'), and Guillaume Racine ('fisicien'). The latter not only prescribed and made up remedies for the king,

[63] K. M. Figg, *The Short Lyric Poems of Jean Froissart: Fixed Forms and the Expression of the Courtly Ideal* (New York and London: Garland, 1994), Appendix A: *Pastourelles*, no. 2, 213.

[64] Forty-one noblemen and forty-two representatives of the major French towns were prescribed by the treaty of Brétigny as hostages. For an important collection of material drawn from the parliamentary records on the status of prisoners and the hostages after Poitiers, see *La Guerre de Cent Ans vue à travers les registres du parlement (1337–1369)*, ed. P.-C. Timbal (Paris: CNRS, 1961), 305–501.

[65] S. A. R. le duc d'Aumale [Henri d'Orléans, duc d'Aumale], 'Notes et documents relatifs à Jean Roi de France et sa captivité en Angleterre', *Miscellanies of the Philobiblon Society*, II (London: Charles Whittingham, 1855–6), item 6, 1–190 and 'Nouveaux documents relatifs à Jean roi de France communiqués, par M. Leon Lacabane', op. cit. V (London: Charles Whittingham, 1858–9), item 2, 1–24. See also J. Deviosse, *Jean le Bon* (Paris: Fayard, 1985), 406–34.

but bought books for him, and various other services. His master chaplain was Gace de la Buigne, who was commissioned by Jean to write the *Roman des Deduis* (1359–77) for the young Philippe de France, to whom Gace also taught falconry.

Among the books Jean bought were a *Romans de Renart*, a *Romans de Loherenc Garin*, and a *Roumans du tournoiement d'Antechrist*.[66] He also paid money to binders, such as 'Marguerite la relieresse' (32 deniers) to cover a French Bible, and Jacques to bind a breviary from the Chapel and also '*un romans de Guilon*'.[67] Jean employed the distinguished painter, Maistre Girart d'Orléans, who had decorated the castle of Vaudreuil in Normandy in 1356. According to the accounts, while Jean was in captivity Girart was commissioned to make several tableaux, a chess set, and to decorate furniture.[68] In short, Jean had a very pleasant time in England, especially to begin with. He stayed in the lavish surroundings of the Savoy for much of the time, did plenty of hunting, was entertained extravagantly by Edward at feasts and tournaments, and received many gifts, such as a present of four greyhounds from Sir John Chandos, venison, and regular game and fish from the countesses of Pembroke and Warren.[69] These two older ladies had married into the English aristocracy from French courtly houses, Châtillon and Bar, and were confidantes of Isabelle, the dowager queen: they visited him often. Isabelle herself lent him books—a *Saint Graal* and a *Lancelot*—and invited him to dinner.[70] Until her death on 23 August 1358 she seems to have been an instrumental figure in a continental French sub-culture that was interwoven within the wider Anglo-French, Anglo-Hainuyer culture of the court. This social whirl was undercut, however, by the failure of the Treaty of London: Edward ordered him to be moved from the Savoy, curtailed his hunting and cut down his retinue. Rather like Lear, he had to haggle over his household knights while the English were besieging Reims.

Jean's presence in England, despite the glamour, has many disturbing aspects. The accounts reveal his constant problems over money. Not only did Edward not give him any kind of allowance to support his regal prisoner's lifestyle, he charged him expenses of 10,000 'réaux' per month for his keep and added them to the ransom demand. Jean wrote many plaintive letters to his subjects asking for help with his costs as well as the ransom; he also had to sell possessions, including some of the presents, with the help of rich London merchants such as Henri Picart, Edward's banker and wine supplier. More

[66] Aumale, 'Notes et documents', 29. See also E. Salter, *English and International: Studies in the Literature, Art and Patronage of Medieval England*, ed. D. Pearsall and N. Zeeman (Cambridge: Cambridge University Press, 1988), 241.

[67] Aumale, 'Notes et documents', 30.

[68] On the tableaux, see Aumale, 'Notes et documents', 31.

[69] On the feasts, see Delachenal, *Histoire de Charles V*, II, 59. S. M. Newton, *Fashion in the Age of the Black Prince: A Study of the Years 1340–1365* (Woodbridge: Boydell, 1980, repr. 1999) gives a richly detailed account of the clothing ordered by and on behalf of Jean II during his captivity and up to his funeral, 57–64, showing how fully he was accommodated within English court practices.

[70] Aumale, 'Notes et documents', 35.

plangently, Jean was caught between two conflicting models of chivalric behaviour: on the one hand he was the dear brother of Edward ('nostre tres chier et ame frere, le roy Dangleterre'), but on the other his sworn enemy ('adversarius noster Franciæ').[71] Two letters, one from Jean to Charles d'Artois and another from Edward to Jean reveal the cracking strains behind the almost overpoweringly proper courtesies of style:

Jean to Charles d'Artois:

Biau cousin, comme nostre tres chier et ame frere, le roy Dangleterre, nous ait par pluseurs fois requis que nous vous feissons retourner en Engleterre tenir vostre prison, nous vous requerons et neantmoins mandons et enjongnons estroictement sur toute lamour, foy et loyaute que vous avez a nous et a la couronne de France que sanz aucun delay et toutes excusacions arrere mises vous vous puissiez ester par devers nostre dit frere au plus tart dedenz la Chandeleur prochaine et gardez que en ce nait aucun deffaut e que vous nen soiez delaians, car il convendroit que nous vous y contraignissions, la quelle chose ne seroit mie vostre honneur.[72]

[Noble cousin, since our very dear and beloved brother, the king of England, has requested us many times that you should return to England to continue your imprisonment, we request and indeed command and enjoin you strictly on all the love, fealty and loyalty that you have to us and to the crown of France that without any delay and putting all excuses behind you, you must be there in front of our aforementioned brother at the very latest by the next feast of the Chandeleur [Feast of the Purification of the Virgin Mary, on 2 February] and be sure that there is no default nor that you are late, for it is necessary that we constrain you there, that this not be against your honour.]

Edward III to Jean II:

Tres chier et tres ame frere, tout plein de foiz devant [ces] heures, vous avons prie molt affectieusement tant de nostre bouche come par noz lettres et messages pur les bosoignes nostre tres chiere mierre de Pennebrok, les qeles nont enkere pris effect, a ce que nous avons entenduz, dont il nous despleyt molt . . . 10 December 1361.[73]

[Very dear and well-beloved brother, full of fealty before these times, we have begged you very affectionately by our own lips as much as by letters and messages about the needs of our beloved mother [Mary of Pembroke], but these have still not taken effect, so we are to understand, which displeases us greatly]

We are a long way from the vitriol of Vitry in these letters. Jean's is an almost painful, doubly, even triply enfolded plea. Because his dear brother the king of England has requested Charles's return to prison, he must in turn request it of Charles. Edward's order is transmuted into an order of his own, but this is

[71] Chaplais, *English Diplomatic Practice*, 107, and n. 191.

[72] P. Chaplais. ed., *Some Documents Regarding the Fulfilment and Interpretation of the Treaty of Brétigny 1361–1369*, Camden Miscellany, XIX (London: Offices of the Royal Historical Society, 1952), 34.

[73] Chaplais, ed., *Some Documents*, item 13, p. 23.

rendered strangely powerless: he has to resort to a long list of verbs—'nous vous requerons . . . mandons . . . enjongnons estroictement'—to match Edward's single and understated word 'requis' and follows it up with a threefold appeal to his feudal obligation—'toute lamour, foy et loyaute que vous avez'—which he expresses as both personal and institutional—'a nous et a la couronne de France'. That hitch between 'nous' and 'la couronne de France' is unfortunate and perhaps telling. Jean cannot now make a command of one of his subjects without revealing his impotence. If you do not imprison yourself willingly to the one who has overpowered me I can do nothing but appeal to your sense of obligation to my now evidently defunct power to command you as *king*.

Edward's letter also reveals a gap between its affection and its anger, but it moves much more swiftly and unembarrassedly from 'tres chier' and 'molt affectieusement' to 'il nous despleyt molt'. But before we assume too cynical a feeling in either king, neither letter, nor any of the large number sent by them during Jean's captivity, merely contradicts the strength of feeling behind their formal expressions of courtesy. Their relationship is indeed closely fraternal, and their inability to let the circumstances of war deny that fraternity is one of the great marvels of Anglo-French kingship in the fourteenth century. Chaplais notes that the more informal and private privy seal, secret seal, and signet letters from Edward to Jean used the subscription 'Vostre frere le roi Dengleterre'.[74] Veering between feasts and colossal debt, elaborate displays of honour and appalling humiliations, Edward III and Jean II lived these profound contradictions in a language that was elastic enough to accommodate them even if it showed subtle signs, at times, of breaking under its own politesse. Delachenal paints a picture of a weak, emotional, rather stage-struck king who succumbs to Edward's superior force of will and larger regal imagination: this perhaps smacks a little of *post hoc* inter-war frustration with the powerlessness of Jean's situation.[75] Jean's ability to maintain linguistic dignity and decorum under such circumstances does not necessarily suggest weakness, but perhaps even a profound mastery of the need to generate a rhetoric sufficient to supply the deficiencies of his situation. It also testifies to the strange tortuousness of a relationship where a bewildering sense of cultural clash is forcing itself clumsily and painfully on to deep fraternal loyalties.

Chaucer's *Knight's Tale* was circulating separately, and probably well before, the larger bulk of the *Canterbury Tales* was completed. The main piece of evidence that attests to this occurs in a reference in the *Prologue* to the *Legend of Good Women* to 'the book that hight . . . al the love of Palamon and Arcite/ Of Thebes' (F, 417–20; G, 405–09). Some lines in Chaucer's short, broken-backed

[74] Chaplais, *English Diplomatic Practice*, 126.

[75] 'Avait-il un tels fonds de vanité naïve, qu'il eût pris le change sur les marques de courtoisie que le vainqueur lui avait prodiguées?' [did he have such depths of naïve vanity that he based the exchange on the marks of courtesy displayed to him by the conqueror?'], Delachenal, *Histoire de Charles V*, II, 50; see also 81.

Anelida and Arcite (24, 25, 29–35, 36–7, 38) share material with some in the *Knight's Tale* (I, 979, 1027 and I, 869, 881–82, 972 respectively): and Sir John Clanvowe's *The Boke of Cupide, God of Love, or the Cuckoo and the Nightingale* cites I, 1785–6 as its first two lines.[76] There is no specific evidence for dating *Anelida*: Clanvowe's poem alludes to the *Parliament of Fowls* and the *Legend of Good Women* and so fits the later 1380s, making the early 1380s likely for this draft of the Theban story.[77] This period in Chaucer's career used to be described as his 'Italian phase' in recognition of two journeys to Italy that he made, the first in 1372 to Genoa and the next in 1378 to Milan, and a flurry of works that show him reading Boccaccio, above all, with intensity.[78] 'Palamon and Arcite' is an example of his close reading of the *Teseida; Troilus and Criseyde,* most famously, of *Il Filostrato.*

To place the *Knight's Tale* in the context of the tense Anglo-French political language of the early 1360s is not to argue for some narrow sense of French influence on Chaucer's writing. Chaucer, some twenty years on, had accumulated a wide store of reading in French, Latin, and Italian which distinguished Chaucerian scholars in their dozens have explored and expounded to great effect. It is rather that the older notions of his poetic progress towards an ultimate Englishness have brought about a fragmentary approach to his reading and writing as if Chaucer were first 'French', then 'Italian', and only then, finally, 'English'. Newer studies, especially of Italian writing, have emphasized, by contrast, that 'French precedents were fundamental to European literary culture'.[79] The powerful influence of the double-authored *Roman de la Rose* is now recognized as working, from Dante's teacher Brunetto Latini's *Tesoretto* in 1266 on, right through the Italian tradition of Dante, Petrarch, and Boccaccio.[80]

It is important also to remember that Boccaccio's four earliest works, including the three that Chaucer drew upon most fully, were all written at the Angevin court of Naples. Boccaccio arrived there in 1327 at the age of fourteen, and by 1341, when he returned (unwillingly) to Florence, had written the *Caccia di Diana* (1334), the *Filostrato* (1335), the *Filocolo* (1336–8?), and the *Teseida* (1339–41?). He was writing in an environment which was very different from the mercantile climate of Florence. The Kingdom of Naples was a uniquely French part of Italy, having been acquired by Charles d'Anjou (who became Carlo I of Naples) in 1266, and retained by the Angevin family through his son Carlo II

[76] D. M. Symons, ed., *Chaucerian Dream Visions and Complaints* (Kalamazoo, MI: TEAMS, 2004): 'The God of Love, a benedicité!/ How myghty and how grete a lorde is he!', 1–2.

[77] Pearsall, *Life of Geoffrey Chaucer*, 153.

[78] Pearsall, *Life of Geoffrey Chaucer*, 102–9.

[79] D. Wallace, 'Chaucer's Italian Inheritance', in *The Cambridge Companion to Chaucer*, ed. P. Boitani and J. Mann, 2nd edn (Cambridge: Cambridge University Press, 2003), 36–57 (53).

[80] See D. Wallace, 'Chaucer and the European Rose', in *SAC. Proceedings, No. 1 1984: Reconstructing Chaucer*, ed. P. Strohm and T. J. Heffernan (Knoxville, TN, 1985), 61–7.

(1285–1309) and his grandson Robert the Wise (1309–43). Between them they created a court in which French, and to a lesser extent Occitan, culture predominated. Carlo I was a patron (when still in France) of Jean de Meun, who refers to him and to Naples in the *Roman de la Rose.* By Robert's reign, the Angevin library was considerable; yet he took pains to enlarge it further. His own interests lay particularly in medical and theological books: but the library was also well equipped with classical, and vernacular Italian and French texts.[81] Boccaccio's reading was very wide: yet, as Vittore Branca emphasizes, his four early works all show the marked influence of French romance, an influence which he would have received as much from his everyday association with Neapolitan aristocrats as from literary sources.[82] In addition to these French sources for the *Filocolo*, the *Filostrato*, and the *Teseida* respectively, David Wallace long ago pointed out that parallels exist between the *Caccia di Diana* and closely contemporary French hunting poems, such as Jehan Acart de Hesdin's *Prise amoureuse* and Raimon Vidal's *Chasse aux médisants.* Seen from a broadly European standpoint, Boccaccio's poetic development presents a significant Italian parallel to fourteenth-century French love narrative and Chaucer's love poetry.

In reading the *Teseida*, then, Chaucer was discovering a work which was very assimilable to Anglo-French appropriation. Most obviously, it clearly struck him as a work about war. It seems hardly necessary to say that the *Knight's Tale* is preoccupied by war, but this has been oddly bypassed in much modern discussion of its articulation of chivalry. Chivalric combat, however, was at the heart of the ideology of war in the medieval period (though it hardly represented its more sordid realities in many circumstances). Here, it is the *Tale's* treatment of clumsy and painful fraternity that stands out.

The poem begins ostensibly with victory and a triumphant homecoming. But almost immediately, Theseus is waylaid by distraught women in black and urged, even before he enters Athens, to begin the whole process again of siege and destruction. Chaucer plunges the reader into the physical horrors of a freshly created battlefield, with its piles of dead bodies being turned over by robbers and corpse-strippers. Here, in this gruesome setting, he locates the bodies of the two young cousins, lying side by side 'thurgh-girt with many a grievous blody wounde' (1010). With heartless narrative pace they are carried away, half dead,

[81] For the contents of the library, see M. Camera, *Annali delle due Sicilie*, (Naples, 1860), II, 402–6; N. F. Faraglia, 'Notizie di molti libri scrittori alluminatori ecc. della Biblioteca del re Roberto', *Archivio storico italiano*, 5th series, 3 (1889), 357–9; F. F. Torraca, 'Giovanni Boccaccio a Napoli (1326–1339)', *Archivio storico per le provincie napoletane*, 39 (1914), 420–23; and also C. C. Coulter, 'The Library of the Angevin Kings at Naples', *Transactions and Proceedings of the American Philological Association*, 75 (1944), 141–55. Camera and Faraglia are convinced of the presence of French romances in the library; Torraca, however, is more sceptical.

[82] As Vittore Branca puts it, 'non a caso il Boccaccio con estrema naturalezza immagina che la sua Fiammetta si diletti di avere letti li franceschi romanzi; (*Fiammetta*, VIII,7,1), e non a caso le sue prime opere narrative sono tessute sulle filigrane del *Floire et Blancheflor*, del *Roman de Troie*, del *Roman* de Thèbes', *Giovanni Boccaccio: profilo biografico* (Florence: G. C. Sansoni, 1977), 38.

half alive, straight into prison: 'perpetuelly—he nolde no raunsoun' (1024). It is a highly dramatic but brutally stripped introduction. We are told only that they are of Theban royal blood 'of sustren two yborn' and in 'angwissh' for evermore. The visual pleasures which follow of Emelye 'the shene' provide temporary relief, but only to trigger the next violent experience of hurt and sorrow as Palamon, and then almost immediately Arcite, are wounded through the eye by her beauty. What follows is an unremittingly wordy representation both of pain and rivalry. For the rest of the entire poem, with at times almost comic insistence, the pair is caught up in wrangling bitterness matched by a highly physical struggle, ended only by the horror of a death caused by disfiguring 'clothered blood' that made Arcite's face go coal black and his body swell with poison.

John Bowers has recently written that the central theme of this chivalric epic is not so much the love of as *between* these two knights.[83] Chaucer certainly reiterates the strength of feeling between them to excessive levels: as many readers have found, their obsessive rivalry subsumes all other emotion until it finally consumes one of them, and Emelye is left rather limply to marry whoever is left. As well as many literary precedents for a romance structured around two closely bound male friends—Amis and Amiloun, Eger and Grime, Tristan and Kahedin, even Orestes and Pylades come to mind—the newly aggressive circumstances of war in which Chaucer was writing throughout his career provide a further model for courtly rivalry in the relationship between Edward III and Jean II. Could it be that the traumatic exchanges between these two kings in the late 1350s and early 1360s, in England as well as across the Channel, also prompted this kind of representation of brothers-in-arms? The prize of female love, or at least of marriage, seems almost irrelevant to the poem at large and is cynically displaced in much contemporary negotiation as well. Instead, there is an excruciatingly concentrated focus on the pair of knights, reduced to a single cipher 'bothe in oon armes'. It does not seem necessary to identify either of them with Edward III or Jean II; in some ways the point is that Arcite and Palamon are indistinguishable and unidentifiable. In collapsing them together, Chaucer is rather showing the intense pressure on fraternity caused by the crushing condition of mutual rivalry:

> This Palamon gan knytte his browes tweye.
> 'It nere', quod he, 'to thee no greet honour
> For to be fals, ne for to be traitor
> To me, that am thy cosyn and thy brother
> Ysworn ful depe, and ech of us til oother,
> That nevere, for to dyen in the peyne,
> Til that the deeth departe shal us tweyne,
> Neither of us in love to hyndre oother
>
> (1128–36)

[83] J. M. Bowers, 'Three Readings of *The Knight's Tale*: Sir John Clanvowe, Geoffrey Chaucer, and James I of Scotland', *JMEMS*, 34 (2004), 279–307 (284) (his italics).

These poignant words, uttered frowningly, distil the pain and bewilderment of many of the cross-channel letters exchanged throughout the fourteenth century. Sworn brothers-in-arms, first cousins by blood, find themselves unable to distinguish hatred from love, treachery from loyalty to death. Their closeness as brothers-in-arms binds each of them to an oath which they spend the rest of their lives seeking to break. Brotherhood-in-arms was a specific contract sometimes drawn up between soldiers concerning ransom costs; Chaucer gives it a sharper twist by reinforcing the bond through blood and love.[84] Richard Firth Green has commented on the English legal context of Palamon's accusation of treason and Arcite's formal pleas in response, pointing out how extreme the recriminations seem to many modern readers, especially in view of Boccaccio's less bitter tone. But perhaps there is a wider parallel in the extensive legal exchanges of the Anglo-French treaties, especially the large amount of documentation post-Brétigny, where the renunciation of power and territory on both sides proved impossible to enact, both verbally and actually. The haste with which the two cousins resort to legal language recalls the impetuosities and retaliations of this diplomatic context, and is repeated when they meet again in the forest using the Anglo-French term 'darreyne' (1609).[85] Their compulsive fighting, at once obsessive and ineffectual, again acts as a figure for the fraught verbal and physical entanglements of the larger war, words enforced but also undermined by physical assault and its failures. Chaucer picks out the strange intimacy of the fighting by describing how they help each other to arm:

> . . . streight, withouten word or rehersyng,
> Everich of hem heelp for to armen oother
> As freendly as he were his owene brother
> And after that, with sharpe speres stronge
> They foynen ech at oother wonder longe.
>
> (1650–4)

Left up to their ankles in blood, they are trapped by the narrator in a violent verbal embrace ('and in this wise I lete hem fightyng dwelle', 1661), and remain that way until the very end of the tale.

Right at the end, however, the tale converts their tussle into a richly elevated account of Arcite's funeral. Prior to this, inserted into the narrative of personal combat, occurs perhaps the most visceral description of war and death in all Chaucer's writing in the scenes painted on the walls of the temple of Mars. Here is the 'darke ymaginyng/ of Felonye', the proverbial 'smylere with the knyf under the cloke', followed by unforgettable images of destruction, some of which,

[84] M. Keen, 'Brotherhood in Arms', *History*, 47 (1962), 1–17, cited in R. F. Green, 'Palamon's Appeal of Treason in the *Knight's Tale*', in E. Steiner and C. Barrington, eds, *The Letter of the Law* (Ithaca and London: Cornell University Press, 2002), 105–14 (106, n. 3).

[85] See *AND* 'dereiner'.

enriched as they are by classical allusion, Chaucer can only have seen in or off the coast of France, wrought by Edward's soldiers:

> The shepne brennynge with the blake smoke;
> The open werre, with woundes al bibledde;
> Contek, with blody knyf and sharp manace.
> Al ful of chirkyng was that sory place.
> The sleere of hymself yet saugh I ther –
> His herte-blood hath bathed al his heer –
> The nayl ydryven in the shode anyght;
> The colde deeth, with mouth gapyng upright . . .
> A thousand slayn, and nat of qualm ystorve . . .
> The toun destroyed, ther was no thyng laft
> Yet saugh I brent the shippes hoppesteres . . .
>
> (2000–8, 2014, 2016–17)

A remarkable shift of tone occurs, however, after the unsparing bodily details of Arcite's long drawn-out death. For, in the midst of his mortal bodily decline, Arcite reverts to the old language of brotherhood and turns the bitter mutual rivalry into a single legacy of love. With Hamlet-like clarity in the face of certain death, he is given the words to unravel the hatred caused by the bond, and reknit it as a quintessentially chivalric relationship:

> 'As in this world right now ne knowe I non
> So worthy to ben loved as Palamon . . .
> Foryet nat Palamon, the gentil man.'
>
> (2793–4, 2797)

This then permits the final union between Palamon and Emelye: but it takes place only after much more verbal delay. It is not just the moving words on death and the human condition uttered by old Aegeus but the elaborate details of the funeral that intervene. The pagan, epic character of this description has received much comment; could there also be more contemporary reverberations in this war poem of the funeral of Jean II? Elaborately described by Froissart and other chroniclers, it was evidently a shocking climax to the Brétigny negotiations. Jean had only returned to England to substitute himself as hostage for one of his sons who had refused to keep his oath. The previous terrible four years had been spent desperately trying to raise his vast ransom and cope with the lawlessness and ruin of post-chevauchée France, swarming with companies of 'self-employed' mercenaries. In September 1363, after entangled and rancorous diplomatic argument about the schedule of repayments and the terms of the hostages, it was finally agreed that the four noble princes (Jean's sons the duc d'Anjou and the duc de Berri, his brother the duc d'Orléans, and the duc de Bourbon) would be returned as far as Calais, awaiting further cash and security against their full release. But Louis d'Anjou abruptly left, when out on parole, and refused to return.

In a move that surprised his contemporaries, Jean decided to return to England himself. Sumption speculates plausibly that he wanted to return to a situation where he and Edward could finally settle things personally, and face to face.[86] He left Boulogne on 3 January 1364; but his health began to decline in March and he died on 8 April. The scale of the funeral in London was huge and spectacular; the body was returned to France in state.[87] It is not just the painstakingly sumptuous details of the ritual that bear comparison with Arcite's funeral, but its peculiar emotional quality. A king dying abroad is always intensely inappropriate; for the French king to die in England in 1364 must have been the ultimate embarrassment, especially since he had voluntarily submitted to the territorial displacement of his person. That death should be the reward for Jean's 'superb gesture' was not only personally cruel but an event that threatened to rock the foundations of the gesture's chivalric meaning. Chivalry could be reclaimed only by an equally expansive act of homage by Edward. In the same way, Palamon's marriage cannot take place until Arcite's funeral has performed an expansive enough gesture in the narrative. In both, Edward's arrangements for Jean's funeral and the Chaucerian extravagance of narrative detail for Arcite's, all in negative hyperbole, there is a consciousness of the excess of feeling required of the survivor to make the necessary recompense for the inequality of death's sudden blow.

If some of these parallels may be granted for the early draft of 'Palamon and Arcite', then, writing the revised *Knight's Tale* in the 1380s, Chaucer had further reasons for exploring the stresses of fraternal relationships. Modern literary historical analysis usually turns for comment on Chaucer's literary decisions to domestic English politics and the turbulence of growing public unease with Richard's reign. Where war is mentioned in relation to the *Knight's Tale*, it is usually in connection with Chaucer's perceived attitude towards war. But the international outlook of the writing suggests different reflections on what it was that pushed Chaucer into such a tortuous yet extensive exploration of war's emotions through this particular literary means.

It seems to have been a decade when several writers from each side and across the Channel began to cast themselves as sharing close, yet fraught literary friendships, in which the experience of antagonism or an anxiety about linguistic identity was never far from the surface. This was a new experience in 'English' writing. Deschamps and Chaucer were one such pairing, Chaucer and Grandson another, Chaucer and Usk, Chaucer and Clanvowe, and Chaucer and Gower were yet others.[88] This was

[86] On the usual impracticability of face to face meetings, see Chaplais, *English Diplomatic Practice*, 76, which implies the rarity and importance of this decision.

[87] Delachenal, *Histoire de Charles V*, III, 17–23.

[88] Guillaume de Deguileville is another writer whose works were circulating in England and in Anglo-French writing more generally from the later fourteenth century (see Chaucer's *ABC* for example).

(probably) the decade of Chaucer's translation of Grandson's five *ballades*; it was certainly the time of Usk's *Testament of Love* written just after Usk switched allegiance (to Nicholas Brembre) in 1384, and of Clanvowe's *Boke of Cupide, God of Loue*. Gower, to whom *Troilus* (usually thought to have been completed about 1386) was co-dedicated in the *envoi*, returned the compliment in a passage spoken by Venus at the end of the *Confessio amantis* (begun *c.*1387) praising Chaucer's 'ditees' and 'songes'. Exile or imprisonment was common to most of these writers (apart from stay-at-home Gower): Grandson's *ballades* were probably written during his imprisonment in Spain in 1372–4,[89] Usk was imprisoned and then hanged, drawn, and beheaded on 3 March 1388, Clanvowe was not exiled as such during his life, but saw much active service in France and died abroad in Greece on his way to Constantinople as part of a crusading mission. Many of them draw on Boethius's *Consolation of Philosophy*, that foundational work of exile and imprisonment, as a guiding text.[90]

One conclusion we may clearly draw from these parallels and pairings is that Chaucer's own reputation was becoming more public, indeed international.[91] But pertinent to the *Knight's Tale* draft is that to pair oneself with another writer is itself becoming a more public activity. Perhaps even sparked by the Deschamps' *ballade* (although dating is very approximate throughout this period), a self-consciousness develops about the art of vernacular composition that involves realizing that another writer has a contemporary purchase on one's own poetry and is also speaking to it. This is very different from the 'universal' or 'common' voice that Anne Middleton once identified in her influential discussion of Ricardian public poetry.[92] She, as many have, dismisses such allusions as 'coterie' references, as a way of writing that Ricardian public poets were trying to repudiate (illustrated by Gower's cancellation of his reference to Chaucer in the Henrician version of the *Confessio*).[93] But, without contradicting the moves towards commonality that Middleton identified, these references can be seen not as an inward form of poetic self-naming amongst a tiny self-enclosed coterie but on the contrary a sign of public recognition that takes us out of the narrow confines of the English court and city. Indeed, it is Middleton's common voice that one might characterize as narrowly English, confined as it is to Langland, Gower, and Chaucer's *Canterbury Tales*, whereas these paired poetic allusions, to which Christine de Pizan is shortly to be added, register a sense of the writer's self that is defined by his, and later, her internationalism.

[89] Wimsatt, *Chaucer and His French Contemporaries*, 213, n. 13.

[90] In particular, Machaut's *Remede de Fortune* and J. Froissart's *Le Paradys d'amour*, ed. P. F. Dembowski, TLF, 339 (Geneva: Droz, 1986).

[91] A classic essay by Glending Olson remains useful here: 'Making and Poetry in the Age of Chaucer', *Comparative Literature*, 31 (1979), 272–90; see also his chapter 'Geoffrey Chaucer' in D. Wallace, ed., *The Cambridge History of Medieval English Literature* (Cambridge: Cambridge University Press, 1999), 566–88 on contemporary contexts for notions of poetry and the poet.

[92] A. Middleton, 'The Idea of Public Poetry in the Reign of Richard II', *Speculum*, 53 (1978), 94–114.

[93] Middleton, 'The Idea of Public Poetry', 107.

To read the *Knight's Tale* draft in this wider community of writers, newly aware of themselves in the 1380s as writers sharing a common enterprise, is to argue that Chaucer's relationship with Deschamps, whatever actual social form it took, provoked reflection on the troubling issues of fraternity that underpinned the whole Anglo-French conflict. This perhaps caused Chaucer to look back, to see, embedded in his own experience, how much the relationship between the two kings of the generation before had represented a larger agonistic tussle between the two cultures. It was now figured for him in his relationship not only with Deschamps, but also with Froissart, Machaut, and Grandson. Each separately but also collectively, began to redefine the borders of international writing in response to the new insecurities central to the Anglo-French negotiations over identity and intellectual property. Clanvowe, and as will later be shown, Gower and Usk, demonstrate that this process of redefinition was happening within England, as well as in the cross-channel exchanges between England and the continent.

ENVOYS AND *TROILUS AND CRISEYDE*

A remarkable coincidence occurs in the fourteenth century between the political and literary circumstances of negotiation. For just as the machinery of diplomatic communication grew more complicated and the person of the envoy was relied upon more extensively, the poetic *envoi*, in the shape of an addition to the strophic pattern of a *chant royal* or *ballade*, reappeared and became a dominant feature of lyric composition. Seth Lerer has set the *envoi* within fifteenth-century English practice and skilfully shown how thoroughly fifteenth-century scribes and compilers drew out a laureate, public Chaucer from his works by means of a culture of lyric rewriting centred on 'Go litel bok' phrases. As Lerer remarks, 'poems such as *Lak of Stedfastnesse, Truth*, and the envoy to Gower and Strode at the close of *Troilus and Criseyde* were among the most popular of Chaucer's texts in the fifteenth century.'[94] Fifteenth-century perceptions of Chaucer do indeed have their own authenticity, and register a long history of scribal and poetic *habitus.*[95] In that sense, the burgeoning genre in the hands of Lydgate and Hoccleve, and the work of Shirley and Stowe and the anonymous poet-scribes who add *envois* to Clanvowe and other 'Chauceriana', are important witnesses to fourteenth-century concerns. Nonetheless, the fourteenth-century context itself for the Chaucerian *envoi* remains relatively unexplored. Explanations of

[94] S. Lerer, *Chaucer and His Readers* (Princeton: Princeton University Press, 1993), 17.

[95] A. Butterfield, '*Mise-en-page* in the *Troilus* Manuscripts: Chaucer and French Manuscript Culture', in *Reading from the Margins: Textual Studies, Chaucer, and Medieval Literature*, ed. S. Lerer (San Marino, CA: Huntington Library, 1996), 49–80 (49–51, 80); [published simultaneously as *Huntington Library Quarterly*, 58 (1995), 49–80].

Chaucer's practice tend to be brief and refer in general terms to French lyrics; it is hard to find much account of his own sense of prior poetic example.[96]

In what sense, then, might it be true to say that diplomatic and literary negotiation follow a symbiotic course? Chaplais has given a wonderfully detailed description of the specific and larger functions and procedures of diplomatic envoys, their missions and types of documentation throughout the later medieval period. His account, along with older work by Joycelyne Dickinson on the Congress of Arras (1435) the indispensable Tout, and the material collected by Perroy, Chaplais himself and, much earlier, Rymer in *Foedera*, provides a wealth of information about the intricacies and practicalities of 'international' communication between England, its significant foreign neighbours and the papacy. A few salient details and conclusions may be added to the picture already outlined earlier in this chapter of some aspects of diplomatic negotiation.

It may be helpful, first, to comment on the envoys themselves: the rank and type of person, their duties and preoccupations. Although, for the most sensitive, high-level business such as the signing of Anglo-French treaties, dukes, bishops, and occasionally even the king himself would be personally involved, for the most part the person sent on a diplomatic mission, including secret missions, would be an ordinary knight or clerk from the king's household, a *familiaris*. As Chaplais puts it, it was more important that a *familiaris* could be trusted than that he had high rank. Moreover, it was a long-standing practice of the English monarch to include 'distinguished foreigners' (and more ordinary ones) in his list of household emissaries. Edward I, for example, had Grandson's great-great-uncle, also called Otho, in his service.[97] This helps put in context the role that Chaucer, Grandson, and others, evidently had as envoys. Chaucer had precisely this role in several journeys between 1376 and 1381. The first, on 23 December 1376, was on the king's secret business ('in secretis negociis domini regis') in the company of Sir John de Burley, the brother of Sir Simon Burley who was a close associate of Chaucer, especially in the 1380s, and became tutor to Richard II.[98] Simon Burley's links with Chaucer are widely rehearsed: it should be added that even as Royal Chamberlain Burley continued to be relied upon by Richard II for top diplomatic missions.[99] It suggests that Chaucer had a continuing and close access to high diplomatic circles despite his relatively lowly status in the household. In Fig. 4, which illustrates Edmund Beaufort giving an audience to two envoys, we see this indirect family link rising into the next generation. Edmund Beaufort, younger brother of John, was a grandson of John of Gaunt and his mistress, later wife, Katherine Swynford, sister to Chaucer's wife, Philippa.

[96] Even Wimsatt, whose analyses of specific poems are excellently detailed, is cautiously unspecific about this point, *Chaucer and His French Contemporaries*, 259.

[97] Chaplais, *English Diplomatic Practice*, 138.

[98] M. Hanly, 'Courtiers and Poets: An International Network of Literary Exchange in Late Fourteenth-Century Italy, France, and England', *Viator*, 28 (1997), 305–32.

[99] Chaplais, *English Diplomatic Practice*, 166.

Figure 4. Edmond Beaufort and the envoys

Paris BnF fr.84, fol.56.

Of the records that survive of subsequent journeys that Chaucer made on Anglo-French diplomatic business, the formula 'in secretis negociis domini regis' occurs repeatedly, on trips to Flanders, Paris, and Montreuil (1377), 'parts of France' (1381), and Calais (1387).[100] What might 'secret business' mean? The exact content of Chaucer's missions is unlikely ever to be uncovered unless further documents come to light; but it is possible from recent research into diplomatic practice and procedures to gain a closer understanding of the nature and character of such business. All confidential matters were normally entrusted to a messenger to be conveyed orally. The general term for diplomatic letter was *nuncium* (*message* in French); for oral messages a credence. The practice of issuing credences involved a subtle sense of the power and yet vulnerability of spoken communication in relation to writing. In essence, the recipient of the oral message needed a guarantee that it had been sent by the king and not simply invented by the envoy. A system of authorization developed that created a secondary written supporting structure to the oral message. The envoy carried a letter (*littera de credencia; lettres de creance/ lettres de credence*; letters of credence [from the early fifteenth century]) which took the form either of a brief summary of the message, or else simply an indication that the messenger had been instructed to give a message.

This may sound simple enough, but in practice the sometimes slippery relation between written letter and oral message, between oral instruction and written letter, and then finally, between oral message and oral or written response could be fraught with social and political weight. Umbrage could be taken if an envoy presumed to deliver an oral message without a letter of credence.[101] Some of the letters of credence took the form of instructions on what to say: these could be more or less detailed, and in some instances, especially from the thirteenth century, were verbatim speeches, such as the credence delivered by Richard de Gravesend, Bishop of London, and two others in July 1293 to Philippe IV of France concerning Edward I's homage for the duché de Guyenne, and the text of his renunciation, sent a year later.[102] It could be argued that such momentous messages could not afford to be left unwritten, although it does raise the question of why they were presented in an oral form at all. Perhaps the issue was one of performance: the renunciation needed to be a performative act, a 'vox viva' not merely a 'vox mortua' in the pre-Derridean words of Pope John XXII in 1326, writing to Edward II.[103] Other messages allowed much more licence to the envoy to expand and interpret brief notes, which became common in Edward III's reign,[104] and others again show a spectrum of positions in between, where

[100] As many biographers have commented, the specific nature of many of these trips remains vague. I leave aside here the trips to Lombardy.

[101] Chaplais, *English Diplomatic Practice*, 190–1.

[102] Chaplais, *English Diplomatic Practice*, 197.

[103] Chaplais, *English Diplomatic Practice*, 75, n. 1.

[104] Chaplais, *English Diplomatic Practice*, 199.

sometimes the normally fairly clear distinction between 'negotiation' (reserved for a procurator or higher level ambassador) and 'speaking a message' (for a humbler envoy) could be blurred.

But this blurring was itself encouraged under certain circumstances. Envoys were sometimes urged to speak 'de eux mesmes'—on their own initiative. This could be useful if the king wished to test the waters over a specific proposal and could do so without its seeming to come directly from him.[105] Other ways of working around the apparently clear demarcations between private and kingly opinion included the delicate matter of whether the envoy initiated his 'off the record' remarks or waited to be prompted by a line of questioning from his listener. For instance, a pair of envoys on a secret mission to Germany in February 1400 were told to take advantage of any informal discussion they might have with Albert of Bavaria, count of Holland, and raise the topic of a possible marriage alliance. Put unofficially like this, the proposal could be considered outside the pressures of public deliberation. The liberty given to envoys to improvise, amplify, and interpret their instructions appears to have become more extensive during the fifteenth century. Guillaume Cuisinot, for example, was told in very broad terms by Henry VI in 1464 to be guided by his own judgement:

Item, fera et dira ledit sire Guillaume Cousinot au surplus tout ce quil verra bon estre et pouvoir servir au bien des matieres dessusdictes.[106]

[Item. The abovementioned Guillaume Cousinot will do and say anything over and above that he can see to be good and will best serve the aforesaid matters.]

The overall impression of reading through such letters and the anecdotes that flesh them out is of the sophistication of this genre of communication. It was a genre under pressure, especially in the atmosphere of the treaty negotiations of the fourteenth and early fifteenth centuries. So much forced attention to the functionality of writing and speaking indicates a culture that was highly sensitive to words, to the possibilities of misinterpretation and of carefully manipulating misinterpretation, to the difference between closing off and opening up a sequence of reactions, to foreclosing outcomes without appearing to do so. In such circles the pressure on the relationship between speaker and audience was immense; it began with the first draftings of an oral message, and with the decisions about how far to proscribe that message and how far to let the uncertainties of a dynamic performance determine its eventual effect.

It is not easy to pinpoint the very first revival of the poetic *envoi* in the fourteenth century. The device is known first in troubadour song, where it often has the term *tornada*, and then becomes more common in the trouvères,

[105] Chaplais, *English Diplomatic Practice*, 203.
[106] Chaplais, *English Diplomatic Practice*, 206.

where it is an important element in *jeux-partis* as well as *chansons d'amour.*[107] *Envois* are not indispensable elements of the *grand chant courtois*, but it is not always clear whether this is because they tended to get mislaid when songs were copied out: some songs even have two or three. They tend to comprise anything from two- to five-line strophic additions to a song, connected by rhyme to the previous strophes. Their function can be hard to summarize. In essence they perform a metatextual role, either addressing the song itself ('Chanson va t'en' [Song, be off!]), the lady ('De cest mien chant, dame, vous fait present'[108] [I make you a gift, lady, of this song of mine]), the patron, or anyone who appears to be in the audience or known to the poet. The following pair of *envois* to the song 'Quant fine amours me prie que je chant' by Gace Brulé are illustrative:

> Envoi 1.
> Par Deu, Gilles, bien me puis esfichier
> Que j'aing dou mont toute la mieuz vaillant,
> La plus cortoise et la mieuz avenant.
>
> Envoi 2.
> Chançon, va t'en, garde ne te targier,
> Et di Noblet que cuers qui se repent
> Ne sent mie ce que li miens cuers sent.
>
> [By God, Gilles, I can boast
> that I love the most worthy lady in the world,
> the most gracious and the most pleasing.
>
> Song, be off! Be sure not to tarry,
> And tell Noblet that a heart that renounces love
> Cannot feel what my heart feels.][109]

Gilles and Noblet are a trouvère and friend respectively of Gace: the two *envois* together direct the song in complex ways to its audience by means of these mediators who, of course, also constitute its audience. As Dragonetti and Poirion indicated, *envois* are messages, and draw on the language of letters, of sending (*envoyer*) and commissioning (*mander*). Their status is often uncertainly authorial: it is not possible to be sure from the manuscript transmission whether an *envoi* has been added by a scribe or whether multiple *envois* indicate separate performance traditions. Such variability in turn raises doubts, which are in any case intrinsic to the song + *envoi* structure, as to whether the *envoi* is inside or outside the song: is it a conclusion or something extra? At first sight, an *envoi* anchors a song to

107 R. Dragonetti, *La Technique poétique des trouvères dans la chanson courtoise* (Geneva: Slatkine, 1979; 1st publ. Bruges, 1960), 304–70.

108 Dragonetti, *La Technique poétique*, 315.

109 Text and translation from *The Lyrics and Melodies of Gace Brulé*, ed. and trans. S. N. Rosenberg and S. Danon, music ed. H. van der Werf (New York and London: Garland, 1985), 114–15.

its historical moment. It fixes it in relation to particular people as well as to the imagined or actual time of performance. But it does so in often unstable ways that unsettle the terms of the performance. By including its own instruction to be sent, the song appears to deny or even discredit its own performance time: only, the *envoi* implies, when the song is finished and has been delivered will it be truly given. In the meantime, the *envoi* causes the song to exist in a limbo between the oral time in which it is sung and that anticipated moment when, as a written object, it is handed to the lady.

The *jeux-partis* include *envois* in perhaps less mysterious ways, but again make subtle play with the relationship between audience and performed poem. Each *jeu-parti* has a debate structure where two 'opponents' alternate strophes. Where they are named, the boundary between participant and audience is overstepped. The other main genre to which envois are attached, the *chant royal*, was characteristic, like the *jeu-parti*, of the town-centred *puy* productions of Arras, Lille, and Valenciennes.[110] These start to appear in the early decades of the fourteenth century: as with all the surviving examples of *formes fixes* it is inherently implausible that one could identify the original example. They consistently have five strophes and an *envoi*, usually addressed to 'Prince', the Prince of the *puy*: one of the earliest may be the five-strophe chanson cited by Nicole de Margival in his *Dit de la Panthère d'amours* (*c.*1290–1328).[111] The adjective 'royal' indicates their *puy* context, since poetic competitions based on *chants royaux* gave a crown to the winning chanson and the title of 'Prince' to the author.[112] Parallel to their composition the *ballade* genre started to settle into the formal three-strophe + refrain pattern that Machaut was to establish emphatically in the mid-century.[113] But although his eight surviving chants royaux all had *envois* it was not Machaut who introduced the *envoi* to the *ballade*. None

[110] As Deschamps explains, *L'Art de dictier*, ed. and trans. D. M. Sinnreich-Levi (East Lansing: Colleagues Press, 1994), 64–5.

[111] Nicole de Margival, *Le Dit de la Panthère*, ed. B. Ribémont, CFMA, 136 (Paris: Champion, 2000).

[112] L. Stewart, 'The Chant-royal, A Study of the Evolution of the Genre', *Romania*, 96 (1973), 431–96.

[113] The so-called origin of the *formes fixes* is a traditionally contentious topic among modern scholars. Since Lawrence Earp's pioneering article, 'Lyrics for Reading and Lyrics for Singing in Late Medieval France: The Development of the Dance Lyric from Adam de la Halle to Guillaume de Machaut', in *The Union of Words and Music*, ed. R. A. Baltzer, T. Cable, and J. I. Wimsatt (Austin: University of Texas Press, 1991), 101–31, newer research, especially on the *ballettes* of Oxford Douce 308 and the works of Adam de la Halle, is sketching out a much more detailed picture than before of the nature and fact of change at the turn of the century and the decades following: M. Atchison, ed., *The Chansonnier of Oxford Bodleian MS Douce 308: Essays and Complete Edition of Texts* (Aldershot: Ashgate, 2005); E. Doss-Quinby and S. N. Rosenburg, eds, with E. Aubrey, *The Old French Ballette: Oxford Bodleian Library, MS Douce 308* (Geneva: Droz, 2006). See Butterfield, *Poetry and Music*, ch. 16; M. Everist, 'Motets, French Tenors, and the Polyphonic Chanson ca.1300', *The Journal of Musicology*, 24 (2007), 365–406.

of his 246 *ballades* has one.[114] The story is very different for Deschamps: over a quarter in total.[115]

Since Deschamps comments in his *L'Art de dictier* that 'ne le soloit on point faire anciennement fors es chancons royaulx' (78–9) ['it was not formerly the custom to compose envoys at all except in chansons royales'], it has been an easy deduction to posit that he was the first to do so. Nonetheless, this third-person remark is not proof. Chaucer also consistently composed *ballades* with *envois* and perhaps began (though dating is only conjectural) at an early date. Wimsatt is keen to argue that Deschamps's *envois* were not a direct model for Chaucer's: rhyme schemes and numbers of lines seem quite independently explored by each author.[116] Evidently both authors on either side of the Channel found it equally natural to pick up and work with a device that articulated poetically a major aspect of their professional lives.[117] Without entering too far into the complex matter of the rise of the *formes fixes*, two developments pertinent to this discussion occurred, both without easy explanation. The formerly lower-style genres originally associated with dance, such as the *rondet de carole* and the *ballette* were taken up as higher-style genres, principally the *ballade* and rondeau; and the formerly higher-style *grand chant courtois* dropped out of fashion and was replaced by the *chant royal* and—though the social context was different—the *ballade.*[118] The use of *envois* thus passed from the *grand chant* to the *chant royal*: and then in a further leap, to the genre that dominated fourteenth-century lyric composition.

These trajectories are worth spelling out because they help explain the hybrid character of the fourteenth-century *ballade* and its compositional relations. Often misleadingly presented as monolithic and 'fixed', the *ballade* is one of the most versatile and inventive genres of the period. It takes on many colours: notably, as we have seen, the elements of dialogue and debate from the *jeu-parti* and of letter or message. Many anthologies testify to the suppleness of the conversations created between poets in *ballade* sequences: in the Pennsylvania MS Codex 902 (formerly MS 15), in Machaut's *Voir Dit* (the double *ballade* between himself and Thomas Paien, as well as the core lyric exchanges with Toute Belle), between Jean de Bucy and Jean de Garancières, Deschamps and Louis d'Orléans (nos 1378–9), Garancières and Charles d'Orléans (no. 77), Guillebert de Lannoy and Jean de Werchin, not to mention the play of exchanges in the *Cent*

[114] The figure is L. Earp's, *Guillaume de Machaut: A Guide to Research* (New York and London: Garland, 1995), 241.

[115] See J. Laidlaw, 'L'Innovation métrique chez Deschamps', in Buschinger, ed., *Autour d'Eustache Deschamps*, 127–40. He reports that 274 out of 916 isometric ballades, and 10 out of 92 heterometric ones, have an *envoi.*

[116] Wimsatt, *Chaucer and His French Contemporaries*, 259.

[117] For further discussion, see also Yeager, 'John Gower's Audience: The Ballades', 85.

[118] Deschamps signals this in *L'Art de dictier*. But note also a confusion in the mss between *chant royal* and ballade: D. Poirion, *Le Poète et le prince* (Paris, 1965; repr. Geneva: Slatkine, 1978), 361.

Ballades, and various links set up by Christine de Pizan.[119] In short, the *ballade* quickly becomes a means not just for technical display but, more significantly, for poets to create a forum for contemporary poetic self-reflection.

In looking back across the Channel at Chaucer's own essays in this medium, they are clearly seeking to engage in the same kinds of conversation. This international lyric language will be discussed more fully in Chapter 7. His work with *envois*, like Deschamps's, is distinctive and exploratory. Just as the process of communicating across the Channel as a diplomatic envoy involved subtle manipulations of speech and writing to flatter status and smooth offence, so Chaucerian poetic *envois* are given the same work. Chaucer's group of philosophical and political lyrics make full use of *envois* and other debate structures (such as the *responsio* alternations of *Fortune*) and, as John Scattergood has shown, are full of links to Deschamps.[120] References to letters ('this lytel writ . . . I sende yow, *Bukton*, 25–6), to prison (*Bukton*), divided loyalties among friends (*Fortune*), the wretchedness and dishonesty of present times (*The Former Age, Truth*), a French song refrain (or perhaps incipit) (*Fortune*), a bille (*The Complaint unto Pity*), to 'Brutes Albyon' (*Complaint to his Purse*) set these poems firmly within the lyric discourse of the Hundred Years War.

Yet it is in a narrative poem that Chaucer gives full licence to the potential in lyric for examining the often tortuous procedures by which language is exchanged across cultures. Readers of *Troilus and Criseyde* have long been aware of its lyric structure: not only are its inset songs and letters consistently marked out in its sixteen surviving manuscripts, often stanza by stanza, but the use of rhyme royal stanzas throughout is also given visual emphasis.[121] Fig. 5 shows the large-scale beautifully decorated initial and border given to Troilus's letter in Book V. A large coloured initial is likewise given to Criseyde's letter in reply (fol.114v). Such a level of decoration is given elsewhere in the manuscript only to the books and proems. The French connection here, given that rhyme royal was the form most commonly used in the French *ballade*, is noticed by a scribe in Cambridge, Corpus Christi College, MS 61 who, by a place where six stanzas are missing (IV, 491, fol.100v), remarks in the margin 'deficuit vi balettes'. From this perspective, *Troilus* appears as a lyric sequence or compilation, like the *Cent Ballades* (*c.*1389). The inset songs and letters, for instance the 'Cantus Troili' (I, 400), 'Cantus Oenonee', and the Boethian/Boccaccian Cantus at the end of Book III take on the role of poetic dialogue through their relation to 'source' lyric or epistolary

[119] On Garancières see J. Taylor, *The Making of Poetry: Late-Medieval French Poetic Anthologies* (Turnhout: Brepols, 2007), 100–1; on Guillebert de Lannoy and Jean de Werchin, see E. Cayley, *Debate and Dialogue: Alain Chartier in his Cultural Context* (Oxford: Oxford University Press, 2006), 46–8.

[120] V. J. Scattergood, 'The Short Poems', in A. J. Minnis, V. J. Scattergood, and J. J. Smith, *Oxford Guides to Chaucer: The Shorter Poems* (Oxford: Clarendon Press, 1995), 483–503.

[121] For details, see Butterfield, '*Mise-en-page*', 52–61.

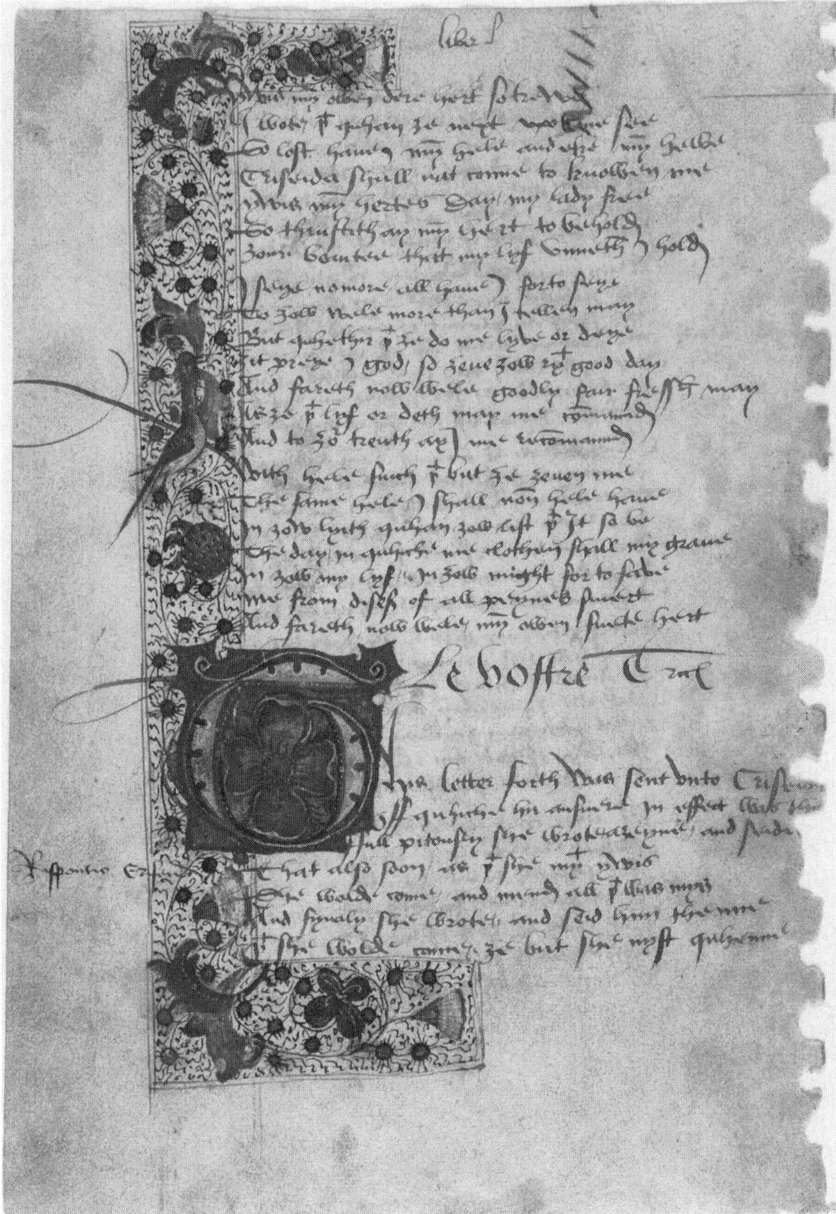

Figure 5. Chaucer, *Troilus and Criseyde*: Troilus's letter, Book V

Oxford Bodleian Library, MS Arch.Selden.B.24, fol.111v. Copyright Bodleian Library: reproduced with permission.

texts, Petrarch's sonnet 88 from his *Canzoniere*, Ovid's *Heroides* 5, and Boethius, *De consolatione*, II, m.8, partly reworked in *Il Filostrato*.

A work of the 1380s, like 'Palamon and Arcite', *Troilus* is another and vastly more extended poem of, about, and immersed in war. The *Cent Ballades*, again, forms a comparison in the dense interweaving of references to tournaments, pitched battles, frontier battles, chevauchées, defensive retreats, and sieges throughout its long debate on love and loyalty. Issues of conflicted fraternity loom large, but not just between two male figures, in this case Troilus and Pandarus, but—in a famously radical decision, departing from Boccaccio—across genders (and generations), between Pandarus and Criseyde. Chaucer further embeds their increasingly strained relationships within a strong sense of overarching family. In that larger textual departure from Boccaccio at the end of Book II, where Pandarus concocts a plan for Troilus to meet Criseyde, the appeals to brotherly and sisterly feeling come thick and fast. Deiphebus is selected by Pandarus as the key to the scheme because he is the brother most loved by Troilus in his 'verray hertes privetee' (1397). Deiphebus enlists the help of his other brother, Hector, and even Helen, cast here as 'his suster, homly . . . com to dyner' (1559–60), gets caught up in the affair. The whole invented story has a peculiar quality because the element of fabrication, hinting at deception, rests on so much genuine feeling. It seems a curious waste of emotional expenditure, paraded by people unaware of the way they are being manipulated in order purely for Crieyde to observe 'wel inough', with an inner delight, her power over Troilus:

> Herde al this thyng Criseyde wel inough,
> And every word gan for to notifie;
> For which with sobre cheere hire herte lough.
> For who is that ne wolde hire glorifie,
> To mowen swich a knyght don lyve or dye?
>
> (II, 1590–4)

So why does Chaucer give so much narrative space to this obscure and emotionally spendthrift digression? One answer may be to build up a powerfully cumulative exposure of the faultlines in fraternal relations in the poem as a whole. Looked at in this light, the scene is full of fragile links and suppressed ruptures: Helen, however 'homly', is the embodiment of betrayal and family tragedy. Criseyde, likewise, is the 'straunge' victim of family betrayal on the part of Calchas, and hence the recipient of so much fellow feeling. Yet she is also the victim who will in turn betray, an act built into her future by the very first lines of the poem. The very strength of the sense of family alliance in this scene has been whipped up on doubly false pretences. This is a profoundly dysfunctional family about to be destroyed by the woman (here Helen and Criseyde blur) it is unnecessarily defending.

This dinner party comes as the climax of Book II of the poem: as readers we have come to it only after the prolonged, teasing, frustrating, bewildering conversation between a suspicious but 'innocent' Criseyde and her artful, knowing uncle. It is here and in Book V that *Troilus* delves most closely into the inscrutable heart of what humans know, or are prepared to admit to knowing, of each other's desires. In both books the pressure on language to reveal is overpowering, and Chaucer ransacks the techniques of linguistic negotiation to expose that pressure and its mechanisms. It is hardly necessary to recall that Book II begins with a proem on linguistic difference: in a passage that has always spoken to and for the modern reader, Chaucer writes of the strangeness of a remote period:

> . . . wordes tho
> That hadden pris, now wonder nyce and straunge
> Us thinketh hem . . .
>
> (II, 23–5)

I have written elsewhere of the way Chaucer presents the encounter between Criseyde and Pandarus as a meditation on the instability of language through history by means of the very unintelligibility of their self-scrutiny.[122] At the same time, of course, he brings this quandary utterly into the present ('now') by insisting that linguistic strangeness is there too; we cannot pretend that our failures to understand one another are the fault of the past ('tho'). The very full sense from the war negotiations of his own time that language is vulnerable to change, that unintelligibility, even, can be used for powerful effect, also enters into the elaborate linguistic ploys of this book. Pandarus has the envoy's charge: indeed Book I shows him leeching it out of Troilus, seeking the commission and, as Edward's or Richard's envoys were required to do, swearing the oath of fealty before he leaves: 'have here my trowthe'.

Immediately, then, Pandarus leaps into that uncertain gap between the wishes of the message-giver and the latitude of the envoy to interpret those instructions. This proves a crucial element in the negotiations that follow since it introduces a deliberate dubiety about his role. Permitted, precisely, to use his own initiative, to speak 'de soi mesme', he cannot ultimately be blamed for any failure of the mission, only given credit for the ways he has manipulated its success. For it is evidently a secret mission, a matter of credence, conducted orally under all the pressures of live performance. The quasi-legal language that emerges in the long narrative hiatus when they eye each other silently sketches out the diplomatic calculation with unsparing acuity:

> Than thought he thus: 'If I my tale endite
> Aught harde, or make a proces any whyle,

[122] 'Chaucer and the Detritus of the City', in A. Butterfield, ed., *Chaucer and the City*, (Cambridge: D. S. Brewer, 2006), 3–22.

She shal no savour have therin but lite,
And trowe I wolde hire in my wil bigyle . . .'
(267–70)

What one notices here is that Pandarus thinks this through as a matter of mutual consideration. It is not just that he has to plan how to say what he has to say, but he has to take into account what her calculations are on the other side of the process. And it is one of the most extraordinary moments in the entire conversation, after Pandarus has broken the silence by talking and talking out his message in the stanzas that follow, to discover that Criseyde's immediate response is not at all that of the emotionally traumatized niece (this comes later), but of the professional negotiator:

Criseyde, which that herde hym in this wise,
Thoughte, 'I shal felen what he meneth, ywis.'
(386–7)

The skill with which the scene unfolds, through this double-sided scrutiny by each character of each of their rhetorical moves, cannot be demonstrated further, though it repays close attention. But it is important to note that Criseyde does have her outburst, before another round of hard negotiation ('It nedeth me ful sleighly for to pleie', 462), and it consists in an agonizing comment on falsity:

. . . 'Allas, for wo! Why nere I deed?
For of this world the feyth is al agoon.
Allas, what sholden straunge to me doon,
Whan he that for my beste frend I wende
Ret me to love, and sholde it me defende?'
(409–13)

In fact, such cries regularly punctuate the scene: the whole is unbearably poignant because Chaucer allows her to give voice to the suppressed tensions that undergird the discussion. These negotiations are not, after all, merely professional, but a matter of dark family abuse pretending to loyalty and affection.

By the time we have reached Book V, war has more fully entered the narrative, and in a cruel twist, Criseyde herself has become the 'transfuge', the 'beste frend' who, following her father, has gone over to the other side. Book IV is saturated with details of contemporary military exchange, with ambassadors, treaties, arrangements for a truce, safe conducts, and a formal exchange of prisoners. Picking up the story after she has gone and Troilus has lost all hope of seeing her return, we find the narrative breaking up into an exchange of letters. It inverts the structure of Book III where a flurry of letter-writing and intermediary work by Pandarus brings them eventually face to face. In Book V, the flurries of mental expectation and disappointment, by bringing on more letter-writing, presage an irrevocable physical loss. The letters thus have the opposite function of a trouvère chanson in that they chart the progressive failure of communication rather than some imagined goal of *joi*. They also flout chanson conventions by including Criseyde's response. At first this is mere detritus: after Troilus's eloquent fifteen-stanza set-piece, Criseyde's reply is crushed into a scant two of indirect summary. When her final full letter is given, it occupies six, painfully evasive stanzas.

As many have commented, these closing epistolary formulas, which act as a form of closure for the whole poem, provide the reader with a formidable interpretative challenge. At this low point, Criseyde seems able only to express her own doom as a literary figure bound to perpetual recrimination. But this view seems itself a failure in the context of the narrative at large. It was an outcome that was never desired, although always anticipated. In using the form and function of the *envoi* Chaucer is able to express something more than mere frustration at this terrible silencing of a woman and the destruction of her reputation. The layered ending, the use of letters in carefully modulated sequence followed by the 'Go litel bok' formula, seems at least in part to be a way of exploring how the language of negotiation betrays itself, even as it seeks to find some point of connection. Where *ballades* and their *envois* / envoys, both poetic and political, learn to utter hard truths about familial loyalties in the context of violence, so Chaucer's *envois* at the end of *Troilus* are an unbearably accurate witness to the ways in which writers were finding their own loyalties compromised and exposed. The 'diversite' in 'the writing of oure tonge' is the problem: formerly familiar, the terms of negotiation are becoming newly unknowable, revealing that the process towards peace is neither secure nor permanent.

6

Trading Languages

The language of invective may encourage us to forget that there were prolonged periods during the Hundred Years War of peaceful interchange between England and the French-speaking continent. The times of truce were often uneasy and shadowed by interminable negotiations, but it is also true in reverse that war was conducted against the backdrop of busy trading links, conducted by those in the highest echelons of society through marriage and ransom deals, right down to the lowest levels of rough barter between soldier and peasant. Fig. 6, from a copy of Froissart's *Chroniques*, shows a herald reading out such a proclamation from a scroll, flanked by the two opposing flags. One of the most glaring examples of the relationship between trade and war is the ransom demand of three million écus d'or made after Poitiers for Jean II, with a first installment of 600,000 écus. The king was permitted to return to France to make arrangements for raising this vast sum through tax, but he met the down payment by selling his eleven-year-old daughter, Isabelle, in marriage to the son of Giangaleazzo Visconti of Milan, for precisely 600,000 écus.[1] This may be the extreme case in aristocratic high finance, but it is not an entirely inaccurate representation of how the extravagant costs and aspirations of war were funded by canny Italian bankers preying on royal women. It also reminds us of how much war was a family business, in every sense of the word.

This chapter combines two kinds of enquiry: into the literary language of trade, especially Chaucer's, and into the kinds of context provided by trade for language use. I am chiefly concerned with the city, and largely with London as the major context in which these two enquiries overlap. Complementing important recent work on the literature of medieval London by Ralph Hanna and others, I will be looking at London English, including Chaucer's, not as an isolated vernacular, but—in a very preliminary way—as one of many competing vernaculars, both oral and written, jostling for space alongside Latin.[2] This

[1] R. Delachenal, *Histoire de Charles V*, 5 vols (Paris: Picard, 1909–31), II, 237.

[2] R. Hanna, *London Literature: 1300–1380* (Cambridge: Cambridge University Press, 2005). See also S. Justice, *Writing and Rebellion: England in 1381* (Berkeley: University of California Press, 1994); D. Wallace, *Chaucerian Polity: Absolutist Lineages and Associational Forms in England and Italy* (Stanford, CA: Stanford University Press, 1997), ch. 6: 'Absent City', 156–81; S. Lindenbaum,

Figure 6. Proclamation of a truce between England and France

Froissart's *Chronicles* (vol. 4, part 1); Bruges, 1470–1475; Master of the Harley Froissart; London BL MS Harley 4379, f.182v. Copyright The British Library: reproduced with permission.

'London Texts and Literate Practice', in D. Wallace, ed., *The Cambridge History of Medieval English Literature* (Cambridge: Cambridge University Press, 1999), 284–309; and the essays in A. Butterfield, ed., *Chaucer and the City* (Cambridge: D. S. Brewer, 2006), and the bibliography cited there. For research on the 'polyglot poetics' of London merchants, see the fine thesis by J. Hsy, 'Polyglot Poetics: Merchants and Literary Production in London, 1300–1500' (University of Pennsylvania: unpublished doctoral dissertation, 2007).

involves taking account of the many ways in which language in the city is characterized, defined, and heard, in so far as we can gauge this from its written forms, and therefore of its variable, mixed, composite, living character. Not far from our concerns is the awareness that so much of city business was shaped by the financial demands of war, either through direct, urgent appeals for money and other supplies from the king, or through sudden releases of tension and inhibition on trading provided by times of truce.[3]

THE STRANGER IN LONDON

London, then as now, was an international polyglot city; by far the largest urban conglomeration in Britain, it was relatively small compared with some continental, and especially Middle Eastern cities and was further decimated by plague during the course of the fourteenth century. Yet it was at the heart of wide and spreading trade networks that stretched right across the known global business routes.[4] Within Britain, London merchants conducted business up and down the country: vintners and woolmongers were trading in Colchester, Bristol, and Cambridge and as far as Durham and Newcastle. Internationally, traders travelled to and from the Low Countries, France, and Italy and also much further afield to Bavaria, the Baltic ports, Constantinople and beyond.[5] As Caroline Barron has remarked, 'London's region increasingly came to include areas overseas': this hints at a view of London, supported by writings on and in London, of a 'porous', open environment, with not only reach and influence on the continent, but one that also possessed satellite financial centres, such as the wine region of Bordeaux, which gave it a presence on foreign soil.[6]

Such ebb and flow meant that people from many continental and other localities lived and worked in the city and Westminster. These included people from areas of the French-speaking continent, from Milan, Genoa, and Florence, the Savoie, Hanse merchants, people from Flanders and Brabant (who settled especially in Westminster and Southwark), Czech-speakers, even a few Greeks.[7] How was such a range of peoples viewed? The terms *alien* or in the vernacular *forein* or *straunge* [*foreyns et estraungers*] were often used, but with more than one meaning. Although *alien* was perhaps the most usual term for a foreigner, that is

[3] See A. Wathey, 'The Peace of 1360–1369 and Anglo-French Musical Relations', *EMH*, 9 (1990), 129–74, and V. Harding, 'Cross-Channel Trade and Cultural Contacts: London and the Low Countries in the Later Fourteenth Century', in C. Barron and N. Saul, eds, *England and the Low Countries in the Late Middle Ages* (Stroud: Alan Sutton, 1995), 153–68.

[4] C. M. Barron, *London in the Later Middle Ages: Government and People, 1200–1500* (Oxford: Oxford University Press, 2004), 237–42; D. Nicholas, *The Later Medieval City, 1300–1500* (London and New York: Longman, 1997), 92–101.

[5] Ibid., 45–52, 76–83 and 84–101.

[6] Ibid., 439.

[7] Ibid., 402–3.

in terms of legal and taxation status 'someone who had been born outside the king's dominions',[8] a *forein* or *alien* was more narrowly someone who was not a freeman (or citizen?) of London; *straunge* could also mean this, but it might as often simply refer to someone who was not from London, but another part of England.[9] One of the main issues in defining people as alien concerned trade: a typical complaint in the Guildhall Pleas and Memoranda Rolls presents:

Marion, þe wif of John Thornton, for a foreyn, retaillyng and byeng as a fre woman. Item we endite Maute kelly and Isabell Sturmyn for foreyn mennes wives retaillyng and byeng as fre wymmen.[10]

Setting oneself up with the trading rights of a citizen when one was a 'forein' or a 'forein' man's wife was thus to invite condemnation. Special alien courts were set up to present cases that affected foreigners, who were sometimes left languishing under charges made by indignant citizens.[11] Nicholas Rudere of Bruges received sympathetic treatment when he tried to escape:

Roll A 27
Membr. 27
20 July 1385

Adam Bamme, late one of the sheriffs of London, was summoned to answer Simon Aylsham, mercer, in a plea of debt, wherein the latter complained that on 24 Nov.1382 in the Sheriffs' Court he sued Nicholas Rudere of Bruges, attorney of Peter Clerk, merchant of Bruges, to render account of £1,000. As the said Nicholas was not a freeman and had no goods in the city, he was taken on a *capias* and brought to Adam's compter in Milk Street, whence he escaped on the Wednesday following.

. . . friends informed John Norhampton, then mayor, that the said Nicholas was a foreigner and had been long in prison, and prayed the mayor to order the defendant, as sheriff, to deliver him according to custom.[12]

In other cases, we hear of Baltazar Oubryak, Lombard (13 July 1386), Bernard Blessyng, a merchant of Bohemia (21 February 1387), and Francis Vyncheguerre, merchant of Lucca (2 March 1387); there are many references to Genoese and to Gascon merchants, and an interesting case (21 February 1393) where

[8] M. Carlin, *Medieval Southwark* (London: Hambledon Press, 1996), 149.

[9] See D. Pearsall, 'Strangers in Fourteenth-Century London', in F. R. P. Akehurst and S. C. Van D'Elden, eds, *The Stranger in Medieval Society*, (Minneapolis: University of Minnesota Press, 1997), 46–62 (46–50).

[10] *A Book of London English 1384–1425* (hereafter *BoLE*), ed. R. W. Chambers and M. Daunt (Oxford: Clarendon Press, 1931), 126.

[11] *Calendar of Select Pleas and Memoranda of the City of London Preserved among the Archives of the Corporation of the City of London at the Guildhall*, ed., A. H. Thomas, 3 vols, I: *Rolls A1a–A9, a.d.1323–1364;* II: *a.d.1364–1381*; III: *a.d.1381–1412* (Cambridge: Cambridge University Press, 1926, 1929, 1932). These alien courts, *pur deliveraunce des foreyns et estraungers* [for the deliverance of aliens and strangers], date from 1221 or earlier: III, 114.

[12] *Calendar of Select Pleas*, ed. Thomas, III, 113–16.

John Lotolli, merchant and burgess of Bordeaux, was heard by a jury of merchants half of whom were English and half Gascon. John Lotolli 'was summoned to answer Robert Normant, master of the ship *Christofre* of Yarmouth, in a plea of debt of £32 1*s* 8*d*, due on a recognisance of 15 April 1388, made at Leybourne [Libourne], a merchant town in Gascony'. The defendant had promised 'to freight the plaintiff's ship with sixty casks of wine at 15*s* the cask to London, Hampton or Sandwich, and 20*s* the cask to Midelburu [Middelburg, Holland] and had failed to do so . . . [He] bound himself to pay to the plaintiff the sum of £30, being half the freight, and also to repay £2 1*s* 8*d* borrowed from the plaintiff in London, the recognisance being attested by the seals of the mayor of Leibourne and Arnaud de Favols, burgess of the same, and witnessed by Bernard de la Barca, Aymeric de Jal Rostit, Amand Leucer, Berthon Dalbiera and Guassias Chivaler, public notary of the duchy of Aquitaine.'[13] We gain a strong impression from such a set of proceedings how thoroughly international merchant business was, and how fully individuals cooperated across the continent from Bordeaux and Aquitaine to Yarmouth and London—with a ship travelling between London and the Kent coast to Holland—to ensure smooth dealings in the transactions of monies and goods.

If these are instances of international fellowship across the business community, then there are plenty of others where implied local resentments come to the surface. The Calendar of Pleas in making complaints about 'foreins' makes certain succinct juxtapositions that make plain the general level of contempt and repudiation in which 'foreins' seem often to have been held:

> Also þat John Tauerner atte bell is a foreyn. Also John Whitlok atte belle atte cartirlane ende and his wyfe be commun baudis . . .
>
> (*BoLE*, 122)

The association between 'baudis' and 'foreins' was well known in Southwark, which had long been a neighbourhood of aliens: 'mercenaries and shipmen, artisans and traders, drifters and settlers'.[14] German- and Dutch- or Flemish-speakers (the 'Doche' or Deutsch) from Flanders and what is now Germany and the Netherlands were particularly numerous, and had the reputation of being largely prostitutes and brewers.[15] A more straightforward reference in the records mentions a boatman named 'lambe' who was regarded as a persistent troublemaker. He is described more than once as 'defectyue' not just for being 'a foreyne & retaylith vitaill' but also 'a chyder, and . . . a baratour with hys neybours, and reble ayeins the kyngys offycyers' (BoLE, 124–5, 133). With names like 'John

[13] *Calendar of Select Pleas*, ed. Thomas, I, 199.

[14] Carlin, *Medieval Southwark*, 149.

[15] Carlin, *Medieval Southwark*, 150, although as she points out, in fact they carried out a number of occupations.

Tauerner' and 'lambe' it seems likely that these 'foreins' were simply non-Londoners, but the following record clearly refers to non-insular peoples:

Item Allard Taillour is an aliand born and holdis hostre, Colouryng many straungers, as Esterlinges and other forains, to grete noisance of his Neghbours.

(*BoLE*, 130)[16]

Allard Taillour does not seem to be creating any specific forms of disturbance to his neighbours, it is rather the mere presence of 'many straungers' that is found to be a nuisance.

Ralph Hanna has written eloquently of the need to attend to 'the local literary culture of discrete places'.[17] That he does so in the context of writing about a London literature is an irony that is not lost on him. There is certainly—as he implies—a danger in stressing London's internationalism so far that one loses sight of the often restrictedly local spur to 'London' writing. Yet one cannot also but acknowledge that urban culture, and especially that of medieval (and modern) London tends to escape such categorization, or at least, in its pockets of self-sufficient inwardness, lives alongside many other communities with a different, outward reach. The Calendar of Pleas is a vivid demonstration of the local and the international brushing shoulders, of an outward-looking business community living (metaphorically if not necessarily actually) on the seaward edge of the city, and a more parochial core looking with suspicion at the outsiders setting up shop on the already crowded streets. It is interesting that Southwark, by contrast, in its role as 'London's scrap-heap, the refuge of its excluded occupations and its rejected residents', was noted for its community spirit; it lacked the official structures and institutions of civic life that were a feature of the city proper on the other side of the Thames but achieved an unlikely solidarity amongst its diverse and motley inhabitants.

The alien presence in London, if one takes London to include as now the 'City' (or financial heart of London) as well as the separate suburban town and royal capital of Westminster,[18] the areas of Southwark, just south of the river, and the built up spaces leading to Westminster in which were located the Inns of Court, Inns of Chancery, large numbers of taverns, and great aristocratic urban

[16] 'Esterlinges' were natives of North Germany or the Hansa towns. 'Colouryng', as Chambers and Daunt gloss it, here means to lend colour to, shelter, or disguise. A perhaps distantly related, but also overtly political sense of the word is used in *Le Songe du Vergier, édité d'après le manuscrit royal 19 C IV de la British Library*, ed. M. Schnerb-Lièvre, 2 vols, Sources d'Histoire Médiévale publiées par l'Institut de Recherche et d'Histoire des Textes (Paris: Editions du CNRS, 1982), where the expression: 'sa possession coulouree' occurs more than once in chapter CXLV, 'Le Clerc'. Schnerb-Lièvre notes that it means 'par couleur et juste titre…*possessio colorata* (*La décrétale Literas*)', I, 270, 272, and 472.

[17] Hanna, *London Literature*, xvii.

[18] See the discussions of 'What is a town?' in G. Rosser, *Medieval Westminster: 1200–1540* (Oxford: Clarendon Press, 1989), 226–9, and in M. Carlin, *Medieval Southwark*, 255–6.

dwellings such as John of Gaunt's Savoy Palace in the Strand, made London both local and international.[19] In 1381, a third of Gaunt's affinity of chamber knights were aliens, including a Scot (Sir John Swynton), two Savoyards (Sir Othon de Grandson and Sir Jean Grivière), the Poitevin Sir Jean Manburni, and Sir Joao Fernandes Andeiro.[20] Medieval London is often now described as fractured and factional, especially in the 1380s and 1390s when riot, rebellion, trade rivalries, and disaffection with royal authority were causing unusual civic upheaval. At the same time, one could argue that these decades also saw remarkable instances of common action, of communities acting together in a concerted way to assert civic desires and frustrations.[21] In short there is a paradox here, familiar to anyone who dwells in a great city, that people can live sharply juxtaposed in virtually autonomous clusters, and yet, given the right spark, suddenly feel a collective identity that is not characterized by kind, race, occupation, or social status but precisely by the common experience of civic dwelling. 'Aliens' are both essential to that experience of commonly shared diversity, and yet can be just as suddenly subject to violent attack from that experience of collective identity. They define the civic, in short, but in so defining it risk being singled out as the face of diversity. The parliament of 13 October 1377 contained a commons' petition demanding the expulsion of enemy aliens from the realm.[22]

It is worth noting that one of the most vivid examples of the representation of city language in Chaucer is emphatically a vision of diverse peoples. Not usually described as a London poem, since it is mostly conducted in the claws of an eagle high up in the stratosphere, the *House of Fame* nonetheless brilliantly renders the noisy chatter of urban life, the simultaneous, competitive and plural voices of public, crowded arenas. Its topic, too, is quintessentially metropolitan: Fame is the classic city value, always chased, always in danger of melting into oblivion:

[19] See R. S. Allen, 'John Gower and Southwark: The Paradox of the Social Self', in J. Boffey and P. King, eds, *London and Europe in the Later Middle Ages* (London: Centre for Medieval and Renaissance Studies, Queen Mary and Westfield College, University of London, 1995), 111–47.

[20] S. Walker, *The Lancastrian Affinity, 1361–1399* (Oxford: Clarendon Press, 1990), 12. As Walker comments, 'the purpose of this last group...imparted to the Lancastrian court a distinctively cosmopolitan glamour and, at the same time, announced that his real ambitions were European rather than English in scope.'

[21] This could be claimed of Richard II's celebrated calming of the 1381 riots, where, in many of the accounts, the mayor is able to command civic support quickly and authoritatively (see, for instance, the accounts by Walsingham and Froissart in R. B. Dobson, ed., *The Peasants' Revolt of 1381* (London: Macmillan, 1970), 179 and 197 respectively.

[22] A. K. McHardy, 'The Alien Priories and the Expulsion of Aliens from England in 1378', *Studies in Church History*, 12 (1975), 133–41 [*Church, Society and Politics*, ed. D. Baker, published for the Ecclesiastical History Society (Oxford: Blackwell, 1975)]. As McHardy notes, however, several of these alien priors worked for Edward III in a diplomatic capacity, and the initial impact of the petition was slight.

. . . of the lettres oon or two
Was molte away of every name,
So unfamous was woxe hir fame

(III, 1144–6)

If we glance in more detail at one of the more exuberant passages describing linguistic noise, we find Chaucer representing it as a vast collection of peoples:

I herde a noyse aprochen blyve,
That ferde as been don in an hive
Ayen her tyme of out-fleynge;
Ryght such a maner murmurynge,
For al the world, hyt semed me.
Tho gan I loke aboute and see
That ther come entryng into the halle
A ryght gret companye withalle,
And that of sondry regiouns,
Of alleskynnes condiciouns
That dwelle in erthe under the mone,
Pore and ryche.

(III, 1521–32)

Crowd after crowd 'of sondry regiouns' and 'alleskynnes condiciouns' approaches Fame to ask for favour: Chaucer is the tourist/anthropologist/historian voyaging through strange scenes in far off locations, seeking to make intelligible what he sees and hears. On the face of it, these seething crowds are hardly inaudible; yet the joke against Geffrey is that he has been brought to hear this confusion of tongues precisely because, in his city life, he hears nothing:

. . . noght oonly fro fer contree
That ther no tydynge cometh to thee,
But of thy verray neyghebores,
That duellen almost at thy dores,
Thou herist neyther that ne this;
For when thy labour doon al ys,
And hast mad alle thy rekenynges,
In stede of reste and newe thynges
Thou goost hom to thy hous anoon,
And, also domb as any stoon,
Thou sittest at another book
Tyl fully daswed ys thy look;
And lyvest thus as an heremyte . . .

(II, 647–59)

Dwelling in the city, with neighbours pressing in on him almost to his door, Geffrey lives an improbably solitary, silent life. Chaucer represents the aporia of the city: the paradox of aphasia or as E. B. White memorably put it of New York, 'the gift of loneliness and the gift of privacy' in the midst of the gossipy excesses of verbal articulation.[23]

This is to qualify somewhat the well-known picture created by Mikhail Bakhtin of the 'language of the marketplace':

> The culture of the common folk idiom was to a great extent a culture of the loud word spoken in the open, in the street and marketplace.[24]

Bakhtin's lively account of Rabelais is famously and rightly attentive to the explosion of languages and registers in Pantagruel's prologue, which includes a curse in Gascon ('le maulubec vous trousque').[25] What Chaucer provides here is more than noise, however; it is a combination of the endless hubbub of urban communication and silence, 'the excitement of participation'[26] and the recognition that what one is hearing may be strange and unintelligible.

THE *BOOK OF LONDON ENGLISH* AND THE 'CUMUNE VOYSE'

The *Book of London English*, compiled by R. W. Chambers and Marjorie Daunt, is a valuable resource of English official documents drawn from various classes of material in the Public Records Office and the Guildhall. It has often been used as a touchstone for understanding the growth of English in public life. Many questions remain about what constitutes 'London' English, and Chambers and Daunt were perhaps purposely over-cautious at times in their estimations of what to include precisely because they sought to distinguish London from official English.[27] My question in this chapter is not so much about the accuracy of the definition of the English as 'London' in the sense of documents 'written by Londoners in London' as in trying to ascertain more about the role of English in an urban context of trade and multilingual diversity. There were many more people living and working in late fourteenth-century London than those specifically registered as citizens—it has been estimated that out of a total population of 40–50,000 there were around 3,000 citizens or about 25 per cent of males over fourteen 'who were not aliens,

[23] E. B. White, *Here is New York* (New York: The Little Bookroom, 1999; 1st pub. 1949), 19.

[24] M. Bakhtin, *Rabelais and his World*, trans. H. Iswolsky (Bloomington and Indianapolis: Indiana University Press, 1984), 182.

[25] Bakhtin, *Rabelais and his World*, 167.

[26] White, *Here is New York*, 22.

[27] See *BoLE*, Preface, 5–10. Research on London English and notions of 'standard' English has been extensive, especially since the landmark publication of A. McIntosh, M. Samuels, and M. Benskin, eds, *A Linguistic Atlas of Late Mediaeval English*, 4 vols (Aberdeen: University Press of Aberdeen, 1986). A full bibliography cannot be given here but see, for further discussion and references, S. Horobin and L. Mooney, 'A *Piers Plowman* Manuscript by the Hengwrt/Ellesmere Scribe and its Implications for London Standard English', *SAC*, 26 (2004), 65–112, and Hanna, *London Literature*, 24–32.

clergy (secular and religious), royal servants or in aristocratic households'.[28] There is no evidence that Chaucer himself was a citizen. The civic nature of London, in other words, although characterized in important ways by those who formed its political community, was much larger and more fluctuating than its bureaucratic core as represented in the official civic documents.

Yet even this core was not narrowly English. An inquiry in 1388 into the practices and financial revenue of all 'misteries and crafts' up and down the country produced a considerable mass of documentary information. Of the over 500 extant responses, forty-two come from London: just six of these survive in English, and one of them from the Gild of St Katherine, Aldersgate, has an opening paragraph in Latin.[29] The records in English, we must recall, give us a tiny proportion of the written linguistic world of the guilds, and even if we are presumably right to assume that the oral sound world was largely English, it was an English used by people who were variously di- or triglossic, either because they were people 'of power' as one guild return puts it,[30] or had a non-English background, such as 'Dederik Johnson, ducheman' who is listed under the 'Fremen and Bretheren' in the accounts of the Brewers' Guild.[31] In trying to understand the significance of the records in English, we need to take account of their status as signs of a linguistic culture that was curiously lopsided, with a dominant but variably competent English oral medium, and a minimally English written medium. The language of the city was far more than English: it was English in a richly mobile and alien setting.[32]

It is with this kind of sense of their wider civic meaning in linguistic terms that we may turn to a fuller reading of the English documents collected by Chambers and Daunt. The longer question concerns how city communities are created through language, and what role a poet plays in creating such notions of consensus. The way particular uses of language relate to particular locations in the world is a way of understanding how kinds of consensus develop. Words are indicative of human habit and custom—they are moral in the root sense of the word (*mos / mores*). The poet participates in the creation of 'usages', or the long accumulated forms of meaning that are part of a word's inheritance.[33] Before

[28] C. Barron, 'London 1300–1540', in D. Palliser, ed., *The Cambridge Urban History of Britain*, vol. 1: *600–1540* (Cambridge: Cambridge University Press, 2000), 395–440 (400).

[29] Barron, *London*, 208. For the six returns in English see *BoLE*, 40–60.

[30] 'to paie', *BoLE*, 49.

[31] *BoLE*, 149.

[32] It is important not to assume that 'literate' means 'English' in the title of Sheila Lindenbaum's influential essay 'London Texts and Literate Practice', in Wallace, ed., *Cambridge History*, 284–309. Her fine essay does not perhaps emphasise clearly enough that the English examples she selects of documentary culture, especially pre-1400, are heavily outweighed by Latin and French. For further discussion, see my Chapter 9 below.

[33] The meaning Chaucer gives to 'usages' (*Troilus and Criseyde*, II, 28) and 'usage' (I, 150) is closely tied to Ovid's 'usus' in the *Ars amatoria* and Horace's 'usus' in his *Ars poetica* as Barbara Nolan shows in an unpublished article, '"Usage" in *Troilus and Criseyde*: A Literary Lineage'.

going on to consider some of Chaucer's 'usages', and observing their embeddedness within city life, I want to see how these instances of public writing in English assume a public knowledge of the English terms in which they are cast. From this we may come closer to understanding some of the common criteria of meaning in his writing and what view he has of English as a language suitable for conveying such meaning, given its context of civic linguistic competition.[34]

The particular shape of this enquiry is not, however, to seek to isolate an 'English' voice from English writing, so much as to recognize how much this notion of 'English' is finding a voice in the midst of other London languages and other European-wide vernacular struggles for authoritative expression. An interesting example is the widely discussed watchword of the rebels in the 1381 rising as reported by the *Anonimalle* chronicler:

> Et les ditz communes avoient entre eux une wache worde en Engleys, 'With whom haldes yow?' et le respouns fuist, 'Wyth kynge Richarde and with the trew communes': et ceux qe ne savoient ne vodroient responder, furount decolles et mys a la mort.[35]

> [And the fore-mentioned commons possessed among themselves a watch word in English: 'With whom do you hold?' and the response was, 'With King Richard and with the true commons': and those who did not know how or did not wish to respond, were decapitated and put to death.]

Here the English has a talismanic force in the French narrative: a chant with two halves, which must be repeated properly at risk of death. Current discussions of vernacularity tend to single out writing in English as evidence of the rise of the vernacular: one might think this an unimpeachable approach, yet before 1400 it is not at all clear that English is the best means for articulating public opinion. In this narrative, it is important to distinguish between the chronicler's use of English to represent the oral speech of the common people and the use of French as his educated writer's choice of language to convey this speech. In writing, in short, English here has a highly circumscribed role. There is some similarity with the case of the Strasbourg Oaths, though the *Anonimalle* chronicler is far less interested in writing English than Nithard is in writing his

[34] David Wallace's *Chaucerian Polity: Absolutist Lineages and Associational Forms in England and Italy* (Stanford: Stanford University Press, 1997) lays the groundwork for such an enquiry within the broad comparative framework of English and Italian urban 'associational forms'. For two, subsequent, more localised studies, see C. Sponsler, 'Alien Nation: London's Aliens and Lydgate's *Mummings* for the Mercers and Goldsmiths', 229–42, and K. Robertson, 'Common Language and Common Profit', 209–28, both in J. J. Cohen, ed., *The Postcolonial Middle Ages* (Basingstoke: Macmillan, 2000). I read both these interesting essays after this chapter had been written and was glad to see how their arguments complement my own more language-based enquiry. To some extent my own approach shares Ralph Hanna's sense that we need to investigate 'the performance that constitutes usage' as well as lexis itself: 'Chaucer and the Future of Language Study', *SAC*, 24 (2002), 309–15 (313). On further political implications of 'common', see also J. E. Howard and P. Strohm, 'The Imaginary "Commons"', *JMEMS*, 37 (2007), 549–77.

[35] *The Anonimalle Chronicle 1333–1381*, ed. V. H. Galbraith (Manchester: Manchester University Press, 1927), 139.

vernacular oaths.[36] One of the most passionate voicings on behalf of the common people was in fact in Latin. John Gower's *Vox Clamantis* takes on—in both senses—the *vox populi*, in a highly learned linguistic register, at once deploring the 1381 rising and claiming to speak for public opinion.[37] The contortedness of Gower's claim needs careful analysis in terms of its linguistic politics. As Siân Echard has well argued, this work warns us away from assuming that, for Gower, Latin stands for a stable and monolithic alternative to the vernacular.[38] Along with the intense play between the Latin and vernacular of *Piers Plowman*, increasingly emerging in modern accounts as a London text, it shows us that there was no straightforward linguistic choice for those seeking to express the common good in the later fourteenth century.[39]

The word 'comune' is naturally of especial interest and it is immediately noticeable how prominently it is used in the English sections of the Calendar of Pleas. Much of the time it is used to establish the grounds for a general tenor of complaint. There are long series of actions which are described in bitterly frequent repetitions as 'noyowse to all þe commune people' . . . 'a grete nosaunce to þe Communes' . . . 'in grete noisaunce of þe commune peple'.[40] When looked at more closely, the notion of 'comune' is very often attached to a sense of free movement along the city's highways. This may be expressed in terms of a hindrance to people's use of 'the comune ground':

> Also the Celer wyndowes in the Rent som tyme Adam Fraunceys in Irmongerlane, for they stonde to moch vp-on the commune grounde, to gret harme to peple passyng forby, defectif.
>
> (*BoLE*, 133)

The complaint expresses a strong awareness of the need for and indeed right of people to be able to move easily along the streets and passages of the city. People are not to encroach upon, let alone occupy, these common thoroughfares ('with empty Pipes and full with vineger'[41]) or a dray or dunghill:

[36] My emphasis here is slightly different from that of P. Strohm, *Hochon's Arrow: The Social Imagination of Fourteenth-Century Texts* (Princeton, NJ: Princeton University Press, 1992), 41, who sees the 'recourse to English' as so rare in contemporary chronicles that it gives the idea of the true commons extra weight.

[37] On the 'comun vois', 'communis vox', and 'vox plebis' in Gower's poetry, see J. Watts, *Henry VI and the Politics of Kingship* (Cambridge: Cambridge University Press, 1996), 'Pressure of the Public', 170 and n. 51.

[38] S. Echard, 'Gower's "bokes of Latin": Language, Politics, and Poetry', *SAC*, 25 (2003), 123–56. See also D. Aers, '*Vox populi* and the literature of 1381', in Wallace, ed., *Cambridge History*, 432–53.

[39] On the circulation of *Piers* in London circles, see Hanna, *London Literature*, 243–304 and Horobin and Mooney, '*A Piers Plowman* Manuscript'. Several essays in K. Lavezzo, ed., *Imagining a Medieval English Nation* (Minneapolis: University of Minnesota Press, 2004), engage with notions of community in later fourteenth-century England. For a thoughtful discussion of Langland's part in the creation of a vernacular politics, see L. Scanlon, 'King, Commons, and Kind Wit: Langland's National Vision and the Rising of 1381', in Lavezzo, ed., *Imagining a Medieval English Nation.*

[40] *BoLE*, 129. [41] Ibid.

Item William Clauson hath stondyng in þe strete a dray þat is hynderyng to þe Pepill bothe day and nyght. Item þer is a donghill in þe watergatestrete anynst Berelane þe whiche is noyowse to all þe commune people, kasting out in-to þis lane ordour of Prevees and other orrible siȝtis.

(*BoLE*, 129)

The vivid sense of continual obstruction created by the present participle in 'hynderyng' reinforced with 'bothe day and nyght' evokes in inverse relief a street scene crowded with busy passers-by at all hours, struggling to get past a large stationary cart. The same active grammar is used of the dunghill: noxious sights and smells 'kasting out in-to þis lane' form just as much of an obstacle to the free flow of city life as a fishmonger's stalls, or a gradually decaying mud wall (*BoLE*, 135).

The extraordinary detail of some of the indictments shows how much anxiety and irritation could be caused by the anticipation of future encumbrances, and not just by existing blockages:

Also the Tymberwek of Fletebrigge is defectif and perilus, and the vndersettyng ther-of vnsufficient, wherby that grete perill is lekly to fall, but zif it be amended. Also the paleyse on the wharf besyde the same brigge is al to-broken and defectif, and otherwhile robous is cast in there, to grete hindryng and lettynge of the streme, because that paleyse is not made. Also j caban made of old bordys at John Broke wexchaundlers shop accrochith vppon the comune grounde and is nuyus to all folk there passyng. (*BoLE*, 135)

The feeling behind this description is that of the daily passer-by, cumulatively troubled by the possibility of being struck by timber that is on the point of collapse, by a permanently unfinished building silting up with rubbish and, with the opposite kind of annoyance, by an illegally built cabin jutting out into the path. This is more than an official record; it is the voice of a city dweller, someone who experiences the physical attributes of city space as part of his own mental as well as physical occupation of that space. The constant references to the need to keep clear and in good repair the common 'hy wey', the 'streme', 'þe comon pauement',[42] the lanes and stairs down to the Thames,[43] all convey an overwhelming perception of the city as not so much a closed in built environment as a great open-air network of public thoroughfares on both land and water. The duty of the urban dweller is defined by reverse implication in these complaints as to preserve and maintain the public space of those highways, in order to allow an unhindered busy movement of traffic.[44]

42 *BoLE*, 132.

43 Ibid., 125, 127–8.

44 On the (rather different) use of urban space in Florence and Rome, see C. Burroughs, 'Spaces of Arbitration and the Organization of Space in Late Medieval Italian Cities', in B. A. Hanawalt and M. Kobialka, eds, *Medieval Practices of Space* (Minneapolis: University of Minnesota, 2000), 64–100.

This then is one particularly powerful sense of 'common' in the public English of these Pleas: the communal ownership of space, and an appeal to a communal desire to keep that space uncluttered. In both cases the term, often extended simply to 'the peple', has no social specificity: collective feeling is invoked or assumed on the basis purely of the shared experience of living in the city, seen here as essentially dynamic. But there are other uses of 'common' that invoke more directly moral assumptions. Margaret, the wife of John Stok, is condemned as 'a comyn scolde', another Mergret as a 'comune strumpet', and Katerine Denys as a 'commune hukster and a resceyvour of euell couynes'.[45] Although there is perhaps some overlap in the sense of public space, here made immorally available by the 'strumpet' in her own person, there is also a wider link between urban space, speech, and trade. It is partly that open quarrelling disturbs public equilibrium in the same way as does a 'grete stenche' from a privy, or a cart standing in the street:

> John Kempe, Cartere, is a Baratour and a commune Scold and hyndryng all the kynges pepill with cartes stondyng in þe strete bothe day and nyȝt.
>
> (*BoLE*, 130)

But the Pleas frequently imply that those who indulge in loud angry talk are bad traders and hence often foreigners too:

> Also we endite Alison herford for a comun scolde and a foreyn, byyng and sellyng as fremen.
>
> (*BoLE*, 132)

Trade is not permitted to be too public; it is not available to everyone, and those who do trade beyond these limits, like Katerine Denys, are likely to be fostering the kind of evil speech that produces conspiracy. The husband of Mergret, the 'comune strumpet', for instance, is 'an vtrer of vnlawfull langage'.[46] The circulation of trade, of crowds of moving people, and of speech, is all connected: a foul obstruction in any one area creates trouble throughout the city's arteries.

The difficulty with reading these Pleas is that we cannot be sure how much they are arguing for a common language that is not really there.[47] The impression we receive from them is highly reversible: on the one hand it presents an effort to express communal frustration with the intrusions and excesses of a minority of urban dwellers, but on the other it implicitly reveals a London that is far from free-flowing but instead plagued by persistently anti-social behaviour that interrupts, encroaches upon, strikes down, trips up, and deceives the

[45] *BoLE*, 126.

[46] Ibid., 132.

[47] For a related argument that the notion of 'common profit' is fractured and contradictory, see L. Farber, *An Anatomy of Trade in Medieval Writing: Value, Consent, and Community* (Ithaca and London: Cornell University Press, 2006), 161–79.

ordinary householder. There is a desire to lay claim to common values, but the sparks of frustration and impatience in the complaints, especially those which remark on a situation which had not changed since the last complaint, suggest that the rhetoric of civic order veiled a much more unruly set of human interactions.[48] As soon as a person, as opposed to a physical object or structure, is marked out as a cause of nuisance, the language of indictment turns very rapidly to xenophobia. Trade protectionism creates a tone of solidarity, but one that can be used in an instant against 'foreins' to create factions rather than a unified standpoint. The number of times a 'forein' is described as being also a 'scolde' or 'baratour' shows how loud words can be a flashpoint, especially when they identify the speaker as different.[49]

We can better appreciate the social reality of this by recalling the extent to which trade was conducted in a medieval city by loud cries. 'Towns were above all markets'[50] and the business of buying and selling was therefore both public and noisy. From the evidence of a slightly later period, it was also a form of public music or chanting. Songs from late fifteenth- and sixteenth-century Paris incorporate versified cries, singing the merits of greens, cabbage, peas, broad beans, turnip, chestnuts; fruit and nuts (cherries, prunes, pears, peaches, oranges, almonds, pine-nuts); herrings and chicken; wine; pies and pastries; matches and candles:

> 'poys vers, poys vers, poys vers'
> 'Marrons de Lyon, Marrons de Lyon'
> 'amendez vous dames, amendez'[51]

According to Truque (1545 collection): there are 'one hundred and seven cries which are cried every day in Paris'.[52] Some of our best evidence from medieval London is to be found in Langland and the anonymous *London Lickpenny*:

> As dykeres and delveres that doon hire dedes ille
> And dryveth forth the longe day with '*Dieu vous save Dame Emme!*'
> Cokes and hire knaves cryden, 'Hote pies, hote!

[48] For the interesting description of complaint as the 'signature form of expression' of late fourteenth-century Londoners, see Lindenbaum, 'London Texts', 288–9. More recent discussion is provided by W. Scase, *Literature and Complaint in England, 1272–1553* (Oxford: Oxford University Press, 2007).

[49] Compare the violent cacophony of noise described in Gower's *Vox clamantis*, I, xi, 797–820, in Macaulay, ed., IV, 44–5 cited, with discussion, in Echard, 'Gower's "bokes of Latin"', 135–6.

[50] J. Schofield and G. Stell, 'The Built Environment 1300–1540', in Palliser, ed., *The Cambridge Urban History*, 371–93 (377).

[51] Early Street cries of Paris, with music from Clément Janequin (c.1485–1558): 'Voulez ouyr les cris de Paris', an *a capella* part song, 1st pub. 1530. See *Chansons polyphoniques*, ed. A. Tillman Merrit and F. Lesure, 6 vols (Monaco: Editions de l'oiseau-lyre, 1956), I, 146–67. The street cries were composed according to a four-line versified form: each cry promoting a specific item for sale. The earliest compilation was by Guillaume de Villeneuve (thirteenth-century); see A. Franklin, *Les rues et les cris de Paris au XIIIe siècle* (Paris: L. Willem, P. Daffis, 1874).

[52] Cited in Bakhtin, *Rabelais*, 181.

Goode gees and grys! Go we dyne, go we!'
Taverners until hem tolden the same:
'Whit wyn of Oseye and wyn of Gascoigne,
Of the Ryn and of the Rochel, the roost to defie!'[53]

Tradespeople created their own verbal and oral space with their cries: these functioned as ways of identifying a particular seller as well as a certain type of goods. As the passage from *Piers Plowman* shows, the street cries were not monolingual. Moreover, the use of French here is attributed firmly to the labouring class. This instance of what was presumably the refrain of a well-known song, '*Dieu vous save Dame Emme!*', is presented by Langland as being sung by workmen digging ditches, not by learned clerics.[54] From the humblest daily talk to the highest echelons of learned composition, via bureaucratic, mercantile, and legal speech and writing, the language of medieval London was a constantly changing mixture of tongues, drawn not only from varieties of English, but also (to differing degrees) from varieties of continental and Anglo-French, Gascon, varieties of Italian, Portuguese, Spanish, Catalan, German, Flemish, Czech, Latin, and even some languages from further east.[55]

TRADING FLEMISH

The presence of a variety of languages and accents can be reported in a benign way as a form of peaceful trading, but in moments of stress it could be a way of identifying people for more menacing purposes, as we saw in the passage from the *Anonimalle Chronicle.* In an often quoted comment from the *Chronicles of London,* the Flemings massacred in the 1381 rising were singled out by the mob for their pronunciation of bread and cheese: they 'koude nat say Breed and Chese, but Case and Brode [*kaas en brood*]'.[56] If we consider evidence from chronicles more broadly from or about Flanders, or nearby Liège, it is striking how many of the violent clashes concerning merchants are told with reference to specific cries and catchphrases. Some of them are battle slogans, such as the war cry of the Flemish weavers and fullers in the 1382 siege of Audenarde: 'Flandre

[53] W. Langland, *The Vision of Piers Plowman: A Critical Edition of the B-Text Based on Trinity College Cambridge MS B.15.17,* ed. A. V. C. Schmidt 2nd edn (London: J. M. Dent, 1995), Prologue, 224–30.

[54] J. A. W. Bennett suggests the song could refer to Emma, wife of Canute. See *Langland, Piers Plowman: The Prologue and Passus I–VII* (Oxford: Clarendon Press, 1972), 103, n. 224 though cp XIII, 340 'of Shordych Dane Emme'.

[55] On mixed-language documents, see L. Wright, 'Trade between England and the Low Countries: Evidence from Historical Linguistics', in Barron and Saul, eds, *England and the Low Countries,* 169–79, her *Sources of London English: Medieval Thames Vocabulary* (Oxford: Clarendon Press, 1996), and the further citations in each; and D. A. Trotter, ed., *Multilingualism in Later Medieval Britain* (Cambridge: D. S. Brewer], 2000).

[56] C. L. Kingsford, ed., *Chronicles of London* (Oxford: Clarendon Press, 1905), 15.

au lion et nos libertés!'[57] and in the battle of Vottem (1346), told by the unnamed *bourgeois de Valenciennes*, where the bourgeois of Liège fight back against the lords with their axes and iron hammers, crying 'Saint-Lambert!'[58] In the latter, the people are reacting to an unannounced attack by the sire de Faucquemont. The chronicler, leaving no doubt where his sympathies lie, explains how the townspeople were interrupted in the midst of their trading:

il s'en ala en l'ost par devers la ville où on vendoit les vitailles et les menues denrées, où il y avoit grant plenté de menu peuple gaignant. Sy se féry le sire de Faucquemont entre eulx, et les commencha à tuer et à décopper. Et qui peut fuyr, il s'enfuy et eschappa, mais touttesfois ils en tuèrent bien environ IIIc, et tout pour attraire les Liégois hors de leur fortresse, mais onques ne s'en murent, et sy avoit si grant noise et sy grant crierye que c'estoit moult très-grant pité à oyr.[59]

[They went in a host towards the town where people were selling food and small amounts of merchandise, where there were great numbers of ordinary people making profits. Then the lord of Faucquemont went among them and began to kill them and cut them down. And anyone who was able to flee made off and escaped, but all the same they killed nearly three hundred, and all for the sake of attracting the Liégois out of their castle, but they never came out, and there was such a huge uproar and such great shouting that it was extremely pitiful to hear it.]

It is the contrast between the busy but undisturbed and, crucially, unarmed—hence the horror and fury in his tone—world of the marketplace and the harsh, abrupt violence of the *gens d'armes* that he brings out so well, almost implying a kind of jealousy felt by the lords towards the peaceful and self-possessed plenty of the people.

One or two Flemish words and phrases can be found in Chaucer, such as the word 'quaad' meaning bad or unlucky.[60] In the introductory banter to the *Cook's Tale*, one of only two *Canterbury Tales* that are set in the city, the 'Cook of Londoun' as he is styled, is satirized by the Host for his reheated pies, 'specials' of leftovers and fly-infested parsley. Roger replies ruefully that these jibes have some point. But he turns the tables with a Flemish proverb:

But 'sooth pley, quaad pley,' as the Flemyng seith.
(I, 4357)

[57] K. de Lettenhove and J. B. M. Constantin, *Histoire de Flandre*, 6 vols, III, *Époque communale 1304–1384 depuis le traité d'Athies jusqu'à la bataille de Roosebeke* (Brussels: Vandale, 1847), see 438 ff. On the violent practices of vendetta practised by the van Arteveldes, see D. Nicholas, *The Van Arteveldes of Ghent: The Varieties of Vendetta and the Hero in History* (Ithaca, NY: Cornell University Press, 1988).

[58] K. de Lettenhove, ed., *Récits d'un bourgeois de Valenciennes (XIVe siècle)* (Louvain: Lefever, 1877), 212. This chronicler also reports that the battle cry of the count of Hainaut against the Frisons was 'Tant m'ayme, sy me sieve en "l'oneur de Dieu et de monseigneur saint Gorge"', 201–3.

[59] Lettenhove, ed., *Récits*, 211.

[60] G. Latré, 'But What Does the Fleming Say?: The Two Flemish Proverbs and their Contexts in Chaucer's Canterbury Tales', *Leeds Studies in English*, 32 (2001), 255–73.

'A true jest is a bad jest', and Roger goes on to say he hopes the Host will not be angry if he 'quits' him with a story about an innkeeper. It is difficult to tease out the resonance of this remark. That a Flemish saying has become part of a Londoner's ironic conversation gives a strong impression of how much the Flemish were an accepted daily presence in urban life. At the same time, the little phrase 'as the Flemyng seith' quietly marks the edge of that acceptance: it is a characterizable and not just an anonymous saying. By contrast, another use of 'quaad' is precisely anonymous and unremarkable. The Host is commenting indignantly on the cheating monk in the *Shipman's Tale*:

> God yeve the monk a thousand last quade yeer!
>
> (VII, 438)

In this context the Flemish word is subsumed into the Host's colloquial idiolect: it has become English. The two examples of Flemish show subtle differences between two kinds of cultural assimilation: the use of the proverb crackles with implicit comment about the distinctiveness of Flemish ways of thinking, whereas the silent appropriation of the same word by the Host shows an unthinking affinity: their language has become his. The phrase has a further resonance. Monday 2 May 1345 was known as 'den quaden maendag', that is 'le mauvais lundi' or Black Monday, so called in a wide range of chronicles after the bloody conflict in Gant (Ghent) between the weavers ('les tisserands', supported by Jacques d'Artevelde) and the fullers ('les foulons').[61] Its literary use by a Southwark publican probably marks not only a sensitivity on Chaucer's part to the density of Flemish speakers in the area, but also (implicitly) a lurking mercantile memory in the community of this disastrous civil war of traders. It may not be too far-fetched to see it as an instance of merchant culture working its way linguistically across the Channel. The wider picture of evidence about Flemish catchphrases suggests that the Flemish carried with them a linguistic charge, that they characterized a certain type of merchant speech that readily passed into other languages.[62]

One further example is revealing in reverse of the way Flemish itself could function as a language that discriminated against foreigners. Gilles li Muisis, in that part of his chronicle where he describes the 1302 rebellion that led to the battle of the Golden Spur at Courtrai, comments that some words in Flemish not known to the French could not be properly pronounced or spoken by them: 'quedam verba in flamingo que nullus nisi sciate flamingum potest perfecte pronuntiare aut dicere'. Those who failed to pronounce them correctly were killed. In his autograph manuscript of the chronicle, the French monk has written 'Et fuerunt verbat' and then left a space. Another hand has copied there the phrase 'scilt en[de] vrient'. We

[61] Nicholas, *The Van Arteveldes of Ghent*, 55–6. Lettenhove and Constantin, *Histoire*.

[62] On the 'distinct discourse of Flanders' see D. Wallace, 'In Flaundres', *Premodern Places: Calais to Surinam, Chaucer to Aphra Behn* (Oxford: Blackwell, 2004), 91–138 (93).

can only speculate on the reasons for this—perhaps Gilles simply did not know how to spell it—but it seems a telling representation of the phrase becoming taboo in written form just as it was orally.[63] Again, from the point of view of this chapter it is interesting that this punning phrase, or password, has such strongly mercantile connotations. The loyalty of the trader, the need for trust (friendship) to accompany the exchange of money (shields)—compare the 'twenty thousand sheeld' (line 331) debt of the merchant in Chaucer's *Shipman's Tale*—is something worth dying and killing for.[64] Flemish merchants were a key cultural presence on the continent and in England for over two centuries: and although they signified, especially for the English, the principal route towards prosperity and expansion, their efforts to conduct business without let or hindrance erupted several times in several cities into scenes of extreme violence.

I have been trying to tease out approaches to several simultaneous, or perhaps consecutive questions. The fundamental enquiry is what kind of commonality English possessed in London. This hard question cannot be answered easily, but one conclusion from the London English records is that they represent not so much a growing swell in the power of English to speak for a community, as a very small effort, in relation to the mass of French and Latin records, to use English to express a desire for that power. This may seem a subtle distinction, but it points to a larger characteristic of medieval city language made up as it is of so many languages, and languages within languages. A proclamation from Letter-book K provides a way of grasping this. It concerns the punishment of one Johannam Cogenho [Ihonet Cogenho] 'be cumune voyse and fame publisshed for a comune desceyuer and begiler of þe people'.[65] The difference in meaning between the first use of 'cumune' and the second has many implications. At first they seem indistinguishable: the proclamation has a commanding ring of authority drawn from its confident knowledge of public opinion. But on closer consideration the first 'cumune' expressing what Jonathan Swift would later satirically call 'the will

[63] Kortrijk, Municipal Library, Cod. 135, f. 28. There is a facsimile of this page in the catalogue of a 1988 exhibition in which this manuscript was displayed: *Jacques Goethals-Vercruysse en Zijn Tijd: Tentoonstelling Stedelijk Museum Kortrijk 29 oktober, 18 december 1988* (Kortrijk, 1988), 70; the ms is described on 181. I am grateful to Gottfried Croenen for his help in tracking down this reference.

[64] 'Scilt' has armorial as well as monetary associations. It seems the meaning of 'coin' is first attested in the 1290s, making it a relatively new 'coinage' by the date of this reference and hence, perhaps, ripe for use as a fashionable slogan. The association of 'scilt' as a unit of exchange with Flemish merchants was no doubt complicated (as it is in Chaucer's *Tale*) by the coin's widespread international usage. I am very grateful to Sjoerd Levelt for also pointing out in private correspondence that the slogan became an important element in nineteenth-century Flemish nationalist mythology, and that 'Scilt' is interesting because it capitalizes not only on the supposed incapacity of foreigners to pronounce it correctly, but also on dialectal differences in the pronunciation of sch-. During the Second World War, in the Netherlands, the shibboleth was 'Scheveningen'.

[65] *Calendar of Letter-Books preserved among the Archives of the Corporation of the City of London at the Guildhall*, ed. R. R. Sharpe, 11 vols (London: J. E. Francis, 1899–1912), *Letter Book K*, 104.

of the people' depends oddly on the second: if Ihonet is a public deceiver, then the people must generally be deceived rather than generally of the view that she is a deceiver. In other words, the proclamation is expressing not a fact so much as a wish or claim. Its own statement is acting out its claim of what 'the cumune voyse' thinks. This is not necessarily *what* the common voice thinks. We know nothing more about this woman, but her name, given in two languages, neither of them English as such, could well be that of a 'forein'. The proclamation publishes a view that it wants the common voice to hold. It wants to wield public opinion against this woman and there's a hint that public opinion is being turned in the very statement that describes it. 'Common' has an insidious power to generate support and not simply (as it claims) to register it.

The question about London English leads on to questions about the use of the vernacular more generally to conduct business, and then about how to understand the complexities of vernacular use when that vernacular is in circulation with several others. The relation between French and Flemish is an instructive comparison in that it reminds us that vernaculars can have a very shifting status depending on context: French was undoubtedly in a dominating position right across England and the continent, but Flemish and some of the Italian dialects were much more assertively used than English on their 'home' soil.[66] But the larger point is that trade is a crucial factor in the ways in which languages circulate in urban contexts. Trade is the medium in which cultural cooperation is negotiated. Foreigners live as foreigners in a city in order to make money, and their presence is tolerated because they are (directly or indirectly) making money for others: to do so they need to come to some kind of linguistic accommodation with their neighbours and this in turn changes the medium itself of linguistic exchange. In a fast-flowing trading environment, language changes as people engage in the process of trusting each other enough to exchange money.

This process is not necessarily, however, a cynical one. These English proclamations and complaints are working in good faith. Their assumptions about collective feeling and their efforts to promote it are not simply desperate means of defying bitter factionalism.[67] Merchants need a double language to conduct business, not because hypocrisy is rife but because the business of creating an atmosphere of mutual trust requires subtlety. Of course, hypocrisy and deceit can hardly be ruled out, but it is more a matter of allowing someone to feel confident that deceit is not in anyone's interest.

[66] See Chapter 4, n. 24.

[67] On the discourses of conflict in medieval London and especially of Chaucer's 'pessimism about social possibility', see M. Turner, *Chaucerian Conflict: Languages of Antagonism in Late Fourteenth-Century London* (Oxford: Clarendon Press, 2007), 7.

CHAUCER'S MERCHANT

Chaucer's portrait of the Merchant famously illustrates the double demeanour of the man of trade, from his forked beard to his 'solempne' proclamations of personal success. It is an extraordinarily concise portrait, one of the briefest in the collection, and in many ways highly understated. All the details are precisely chosen, yet, in contrast to the Friar and Clerk on either side, the Merchant remains hidden in the depths of his carefully lineated type. Chaucer's own poetic method is likewise purposely obscure: we are given all the small messages of quiet prosperity, the Flemish beaver hat, elegant boot clasps, polished phrases advertising his predictable opinions and financial reliability with a dash of finesse, only then for the pen to strike at the heart of his cultivated image and expose the well concealed fact of his debts. But the timing of the exposure leaves room for the last few remarks to float in a wittily poised atmosphere that does not quite succumb either to condemnation or endorsement:

> This worthy man ful wel his wit bisette:
> Ther wiste no wight that he was in dette,
> So estatly was he of his governaunce
> With his bargaynes and with his chevyssaunce.
> For sothe he was a worthy man with alle,
> But, sooth to seyn, I noot how men hym calle.
>
> (I, 279–84)

It is commonplace to remark on these features of Chaucer's description, and especially, among an older generation, to see them as instances of his celebrated irony. Yet the point here is less to do with an idiosyncratic poetic vision than whether Chaucer's English is part of some broader London articulation of merchant behaviour. Two details might catch our attention: the 'Flaundryssh bever hat' and his skill at exchange:

> Wel coude he in eschaunge sheeldes selle. (I, 278)

His wearing of a Flemish hat is intriguing: is he Flemish? We assume not, since there are no overt signals from the narrator that he is reacting to a 'forein'. Yet when we stop to think about it, the very looseness of what would in a later century be called 'point of view' means that we cannot be sure whether the Merchant himself or the narrator is describing the hat as 'Flemish'. This doubt creates a lingering question because our sense of him as 'English' depends on assuming that the Merchant himself is using the epithet 'Flemish' in that slightly, but crucially, distanced way. He is putting on 'Flandryssh' garb and thus aligning himself with fellow traders who are part of a predominantly Flemish culture. Yet if it is the narrator's word then there is nothing to prevent the Merchant from being indeed Flemish, or as Flemish (or English) as someone has become after years of trading between the English and Flemish coasts. The Merchant may be precisely a figure who has become so skilled at 'eschaunge' that he typifies the kind of international businessman who is not readily categorized. To put it another way, once again that signifier 'Flemish' functions in a double way, both to point out a sense of difference, but also to articulate a wider perception of the merchant as a primary representative of cross-channel and cross-continental relationships.

If this does not already seem over-subtle, then one might be tempted to add that Chaucer's own perspective cunningly represents a further act of exchange. The word 'eschaunge' is Anglo-French: that is, it has a tradition of being spelled differently from continental French 'changer', and also of carrying a wider range of meanings specifically to do with buying and selling.[68] It is thus a word that stands on the edge of English and French, passing between them and also signifying independently that quintessentially trading perspective of the middle man. Chaucer's reticence in his portrait is thus in itself a mercantile sleight of hand. He both characterizes his Merchant as Flemish and leaves his characterization totally undetermined and unnamed; his meaning is covert, calm on the surface, concealing unquantifiable debts beneath. His linguistic manoeuvrings share something with the English Pleas and proclamations in the way they appeal to common perspectives while also subtly turning them. It is a use of English, as we know well from the General Prologue as a whole, that covers the face of bad practices, difficult customers, and dodgy deals. It is a use of English that trades between plural cultures.

THE SHIPMAN'S TALE: THE 'FAMYLIER ENEMY'

Henry V ordered a proclamation to be issued in 1415[69] summoning aid for the siege of Harfleur. Entitled 'A crye made for comune passage toward Hareflieu', it is addressed to:

> all maner of men, marchauntz, artificers, or other, or what estat, degre or condicion that euere they be, that willen toward oure liege lord the kyng . . . that god him spede, with corne, brede, mele, or flour, wyne, ale, or bier, fyssh, flessh or any other viteill, clothe, lynnen, wollen or eny merchaundise, shertys, breches, doublettys, hosen, shone' . . . and that they 'make redy . . . their bodyes, goodes, merchaundyses, ware, stoffur, viteill, what euer it be; and in the mene while come to the Mair, and he shall dispose and assigne theym redy shippyng and passage vnto the forseide costes.[70]

[68] The word *eschaunge* occurs (with variant spellings) in both the *AND* and the *MED* with a similar range of meanings including the exchange of persons, prisoners of war, property and money.

[69] On the alternative date of May 1416, see *BoLE*, 64.

[70] *BoLE*, 64.

Although ostensibly calling 'all maner of men' this is a proclamation that singles out merchants with special care. The king does not just want merchants, he wants their goods, and indeed his phrasing makes them synonymous with their goods ('their bodyes, goodes, merchaundyses, ware, stoffur, viteill, what euer it be'). In offering them 'redy shippyng' or free passage to the continent, he hopes to induce them to give him their merchandise. The idea is that they gain a 'comune passage' for the common profit. It is a curious mixture of the old language of feudal obligation ('that willen toward oure liege lord the kyng') and a newer recognition of the pecuniary drive that is compelling both the king and his subjects into battle. Other proclamations target different classes of people: 'alle maner of lordes knyghtys and Squiyers',[71] 'all maner of mariners' . . . 'all manere of Shipmen',[72] and 'al maner of Knyghtes'.[73]

The portrait of the Merchant is part of a larger, though not entirely expected sequence of portraits of mercantile culture in the *Canterbury Tales*. In the event, the story about trading is not given to the Merchant but to the Shipman, and in retrospect it seems no accident that the Merchant is preceded by the Friar in the General Prologue since a merchant and a professional man of religion are the two main male players in the *Shipman's Tale*. The portrait of the rough and rather dangerous Shipman stands somewhat apart both from the urbane *Tale* that carries his name and the so-called *Merchant's Tale*, whose central character is not a merchant but a knight. It is easy enough to find rationalizations of these decisions, and many readers have done so: for instance the attribution of a tale about a knight to the Merchant is usually held to be revealing of an aspiration towards gentrification that is typical of the late fourteenth-century affluent urban middle class. The *Shipman's Tale* is often left out of these assessments. It is not one of Chaucer's most admired or widely discussed *Tales*. It tends to be dismissed as a very smoothly accomplished and cleverly plotted but somehow rather standard fabliau. The moral issues it raises do not appear to have excited much passion: its particular version of sex and money among merchants and monks, however neat, has not seemed especially multi-faceted, unlike say, the *Miller's Tale*.[74]

However, I would like to suggest another way of reading the familiar fabliau triangulation of the *Tale* as not just a social affair (in both senses of the word) but as a subtle, and beguilingly local representation of the contorted triangular cross-channel relationships of the late fourteenth century. It gives literary life to the experience of trading cultures, languages, and goods across a tensely guarded

[71] *BoLE*, 64.

[72] *BoLE*, 65.

[73] *BoLE*, 66.

[74] However, two recent fine discussions signal a new interest in this *Tale*: K Taylor, 'Social Aesthetics and the Emergence of Civic Discourse from the *Shipman's Tale* to *Melibee*', *Chaucer Review*, 39 (2005), 298–322 and E. Kendall, 'The Great Household in the City: the *Shipman's Tale*' in Butterfield, ed., *Chaucer and the City*, 145–61.

space of friendship and enmity. It is told by a Devonshire shipman, of considerable cross-channel experience, of a French merchant, living in St-Denis (just outside Paris), who travels to Bruges in Flanders. In a sense, the whole of it can be conveyed in just two words, a 'famylier enemy'.[75] (I will be discussing this phrase in more detail in Chapter 8.) To recall: there is no specific source or even analogue for the *Tale.* It borrows the general structure of the 'lover's gift regained' but the nearest version of this in Boccaccio is not especially close. Chaucer embeds the exchange structure within a markedly familial, even incestuous set of friendships. He seems to use a special set of 'new' words in almost every work he writes[76]—here the key new word is 'cozen', and 'cosynage', closely crowded by 'famulier', 'brotherheede', 'alliaunce', and, finally, 'taile/taille'.

This yonge monk, that was so fair of face,
Aqueynted was so with the goode man,
Sith that hir firste knoweliche bigan,
That in his hous as famulier was he
As it is possible any freend to be.
And for as muchel as this goode man,
And eek this monk of which that I bigan,
Were bothe two yborn in o village,
The monk hym claymeth as for cosynage,
And he agayn; he seith nat ones nay,
But was as glad therof as fowel of day,
For to his herte it was a greet plesaunce.
Thus been they knyt with eterne alliaunce,
And ech of hem gan oother for t'assure
Of bretherhede whil that hir lyf may dure.

(VII, 28–42)

This is full of Chaucer's characteristically double-sided linguistic gestures. Every seemingly casual adjective, every phrase, counts (the monk is 'yonge' and 'fair of face') and especially every particle: 'as' ('as famulier as it is possible . . . ' and 'gan'). The word 'famulier' is fraught with awkwardness: occurring partly because a strain of hyperbole is put on it—where to be 'over-familiar' is less rather than more desirable—and partly because the word 'freend' is placed at the other end of the scale. If a 'famulier' is a member of the household, then friendship is not entirely equivalent or appropriate: there is enough slippage between the two

[75] See Chaucer's translation of Book 3 of Boethius's *De Consolatione*: 'Certes swiche folk as weleful fortune maketh frendes, contraryous fortune maketh hem enemys. And what pestilence is more myghty for to anoye a wyght than a famylier enemy? (*Boece*, 3 pr 5.68–70).

[76] See C. Cannon, *The Making of Chaucer's English* (Cambridge: Cambridge University Press, 1998).

to make one wonder just how familiar it is possible for a friend to be, or conversely just how friendly one can be with someone in the family.

Raising the stakes even higher, the monk 'hym claymeth *as* for cosynage'. Again this is full of doubt: the grounds for kinship are to do with birthplace rather than blood. As so often with Chaucer, the denial of a proposition admits rather than rejects the possibility of the proposition being true; so the merchant 'he seith nat ones nay' makes it quite clear that he does not think for a moment that they are related. He is shown beautifully caught in both his minds, the denial of the doubt sharing the same line as his affirmation 'And he agayn'. They go on, in any case, riding through any quibbles, to 'knyt' themselves 'with eterne alliaunce' and sworn brotherhood. This range of relationships is cumulatively confusing rather than reassuring, and it is not helped when the monk calls the merchant's wife 'nece' (VII, 100) and she addresses him as 'deere love' (VII, 158).

But the point is not merely that they are playing a cynical game of marital deception. The questions over these words, and the relationships they imply, echo some of the central questions of the period about allegiance and betrayal, trust and friendship, kinship and foreignness. It is not just a matter of playing bedtricks; the language of family relationships is a crucial register of political allegiance and negotiation. At an aristocratic level, perhaps the most resonant case is that with which we began and also discussed at length in the previous chapter, of Jean II after Poitiers, brought captive as a hostage back to London by the Black Prince, treated with utmost courtesy and kinship by Edward III, and even given a palace of his own, while simultaneously being required by Edward to negotiate away his territorial possessions, financial resources, and personal power. Although the advantages won by Edward were eroded in the next decade, the language of diplomacy in Richard II's letters to Charles VI of France maintains the same formulas:

A treshaut et puissant prince C. par le grace de Dieu notre treschier et tresame frere et cousin de ffrance, R. par ycelle mesme grace roy dEngleterre etc., salut et entiere dilectioun.[77]

[To the very high and powerful prince C. by the grace of God our very dear and well-beloved brother and cousin of France, R. by the same grace King of England etc., greetings and great love.]

When in some letters, Richard styles himself 'Roy dEngleterre et de ffrance et seigneur dIrlande,' the pressure on 'frere et cousin de ffrance', repeated many times in separate letters, observably increases. Similar pressures weigh on the later

[77] *The Diplomatic Correspondence of Richard II*, ed. E. Perroy, Camden Third Series, 48, Royal Historical Society (London: Offices of the Society, 1933), no. 223 (Frontispiece): Langley Manor, 30 September [1395]—Richard II to Charles VI, King of France. Paris, Arch. Nat. J.644, no. 35/5.

phrases of kinship and trust used by Henry V towards the duc de bourgogne, soon to turn his back on the English and make a fresh alliance with the dauphin:

> the whiche oure brother of Burgoigne we fynde right a trusty, louyng, and faithful brother vnto us in al thing.[78]

The diplomatic context for the word 'familiar' is also worth noting: as we discussed in the previous chapter, all the king's subjects had to apply for letters of safe conduct when they travelled abroad. When a traveller was particularly dear to the king, then he was issued with *litterae de familiaritate*, a special commendation written to all princes of the world. The king's familiars would often be sent on difficult or delicate missions involving matters of potential dispute or antagonism.[79] Philippa of Hainaut described Froissart as 'uns de ses clers et familiiers'.[80]

The point is that the particular character of the English–French war involved constant uncertainties even, or especially within, close relationships. Aggression and intimacy often went hand in hand, as in the expulsion of alien monks from priories in 1378, several of whom had worked for Edward III in various diplomatic capacities.[81] The famous story of the burghers of Calais provides an example within civic or mercantile milieus of allegiance and extreme resistance colliding in an astonishingly abrupt way, since three or four of the original six afterwards entered Edward's service.[82] When the monk meets the Merchant's wife in the garden, they pass quickly and seamlessly from swearing each other to secrecy on their 'love and affiaunce' (VII, 140) and 'for no cosynage ne alliance' (VII, 139), to the outright renunciation by the monk of any claim of relationship to the merchant:

> He is na moore cosyn unto me
> Than is this leef that hangeth on the tree!
> I clepe hym so, by Seint Denys of Fraunce,
> To have the moore cause of aqueyntaunce
> Of yow, which I have loved specially
> Aboven alle wommen, sikerly.
>
> (VII, 149–54)

78 *Letter book I*, 12 July 1421: Letter from the King to the Mayor and Aldermen, *BoLE*, 84.

79 See *The Diplomatic Correspondence of Richard II*, ed. Perroy, x; and Chaplais, *English Diplomatic Practice in the Middle Ages*, 92–3 and Chapter 5 above, p. 188.

80 Froissart, *Livre I Rome MS*, 127–8; see G. Croenen, 'Froissart et ses mécènes: quelques problems biographiques', in O. Bombarde, ed., *Froissart dans sa forge: Colloque réuni à Paris, du 4 au 6 novembre 2004 par M. Michel Zink, professeur au Collège de France, membre de l'Académie des Inscriptions et Belles-Lettres*, (Paris: Académie des Inscriptions et Belles-Lettres, 2006), 9–32 (12).

81 McHardy, 'The Alien Priories'.

82 For an absorbing study of the mythologies of the siege of Calais, see Moeglin, *Les Bourgeois de Calais*.

His swearing by 'Seint Denys of Fraunce' (and the wife's reference later to 'Genylon of Fraunce' [VII, 194]) just as he betrays his friend, his 'frere et cousin', in a *Tale* set in St-Denis, the abbey town outside Paris where the holy relics of this patron saint of France were kept, seems pointed: at any moment, the passage implies, claims of allegiance are always under pressure to succumb to other claims. Moreover, claims of allegiance to a king or a saint are hard to disentangle from the immediate desires and needs of local friends and strangers. Deschamps, as we recall from Chapter 4, writes about such things more frankly than Chaucer. He shows so brilliantly from the other side how friendship can hang in the balance: the suspense in the Calais poem over whether Grandson will leave him to be arrested lingers like an aftertaste. Their cross-cultural friendship depends on recognizing the limits of what they have in common, and on not taking anything for granted.

A feature of the 'new' words in the *Shipman's Tale* is that they are also puns. One of the main topics of critical conversation about this *Tale* has concerned the question of whether there is a pun on cozen ('to cheat') and cosynage.[83] As far as I know, no one has yet come up with an earlier or contemporary reference in English with exactly this meaning.[84] References have been found in French, but most also date from the fifteenth century.[85] However, if we look earlier into French and Anglo-French, there are intriguing sightings in the thirteenth-century *Roman de Renart* and the Anglo-French *Horn* (*c.*1170).[86] The *Renart* example is interesting because it sets the word in the larger context of deception. Renart, the arch-deceiver, is being cursed by Chantecler:

> Cousins Renart, dist Chantecler,
> nus ne se doit en vos fiër:
> dahez ait vostre cousinage!
> torner me dut a grant domage.
>
> (lines 4443–6)

[83] R. M. Fisher, 'Cosyn and Cosynage: Complicated Punning in Chaucer's "Shipman's Tale"', *Notes and Queries*, 210 (1965), 168–70; R. J. Pearcy, 'Punning on "cosyn" and "cosynage" in Chaucer's Shipman's Tale', *American Notes and Queries*, 17 (1979), 70–71; G. Joseph, 'Chaucer's Coinage: Foreign Exchange and the Puns of The *Shipman's Tale*', *Chaucer Review*, 17 (1983), 341–57; T. Hahn, 'Money, Sexuality, Wordplay, and Context in the Shipman's Tale', in *Chaucer in the Eighties*, ed. J. N. Wasserman and R. J. Blanch (Syracuse, NY.: Syracuse University Press, 1986), 235–49; and Taylor, 'Social Aesthetics,' 302–10.

[84] The earliest reference given by the *MED* is fifteenth-century: *cosin* n., 'fraud, trickery' (1453).

[85] Ruth Fisher points to a reference (noted in Godefroy) to *cosin* in *Les Cent Nouvelles Nouvelles* (1456), and to *cousine* meaning 'courtesan' in thirteenth-century fabliau usage ('Le Chevalier qui faisoit parler les cons et les culs'), 'Cosyn and Cosynage', 169. Roy Pearcy finds an example in a 1575 copy of a Brabant *chanson de mal mariée* that probably originates much earlier, 'Punning on "cosyn" and "cosynage"'. Karla Taylor also notes the collocation of '*coçonage* (commercial dealings, often shady) with *cosinage* (kinship)' in fourteenth-century French ('Social Aesthetics', 308 and 319 n. 24).

[86] On *Le Roman de Renart*, see L. Patterson, *Chaucer and the Subject of History* (London: Routledge, 1991). As far as I am aware, the citation in *Horn* has not received published comment in this context.

['Cousin Renart,' said Chantecler, 'No one must trust in you: a curse on your 'cousinship'! It made me fall into great trouble.']

The author plays here with the distance between 'cousins' and 'cousinage': Renart has been claiming repeatedly that he and Chantecler are first cousins, and that the Cock has therefore no reason to fear him. He would rather lose a paw than see him get hurt as they are so closely related. But once the Cock narrowly escapes from the Fox's jaws, he angrily denounces the terms of this false relationship. It is of course absurd, zoologically speaking, for the Cock to call the Fox 'Cousin' (though to do so is central to the Aesopic mode of the fable). But here the usually ignored dark humour of their specious familiarity is suddenly exposed as the Cock angrily denounces its terms. Likewise, in the Anglo-Norman *Horn* there is an instance of the phrase 'Ne tenir pur cosin': 'ne l'esparnia, ki nel tint pur cosin. Ainz li trencha le chief' [He did not spare him, having no love for him, but cut off his head like this] (line 1535).[87] The *Anglo-Norman Dictionary* gives two glosses: 'to be ruthless with' and in the revised entry in the online version 'to have no love for'.[88] It is striking that the meaning emerges out of ironic understatement, evoking a world where the mere fact of kinship is all that prevents routine violence.

For my money, I have no doubt that Chaucer is indeed working with a cluster of meanings around cozen that makes ironic reference to kinship and trust by means of closeness and falsity, and payment for sex. It may well be that he is the first in English to do so. But a glance across the other languages of England, as well as over the Channel, shows that the issue of linguistic exchange is in any case alive with richer cross-cultural implication than has so far been remarked. In discussing the meanings of cosyn, Chaucerians have always worried over it as an English problem: when did its meaning of 'deceive' enter English? Yet languages, especially those of medieval London, did not always observe post-medieval national boundaries. The particular interest of finding relevant meanings in Anglo-French is that this is hardly a foreign language for an English poet. As work on the *Anglo-Norman Dictionary* has progressed, it has become clear to the compilers that the border between English and French is often indistinct'.[89] In a linguistic context where English and French (to name no other languages) are in daily use of a pragmatic, domestic, legal, and financial kind, and where French is the culturally dominant medium for vernacular poetry, the traffic of meanings across languages is constant and mutually enriching. But in any case, there is a kind of joke about the way the

87 *The Romance of Horn by Thomas*, ed. M. K. Pope and T. B. W. Reid, Anglo-Norman Texts, 9–10, 12–13, 2 vols (Oxford: Blackwell, 1955–64), I, 51.

88 *AND* cosin[1] cosinage s. 1 kinship, blood relationship, consanguinity; affinity, relationship; close friendship 2 behaviour befitting a kinsman 3 kindred, kinsfolk 4 race.

89 D. A. Trotter, 'Language Contact, Multilingualism and the Evidence Problem', in U. Schaefer, ed., *The Beginnings of Standardization: Language and Culture in Fourteenth-Century England* (Frankfurt: Peter Lang, 2006), 73–90.

tale so successfully introduces the possibility of deception even about its own puns: if Chaucer does not mean 'to deceive' by cosyn, then his tale shows how close language can come to coining new meanings even when the process is not recognized. A word can hover on the border of being recognized: one moment it is a foreign word, autonomous if not independent; the next it has become unnoticeably English, unthinkingly possessed and used.

It becomes hard to avoid economic metaphors when discussing processes of linguistic exchange, and, as many commentators have remarked, the *Shipman's Tale* is itself saturated with them. Notably, it uses a language of financial transaction to scrutinize larger issues of trust in and through language. In his fine article on 'Foreign Exchange and the Puns of the *Shipman's Tale*', Gerhard Joseph writes acutely of the poem that 'both money and language undergo a foreign exchange'.[90] The many bilingual puns in the *Shipman's Tale* function in just this way. I will consider one more: Taille n., also tail(e, taiel, tayille, teil(e, tale (*MED*). At the end of the tale, the wife asks her husband to 'score' her debt 'upon my taille' (VII, 416). The reference is to a tally or 'a scored wooden stick for recordkeeping' (*MED* 3). The very last two lines, spoken presumably by the Shipman, repeat the word twice more in the work's famous final inscription:

> Thus endeth my tale, and God us sende
> Taillynge ynough unto oure lyves ende. Amen.
>
> (VII, 433–4)

So far, the consensus of Chaucerian scholarship has totted up three punning meanings: 'tally', 'sexual member', and 'tale or story'. Karla Taylor has also very persuasively commented on the correspondence in this twist in the final couplet from 'tale' to 'taillynge' 'to the play common in French fabliaux on con/conte as female genitalia and story'.[91] There may be two further associations, each of which has larger implications for our understanding of Chaucer's use of a French-inflected English.

One concerns the wider sense of *tallage* as tax, especially as applied to alien merchants, and *tailles* as war taxes.[92] Could there be yet another, a 'flexible hanging appendage' as the *MED* puts it, hanging onto the end of this cross-channel, cross-lingual story? One possibility is that 'tale' and 'taillynge' in the *Shipman's Tale* allude to the slur that the English have tails. The tale ends with tails, and the 'taillynge ynough' could be a self-mocking comment by the Shipman as he hopes for more false trading, more *usure*, across the Channel. It seems likely that this meaning was available, like the wife, for possession. To bring in Deschamps, once more: one of the five or six poems which play with the

[90] Joseph, 'Chaucer's Coinage', 343.

[91] Taylor, 'Social Aesthetics', 304.

[92] On *tallage* as applied to alien merchants and *tailles* as war taxes, see, respectively, T. H. Lloyd, *Alien Merchants in England in the High Middle Ages* (Brighton: Harvester, 1982), Appendix II, and Contamine, *War in the Middle Ages*, 150–65 (156).

tail story about the Anglais, Balade no. 868, uses the same transliterated English as the Calais–Grandson *ballade*, and the same old link with drunkenness that we saw in Jacques de Vitry:

> Franche dogue, dist un Anglois,
> Vous ne faictes que boire vin.
>
> French dog, said an Englishman,
> You do nothing except drink wine.

The joke works on several levels including cowardice, drunkenness, sex, scatology, and bestiality, with puns on 'queue' in the refrain 'Levez vostre queue, levez!' meaning a measure of liquid as well as a tail.[93]

But I do not just want to argue for another pun. Understanding the circulation of meaning in this period involves observing processes of deception and deliberate failures of communication as well as sincere protestations of friendship and alliance. That this was also happening over the borders of 'English', 'French', and 'Flemish' (as well as many other linguistic family groupings) was a source of anger, humour, anxiety, and wit to many vernacular writers. The creation of false friends, both fictionally and linguistically, shows how daily professional life in the late fourteenth century could be represented as bordering constantly on conflict, even treachery, while it also depended on shared jokes and meanings.

In a passage in *Monolinguisme*, Derrida recalls the commercial undertow of his 'Exergue' in a way that has remarkable reverberations with the linguistic trading practices of the *Shipman's Tale*. It happens to be one of Derrida's more medieval moments: talking of his fear at the sound of his own accent, his first-person speaker describes how he was harpooned by 'pure' French:

> j'ai été comme harponné par la littérature et par la philosophie françaises, l'une et l'autre, l'une ou l'autre: flèches de métal ou de bois, corps pénétrant de paroles enviables, redoutables, inaccessibles alors meme qu'elles entraient en moi, phrases qu'il fallait à la fois s'approprier, domestiquer, *amadouer*, c'est-à-dire aimer en enflammant, brûler (l'amadou n'est jamais loin), peut-être détruire, en tout cas marquer, transformer, tailler, entailler, forger, greffer au feu, faire venir autrement, autrement dit, à soi en soi.[94]
>
> [I seemed to be harpooned by French philosophy and literature, the one and the other ... wooden or metallic darts ..., a penetrating body of enviable, formidable, and inaccessible words even when they were entering me, sentences which it was necessary to appropriate, domesticate, coax ..., that is to say, love by setting on fire, burn ['tinder'

93 It is not necessary to my argument that Chaucer should have known this or indeed any of the '*Anglois coué*' Deschamps *ballades*, although the late date usually assumed for the *Shipman's Tale* does not rule it out.

94 J. Derrida, *Monolinguisme de l'autre ou la prothèse d'origine* (Paris: Galilée, 1996), 84; translations are cited from *Monolingualism of the Other, or, the Prosthesis of Origin*, trans. P. Mensah (Stanford, CA: Stanford University Press, 1998), 50–1.

. . . is never far away], perhaps destroy, in all events mark, transform, prune, cut, forge, graft at the fire, let come in another way, in other words, to itself in itself.]

In terms reminiscent of *Le Roman de la Rose*, where Cupid's arrow pierces the first-person lover, Derrida's speaker finds his body of speech penetrated by what he earlier calls 'le modèle dit scolaire, grammatical ou littéraire' ['the model called academic, grammatical, or literary'].[95] As the sentence continues, his violent sexual metaphor turns gradually into a new set of sliding, punning terms. His inclusion of 'tailler' in a sequence that puns on *entailler* and ends with the self 'à soi en soi' is of course wonderfully coincident to Chaucer, and it also has the happy consequence of reminding us that the process of trading languages is part of a monolingual experience too. It is partly that shaping, crafting, tailoring, and calculating are all transforming elements in telling the story of the self. But the crucial element occurs near the end in the sequence 'faire venir autrement, autrement dit': the discovery of one's self ['sa propre identité'] is a matter of allowing this strange other idiom of one's 'own' language to be overpowering.

Deschamps serves once more as a point of comparison with Chaucer because they each seem to respond very differently, though with equal cleverness, to the challenges of cross-lingual travel.[96] Deschamps wanted to trade insults actively and loudly, enjoying the frisson of offence. Chaucer, in a period of occasionally extreme civic disturbance, was apparently less inclined to show his hand. We must remember that the French experience of the English 'at home' on the continent was much more violent than it was for the English of the French in England: as a practising soldier, Deschamps had every motive to accentuate differences and sharpen the edges of cultural confrontation. Chaucer's game, however, was perhaps no less blatant in the end. The daylight robbery of English appropriation from French culture was a daily domestic, cultural activity. Cozening, as we know from Elizabethan and especially Restoration drama, is a process of establishing the kind of familiarity with someone that creates the possibility of deceiving him or her. The English assumption of close family ties in order to gain a quick buck was unsurprisingly resented by the French who had to endure the indignity of living under threat from those whose vernacular was weak and culturally dependent on theirs.

[95] Derrida, *Monolinguisme*, 75; *Monolingualism*, 44.

[96] As discussed in Chapter 4, Deschamps wrote many poems about the experience of travelling, usually in intense discomfort on military campaigns across Europe, where Flemings, the English, the Lombards and the Germans/Moravians/Bohemians all receive barbed comment.

THE MERCHANT'S TALE

The 1415 proclamation by Henry V that we considered earlier of course postdates the composition of the *Canterbury Tales*, yet it gives us an insight into the ways in which the population was categorized that is quite separate from estates satire, and has interesting points of contact with Chaucer's associations of Merchant, Shipman, Knight, and Squire. The English royalty were in constant need of men, goods, and money throughout the extended war period, and were happy to receive all offers. But it is clear from the various public appeals that merchants, mariners, knights, and squires were particularly important target constituencies for the war effort. There is an implicit equivalence here which we also find in Chaucer's subtle interlacing of portraits and tellers. One common thread is the attention to local treachery. Chaucer makes small but significant verbal links across this cluster of tales and portraits. Thus the Friar in the *General Prologue*, anticipating the intimate antics of the Monk in the *Shipman's Tale*, is described as:

> Ful wel biloved and famulier was he
> With frankeleyns over al in his contree,
> And eek with worthy wommen of the town;
>
> (I, 215–17)

This Friar is presented as chiefly interested in profit; he exploits his allegedly vulnerable position as someone who cannot earn his living, by mixing entirely with traders of upper pretensions:

> But al with riche and selleres of vitaile.
> And over al, ther as profit sholde arise,
> Curteis he was and lowely of servyse.
>
> (I, 248–50)

'Esy' trading is practised most efficiently by the household familiar: he shares people's confidences in exchange for sweet confessions and a pleasant life.

This role in the *Merchant's Tale* is played by January's squire, Damian. One of the narrator's more high-pitched observations spills over into this condemnation of Damian's betrayal:

> O perilous fyr, that in the bedstraw bredeth!
> O famulier foo, that his servyce bedeth!
> O servant traytour, false hoomly hewe,
> Lyk to the naddre in bosom sly untrewe,
> God shilde us alle from youre aqueyntaunce!
> O Januarie, dronken in plesaunce
> In mariage, se how thy Damyan,
> Thyn owene squier and thy borne man,

Entendeth for to do thee vileynye.
God graunte thee thyn hoomly fo t'espye!
For in this world nys worse pestilence
Than hoomly foo al day in thy presence.
(IV, 1783–94)

Here the shock of the familiar traitor (picked up again from *Boece*) is transposed socially from the relatively high-ranking guest posing as cousin and brother in the *Shipman's Tale* to the servant, January's 'owene squier', turning against his master and liege lord. This is a different and even more insidious definition of the alien from others we have considered since the 'foo' turns out to be not just 'hoomly', like Helen in *Troilus*, but invisible. January is blind to the theft being planned under his nose, but this foe, with his 'false hoomly hewe', seems likely to have escaped notice by even the sharp-eyed. Unlike Allard Taillour in the English Plea who 'holdis hostre, Colouryng many straungers', Damian has the colouring of the innocent 'borne man' and thus avoids detection.

The broad equivalence of merchant, knight, shipman, and squire seems to inform Chaucer's perception of the common practices of piracy and international trading, war and financial exchange on a large as well as very local scale. His famous description of January searching for female goods in the brightly polished mirror of the 'commune market-place', as many have observed, cruelly and wittily debases the coinage of knightly behaviour. Read in the wider context of medieval mercantile culture and especially against the subtle punning of the *Shipman's Tale*, however, it seems more than merely condemnatory. Gilles li Muisis, in his poem *C'est des marchéans*, evenhandedly comments:

marchandises sont partout par maintes guises.
Aucunes sont loaius et loyalment acquises;
Les autres sont doutavles et en fauseté quises', 2–4[97]

[merchandise is everywhere under many guises; some [merchants] are loyal and their goods faithfully acquired; others are untrustworthy and obtain their goods under false practices,]]

The new world of negotiation opened up by the hugely influential practices of war makes trade the primary international medium for cooperation as well as confrontation. It is also the best means city dwellers have for creating peace and prosperity, even if the rougher business challenges that effort. Chaucer is too astute a writer not to realize (in both senses) the 'common profit' of the vernacular in a linguistic world where the trading is easy.

[97] G. li Muisis, *Poésies*, ed. K. de Lettenhove, 2 vols (Louvain: Lefever, 1882), II, 57–9 (57).

7

Lingua franca: The International Language of Love

CROSS-CHANNEL POETIC COMMUNITIES

Medieval love poetry, seen as the quintessence of courtly discourse, is often felt to belong to a different world from the busy urban 'common' parlance of the previous chapter. A picture such as the carole scene in a fourteenth-century manuscript of Machaut's *Remede de Fortune* (BnF fr.1586, fol.51r), colludes in this by creating an image of a wealthy, leisured, secluded style of life set in a beautiful, cultivated landscape that seems to exist precisely in order to be represented in this kind of delicate, expensive medium.[1] Yet the grains of truth in this assumption, as many have recently argued, need to be countered with the realization that throughout the thirteenth century urban communities expanded rapidly around and adjacent to seigneurial holdings. The space where a castle might once have been on the outskirts of a city wall became part of a growing urban complex, a situation as true of London as it was of continental towns such as Arras, Bruges, or Florence. To speak of the court is not necessarily to preclude the urban; on the contrary, courtliness can often only be understood as an urban phenomenon.[2] The seemingly quiet, inwardly refined, 'precious' language of the courtly lyric likewise has a closer relation than it might seem to the mercantile cut and thrust of civic communities, and a hidden undertow of linguistic trading. This is well illustrated by the London *puy*.[3] As Anne Sutton has convincingly

[1] A. Butterfield, 'Le tradizioni della canzone cortese medievale', *Enciclopedia della musica (The Einaudi Encyclopedia of Music)*, gen. ed. Jean-Jacques Nattiez with Margaret Bent, Rossana Dalmonte, and Mario Baroni, 4 vols, IV: *Storia della musica europea* (Turin: Einaudi, 2004), 130–51; translated as 'Les traditions du chant courtois médiéval', *Musiques: Une encyclopédie pour le XXIème siècle*, gen. ed. Jean-Jacques Nattiez, Histoires des musiques européennes 4 (Paris: Editions Actes Sud and Cité de Musique, 2006).

[2] See C. Page, 'Court and City in France, 1100–1300', in James McKinnon, ed., *Antiquity and the Middle Ages from Ancient Greece to the 15th Century* (Basingstoke and London: Macmillan, 1990), 197–217; and, for some comments on London, M. Vale, *The Princely Court: Medieval Courts and Culture in North-West Europe* (Oxford: Oxford University Press, 2001), 138–40.

[3] H. T. Riley, ed., 'Regulations of the Feste de Pui', *Munimenta gildhallae Londoniensis*, Rolls Series, 3 vols (London: Longman, Brown, Green, Longmans, and Roberts, 1859–62), II: i, *Liber customarum*, 216–28*puy*.

shown, this flourished in the last quarter of the thirteenth century but did not survive much beyond 1300.[4] The complaints of extravagance amongst certain members in the second set of statutes give some clue as to the atmosphere which led to its dispersal. The character of the London *puy* draws its inspiration, and probably its origin, from the well-established northern French *puys* and *confreries* of Arras, Lille, Valenciennes, and Abbeville.[5] These were poetic guilds, usually founded from a religious or charitable motive, which met to hold poetic contests. A *puy*'s members would elect a yearly *prince* or *maître* who would preside over a feast in which the submitted poems would be judged and the winner awarded a silver crown. Several poems survive in manuscript with a crown drawn by the winners to indicate their status.[6] The significance of the London *puy* in the present discussion is that it represents a lyric cultural import from France into the heart of the London mercantile community. Its members included mercers, mayors, aldermen, sheriffs, learned clerks, and royal collegiate clergy, some of whom were among the wealthiest merchants in the city. One of the reasons for participating in the *puy* is given in the regulations as 'for the renown of London' the composition of French chansons, on the model of French *puys*, amongst bourgeois businessmen, is seen as a means of enhancing the self-image of England's prime urban centre.

It is not entirely clear from the surviving records whether the London *puy* was an expatriate concern, partly run by foreign businessmen in their own cultural

[4] A. F. Sutton, 'Merchants, Music and Social Harmony: the London *Puy* and its French and London Contexts, circa 1300', *The London Journal*, 17 (1992), 1–17 and her 'The *Tumbling Bear* and Its Patrons: A Venue for the London *Puy* and Mercery', in J. Boffey and P. King, eds, *London and Europe in the Later Middle Ages* (London: Centre for Medieval and Renaissance Studies, Queen Mary and Westfield College, University of London, 1995), 85–110.

[5] On the *puy* in general, see A. Butterfield, '*Puy*', *Medieval France: An Encyclopaedia*, gen. ed. W. W. Kibler (New York: Garland Press, 1995), 771; more detailed accounts of the thirteenth-century Arras context include Butterfield, *Poetry and Music in Medieval France from Jean Renart to Guillaume de Machaut* (Cambridge: Cambridge University Press, 2002), ch. 8, 133–50; and C. Symes, *A Common Stage: Theater and Public Life in Medieval Arras* (Ithaca: Cornell University Press, 2007). For the fourteenth century and later, see J. I. Wimsatt, *Chaucer and His French Contemporaries: Natural Music in the Fourteenth Century* (Toronto: University of Toronto Press, 1992), 274–81; G. Gros, *Le Poète, la Vierge et le prince du Puy. Etude sur les Puys marials de la France du Nord du XIVe siècle à la Renaissance* (Paris: Klincksieck, 1992); and J. Taylor, *The Making of Poetry: Late-Medieval French Poetic Anthologies* (Turnhout: Brepols, 2007), 13–18.

[6] For example, the chanson 'J'ai un iolif souvenir' by Perrin d'Angecort has a crown drawn round the marginal rubric 'coronee' in BnF n.a.fr.1050, fol.112r; five of Froissart's chansons have the same rubric (Wimsatt, *Chaucer and His French Contemporaries*, 276). Only one *chanson couronnée* appears to have survived in English sources, and even this is not conclusively associated with the London *puy* since the attributed author has not been identified in the *puy* records, and the song text does not match the regulations specified for the *puy* competition. For a recent edition of this song and a facsimile plate showing the crown, see H. Cooper, 'London and Southwark Poetic Companies: "Si tost c'amis" and the Canterbury Tales: Appendix: An Edition and Translation of Renaus de Hoiland, "Si tost c'amis"', music edn by H. Deeming, in A. Butterfield, ed., *Chaucer and the City* (Cambridge: D. S. Brewer, 2006), 109–25 (117–25).

On the *cantus coronatus* more broadly, see C. Page, *Voices and Instruments of the Middle Ages* (London: Dent, 1987), 196–201.

style, or an attempt by English merchants to emulate the social activities of their counterparts in northern France. Even this distinction is probably a false one, in that Henry le Waleys, one of the wealthiest members, was a past mayor of Bordeaux as well as of London, and thus can hardly be characterized as having a narrowly English outlook.[7] The point is rather that then, as now, London was run by a large international community, and that it was natural to turn to French practice for an international model of a literary society. There seems to have been no question of such an organization existing to promote the amateur writing of lyric poetry in English: amateur, vernacular poetry in London at this date was pre-eminently French.

The attempts to link Gower and even Chaucer, Froissart, and Othon de Grandson with the London *puy* by postulating its shadowy (and undocumented) existence right through the century are far-fetched.[8] But Jehan de le Mote and Froissart certainly wrote for continental *puys*, and Deschamps is named in the list of participants in the *Cour amoureuse*, a perhaps parodic courtly imitation of a *puy* apparently founded by Charles VI in 1400.[9] It would not be misleading to see the model of the *puy* as informing the character and practice of most fourteenth-century lyric writing in its emphasis on public competition and poetic prowess. *Puys* form part of the narrative in Jehan de le Mote's *Le Parfait du Paon* and his *Regret Guillaume:* the *Parfait* even includes detailed comments on the process of adjudication and the literary criticism performed on each *ballade* entry by the judges.[10] Perhaps the most significant feature for our purposes is the use of the refrain: the challenge would normally consist in trying to write the best *chant royal* and later, *ballade*, on a set refrain.[11] Many poems of the period thus share refrains, and even where there is no specific social link known to us now between the poets concerned, the network of poetic correspondences is broad.[12]

[7] For further references confirming the French connections of several of the merchants named in the London *Puy* statutes, see Sutton, 'The *Tumbling Bear*', esp. 90–3.

[8] John H. Fisher, *John Gower: Moral Philosopher and Friend of Chaucer* (London: Methuen, 1965), 78–83, cautiously echoed by Wimsatt, *Chaucer and His French Contemporaries*, 276 and n. 7.

[9] *La Cour amoureuse dite de Charles VI*, ed. Carla Bozzolo and Hélène Loyau, 2 vols (Paris: Léopard d'Or, 1982–92). This supplements the earlier study by A. Piaget, 'La Cour amoureuse dite de Charles VI', *Romania*, 20 (1891), 417–54. All that survives is a single copy of the charter: it is not clear that its elaborately prescribed events ever took place. For recent discussion, see Taylor, *The Making of Poetry*, 13–18.

[10] See Taylor's discussion of the *Parfait, The Making of Poetry*, 28–33.

[11] See the regulations for the *puy* at Amiens, for instance, which specify that the *puy* 'Maistre' must give out to the other members (rhétoriciens) a refrain praising the Virgin eight to fifteen days before each of the main feasts, for them to compose a *ballade* and compete for a prize to be awarded at the subsequent feast ('ung pris tel que bon luy samblera a cely qui ara la meilleure balade selon le reffrain du jour', V. de Beauvillé, *Recueil de documents concernant la Picardie*, 5 vols (Paris, 1860), I, xiv–xv, 139–54 (141) and A. Breuil, 'La Confrérie de Notre-Dame du Puy, d'Amiens', in *Mémoires de la Société des antiquaires de Picardie*, 2e série, III (1854), 485–680, (610).

[12] On the musical as well as poetic networks of the late fourteenth- and fifteenth-century French and Flemish Ars Nova and Ars Subtilior chansons, see R. Strohm, 'The *ars nova* Fragments of Ghent', *Tijdschrift van de Vereniging voor Nederlandse Musiekgeschiedenis*, 34 (1984), 109–31; and

Puys are therefore a further important context for the *ballade* exchanges between de le Mote and Vitry, and then from Deschamps to Chaucer. This chapter shifts focus slightly from the conflict-induced flashes of invective in lyric to the very substantial range of material in both French and English in which the poetic transfers are less overtly tense. *Puys* are a helpful reminder that poets of the period had a guild-inspired framework for writing poetry as well as that provided by their professional roles as soldiers, diplomats, and envoys. In some sense this is to return to the more usual ground of discussion of what is normally described as the dependence of English courtly writing on French. This is the category of the 'literary', the sense poets had of each other as writers. This body of material gives us ample resources for such an investigation, conducted here less in terms of personal response and counter-response than of the very close detail of verbal exchange. A large number of lyrics and narratives provide the means to observe at close quarters how language was carried back and forth into English from French and into Anglo-French from continental French. What is 'really' happening in this process of exchange?

We saw that de le Mote was accused of treachery for speaking French *for* the English. Chaucer, in a similar vein, was accused by Deschamps of being a translator. From the continent, then, or at least from Deschamps in certain moods, English looked like a kind of French, an ambassador for French, yes, but a potentially disloyal one. Did this make sense from the English coastline? What was the broader view of English writing from other francophone writers with other allegiances? To answer this it is necessary to study both English and Anglo-French examples.

The Chaucer lyrics seem an obvious place to turn for a variety of reasons. It is partly because they are so heavily 'French'.[13] Chaucer's are the first fourteenth-century *ballades* in English.[14] There is early recognition of Chaucer's pioneering status as a writer of *ballades* in George Ashby's *Active Policy of a Prince* (*c.*1463). Ashby's praise is notable for the way it links the composition of *ballades* to that of

his *The Rise of European Music 1380–1500* (Cambridge: Cambridge University Press, 1993); and more recently, a range of articles by Y. Plumley, 'Citation and Allusion in the Late *Ars nova*: The Case of *Esperance* and the *En attendant* songs', *EMH*, 18 (1999), 287–363; and her 'Crossing Borderlines: Points of Contact between the Late-Fourteenth Century Song and Lyric Repertories', *Acta Musicologica*, 76 (2004), 201–21; 'Intertextuality in the Fourteenth-Century Chanson', *Music and Letters*, 84 (2003), 355–77; and 'Playing the Citation Game in the Late-Fourteenth Century', *Early Music*, 31 (2003), 20–39.

[13] They have traditionally been taken by modern editors as 'early' poetry, except for the moral lyrics. There is a circularity here which, as I have argued elsewhere, derives from an assumption that Chaucer 'moves on' from his French phase.

[14] On the group of twenty-three religious lyrics with *ballade*-derived three-stanza forms in the last quire of the Vernon MS, likely to date from the last quarter of the century, see J. Burrow, 'The Shape of the Vernon Refrain Lyrics', in D. Pearsall, ed., *Studies in the Vernon Manuscript*, (Cambridge: D.S. Brewer, 1990), 187–99.

'fresshe, douce englisshe', and Chaucer to Gower and Lydgate, all of whom, he says, were

> Firste finders to oure consolacion
> Off fresshe, douce Englisshe and formacioun
> Of newe balades not vsed before.[15]

Chaucer's lyrics have thus figured large in the long history of 'Chaucer and the French Tradition'.[16] They also provide a generic echo of what Deschamps was composing, and in that sense help us to compare like with like. But, following Ashby's cue, in order to compare like with like even more fully, they will be put alongside that other major body of later fourteenth-century love lyric poetry written in England—more significant in many respects than that ascribed to Chaucer—John Gower's *Cinkante Balades.*[17] Moreover, once we scratch the surface of connection between Chaucer and Gower we find that the poetic community outlined in Chapter 5, the international cross-channel exchanges between Chaucer and Grandson, Deschamps, Froissart and Machaut, constitutes a *puy*-like forum in its own right and one worth exploring in some detail.

This chapter thus has two goals: to develop our sense of the way late fourteenth-century lyric discourse moves easily not just between poets, but also between languages, and second, to use this close reading as a means of rethinking our models—source study, citation, intertextuality, translation—for understanding textual relationships. The *Cinkante Balades* prove to be a central vantage point for observing many instances of cross-lingual verbal exchange, of intricate verbal networks that are a symptom of mutual and widely influential cultural imaginings.

GOWER'S FRENCH AND THE CONTINENT

Comparisons between Chaucer and Gower have been relatively frequent, but they are nearly all confined to their handling of narrative in English or, more recently, to questions of political circumstance. Their work as lyric poets has attracted very little commentary.[18] It may be that the practice of source criticism that has so dominated the study of Chaucer's lyrics is oddly responsible: the continental French of the *Rose*, Machaut, and Froissart is assumed to be distinct or 'other' enough from Chaucer's English to be considered a source in a way that Gower's Anglo-French is not. Chronological considerations also apply:

[15] *Idea of the Vernacular*, 59.

[16] It is worth remarking that Muscatine, however, does *not* talk about them: his French Chaucer is dominated by narrative.

[17] There is not space unfortunately to treat the *Traitié* as well here, though some reference will be made to this smaller collection in Chapter 8.

[18] Wimsatt claims 'there is . . . no particular discernible connection between Chaucer's and Gower's lyrics': *Chaucer and His French Contemporaries*, 337, n. 49.

Chaucer's lyrics have usually been taken to be early works; Gower's to be late. But as Kathryn Lynch, amongst others, has pointed out, there is a difference between traditions that have grown up about the dating of Chaucer's works and the status of the evidence: we know very little for certain.[19] There may be a further reason to do with Gower's French.

The status of his French, and indeed of fourteenth-century French writing in England, remains obscure in modern scholarly assessments of the period.[20] This obscurity has its roots in the convoluted historical inhibitions at work in the current conventional view of Early Medieval literature in England as sparse. To think of early Middle English writers as existing in 'splendid isolation from vernacular inspiration', as they have recently been described, is to excise French from the definition of insular vernacularity.[21] And yet, as earlier chapters of this book have argued, this makes little sense in terms of the multilingual habits and competences of thirteenth-century writers and their audiences. Vernacular is not a term that can be accurately used in the singular of medieval writing in England. Writers of Anglo-French had audiences that had a far from isolated 'English' perspective. If these writers were 'English' too, then writers of Middle English cannot have had an exclusive sense of writing English. To put it more starkly in linguistic terms, anyone capable of putting English into writing had prior competence in Latin, and most likely, French. Their knowledge of, and assumptions about, English as a written language were shaped by their acquisition of other insular languages. Caution should be exercised in any assumptions about how distinct, let alone how isolated, languages (or literatures) seemed to medieval writers. The post-Victorian tendency to translate 'English' as a linguistic category into 'English' as a national one may be one source of confusion. Once it is realized that medieval writers readily identified what was 'English' as a social label with, and by means of, the linguistic category of French, then it becomes less evident that they necessarily perceived the use of English as a proto-nationalist act.

To think through what all this might mean for writing in the several languages of England in the medieval period holds many challenges. Having taken up the issue with respect to some thirteenth-century instances of Anglo-French, I continue it both into the fourteenth century and into English. The comparison between Chaucer and Gower serves to develop various lines of enquiry. It hardly needs saying that Gower occupies less of the foreground as an 'English' poet than Chaucer: the caption 'Father of English Poetry' does not belong to him in the way it has seemed naturally to have been possessed by

[19] 'In general it can be said that the dating of the short poems has grown steadily *less* certain since nineteenth-century scholars distributed them among four distinct periods' (*Geoffrey Chaucer: The Minor Poems*, ed. G. B. Pace and A. David (Norman: University of Oklahoma Press, 1982), 8; K. Lynch, 'Dating Chaucer', *The Chaucer Review*, 42 (2007), 1–22.

[20] However, given the broader emphasis on Gower's French and Latin writing in the 600th anniversary conference held in July 2008, there are signs that this will change.

[21] C. Cannon, *The Grounds of English Literature* (Oxford: Oxford University Press, 2004), 11.

Chaucer.[22] One very simple reason for this is that he did not write exclusively in English. As Siân Echard has remarked, the early modern and later reception of Gower has been curiously ambivalent about his 'adventures in languages other than English'.[23] His decision to write major works in three languages has always been a thorn in the flesh for a post-Chaucer, post-triumph of English perspective on English literature. The assumption, from that perspective, that Chaucer progressed towards Englishness in his own writing does not work well for Gower.[24] The most recent discussion of the dating of the *Cinkante Balades* and *Traitié* has convincingly reiterated on new grounds a broad case for their position towards the end of Gower's poetic career.[25] The very fact that the *Traitié* acts as a coda to the *Confessio amantis* in several manuscripts indicates that Gower did not even make English the last word of the *Confessio*.[26] Such evidence, and the fact that all three books were placed on his tombstone, imply that Gower did not seek, and certainly did not achieve, a single linguistic identity as far as his contemporaries saw it.[27] To return to a question that was posed in Chapter 1, what then are the stakes involved in describing him as 'French'? Why has he been largely ignored by French scholars, in England, let alone on the continent?[28] To put it another way, how 'English' is he? What does either 'French' or 'English' mean in the later fourteenth century? And to press the other concern of this book, what of the perspective from which these questions are asked? Gower, as I have been suggesting, has traditionally been considered from an almost exclusively

[22] The standard sources for a historical conspectus of Chaucer criticism in which this caption quickly becomes a leitmotif are Caroline F. E. Spurgeon, ed., *Five Hundred Years of Chaucer Criticism and Allusion 1357–1900*, 3 vols (Cambridge: Cambridge University Press, 1925), now updated and supplemented by J. C. Boswell and S. W. Holton, eds, *Chaucer's Fame in England: STC Chauceriana, 1475–1640* (New York: MLA, 2004); and D. S. Brewer, ed., *Chaucer: The Critical Heritage*, 2 vols (London: Routledge & Kegan Paul, 1978).

[23] 'Introduction', in Echard, ed., *A Companion to Gower*, 12. See also her essay on 'Gower in Print', ibid., 115–35, which ponders the different ways printers have responded (or failed to respond) to the trilingual challenges of his oeuvre.

[24] Gower scholars have been very aware of this, and more sceptical of the Chaucerian progression towards Englishness as a result. Nonetheless, it does seem to influence arguments about the chronology and character of Gower's own writing career: see R. F. Yeager on 'Gower was wrong' (142) and his unsupported assertion that 'English court tastes during Richard II's minority were unfocussed, and those of Richard himself, as he grew into power, were less and less 'French' ('John Gower's French', in Echard, ed., *A Companion to Gower*, 145).

[25] See R. F. Yeager's fine discussion in 'John Gower's Audience: The Ballades', *Chaucer Review*, 40 (2005), 81–105'.

[26] See A. Butterfield, 'French Culture and the Ricardian Court', in A. Minnis, C. Morse, and T. Turville-Petre, eds, *Essays on Ricardian Literature in Honour of J.A. Burrow* (Oxford: Clarendon Press, 1997), 82–121.

[27] Attempts by Yeager to deduce anything conclusive from the order of the books on the tombstone, for example, seem doubtful.

[28] For an important exception, see J. Gilbert, 'Men Behaving Badly: Linguistic Purity and Sexual Perversity in Derrida's *Le Monolinguisme de l'autre* and Gower's *Traitié pour essampler les amantz marietz', Romance Studies*, 24 (2006), 77–89.

(and retrospectively) 'English' point of view.[29] How would *he* have looked from the continent?

Gower, as no other English writer of the fourteenth century, makes us question Englishness.

RETHINKING SOURCE STUDY

In order to attempt a preliminary answer to this last question, this chapter places the comparison between Chaucer and Gower within a wider network of continental and insular writing. In part this is to follow a *puy*-inspired route of tracing citations and allusions across a community of linked writers.[30] This journey leads through the large territory of source study and translation. Much modern research on Chaucer's lyrics, indeed on Chaucer's relation to French writings more generally, has emphasized their character as works of translation. There have been excellent studies, for example, of Chaucer's 'worde by worde' handling of Grandson's *ballades* in his so-called *Complaint of Venus*.[31] However, as Ruth Evans has powerfully argued, there are further, and perhaps other, ways of thinking about translation. She urges, with acknowledgement of Rita Copeland's work on rhetoric, that it is important for modern readers of medieval texts to see translation as a matter of shaping ideology as well as of style or local verbal transfer.[32]

Since her 1994 essay, a pioneering (though not uncritical) attempt to draw colonial discourse theory into research on medieval translation practices, much further thinking has taken place, and new perspectives on both the medieval and the colonial sides of translation are continuing to develop. I will return to this in the next section of the book, with discussion of Chaucer as 'The English Subject'. Here, my effort is initially exploratory. For this range of lyrics in French and English poses many questions about methodology. The relationships between them slip fluidly and even confusingly between several kinds of current critical approach: translation, source study, intertextuality, and citation.

Source study has been the traditional means of establishing connections between writers for many decades of modern scholarship. One of the outstanding exponents of this approach in relation to Chaucer's knowledge of French writing

[29] Scholars such as Yeager and Echard, by contrast, have worked tirelessly in the face of this tradition to enable the non-English works of Gower to be available for wider scholarly appreciation.

[30] My own long-standing interests in French refrains converge here (from a different starting-point) with Yeager's; see his chapter 'Gower's lines', in his *John Gower's Poetic: The Search for a New Arion* (Cambridge: D. S. Brewer, 1990), 45–113.

[31] See, in particular, H. Phillips, '*The Complaint of Venus*: Chaucer and de Graunson', in R. Ellis and R. Evans, eds, *The Medieval Translator* (Exeter: University of Exeter Press, 1994), 86–103 and J. Scattergood, 'Chaucer's *Complaint of Venus* and the "Curiosite" of Graunson', *Essays in Criticism*, 44 (1994), 171–89.

[32] R. Evans, 'Translating Past Cultures?', in Ellis and Evans, *The Medieval Translator*, 20–45.

is James Wimsatt. It clearly remains very useful to be able to identify exact quotations, allusions, and instances of close or direct translation, and many critical arguments continue to depend profitably on it. Nonetheless, as Seth Lerer has recently remarked, it is an academic approach that now seems rooted in the mid-twentieth century (along, more arguably, with 'critical appreciation and close verbal analysis').[33] Even on its own terms, and within its own critical assumptions, source study exponents have worried over the often false specificity of the approach.[34] It seems we can only be really sure a writer has read another writer if we home in on closer and closer correspondences, but the difficulty is that this presupposes a very limited model of both writing and reading.[35]

The ideal end point of the search, in fact, for a source hunter is translation, in the sense of a text transferred word by word, sense by sense into another text, for here the tangibility of the source text seems no longer an issue. But even this comes up against difficulties when the linguistic field of the texts under comparison is narrow and fairly self-contained, as it is in the case of the language of love.[36] One very quickly finds oneself stumbling over such questions as how to distinguish between the formulaic and the 'original', the specific citation and the common memory.[37]

And if, at first sight, the model of intertextuality seems the obvious antidote to such concerns, on closer consideration the promise it holds becomes a mirage. A plunge into that 'mosaic of quotations' as Julia Kristeva defined 'any text' very quickly becomes disorientating. If we are seeking clues to the compositional process, or to how authors seek to understand and control the meaning of their texts, then we will be as interested in the tiny, local moments of (apparent) choice as in the indiscriminate forces of textual determinism that are certainly present in any one textual instance but indescribable in their vast effect.[38]

Poets do not merely use the same genre of learned love language, they also specifically cite one another's phrases and lines in direct riposte. Citation resists intertextuality in alerting us to explicit attempts by poets to create poetic lineages, to pose as citers and make visible gestures of authorial control. In this they are engaged in something more than source study and less than translation: or rather,

[33] 'Introduction', in S. Lerer, ed., *The Yale Companion to Chaucer* (New Haven and London: Yale University Press, 2006), 5.

[34] For a recent, wide-ranging discussion of some of these issues, see 'Colloquium: The Afterlife of Origins', *SAC*, 28 (2006), 217–70.

[35] For a proposal to widen the traditional terms of 'source' and 'analogue' with 'hard' and 'soft', see P. G. Beidler, 'New Terminology for Sources and Analogues', *SAC*, 28 (2006), 225–35.

[36] The *locus classicus* for this observation is P. Zumthor's *Essai de poétique médiévale* (Paris: Éditions du Seuil, 1972).

[37] A. Butterfield, 'The Art of Repetition: Machaut's *Ballade* 33 "Nes qu'on porroit"', in T. Knighton and J. Milsom, eds, *Close Readings: Essays in Honour of John Stevens and Philip Brett*, Special Issue of *Early Music*, 31 (August 2003), 346–60.

[38] Ruth Evans's reference to 'genetic criticism' may have potential application here: 'The Afterword of Origins: A Response', *SAC*, 28 (2006), 263–70 (266).

observing their practice closely may give us the opportunity to see at what level translation is taking place, and with what ideological consequences. Nonetheless, the degree of purposive control implied in citation can be very hard to trace, and directs us, once more, towards more open models of textual exchange.

The lyric clusters that are the subject of this chapter show that notions of translation, intertextuality, source study, and citation are mutually disruptive. My concern is not to rely on any of them, but rather to go back behind the assumptions that they carry. This is pressed on us by the complexly shared—and complexly distinct—character of the material in which relationships are set up between poets writing in English and French, in English and Anglo-French, and in French and Anglo-French.

Translation is both the largest framework and the most detailed, since it can imply the broadest cultural transfer and the most particular verbal transfer, perhaps at the same moment. But what *kinds* of transfer are involved in moving across these closely connected boundaries? *Is* there a boundary between Gower's French and Machaut's French? Is it possible to perceive it, and if so on what terms?

Each notion is in some way potentially illuminating of this Anglo-French lyric poetic practice, but all are powerfully complicated by the fact that the material for comparison involves translations within as well as across languages. In comparing the discourse used by love poets writing in different languages in different locations, in seeking to discern the direction of cultural flow, the sense of relative linguistic status and of authorial prestige in the shared vocabularies and mythologies, we need to be aware of this crucial diglossia.

One way forward may be contained in newer approaches to citation in the fields of French literature and music. They have been stimulated by attention to the large repertory of French refrains that was copied from the thirteenth century onwards. French refrains both provoke and revoke distinctions between the formulaic and the individually crafted utterance. Some two thousand survive—they circulate, often with music, in a wide variety of genres, and there are many instances of the same one- or two-line tag being cited in as many as four or five different works. Studying refrain citation on a wide basis is revealing about medieval creative practices: vernacular writers and composers show much subtlety and ingenuity in exploring the borderland between the already known (the *déjà dit*) and the newly coined, what one might call the newly known.[39]

The relevance of this to Gower is both specific and more general. Specifically, his French *ballades* connect directly to this tradition by themselves citing refrains. One of the most current, with over twenty-five citations from the thirteenth to the fifteenth century—'*Qui bien aime a tart oblié*' [He who loves well forgets slowly]—acts as the refrain to his *Ballade* 25; several others circulate refrains and

[39] On the refrain, see N. H. J. van den Boogaard, ed., *Rondeaux et refrains du XIIe siècle au début du XIVe* (Paris: Klincksieck, 1969); E. Doss-Quinby, *Les refrains chez les trouvères du XIIe siècle au début du XIVe* (New York: Peter Lang, 1984); Butterfield, *Poetry and Music*, 75–102.

other lines in the classic French manner. I will discuss some examples shortly. More generally, the use of these snippets of shared language provides a way of grasping some of the parameters of this language, and hence of the wider linguistic community within which Gower was writing. They do so not necessarily in the terms of elevated allusion, but rather, more fundamentally, in terms of a shared koiné, an exchange of linguistic material that is at once at the lowest level of style and the most visible expression of that style.

THE *CINKANTE BALADES*: FIVE ANGLO-FRENCH TEXTUAL PERFORMANCES

Apart from Fisher, only R. F. Yeager has given Gower's *Cinkante Balades* as a group any serious study. Gower studies have fortunately moved on considerably since Fisher's manifestly mistaken assertion that 'Chaucer . . . reveals a profound influence from the French court poets, whereas Gower shows little, if any, knowledge of them'.[40] In a 2003 paper, for instance, Brian Merrilees made an important demonstration of the extent to which Gower's French vocabulary, far from being narrowly Anglo-Norman, reflects the newest trends in continental French.[41] It seems clear that there is much more to be asked and answered about the linguistic and social context of Gower's French—about where he acquired it and used it, by what means new vocabulary circulated, and by and for whom.

Some answers may be obtained by following through some of the analogues to the *Cinkante Balades* as a collection. First, there are no collections surviving in English at or before this date. In fourteenth-century French, the closest examples (though on a much larger scale) include the collection of around 282 fixed-form poems in Machaut's *La Louange des Dames*, collected throughout his life in several codices from *c.*1324 to the 1370s, the Pennsylvania MS Codex 902 (formerly MS 15) anthology of 310 lyrics, copied *c.*1400, and the *Les Cent Ballades* by Jean le Seneschal and fellow knights (probably of the late 1380s and early 1390s, of which the earliest surviving copy is BnF fr.2360,

[40] Fisher, *John Gower*, 74. Since J. A. Burrow's pioneering essay, 'The Portrayal of Amans in *Confessio Amantis*', in *Gower's Confessio Amantis: Responses and Reassessments*, ed. A. J. Minnis (Cambridge: D. S. Brewer, 1983), 5–24, Gower's relation to his French contemporaries has been discussed in R. F. Yeager, *John Gower's Poetic*, W. Calin, *The French Tradition and the Literature of Medieval England* (Toronto: University of Toronto Press, 1994), 380–5; Butterfield, 'French Culture and the Ricardian Court'; Butterfield, '*Confessio amantis* and the French Tradition', in Eichard, ed., *A Companion to Gower*, 165–80; and, Butterfield, 'Articulating the Author: Gower and the French Vernacular Codex', *The Yearbook of English Studies*, 33, Special Number: *Medieval and Early Modern Miscellanies and Anthologies*, ed. Phillipa Hardman (MHRA, 2003), 80–96. On Gower's own French writing see Yeager, 'John Gower's French' and 'John Gower's Audience'.

[41] 'John Gower's French Vocabulary', paper presented at 'Gower and the hypertext', Senate House, University of London, 28–30 July 2003. I am very grateful to Brian Merrilees for kindly sending a copy of this paper to me.

from the end of the fourteenth century).[42] Other anthologies that might be mentioned in this context include Westminster Abbey MS 21 and BnF n.a.fr. 6221 (first half of the fifteenth century);[43] and the two collections of Graunson's lyrics in BnF fr. 2201 and Neuchâtel, Bibl. Arthur Piaget VIII, respectively. The *Trésor amoureux*, late fourteenth century, once tentatively ascribed to Froissart, offers a further comparison: a lyric anthology divided into four narrative sections, in between which occur groups of *ballades*: the first has forty-four, the second forty, and the third another forty-four.[44] These *ballade* clusters are in turn divided by sets of rondeaux, in three groups of twelve. Much smaller groupings of lyrics occur in sporadic clusters throughout such narrative works as Machaut's *Voir Dit* and *Remede de Fortune*, and Froissart's imitative *L'Espinette amoureuse, La Prison Amoureuse*, and *Le Joli Buisson de Jonece*. A generation before Froissart, Jehan de le Mote gathered lyric sequences into his *Regret Guillaume* and *Parfait du Paon*.[45]

The *Cinkante Balades* is unusual in being a single-author collection of precisely the size that it is: in a sense it is a model in miniature of the *Louange*, and, as its title indicates, a half-size version of the *Les Cent Ballades*. The latter seems to have been a cult work of the 1390s, and copied in conception by Christine de Pizan's *Cent Ballades d'Amant et de Dame* and, in due course, Charles d'Orléans's sequences. We have no hard evidence for determining the date of the *Cinkante Balades*; R. F. Yeager has reconsidered the options with care and erudition and made several interesting suggestions.[46] One might add that the types of analogue fall into two broad types: love narratives with skeins of inset lyrics, and lyric sequences (one or two works such as the *Trésor* fall between the two). Gower was very much part of a growing trend in compiling self-authored lyric sequences that was sparked by Machaut, taken up by Gower and then, as the genre of the anthology attracted the involvement of a range of authors, became the cross-channel poetic activity *du jour*.[47] We do not know exact chronologies: but there

[42] See *La Louange des Dames by Guillaume de Machaut*, ed. Nigel Wilkins (Edinburgh: Scottish Academic Press, 1972), with discussion of the individual pieces including chronological issues in L. Earp, *Guillaume de Machaut: A Guide to Research* (New York and London: Garland, 1995); J. I. Wimsatt, *Chaucer and the Poems of 'Ch' in University of Pennsylvania MS French 15* (Cambridge: D.S. Brewer, 1982); Jean le Seneschal, *Les Cent Ballades*.

[43] On BnF n.a.fr. 6221 see Wimsatt, *Chaucer and the Poems of 'Ch'*, 60–1, and his 'Collections of French Lyrics Chaucer May Have Known', in A. Crépin, ed., *L'Imagination médiévale: Chaucer et ses contemporains: Actes du Colloque en Sorbonne*, Publications de l'Association des Médiévistes Anglicistes de l'Enseignement Supérieur, 16 (Paris: Publications de l'AMAES, 1991), 33–51.

[44] *Le Trésor amoureux, Oeuvres de Froissart: Poésies*, ed. A. Scheler, III, 52–305.

[45] Some seventy narratives with lyric insertions survive from the thirteenth to the fifteenth centuries: there is a convenient list in M. B. M. Boulton, *The Song in the Story: Lyric Insertions in French Narrative Fiction, 1200–1400* (Philadelphia: University of Pennsylvania Press, 1993) (though the numbers of lyrics given should be treated with caution). See also Butterfield, *Poetry and Music*, Appendix 1.

[46] Yeager, 'John Gower's Audience'.

[47] There seems to have been a particular interest in hundreds: compare Machaut's 100–rhyme complaint in the *Fontaine amoureuse*, and Froissart's in *L'Espinette amoureuse* (Taylor, *The Making*

is no reason to leave Gower out simply because he was writing on the English side of the water. The connections with the *Louange* concern the use of refrains and interlinking lines (as the later part of this chapter will discuss in detail), and the structuring of mini episodes within the larger layout. This is also a feature of the Penn anthology, here made more complex by the sets of dialogue set up between different authors.

Chapter 4 considered the atmosphere of exchange in some of the smaller groups of *ballades*, such as those sent between Philippe de Vitry and Jean de la Mote in the 1350s. These much more ambitious sequences await full analysis, but even on a cursory glance reveal great subtlety in their treatment of language as an almost transparent medium, each line a palimpsest of other lines. My particular interest here in the *Cinkante Balades* lies in the several moments of linguistic exchange that, like the Vitry and de la Mote group, involve a passage of words across Anglo-French boundaries. I will describe five of them, some of which have been noted before, some put forward here for comment for the first time as far as I am aware, and then single out one for more detailed discussion. Each instance has its own characteristics as a form of textual link and my effort will be questioning and exploratory, endeavouring to consider what each can teach us about the possible significance of such connections.

Ballade No. 25 and '*Qui bien aime*'

As soon as one starts to read the *Cinkante Balades* more closely, then far more than five of these cross-lingual events begin to show themselves. This account is not at all exhaustive, in short, but rather a set of vistas revealing the potential for the multiple kinds of linguistic exchange that are latent in these texts. Let me begin with *Ballade* 25 and its refrain '*Qui bien aime a tart oblie*'. Gower's use of this refrain places him in a chronology of citation that reaches back to the thirteenth century and forward to the fifteenth on both sides of the Channel.[48] '*Qui bien aime*' functions as a trouvère song refrain, surviving with and without music, as a line cited in various polyphonic motets, romances and *dits*, as a proverb in proverb collections, and then from the fourteenth century, in several works by Machaut, in *Le Songe du vieil pelerin* by Philippe de Mèzières, in Deschamps, in place of the announced roundel in several manuscripts of Chaucer's *Parliament of Fowls*, the *Parliament of Birds*, a poem by Jean Régnier, and another by Jean Molinet. It often occurs scribbled as a pen trial or simply (one presumes) as a favourite saying in the

of Poetry, 38); and a parallel trend in narrative with Boccaccio's *Decameron* and *Les Cents Nouvelles Nouvelles.*

[48] Butterfield, 'French Culture and the Ricardian Court', 99–107 (101–03) I have collected some twenty-five to thirty citations of this refrain, as part of an ongoing study. Gower's ballades are cited from *The Complete Works of John Gower*, ed. G. C. Macaulay, 4 vols (Oxford: Clarendon Press, 1899–1902), *I: The French Works*, 335–78.

margins of manuscripts; Gower cites the line in his *Miroir de l'Omme* (line 27867) as well as the *Balades*.

'*Qui bien aime*' can serve as a primary instance of how illimitable the textual search for connection becomes. Its prolific history of citation represents the ever-expanding network of textual traces that rush outwards from any text like stars in the expanding universe. In general, no doubt, this history was invisible to many of its participants, but there do seem to be some specific moments, especially in Machaut, where greater self-consciousness enters the picture. Is Gower's usage one such example? How do we decide? And what kind of self-consciousness? We might note first of all that it occurs at the centre of the sequence, the twenty-fifth *ballade* of fifty,[49] and marks the first moment in which the discussion of love takes a more anxious, even bitter turn with the reference to the *mesdisants*, those perennial spoilers of love's joys. This is a *ballade* which makes particular reference to prior talk, to the way in which every love affair is entangled in a prior linguistic history that threatens to destroy it. In that sense '*Qui bien aime*' could have a double meaning for the sequence: in citing it Gower sets his own work of love lyrics firmly and centrally within an all-embracing history of love language, yet he also allows the citation to signal an anxiety about the future loss and decay of that language.

Yeager, in discussing this quotation, argues that this, and other lines throughout the *Cinkante Balades* 'echo and "correct" the traditional "voice" of French courtly lyric by calling its implications to account' (111). The ultimate purpose then of all these citations and lines like them is to draw attention to 'the dangerous writing of the courtly lyric' (112). Gower is using this language 'against itself'. Yeager's case is carefully made, and is part of a broad and searching discussion of Gower as moralist. But it is important to register that arguments about the meaning of particular citations are vulnerable to the sheer scale of the process. '*Qui bien aime*' already has so long and wide a history in French that any new citations cannot distinguish themselves wholly from that. Another way of saying this is that in citing '*Qui bien aime*' at all any author, any citer, is implicitly drawing attention to love's capacity to change and die, and is thereby already using language to comment against itself.

We can see this from the many parallels with Machaut's *Voir Dit*, which permeate the *Cinkante Balades*. In Machaut's work, the poet, played seemingly for real as an old man, is engaged in exchanging lyrics and letters throughout a long verse narrative with a young female admirer, Toute Belle. Several of Gower's *ballades* echo moments in the *Voir Dit*, such as No. 28 which, in asking for a response from the lady, actually requests some writing:

49 Strictly speaking, there are fifty-four, since the sequence has two dedicatory *ballades* to Henry IV, two *ballades* are marked No. IIII, and a final *ballade* dedicated to the Virgin.

Prenetz ceo dit de moi pour remembrer,
Et mandetz moi de vos beals ditz auci . . .

(23–4)

[Receive this poem from me as remembrance,
And send me also a beautiful poem of yours . . .]

Then, in the next, the speaker refers to tales of rumour that she has been angry with him after he has deliberately stayed away, which recalls the section in the *Voir Dit* where the lovers become temporarily estranged. More instances of textual reminiscence could be readily found and of course these would include the three citations of '*Qui bien aime*' itself, but the larger issue concerns the question of what kind of identity '*Qui bien aime*' had for Gower. Machaut has already so thoroughly explored the vulnerability of love language in the *Voir Dit* for both poet and lady that Gower can hardly be offering this as a perspective on its own terms that somehow trumps Machaut. Yeager's view implies that Gower must be reacting *against* Machaut and Deschamps (against whom he 'takes aim' [113]), in using the same language and saying the same lines. For Yeager, the reaction comes because he is writing from an *English* perspective.

It is illuminating in this context to put Gower's response to '*Qui bien aime*' alongside the Chaucer citation. '*Qui bien aime*' occurs in place of the announced roundel at the end of some of the manuscripts of Chaucer's *Parliament of Fowls* and also as a refrain in the stanzaic *Parliament of Birds*, a fifteenth-century response to Chaucer's *Parliament* copied into Cambridge University Library MS Gg.4.27 in a sequence with Chaucer's *ABC*, his *Envoy to Scogan* and two anonymous macaronic lyrics. In these two places the presence of '*Qui bien aime*' gains a lively Anglo-French meaning. Again the issues and responses are complex. For most modern Chaucerian editors, the existence of a French refrain here is something of an embarrassment. It does not fit the modern editorial image of an exclusively English Chaucer which is better served by the single, later fifteenth-century attempt to plug the gap with a roundel text in English.[50] Yet to find the French refrain in these Chaucerian manuscripts testifies to the pervasive Anglo-French rather than narrowly English culture of the late fourteenth and fifteenth centuries. That it was natural for a scribe or compiler to insert a French refrain in the space left by the English text for a song should not cause surprise, especially when we remember Chaucer's cue 'The note, I trowe, imaked was in Fraunce'. But more than this, the *Parliament of Birds*, stimulated as it seems to be by the macaronic ending of Chaucer's *Parliament* gives us a glimpse both of how this Anglo-French culture was writing itself ever more thoroughly into 'English' love

[50] Ralph Hanna III, 'Presenting Chaucer as Author', in T. W. Machan, ed., *Medieval Literature: Texts and Interpretation* (Binghamton: Medieval & Renaissance Texts & Studies, 1991), 17–39. Hanna dates the addition in Gg to 'no earlier than circa 1460–1470 and likely later still' (30); the earliest version of the roundel is in J ('near mid-century').

poetry, and how Chaucer's own work seems to have prompted it.[51] It is structured in fifteen English stanzas, each (except in two instances) concluding with a different French refrain. In the two anomalous stanzas the cuckoo and the starling burst out against French, admitting they cannot speak it well ('I can no french soþ for to seyne' [cuckoo] . . . I can no skille of swich french fare/ To speke in engelych I haue more deynte [starling]', and utter one English refrain each as part of their rebellion. This is raucously comic: the poet allows in a dissident view of French but by the least civilized members of the parliament, and not only turns back to French but gives it the last word.

'*Qui bien aime*' takes its place after the fourth stanza, ostensibly as one of the quietly assertive French refrains; but again its history cannot but speak of the larger practice that lies behind such a citation. The interest of the Gower example is that it seems to mark a very early moment in the cross-channel career of '*Qui bien aime*'. Could it have been the first citation on English soil? We cannot tell much about the earliest state of the *Parliament of Fowls*, except that perhaps the very variability in the manuscripts indicates that there was some kind of gap. The 'original' poem, however little we like to remember this, seems likely to have finished without a *written* conclusion. Assuming that the *Cinkante Balades* are late in date, could Gower have seen '*Qui bien aime*' in a Chaucer manuscript? Could he have heard a Chaucerian roundel sung to a French tune? Perhaps, though whether it is a fifteenth-century gloss or a record of a performance cue is hard to tell. But either way, are we right to hear Gower say it with an English accent?

The Chaucerian, followed by the Chauceriana context, suggests a different conclusion. It seems to show that '*Qui bien aime*' did not seem 'French' until later in the fifteenth century. Even then, 'French' refrains held sway, and it was the attempt to write and speak in English equivalents that was worth gentle comedy. It is very hard to get inside these citations, but the extraordinary, yet also ordinary fluidity of this unassuming proverbial line not just across contexts but across languages, and (although there is no space to discuss it here) across language and music, should hold us back from making too swift a cultural judgement. In a way that we have come to recognize to be typical yet still remarkable about refrains, '*Qui bien aime*' both recedes into the background and stands out as pivotal. This is nowhere more true than Gower's decision to place '*Qui bien aime*' at the very centre of his sequence.[52] The very breadth of

[51] Gg itself doesn't have the French refrain, but the sole copy of an eight-line version of the song.

[52] On the significance of mid-points, see Karl D. Uitti, 'From Clerc to Poète: The Relevance of the *Romance of the Rose* to Machaut's World', in M. P. Cosman and B. Chandler, eds, *Machaut's World: Science and Art in the Fourteenth Century*, Annals of the New York Academy of Sciences, 314 (New York: New York Academy of Sciences, 1978), 209–16; S. Huot, *From Song to Book: The Poetics of Writing in Old French Lyric and Lyrical Narrative Poetry* (Ithaca and London: Cornell University Press, 1987), 69, 72–73, 90; and, in relation to *Fauvel*, Butterfield, *Poetry and Music*, 204–05.

reference contained in '*Qui bien aime*' suggests that it was precisely that openness which attracted Gower rather than a desire to close it down ethically. Perhaps the wider point embodied in '*Qui bien aime*' is that it helps us see something about the communal character of a certain type of poetic production. Moreover, it was a communal practice that ranged with ease across English and French and across the insular and the continental. It was a practice that was open, public, and generative.

Ballades Nos 34 and 35: Valentine poetry

My second case involves the two Valentine *ballades*, Nos 34 and 35. They follow on naturally from the previous example since there are connections with Chaucer, bird parliaments, and song. Let us begin with the immediate Chaucer parallels. Thus the first one opens:

Saint Valentin l'amour et la nature
De toutz oiseals ad en governement;
Dont chascun d'eaux semblable a sa mesure
Une compaigne honeste a son talent
Eslist tout d'un accord et d'un assent:
Pour celle soule laist a covenir
Toutes les autres, car nature aprent,
U li coers est, le corps falt obëir.

(1–8)

St Valentine has the love and nature
Of all birds under governance;
Wherefore each one of them,
All with one accord and one assent,
Elects a companion honest in its inclination,
Like to its own estimation.
For that one alone it gladly leaves aside
All others, for nature teaches that
Where the heart is, the body must follow.[53]

Although in Chaucer it is Nature rather than the saint who organizes the mating 'thorgh [her] governaunce' (387), she has the same emphasis on 'acord' (381) and assent (526). The second *ballade* has an even closer link, especially in the third stanza where the speaker comments wistfully:

O com nature est pleine de favour
A ceos oiseals q'ont lour eleccion!

(15–16)

[53] The translations are mine; I have benefitted from R. F. Yeager's generosity in making available to me his forthcoming translation of Gower's *Cinkante Ballades* and *Traitié*.

[Oh how nature is full of favor
To those birds who have their choice!]

He alone does not have the one he would choose, although 'chascun Tarcel gentil ad sa falcoun' (22) [Each noble tercel has her falcon]. The poem even ends with song, in fact with a song followed by the mournful refrain of the one lover who remains single:

Ma dame, c'est le fin de mon chançoun,
Qui soul remaint ne poet avoir grant joie.
(24–5)

[My lady, this is the end of my song,
Whosoever remains alone cannot have great joy.]

If we follow the ordinary logic of source study then we would need to establish who first came up with the idea of a Valentine setting for a love poem. Despite exhaustive discussion by Fisher and especially H. A. Kelly, no conclusion has been reached on whether this accolade falls to Chaucer, Gower, or Graunson.[54] But uncertainty has many useful consequences. It means that we are immediately required to avoid a linear, chronological approach and see this theme as cooperatively generated, which it undoubtedly was. This in turn helps us to take a less Chaucer-centred view of the material. It was actually Graunson who was the most prolific on the subject, producing nine poems that refer to the saint.[55] This has significance because it gives us a body of francophone material, neither exactly French nor English, to put alongside Gower's Anglo-French and Chaucer's English. One of two Savoyard knights in Gaunt's service, whom we have already seen represented as a cruelly teasing friend of Deschamps, Graunson had a privileged and flamboyant role as an international courtly personality, widely reputed for his chivalry, prowess in battle, and skills as a diplomat and poet. Like the blind Jean de Luxembourg who rode to his death in Crécy, he even had (though this sounds callous) a textbook death in his early fifties defending his honour in a duel. The shock with which his death was received was matched by the sense that this was the ultimate act of chivalric self-immolation.[56]

Graunson was thus also the ultimate cross-channel poet, someone who cannot be fitted neatly into an insular versus continental polarity. Freed from the need to

[54] H. A. Kelly, *Chaucer and the Cult of Saint Valentine* (Leiden: Brill, 1986) eventually presents the hypothesis that Chaucer was indeed the first, but it rests on a complex series of circumstantial arguments.

[55] *Balade de Saint Valentin double, Balade de Saint Valentin,* 2 *Complaintes de Saint Valentin, Complainte amoureuse de Sainct Valentin, Souhait de Saint Valentin, Songe Saint Valentin* and *Complainte* from his *Livre Messire Ode*, which takes place on Valentine's Day.

[56] For recent discussion, see *Othon de Grandson, chevalier et poète: Etudes*, ed. Jean-François Kosta-Théfaine, Medievalia, 63 (Orléans: Paradigme, 2007).

argue either that he borrowed from Chaucer or that Chaucer borrowed from him, and with the presence of Gower to thicken the relationships further, we can come closer than usual to a sense of poetry as an activity fostered by writers who, despite choosing apparently different linguistic matrices, had similar sources of inspiration and sought similar patterns of language to express them. This will now be illustrated with brief reference to two more examples before finishing with a more detailed consideration of an intricately plotted network of *ballade* interchanges.

Ballades Nos 41–4 and 46: a female voice, Graunson, and Chaucer

The third of my Anglo-French 'events' works outward from Gower's *ballades* 41–4 and 46. It marks a strange and rather tense moment of torque in the sequence where Gower's male poet-narrator is suddenly replaced by a bitter female narrator. He builds up to the change of speaker in *Ballade* 40 by first introducing a new, sour note of accusation from the male lover: his lady speaks affectionately but her deeds are unreliable. She is like Helen, a betrayer and two-timer, leaving him vainly asserting the value of loyalty in the repeated refrain:

Loials amours se provont a l'essai.

[Loyal lovers prove themselves at the test.]

In retort, the next *ballade* strikes back with a female response: 'Des fals amantz tantz sont au jour present' ['There are so many false lovers today']. She reverses all the complaints of the previous *ballade*: she is the speaker of truth 'Jeo sui de celles une, a dire voir' (5) ['I am one of those, to speak truth']) and he the false lover, a hypocrite who is one thing in the morning and quite another in the evening. Once more the range of allusion seems both deep and wide, to the *Voir Dit*, and to the Troilus story (references to which are laced through the *Cinkante Balades* and the *Traitié*).[57] The next two *ballades* (Nos 42–3) reinforce her message with mythical references to male treachery, and then, just as abruptly, Gower produces a *ballade* with a female speaker who praises her lover extravagantly for his loyalty. After this we are back with the usual male speaker for one *ballade* (No. 45) only to switch again to the praising female (No. 46), before finishing with a group of four that become increasingly more generalized in theme.

This section of the *Cinkante Balades* is not only rich in reference but also makes these references in a wide range of ways. Perhaps the broadest but still clearly outlined framework of comparison is to the *ballade* exchange between Grandson and Chaucer. The object of much detailed modern commentary, this

[57] Compare Froissart's *Le Paradys d'Amour*, 974; and Machaut's *Fontaine Amoureuse*, 1336–40, 1952.

exchange has Chaucer translate five *ballades* by Grandson entitled in one manuscript (Paris BnF, fr.2201, fol.75v-77v) *Les cinq balades ensievans.*[58] The best guess is that Grandson probably composed them while he was imprisoned in Spain in 1372–4, and that he brought them back with him to England on entering Gaunt's service in 1374. Even if this were more than conjecture, it still leaves the date of Chaucer's poems very open.[59] Chaucer translates the 1st, 4th and 5th (using some material from the 2nd and 3rd), changes the speaker from male to female and adds an *envoi.* Four of the ten manuscripts in which his *ballades* are copied give them the title *The Compleynte of Venus.* At first sight, we at last have a solid example of a source relationship with an object text and its translated partner. Yet in some respects the Grandson—Chaucer exchange adds to rather than lessens the interpretative challenge of Gower's switches of gender. Commentators have not after all found it easy to ascertain the direction and purpose of Chaucer's changes to Grandson and even the most recent persuasive account by Helen Phillips finds itself observing a contortion in Chaucer's apparent decision to present female passivity as a model for authorial practice.[60] Yet again, in trying to understand one author—Gower—we find that the textual model which might seem to provide a stable comparison is itself unstable and full of variance.[61]

Nonetheless, the parallel between the two textual actions is full of latent implication and offers tantalizing possibilities for this chapter's attempt to observe Anglo-French dialogue at close quarters. For underlying each swerving, skewing gender reversal is one of the key texts of Anglo-French text creation in the period: Chaucer's difficult, self-contradictory, self-abasing *envoi*:

> Princes, receyveth this compleynt in gre,
> Unto your excelent benignite
> Direct after my litel suffisaunce.
> For elde, that in my spirit dulleth me,
> Hath of endyting al the subtilte
> Wel nygh bereft out of my remembraunce,
> And eke to me hit ys a grete penaunce,
> Syth rym in Englissh hath such skarsete,
> To folowe worde by worde the curiosite
> Of Graunson, flour of hem that make in Fraunce.
>
> (*The Complaint of Venus*, 73–82)

The puzzles are many. As Wimsatt points out, the form of this *envoi* is anomalous: unlike most *envois* its versification is different from the preceding

[58] These occur in the same order but with no title in the Penn MS.

[59] Wimsatt proposes any time between 1374 and 1392: *Chaucer and His French Contemporaries*, 213–14.

[60] Phillips, '*The Complaint of Venus*'.

[61] Compare Chaucer's *Complaint to Mars* and *Complaynt d'amours.*

ballade stanzas, it has a larger number of lines than any French *envoi* and does not in any case have a *ballade*-type rhyme scheme. The complaint that English rhymes are scarce is whimsical. In fact Chaucer, by using only two rhyme sounds in the whole stanza performs a much more difficult (and characteristically French) feat than either he or Grandson attempts in the *ballades* themselves. Then the reference to 'Elde' is also provocative. It has the same ring as his self-mocking exclamation in the *Lenvoy de Chaucer a Scogan*:

> But wel I wot, thow wolt answere and saye,
> 'Lo, olde Grisel lyst to ryme and playe!' (34–5)

But in *Venus* he is even older: where the *Scogan* Chaucer suffers perhaps only from middle-aged spread ('hoor and rounde of shap'), this one is sinking into the torpor and memory loss of old age: his spirit is becoming dull and the subtle arts of composition are vanishing from his memory. The image is conveyed here of an elderly poet struggling to match the virtuosity of his Savoyard francophone colleague. If we were to take this image at its word then it suggests a poet in awe of French 'curiosite' into his old age and more aware than ever of English's inadequacies as a vernacular in waiting.

It is always unwise to lean too gratefully on any single Chaucer remark. And as we have just seen, Chaucer's poetic powers, at least on the evidence of his ability to find rhymes, are not drowning but waving. Also, the word 'curiosite' has much behind and around it, and will be considered more fully later in the book. This *envoi* forms a piece with Chaucer's practice in *envoi*-writing more generally, where layered writing enables twisting and turning perspectives to be grafted into a work, such as the so-called *Lenvoy de Chaucer* at the end of the *Clerk's Tale* as well as the ending of *Troilus*. The hiccups and gender reversals of voice in the relationships between all these interlinked texts seem to point to some internal understanding (that after all goes back as far as the troubadours) between all three poets, Chaucer, Grandson, and Gower. It involves recognizing that love language—a figure for poetic language—has a central need to undercut itself, and that to introduce the radically other perspective of the usually silent woman is a key means of achieving this. For all three poets this also involves negotiating the otherness of language: female and French have uncannily similar qualities in this debate, for both are familiar, so familiar that they can afford to be ignored, yet so strange that they suddenly also speak up and disrupt. As Gower wryly observes in *Ballade* No. 17, 'Ma dame . . . sciet langage a plentée', 17 [My lady . . . has a full command of language].[62]

[62] Christine de Pizan's use of male-female dialogues, for instance in her *Cent ballades d'amant et de dame*, develops this point in important respects.

Ballade No. 45 and 'To Rosemounde'

The last two 'events' both come from this final section of the *Cinkante Balades*. *Ballade* No. 45 is oddly placed, as I remarked earlier, in interloping as a male-voiced *ballade* in between the new short sequence of female-voiced ones. As one reads it is difficult to avoid recalling Chaucer's *To Rosamunde*. I present the most immediately recognizable parallels below:

Madame, ye ben of al beaute shryne
As fer as circled is the mapemounde,
For as the cristal glorious ye shyne (Chaucer, 1–3)
Ma dame, jeo vous doi bien comparer
Au cristall, qe les autres eslumine; (Gower, 1–2)[63]

And lyke ruby ben your chekes rounde (Chaucer, 4)
Vostre figure auci pour deviser,
La chiere avetz et belle et femeline (Gower, 7–8)[64]

It is an oynement unto my wounde (Chaucer, 7)
Car celle piere qui la poet toucher
De sa vertu reçoit sa medicine,
Si en devient plus preciouse et fine:
Ensi pour vo bounté considerer
Toutz les amantz se porront amender. (Gower, 3–7)[65]

Jeo sui constreint, ensi com de famine
Pour vous amer de tiele discipline . . . (Gower, 11–12)[66]
[Your semy voys that ye so small out twyne]
Maketh my thoght in joy and blis habounde.
So curtaysly I go with love bounde (Chaucer, 11–13)

What force might these parallels have? The one word that really stands out for its unlikely likeness is 'cristall' which is fairly rare at this date, and in insular sources is largely to be found only in Gower and Chaucer.[67] The line in Gower, 'Ma

[63] [My lady, I well ought to compare you
To crystal, that illumines the others]

[64] [In order also to describe your appearance:
You have a face that is beautiful and feminine.]

[65] [Because whoever is able to touch that stone
Through its power receives a cure,
So it becomes more precious and refined:
Thus by reflecting on your goodness,
All lovers will be able to improve themselves.]

[66] [I am constrained so strictly by famine,
To love you just as if...]

[67] References from the *MED* include (a1393) Gower *Confessio Amantis* (Frf 3) 5.5066: A Ston mor briht than a cristall Out of hir mouth..Sche let doun falle; a1425 Gower *Confessio Amantis* (Bod 902) 4.1322: The beaute of hire face schon Wel bryhtere þan þe Cristall ston. *c.*1400(?*c.*1380) *Pearl*

dame, jeo vois doi bien comparer', has some interesting links with *ballades* by Machaut and Froissart. Machaut's *Ballade* Wilk.115 (B28)=Lo203 shares this same opening line, as does his *Dit de la Harpe* and two *ballades* by Froissart.[68] Altogether the links draw on the much-rehearsed topoi of female shapeliness, love sickness, and the metaphor of constraint applied to the lover. Seemingly instigated by Machaut, this specific poetic trigger of female address passes through several French pieces as well as being turned into English. And the parallels between the Gower and the Chaucer poems seem to cluster together in enough of a critical mass and order to suggest that we have a parallel compositional sequence in each poem and not a merely coincidental collocation of images and phrases. But again, one would be hard pressed to decide who was borrowing from whom. The vividly comic extravagance of Chaucer's version could perhaps more easily be seen as a faintly satiric response to Gower's more serious metaphoric excursions than Gower's a sober rendition of Chaucer's, but these assumptions are naturally speculative and probably worth very little. Of greater importance to the larger argument of this chapter is that the language is so overlapping. That English—French boundary is almost transparent here: like the word crystal, it is both English and French and it makes little sense to claim it as either.

Ballade No. 43: Machaut, Thomas de Paien, Grandson, Froissart, Chaucer

The final example brings us back to a very large network of connections, this time not through a single refrain like '*Qui bien aime*' but through several lines, including refrains, all of which act with the generative potential of refrains.

Ballade No. 43, 'Plus tricherous qe Jason a Medée' [More treacherous than Jason to Medea], hooks to four other *ballades*, with many more in the near distance. Let me go through the complex of pieces. To find the heart of the web we need to follow the trail to Machaut. First, then, Gower's refrain '*C'est ma dolour, qe fuist ainçois ma joie*' [It is my grief, that once was my joy] is verbally close to the refrain *'Cest ma dolour et la fin de ma joie'* [It is my woe and the end/ goal of my joy] of Machaut's *Ballade* Wilk.166=Lo34 from the *Louange des dames* 'Pour Dieu vous pri que de moy vous souveingne' [For God's sake I beg you to remember me]. On the face of it the two make a contrary pairing. Machaut's song is uttered by a male lover full of wonder at his lady's beauty

(Nero A.10) 74: Dubbed wern alle þo downez sydez Wyth crystal klyffez so cler of kynde. *c.*1400(? *c.*1380) *Pearl* (Nero A.10) 159: I se3..A crystal clyffe.

[68] Nos. 17 and 35 in Baudouin, ed. and two Cypriot-French *ballades* (Earp, *Machaut: A Guide*, 333). For Machaut's lyrics I follow Earp in that 'Lo' numbers refer to the numbers assigned by Chichmaref, *Poésies lyriques*, 'Wilk' to those by Wilkins, ed., *Louange des Dames*. (See bibliographical note, p. xiv.)

and shyly insisting on his loyalty and sincerity: 'Ne penz ja pour ce que je me feingne/D'amer' [Do not think that it is because I feign love]. The refrain expresses the classic simultaneous pain and joy of his as yet unrequited condition. Gower's slight change of grammar as well as voice ('*qe fuist ainçois*') speaks volumes: the pain and joy are now put into a temporal sequence with female joy cruelly turned to pain by male treachery.

But it is through its opening line that Gower's 'Plus tricherous qe Jason a Medée' links up most widely with other *ballades*. A first port of call is Froissart's 'Ne quier veoir Medee ne Jason' [I have no wish to see Medea or Jason]. From here we find the concatenating 'Ne quier vëoir la biauté d'Absalon'. This *ballade* by Machaut turns out to be one of a pair set into the *Voir Dit*, in which the other, ascribed to Thomas de Paien, has been built round the same refrain: '*Je voi assez, puis que je voi ma dame*' ['I see enough when I see my lady']. This refrain brings us back full circle to Froissart whose 'Ne quier veoir Medee ne Jason' also shares this refrain: '*Je voi assés, puis que je voi ma dame*'. In yet another direction, this refrain turns out to exist in English '*My lady cometh, that al this may disteyne*' as the refrain to Chaucer's *ballade* 'Hyd, Absolon, thy gilte tresses clere'.[69] The links between the Machaut and de Paien *ballades*, Froissart, and Chaucer are well known, and have been discussed by various commentators, perhaps most thoroughly by James Wimsatt.[70] The connection with Gower, however, has attracted rather less notice, and although Fisher and, following him, Yeager, have put Gower and Grandson together, the further links with the rest were not part of either of their arguments.

Once more, the purpose of the discussion here is to try to clarify the nature of the textual relationships. Are any of them sources? Imitations? Translations? Witting or unwitting participators in a common trope? In what terms are they best discussed?

It is possible, as ever, to discern several types of relation. Machaut's *ballade* pairing with Thomas de Paien is the clearest instance of a planned partnership. It is an unusual instance in the *Voir Dit* of a double *ballade*: the first, which has 'Thommas' in the margin of several of the manuscripts, is immediately followed by 'Response G. de Machau': each has the same refrain, the same rhyme scheme, and, most remarkably, a combined musical setting.[71] I give here the first stanza of each:

[69] According to Fisher, *John Gower*, 76, there is a further parallel to Gower's first line in Grandson's 'Ho doulce Yseult, qui a la fontaine/Avec Tristan, Jason et Medea'. This couplet is actually part of Balade 77, p.379, lines 17–18, 'Se Lucresse, la, tresvaillant romaine'.

[70] Wimsatt, *Chaucer and His French Contemporaries*, 181–2. It must be noted, however, that he gets the attributions the wrong way round.

[71] *Le Livre du Voir Dit*, ed. P. Imbs and J. Cerquiglini-Toulet (Paris: Librairie Générale Française, 1999), 6421–44; 6445–68; 6494–517.

Balade

Thommas

Quant Theseüs et *Hercules* et *Jason*
Chercherent tout et terre et mer parfonde
Pour accroistre leur pris et leur renon
Et pour vëoir bien tout l'estat du monde,
Moult furent digne d'onnour;
Mais quant je voi de biauté l'umble flour
Assevis suit de tout, si que, *par m'ame,*
Je voi assez, puis que je voi ma dame.
(6421–8)

[When Theseus, Hercules, and Jason
Travelled all over the earth and the deep ocean
To increase their valor and renown
And see the whole condition of the world,
They were greatly worthy of honor.
But when I see beauty's humble flower,
I am so fully satisfied that by my soul
I see enough, when I see my lady].

Balade, et y a chant

Response G. de Machau

Ne quier vëoir la biauté *d'Absalon,*
Ne de Ulixes le sens et la faconde,
Në esprouver la force de Sanson,
Ne regarder, que Dalida le tonde,
Ne cure n'ai par nul tour
Des ieus Argus ne de joie grignour,
Car pour plaisance et sans aÿde *d'ame*
Je voi assez, puis que je voi ma dame.
(6445–52)

[I do not seek to look upon Absalom's beauty
Or the cunning and eloquence of Ulysses,
Or to test the strength of Samson,
Or to see Delilah cut his hair.
I give no thought at all
To the eyes of Argus or to greater joy,
Since for pleasure and without help from anyone
I see enough, when I see my lady.

Because they are set into a narrative poem we learn more than usual about the (alleged) circumstances of their composition. Toute Belle remarks, for instance, in a letter (No. 38) that she prefers Guillaume's poem. This plays up to what is evidently a competitive, *puy*-like challenge, in which, as Guillaume describes in

Letter 35, the poet who goes first has the advantage because he is able to cream off the best choice of rhymes ('il fist devant et prinst toute la graisse du pot a son pooir, et je fis après: si en jugerés s'il vous plaist, mais vraiement il havoit l'avantage de trop', p. 572 [he went first and creamed off as much fat from the pot as he could, and I came after: judge if you wish, but he really had the advantage by far]) In a sense they are entirely equivalent pieces. On the same theme, and using a tightly prescribed framework of rhymes, each simply chooses slightly different rhetorical routes towards each repetition of the refrain. The two together present a beautifully clear illustration of the sense of shape and space of a fourteenth-century *ballade*: to borrow the Pygmalion metaphor used in Machaut's second stanza, they provide an almost palpable sense of form that can be moulded into slightly different figurations, caught in the simultaneity of a single musical period that encompasses both texts.

Froissart's *ballade* develops this in a very similar direction: but the first oddity is that its hybrid text is much closer to each separately than either is to the other. Froissart starts with the same anaphoric gesture as Machaut, 'Ne quier veoir', but with a classical reference partly taken from Paien in that he substitutes Medea and Jason for Absalon:

Ne quier veoir Medee ne Jason,
Ne trop avant lire ens ou mapemonde,
Ne le musique Orpheüs ne le son,
Ne Hercules qui cerqua tout le monde,
Ne Lucresse qui tant fu bonne et monde,
Ne Penelope ossi, car, par saint Jame,
Je voi assés, puis que je voi ma dame.[72]

[I do not seek to see Medea or Jason,
Or read too much into the map of the world,
Or the music of Orpheus or its sound,
Or Hercules, who travelled all over the world,
Or Lucretia, who was so good and pure,
Or even Penelope, for by Saint James
I see enough when I see my lady.]

He keeps the gesture going for the whole stanza (Ne . . . Ne . . . Ne . . .), (he uses rhyme royal rather than their eight-line structure), and most strikingly repeats 'Ne quier veoir' at the start of each stanza. A further exact correspondence occurs in lines 3–4 of the third stanza which are the same as lines 1–2 of Machaut's second stanza:

Ne l'ymage que fist Pymalion,
Qui n'eut parel premiere ne seconde (Froissart, 17–18)
[D]e l'ymage que fist Pymalion
Elle n'avoit pareille ne seconde; (Machaut, 6453–4)

[72] Froissart, *Ballade* No.6, *Ballades et Rondeaux*, ed. R. S. Baudouin (Geneva and Paris: Droz, 1978).

[Nor do I wish to see the image Pygmalion made,
Who had no equal or near equal;]

Yet even with such discipline in the versification and rhetorical patterning, Froissart's poem shows wonderful freedom with the classical references. Pegasus in the third stanza takes off ecstatically, an image which exactly represents the underlying combination contained by the poem of tight verbal contact with the double *ballade* and soaring, expansive, allusive flights.[73] Chaucer's 'Hyd Absolon' picking up from Froissart the rhyme royal and the refrain (slightly modified) has the same device of a rhetorical anchor ('hyd . . . ') that echoes throughout the poem. At the same time, he borrows Froissart's freedom with classical names, pouring off pair after pair of passionate, often wronged women (though beginning with Absalon and Jonathan):

Herro, *Dido*, Laudomia, alle yfere,
And *Phillis*, hangyng for thy *Demophoun*,
And Canace, espied by thy chere,
Ysiphile, betrayed with *Jasoun*,
Maketh of your trouthe neythir boost ne soun;
Nor Ypermystre or Adriane, ye tweyne:
My lady cometh, that al this may disteyne.

(Chaucer, *Prologue* to the *Legend of Good Women*, F, 263–9)

The composition gives the powerful impression, once more, of a stable framework in which substitution is the main creative impetus. It is tempting to connect this practice with two of the poems by 'Ch': 'Humble Hester' and 'Venez veoir', the first of which has a stanza apostrophizing famous women and the second of which is structured upon a strict anaphoric sequence so that the first four stanzas of this chant royal are each built incrementally upon the phrases 'Venez veoir', 'Avisez bien', 'Ymaginez', and 'C'est' respectively.

This particular group of *ballades* (by Machaut, Froissart, and Chaucer) shows such strong internal links that one feels fairly confident as a reader of the moments of reaction back and forth between them. Gower's and Grandson's, in having slightly more glancing points of contact, in a sense make the discussion even more interesting because we are required to scrutinize the terms of comparison more closely. Fastening on Gower: what exactly does his poem share with any of the others? One feature is the rhetorical anchor (Plus . . . que . . .) used like Froissart and Chaucer to structure a whole stanza; another is his own freedom with the classical references. Although he is illustrating a new point of view, that of the spurned lady,

[73] J. Cerquiglini-Toulet, 'Démembrement et dévoration: une structure de l'imaginaire poétique de Jean Froissart', in O. Bombarde, ed., *Froissart dans sa forge…* (Paris: Académie des Inscriptions et Belles-Lettres, 2006), 91–103.

this is set in motion by the same choice of lovers as in Froissart (Jason and Medea). One difference, however, may be found in Gower's addition of an *envoi.*

We may still feel, though, that the Jason and Medea allusion is not quite enough to bring Gower's work in this *ballade* fully into focus against the other examples. How specifically does it refer to any of these other instances? Is it not the kind of reference that is so widely shared that it cannot be exactly attributable to any one poet? Fisher, for instance, is dismissive: 'in the context of the tradition, such verbal echoes as these are trifling'.[74] In the case of Machaut, for example, one trips over further references almost without looking to Absalon (ll.2138–9) and Medea and Jason (letter 40) in the narrative of the *Voir Dit*; or in the poems of 'Ch', as in 'Fauls Apyus' and 'Humble Hester'.[75] One of the *Traitié ballades* (No. 8) is focused entirely on the myth. Their very commonness seems to tell against an argument that Gower is citing anyone in mentioning them as well. Yet is not Fisher's objection itself tellingly contradictory? It is precisely the sense of a tradition that makes verbal echoes significant. There is a paradox, once more, for any echo sets up a notion that the prior textual sound was worth hearing and recalling: a tradition is no more than such a process writ large. At what point, then, an echo becomes trivial is moot: one might argue in reverse that the echo can only become more resonant the more frequently it sounds.

Further investigation into Machaut's creative practices reveals rampant cross-reference, self-citation, and repetition of all kinds on a grand scale. His *Ballade* 33, 'Nes qu'on porroit' [No more than one could . . .], is a tissue of citations built up from the preceding letters and narrative of the *Voir Dit.*[76] To take only the *Louange des Dames,* many refrains and first lines are shared among the lyrics. For instance, line 1 of Rondeau Wilk. 221=Lo168 *'Dame de moy tres loyaument amée'* [Lady very loyally loved by me] is the same as line 1 of *Ballade* Wilk.33=Lo100: 'Dame de moy tres loyaument amée'; and, reaching out further to other works and other authors, Chant Royal no.7=Lo48 and Pennsylvania MS Codex 902, No. 115, fol. 33b have the same opening line 'Se trestuit cil qui sont et ont esté' [If all those who are and have been] as a *ballade* by Le Mote in his *Parfait du paon.* Ballade Wilk.115 (B28)= Lo103 has the same opening line as his *Dit de la Harpe* and 2 ballades by Froissart: 'Je puis trop bien ma dame comparer' [I can compare my lady too well];[77] it has further links with two Cypriot-French ballades. *Ballade* Wilk.92=Lo53 has the same opening as a ballade by Graunson (Piaget, No.26, p. 277), and Machaut's own motet M12 'Helas! Pour quoy virent onques mi oueil' [Alas! Why do my eyes never see].[78] *Ballade* Wilk.181=Lo162 has a similar opening line 'Se Diex me doint de ma dame

[74] Fisher, *John Gower,* 76.

[75] Wimsatt, *Chaucer and the Poems of 'Ch',* No. V, 20, lines 27 and 32; and No. IX, 32, line 3. See also 'Dur Moïses', 44, lines 9–10. This is hardly an exhaustive list.

[76] Butterfield, 'The Art of Repetition'.

[77] Earp, *Machaut: A Guide,* 333. See the discussion of Gower ballade No. 45 above.

[78] Earp, *Machaut,* 326.

joïr' [If God would give me my lady to enjoy] as a *ballade* in Penn, fol.26a 'Se dieu me doint de vostre amour jouir'. As for refrain connections: two rondeaux, Wilk. 270=Lo68 and Wilk.271=Lo247 share the refrain '*Se vos courrous me dure longuement*' [If your anger endures long against me], as do two *ballades* Wilk.148=Lo61 'Nuls ne me doit d'ore en avant reprendre' [No one must from now on blame me] and *Ballade* Wilk.155=Lo38 'On verroit maint amant desesperer' [One would see many lovers despair], which share the refrain '*Loyal amour et ma dame sans per*' [Loyal love and my matchless lady]. In a larger complex, the refrain of *Ballade* Wilk.77=Lo5 'Gent corps, faitis, cointe, apert et joli' [Noble figure, well-formed, elegant, open and honest, and pretty] (which is also cited in the *Voir Dit*) '*Qu'autre de vous jamais ne quier amer*' [that any other than you I do not seek to love] is the same as that of 'De toutes flours' [Of all flowers]=B31 '*Autre après li ja mais avoir ne quier*' [any other after this one I will never have or desire] and as that of Wilk.209=Lo225 '*Qu'autre de li jamais avoir ne quier*'. It is also related to the first line of a *ballade* in Turin MS L.IV.3, fol.160.[79]

Sometimes the refrain and opening lines swap positions: thus, in another cluster of pieces the refrain '*Dame, comment que vous soie lonteins*' [Lady, how may you be so far away] of Wilk.149=Lo14 'On dist souvent que longue demourée' [One often says that a long parting] is the same as the refrain of Wilk.141=Lo129 'Ne cuidiez pas que d'amer me repente' [Don't think that I repent of love]. This refrain '*Dame, comment que vous soie lonteins*' is in turn the same as the incipit of two *Ballades* Wilk.31=Lo130 and Wilk.32=Lo13; 'Dame, comment que souvent ne vous voie'/ 'Dame, comment que vous soie lonteins' . . . [Lady, how is it that I do not see you often] each of which share another refrain: *Ne me [soiez] de vostre amour lonteinne* [Do not let your love be far from me].

Likewise, line 1 of Wilk.188=Lo135 'Selonc ce que j'aim chierement' [according to the one I love dearly] is the same line as the refrain of *Ballade* Wilk.206=Lo136 'Tres douce dame debonnaire' [Very sweet, gracious lady]. Wilk.188 triggers a celebrated tour de force of citation, since in addition to the re-use of its opening line, its eighth line, 'Trop compere amours chierement' [Love compares too dearly] is the refrain of Wilk. 12=Lo137 'Amis, vostre demourée' [Friend, your stay], its fifteenth line 'Et se vo douce chiere ment' [And if your sweet appearance lies] is the refrain of Wilk. 34 =Lo138 'Dame, de tous biens assevie' [Lady, perfected in all good qualities] and finally line 20 'Onques amour ne fu si chiere' [Love was never so dear] is the refrain of Wilk.49=Lo139 'Douce dame, je vous requier mercy' [Sweet lady, I beg mercy of you]. In what seem to be quite random repetitions, individual lines buried within stanzas will turn up again in another *ballade*, such as line 8 'car je suis cils qui cuer et corps ottri' [for I am he who has granted his heart and body] of Wilk. 49 =Lo139 'Douce dame, je vous requier mercy' [Sweet lady, I beg mercy of you]

[79] See A. Piaget, *Oton de Grandson sa vie et ses poésies* (Lausanne: Librairie Payot, 1941), 291; Earp, *Machaut: A Guide*, 258.

which turns up as line 17 of Wilk. 39=Lo144 'Dame, pour Dieu, ne metez en oubli' [Lady, for God's sake, do not forget]; and line16 'Qui me povez dou tout faire ou deffaire' [Who can make or destroy everything in me] of Wilk.141=Lo129 'Ne cuidiez pas que d'amer me repente' [Do not think that I repent of love] which is like line 11 'Qu'elle a pooir de mi faire et deffaire' [that she has the power to make or destroy me] of Wilk.121=Lo70 'Las! J'ay failli à mon tres dous desir' [Alas! I have lost my very sweet desire]. We even find the re-use of a whole stanza, since Wilk.86=Lo121 'Helas! dolens, que porray devenir' [Alas!, wretch, what will become of me?] has the same 3rd stanza as Wilk.93= Lo127 'Hé! mesdisans, com je vous doy haïr' [Hey! Backbiter, how I must hate you] (though with a different refrain attached).

It may seem very laborious to list these examples so fully. In fact, I have barely scratched the surface. Recent work has started to uncover layers of trouvère reference in Machaut, and there are many, many more cross-references to be observed within the corpus of fourteenth-century lyric that are only newly being traced and discussed.[80] One small example: the line 'la belle qui m'a en sa prison' [the pretty one who has me in her prison] in the second stanza of Machaut's 'Ne quier veoir' [I do not ask to see] occurs in Baudouin de Condé, *Li Prisons d'amours*.[81] This kind of practice has long been observed of the later fifteenth-century and early sixteenth-century rhetoricians such as Molinet and Jean Marot.[82] It has been less clear until recent work that it extends back into the fourteenth and thirteenth centuries, and scholars are still at the early stages of developing a suitable approach to the issues which arise out of these discoveries, including the role of memory, music, and non-literate processes in establishing connections between works, authors, and audiences. Work on rhetoric in performance and on gesture has the potential to be illuminating about poetic as well as

[80] For a longer list of such correspondences, see Earp, *Machaut: A Guide*, 258–65, whose work synthesises that of Poirion, *Le Poète et le prince*, 204, 543n.127; *Louange des Dames*, ed. Wilkins, 14–16 and J. Cerquiglini, 'Le lyrisme en mouvement', *Perspectives médiévales*, 6 (1980), 75–86 and her *'Un Engin si Soutil': Guillaume de Machaut et l'écriture au XIVe siècle* (Paris: Champion, 1985), 34–37, 96–99. Such work has been developed more recently on both verbal and melodic cross-references by Plumley, 'Citation and Allusion'; E. E. Leach, 'Fortune's Demesne: The Interrelation of Text and Music in Machaut's *Il Mest Avis* (B22), *De Fortune* (B23) and Two Related Anonymous Balades', *EMH*, 19 (2000), 47–79; and J. Boogaart, 'Encompassing Past and Present: Quotations and their Function in Machaut's Motets', *EMH*, 20 (2001), 1–86; M. Bent, 'Words and Music in Machaut's Motet 9', *Early Music*, 31 (2003), 363–88; K. S. Brownlee, 'Fire, Desire, Duration, Death: Machaut's Motet 10', in S. Clark and E. E. Leach, eds, *Citation and Authority in Medieval and Renaissance Musical Culture: Learning from the Learned*, (Woodbridge: Boydell Press, 2005), 79–93; and A. Clark, 'Machaut reading Machaut: Self-borrowing and Reinterpretation in Motets 8 and 21', in Clark and Leach, eds, *Citation and Authority*, 94–101. A project entitled 'Citation and allusion in fourteenth-century French lyric and song' led by Yolanda Plumley is currently under way at the Centre for Medieval Studies at the University of Exeter (funded by the Arts and Humanities Research Council).

[81] Butterfield, *Poetry and Music*, 252–6.

[82] P. Zumthor, 'Le Carrefour des rhétoriqueurs: Intertextualité et Rhétorique', *Poétique*, 27 (1976), 317–37.

musical creative practices in the period.[83] Genres such as the motet, and in particular the *motet enté*, provide analogous examples of the intricate forms of repetition and citation so common in Machaut. The larger point in relation to Gower is that, although we may find it hard sometimes to find the literary (or musical) reasons for these densely woven references, the practice itself was clearly endemic in this genre of poetry. Gower is not making atypical moves in citing so broadly; he is acting entirely within an established international practice.

RHETORICAL CONCLUSIONS

There are many threads to pull together at the end of this discussion of Gower and Chaucer and their 'French' contemporaries. The elaborate criss-crossing of material across the late fourteenth-century lyric may speak to the growing sense for a while, particularly among Chaucerians, that source study needs fresh thinking. In trying to understand 'what Chaucer's language is', we clearly need to take account of the way it interacts with texts that are using the same stylistic language but in another language. Linear models of relationship between one lyric text and another do not seem adequate as ways of describing a level of interconnection between texts that we have seen to be so thorough-going and pervasive as often to defy specificity. It is profoundly important to be aware of the sheer density of reference in this love language. As Zumthor long ago demonstrated, this is a tightly circumscribed language, with a relatively small vocabulary.[84] For this reason, we need to find a different way of talking about it from 'original' or its converse, 'borrowed'. All of it is borrowed; none of it is original. Yet this is not even a specifically medieval condition of love language. It is true of love language transhistorically. Moreover, recognizing this does not mean that we deny ourselves the opportunity to observe very particular creative moves and reactions. The metaphor of exchange, so frequently part of the lyric language itself, is revealing of the anxieties as well as the pleasure of medieval lyric production. The formation of these *ballades* is not a case of moments of originality acting as sources for other poets, but a more collective and collusive generative impulse. Each *ballade*, or each topos behind a cluster of *ballades*, is less an individual work or works—a source and an imitation—and more a nodal cluster of ideas and linguistic phrases, core creative pools of verbal inspiration, fluid memorial 'sources' (in the classical and French meaning of fountain) in which many poets drank.

A further implication of such material is that it shows us another model of how language is exchanged. It is particularly pertinent to the larger argument of this

[83] As was evident in a stimulating workshop, led by Mary Carruthers, on 'Rhetoric and the Non-verbal Arts' on 25–26 March, 2006 in Balliol College, Oxford.

[84] Zumthor, *Essai de poétique médiévale.*

book that these examples of cross-reference pass between authors that we now categorize as English and French, but that then had a much looser identity. We have many examples here of a common language that is crossing between a wide range of cultural perspectives: from French-to-French (Machaut and Paien); English-to-English—in *French* (Froissart and Gower); Anglo/Savoyard French-to-English (Grandson and Chaucer), and English (in French)-to-English (in English) (Gower and Chaucer). There are probably more permutations to be invented even than these, but the real argument is that their very plurality undermines the attempt to categorize. Rather than start from a notion that we have two texts, an object text, and either—working backwards—its source or else—working forwards—its point of arrival in a transformed text, these ballades offer a cooperative, open text. Instead of a stable object each poem is more like a set of dynamic, reactive textual relationships. Working across different kinds of English and different kinds of French they collectively show both languages engaged in new processes of cultural formation. In short, the categories of English and French in the late fourteenth century are more porous than source study usually implies, and the linguistic and literary relationships are conducted by means of, and sometimes against the grain of, many subtle distinctions of position, status, and cultural ambition that are not adequately rendered by the single opposition English and French.

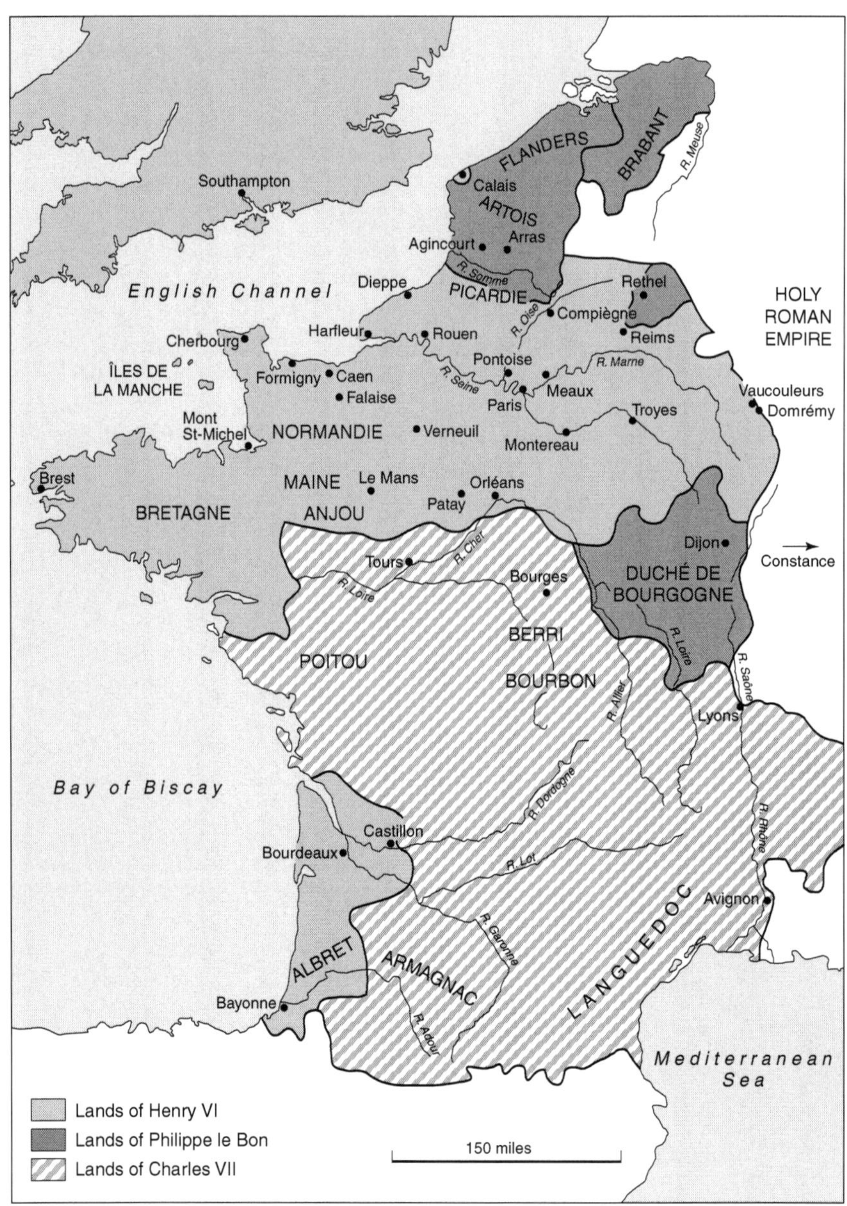

Map 3. France in 1429

PART III
VERNACULAR SUBJECTS

Part III now turns more directly to the creative frustrations and achievements of English as a medium for vernacular literature from the fourteenth century onwards.

Chapter 8, 'The English Subject', investigates the role widely ascribed to *The Book of the Duchess*, Chaucer's first surviving narrative poem, as a polemically 'English' work. It sees it instead as a poem steeped in multilingualism, both on Chaucer's own part as a professional civil servant and francophone reader, and also as the product of centuries of Anglo-French cultural interchange. Rather than see Chaucer as 'English' in resistance to 'French', we can develop a more nuanced appreciation of the ways in which cultural meanings pass from one language into another, and can be shared as well as denied or misunderstood across languages. *The Book of the Duchess* is compared not just with its direct models by Machaut and Froissart, and the older *Rose*, but with the transpositions of Boethius via Boccaccio and the tradition of thirteenth-century French romance represented by Jean Renart, in *Troilus and Criseyde*. What has been conventionally heralded by modern critics as the new subjectivity of Chaucer's love vision is reassessed in terms of an overt, and long-standing debate about English and its capacity to express a discourse of subjective desire in the face of French's acknowledged subtlety. The chapter concludes with Charles d'Orléans, perhaps the most riven example of a vernacular subject in English literary history, an exile and royal prisoner, writing in a borrowed vernacular as well as his own, fated to survive, poetically, in a shadowy interwar zone of linguistic hybridity.

Chapter 9, 'Mother Tongues', in conscious debate with the notion of 'Father Chaucer', considers the underlying role of women in the inheritance and propagation of vernacular languages. It reassesses the evidence for the status of English through historical and linguistic evidence and such contemporary supporters of English as Higden and Trevisa, by setting it alongside the growing importance of French as a language required by the English in their renewed assertion of rule in France. Through a detailed discussion of two works, a remarkable fifteenth-century teaching document, known as the *Femina nova*, in which a teacher of French has revised an earlier treatise by Walter Bibbesworth, and the dialogues known as the *Manières de Langage*, it considers the increased cultural importance attached to French by the efforts to teach it using the apparatus of Latin grammar. It goes on to review contemporary writings about English in the shape of the rising genre of the vernacular prologue, with special attention to Usk and such ideologically charged words as 'symple' and 'straunge', and sets this in the context of a wider discourse about mother tongues. Finishing with Christine de Pizan, a spokeswoman in the later stages of the war for female participation in the powerful culture of poetic exchange sketched in previous chapters, and her translator into English, William Caxton, the chapter argues that both English and French are caught up in a conflictual set of associations between the vernacular and the value of natural as against artificial languages.

Chapter 10, 'Betrayal and Nation', concludes the book by moving on still further, first into the atmosphere of tortured and torturous recrimination of a fractured France under fifteenth-century English rule, and then, irresistibly, to Shakespeare. Following on from Christine de Pizan, it centres firstly on the extraordinary figure she championed, Jeanne d'Arc. Undoubtedly the single most celebrated symbol of Anglo-French rivalry, her story, occurring as it does in the last stages of the Hundred Years War, and also in a period where early modern historians have conventionally sought to locate the birth of nationhood, is riven with contradiction. Negotiating between the volatile identities of the French and the English, Jeanne's own volatile identity epitomizes a period in which conflicting pressures were placed both on individual and collective allegiance. Her life has particular interest for the topic of this book in the way its various contemporary narrative and legal representations demonstrate the intricate processes of retrospection. Reclaimed repeatedly for different ideological ends, her story offers a remarkable insight into the contradictions and ironies of nationalist assertion. It also pays attention to the way the story's original location in uneducated female speech has passed into French national history.

If Jeanne represents the archetype of national betrayal, Shakespeare, finally, acts as the archetype of postmodern Englishness. I examine how his use of Henry V's marriage to articulate a drama of nation has proved infinitely appropriable to modern histories of English and Englishness. Just as Chaucer has been used retrospectively to create an incipient Englishness well before its time, so Shakespeare's French Catherine has served all too easily (for the English) as a type of subservient Frenchness to an inflated English patriotism. Yet in both writers we see an embedded history of powerfully creative linguistic friction that bears witness to the contrariness of the categories of 'English' and 'French' throughout the medieval period, and well beyond.

8
The English Subject

For many readers, Chaucer's *The Book of the Duchess* marks the moment when literary English was born. Inescapably, however, this makes English a product of French. The *Duchess* has long seemed to possess a special originary status because it is Chaucer's first surviving narrative poem. Chaucer's birth as a narrative poet, the birth of the English love narrative, and the birth of English literary history all coalesce. That the poem starts with 'I', again for the first time in an English love narrative, makes an even more powerful statement of English assertion: here, now, the first English poet makes his first utterance. I show this 'I' in one of the three surviving later fifteenth-century manuscripts, in this case Fairfax 16 (see Fig. 7). But intertwined with such claims lurks an awareness of how deeply the *Duchess* relies on French models. The poem represents the first encounter not just of Chaucer but of any English poet with first-person French love narrative. Paradoxically a French tradition determines this very English event. The *Book of the Duchess* thus represents a key instance in, and yet simultaneously a stumbling block to, any attempt to yoke Chaucer to Englishness.

I want to ponder this strange cross-cultural situation from various points of view, beginning with the notion of origin as it attaches to the *Book of the Duchess.* Many Chaucer scholars seem to have found the presence of French in this primal history of English literature not only awkward but in need of repudiation. Gayle Margherita, in her study, *The Romance of Origins: Language and Sexual Difference in Middle English Literature,* was one of the first to take a psychoanalytic approach to the *Book of the Duchess* and literary fatherhood. For Margherita, the *Book of the Duchess* represents the site of 'originary fantasies'. Chaucer is creating through it 'an ideological intervention on behalf of a national vernacular that was finally gaining ascendency'. The moment of origin, then, occurs in Chaucer's desire to create 'a specifically English literary tradition that might rival that of the continent'. Since 'the *Duchess* is in fact a mélange of conventional moments borrowed from Machaut, Froissart, and Guillaume de Lorris', it is Chaucer's 'appropriation and "Englishing" of these conventional texts' that marks the moment of his attempt to found a patrilinear tradition. In this reading, the French texts serve as the object of rejection as Chaucer makes a conscious decision to inaugurate a new literary line.[1]

[1] G. Margherita, *The Romance Origins: Language and Sexual Difference in Middle English Literature* (Philadelphia: University of Pennsylvania Press, 1994), 85.

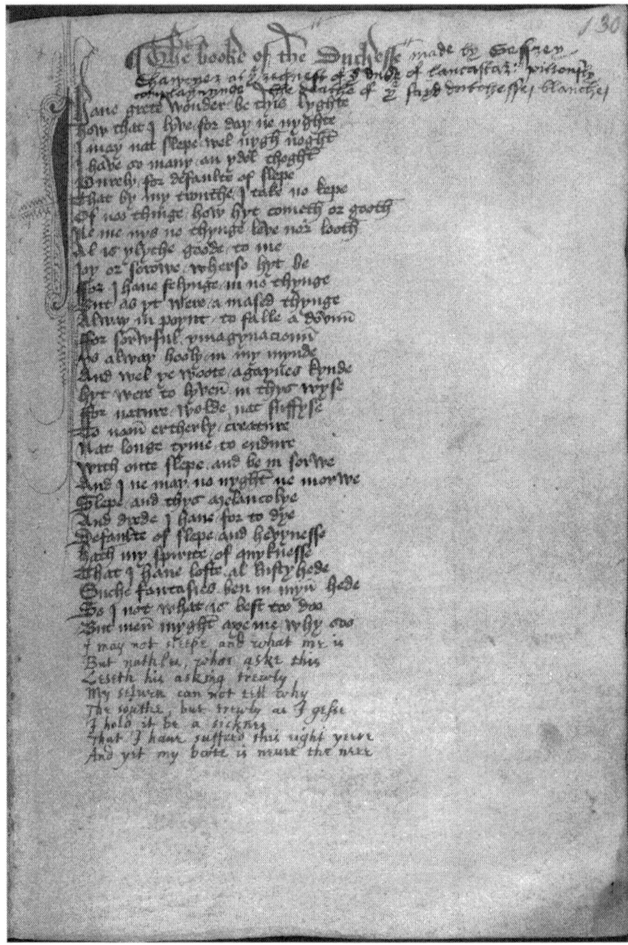

Figure 7. Chaucer, *Book of the Duchess*: opening lines

Oxford Bodleian Library, MS Fairfax 16, fol.130r. Copyright Bodleian Library: reproduced with permission.

Steven B. Davis, although more sympathetic in principle to French writing, takes this point even further. He argues that it was Chaucer himself who conspired to create a negative image of French poetry in order to assure his 'own authority as fons et origo': 'Chaucer defined for the English a French poetic tradition that shall hereafter seem two-dimensional, narrow in scope and appeal, lacking serious historical reference, read primarily for diversion not reflection.'[2] This intriguing suggestion blames not the insensitivity of modern readers, but

[2] S. Davis, 'Guillaume de Machaut, Chaucer's *Book of the Duchess*, and the Chaucer Tradition', *The Chaucer Review*, 36 (2002), 391–405 (403, 395, 402).

Chaucer's own calculated shaping of his heritage for the modern failure to give Machaut and Froissart their due. In short, it is our sensitivity as readers of Chaucer that has led us to undervalue Machaut. Milder versions of these arguments are pandemic in Chaucer criticism. The tension between a desire to promote the *Duchess* as English and original and yet to see it as French and derivative can be perceived in two further widespread responses to the poem. Those who admire it see it as a work which manages to 'transform' its sources. Barry Windeatt perhaps puts it most overtly:

> Knowledge of the French poems that were in Chaucer's mind should not diminish admiration for Chaucer's originality simply understood, but can focus attention on the sphere in which his originality really operates, by laying bare to us some of the process of co-ordinating, extending, crystallizing, by which Chaucer's imagination sees how much more he can do with the materials left by the French poets.[3]

We must overcome any 'tinge of disappointment' in discovering a line from Chaucer to be not original but one translated from Machaut or Froissart and instead decide that his 'essential originality' remains undimmed because he is able to work so much more creatively than the French poets were able to do with the same materials. Alternatively, there is a view of the poem from Wolfgang Clemen onwards as brilliant in places but often rough and immature, exhibiting in its youthfulness characteristics that Chaucer later improved and refined. Here, even more easily, the French sources are taken to be part of this early phase, and by extension an inferior kind of writing from which Chaucer learnt to move on.[4]

It is odd, given how quick medieval scholars are in other circumstances to insist on its anachronism, that this marked strain of post-romantic versions of originality should linger in so many discussions of the *Book of the Duchess*. From the straightforward equations of original with 'individual' and 'creative' to the more sophisticated psychoanalytic connections of original to 'originary fantasies' there is a powerful desire to explain Chaucer's achievement in this poem as a form of battle of the books. Ultimately, it seems to be a matter of thinly disguised English/Germanic amour propre determined to win through against the French.

But the tension here, to reiterate, is that Chaucer is *not* being original. As the earliest scholarship on Chaucer's reading discovered, and Charles Muscatine and James Wimsatt have classically demonstrated, the *Book of the Duchess* is a mosaic of citations and larger structural borrowings, principally from the *Roman de la Rose*, Guillaume de Machaut, and Jean Froissart, but also from a wide range of other French authors from Watriquet de Couvin to Jean de le Mote.[5] More particularly, even that opening 'I' is a translation:

[3] B. A. Windeatt, ed. and trans., *Chaucer's Dream Poetry: Sources and Analogues* (Cambridge: D. S. Brewer, 1982), x.

[4] W. Clemen, *Chaucer's Early Poetry*, trans. C. A. M. Sym (London: Methuen, 1963).

[5] On the older scholarship, see Windeatt's bibliography in *Chaucer's Dream Poetry;* C. Muscatine, *Chaucer and the French Tradition: A Study in Style and Meaning* (Berkeley:

I have gret wonder, be this lyght,
How that I lyve . . .

(lines 1–2)

This, as Wimsatt's sterling studies have made deeply familiar, is the start of Froissart's *Le Paradys d'amour*:

Je suis de moi en grant mervelle
Comment tant vifs . . .

(lines 1–2)[6]

I marvel greatly at how I stay alive . . .

Neither the core material of the *Duchess* nor its first person statement of Englishness is thus original to Chaucer. Indeed, Chaucer's 'I' is less emphatic than the more explicitly nationalist statement by John Gower at the end of his *ballade* sequence *Traitié pour essampler les amantz marietz*:

Jeo sui Englois, si quier par tiele voie
Estre excusé;[7]

[I am English, and seek in this way to be excused.]

But Gower's *Traitié* has proved even harder to reconcile with a notion of Englishness than the *Duchess*: to say *in French* that one is English has not seemed relevant to anyone seeking to locate the origin of English literature and so Gower's remark has been quietly ignored, along with Henry of Lancaster's equally counter-cultural 'jeo sui engleis [et n'ai pas moelt hauntee le franceis]'.[8] Nonetheless, English was evidently not the only language in the late fourteenth century in which to think of oneself as English, and this further undermines the unique status of Chaucer's 'I'.

University of California Press, 1957) and J. I. Wimsatt, *Chaucer and the French Love Poets* and *Chaucer and his French Contemporaries: Natural Music in the Fourteenth Century* (Toronto: University of Toronto Press, 1992). *The Literary Background of 'The Book of the Duchess'* (Chapel Hill: University of North Carolina Press, 1968).

[6] Jean Froissart, *Le Paradis d'Amour*, *L'Orloge amoureus*, ed. P. Dembowski TLF, 339 (Geneva; Avoz, 1986) J. I. Wimsatt, *Chaucer and the French Love Poets: The Literary Background of 'The Book of the Duchess'* (Chapel Hill: University of North Carolina Press, 1968), 118–33 and *Chaucer and His French Contemporaries*, 174–209.

[7] John Gower, *The Complete Works*, ed. G. C. Macaulay, 4 vols, (Oxford: Clarendon Press, 1899–1902), vol. 1: *The French Works*, 391.

[8] *Le Livre de Seyntz medicines: The Unpublished Devotional Treatise of Henry of Lancaster*, ed. E. J. Arnould (Oxford: Basil Blackwell, 1940). This remark forms part of the apologia in the Epilogue (239). It is important not to take its self-deprecation at face value, since Henry's treatise shows high linguistic competence (see further, W. Rothwell, 'Henry of Lancaster and Geoffrey Chaucer: Anglo-French and Middle English in Fourteenth-Century England', *MLR*, 99 (2004), 313–27).

It might be objected that all this is to miss the point. Surely the *Duchess* is a key text in the history of English precisely because Chaucer decided to write it *in English*. Unlike Gower, moreover, Chaucer appears to have made an exclusive linguistic choice. I remarked in Chapter 1 that this is not a counter-argument because it imputes to 'English' an identity that needs re-examining. This chapter returns to that remark to bring to the surface the implications of that re-examination. It seeks to re-evaluate the significance of Chaucer's choice of English by continuing to explore how far Englishness includes Frenchness. I will be arguing, first, that English was not the exclusive choice it appears to be but a language that collaborated at a deep level with the dominant *lingua franca* of French. But second, this collaboration was complicated by the diversity of French: as a homely as well as foreign language for Chaucer, his relationship to French cannot have been one of either straightforward acceptance or rejection. This will take me, third, to issues of linguistic subjectivity and, fourth, carrying on from the last chapter, translation. How far, in short, does Chaucer's choice of English represent some kind of fashioning of an 'English' literary self and how do we reconcile this with the complexly double vernacularity that he and his poetic contemporaries experienced and practised? Finally, discussion of 'the English subject' will turn to Charles d'Orléans, perhaps the most conflicted example of a vernacular subject in English literary history, to glance ahead at the linguistic privations of an exile and royal prisoner, writing, in a reverse direction from Chaucer, an English that was for him a homely and foreign vernacular of both lesser and greater fluency than his own.

THE *BOOK OF THE DUCHESS* AND THE ASSERTION OF ENGLISH

It may seem odd to have postponed the topic of Chaucer's Englishness this far in a book entitled *The Familiar Enemy*. There are arguments for postponing it even further. For as I have tried to show, the need to unravel the assumptions behind Chaucer's Englishness runs so deep that it might be better to avoid saddling him with the notion altogether. This chapter will continue to seek to denaturalize 'English', all the more as the word comes into close contact with Chaucer. It cannot agree with Thorlac Turville-Petre's assertion that the absence 'of national feeling or sense of national identity' that Derek Pearsall finds in Chaucer 'indicates that the battle for English that preoccupied writers early in the century had been won'.[9] It argues, by contrast, that Chaucer and his English

[9] T. Turville-Petre, 'Afterword', in K. Lavezzo, ed., *Imagining a Medieval English Nation* (Minneapolis: University of Minnesota Press, 2004), 340–6 (341).

contemporaries and immediate followers were all too aware of the humble status of this vernacular and indeed that this consciousness permeated English culture for perhaps at least two further centuries. The absence of linguistic jingoism in Chaucer comes not from comfortable security in English's internationalism but quite the reverse, from realizing that English could never achieve cultural status in its own right without seeking to participate as fully as it could in the dominant *lingua franca* of French.

As the previous chapter has argued, love poetry, in particular, was a public, international, collective, and openly generative activity. This can be demonstrated by a closer look at the 'je' from Froissart's *Paradys* that underlies Chaucer's 'I'. For Froissart, too, is innovating. French chroniclers began to use 'je' (as opposed to the third-person 'cil') in their prologues from around 1300:[10]

> je, Jehan sire de Joyngville, seneschal de Champaigne, faiz escrire . . .
>
> [I, John, Lord of Joinville, seneschal of Champagne, cause to be written . . .][11]

> Je, Guillaume Guiart,
> D'Orliens né, de la Guillerie
> . . .
> Ai ci en cest mien romans mise
> M'entente a trouver.

[I, Guillaume Guiart, born in Orleans, . . . have here put my intention to compose in this vernacular [narrative].][12]

By contrast, the use of 'je' to start a narrative *dit* is far rarer until the late fourteenth century and again, though no doubt this is another hostage to fortune, I cannot find an earlier example than the *Paradys*.[13] Importantly, Froissart is not

[10] C. Marchello-Nizia, 'L'Historien et son prologue: forme littéraire et stratégies discursives', in D. Poirion, ed., *La Chronique et l'histoire au moyen âge: colloque des 24 et 25 mai, 1982*, Cultures et civilisations médiévales II (Paris: Presses de l'Université de Paris-Sorbonne, n.d.), 13–25.

[11] *Jean de Joinville: Mémoires ou Vie de saint Louis*, ed. J. Monfrin (Paris: Garnier Flammarion, 1998).

[12] *Branche des Royaux Lignages, Chronique métrique de Guillaume Guiart*, ed. J. A. Buchon, Collection des chroniques nationales françaises, 7 (Paris: Verdière, 1828), 6 (lines 30–1, 33–4). See also lines 485–92: 'Je, qui tant sui povres oms, ose/Emprendre si pénible chose...' ['I, who am such a humble man, dare to undertake so laborious a thing'].

[13] My reference set includes Rutebeuf, Watriquet de Couvin, Baudouin, and Jean de Condé, Jehan de le Mote, Adam de la Halle, Jehan Acart de Hesdin, Guillaume de Machaut, and numerous thirteenth-century narratives. The one precedent I have (so far) found occurs in 'C'est de la Povretei Rutebeuf', 2:420 (lines 1–2): 'Je ne sai par ou je coumance / Tant ai de matyere abondance' ['I do not know where I should begin I have so much subject-matter'], but this is a four-stanza chanson and not a narrative *dit* as such. The use of the first-person construction does occur, for example, in Jean de Meun's continuation of the *Roman de la Rose*; in Watriquet de Couvin's *Li Despis du Monde*, 155 (line 1): 'Dit vous ai d'armes et d'amours' ['I have told you of deeds of arms and of love']; in Phillippe de Remi, *Le Roman de Manekine*; and in Raoul de Houdence, *Il Roman des Eles*. But in none of these is the first word 'je'.

writing as a 'François': not only was the *Paradys* almost certainly composed in England, it is misleading, as we have discussed, to treat this celebrated Hainuyer as having 'French background' here.[14] On the contrary, the very prevalence of these subjective assertions in England across English, Anglo-French, and an imported continental French suggests that Chaucer is working *with* the grain of a larger vernacular poetic enterprise, and therefore not standing out in an independent bid to make different, special claims for Englishness.

Further evidence of the open character of the *Duchess* is written all over its allusive relationship with French writings. But as we have seen, it is vital to understand this relationship as triangular rather than binary. Chaucer's writings do not display a single relationship between two languages, English and French, but a set of relationships between several language boundaries that are played out within England as much as they are across the Channel. The dialogue between English and continental French is indeed crucial, but it cannot be studied in isolation from that between English and French within the islands (here including Ireland as well as Wales and Scotland), and between insular French and continental French across the Channel.

Before looking at some examples in detail the many issues at stake here need reiteration and further clarification in this Chaucerian context. Perhaps the most important argument first of all is that vernacular in England does not mean only English. It has become an almost completely shared practice in current medieval scholarship to use the word 'vernacular' to mean only English. But just as we have learned that we must disengage ourselves from too easy an equation between Chaucer and the rise of English, so now perhaps we are ready to see how powerfully the retrospective image of Chaucer as 'English' has repressed any desire to recognize that he was not working only with English. He was also engaged with a second vernacular that was both his and the enemy's, used both within the English court and to articulate the Anglo-French war that was a constant feature throughout his lifetime (and before and beyond).

But to call this vernacular 'French' is also perhaps too easy. Allowing due status to Anglo-French in our enquiries helps us to realize that French is a plural category, with boundaries that shift and reposition themselves the longer we study them. French and Latin, in England, are not 'non-English', any more than English is straightforwardly non-French. That instinct to separate, in a sense a casualty of modern lexicographical practice, must be resisted and questioned at every opportunity.[15] It is important to add that this argument applies equally to

[14] See J. Devaux, 'From the Court of Hainault to the Court of England: The Example of Jean Froissart', in C. Allmand, ed., *War, Government and Power in Late Medieval France (Power in Late Medieval France)* (Liverpool: Liverpool University Press, 2000), 1–20.

[15] An approach everywhere demonstrated in J. N. Adams, *Bilingualism and the Latin Language* (Cambridge: Cambridge University Press, 2003).

continental French. There is no norm or standard of Parisian French until the use of French in the *chancellerie royale* began to increase dramatically in the fourteenth century, and the influence of French was so wide, from what is now the Netherlands and Belgium down to the Languedoc and Italy and east into the Mediterranean and beyond, that many kinds of French were in use.[16] Italian, likewise, as Dante implicitly reveals in his *De vulgari eloquentia*, had no common spoken form until reunification in the late nineteenth century.

ENGLISH AND FRENCH SUBJECTS

All these issues lead me to argue that we need to be alive to the moments when continental French becomes Anglo-French and then gains a newer continental French resonance, and all this in an 'English' context. Something like this happens in the *Book of the Duchess* in its connections with Machaut, Froissart, and the *Rose*. Chaucer's 'I' in the *Book of the Duchess* (after 1368) is part of a triangular relationship between the 'je' of Machaut's *La Fontaine amoureuse* (end of 1360), and that of Froissart's *Le Paradys d'amour* (1361–2). The *Fontaine amoureuse* is a highly political poem, written during the closing stages of the Treaty of Brétigny for Jean, duc de Berri who was sent to England as a hostage. It is not usually read in this way, especially in relation to Chaucer, but to recall this somewhat tense context for Machaut's work deepens our sense of the terms of linguistic exchange. Machaut's sophisticated deployment of a first-person voice throughout his poetry has received well-deserved attention: of particular remark in the *Fontaine amoureuse* is his artful intersection of the poet's 'je' and that of his patron.[17] After a brief prologue introducing the poem and his role as poet, his patron and their coded names, Machaut turns to his 'matiere'. Unable to sleep he hears through the window of his room another insomniac, at first groaning in despair at the prospect of having to part from his lady, and then reciting a complaint he has composed for her. Machaut sits at his inlaid ivory desk, takes up his pen, and transcribes the complaint, word for word. At daybreak he goes to meet the lord and they walk out to a beautiful park and rest by a marvellously carved fountain. Here the patron discovers that Machaut has copied out his complaint: he is

[16] Lusignan, *La langue des rois au Moyen Âge: le français en France et en Angleterre* (Paris: PUF, 2004), 95–153 (esp. 119–22).

[17] Classic accounts include W. Calin, *A Poet at the Fountain: Essays on the Narrative Verse of Guillaume de Machaut* (Lexington: University Press of Kentucky, 1974), K. S. Brownlee, *Poetic Identity in Guillaume de Machaut* (Madison: University of Wisconsin Press, 1984), J. Cerquiglini, *'Un Engin si Soutil: Guillaume de Machaut et l'écriture au XIVe siècle'* (Paris: Champion, 1985), and S. Huot, *From Song to Book: The Poetics of Writing in Old French Lyric and Lyrical Narrative Poetry* (Ithaca and London: Cornell University Press, 1987).

surprised and pleased to be given the poem. Almost immediately he then falls asleep, the poet follows suit, and together they dream the same dream as they realize on waking.

In this careful, clever double subjectivity Machaut and the duc both split and redouble their roles. The duc turns out to supplant the poet by composing his own complaint; this conversely makes the poet a patron since he has created the opportunity for the duc to compose. And then by sharing the dream they each usurp the lone space of a dreaming subject and make it double. Inspired by the double-authored *Roman de la Rose* and the ingenious means by which Jean de Meun both supplants and humbly submits to Guillaume de Lorris, Machaut performs a similar trick on the poet—patron relationship. The duc is allowed to speak as if in his own right but his words of complaint are given back to him by the poet, who has himself pretended that his own act of composition was really an act of transcription. So much has often been observed of the poem. But the special plangency of the *Fontaine amoureuse* is that, as a poem of war, the duke's 'je' is not that of the ordinary lover but of a hostage about to be handed over to English control. References to war abound as indeed they do in many of Machaut's writings. Near the start, the poet keeps up a steady stream of anecdotes about his own conduct in war, how fearful he is on the battlefield when enemy blows are in prospect, and how hard it is to follow one's king into 'sauvage' lands where one does not know the language:

Car le païs m'estoit sauvage
Et ne savoie le langage,
Et s'estoie certeinnement
Dalés lui plus seürement
Que long de li; . . .

(149–53)

For the country was unfamiliar to me,
And I did not know the language,
And I was certainly
Safer by his side
than far from him . . .

(pp. 96–7)[18]

This echoes a similar passage in *Le Confort d'ami*, where, along with advice on how to conduct oneself in war during truces, on treating hostages, avoiding sieges, on the importance of good spies and how to accept invasion (lines 3113–end), he comments (slightly extravagantly) on what it would be like to be a prisoner in England:

[18] Cited from Guillaume de Machaut, *Le livre de la Fontaine amoureuse* ed. and trans. J. Cerquiglini-Toulet (Paris: Stock, 1993) 1993).

Ou tu fusses en Engleterre
En prison sous clef et sous serre,
Ne peüsses venir n'aler,
Et n'eüsses a qui parler
Se n'apreïsses le langage
En ta prison et en ta cage.
Mais ce n'est pas chose legiere
De l'apenre en tele maniere. . . .

(2843–50; pp. 148–9)

[Now if you'd been in England,
Imprisoned under lock and key,
You couldn't have come or gone,
And you'd have had no one to talk to
Unless you learned the language
In your prison, in your cell.
But it's no easy thing
To learn under such circumstances. . . .][19]

Machaut's sense of the troubles of war includes an anxiety about language as a prisoner in an enemy's country: how far would one be understood?[20] More indirectly, he turns some of the familiar complaints of the troubadour crusader lyric into living metaphors of contemporary stories of separation. The phrase 'soit deça mer, soit dela mer' (1364, 821, 493, 106) or 'se je te sui lonteinne' (2287) expresses not merely a figurative longing from the past but the fear of an imminent voyage across the Channel and an exile of uncertain duration:

. . . tu as doubtance
Que jamais ne veingnes en France . . .

(*La Fontaine amoureuse*, 2320–1)

. . . a fear
That you would never return to France . . .]

As a hostage ('en ostage/ suis' 398–9), the duc will lose his sovereignty and even his subjectivity in the sense that he loses the conditions under which that notion of personal jurisdiction had political meaning. As an unwilling subject of the king of England, Jean duc de Berri, along with the other royal French princes, and of course Jean II himself, could no longer be defined in the same way. Machaut's splitting and doubling games with the first person take on a potential urgency and gravity in this light: they are not trifling with the metaphors of love

[19] Cited from Guillaume de Machaut, *Le Confort d'ami (Comfort for a Friend)*, ed. and trans. R. Barton Palmer, Garland Library, 67, Series A (New York and London: Garland, 1992).

[20] Although it is likely that Machaut travelled with the king of Bohemia to places where he did not know the language, it seems either a rhetorical sleight of hand to claim that England was in the same category or a story from the trenches.

but reveal an almost obsessive concern with the fracture and dissolution of the French princely subject created by the fiasco of Poitiers.[21]

Froissart, by contrast, had no such tensions. Living and working in England from 1362 as a protégée of Philippa of Hainault, his position at the English court was evidently warmly promoted.[22] His *Paradys d'amour* is saturated with ideas, images and rhymes from the *Fontaine amoureuse* and also from Machaut's earlier *Remede de Fortune.*[23] If Machaut's *Fontaine amoureuse* was written on the brink of the duc de Berri's departure for England, the *Paradys* was written as Froissart arrived in England. It was his first English poem. Although it ostensibly centres on the pain of a lover, the *Paradys* soon reveals itself to be a sparkling celebration of the art of lyric composition, in which the sheer pleasure of poetic virtuosity is affirmed through a range of inset lyrics. To reinforce the point that the pleasure provided by the lyrics has its own value, Froissart is assiduous in providing appreciative responses to the lyrics from within the poem. For instance, Plaisance remarks each time on the quality of the four lyrics she asks the narrator to perform:

> Sitost que lor och recordé,
> Dist Plaisance: 'Par le corps Dé,
> Moult bien me plaist en tous endrois.'
>
> (860–2)

> [As soon as I had recited (recorded it) for them,
> Pleasure said, 'By God's body,
> This pleases me greatly in every way.]

She even uses the first *rondelet* to aid her judgement of the second:

> Lors que j'euch fait, Plaisance dist:
> 'Chils rondelés bien me souffist,
> Je le prise bien autrement
> Com chils qui est fais par devant.'
>
> (897–900)

> [When I had finished, Pleasure said,
> 'This rondeau satisfies me very much;
> I have a very different appreciation of it
> From the one that was done before.']

[21] Other war references in the *Fontaine amoureuse* include: lines 923ff, 'en ostage/ suis' 398–9, 204–5, 'en la bataille' 2440ff.

[22] See the commemorative lines by Froissart on both Philippa and Blanche in his *dit, Le Joli Buisson de Jonece,* ed. A. Fourrier (Geneva: Droz, 1975), lines 231–4, 241–3, 246–50. On the date 1362, see Chapter 5, n. 61.

[23] See the list of parallels in Wimsatt, *Chaucer and the French Love Poets,* 155–62.

The standard being applied to the lyrics in these cases consists in the degree of pleasure they inspire. Froissart intends in his poem not merely to give pleasure, but to affirm a principle of pleasure.[24] The poem ends not only by gratified musings on the dream comforts of the lady's mercy but by thanking Orpheus for his help in the composition of all the songs:

> Si l'en grasci et Orpheüs,
> Qui me monstra et l'art et l'us
> De canter balade et rondiel
> Et virelay fait la nouvel
> Et le lay qui a bien maniere.
>
> (1712–16)

> [Thus I thank him and Orpheus
> Who showed me the art and the practice
> Of singing ballades and rondeaux
> And the newly-composed virelai
> And the well constructed lai.]

That quality of writing to please—both himself and his audience—also manifests itself in the frequent comments on his own newness as a writer. Such claims are frequent in the troubadours and are embedded in the practice of composing love poetry. But I think Froissart's love poetry is indeed radical and experimental in ways for which it has not always been credited. One particular feature is his use of the first person. Where Machaut develops the practice of substitution, Froissart pushes the first-person mode itself further into the spotlight. Not only does the poem start with 'Je sui de moi en grant mervelle', a boldly public introspection, but it follows this up with many other lines beginning with 'je' and revolving around 'je': in the introductory section before the *complainte* begins, six lines begin with 'je' and some of these appose this 'je' with another in the same line or same couplet:

> Pour quelle amour en ce travel
> Je sui entrés et tant je vel.
>
> (11–12)

> [For whose love I have entered
> into this suffering and lie awake so much.]

> Je ne sçai le pertuis par u,
> Je m'endormi en tells pensees
> Que chi vous seront recensees.
>
> (30–2)

[24] Compare *La Prison Amoureuse*, 273–89.

[I do not know through what chink he came in
I fell asleep in these very thoughts
That will be represented to you.]

The point is not his use of the first person per se: obviously the very genre of the *dit* can be defined as an exploration of the lyric first person in a more extended expository verse narrative form. However, we can see the difference more clearly in Froissart if we compare the opening of Machaut's *Fontaine amoureuse*:

Pour moy deduire et soulacier
Et pour ma pensee lacier
En loial amour qui me lace
En ses las, ou point ne me lasse
Car jamais ne seroie las
D'estre y, ne n'en diroie 'helas',
Vueil commencier a chiere lie . . .
(1–7)

[To delight and entertain myself,
And to lace my thoughts
In the faithful love which ties me
In its bonds (and these never tire me,
For I would never weary
Of being there, nor say 'alas')
I wish to begin with a cheerful expression . . .]

Grammatically, this is far more indirect than Froissart: not only is there a Virgilian syntactic inversion with the first clause not appearing until line 7, but the whole structure of the sentence, created to make a sounding interlace of assonance, is more like the older third-person mode of the chronicler, full of detours and sidesteps. Froissart, by contrast, gives his first person a far more active and direct function. He is not necessarily more heavily characterized than Machaut's, or dramatic; it is rather that his grammatical control is more visible and his textual manipulations more emphatic.

For many modern Chaucerian scholars, as I remarked in Chapter 1, the use of French in England in the fourteenth century is confined to 'Anglo-Norman' and is already anachronistic: English writing is defined by writing in English, and anyone writing in French is doing something inherently marginal.[25] But this leaves out the several poets writing in continental French in England, such as Jehan de le Mote, Gace de le Buigne, Othon de Grandson, and Jean de Garancières.

[25] The stringent efforts of Rothwell in a large series of articles to argue otherwise are, however, beginning to make inroads on these perspectives. See, in particular, as well as the article cited in note 8 above, 'The Trilingual England of Geoffrey Chaucer', *SAC*, 16 (1994), 45–67, and 'The Teaching and Learning of French in Later Medieval England', *Zeitschrift für französische Sprache and Literature*, 111 (2001), 1–18. Serge Lusignan's groundbreaking work is also gaining recognition.

Moreover, Froissart's special position as a *picard* writer in the English court meant that his work of this period—which includes most of his verse love narratives—has some claim to be as English as Chaucer's, even if it cannot exactly be called 'Anglo-Norman'. One might even say Froissart had a greater claim to be regarded as an English court poet, since his function as such in Philippa's household is clearly attested, in contrast to Chaucer, for whose writings we have very little evidence of patronage.[26] It was he, rather than Chaucer, for instance, who wrote an epithalamion, *Le Temple d'Honneur*, for Humphrey X of Bohun and Jeanne d'Arundel.[27] In a sense we could regard the *Book of the Duchess*, written soon after Froissart's departure from England, as Chaucer's bid to borrow his mantle.

It is unsurprising, in any case, that Chaucer should have been so influenced both by Froissart and by Froissart's own poetic mentors. My suggestion is that his opening word-for-word translation of the *Paradys* represents a complex negotiation on his part between Froissart and Machaut, an intervention in their debate about subjectivity. We might first note the dominant strand of linguistic anxiety in the *Book of the Duchess*. This anxiety takes several forms, one about his own articulacy in English, and others that include the lack of response to the abruptly terminated story of Ceyx and Alcyone as well as the cross-firing misunderstandings between the 'man in blak' and the poet's 'I'. At first sight, Chaucer does seem to be expressing the classic symptoms of cultural inadequacy:

> Me lakketh both Englyssh and wit
> For to undo hyt at the fulle
>
> (897–8)

This comment along with occasional very visible moments of translation, such as the word *attempre*:

> And ful attempre for soothe hyt was;
> For nother to cold nor hoot yt nas
>
> (341–2)

indicates that the process of Englishing is certainly self-conscious. But it would be a mistake to see this as evidence of his stumbling immaturity as a writer. In part this is because, as A. C. Spearing, amongst others, has beautifully described, such moments link together with other more profound hesitations over what words to use in response to death and the anguish of another's bereavement.

[26] For an excellent recent re-evaluation of the evidence for Froissart's relationships with his patrons, see G. Croenen, 'Froissart et ses mécènes: quelques problems biographiques', in O. Bombarde, ed., *Froissart dans sa forge...* (Paris: Académie des Inscriptions et Belles-Lettres, 2006), 9–32.

[27] *Le Paradis d'amour*, ed. P. F. Dembowski, 12. The accounts of Jeanne, Duchess of Brabant, refer to 'uni Frissardo, dictori, qui est cum regina Anglie', 15, n. 32 and 16, n. 35.

I would like to build on this by suggesting that Chaucer is working between two different models of linguistic assertion in Machaut and Froissart. Machaut (and Froissart too, of course) makes him fully aware of the cultural status of French: his subtle reinterpretation of the *Rose*'s double authority shows Chaucer a vernacular literary history of immense collaborative power of which, as yet, there is no echo in English. Chaucer's response, to translate Froissart's bold initiating 'je' is not, however, particularly humble. It is instead brilliantly ambiguous. For it does make an English statement: it appropriates that French subject as if on behalf of Edward III for new cultural ends. But it does so in the form of a translation. This English 'I' is at once new and borrowed. Chaucer is the new 'speaking' subject of an English *dit*, and a humble translator.

The word *deffaut/defaut* provides an example at close quarters of the three-way linguistic exchanges taking place. Chaucer seems obsessed by it, particularly at the start of the poem where it describes a lack of sleep:

I have so many an ydel thoght
Purely for defaute of slep (4–5)

Defaute of slep and hevynesse
Hath sleyn my spirit of quyknesse (25–6)

I had be dolven everydel
And ded, ryght thurgh defaute of slep (222–3)

Rather then that y shulde deye
Thorgh defaute of slepynge thus (240–1)

Once again, it is tempting to read this figuratively as a symptom of the poet's sense of absence, of a literary void in English that he must fill. It seems to go hand in hand with his equally obsessive use of 'nothyng' (795, 1106) or just 'thing' (869), his insistence that death is just the other side of sleeplessness, with the lack of music for the song ('a maner song/ . . . withoute song' 471–2), with the failure of the hounds to find their prey (384).[28] Was there a continental French trigger for this word? Machaut uses it twice, Froissart not at all. In Machaut it occurs near the end of the *Fontaine amoureuse* where the duc is describing his departure from France:

. . . y me faut
Demain partir sans nul deffaut
(2773–4)[29]

Here it has the precise legal meaning of the treaty: as a hostage he must leave without defaulting on the terms agreed. Is it possible that Chaucer found himself drawn to this word because it represented so perfectly the cultural cleft stick of his poetic act? For him *defaut*, an Anglo-French word with a long legal history,

[28] A further reference to 'fayle (to rekene)' occurs at line 441.
[29] See also 'Jamais deffaut' (*Fontaine amoureuse*, 802).

marked his own lack as a poet of English trying to compete with the Picard Froissart; yet it was also the one word in the *Fontaine amoureuse* which marked the new vulnerability of continental French. In the translation from continental French to English, *defaut* simultaneously means French cultural power and its concomitant English weakness, and English political power and its concomitant French weakness.

THE MONOLINGUAL TURN

Derrida's *Le monolinguisme de l'autre* is profoundly illuminating about the further complexities of this linguistic situation.[30] It is worth recalling his (somewhat tongue-in-cheek) propositions discussed in Chapter 3:

> *On ne parle jamais qu'une seule langue.*
> *On ne parle jamais une seule langue.*
>
> *[you only ever speak one language*
> *you never speak only one language]*

To which he adds a third: '*Oui, je n'ai qu'une langue, or ce n'est pas la mienne.*' ['*Yes, I only have one language, and it is not mine.*'][31]

A couple of points have particular relevance to the present discussion. One concerns the peculiar quality, as Derrida presents it, of the first-person voice and its relation to its own language ('ma langue' (47), 'l'ipséité' (32)). Derrida plays with his text's formal representation of this relation. As Jane Gilbert has astutely noted, 'it may (or may not) be significant that the quotation mark which begins halfway down the first page of text ("Je suis monolingue", 13) is never formally closed.'[32] To use a language is not necessarily to adopt a position of power towards that language. On the contrary, it may be a sign of utter submission; yet he seems to be saying that this very experience of language being 'au bord', not 'la mienne', 'ni en lui ni hors de lui' (14) makes articulation possible. That sense of being permanently forbidden to speak, forbidden to feel in one's natural element, is an all-encompassing pressure of speech:

> Le monolinguisme dans lequel je respire, même, c'est pour moi l'élément. Non pas un élément naturel, non pas la transparence de l'éther mais un milieu absolu. (13)

> The monolingualism in which I draw my very breath is, for me, my element. Not a natural element, nor the transparency of the ether, but an absolute habitat (1)

[30] J. Derrida, *Le monolinguisme de l'autre ou la prothèse d'origine* (Paris: Galilée, 1996).
[31] See Chapter 3 above, p. 98–9.
[32] J. Gilbert, 'Men Behaving Badly: Linguistic Purity and Sexual Perversity in Derrida's *Le Monolinguisme de l'autre* and Gower's *Traitié pour essampler les amantz marietz*', *Romance Studies*, 24 (2006), 88, n. 3.

This both leaves one unable to experience a distance from one's language and yet always alien from it:

> Cette structure d'aliénation sans aliénation, cette aliénation inaliénable n'est pas seulement l'origine de notre responsabilité, elle structure le propre et la propriété de la langue. (48)

> [This structure of alienation without alienation, this inalienable alienation, is not only the origin of our responsibility, it also structures the peculiarity and property of language.] (25)

This may well seem too intense a comparison to fit with Chaucer's position as a writer of English in the 1360s. But some connections may be made. Most broadly, perhaps, Derrida shows that monolingualism is a far from singular condition. Chaucer may have written in English, but English was not a single language for him, a multilingual speaker if (in terms of what has survived) a monolingual author. There was nothing isolated or autonomous about fourteenth-century written English, and to use it was to be not only profoundly aware of other languages, but also to be thinking across and among and between other languages. More intimately, Derrida reminds us of the strains and tensions involved in the politics of linguistic 'choice'. No poet in England in the later fourteenth century had only one language: yet a writer of English may well have felt that English was not 'his' language, in that it was not a language yet available as a way of uttering 'Je'.[33] Gower's 'Jeo sui Englois' speaks this with devastating succinctness. But it was not as if 'Je', at least as a way of initiating a whole written discourse, is an untroubled locution either. Froissart's 'Je', located in 'English' courtly discourse, is not exactly equivalent to Gower's 'Je' let alone to Chaucer's 'I'. All three authors speak with a subtly different boldness, each laying claim to a language that is not theirs.

For these reasons Chaucer's use of English in the *Book of the Duchess* is not a nationalist reaction against French but a profound gesture of subjectedness as well as of subjectivity. In a sense it mirrors the French position where, as we have seen, from a different political context, Jean II was forced into subjection while also being granted the courtesies of fraternal royal honour. The situation is therefore not one of English repudiation or triumph over French but rather a recognition that the asymmetries of power between French and English made each side vulnerable as well as dominant. Too much connected them to make easy gestures of superiority, whether political or cultural, either possible or desirable.

The fact that the language of origins attaches itself so readily to Chaucer means that it is easy to elide the claims of other contemporary English writing as newly 'English'. In trying to understand Chaucer's purchase on English I do not wish to imply that he was the only writer of English to engage with French internationalism in the reign of

[33] On the use of 'je' to signal vernacular poetic authority, see K. S. Brownlee, *Poetic Identity in Guillaume de Machaut* (Madison: University of Wisconsin Press, 1984).

Edward III. There is too much uncertainty over dates to know whether the *Book of the Duchess* came before Langland's earliest efforts to compose the prologue of *Piers Plowman* or, for that matter, the initial imaginative shapings of the poet of the *Gawain*-manuscript. *Piers, Pearl,* and *Sir Gawain and the Green Knight* all show considerable influence from French love narrative and *Piers* and *Pearl,* in particular, from the dream device that is prominent in the French tradition. It would be foolish to claim that Chaucer was creating an English subjectivity single-handed:[34] but, on the other hand, the detail of his work as a translator of the French *dit* and his position in successive courtly households undoubtedly meant he had especially close access to French literary modes of textual production and to the physical translation of several of their key patrons into English hands. To put it another way, he had the perspective through his international contacts to recognize how English was viewed from the continent; and this may be one reason why he was uniquely placed to reinvent it.

TRANSLATING ENGLISH

We should now reflect further on the process and detail of translation in the *Book of the Duchess.* Muscatine and Wimsatt, along with earlier twentieth-century scholars, have provided important insights into the structural and verbal debts of Chaucer to a wide range of writings, including Ovid and the Bible as well as vernacular French. This puts us in a strong position to build up further perspectives on his work as a translator. As I indicated in Chapter 7, our understanding of translation has developed in many directions from the word-for-word model with which we are most familiar, especially in relation to Chaucer's French reading. Substantial new work on biblical translation, in particular, has touched on ideas of Englishness by investigating the character and practices of Lollard efforts to broaden access to the Bible itself and to the academic discussions associated with those controversial aims.[35] In this story, as Sarah Stanbury rather wickedly put it, English is sometimes given a 'heroic agency', cast as 'a powerfully oppositional voice' to the claims of the clerical exclusivity of Latin as if employing English was 'an ethical good', as if 'English was conscious of itself' (98). In her excellent joke, Englishness becomes 'a kind of materna lingua semiotic or

[34] A. C. Spearing, *Textual Subjectivity: The Encoding of Subjectivity in Medieval Narratives and Lyrics* (Oxford: Oxford University Press, 2005): 'we do not know how to write such a history', 31.

[35] For a useful conspectus, see V. Gillespie, 'Vernacular Theology', in P. Strohm, ed., *Middle English,* Oxford Twenty-First century Approaches to Literature (Oxford: Oxford University Press, 2007), 401–20, Further Reading: (419–20); and A. Cole, 'Heresy and Humanism', in Strohm, ed., *Middle English,* 421–37.

amniotic' (99–100).[36] French, if it appears at all in this theological narrative, is one of the repressors, or at best, mediators, a means, but little more, towards the larger process of Englishing. Much remains to be considered in relating these debates over translation from Latin to models of vernacular translation, that is, translation from one vernacular to another. Although this task lies beyond the scope of this book, the relationship between English and French is a rich but still neglected resource for considering the broader ideologies of vernacular translation in England.[37]

In the next chapter I will look more closely at the complex evidence for the status of English in relation to French at and after Chaucer's time. Here comes a more immediate question: given his own double vernacularity, how does Chaucer's bilingualism (I leave aside for the present his knowledge of other languages, such as Genoese, Tuscan, Flemish, and Latin) affect our understanding of his work as a writer? Does it make a difference to our understanding of him as a translator to recognize that he was working between two vernaculars that he—in different ways—could regard as his own? Do we, to put it bluntly, need to think in further, different ways about translation?

It seems clear that the *Book of the Duchess* is preoccupied by issues of eloquence, or perhaps one should say inarticulacy. I want to revisit several of them, notably the ending of the Ceyx and Alcyone story, the Black Knight's first song, and aspects of the conversation between dreamer and knight. As is well known, Chaucer's version of the Ceyx and Alcyone story ends by breaking off before the metamorphosis of the married couple into birds. He probably knew the Ovid direct but the detail of the narrative comes from Machaut, whose long, zestful account in the *complainte d'amant* of the *Fontaine amoureuse* is also borrowed by Froissart.[38] Machaut keeps the metamorphosis, but for him the point of the story is not only to keep the image of faithful love flying for as long as possible but also to linger on the maritime scene. He adds the further interpretative transformation of the uncertain meaning of these birds for sailors:

[36] S. Stanbury, 'Vernacular Nostalgia and the Cambridge History of Medieval English Literature', *Texas Studies in Lit and Lang*, 44/1 (2002) 92–107. J. D. Burnley, 'Sources of Standardisation in Later Middle English', in J. B. Trahern, Jr., ed., *Standardizing English* (Knoxville: University of Tennessee Press, 1989), 23–41.

[37] Stanbury's comments do, I think, apply to certain perspectives in the *Cambridge History*, but it would be misleading to understand them as true of the larger editorial aims of that *History* which are deeply European in outlook.

[38] That both Machaut and Chaucer were also using the *Ovide moralisée* as well as the *Metamorphoses* is suggested by Wimsatt, who includes the former in his 'Appendix: Sources of the Diction of the *Book of the Duchess*', in his *Chaucer and the French Love Poets*, 155–62; for further discussion, see A. Minnis, 'A Note on Chaucer and the *Ovide Moralisée*', *Medium Aevum*, 48 (1979), 254–7.

Quant d'eaus voient ces oiselés prochains,
D'avoir fortune ou tempeste certeins
Les font souvent.

(696–8)

[When they see these birds near them,
They are often certain of having a stroke of luck
Or a storm.]

The *Fontaine amoureuse* ends with the duc at a small seaside town:

. . . sus la mer nous trouvames
En une ville petiote,
De barat pleinne et de riote.
Or la nommez, se vous volez,
Car il y a moult d'avolez.

(2808–12)

. . . we found ourselves by the sea
In a very small town,
A place full of uproar and riotous behaviour.
Name it now if you like,
For the town is full of strangers.

He sings a final *rondel*, the refrain of which prays that his heart's joy will remain in the country where his lady has to stay, and then sets sail, leaving the poet on the shore:

Si s'en ala par mer nagent . . .
Ensi parti. Je pris congié.

(2841, 2847)

[And thus departed, sailing across the sea . . .
And thus he left. I took my leave.]

Thus the couple are parted by the sea if not yet by death, and the memory of the Ovidian mythology returns only to underline the risk of a journey by sea and the certain tempests of exile to come.

In Chaucer's hands, the story ends with the unalleviated horror of bereavement: Alcyone's eyes roll up and lose the power to see and after one cry, 'Allas!', she dies within three days. The same blankness induced by emotional saturation has been a characteristic of the sleepless poet and will shortly be observed in the knight:

he herde me noght;
For he had wel nygh lost hys mynde.

(510–11)

The very intensity of these moments makes them more than representations of verbal failure. Chaucer pitches them so high that we are taken beyond the painfulness of the emotion and drawn into the reasons for such verbal failure. He takes us back repeatedly, in other words, to the Machauldian position of the poet standing alongside, watching an extreme outpouring of love and grief and seeking to transcribe it. But whereas for Machaut the poet never loses his skill—in fact his artistry redoubles—for Chaucer these moments seem all the more self-lacerating. His use of a refrain is a further example: auto-citation in Machaut is a sign of the poet's confidence in his own powers of poetic authority, but in the *Book of the Duchess* it reiterates, with brutal honesty, that the transcription has failed:

'Why so?' quod he, 'hyt ys nat soo,'
Thou wost ful lytel what thou menest;
I have lost more than thow wenest.'

(742–4, 1137–8, 1305–6)

Nowhere does this seem to be more true than of the knight's first little song, apparently so glaringly ignored by the dreamer. It has been well argued by A. C. Spearing that arguments about characterization here are misplaced. This very textual moment does not need explaining away, and indeed has never been very well explained if we rely on trying to identify the poem's 'experiencing "I"' and 'narrating "I"'.[39] I focus instead on its opening 'I':

I have of sorwe so gret won
That joye gete I never non
Now that I see my lady bryght,
Which I have loved with al my myght,
Is fro me ded and ys agoon.

(475–9)

Once again, Chaucer uses the lyric subject but only somehow to veil and obscure its force. The true meaning of the lyric, deprived of its 'noote', is exposed at the end in the reiterated: 'She ys ded!' In between, the dreamer/'experiencing "I"' is repeatedly rebuffed:

he loked on me asyde,
as who sayth, 'Nay, that wol not be'

(558–9)

But it is also notable that the knight rebuffs himself as often: 'Need? Nay, trewly, I gabbe now' and descries his own stammering awkward speech to his lady:

[39] Spearing adopts these terms from F. K. Stanzel; see A. C. Spearing, *Textual Subjectivity: The Encoding of Subjectivity in Medieval Narratives and Lyrics* (Oxford: Oxford University Press, 2005), 150, 154–5.

For many a word I over-skipte
In my tale, for pure fere
Lest my wordes mysset were.
(1208–10)

I seyde 'Mercy!' and no more.
(1220)

. . . she sayde 'Nay'
Al outerly. . . .
(1243–4)

One way of reading these moments is to see them as part of a strategy of plain speaking. It is tempting to see this as an opposition between English and French: French artifice is shown up by English plain speaking. I will be showing in the next chapter how fully (and contortedly) this develops as a way of speaking about the two vernaculars in the fifteenth century and later. But I wonder whether in the late 1360s or early 1370s this is to anticipate, at least in these terms. These seem to me to be more like moments described by Dipesh Chakravarty as 'rough translation', or in more detail by Gayatri Spivak as 'the founding violence of the silence at work within rhetoric'.[40] Both Chakravarty and Spivak (from whom he draws much), both Bengali intellectuals, are thinking through two problems of cultural translation, in Spivak's case of the other-languaged female whose 'texts must be made to speak English' and in Chakrabarty's of the modern Indian peasant (his term) and how his or her voice might speak in a Western model of historical narrative. They both talk of the 'scandal' of translation: of the way in which the discipline of modern Western secular academic history cannot deal, for instance, with a peasant who claims that his prayers to the gods provoked him into rebellion. The peasant's prayers are untranslateable as a form of history: in their own terms the prayers tear that history apart since they destroy its explanatory coherence and its ability to tell an event sequentially.[41] So they are translated into quite different terms: economic, social, or psychological. Any attempt to allow the peasant's explanation its own force would not make academic sense. For that kind of translation to happen, we need a new system of exchange, and one that recognizes the impossibility of the old.

The painful silences in the *Book of the Duchess*, the awkward sense between dreamer and knight that a phrase has just been spoken in an incomprehensible language, correspond to a passage in her essay on the 'Politics of Translation'

[40] D. Chakrabarty, *Provincializing Europe: Postcolonial Thought and Historical Difference* (Princeton: Princeton University Press, 2000), 17; G. C. Spivak, *Outside in the Teaching Machine* (New York and London: Routledge, 1993), 179–200 (181).

[41] Cf.: 'The archives thus help bring to view the disjointed nature of any particular 'now' one may inhabit; that is the function of subaltern pasts' (Chakrabarty, *Provincializing Europe*, 108).

where Spivak describes the relations between rhetoric, logic, and silence. Rhetoric disrupts logic:

> Logic allows us to jump from word to word by means of clearly indicated connections. Rhetoric must work in the silence between and around words in order to see what works and how much. The jagged relationship between rhetoric and logic, condition and effect of knowing, is a relationship by which a world is made for the agent, so that the agent can act in an ethical way, a political way, a day-to-day way; so that the agent can be alive, in a human way, in the world. Unless one can at least construct a model of this for the other language, there is no real translation . . . Without a sense of the rhetoricity of language, a species of neocolonialist construction of the non-Western scene is afoot.[42]

This is not entirely easy to follow, but perhaps Spivak is alluding to the necessary but impossible task of a translator to do more than follow the strict logic of the words being translated. It is all the things that are not said that also need to be translated. The analogy with the *Book of the Duchess* is far from perfect but her remarks may point to the possibility that Chaucer is likewise working with a mode—dream—that encourages logical leaps, and also a system of imperfect exchange, between a language honed for its specific courtly task and another that has up to now had an inferior and different position. The fact that it is the subject 'I' which Chaucer regularly presents as veiled, gagged, or simply, loudly, silent suggests that he was sensitive to the instances where one kind of discourse will not translate into another, not unless that silence or failure can itself be taken as a form of unequal exchange.

Quoting Spivak again,

> yet language is not everything. It is only a vital clue to where the self loses its boundaries. . . . by juggling the disruptive rhetoricity that breaks the surface in not necessarily connected ways, we feel the selvedges of the language-textile give way, fray into frayages or facilitations.[43]

This strikes me as a way of describing (quite unsuspectingly) the first forty lines of the *Book of the Duchess*, where Chaucer's English self frays around the words 'thing' and 'nothing', 'defaut', and 'slep', and the last forty, around the extraordinary rhetorical disruptions of:

> 'She ys ded!' 'Nay!' 'Yis, be my trouthe!'
> 'Is that youre los? Be God, hyt ys routhe!'
> (1308–9)

[42] G. C. Spivak, 'The Politics of Translation', in *Outside in the Teaching Machine* (New York and London: Routledge, 1993), 179–200 (181).

[43] Spivak, 'The Politics of Translation', 180. She comments here that 'facilitation' is the English translation of the Freudian term *Bahnung* (pathing) which is translated *frayage* in French.

ENGLISH AS A FOREIGN LANGUAGE

I have been arguing that English is newly poised, with the *Book of the Duchess*, to accommodate translation. Far from being ready to emerge as a self-contained 'triumphal' language it is open to being transformed through French. A similar history can be traced of Italian. This process is much more characteristic of Western languages or language situations in general throughout the medieval period and into the present than the narrower nationalist arguments that have become so current since the 1870s. As we know well from other kinds of linguistic arguments, the struggle to find 'pure' languages is very recent and fights against the natural condition of languages to blend, change, and resist standardization. Translation is in fact the natural condition of European languages and modern neuroses about linguistic identity are a falsification of a linguistically plural continental history. The struggle to see Italian as Italian is even more recent than that to see English as English, and the controversies are beginning anew with French and *la francophonie*, only officially recognized as 'French' in a dossier issued by the Ministère de la culture et communication in September 2003.[44] Bernard Cerquiglini has led a move towards reassessing the post-François 1er tight link between language and state as '*les langues* de France' where the plural gains sharp political meaning.[45] We can see many parallels with the sixth- to ninth-century devolutions from Latin (or a range of Latins) into the romance vernaculars discussed in Chapter 2, and of course Latin itself, as Adams has brilliantly demonstrated, was a vastly complex process of accommodation with Greek.

The argument about English in the last quarter of the fourteenth century can perhaps be pushed a little further by means of Chaucer's relationship to Machaut and Froissart. Chaucer's *Book of the Duchess* seems to show English in the midst of realizing that when one *can* translate, one can start recognizing linguistic difference. Until the mid-fourteenth century it was not clear that translation into English was necessary. The first port of call from Latin was the other English vernacular, French. This is not to say, of course, that no translations into English existed before Chaucer, but the efforts were local and individual rather than about 'English'.[46] One might even say that it was not before Froissart's *Le Paradys d'amour* that English began to look as if it could speak an international language, and perhaps it was because Froissart's language was not either Anglo-Norman or Parisian, but *picard*. For Chaucer, a *picard* poem written in England for an English courtly

[44] 'Les premiers assises nationales des langues de France', Dossier, Ministère de la culture et communication, No.109, Sept. 2003. See <http://www.culture.gouv.fr>.

[45] B. Cerquiglini, ed., *Les Langues de France* (Paris: PUF, 2003).

[46] See *Idea of the Vernacular*, 332; this seems especially the case with Robert Mannyng and the *Cursor Mundi*.

household was just foreign enough to impel him imaginatively into his own effort at English, in English. In that sense, Froissart in *Le Paradys*, like Jean de le Mote before him, is translating from the language of the enemy into Anglo-French. Chaucer's *Book of the Duchess* is the natural next step. It reflects a negotiation with just how foreign French is having to seem to an Anglo-French courtier and poet by the closing stages of a century dominated by war, and how far English is capable of becoming both francophone and of distancing itself enough from French to have independent authority as a vernacular.

It is in *Troilus and Criseyde* rather than the *Book of the Duchess* that Chaucer seems to find this mode for English and in the Prologue to the *Legend of Good Women* that he articulates his perception most explicitly. Before substantiating this with some examples I argue that a crucial stage in Chaucer's apprehension of the linguistic difference of English takes place in his translation of Boethius's *De Consolatione.*

Chakravarty's phrase 'rough translation' can be taken (roughly) to convey a common view of Chaucer's *Boece.* Described in the G version of the Prologue to the *Legend of Good Women* as 'besynesse' (the F version gives 'holynesse'),[47] Chaucer's activity as a translator has occasioned both respect and puzzlement, the latter veering into criticism (Fisher described it as 'fumbling').[48] Tim Machan's recent editions both of the prose itself and of its sources have given us ample materials to judge whether this is a raw, rough English rendering or a more artful set of responses to the linguistic challenges of a work of philosophy that clearly shaped his thinking in profound ways. *Boece* is of interest here for a variety of reasons: it happens to be the only work of Chaucer's that employs the adjective 'forein',[49] and does so eighteen times.[50] That it occurs in a work that Chaucer is producing out of Latin, a French translation and a Latin commentary (or two) provides the opportunity to observe him close up working with all three languages as he endeavours to make sense of Philosophy's exposition. It is not just that we can observe Chaucer as a translator in another context from the *Duchess*, but that the *Boece* tells us more about what Chaucer thought about English. His uses of 'forein' are indices of an education in linguistic and philosophical strangeness that Chaucer began in the *Book of the Duchess* and then developed elsewhere in his writings.

Chaucer's engagement with the 'forein' begins early in the translation in Book 1, m.2, where Boethius builds up a powerful picture of mental darkness. Chaucer's text is here quoted alongside Boethius in Latin and Jean de Meun's French translation.

[47] See G, 412–13, F, 424–5.

[48] Cited in T. W. Machan, *Techniques of Translation: Chaucer's Boece* (Norman, Okla.: Pilgrim Books, 1985), 27.

[49] I discount LGW 1962 where it means privy.

[50] Bo1 m2,4; Bo1 pr4,113; Bo2,pr2,25; Bo2,pr5,73; Bo2,pr5,96; Bo2,pr5,126; Bo3,pr3,70; Bo3,pr3,80; Bo3,pr6,37; Bo3,pr6,45; Bo3,pr9,29; Bo3,pr9,71; Bo3,m9,7; Bo3,pr12,191; Bo4, pr3,25; Bo4,pr3,105; Bo4,pr4,199; Bo5,pr4,216.

'Allas! How the thowht of man, dreynt in overthrowynge depnesse, dulleth and forletith his proper cleernesse, myntynge to goon into foreyne dyrknesses as ofte as his anoyos bysynesse wexeth withowte mesure, that is dryven to and fro with wordely wyndes!

(lines 1–4)[51]

'Ha lasse! comme la pensee de cestui, plungiee en trebuichable parfondece, rebouche et, sa propre clarté delaissiee, [tendant] a aler en foraines tenebres et sa nuisable cure, par quantes foiz [est elle] demenee par les vens terriens, craist elle sens fin.

'Heu quam precipiti mersa profundo
Mens ebet et propria luce relicta
Tendit in externas ire tenebras,
Terrenis quociens flatibus aucta
Cressit in immensum noxia cura.

Chaucer's own rendering of the French seems to respond to Jean de Meun's own heightened response to the Latin. Jean uses the word 'trebuichable'[52]—a precise but also vividly metaphoric realization of the Latin idea of falling—which Chaucer gives as 'overthrowynge'. This sets up the severe disorientation to come of 'foreyne dyrknesses' ['foraines tenebres']. In both the French and then the English, 'forein' comes as a sharpened version of 'externas': it adds a notion of incomprehension to that of distance which seems to increase its horrors. From here on in Books 2 and 3 'forein' becomes part of an increasingly political discussion of worldly power. Latin 'externa' is rendered as 'forein' and now also '[e]strange': it is not just that one must cast away worldly goods, but they must come to seem strange. Their very nature must be 'maked foreyne fro the', that is, recognized to have characteristics that owe nothing to you and hence do not in any way belong to you.

Although this might seem to be simply a strong way of expressing a form of detachment, the *Consolatio* goes on to show that human disengagement takes complex forms. There is space to comment on just one instance. It strikes home at Boethius's own situation of being a trusted advisor, or as Chaucer puts it a 'familier', who finds himself in prison. Philosophy, with piercing frankness, exposes this relationship, supposedly of trust and confident personal knowledge, as fragile. Having held the two terms 'familiar' and 'tyrant' apart throughout the passage, she suddenly drives them devastatingly into collision:

And what pestylence is moore myhty for to anoye a wyht than a famylier enemy?

(*Boece*, 3 pr.5. 39–40 (p. 41))

[51] *Chaucer's Boece: A Critical Edition Based on Cambridge University Library, MS Ii.3.21,ff. 9r–180v*, ed. Tim Machan (Heidelberg: Winter, 2008), p. 5. Jean de Meun's translation and the Latin are quoted from *Sources of the Boece*, ed. T. Machan (Athens and London: University of Georgia Press, 2005), pp. 28–9.

[52] See *trebuchable* [TL: 'Qui fait trébucher, périlleux'] = causes one to stumble, dangerous.

Et quelle pestilance est plus puissant a nuire que familiers anemis? (p. 105)
Que vero pestis efficacior ad nocendum quam familiaris inimicus? (p. 102)

This comes at the heart of a long and difficult lesson in how to harden oneself away from familiarity into foreignness. Chaucer learns it twofold, ethically and linguistically. For the words 'forein' and 'strange' become strange to him as he translates. They are well known to him, part of his Anglo-French linguistic heritage. But here, in the act of translating the bitterly painful history of a man whose sense of integrity was traduced, who found familiarity turn incomprehensibly into hostility, Chaucer himself learns to use 'forein' and 'strange' as foreign words, as words that he translates into English in their own guise, unchanged, yet alienated. Like 'defaut' [or 'fraunchise'], translation takes place across a semantic gap that opens up within a word rather than between one word and its chosen linguistic other.[53]

There is a connection between Philosophy's question and her earlier references to 'nacioun' in Book 2. Here she is trying to provide a rational corrective to the human desire for fame: earthly renown, she says, is after all very limited. There is so 'many a nasyoun, diverse of tonge a[n]d of maneres and ek of resoun of hir lyvynge' that the reputation of exceptional men, or even of famous cities may not reach them:

to the whiche naciouns, what for deficulte of weyes and what for [diversite] of langages and what [for] defawte of unusage and entrecomunynge of marchaundise, nat only the names of syngler men ne may nat strecchen, but ek the fame of cytes ne may nat strecchen.

(Machan, 2 pr.7. 29–32, p. 30)

This rather awkwardly written passage (which is only a small part of a much longer section) raises some important issues in its very awkwardness. It advertises

[53] '*Forein*' is attested in the *AND* under the following spellings: *forein, foreyn, forain, forayn, foran, foren, foreint, forien; forrein; foreyin, foreigne; furain, furein; ferein, f. foreynne (farein)*. Its meanings include as an adjective: 1.'extraneous, alien', (law): situated outside the jurisdiction of a town etc, not local; 2.outer, exterior; outer, secular 3. Foreign, distant, geographically distant, remote in blood 4. (of time) distant, and as a noun: 1. Foreigner, alien; (of guild) non-member 2. Outskirts, area outside city walls 3. (law): Forinsec (that is, foreign) service 4. Latrine, privy. In Middle English, spellings attested are: *forein* (adj.) Also *foren, foran, forren, furren, ferren* (and as noun: *forin*). The meanings are closely similar, though with more emphasis on a *forein* as 'one born in another country or belonging to a different nation', a stranger, a traveller. As an adjective, *forein* has additional meanings including 3. *forein womman* meaning prostitute, also alien to one's nature, contrary, inimical and 4. Public, and also inferior. In Middle French (*DMF forein aforain*), *forein* is only attested once in Machaut, meaning external; otherwise the more common attestation is *aforain* (Picardie, Wallonie), meaning 1. a stranger, someone who lives outside the jurisdiction of a lordship, kingdom or the franchise of a town and 2. Exterior, not relevant.

For *estrange*, the *AND* also lists *estraunge; estrangne, estraigne; estraunger; strange, straunge, straunger*. The meanings overlap considerably with *forein*, although they also include 4. Outside one's experience, with meanings ranging from wondrous, marvellous, unusual to hostile, harsh, dreadful. In the *MED straunge* is listed with *straung, strang(e, straunche, straunce, strounge, strong(e, (?gen.) stranges & (error) storge; pl. stra(u)nges, stranghis, (?gen.) straungene* and again the overlap of meanings is high. There are more attested applications to dress, food, astronomy, and language.

itself as a 'rough' translation. The long, sometimes clumsy words and phrases clog the syntax. A discussion of the foreignness of the strange customs of people who live far away is itself being conducted through the effort of translation from other tongues. The examples of 'translationese' ('defawte of unusage and entrecomunynge of marchaundise') make us simultaneously aware that this is not plain English even though it is no longer Latin or French. Once again the word 'defawte' in the uneasy neologism 'defawte of unusage' is central to this tension between the attempt to find a 'naturel' language for these thoughts and the sense that they are too foreign to convey naturally.[54]

This conjunction impressed upon Chaucer in the *Boece* between the estranged prisoner's intellectual history, the forcing on him via Jean de Meun of the word 'forein' and the hard activity of translating took deep root in his writings, indeed in his own philosophy. We can trace it through his 'Boethian' and other lyrics, through the *Legend of Good Women, Troilus and Criseyde*, and much else such as the *Knight's, Clerk's, Shipman's*, and *Manciple's Tales.*

TROILUS AND CRISEYDE AND ENGLISH VERNACULAR AUTHORITY

It is *Troilus and Criseyde* that most clearly and magnificently shows the imprint of this Boethian lesson in translation. As many other Chaucerian readers have eloquently described, Chaucer finds in Boethius a way of translating Boccaccio. My contention is that he articulates hard truths about detachment by seeing Boccaccio's *Il Filostrato* as a francophone rather than purely 'Italian' work. Boccaccio helped Chaucer distance English from French as well as enable English to gain new heights of francophone internationalism by his own relationship to French writing. For his own Neapolitan context for composing *Il Filostrato* meant that Boccaccio was trying out French-inspired lyric gestures from the trouvères and a newly intense first-person exploration of love from the *Rose.*[55] Observing this accommodation at close quarters in Boccaccio's Tuscan dialect seems to have given Chaucer enough distance to develop further his own English vernacular's authority. The further step of the argument is that it is through his use of inset song that Chaucer often pauses to reflect on the process of

[54] 'Unusage' is not recorded elsewhere in the *MED.*

[55] Details of interaction between the court at Naples and French poets of importance are in fact numerous. For instance, we can continue to trace an Arrageois association into the fourteenth century with the presence in Carlo II's court in 1302 of Nevelon Amiot, whose *Vers d'Amour* contains French *refrains*: F. Sabatini, *Napoli angioina: cultura e società* (Naples: Edizioni Scientifiche Italiane, 1975), 38. More notably, Carlo I was a patron (when still in France) of Jean de Meun, who refers to him and to Naples in the *Roman de la Rose.* S. Asperti, *Carlo I d'Angio e i trovatori: componenti 'provenzali' e angioine nella tradizione manoscritta della lirica trobadorica* (Ravenna: Longo Editore, 1995).

translation, and hence on the nature of poetic language. In this the prosimetrum genre of the *Consolation* is generative. Chaucer is influenced not only by Boethius's philosophy but by his formal alternation of song and prose. Chaucer used Boethius specifically to amplify and modify Boccaccio's allusions to French love narrative, in particular to his use of song. Chaucer's structural placing of song in relation to internal debate derives from Boethius's use of song in the dialectical structure of the *Consolation.*

There is a circularity here in that the *Consolation* was itself a major influence on Machaut and Froissart. Moreover, in the hands of French translators it prompted something more than slavish translation, amounting to works in the vernacular of a metrical ingenuity that aspired to poetic status. The close association of these 'mixed' (that is verse and prose) translations with love narratives containing songs is demonstrated physically in one of the manuscripts of the revision of Renaut's translation carried out *c.*1380 by an anonymous Benedictine monk. The manuscript, Cambridge, Trinity Hall MS 12, is well known for its numerous lively drawings.[56] But it is also remarkable for the way in which French *ballades* have been inserted into the translation at the end of Books I, II, IV, and V.[57] They are not part of the translation, but distinct from it; no other copies of them have been found elsewhere, although, as Dwyer has pointed out, the refrain of the third *ballade* ('Je meurs de soif au pres de la fontaine') is identical to the first line of a group of ten *ballades* by Charles d'Orléans.[58] Thus not only are the *metra* rendered in varying French metres, they are supplemented by actual courtly lyrics. Since each book of the *Consolation* except the last ends with a *metrum,* the *metra* and the *ballades* are directly juxtaposed. The courtly tone imparted to the *Consolation* by the *ballades* is confirmed by the illustrator. Alongside his drawings of scenes from the *Consolation,* he includes an illustration next to the second *ballade* of the King of Love, enthroned, with two arrows in each hand, and a man and a woman kneeling before him.[59] This, together with his picture of Dame Musique carrying a scroll (fol.16), is characteristic of the kind of picture which decorates, for instance, the Machaut manuscripts.[60] This early fifteenth-century manuscript witnesses the way in which the *Consolation* had been increasingly assimilated throughout the fourteenth century into French

[56] See the detailed description by M. R. James, *A Descriptive Catalogue of the Manuscripts in the library of Trinity Hall, Cambridge* (Cambridge: Cambridge University Press, 1907), 14–32, and the discussion in R. A. Dwyer, *Boethian Fictions: Narratives in the Medieval French Versions of the Consolatio philosophiae* (Cambridge, MA: Mediaeval Academy of America, 1976), 27–9.

[57] Dwyer's description of the ballades as 'interspersed between the latter books of the *Consolatio* and following works' (72) is therefore not strictly accurate.

[58] R. A. Dwyer, 'Je meurs de soif auprès de la fontaine', *French Studies,* 23 (1969), 225–8.

[59] Trinity Hall, MS 12, fol.31b.

[60] For much useful information and bibliography, see L, Earp, 'The Miniatures', in his *Guillaume de Machaut: A Guide to Research* (New York and London: Garland, 1995), 129–88.

court culture.[61] Chaucer's own verse renderings of the *Consolation* were part of that process.[62]

For Chaucer, both *Il Filostrato* and the *Consolation* had a French courtly aspect. We see this if we trace some of the instances in *Troilus* where the Boethian use of song turns out to be decisive. *Troilus* makes constant negotiations with foreign languages. Ranging across five sources (Dares, Dictys, Benoit, Guido, Boccaccio) in as many languages (Latin and Greek, French, Italian, and English) its narrator constantly seeks in the implied cultural tussle between them to speak 'in the space of the other'. In perhaps the most celebrated of the songs, the *Canticus Troili* of Book I which mysteriously translates a Petrarch sonnet 150 years before anyone else in England, we see a classic example of Chaucer's double impulse to translate, not Italian into English so much as Franco-Italian to Anglo-French. In the narrative process that leads up to the song, Chaucer intensifies Troilus's mental reaction to his new experience of love in a specifically French direction. Where Troiolo only imagines Criseida's appearance, Troilus makes 'a mirour of his mynde / In which he saugh al holly hire figure', a phrase also used to translate the role of Dous Penser in the *Romaunt*:

For Thought anoon thanne shall bygynne,
As fer, God wot, as he can fynde,
To make a mirrour of his mynde;
For to biholde he wole not lette.
Hir persone he shall afore hym sette . . .

(*Romaunt*, 2804–8)

The way in which the song crystallizes the sense of mental turbulence in Troilus bears some resemblance to certain passages in thirteenth-century French romance, where, for instance, in Jean Renart's *Le Roman de la Rose*, the Emperor Conrad also sings or hears songs which represent his state of mind (3180–95 and 4127–40).[63] When the song actually comes, it has been translated out of sonnet

[61] A second feature of the manuscript, not commented upon by Dwyer, puts the *Consolation* into a markedly close relation with a courtly romance into which a song had already been incorporated by the poet. The work which immediately follows the *Consolation* in the manuscript is *La Chastelaine de Vergi*, written, it seems, in the same hand (see fols.90–96b). The juxtaposition of the two works is itself telling: yet, in addition, the scribe inserts a further *ballade* at the end of the French poem. Not only is the *ballade* similar in style and structure to the *ballades* interpolated into the *Consolation*, but the second line ('Je meurt de soif *et* suy a la fo*n*taine'), is almost identical with the refrain of the third ballade. *La Chastelaine de Vergi* contains in any case a stanza from a *chanson* by the Chastelain de Couci; the scribe, however, seems determined to make his own contribution to the process of lyric interpolation already exemplified in the poem, just as he has done to the *Consolation*. Thus he yokes the two works firmly together.

[62] Both 'The Former Age' and 'Fortune' occur copied in a sequence after Book 2, m.5 of CUL Ii.3.21, a copy of *Boece*.

[63] See Huot, *From Song to Book*, 108–16 and A. Butterfield, *Poetry and Music in Medieval France from Jean Renart to Guillaume de Machaut* (Cambridge: Cambridge University Press, 2002), 64–71.

form into a three-stanza *ballade* shape (sans refrain of course). But the technique of allowing the song to arise out of the debate, and provide a pause in which Troilus can comment upon his own state of mind finds its closest precedent in the *Consolation.* The *Consolation* provided a model for many kinds of use of song in the process of debate. In particular, just as Troilus's song represents a pause in his thinking in order to reflect upon his own thoughts, several of the early *metra* (such as I, m.2 and m.7) represent a static analysis of Boethius's state of mind, caught as it is between his feelings of sorrow and his desire to clarify his confusion. The Latin structural sub-text stimulates an extra, doubled desire to translate, to make in English a francophone articulation of this quasi-troubadour song.

So many readers have commented on the two stanzas that immediately precede the song that it may seem otiose to add anything more. But we might note first, that it is lyric that stimulates the discussion of vernacular poetic translation just as it did between Jehan de le Mote and Vitry, Deschamps, and Chaucer, and second, that Chaucer seems particularly exercised by this issue of linguistic difference ('oure tonges difference'):

And of his song naught only the sentence,
As writ myn auctour called Lollius,
But pleinly, saue oure tonges difference,
I dar wel seyn, in al, that Troilus
Seyde in his song, loo, every word right thus
As I shal seyn; and whoso list it here,
Loo, next this vers he may it fynden here.

(I, 386–99)

Commentators usually rightly draw attention to the link with the Proem to Book II where Chaucer writes of the 'chaunge' . . . 'in forme of speche' . . . / Withinne a thousand yeer' (II, 22–3). The self-consciousness is marked along with an extraordinary sensitivity to the problems of historical translation. Chaucer appears acutely aware of the temporal oddity of this attempt to render into contemporary English a story that has already had so much temporizing linguistic history.

Antigone's song later in Book II demonstrates the Boethian leverage to this kind of reflection even more conspicuously. Criseyde's private reflections about Troilus have come to a crisis of indecision: to distract herself she decides to join her three nieces in the garden. In the midst of this period of relaxation, one of them, Antigone, sings a song in celebration of Love. For Criseyde, the impact of the song is at last decisive: from this moment on she begins less to fear love than to welcome it.[64] *Il Filostrato* is significant more here as an absence than as a presence. Criseida also shows reluctance to accede to Troiolo, and considerable

[64] Wimsatt points out that it is not derived from the lay *Le Paradis d'Amours* alone, as Kittredge maintained, but that there are several similarities with another four of Machaut's lyrics, especially

anxiety about the loss of honour that she feels will inevitably ensue. But the process by which she does eventually succumb takes place, not through the external stimulus of a song but under the pressure of her own desire: attracted to

'. . . le maniere sue,
gli atti piacevoli e la cortesia.
E si subitamente presa fue,
che sopra ogni altro bene lui disia,
e duolle forte del tempo perduto,
che 'l suo amor non avea conosciuto.

(Stanza 83)

. . . his manners, his pleasing behaviour and his courtesy. And she was so rapidly overcome that she desired him more than any other kind of happiness and greatly regretted the time that had been wasted when she had not known about his love.[65]

The whole episode in the garden in Chaucer's story thus creates extra narrative space in Boccaccio's story: in this sense the *Filostrato* acts here not as a source so much as a model of narrative procedure, as a shaping mental constraint which gives specific form to Chaucer's distinctive treatment of it.

Whether Chaucer was aware of it or not, the narrative context of his song once again harks back with remarkable directness to thirteenth-century romance (a debt also visible in Boccaccio). Like the Emperor Conrad in Renart's *Rose*, who hears most of his songs (if he does not sing them himself) from a (male or female) performer in the company of a select group of courtiers, Criseyde goes down into her garden 'to pleyen' with her three nieces and a large company of her women. The song sung by her niece Antigone is thus part of the general atmosphere of 'pleyinge', not directly prompted by Criseyde's feelings in any way.[66] Chaucer creates extra time for Criseyde, seemingly extraneous time, for her conversion to love. For this Boethius is the prime mover. The third song in the Consolation has a particularly remarkable structural function. Boethius's eyes are so filled with tears that he becomes unable to respond coherently to Philosophy. Seeing this, she stops talking and wipes his tears with a fold of her dress. A song follows, describing the dazzling heavenly light that causes darkness to flee. Immediately afterwards, as Boethius comments, his eyes and his mind clear: the song's words, as they describe the power of light to pierce through the shadows, in this way perform their own meaning upon him.

with his lay *Mireoir amoureux*: 'Guillaume de Machaut and Chaucer's *Troilus and Criseyde*', *Medium Aevum*, 45 (1976), 277–92 (288–91).

65 *Geoffrey Chaucer, Troilus and Criseyde: A new edition of The Book of Troilus*', ed. B. A. Windeatt (London and New York: Longman, 1984), p. 200. *Chaucer's Boccaccio: Sources of Troilus and the Knight's and Franklin's Tales*, ed. and trans. N. R. Havely (Cambridge: D. S. Brewer, 1980), 39.

66 The public performance of song by aristocratic ladies is well documented in French romance: for example, Fresne in *Galeran de Bretagne*, Lïenor in *Guillaume de Dole*, Euriaut in the *Roman de la Violette*, and Marthes in *Ysaye le Triste*.

There is an evident analogy between the action of Antigone's song on Criseyde and the action of the song on Boethius: both occur at a moment of mental crisis, and both succeed in resolving that crisis. But the textual presence of the *Consolation of Philosophy* is even more insistent. If we follow through all the twists and turns of Criseyde's inner argument, we find that suddenly, in the midst of it, she appears to decide firmly in Troilus's favour. Beginning a stanza with a rush of questions, by the end she has answered them boldly:

'What shal I doon? to what fyn lyve I thus?
Shal I nat love, in cas if that me leste?
What, pardieux! I am naught religious.
And though that I myn herte sette at reste
Upon this knyght, that is the worthieste,
And kepe alwey myn honour and my name,
By alle right, it may do me no shame.'

(II, 757–63)

But then just here, at this apparent moment of resolve, Chaucer interposes a stanza of deeply Boethian resonance:

But right as when the sonne shyneth brighte
In March, that chaungeth ofte tyme his face,
And that a cloude is put with wynd to flighte,
Which oversprat the sonne as for a space,
A cloudy thought gan thorugh hire soule pace,
That ouerspradde hire brighte thoughtes alle,
So that for feere almost she gan to falle.

(764–70)

This is an allusion in reverse: where the description of the sun shining through clouds of darkness in Boethius acts to dispel his mental obscurity, in Chaucer the same description signals a transition in Criseyde's mind from clarity to a sudden onset of anguish. Chaucer is not simply borrowing a simile, he is imitating a larger structural process. By taking a simile from a song, and one in which the troubled Boethius passes from misery to calmer self-possession, Chaucer hints at the future effect on Criseyde of the song by Antigone which is yet to come. The process of consolation for Criseyde is delayed until Antigone sings: Chaucer suspends the action of the Boethian song so that at first it represents only the doubt in Criseyde's mind, not its resolution.[67]

If the *Filostrato* gives form, in its very absence, to the narrative space Chaucer has created between Criseyde's state of indecision and her eventual emotional

[67] As her period of internal debate comes to a close, however, the imagery of the *metrum* is briefly recalled: 'And after that, hire thought gan for to clere' (806).

surrender, then the *Consolation of Philosophy* offers Chaucer a means of structural transition within that space. When we finally come to Antigone's song, we encounter a further, French set of textual relations. The song itself has verbal links with a group of songs by Machaut. Perhaps more important still are the similarities between the setting of the song and the contexts of songs in thirteenth-century French romances, works in which the public performance of songs takes on a particular significance.[68]

Taking this French presence into account, as well as the Latin and Italian, Chaucer's handling of Antigone's song is revealed as an intricately woven fabric of references. As if she were in a thirteenth-century French romance, Criseyde hears the fourteenth-century French song in a garden as a form of incidental public entertainment, her reactions open to public scrutiny. The timing of the song, however, is Boethian in that it occurs precisely when Criseyde is trying to distract herself from a moment of intellectual suspension. The song comes at the peak of a process of indecision. However, unlike the *Cantici Troili*, she hears it only incidentally. It comes unexpectedly, and at a time when Criseyde is deliberately trying to distract herself from a suspended point of argument. The effect of this upon her is strikingly analogous to the effect of the *metra* in the *Consolation* upon Boethius. In the *Consolation*, the *metra* provide the argument as a whole with considerable flexibility of movement. The hiatus between a *prosa* and a *metra* allows the argument to take a leap forward. Yet it does so, especially in the early *metra*, precisely because the *metra* are seemingly designed pleasurably to distract Boethius. It is the very time spent away from the philosophical argument that Boethius finds helps him to be attracted more towards it. Likewise, Criseyde suddenly receives through the song the very impetus towards love which she had so far restrained and constrained in argument. By proclaiming the joys of love with such a lack of reserve, Antigone's song releases Criseyde from the embarrassment of having to give in to love consciously. But the French song works on Criseyde through a Latin mechanism: or, to put it the other way round, the suspended process of consolation signalled by the first allusion to Boethius is released, not by a return to Boethius but by a French-type lyric.

Chaucer interposes that Boethian stanza in a way which not only causes Criseyde's psychological process exactly to mirror Boethius's in the *Consolation of Philosophy*, but also to mirror Boethius's strategy of presenting that process. Boethius's use of song acts as a model for the way in which this whole play of textual authorities traces the delicately impulsive stages of Criseyde's progress from anguished indecision to consoled emotional quiescence:

> But every word which that she of hire herde,
> She gan to prenten in hire herte faste,
> And ay gan love hire lasse for t'agaste

[68] See n. 66 above.

Than it dide erst and synken in hire herte,
That she wex somwhat able to converte.

(II, 899–903)

Such careful deployment of Boethius continues throughout the poem. Chaucer repeatedly constructs situations where the process of translation, here having the benign effect of enacting the inexplicable moment when Criseyde begins to (was already in?) love shows a gap or hiatus, but elsewhere, as the tragedy deepens, an enforced estrangement. Cracks appear early, perhaps most clearly in their first dawn parting in Book III, where Troilus asks to know 'outrely' whether he was set as firmly in her heart as she in his (1486–91). Her extraordinary reply has a confident eloquence of which any vernacular poet in any period could be proud: it emerges, I would argue, out of the pressure of rising to the challenge of a reply suitable to the high courtly stakes of the question. It is a masterpiece of largely monosyllabic plain speaking, which manages to place every plain word in jeopardy since we know how every word will be gainsaid:

'Ye ben so depe in-with myn herte grave,
That, though I wolde it torne out of my thought . . .
To dyen in the peyne, I koude nought . . .
As fayn wolde I as ye that it were so . . .

(III, 1499–1500, 1502, 1517)

Criseyde's second letter (V, 1590–1631) plumbs even lower depths of self-estrangement. What Chaucer achieves in it is the culmination (though not of course the end point) of a long journey in English subjectivity. Its lesson has involved detaching any comfortable notion of self from language. Criseyde's confusions, her incomplete syntax, the desperate silences in the 'jagged relationship between rhetoric and logic' reveal a first-person that has broken free from itself. If this is an English moment then it is only because Chaucer has found a way of giving this language an acute sense of its own self-estrangement.

Near the end of Book V Chaucer makes his famously grandiloquent claim to poetic fame:

Go, litel bok, go, litel myn tragedye,
Ther God thi makere yet, er that he dye,
So sende myght to make in som comedye!
But, litel book, no makyng thow n'envie,
But subgit be to alle poesye;
And kis the steppes where as thow seest pace
Virgile, Ovide, Omer, Lucan, and Stace.

(V, 1786–92)

I mentioned in Chapter 5 that this stanza has the function of an *envoi.* As such, it participates in the curious and often wrenchingly awkward linguistic negotiations that are characteristic of Chaucer's *envois*. Its public mission is to set Chaucer in fame's row as the six of sixth among the greatest classical poets he or any age has known. But it hardly does so unambiguously. The puzzlingly self-deprecating reflex 'litel' is a frequent one in Chaucer; it occurs for instance in Book IV where he disclaims his 'litel tonge's' ability to transcribe Criseyde's 'heigh compleynte' (IV, 799–805). Repeated with careful, rhetorical deliberation, here it carries out the same manoeuvre that was writ large in the *Book of the Duchess* of subjectedness as well as subjectivity. Chaucer's assertions of vernacular supremacy are not complete without an accompanying gesture of submission. His 'litel book' must be 'subgit . . . to alle poesye', otherwise it cannot reach for the temple steps.

He follows this through in the next stanza, admitting with epic eloquence to the limitations of his own humble vernacular:

> And for ther is so gret diversite
> In Englissh and in writyng of oure tonge,
> So prey I God that non myswrite the,
> Ne the mysmetre for defaute of tonge;
> And red wherso thow be, or elles songe,
> That thow be understonde, God I biseche!
>
> (1793–8)

This is not ironic, at least not straightforwardly. The two stanzas are written as a tightly connected sequence. The 'defaute of tonge' is real, and so is the 'diversite' and lack of understanding: the fame of fourteenth-century English 'may nat strecchen' to many nations, 'what for difficulte of weyes, and what for diversite of langages, and what for defaute of unusage'. But this does not stop Chaucer from brilliantly trying out eloquence on a previously unattempted scale, with a vernacular that understood its own limitations by virtue of its need to translate its other.

CHARLES D'ORLÉANS AND THE ENGLISH SUBJECT

Machaut's gloomy prognostications in *Le Confort d'ami* of what life would be like for a French prisoner in England seem to have been far off the mark at least in relation to Charles d'Orléans. Dragged at Agincourt out of the bloody mire of a battlefield, like the fictional Palamon and Arcite a generation earlier, he was kept in captivity in England for twenty-five years. Although passed between many wardens, his conditions were those of his English aristocratic peers and their associates, and he had access to many books. During this period his own ducal city was besieged by the English (against chivalric convention), and spectacularly won back for the dauphin on 8 May 1429 by a previously unknown and unanticipated girl with no experience of battle, Jeanne d'Arc. Charles was not merely a passive, captive observer of the war but worked hard diplomatically and corresponded widely. On his eventual release he married again and had another young family. He regained a vigorous political life in France; one of his new children became Louis XII.

In England he wrote a large collection of French poetry and another set of English poetry: the French poems survive in many copies, including an autograph version (BNF fr.25458), the English in a unique manuscript (BL Harley 682) that appears to follow the layout of the French book closely.[69] Approximately half of them have an equivalent in the French collection; the rest are independent pieces. He left the English book in England on his return to France in 1440, and wrote more French poetry. In France he also arranged for a new compilation of his poetic oeuvre to be made in which his poems were translated into Latin. This manuscript, Grenoble MS 873, presents his French poetry in facing columns with translations by Antonio Astesano.[70] Not since Gower had a poet in England constructed so careful a trilingual oeuvre. As A. C. Coldiron has remarked, this extraordinary book 'aims to be public "world lyric" for all time' (119). But just as startlingly, Charles was the first continental French poet to translate into English. This only happened through the political accident of war, since it would be a long time before English writing had that international cachet. Yet of course that political accident shaped its character. Charles's project of English translation acts as an exact counterpart to Chaucer's decision to write the *Book of the Duchess* in English. With his reliance on the *Troilus* rhyme royal stanza, Charles's lyric sequences also form a counterpoint to *Troilus and Criseyde.*

If Chaucer was seeking to make English a vernacular of equal importance to French, then Charles presents us with the absorbing, and unexpected, spectacle of a French writer trying his hand at English.[71] It is intriguing to speculate what his purpose was in doing so, and how he and his French and English contemporaries viewed both his decision and the poems themselves. One comment by René d'Anjou in his *Livre du Cuer d'Amours espris* (1457) indicates that there was some French awareness of his activity:

> Car prins fuz des Anglois et mene en seruaige
> Et tant y demouray qu'en aprins le langaige[72]

> [For I was captured by the English and led into servitude
> And stayed there so long that I learnt their language]

[69] M.-J. Arn, 'Two Manuscripts, One Mind: Charles d'Orléans and the Production of Manuscripts in Two Languages (Paris BNF MS fr.25458 and London, BL MS Harley 682)', in eadem, ed., *Charles d'Orléans in England* (Cambridge: D.S. Brewer, 2000), 61–78.

[70] A. E. B. Coldiron, *Canon, Period, and the Poetry of Charles of Orleans: Found in Translation* (Ann Arbor: University of Michigan Press, 2000), 112.

[71] Compare the later example of Voltaire in his *Letters to a Nation.*

[72] R. Steele and M. Day, eds., *The English Poems of Charles d'Orléans*, 2 vols, EETS, os 215 (London: Oxford University Press, 1941), xiv.

From an English perspective there was appreciation, sometimes expressed as concern in the negotiations over his release, of his knowledge of English customs and law as well as the language. Holinshed's *Chronicle* evidently draws on a popular opinion in saying that Charles 'was deliuered out of Englande into Fraunce . . . speaking better Englishe than Frenche'.[73] But the political realities of such descriptions of Charles as having 'gret subtilite' and being a 'great and felle-witted man' were that he remained a powerful threat to English interests and therefore was retained for an unconscionably long life sentence.[74] The fact that he left the poems in England may tell us something about his sense of their wider interest; it may also more simply indicate a desire to shake English dust off his feet. But that he wrote them at all is evidence of a linguistic curiosity that went beyond mere chauvinism.

One brief example must suffice. It occurs in an *envoi.* It is a case where only the English version of the poem has an *envoi*: the French has a crisper three stanzas. As A.C. Coldiron points out, all the English *ballades* have *envois* (whereas around one quarter of the French lack them).[75] This particular *ballade*, No. 39, is a good example of Charles's employment of a looser, longer line in English than in French (seven syllables). If it is less easy to describe the metrical character of his English poetry, then this appears to be the point. The *envoi* draws attention to its 'dark furdullid rude myture':

> O goo thou derke fordullid rude myture
> And say for trouthe forwhi hit is no lese
> That y haue chose withouten departure
> As for my souereyne lady and maystres.[76]

Charles's self-deprecation here is many-sided and goes beyond matters of metre. Modern appreciation of his English writing, resisting older dismissal of it, has had to find new approaches towards understanding his inventive approach to English, his odd neologisms and the uneven line lengths and rhythms. This poem contains the unique 'oxyan' for 'ocean' and a remarkable line where the central syllable is repeated: 'Hope hath bihight ye ye ye but he . . . '. In part, then, he parades his English as distinctive and self-generated: its very pecularities work against the grain of the French. His use of the *envoi*, particularly in this instance, seems calculated to give poetic, formal voice to that passage from one language to

[73] R. Holinshed, *The Third volume of Chronicles* (London: Henry Denham, 1586), f.618.

[74] M. K. Jones, '"Gardez mon corps, sauvez ma terre"—Immunity from War and the Lands of a Captive Knight: The Siege of Orléans (1428–29) Revisited', in Arn, ed., *Charles d'Orléans in England*, 9–26 (13).

[75] Coldiron, *Canon, Period*, 46. Her fine account discusses the relationship between many of his English and French lyrics. For references to Arn's pioneering work on this topic, see the bibliography listed in Arn, ed., *Charles d'Orléans in England*, 215.

[76] I cite from M.-J. Arn, ed., *Fortunes Stabilnes: Charles d'Orléans's English Book of Love* (Binghamton, NY: Medieval and Renaissance Text Society, 1994).

another. Another quatrain, this time in French, offers some clue to his sense of this process:

> Le trucheman de ma pensee,
> Qui parle maint divers langaige,
> M'a rapporté chose sauvaige
> Que je n'ai point acoustumee.
> En francoys la m'a translatee[77]
>
> [The interpreter of my thought,
> who speaks many different languages,
> has brought me back something primitive (strange, wild)
> to which I am completely unaccustomed.
> He translated it into French for me . . .]

A medium, an interpreter (compare the 'drugemans' mentioned by Froissart), but also a trickster, the strange position in which Charles finds himself, culturally and linguistically, corresponds to all these roles. He asks for his French to be translated back to him: 'En francoys la m'a translatee'. In this extraordinary turn, he is now a stranger to his own language, exiled from it as he returns from captivity.[78]

Both Charles and Chaucer indicate the ways in which the deep linguistic rivalries of prolonged Anglo-French hostilities had created aberrant conditions for change. Returning once more to Chakrabarty's notion of 'rough translation', they both exemplify a kind of 'subaltern disjointedness' in their activities as translators. In discussing what is minor about the 'minority' of some particular pasts, Chakrabarty describes how 'these are pasts that are treated, to use an expression of Kant's, as instances of human "immaturity"'.[79] This has consistently been the fate of the *Book of the Duchess* and Charles's English poems, each dismissed as juvenilia in their roughness. But, he goes on, 'the archives thus help bring to view the disjointed nature of any particular "now" one may inhabit; that is the function of subaltern pasts'.[80] Chaucer's English in the late 1360s or 1370s was in a disjointed 'now': it made an exchange with French that involved subjection but also a claim on the future that its political ambitions sought. It was ironic that Charles should make a similar exchange, again in a temporal warp, but in the reverse condition of subjection. By then, however, it was a sign that both languages were different enough to be translated by the same person.

[77] Jean-Claude Mühlethaler, ed., *Charles d'Orléans: Ballades et Rondeaux: édition du manuscrit 25458 du fonds français de la Bibliothèque Nationale de Paris*, 2nd edn (Paris: Livre du Poche, 1992), 514, Rondeau 168, lines 1–4.

[78] See also the discussion by Jacqueline Cerquiglini, *The Colour of Melancholy: The Use of Books in the Fourteenth Century*, trans. Lydia G. Cochrane (Baltimore and London: Johns Hopkins University Press, 1997), 14–15.

[79] Chakrabarty, *Provincializing Europe*, 101.

[80] Chakrabarty, *Provincializing Europe*, 108.

9

Mother Tongues: English and French in fifteenth-century England

If 'father' is the commonest early trope attached to Chaucer, then English also in due course gathers to itself the description of 'mother'. This chapter continues the discussion of the status of English in relation to French into the fifteenth century by investigating this seemingly contradictory notion of English as a mother tongue or *materna lingua*. English's role as a vernacular in the fifteenth century is told in different, conflicting accounts. Perhaps the most influential linguistic argument is that of John Fisher, who makes the double case first for the rise of what he has called 'Chancery English' and, second, for the deliberate promotion of English by Henry V as part of a larger Lancastrian polity.[1] But other narratives as well currently jostle, perhaps more palpably, for our attention: the actions against heresy in Arundel's *Constitutions*; the vicissitudes in political action and language caused by the deposition and probable murder of Richard II and the regal establishing of Henry Bolingbroke and his successors; and the anxious establishment of Chaucer as laureate by *his* poetic successors.[2] The renaissance of interest in the fifteenth century among literary scholars has been driven at least partly by a profound dissatisfaction with the perception of the fifteenth century as 'dull'. We have learnt to see that the literary description 'dull' is artfully claimed by fifteenth-century poets, and hides a wealth of political self-fashioning.[3] The change of perspective has also been impelled by a richer engagement with history. This brings the disciplines closer together, but perhaps still only half-way.

[1] J. H. Fisher, 'Chancery and the Emergence of Standard Written English in the Fifteenth Century', *Speculum*, 52 (1977), 870–99; and 'A Language Policy for Lancastrian England', *PMLA*, 107 (1992), 1168–80. See also M. Richardson, 'Henry V, the English Chancery, and Chancery English', *Speculum*, 55 (1980), 726–50; and J. H. Fisher, M. Richardson, and J. L. Fisher, eds, *An Anthology of Chancery English* (Knoxville: University of Tennessee Press, 1984).

[2] See, most influentially, P. Strohm, *England's Empty Throne: Usurpation and the Language of Legitimation 1399–1422* (New Haven and London: Yale University Press, 1998), and *Politique: Languages of Statecraft between Chaucer and Shakespeare* (Notre Dame, IN: University of Notre Dame Press, 2005); J. Simpson, *Reform and Cultural Revolution* (Oxford: Oxford University Press, 2002); S. Lerer, *Chaucer and His Readers* (Princeton: Princeton University Press, 1993).

[3] For an influential exposition of this view, see D. Lawton, 'Dullness and the Fifteenth Century', *English Literary History*, 54 (1987), 761–99.

The fifteenth century has never seemed remotely self-deprecating to a historian interested in the Tudor wars of succession and the Hundred Years War.

Paul Strohm, most notably, has made it impossible for literary scholars now to ignore the deep historicities of Tudor imaginings. Yet for the historian and the student of nation the overriding event of the early fifteenth century was the battle of Agincourt. This historical perspective has not come fully into view for those interested in the textual vicissitudes of the fifteenth century. Now that we have learnt to read fifteenth-century English narratives of power, counsel, and report with a new kind of attention to their place within a densely woven network of events and words, it may be possible to engage more fully with that other pressing narrative of power as it was exercised by Tudor rulers on the continent. This unlikely but devastating English military success urges itself upon our attention in this book because it underpins a broader historical sense of the first half of the fifteenth century as one of triumphal achievement and hence of burgeoning national pride. It also underpins Fisher's proposition that English was specifically 'encouraged by Henry IV, and even more by Henry V' . . . 'as a deliberately instigated activity that laid the groundwork for the political actions of 1416–22'.[4]

This chapter seeks to connect these claims with our other understandings of fifteenth-century language and politics by setting them within the long history of English engagement with French. Its larger effort is thus to think through in a preliminary way some of the implications for our sense of English literary history of the narratives, both medieval and modern, that encircle Agincourt. Its working assumption, to put it briefly, is that Agincourt is not merely important but intrinsic to the history of English, though not in the way it is usually told. It seems no accident that the author, probably the Oxford teacher William Kingsmill, of the 1415 version of the *Manières de langage* should include a description of the battle as part of his pedagogic instruction to an English audience on how to speak French (see Fig. 8 below).[5]

While Fisher is careful to stress that French was important until after 1400, the more generally held assumption is that English makes huge strides in the fourteenth century. On literary grounds, the outstanding landmarks include the Auchinleck Manuscript, followed by the cluster of major 'Ricardian' poets in English (Chaucer, Langland, Gower, and the *Gawain*-manuscript). Their achievements are held to be buttressed by such political decisions as the 1362 Statute of Pleading which declared that English should be used in preference to French in court pleas and the delivery in the same year of the opening Speech to Parliament in English. I propose in this chapter to go over this ground in some detail, partly in the light of revisionary research by Serge Lusignan and Mark Ormrod, and partly by juxtaposing the rise of French teaching manuals with that of the English

[4] Fisher, 'A Language Policy for Lancastrian England', 1170, 1174.

[5] *Manières de Langage (1396, 1399, 1415)*, ed. A. M. Kristol (London: ANTS, 1995), 70.

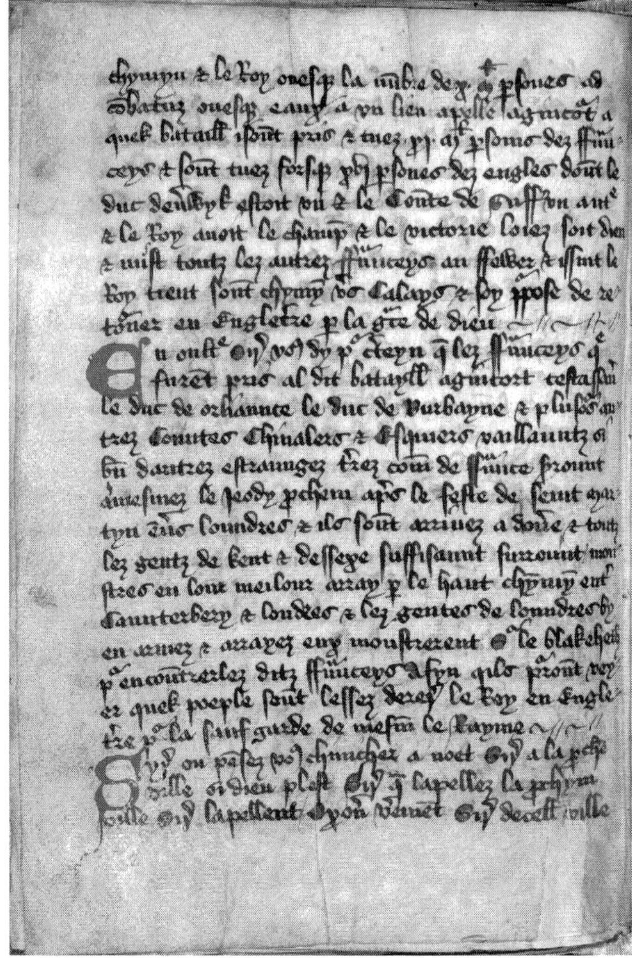

Figure 8. *Les Manières de langage*, fifteenth-century language treatise, dialogue on the battle of Agincourt

Trinity College, Cambridge MS B.14. 40, fol.149r.

vernacular prologue and its developing discourse of and about the use of English. The juxtaposition brings out the ways in which the relationship between English and French brings rich new perspectives to our sense of the literary and historiographical narratives of the period. The discussion of French in relation to English serves to underline the continuing importance of French in English culture between the mid-fourteenth and sixteenth centuries.

AGINCOURT AND ITS EFFECTS

It may be worth reminding ourselves (with necessary brevity) of the international context for the status of English and French across the fourteenth and into the fifteenth century. We have subtle accounts of the internal insecurities of polity and of language;[6] however, more attention to the wider efforts of the Lancastrian rulers to exert influence on the continental mainland brings different emphases to such perspectives. One reason why literary accounts of the late fourteenth century often sideline the Hundred Years War is because of the often-repeated view that Richard II was not only against war himself but surrounded by advisors who, on both sides of the Channel, were urging peace. Philippe de Mezières is the major figure of this period who sought to end the Anglo-French conflict through personal diplomacy and long, argued treatises addressed to Charles VI and Richard, as well as other members of the international aristocracy.[7] Yet Philippe's aims were far from pacifist; he wished to reorient the purpose of European warfare away from what might be called a civil war and towards a holy struggle to recapture Jerusalem from the Ottoman Turks. Richard certainly did not seem to have the desire of his father or grandfather to prosecute war on the continent, but the treaty of 1396 was less of a high water mark representing a new period of calm and recuperation in the Anglo-French conflict than a 'simple suspension of hostilities' that recognized an existing stalemate.[8] It was also the by-product of continental despair at the Great Schism and the crushing failure to date of the Christian west in resisting the increasing military strength of the Turks. Just two months before Richard's marriage in November 1396 to Isabella, the six-year-old daughter of Charles VI, the entire Crusading army was wiped out at Nicopolis.

Moreover, only three years later, the murky circumstances around Richard's deposition and death and the consequent shipping of Isabella back to France combined to upset any notions of long-term peace. Although Bolingbroke had had some support in France for his exile and the forfeiting of his lands by Richard, this evaporated with the shocking news of kingly usurpation and the snub to Isabella. The new Henry IV received two personal challenges from Louis d'Orléans, an attack on Gascony, and piracy escalating into sea battles in the

[6] See, in particular, Strohm, *Politique*. For a densely historicized argument connecting Ricardian courtly language with that of Charles V and the broader French literature of kingship, see L. Staley, *Languages of Power in the Age of Richard II* (Pennsylvania: Pennsylvania State University Press, 2005).

[7] His major treatises include in 1388–9 *Le Songe du Vieil Pèlerin*, ed. and trans. G. W. Coopland, 2 vols (Cambridge: Cambridge University Press, 1969); in 1389 *Epistre au Roi Richart/Letter to King Richard II*, ed. and trans. G. W. Coopland (Liverpool: Liverpool University Press, 1975); and his writings on the Order of the Passion, notably *De la Chevallerie de la Passion de Jhesu Crist* (1396). The dates are from Coopland; see also the concise yet wide-ranging discussion of his career and works by Staley, *Languages of Power*, 129–36.

[8] G. Harriss, *Shaping the Nation: England 1360–1461* (Oxford: Clarendon Press, 2005), 423.

Channel. Richard's fall was witnessed by the French esquire, chronicler and lyric composer Jean Creton, who decided to come over from Paris to spend some time in Richard's household in May 1399, and found himself present both during Richard's expedition to Ireland and then his capture at Conway. Creton, a friend of John de Montagu, earl of Salisbury, who invited him to join his party 'pour rire & pour chanter' (314) wrote in outraged tones in his *Histoire du Roy d'Angleterre Richard Traictant particulierement la Rebellion de ses subiectz et prinse de sa personne* of 'la traison mortelle' that was inflicted on Richard by those who had sworn loyal allegiance to him.[9] Creton's position is revealing of the multi-layered contortions that marked the Anglo-French relationship at this date. Although his chronicle is often described as a form of propaganda, the anomaly of its pro-Ricardian bias deserves comment.[10] It clearly suited the interests of Charles VI and Philippe, duc de Bourgogne to have material that denigrated Henry IV, yet Creton was no puppet.[11] He and Salisbury evidently shared an interest in lyric composition (Creton praises Salisbury's facility in creating 'balades & chancons,/Rondeaulx & laiz'[12]), and his seemingly spontaneous whim to travel to England for a spring break, even if embellished to suit his *dit amoureux*-inspired verse opening, implies a world in which such cross-channel visits were plausible and even common. The ease with which he and his companion are able to join Richard's household is shown up in relief when Henry comes to seize Richard. They were terrified, writes Creton, now writing in vivid prose, and asked the herald, Lancaster, to intercede with Henry to spare their lives:

A lentree du chastel nous mena lancastre le herault devāt le duc agenoilliez a terre, et lui dist le dit herault en langage englesch, que nous estions de france, et que le roy nous avoit envoie avecques le roy richart en irlande pour esbatre & pour veoir le pays, et que pour dieu il nous voulfist sauver la vie. Et lors nous respondi le duc en francoiz, Mes enfans . . .[13]

[At the entrance of the castle Lancaster the herald led us in front of the duke, kneeling on the ground, and the aforementioned herald said to him in the English language that we were from France, and that the king had sent us to go with king Richard to Ireland to enjoy ourselves and see the country, and that for God's sake he wanted to spare our lives. Then the duke replied in French to us, 'My children . . .']

In a pantomime of fearful supplication they get the herald to speak to Henry in English, explaining that they are merely tourists caught up in the fray. But Henry

[9] *Metrical History of the Deposition of King Richard II*, ed., J. Webb, *Archaeologia*, 20 (1824), 1–423.

[10] See the discussion in A. Gransden, *Historical Writing in England II c.1307 to the Early Sixteenth Century* (London: Routledge & Kegan Paul, 1982), 188–93.

[11] Philippe le Hardi paid Creton 60 écus for a book on Richard II that is most likely the chronicle (Gransden, *Historical Writing*, 161, n. 21); Charles III of Anjou (1414–72) also owned a fine illustrated copy (Gransden, *Historical Writing*, 189).

[12] Creton, *Metrical History*, 320.

[13] Creton, *Metrical History*, 373.

of course replies in French, a gesture which seems designed to confirm that he knows perfectly well both how to tantalize them with his anti-French status as a new claimant to the English throne and yet to show—from within their own language—that he understands their newly uncertain apprehension of their status in an English court. In this moment of stress, in other words, the French guests suddenly feel they have to submit to English as the medium of communication with an English figure of power: yet the anecdote reveals that this is an artificial piece of linguistic politics since they seem to have had no need to trouble themselves with English in Richard's court up to now.

Creton's account shows partiality to Richard because Creton himself was warmly received and well liked in the English royal household: whatever political capital was made of that in relation to Henry does not detract from the sense we gain both of the close family ties between Richard and his father-in-law, and of the relaxed easiness which characterized the wider network of friendly associations among Anglo-French personnel a little lower down the social scale. It was because of that closeness that the affront of Isabella's return to France was felt so keenly: cordial feelings and high dudgeon were never far apart. The change of ruler nonetheless marked the beginning of a new phase of conflict which was exposed when Henry V's sensational win at Agincourt coincided with the major ecclesiastical council held at Constance in 1416, just after the battle. This gave England a highly public, international arena in which to parade its political supremacy over France, and this served to consolidate Henry's plans to conquer France through settlement and not only through piecemeal warfare. For the first time, English settlers, especially in Normandy, were encouraged to take a long view of their residence in France and this was matched in reverse by the long-term forced residence in England of a large number of French aristocratic captives, most famously Charles d'Orléans. Such settlement created complex conditions for vernacular identity, since on both sides bilingualism was perpetuated, but with different pressures being placed on the hierarchical relationship between the two languages. More pragmatically than ever, French was needed by English diplomats, merchants, and settlers as they colonized Normandy and Paris;[14] conversely, as English gained ground in England, a consciousness began to develop of its continuing insignificance on the international stage.[15]

14 The most well-known account of the Parisian occupation is the anonymous *Journal d'un bourgeois de Paris, 1405–1449*, ed. A. Tuetey, Société de l'Histoire de Paris (Paris: Nogent-le-Rotrou, 1881), translated by J. Shirley, *A Parisian Journal (1405–1449)* (Oxford: Clarendon Press, 1968). New information on language practices during the occupation is emerging from the ongoing AHRC project *The Soldier in Later Medieval England*, directed by Anne Curry, as evidenced in her unpublished paper 'Languages in the military profession in the later middle ages', presented at *Language Over Time: A Symposium On Anglo-Norman In The Context Of Medieval French Language Use*, Birmingham City University, 19 January 2008.

15 Some of the individuals who invested most—personally, financially and legally—in the English occupation include Sir William Oldhall, Sir John Handford, Sir John Fastolf, Walter, Lord Fitzwalter and others, litigants to the *Parlement* of Paris: see C. T. Allmand and

Yet even this period of English dominance was thrown into uncertainty by the unexpectedly abrupt death of Henry in 1422, leaving a baby of nine months as his heir. Henry had made great gains on a variety of fronts: negotiating artfully between the rival French ducs of Bourgogne and Orléans, and the mentally unstable Valois king, Charles VI, he had seized the opportunities created by their bitter feuds. Jean Sans Peur of Bourgogne had Orléans assassinated in 1407; this led to an alliance of dukes against Jean Sans Peur who became known as the Armagnacs after they were joined by Bernard, comte d'Armagnac in 1410. The English mostly supported the Burgundians, and Jean Sans Peur was conspicuously absent from Agincourt. After Agincourt Henry V and Jean worked in a kind of tandem to obtain control over Normandy and Paris respectively. But then in a dramatic turn, Jean, seeking to resist the spread of Henry's ambition by reassessing his relationship with the dauphin, the future Charles VII, was himself murdered by the dauphin's guard in 1419 in a meeting at Montereau. This opened a route for Henry to fill the vacuum left by Jean. He not only offered support to the Burgundian garrison in Paris, but, arguing that the dauphin's brutal crime had disbarred him from the French throne, claimed his own right to become Charles VI's heir. Burgundians and Valois caught alike in a cleft stick, each feared Henry's alliance with the other. Henry's scheme thus succeeded and in the Treaty of Troyes in 1420, with the backing of Philip, Jean's successor, the dauphin's son was disinherited and Henry's own claim to the throne was sealed with his marriage to Charles's daughter, Catherine.

As Christopher Allmand has persuasively argued, this Treaty 'was the most important treaty of the Hundred Years War'.[16] Unlike any previous English assertion of right over French territory, Henry set himself up to be a joint ruler of two separate kingdoms, France and England. Piecemeal possession—of the fluctuating borders of Aquitaine, Calais, and the Crécy region, and more recently Normandy and Paris—changed to a larger claim over France itself. The astonishing audacity of Troyes could even be said to precipitate a new sense of what 'France' and 'England' meant. It is tempting to hail this as a nation-shaping moment. Yet the situation was full of contortions and complexities. On one side, the treaty could indeed be thought to create a notion of a unified France. It took an English monarch, in other words, to give cohesive shape to an otherwise bitterly fractured territorial and conceptual space in which ducal power had proved to be far more dominant than that of kingship.[17] An English perception that the way to govern France was to subsume all that division under a foreign

C. A. J. Armstrong, eds, *English Suits before the Parlement of Paris 1420–1436*, Camden Fourth Series, 26 (London: Offices of the Royal Historical Society, 1982), Appendix II, 290–309.

[16] C. Allmand, *The Hundred Years War: England and France at War c.1300–c.1450* (Cambridge: Cambridge University Press, 1988), 30.

[17] On the significance of Bedford's decision as regent to reunite the duchy of Normandy with the French crown, see Allmand and Armstrong, eds, *English Suits*, 4.

ruler seemed oddly persuasive, partly, of course, because of his military strength but also perhaps because this ruler was not 'foreign' in any straightforward sense. It was not just that in marrying Catherine Henry was creating a familial basis for joint rule, but that this marriage renewed the genealogical links between Henry and his grandfather, Edward III, through whom the dynastic rights over France (at least from an English point of view) were shared with, rather than presumed upon, the Valois.

Henry's death in 1422 naturally disturbed the stability promised by this treaty, especially since it was followed shortly after by the death of Charles VI. In a curiously circular historical twist, the baby assumed the double monarchy in a situation reminiscent of the death of Louis X in June 1316, whose son was born posthumously in November but survived only a few days. In claiming the throne, Philippe, Louis's brother, laid himself open to accusations of usurpation that Edward III was later to exploit. Bedford, brother of Henry V, like Philippe a century previously, became ruler of France and laid himself open to the rival claims of the disinherited dauphin. Bedford was content to be regent rather than king, but the historical similarities of the situation show just how intertwined the regnal histories of France and England were across many generations, and how the issues of dynastic right were exceptionally finely balanced. In the event, then, it was Bedford rather than an English king as such who, winning his own Agincourt at Verneuil in 1423, presided over the most extended period of English rule in France and gave English its most settled sense of itself as occupying a place on the continent.[18] The difference between this context for English occupation and Aquitaine or Calais was partly a matter of distance—Aquitaine had its own cultural world far from, and much more independent of Paris, and Calais was a small port whose crucial importance functioned very differently. It was also legal, linguistic, and cultural. Bedford's keen attention to the *Cour du Conseil* at Rouen established a network of property rights for English settlers such as Sir John Fastolf that bound them tightly to a region that was close to the English south coast, and hence created conditions for language use that had long-term ties to the continent, among individuals whose concerns straddled both continent and island.

This new post-Ricardian phase of the war thus created new conditions for the vernacular reach of both English and French. In attempting to define them, or at least clarify them, there are a great many factors to take into account. Perhaps most important is to realize the manner in which English settlement in France affected the nature of English as a continental export. Research into the language of the settlers is still in its very early stages, but what there is suggests that English

[18] The classic study is C. Allmand, *Lancastrian Normandy, 1415–1450: The History of a Medieval Occupation* (Oxford: Clarendon Press, 1983); more recently Anne Curry has also concentrated on this period: see her *Agincourt: A New History* (Stroud: Tempus, 2005) and the references cited there.

continued to have limited currency as an international language. The Henrys and Bedford ruled as French regents; although they encouraged English immigration, they did not seek to impose the English language on the French.[19] This is unsurprising in view of the arguments traced by this book thus far: the English had used French in France for centuries, having been themselves at least partially identified with French. At the same time, the increasing strength of English as a vernacular in England meant that English power abroad was increasingly purposively signified as English even if this was articulated in French. A rather crushing example of this is the description of the Agincourt victory in the 1415 *Manière*.[20] Conversely, the hostages brought back to England were confronted by this other vernacular, even if the more socially elevated of them were spoken and written to in French. We therefore have a complex situation in which both vernaculars persisted, yet their signifying value was changing. Moreover, they persisted on both sides of the Channel.

This brief historical purview must allude finally to the extraordinary way in which a seemingly very male history of division and conquest was itself challenged by a woman who carried out her revenge on the English in the guise of a male soldier. I will be discussing Jeanne d'Arc at greater length in the next and final chapter: here Jeanne serves to remind us that these issues of language and nation in the fifteenth century set male and female in large-scale opposition. Chaucer as 'father' works in a very different way from language as 'mother'; likewise, the two polar historical figures of the English and French fifteenth century—Henry V and Jeanne d'Arc—conjure supremely conflicting images of nation and of history. Jeanne's great effort to get Charles crowned, against all the odds, did succeed and, although she was put to death in the process, that coronation marked the most significant turning point of the war. Indirectly then, in this chapter she figures, like Blanche in the *Book of the Duchess* or Griselda in Boccaccio, Petrarch, Philippe de Mezières, and Chaucer, as a silenced woman whose eloquence speaks loudly in the halls of history.[21] It is a further argument of this chapter that the figuring of the vernacular as female had a vital, if tortuous, role in the developing discourse concerning vernacular authority in England.

[19] They also ruled as 'roys de France' and therefore 'ruled in their French territories according to French law', S. H. Cuttler, *The Law of Treason and Treason Trials in Later Medieval France* (Cambridge: Cambridge University Press, 1981), 40. Denise Angers reports that in Normandy in the fifteenth century out of 1063 actes covering 1418–21, 932 are in Latin, 129 in French and just 2 in English ('La guerre et le pluralisme linguistique', 133).

[20] *Manières de Langage*, ed. Kristol, 70.

[21] For a brief reference by Philippe de Mezières to the story of Griselda, see *Letter to King Richard II*, ed. Coopland, 115 (French), 42 (trans.); xxix, n. 53; his full retelling in the *Livre de la Vertu* is discussed by Staley, *Languages of Power*, 285–8.

THE STATUS OF ENGLISH

I return here to some of the issues that were raised in Chapter 2 about the status of the vernaculars in England, there focusing on the twelfth and thirteenth centuries. My argument there was that although the disciplinary histories of Anglo-Norman and continental French suggest otherwise, the changing character of insular French has much more in common with changes in continental French than is usually allowed. The corollary is that writing in English, especially in the period before the mid-fourteenth century, but also thereafter, is not isolated but richly engaged with England's other vernacular. English literature before the fourteenth century has been described as 'an "unstable continuum", a shape in which the spaces between texts are more common—and therefore seem more definitive—than writings themselves'.[22] It follows that to agree with this description one must predefine English as English. But if one does not so predefine English, what seems so natural as to be a tautology (English as English) no longer appears so. The barren desert in which a few oases of English miraculously hide awaiting charmed discovery vanishes, and is replaced by a fertile profusion of literature in which English finds its place among the far greater riches of French and Latin. Christopher Cannon has rightly commented that such a 'shape' of English literary history is 'necessarily the product of a kind of attention'.[23] It is the continuing argument of this book that if we broaden our attention to English vernacularity and see it as including French then English precisely changes its shape.

The other corollary is that we no longer need to privilege 'English' moments in our literary history, or at least we can re-examine the kinds of pressure that have been placed on such moments. Accounts of the rise of English, and their obverse narratives of the decline of French have been particularly prone to the collecting of anecdotes that are read as evidence of linguistic practice and status. Certain anecdotes have accumulated a venerable tradition of modern citation, such as—on the French side—Walter Map's apparently sneering comment about 'Marlborough French'[24] or the nun of Barking's reference to 'un faus franceis', through to Ranulph Higden's *Polychronicon* as translated by John Trevisa, Chaucer's Prioress, and Froissart on Richard II, and—on the English side—Trevisa again, the 1362 Statute of Pleading and the opening of Parliament in

[22] C. Cannon, *The Grounds of English Literature* (Oxford: Oxford University Press, 2004), 19, citing G. Shepherd, 'Early Middle English', in *The Middle Ages*, ed. W. F. Bolton (London: Barrie & Jenkins, Sphere, 1970), 81–117 (81).

[23] Cannon, *The Grounds of English Literature*, 20.

[24] A. M. Kristol's article 'La prononciation du français en Angleterre au XVe siècle', in *Mélanges de philologie et de littérature médiévales offerts à Michel Burger*, ed. J. Cerquiglini-Toulet and O. Collet (Geneva: Droz, 1994), 67–87, provides an important revisionary account of many of these examples.

English, Henry IV's use of his *materna lingua* in his maiden speech as king in 1399, and the Brewers' Craft declaration in 1422.[25] But the context for these anecdotes is rarely discussed in detail, and large generalizations are usually made to hang on them, some of them contradictory: thus a recent survey states 'from the middle of the twelfth century at the latest, most members of the aristocracy were bilingual. And what is more their mother tongue is likely to have been English; there can have been very few, if any, monolingual French speakers by that point.'[26] Yet, in another account, one finds: 'during the twelfth century there were still many French speakers in England, including people who moved between England and France like the aristocracy, the higher clergy, and their servants'.[27] The former appears to be speculating about 'English' aristocracy, yet numerous members of this social group were international figures who, as Nicholas Orme suggests in the second remark, were frequent travellers across the Channel and cannot easily be described as 'English'.[28] Speculation that hardens into assertion has unfortunately been characteristic of much standardly referenced discussion of the languages of England, where a single chance remark is often made to yield a fact about a whole social group, or even an entire population.[29] And as we saw in Chapter 3, remarks about dialect are especially hard to interpret, and may be very misleading as evidence of 'corrupt' usage.[30]

Three kinds of alternative argument will be made. The first is that we need to rethink our model of insular French to account for some of the complexities of language contact that are now being uncovered.[31] It is no longer adequate to say that either insular French was a mother tongue or else it was dead, especially of the fourteenth and even fifteenth centuries. Second, our narratives about the status of English need to accommodate the new point that is emerging: French was actually increasing its vernacular profile through the latter part of this period, obviously most emphatically on the continent but in England as well. As I will discuss below, the English played a crucial role in promoting French at the turn of the fourteenth century and into the fifteenth through the development of vernacular grammars and other materials for teaching French. Third, some of the

[25] For references to these instances, see below. N. Orme, *Medieval Schools from Roman Britain to Renaissance England* (New Haven, CT: Yale University Press, 2006), see 74–8; de Mezières, *Letter to King Richard II*, ed. Coopland, xvii; A. G. Rigg and E. S. Moore, 'The Latin Works: Politics, Lament, Praise', in S. Echard, ed., *Companion to Gower* (Woodbridge: D. S. Brewer, 2004), 153–64 (154).

[26] M. Townend, 'Contacts and Conflicts: Latin, Norse, and French', in *The Oxford History of English*, ed. L. Mugglestone (Oxford: Oxford University Press, 2006), 61–85 (67).

[27] Orme, *Medieval Schools*, 74.

[28] See R. Bartlett, 'The Cross-Channel Realm', *England Under the Norman and Angevin Kings 1075–1225* (Oxford: Clarendon Press, 2000), 11–28.

[29] For a survey of such references to the 1362 Statute of pleading, for example, see W. M. Ormrod, 'The Use of English: Language, Law, and Political Culture in Fourteenth-Century England', *Speculum*, 78 (2003), 750–87, n. 2.

[30] For a survey of scholarship on insular French, see Chapter 2, n. 42 and 46.

[31] See Chapter 2 and the work of Trotter, Rothwell, Ingham, and Wright cited there.

implications of this vernacular growth of French can be traced in the developing genre of the English vernacular prologue and the mother tongue discourse which becomes more prominent in English in the fifteenth century. English ideas about *materna lingua* were convoluted, even self-undermining, not least because of its associations with a feminized image of French.

An enormous amount has been written on the development of English in the late fourteenth and fifteenth centuries. It is true to say, though, that there is far from being a consensus about the finer details of this process, and indeed some recent work, notably by W. M. Ormrod on the 1362 Statute of Pleading, has called into question many of the traditional pieties. Ormrod has been reinvestigating evidence from a historian's perspective: here I will be suggesting that a rich area for further research lies in the relationship between English and French linguistic usage in this period. Much of the current, and very invigorating work on Chancery English, on law, on Lollardy and the English Bible and vernacular theology more broadly, and on women's literacy, perhaps naturally takes an English line. The evidence for change and growth—one might think hardly surprisingly—is taken from writings *in English*, from Prologues to English translations of devotional and didactic material, collected together in the pioneering compilation by Jocelyn Wogan-Browne, Ruth Evans, and Nicholas Watson, or from chancery and guild records, petitions, letters, chronicles, even literature.

Yet one could argue that this is only half, or perhaps even only a third, of the picture. Our perspective on the use of English will be limited if we do not take into account the ways in which writers of English are working alongside, through, across, and sometimes against, the far more culturally dominant languages of French and Latin. French is of particular relevance and interest because it is also an English vernacular. Writing in English rarely happens in a linguistic vacuum: with few exceptions (to reiterate conclusions from earlier chapters), writers of English in the texts that have come down to us developed their sense of language through Latin and French. Their use of English, then, is implicated in, trammelled by, contexts in which English is far from being an accepted or current linguistic medium.[32]

My argument in detail is that the two narratives, the rise of English and the decline of French, need to be at once disentangled and re-entangled. Currently the one is predicated on the other: proof of English's rise can be found in the decline of French and vice versa. But this leads to distortions and the overvaluing of specific moments of linguistic assertion or denigration. The obituary of French in the later period has been prematurely written. Instead, the evidence points overwhelmingly to a linguistic situation in which English's rise as a vernacular can be understood only by recognizing how deeply it was pressured,

[32] The historian J. Catto, 'Written English: The Making of the Language 1370–1400', *Past and Present*, 179 (2003), 24–59 has recently made a pungent case along these lines.

enveloped, and stimulated by the concurrent changes in the status of French right through the medieval period and, as I will also argue, well into the early modern. Looking at the two vernaculars together gives us a much richer context for understanding vernacularity than attempts to find evidence of English's newly acquired authority, or, for that matter, to visit decline upon French. The new surge in English power and presence on the continent under the Lancastrians brought with it a complex renegotiation of identity through language, and this manifests itself in an absorbing playoff between two models of vernacular power.

Ormrod has sought to make some important and overdue distinctions between oral and written usage of both English and French.[33] In essence he argues that English took longer to gain authority as a *written* vernacular than is often assumed, and that the role of French in sustaining the written record of government, parliament, trade, and law was both longstanding and enduring. His careful reading of the 1362 Statute in both its surviving Anglo-French versions as a parliament roll and a statute roll argues convincingly that it had a symbolic rather than a substantive status. Noting that the final day of business of the parliament coincided with Edward III's fiftieth birthday, Ormrod concludes that it was part of a wider set of initiatives to demonstrate the king's goodwill to his subjects and was 'ultimately accepted by most of its potential beneficiaries as something of a fleeting fancy'.[34] Whether or not this is supportable, Ormrod's effort to reassess the documents at the very least makes clear that only the most patient contextual work will make sense of their wider social and historical implications. The larger point is that the Statute does not, as is so often claimed, seal the process by which English became an official language. Serge Lusignan has detailed how French remained the language of law and of administration until well into the fifteenth century (and in the case of law very much longer) and the scattered references to the use of English in public, official documents or public speaking need to be placed in that context. The very fact that the Statute itself was recorded in French, though obvious enough, reminds us that, rather like *De Vulgari eloquentia* where Dante wrote his support for Tuscan in Latin, the Statute may have called for the use of English but enacted that call in French.

Law French, established since the reign of Henry II as the spoken language of the royal courts, was applied more widely than ever from the 1360s.[35] Yet we must not assume too readily that this meant it was only a written language. It is widely asserted by modern scholars that French ceased to be used as a spoken

[33] Ormrod, 'The Use of English'. I have learnt much from this important article, which was anticipated in part by W. Rothwell, 'English and French in England after 1362', *English Studies*, 6 (2001), 539–59, but differ from certain of its claims and deductions.

[34] Ormrod, 'The Use of English', 763.

[35] Brand, 'The Languages of the Law', 72–3, touches on the later fourteenth-century evidence, though his main argument concerns the thirteenth century.

vernacular in England from as early as the thirteenth century, or perhaps even earlier.[36] Even Ormrod believes:

It was the very fact that so few people in England actually spoke French after the thirteenth century that itself accounted for the development, during the later thirteenth and early fourteenth century, of law French as the official language of disputation in the courts and of Anglo-Norman as an accepted language of written communication in royal and civic government. In other words, the employment of French as a formal and authoritative language of process actually increased in inverse proportion to its use as a language of generalized social exchange.[37]

But the evidence adduced for the lack of spoken French rests largely on the survival of the first teaching treatise on French by one Walter Bibbesworth in the thirteenth century, on the somewhat curious grounds that its existence proves that people in England no longer spoke French.[38] As I will shortly discuss of this and other teaching material, especially of the *Femina nova*, a teaching text recast from Bibbesworth in the fifteenth century, this is a highly misleading deduction both of the state of French in the thirteenth century, and of its implied obsolescence thereafter. One of the problems is that there is no recognition that many kinds of French may be in use, varying between monolingual 'mother tongue' usage, second language acquisition on varying levels, and bilingual users who may have only written competence in French but do not use it orally, or vice versa. A further complication—as we can see from the *Manières*—is that many of these insular users of French, especially those who worked in areas of cross-channel business, were frequently exposed to continental French, both oral and written. After the onset of war under Edward III, French in all these varieties, insular, continental, and hybrid, actually gained a stronger oral and written presence in England in the fourteenth century and into the fifteenth, from various directions: the increase in legal and diplomatic business, the increase in cross-channel travel for military personnel and merchants as well as the higher ranking clerks, clerics and diplomats, and the presence of political prisoners,

[36] Rothwell, 'English and French'; Short, 'On Bilingualism', 468.

[37] Ormrod, 'The Use of English', 755.

[38] This treatise, Walter of Bibbesworth, *Le Tretiz*, ANTS, Plain Texts Series 6 (London: ANTS) was edited by William Rothwell in 1990, and republished, with minor corrections, in 2002, downloadable on <http://www.anglo-norman.net/sources/>. A new edition of the Trinity MS B.14.40 version of *Femina* is also now available online, ed. W. Rothwell (Swansea and Aberystwyth: Anglo-Norman Online Hub, 2005). On Bibbesworth, see W. Rothwell, 'The Place of *Femina* in Anglo-Norman Studies', *Studia Neophilologica*, 70 (1998), 55–82; W. Rothwell, 'Anglo-French and Middle English Vocabulary in *Femina Nova*', *Medium Aevum*, 69 (2000), 34–58; W. Rothwell, 'The Teaching and Learning of French in Later Medieval England', *Zeitschrift für französische Sprache and Literature*, 111 (2001), 1–18; S. Lusignan, *La Langue des rois au Moyen âge: le français en France et en Angleterre* (Paris: PUF, 2004), 191–4, and R. Haas, '*Femina*: Female Roots of "Foreign" Language Teaching and the Rise of Mother-Tongue Ideologies', *Exemplaria*, 19 (2007), 139–62.

including—in the case of those who were of high social status—their retinues and household associates.[39]

It might be objected that these factors are a separate matter from the speaking of French as an insular vernacular. But evidence of the nature of vernacular speech is notoriously hard to gather, and we should be wary of assuming that the various linguistic worlds of French—legal, financial and courtly, insular and continental—did not bleed into each other, nor that oral and written practice in any of these areas were necessarily kept separate. We do not need to assume, in other words, that the absence of monolingual 'mother tongue' speakers of insular French would necessarily mean that French did not have an oral presence in late medieval England. This was created in part by law French: the high competence of English lawyers in oral pleading in French did not happen in secluded corners; it was an audible aspect of many kinds of transaction from property deals, claims against disorderly conduct, improper trade practices, and so on. And it was also created by the influx of hostages after the Treaty of Brétigny, which, since it contributed to an increase in the number of monolingual continental French users in England, put pressure on English courtiers to use more French, and a French that was, as a result, responding directly to continental French.

It follows that this world of mixed language use in both spoken and written contexts was full of highly volatile linguistic competence. We cannot then pronounce too quickly on matters of oral decline or increase, especially when relying on written evidence. In the case of Parliament, where we have a closely defined public arena for speech, Ormrod has rightly insisted that 'changes in the language of the *written* text on the parliament rolls—from Latin to French in the early fourteenth century and from French to a combination of Latin, French, and English in the fifteenth century—provide little or no indication in themselves of any precise timing in the shifts of *spoken* language' (777).[40] Even Ormrod, then, by his own account, is guilty of exaggerated speculation when he writes of the downward trend of French in 'generalized social exchange'. We cannot speak substantively of a general situation; and the social exchange among certain select classes (though of course not among others) with plenty of cross-channel contact was evidently full of French. Moreover, the influx of continental French speakers and writers, as earlier chapters have discussed, had an undoubted influence, in the case of Gower, for instance, upon the character of *written* insular French.[41] It also influenced English.

Ormrod's larger argument, in short, is not only convincing but can be taken further. The increasing oral strength of English is taking place in an environment

[39] As well as references cited in earlier chapters, see, concerning musical contacts, A. Wathey, 'The Marriage of Edward III and the Transmission of French Motets to England', *Journal of the American Musicological Society*, 45 (1992), 1–29.

[40] Ormrod, 'The Use of English', 777.

[41] See Chapter 7, n. 41 above.

where French is also increasing its oral presence. Where this occurs among literate personnel, trained increasingly in *writing* French as well as Latin, then the potential for language contact and exchange is high. It also perhaps puts pressure on English to perform with more public dignity. To give further context to this, it is worth recalling that the 1362 Statute follows a period in France when Charles, then duc de Normandie but shortly to accede as king on the death of his father Jean II in 1364, transformed the use of the vernacular in royal government. Required to act as regent after the capture of his father at Poitiers, Charles presided over a radical administrative overhaul in which the percentage of *rémissions* granted in French as opposed to Latin grew from around 10 per cent in 1356, to 60 per cent in 1358 and more than 80 per cent in 1359–60.[42] The use of French dropped dramatically again once Jean II returned from captivity in 1360, but, as king, Charles energetically resumed his vernacular project, and began also commissioning translations of scientific, devotional, and historical material on a large scale.[43] Lusignan suggests that one reason for Charles's interest in promoting French was his own weakness in Latin;[44] be that as it may, it seems possible that the impulse for the English Statute may have arisen in part from a post-Poitiers desire to assert English in the courts and perhaps even to compete with Charles's reforms.[45] But there is no need to posit any sense of direct response from English officials to French administrative procedures, to suspect that both English and French judiciary were acting in parallel to conditions mutually enforced on both sides by the war. The difference between the two situations is that English did not yet have the written authority of French, and so the Statute alludes only to oral pleading and its injunctions were never carried out.[46] It was not until the reign of Henry V that written English was adopted for use, and then only in his signet correspondence (the first securely dated letter is from 1417) rather than under the privy seal or in chancery.[47] Not a single document in Hoccleve's privy seal formulary is in English (they are all in French); chancery continued to function in French and (perhaps surprisingly) increasingly in Latin throughout the fifteenth century.[48]

[42] Lusignan, *La Langue des rois*, 121.

[43] See Staley, *Languages of Power*, 270, as part of her chapter 'French Georgics and English ripostes', 265–338.

[44] Lusignan, *La Langue des rois*, 122–3.

[45] Lusignan posits a similar argument to Ormrod's about the use of the vernacular to deal with fallout from the war, in France from the États (Lusignan, *La Langue des rois*, 120–21) and in England from the labour crises (Ormrod, 'The Use of English', 769).

[46] Fisher, Richardson, and Fisher, eds, *Anthology of Chancery English*, xv. Ormrod oddly castigates Devaux for citing the unenforcement of the statute as 'evidence of the enduring influence of French', although his own essay contributes to that assessment, 'The Use of English', 750, n. 2. My wider case could be said to support Devaux, though it seeks not to pit one language against the other but rather to consider their mutual influence on linguistic practices and assumptions.

[47] Fisher, Richardson, and Fisher, eds, *Anthology of Chancery English*, 84–5.

[48] Fisher, Richardson, and Fisher, eds, *Anthology of Chancery English*, 20.

One of the sources of special assertion (both medieval and modern) about English as a written language is the Wycliffite Bible. Much emphasis has been placed in recent scholarship on the role of this translation in affirming the authority of English.[49] Put simply, many scholars have argued that the decision to render the Bible in English was the catalyst which enabled English to start taking itself seriously. Building on the many links between Lollardy and the members of Chaucer's circle, Andrew Cole has further argued that the Wycliffite General Prologue had a direct influence upon Chaucer's Prologue to *The Treatise on the Astrolabe*, and hence upon Chaucer's sense of his place among English translators, that is, translators into English. Whether or not the specific link between Chaucer and the Wycliffite General Prologue is accepted, the existence of a Bible in English was clearly of enormous significance to the growth of the vernacular. Ironically, however, this cut both ways. For, as is well known, the initial support for Lollardy among the more powerful members of the court and metropolitan circles in the fourteenth century changed to anxiety and hostility: certainly, as Nicholas Watson emphasized in the mid-1990s, by 1409 'the close connections between Lollardy and the vernacular had come . . . to be a major focus of institutional concern'.[50] But even before then, there are signs that writing in English was certainly not advanced, and perhaps even suppressed in official circles: Caroline Barron has pointed to the gap in the London Letter Books, and we might add to this the absence of consolidation in terms of written practices of the apparent new push towards English in the Statute and parliamentary speech.[51] Thus although the records state that the next two parliaments in 1363 and 1365 were also opened in English, this did not lead to the adoption of English as a language of record, a situation which did not change until the 1420s.

The picture that is emerging has much in agreement with Andrew Cole's finely nuanced account of English as subject to many pressures and vicissitudes. Taking more direct account of the similar pressures upon French means, however, that we can be clearer about the relative lack of written status possessed by English. It might even suggest that the undoubted importance of the new writers in English, Chaucer and Langland pre-eminent among them, was still based more heavily upon their oral circulation than we have tended to assume.[52]

[49] A. Cole, 'Chaucer's English Lesson', *Speculum*, 77 (2002), 1128–67.

[50] N. Watson, 'Censorship and Cultural Change in Late-Medieval England: Vernacular Theology, the Oxford translation debate, and Arundel's Constitutions of 1409', *Speculum*, 70 (1995), 822–64 (829).

[51] In an unpublished paper delivered during a session on Medieval London at the 41st International Congress on Medieval Studies, Kalamazoo, 4–7 May 2006.

[52] This might be said to be especially true of the unfixed character of *Piers Plowman* manuscripts.

A single remark by Trevisa, whose time at The Queen's College, Oxford partly overlapped with that of Wycliff,[53] is widely used as 'evidence' that French ceased to be a language of importance in England from 1385.[54] It occurs in the famous description in chapter 59 ('De incolarum linguis' or 'Of the langage of the inhabitores of Englonde' as the BL MS Harley 2261 copy translates the title) of Trevisa's glossed translation of Higden's *Polychronicon.* Trevisa says:

Iohn Cornwaile, a maister of grammer, chaunged þe lore in gramer scole and construccioun of Frensche in to Englische; and Richard Pencriche lerned þe manere techynge of hym and of oþere men of Pencrich; so þat now, the ȝere of oure Lorde a þowsand þre hundred and foure score and fyue, and of the secounde kyng Richard after þe conquest nyne, in alle þe gramere scoles of Engelond, children leueþ Frensche and construeþ and lerneþ an Englische[55]

This passage has caused confusion, and indeed it contains some ambiguities. Even before we try to attend to the facts that Trevisa may or may not be asserting, it seems important to register that his style is hyperbolic. As Tim Machan has pointed out, we must not take Trevisa's extravagant rhetoric at face value: it is implausible that Trevisa could know, in any specific factual sense, what 'alle the gramere scoles of Engelond' were teaching.[56] Andrew Galloway is surely right that Trevisa's interest in the date 1385 is bound up with making the date of his own writing into an 'epochal' event, and we must be wary of mistaking it for sober description.[57] Trying to deduce what was really going on in English grammar schools is not easy. Ostensibly Trevisa is referring to the teaching of Latin grammar, and claiming that from 1385 all grammar school boys in England were being taught Latin through the medium of English rather than French. Yet this seems very unlikely to be the case in general. Evidence from the pedagogical material suggests that throughout the fourteenth century a mixture of teaching in a mixture of languages took place, but that the primary goal of language teaching remained to instruct pupils in the reading and writing of Latin. This process was evidently aided from the thirteenth century on with

[53] R. Waldron, 'Trevisa, John (b. *c.*1342, d. in or before 1402)', *Oxford Dictionary of National Biography* (Oxford University Press, 2004); <http://0-www.oxforddnb.com.catalogue.ulrls.lon.ac.uk:80/view/article/27722> (accessed 3 December 2008).

[54] See, among many others, J. Coleman, *Medieval Readers and Writers: English Literature in History 1350–1400* (London: Hutchinson, 1981), 30; Kibbee, *For to Speke Frenche Trewely*, 55–6; J. Burrow, 'The Languages of Medieval England', in *The Oxford History of Literary Translation in English Volume 1: To 1500*, ed. R. Ellis (Oxford: Oxford University Press, 2008), 23.

[55] *Polychronicon Ranulphi Higden monachi Cestrensis*, ed. C. Babington and J. R. Lumby, 9 vols, Rolls Series 41 (London: Longman, Green, Longman, Roberts, and Green, 1865–86), II, 161.

[56] T. W. Machan, *English in the Middle Ages* (Oxford: Oxford University Press, 2003), 84.

[57] A. Galloway, 'Latin England', in K. Lavezzo, ed., *Imagining a Medieval English Nation* (Minneapolis: University of Minnesota Press, 2004), 41–95 (47). It might be worth pointing out that despite the rhetoric, only fourteen manuscripts survive of Trevisa's translation of Higden as opposed to 118 manuscripts in Latin, which contributes to a sense of Trevisa's special pleading about the importance of English.

vernacular glossing, with some English but largely in French.[58] Two groups of orthographical treatises, one originally dating from *c.*1300 and the other *c.*1400 show that French was also being taught, again with occasional reference to English but largely through the medium of Latin.[59] Interestingly, some of the same pedagogic material for teaching French was being used both in England and on the continent.[60] The balance between written and spoken instruction is not entirely clear for French, and must have varied. The teaching of French seems to have had a range of audiences: from the specific pragmatic needs of thirteenth-century aristocratic families in administering estates (the target of Bibbesworth's *Tretiz*) to those in the fourteenth century and later, who were already schooled in Latin and were seeking to improve their legal or diplomatic writing as well as speaking skills in French.

However, beyond the immediate question of what was being taught and when, in the context of the whole chapter Trevisa's larger point is rather different from the nationalistic promotion of English that is usually assumed.[61] He has just described, with equal extravagance, that before 'the deth' (that is, the Black Death), children were learning French from the cradle:

children in scole aȝenst þe vsage and manere of alle oþere naciouns beeþ compelled for to leue hire owne langage, and for to construe hir lessouns and here þynges in Frensche . . . Also gentil men children beeþ i-tauȝt to speke Frensche from þe tyme þat þey beeþ i-rokked in here cradel, and kunneþ speke and playe wiþ a childes broche; and vplondisshe men wil likne hym self to gentil men, and fondeþ wiþ greet besynesse for to speke Frensce, for to be i-tolde of.[62]

Not just the gentle classes but 'vplondisshe men' are alike saturating their children with French. What he then pictures as a contrasting dearth of French is not to be welcomed but deplored. This situation, he writes, has 'auauntage in

[58] T. Hunt, ed., *Teaching and Learning Latin in Thirteenth-Century England*, 3 vols (Cambridge: D. S. Brewer, 1991). Fisher writes: 'every reference that I have found to school books or subjects taught in the formal curriculum in the fourteenth and fifteenth centuries is to Latin', 'Chancery', 893.

[59] Kibbee, *For to Speke Frenche Trewely*, 47–57. Evidence for the use of English primers in schools is sparse and 'not very satisfactory', J. A. Hoeppner Moran, *The Growth of English Schooling, 1340–1548: Learning Literacy and Laicization in Pre-Reformation York Diocese* (Princeton: Princeton University Press, 1985), 45. Moran reports that Oxford University statutes *c.*1380 required grammar school teachers to use English and French; however very few English primers survive before the fifteenth century: she cites just one, 43–9. Her evidence (37, n. 46) that grammar school children learnt to compose Latin in an English rather than French medium from 'as early as the 1340s' is, once more, from Trevisa.

[60] B. Merrilees, 'Donatus and the Teaching of French in Medieval England', in *Anglo-Norman Anniversary Essays*, ed. I. Short, ANTS Occasional publications 2 (London: ANTS, 1993), 273–91 (276–7).

[61] I differ here from Andrew Galloway, who sees Trevisa as pronouncing 'the birth of a fully, irrevocably unifying and isolating, national language, springing forth full-born from the grammar masters of his own native Cornwall', 'Latin England', 48.

[62] *Polychronicon Ranulphi Higden*, ed. Babington and Lumby, II, 159.

oon side and disauauntage in another side'. The advantage is that children learn grammar more quickly, but the disadvantage is:

þat now children of gramer scole conneþ na more Frensche þan can hir lift heele, and þat is harme for hem and þey schulle passe þe see and trauaille in straunge landes and in many oþer places. Also gentil men haueþ now moche i-left for to teche here children Frensche. (161)

In tones prefiguring laments about the state of language teaching in twenty-first-century Britain, we find here a cue for the *Femina nova.* Trevisa reveals that in his view, and those of 'gentil men', the acquisition of French was still extremely desirable, and indeed an unquestioned necessity since, after the Black Death, the 'gentil men' had to strive all the harder to achieve it. That this was not an aspiration confined to 'gentil men' is suggested by Langland's complaint, voiced through Anima, that there is 'nought oon among an hundred [of these new clerks] that an auctour kan construwe, / Ne rede a lettre in any language but in Latyn or in Englissh'.[63] If we move on from trying to take Trevisa literally in his comments on grammar schools, the chapter turns out to be a much more broadly revealing window on language perception.[64] For Trevisa's trenchantly expressed observations indicate that attitudes towards French are becoming more varied and subject to changing social conditions. The expectation that educated (and aspirant) children will 'passe the see and trauaille in straunge landes' gives a new impetus to French, since English is evidently of no use abroad. What Trevisa seems to be registering, in fact, is that there is a renewed interest in continental French.

The rest of the chapter muses in fascinating ways about his realization that these international considerations are changing the way people think about language. We see this in the way the dialogue (created by Trevisa) between Higden and Trevisa in his gloss develops. Higden, as it were, responds thoughtfully:

Hit semeþ a greet wonder how Englische, [þat is þe burþe tonge of Englisshe] men and her owne langage and tonge, is so dyuerse of sown in þis oon ilond, and þe langage of Normandie is comlynge of anoþer londe, and hath oon manere soun among alle men þat spekeþ hit ariȝt in Engelond. (161)

But this stimulates Trevisa to the very sharply perceptive cross-channel observation that:

[63] W. Langland, *Piers Plowman: The Prologue and Passus I–VII*, ed. J. A. W. Bennett (Oxford: Clarendon Press, 1972), XV, 374–5.

[64] Kibbee's remarks concerning this statute are particularly unsatisfactory, and often inaccurate, *For to Speke Frenche Trewely*, 58–9. He is wrong, for instance, about the decline in French in the legal system, and outdoes Trevisa's rhetoric in claiming that the plague killed French as well as people: 'this devastating disease struck the final blows against the French language, weakening the former strongholds of that language to the point where they could no longer resist the advance of English', *For to Speke Frenche Trewely*, 58.

Neuerþeles þere is as many dyuers manere Frensche in þe reem of Fraunce as is dyuers manere Englische in þe reem of Engelond. (161)

Against the grain, perhaps, Trevisa finds himself admitting that English, 'burþe tonge' or no, is not emerging as the unified superior alternative to French. On the contrary, it looks more 'dyuerse' than ever. It is French, by contrast, that seems to have unifying force in England: 'oon manere soun'. But a moment's reflection reminds him that French, too, is 'dyuerse'. The more pressure increases for the English to speak French abroad, the more they realize that 'their' French is only one of many.

This is an extraordinary set of comments, and, amongst other things, the chapter as a whole, with its famous remarks on the 'scharp, slitting, and frotyng' (163) character of English in York, betrays an awareness that whatever one may think about one's 'owne langage and tonge', the reality of linguistic practice disrupts the rhetoric of unity. For our purposes, it is especially significant that Trevisa does not make this argument on an insular basis. He understands language use in England to be as much a matter of negotiation between the island and the continent as it is between different regions of the north, south, and west. His sensitivity to sound and accent—to 'straunge wlafferynge, chiterynge, harrynge, and garrynge grisbayting' (159)—manifests itself not only in this vividly onomatopoeic vocabulary but as a comment about language perception. He is torn between wanting to assert a simplicity for English, 'that natif langage', but actually expressing with considerable linguistic sophistication that language is heard and spoken in England, now just as much in the past, with a bewildering intralingual diversity. But the international context for his reflections shows him aware that English's relationship to French is developing out of an insular model of historical polyglossia (as first outlined by Bede) into an even more complexly shifting modern diglossia, in which insular Englishes and Frenches are revealed as such (that is, precisely as plural) by their contact with continental French diversity.

Far from deserting French, the aspiring gentles created an exceptional moment in the history of vernacular language. For the date of Trevisa's chapter corresponds to a new wave of French teaching manuals. Let us examine these now more closely to see what kinds of assumptions they bring to bear upon the character of English and French at the turn of the fourteenth century, and how they influence it.

TEACHING FRENCH IN ENGLAND

The first model letters in French and Latin survive from the 1350s, just after the Black Death, by the Oxford teacher Thomas Sampson.[65] They, and various other

[65] Kibbee, *For to Speke Frenche Trewely*, 84. For information on the Oxford teachers, see a series of articles by H. G. Richardson, 'An Oxford Teacher of the Fifteenth Century', in *Bulletin of the*

written materials designed for teaching French which appear at the end of the fourteenth and into the fifteenth centuries, have been studied from several perspectives.[66] My purpose here is to ponder their significance for the linguistic tensions of the later stages of the war, and in particular by setting them in the context of the Anglo-French jargon texts that have been a focus of earlier chapters of this book. In the case of the jargon texts specific issues arise about the perceptions each side had of each other's use of language. The teaching manuals are very much part of this tradition in one sense, since they are engaged precisely in conveying an image of French to their readers. At the same time they have a pedagogic purpose which affects the tone and style of the writing: it has the potential to unlock—even without the same kind of cunningly manipulated ironies—various cultural perceptions about language in England at the end of the fourteenth and well into the fifteenth centuries.

Here is a brief sketch of the materials. They can be considered as falling into eight categories: simple interlinear glosses; more extensive nominalia, glossaries, and word lists; the Bibbesworth *Tretiz*; works of grammar, including verb conjugation tables; treatises on orthography; the *manières* or dialogues; model letters (*ars dictaminis*), and finally, legal treatises.[67] These have a broadly chronological development: the glosses started appearing in the twelfth century where their function evidently concerned learning Latin rather than teaching French.[68] Trilingual glosses and the first French–English wordlists appear in the second half of the thirteenth century, in which we can include Bibbesworth's *Tretiz* as the most extensive and sophisticated example. Towards the end of the fourteenth century a much wider set of materials begins to emerge which gives French the apparatus of Latin grammar teaching. Bibbesworth's treatise, which survives in two thirteenth-century and eleven fourteenth- and early fifteenth-century manuscripts[69] was repackaged in the fifteenth century in a further three manuscripts, Trinity College Cambridge B 14.39/40; London, British Library MS Sloane 513; and Oxford, All Souls College MS 182. While Sloane 513 and All

John Rylands Library, 23 (1939), 436–57; 'Letters of the Oxford Dictatores', in *Oxford History Society*, New Series, 5 (1942), 360–416; 'Cistercian formularies', in *Formularies which bear on the History of Oxford c.1204–1420*, ed. H. E. Salter, et al., 2 vols (Oxford: Clarendon Press, 1942), II, 281–327; 'Business training in Medieval Oxford', *The American Historical Review*, 46 (1941), 259–79.

[66] The work of editing and describing these materials has been carried out by William Rothwell, Tony Hunt, Andreas Kristol, Brian Merrilees, and Serge Lusignan, building on work by M. Dominica Legge and other scholars.

[67] These categories are outlined by Kristol in his compendium of sources in 'L'enseignement du français en Angleterre (XIIIe-XVe siècles): Les sources manuscrites', *Romania*, 111 (1990), 289–330.

[68] Hunt, ed., *Teaching and Learning*. Kristol suggests that the Oxford, Bodleian Library MS Douce 88 *Nominalia* was designed for those wishing to acquire French to a similar level of attainment as their (obviously good) Latin, 'L'enseignement du français', 300.

[69] I take these identifications from Kristol, 'L'enseignement du français'; see also R. Dean and M. B. M. Boulton, *Anglo-Norman Literature: A Guide to Texts and Manuscripts* (London: ANTS, 1999), nos 285 and 286.

Souls 182 are simply abbreviated 'mixed' recensions of Bibbesworth's original treatise, the version in TCC B 14.39/40 is uniquely reshaped, in a version known as *Femina nova.* In this latter revision, where it occurs together with an extract from *Urban le Courtois*, Bozon's *Proverbes de bon enseignement*, and a three-column vocabulary list, it becomes a combination of word list, dialogue, grammar, pronunciation guide, and courtesy or estate book, combined with Bibbesworth's fascinating excursions into homonyms and puns.[70]

BL Sloane 513 and All Souls College 182 both contain a mixture of teaching materials.[71] As well as Bibbesworth's *Tretiz*, they contain the first proper vernacular grammar which was commissioned (before 1409) by John Barton, *escolier de Paris*, and a wide range of letters and dialogues.[72] Dialogues became increasingly popular, with three 'manières' dated 1396, 1399, and 1415, a tradition taken up into print by Caxton, whose 1483 *Dialogues* are probably based on the *Livre des mestiers*, an Anglo-Flemish dialogue.[73]

This efflorescence of pedagogic writings is a powerful testament to the kinds of desire for French expressed by Trevisa. Scholars have been quick to dismiss them as a last-ditch effort to shore up a language that had gone into irreversible decline.[74] The usual assumption is that French was fading fast as one of England's vernaculars, and these teaching manuals are a final proof of it. If they were necessary, then people cannot have known French any more, even to quite a basic level. Yet this imposes a retrospective teleology about French which, as I have argued, distorts these texts and their purposes. Other conclusions are also possible as we think more broadly about the international pressures on both English and French at the turn of the fifteenth century. To turn the case round,

[70] There is a potentially confusing proliferation of modern titles for these treatises. Since Bibbesworth's *Tretiz* is sometimes also called *Femina* (from the opening rubric), the unique Trinity College version is sometimes referred to by the title *Femina nova* (see Dean and Boulton, *Anglo-Norman Literature*, nos 285 and 286), a practice which I follow in this book. Rothwell, however, retains *Femina* as a title for the Trinity College version.

[71] For descriptive comment on their contents, see Legge, *Anglo-Norman Letters and Petitions*, ix–x and Merrilees, 'Donatus and the Teaching of French', 280.

[72] Rothwell calls this 'the first genuine grammar of French to be written in French by Frenchmen for use by Englishmen' ('English and French', 547). Two other grammars survive, the former produced under the auspices of another Oxford schoolteacher, William Kingsmill (1415–30): *Liber donati: A Fifteenth-Century Manual of French* (*c.*1415), ed. B. Merrilees and B. Sitartz-Fitzpatrick, ANTS, Plain Texts Series 9 (London: ANTS, 1993); *Donait soloum douce franceis de Paris* (*c.*1410), ed. B. Merrilees, in *Anglo-Norman Anniversary Essays*, ed. Short, 273–91.

[73] *Manières de Langage*, ed. Kristol; the *Dialogues in French and English by William Caxton*, ed. H. Bradley, EETS, ES 79 (London: Kegan Paul, Trench, Trübner, 1900) were printed by Richard Pynson, native of Normandy and student of Paris. Wynkyn de Worde, native of Alsace, probably came to work with Caxton from Bruges in 1476. *Le Livre des Mestiers* was first published by H.-V. Michelant, ed., *Le Livre des Mestiers: Dialogues Français-Flamands composés au XIVe siècle par un maître d'école de la ville de Bruges* (Paris: Librairie Tross, 1875): he took it from BnF Ms 16 Neerl. See also L. H. Cooper, 'Urban Utterances: Merchants, Artisans, and the Alphabet in Caxton's Dialogues in French and English', *NML*, 7 (2005), 127–61.

[74] See W. Ayres-Bennett, *A History of the French Language through Texts* (London: Routledge, 1996), 137, for this perspective from French studies.

this treatment of French, as Serge Lusignan has insisted, is a remarkable moment in the history of Western vernaculars.[75] Uniquely for a vernacular language, French was given school status, and thus treated not so differently from Latin. That it should be the English who created this pedagogic image of French is of prime ironic importance. Well before indigenous grammars were produced in France (from the 1550s), French was cast as a grammatical language by the English.[76] The English created for French the main tools that were used in teaching Latin: *nominalia, artes dictaminis*, and a *donat/donatus*. Lusignan traces the developing consciousness of French in the later Middle Ages as a language capable of philosophical enquiry in its own right: it was the English who played a crucial role in giving it cultural value and power.

These observations gain further significance when they are related to the changing status of English. We might well wonder why the English start to promote French when English is supposedly in its 'triumphant' phase? That this should happen in the decades when England was most fully confident of its political and military power on the French mainland is worth pondering: these decades also coincide with a stream of invective (from both sides). The complex and at times contrary twists and turns with which language use represents status are very visible here. Whatever happened in the *longue durée*, English confidence, as Shakespeare's *Henry V* so subtly argues, manifested itself, at least for a while, in the promotion of French rather than of English.

There are two ways of responding to this conundrum that I briefly develop in the next part of this chapter. One concerns the perspective provided by the *Manières*. If we look at these in the first instance rather than the more overtly schematic or systematic books, they remind us quite sharply of the importance of thinking about French in oral as well as literate terms. The *Manières* do not teach grammar, they demonstrate speech. This is true of the *Femina nova* as well. William Rothwell has itemized with characteristic thoroughness some of the mistakes displayed in the *Femina nova*, for example, where the scribe 'sets down utter nonsense in both French and English' . . . 'casting serious doubt on the scribe's competence in French and demonstrating his propensity for having recourse to Latin'.[77] Yet I would like to suggest different ways of looking at these 'gross blunders'.[78] Rothwell's sense of offended correctness when he analyses the language of the *Femina nova* may be in danger of obscuring the larger interest of the work. One of its most intriguing features is located in the bottom margins and in the final three columns. In the margin the scribe has

[75] *Parler vulgairement: Les Intellectuels et la langue française aux XIIIe et XIVe siècles* (Paris; Montréal: Vrin; Les Presses de l'Université de Montréal, 1986), 101.

[76] Michelle R. Warren is incorrect in her assertion that John Palsgrave's was the first grammar, 'Post-Philology', in *Postcolonial Moves: Medieval Through Modern*, ed. P. C. Ingham and M. R. Warren (Basingstoke: Palgrave Macmillan, 2003), 19–45 (35).

[77] Rothwell, 'Anglo-French and Middle English Vocabulary', 46.

[78] Rothwell, 'Anglo-French and Middle English Vocabulary' 47.

placed a pronunciation guide keyed in to words in the text: each couplet in French is followed by a translation into English:[79]

> Beau[a] enfant[b] pur apprendre
> En franceis[c] devez bien[d] entendre
> ffayre chyld for to lerne
> In frensh 3e schal wel understande

This continues in four-line macaronic stanzas. The little letter annotations (in red) are keyed to the bottom of the page:

> **a** Beau debet legi beu **b** enfaunt **c** fraunceys **d** bein

Likewise, the columnar wordlists at the end contain a list of French words, followed by the same words spelled according to the way they should be pronounced, and finally a list translating them into English. These could be described as earnest versions of the pronunciation jokes in *Des Deus Anglois et de l'Anel* or *La Male Honte.* Although they have a quite different function from the fabliaux they testify to a similar preoccupation with how different versions of the same language sound. A century and a half on, the relationship between English and French has indeed changed: this is evident from the change in genre (although of course the *Femina nova* is worked from a thirteenth-century text). Yet there is still the same perception that somehow pronunciation marks out the borders of people's sense of possession of a language. It does so, in these teaching manuals as well as in the fabliaux, with an awareness that the borders look different from either side, and are therefore demarcated according to different principles. What is new in the fifteenth century is a clearer focus on English as a growing language of power. But it is complicated by the need to use French more than ever as a means of asserting English power on the continent, and therefore to change the English model of French from insular to continental.

When *does* French become a 'foreign language' in England? Perhaps we are seeing signs of this in the attempt to mould insular French into a continental language. Here are the first two quatrains in full:

> Beau enfaunt pur apprendre
> En franceis devez bien entendre
> ffayre chyld for to lerne
> In frensh ȝe shal wel understande
>
> Coment vous parlerez bealment
> Et devant les sagez naturalment
> How ȝe schal speke fayre
> And afore þyze wyzemen kyndely

[79] I cite from W. Rothwell, *Femina* (2005), checked against the manuscript.

To speak French 'fayre' is crucially ambiguous: the young must learn to speak in ways that convince a discerning audience that they possess French 'naturalment' / 'kyndely' rather than are possessed by it.

Yet this process of estrangement ironically involves an ever greater attempt to control its sounds and idioms. We can see this in a curious piece of self-reflexive dialogue entitled: 'La manere du parler a un estrange homme qui vient de loigne pais'.[80] The first man comes from Venice, but the second from Paris, which he describes as the most beautiful city he has seen in his life. The interlocutor exclaims with sycophantic delight that this is true, and that this man is speaking the sweetest French he has ever heard: 'quar est le plus gracious parler que soit en monde et de toutz gentz meulx preisés et amee que nulle autre' [for it is the most gracious speech that there could be in the world and all people prize it best and love it above any other]. He wishes he could speak as well and graciously. 'No, no,' replies the Parisian, 'your French is very good. You must have lived there a long time.' 'But I have never been there.' 'So how do you know how to speak so well?' 'Veraiment, sir, sicom je m'ay coustumé a parler entre les gentz de ce pays icy' [Truly, sir, in the way that I have learnt to speak among the people of this country here].[81] An English anxiety about speaking Parisian French is matched here by an English desire to assert that it is exactly like Anglo-French. Of course this is what the teacher wants his pupil to think; but what is of interest here is not so much whether there *is* a difference between the two kinds of French, as the attempt to create an Anglo-French that denies that difference.

Another little snippet of dialogue denies difference in tellingly other terms:

– Hé, mon amy . . . De quele pays esties vous? Ou fuistes vous nee?
– Mon sire, je su de Henoude.
– Que dea, vous esties un Englois donques!
– Nonil dea, mais nous aymons bien les Engloys a cause que les plus vaillantz seignours de ceste pais la sont de nostre linage.[82]

[– Hey, my friend . . . from what country are you? Where were you born?
– Sir, I am from Hainault.
– Good lord, you are an Englishman then!
– Not at all, but we love the English well because the most noble lords of this country are of our lineage.]

There is no attempt here to reconstruct the sound of Hainuyer French; instead, the joke is that the Hainuyer are really English since the English are descended from them. This may even be a submerged clue that what is really going on in the later passage is that a Parisian might equate an Anglo-French accent with that of a

80 *Manière de 1396*, ed. Kristol, 32–4.
81 *Manière de 1396*, ed. Kristol, 32–3.
82 *Manière de 1396*, ed. Kristol, 23.

Hainuyer. Speaking Hainuyer on the continent is apparently no bar to being taken as 'English'.

Perhaps the most vivid example of the position of the *Manières* as documents of orality is the song cited in the 1396 *Manière*. The knight is told what to do as he rides along: what else but sing?

Tresdoulz regart amerousement trait
Tant de doulceur fera mon cuer entrer
Quant les miens yeulx te pevent racontrer
Que tout mon sang me fuit et vers toi trait (9)

[Very sweet look, carried by love, will make so much sweetness enter my heart when my own eyes can meet you, that all my blood flees from me and draws towards you . . .][83]

Many of the vignettes are written with a keen sense of wry social humour, as in this dialogue about how to deal with children's quarrels:

Ore je vous moustray la manere de parler a un enfant.
Quant vous orrés ou verrés un enfant plorer ou gemyr, vous dirrés ainsi:
– Qu'as tu, mon enfant? *Ou si*: Qu'avés vous, mon amy? *Ou si*: Qui te meffait, beau fils? *Ou si*: Qui t'a fait plorer, beau doulx enfant?
– Mon seigneur, vostre petit garcion m'a ainsi froté, acraché, bufaté et batu q'il me fist sangnier la noise.
– Hé, beau fils, ne vous chaille, car je l'amendray bien a point, et il serra tresbien batu sur le cuil pur l'amour de vous. Et puis il ne serra plus si hardif de vous meffair decy en avant.
– Grant mercy, mon seignour.[84]

[Now I am going to show you the way of speaking to a child.
When you will hear or see a child cry or groan, you will speak like this:
'What is wrong, my child? Or this: What is wrong, my friend? Or this: Who is mistreating you, noble son? Or this: Who has made you cry, noble, sweet child?
My lord, your little boy has scraped, spat on, battered, and beat me so that he has made my nose bleed.
Hey, noble son, don't worry, for I will put this right immediately, and he will be very well beaten on the backside for love of you. And then he will not be so bold as to mistreat you like this beforehand.
Thank you, my lord.]

We can see from such a passage that the *Manières* actually imply a rather developed knowledge of French—it is not a basic phrase book but a guide to something more subtle: to social register. At the higher echelons of this linguistic

[83] Four out of five of the manuscripts of the *Manière 1396* have this text; the fifth has a drinking song in the same place, but 'Tresdoulz' later; the All Souls copy has another unique rondeau as well. See E. E. Leach, 'Learning French by Singing in 14th-century England', *Early Music*, 33 (2005), 253–70.

[84] *Manière de 1396*, ed. Kristol, 24.

guide, the types of speech approximate to types of vernacular fiction—to courtly song, to romance (chevaliers have been singing songs on a journey in romances prior to this for several hundred years), and to epistolary accomplishment. We come full circle with our comparison with the thirteenth-century Anglo-French jargon texts in finding an inset 'fabliau': 'Le mari battu, cocu et content'.[85]

In short, the presumed audience of the *Manières* contains already competent users of French who want to acquire more finesse and social acumen through language. This implies in turn that the grammars are not so much a sign of an imperfect and fading grasp of French trying vainly to resurrect itself as a lively knowledge, but rather of a radical desire to re-ground an existing lively oral knowledge of French as a knowledge capable of being transmitted *through writing*. The *1415 Manières* even seems to function as a kind of broadsheet, relaying news hot off the press about the extraordinary losses of the French first at Harfleur and then Agincourt (see Fig. 8). It is in this context that I now want to consider some of the writings *about* English, particularly (though not exclusively) in the genre of the translator's prologue. This will in turn act as a preface to a discussion about mother tongues, as perceived by French as well as English writers.[86]

ENGLISH VERNACULAR PROLOGUES: SIMPLE AND STRANGE

The provocative yet carefully nuanced essays that accompany the material selected by Jocelyn Wogan-Browne, Ruth Evans, and Nicholas Watson to represent 'the idea of the vernacular' provide an essential framework for the interpretation of this material. To a large extent they avoid what must be described as the somewhat imprisoning teleology that has characterized discussions of English and Englishness from the earliest days of disciplinary English. English is always progressing inexorably to a glorious and indeed, in due course, imperial end. Where earlier discussions tended, as we have also observed in the case of French, to fasten on the same, widely cited anecdotes and assertions taken from such sources as Robert Mannyng's *Chronicle* or the *Cursor Mundi* to demonstrate early consciousness of English as a national language, and the earlier the better, Wogan-Browne, Evans, and Watson provide a much broader range of extracts, thoughtfully arranged and rearranged to enable fresh juxtapositions and deductions.

85 *Manière de 1396*, ed. Kristol, 13–16.

86 If space permitted, it would be interesting to compare the *Manières* with Deschamps's *L'Art de Dictier*, the first *ars poetica* in French and a work that is exclusively concerned with the vernacular, both as performed orally and read.

It is in this spirit that I want to make my own necessarily abbreviated selection of material, focusing on a central opposition, between the 'simple' and the 'strange', the latter a word that has already preoccupied us in relation to Chaucer. I will be going back to the fourteenth century in order to build up a sense of how the arguments develop. Time and again, writers voice a perceived distinction, between 'symple speche . . . That is lightest in mannes mouth' (lines 35–6) and 'strange Inglis' (lines 40, 41, 57); 'strangere' (line 48).[87] I am quoting here from Robert Mannyng, a writer who has become a staple starting point of ideas of English and Englishness, the writer who also starts off the *Idea of the Vernacular* anthology. It is tempting to see Mannyng as a kind of 'working-class hero who championed straightforward English poetic forms and language'.[88] These words are from a study of Mannyng by Joyce Coleman who has argued, to the contrary, that far from writing for a common man, Mannyng is addressing an elite gentry audience. Even more radically, she suggests that this audience was not English but assimilated Anglo-Norman, and the issue devolves around his—and their—anxieties about their ability to cope with sophisticatedly fashioned English. Developing this, I will attempt to argue that 'strange', although it may seem to apply to 'Inglis', is in fact a (somewhat contorted) reference to French.

Reading more widely, we see this opposition between 'simple' and 'strange' aligning itself explicitly with an English–French issue. It may be helpful first to comment on the range of meanings of 'strange' and the cluster of related terms on either side of the distinction. 'Straunge' is, of course, more usually 'foreign' or 'unfamiliar' (compare *straunge strondes* from Chaucer's *General Prologue* (line 13), or when Trevisa remarks of the Flemmyngs of western Wales that they 'haueþ i-left her straunge speche and spekeþ Saxonliche i-now')[89] as well as 'recondite' or 'obscure' and 'elaborate, fancy, curious, ingeniously wrought', which the *MED*, slightly oddly, given its own range of citations which are heavily to do with language, ascribes to contexts of food or dress rather than language. So in a sense the collocation 'strange Inglis' means foreign English, an interestingly intricate concept, and one that is worth unravelling. 'Strange', as we discussed in relation to Chaucer's translation of Boethius, is in some sense itself foreign English, in that it is first and most widely attested in Anglo-French, as *estrange* but also as *strange* and *straunge*, where the meanings refer quite broadly to 'outside one's experience', including outside a community such as a family or guild, or legally without status.[90]

[87] J. Wogan-Browne, N. Watson, A. Taylor, and R. Evans, eds, *The Idea of the Vernacular: An Anthology of Middle English Literary Theory 1280–1520* (hereafter *Idea of the Vernacular*) (Exeter: University of Exeter Press, 1999), 21.

[88] J. Coleman, 'Strange Rhyme: Prosody and Nationhood in Robert Mannyng's Story of England', *Speculum*, 78 (2003), 1214–38 (1214).

[89] *Polychronicon Ranulphi Higden*, ed. Babington and Lumby, II, 159.

[90] For the full range of meanings for *forein* and *straunge*, see Chapter 8, n. 53.

'Strange' comes with a rich supporting lexis, quite a few of them Chaucerian: 'subtilite', 'curiosite'—both words picked up by Walton[91]—'queynt', 'privy', 'fantasye', 'faire', and 'festisly'. To recall, these are all comments about French: 'the curiosite/Of Graunson',[92] of the Prioress 'And Frenssh she spak ful faire and festisly' (*General Prologue*, I, 124), and 'queynt knyttyng coloures' and 'privy termes in Frenche', both used by Usk in the Prologue to his *Testament of Love*.[93] But they derive the full strength of their meaning from being set against another word-hoard, this time applied to English—'English' English as one might say: English is not only 'simple', it is 'light', 'naked', 'clear', 'open', 'lewed', 'ignorant' (that is Hoccleve), 'homely', 'commune, playne, rounde Englisshe' (Fox, *The Rule of Seynt Benet*), 'boystous' (Usk again), and 'rewde'. The contrast between these two vocabularies may be easy enough to observe, but the relation between them, the tone, the implied relative value is not at all straightforward.

It is Usk who gives the most developed yet also absorbingly obscure commentary on linguistic strangeness. The Prologue ostensibly begins with the usual deprecations. But it is very hard to know in which direction the praise and blame is falling, and indeed what is praise and what is blame. The first sentence immediately sounds a little accusing:

> Many men there ben that, with eeres openly sprad, so moche swalowen the delyciousnesse of jestes and of ryme, by queynt knytting coloures, that of the goodnesse or of the badnesse of the sentence take they lytel hede, or els non.[94]

But who is being accused? It seems to be the men with 'openly sprad' ears. But these individuals are not wholly culpable since they are being led astray by clever rhetoric. In an oddly—clumsily—mixed metaphor, they swallow (through their ears?) delicious jokes and rhymes in 'queynt knytting coloures'. The ambivalence already established over 'queynt' and 'delycious'—how could one complain of something delicious?—is carried over into the next paragraph, where the speaker describes himself as too 'dul' of wit and too troubled to be acquainted with 'the craft of endyting'. Instead, he argues, since 'rude wordes and boystous' pierce the heart of the listener, this book, lacking 'the greet floode of wit' and 'semelych colours', will dig deep with such 'rude wordes and boystous' so that its sentence can be seized.[95]

So far, despite some oddities, we are given a fairly recognizable set of critical and ethical dichotomies, between the truth, set deep down at the heart of the matter, and superficial glamour, between deliciously crafted humour and serious sentence. Borrowing the metaphorical association of 'dolven', Usk manages to

[91] *Idea of the Vernacular*, 36, lines 9–11.
[92] Chaucer, *Complaint of Venus*: Envoy, in *Idea of the Vernacular*, 28, lines 10–11.
[93] *Idea of the Vernacular*, 29–30, lines 2, 25.
[94] *Idea of the Vernacular*, 29, lines 1–3.
[95] *Idea of the Vernacular*, 29–30, lines 4–10.

imply that 'rude wordes and boystous' (a phrase he repeats with awkwardly mimetic emphasis) are honest labour unlike the colours of the frivolous. In a manoeuvre also used by Chaucer's Franklin and others, the self-deprecation twists in two directions simultaneously: the author sets himself up as a weak rhetorician unable to hold his own in exalted company. On the other hand, suddenly revealing some bite, plain speaking is better, he says, because it avoids the pretensions and distractions of the learned and takes its audience straight to the truth.

The next paragraph, however, throws much into deliberate disarray. For what could have been understood to be a contrast between two types of English, the learned and rhetorically elaborate versus the plain and unsubtle, turns into a much more entangled disquisition on French and Latin as well as English. He begins by changing the metaphors again, now introducing the material occupation of the professional illuminator, where 'colours ryche' and 'red ynke' are contrasted with 'coles and chalke'.[96] Mixed in with this is a reference to verse (Some . . . peynten with colours ryche, and some with vers, as with red ynke')[97] which presumably leaves prose as the 'coles and chalke'. But the logic of the next few remarks is not transparent. The 'leude', he says, will find good matere in 'thilke chalky purtreyture, as hem thynketh for the tyme' but afterwards the sight of the 'better colours' will give them more joy than their original 'leudeness'. So the chalky style of writing, 'this leude clowdy occupacion' is not actually praiseworthy; only the 'leude' do this: 'for comenly leude leudeness commendeth'. The real purpose of 'coles and chalke' is to lead the 'leude' on towards more precious things.[98] This makes sense, but only through the large concession that grey plainness is of *less* value than colourful elaboration. Those early protestations were not to be believed, then.

Further complications ensue from Usk's own style. For someone so apparently eager, at least initially, to praise the 'rude . . . and boystous', his own language is full of extravagant and whimsical details, chasing down a torrent of physical metaphors to do with hearing, taste, and sight, mining, grafting, digging, sketching, and painting. It is perhaps a moot point whether this represents rhetorical skill or gauche ambition: the phrase 'for comenly leude leudeness commendeth' captures this uncertainty in its half- punning, half-clever chiasmic

[96] *Idea of the Vernacular*, 30, lines 11–12.

[97] This is an interesting locution, equating the colours used for illumination, not with the red ink used for verse but with the verse itself. Red ink is used for verse in both French and English vernacular manuscripts, and also in sermons, see A. Butterfield, *Poetry and Music in Medieval France from Jean Renart to Guillaume de Machaut* (Cambridge: Cambridge University Press, 2002), 184. Red is also used for the Latin argument in many of the Gower, *Confessio amantis* manuscripts: see, for instance, London BL MS Stowe 950 and BL MS Harley 3869. On inset verse as itself a form of ornament, see Butterfield, *Poetry and Music*, 105.

[98] *Idea of the Vernacular*, 30, lines 13–16.

repetition of 'comenly' and 'commendeth'. Is this a 'leude comendacioun' or a learned one?

But it is the next move that is the most significant for my purposes. Caught hedging, undecided whether to claim virtue in his plainness or assert rhetorical mastery through the extravagance of those claims, he changes the terms of the discussion again by displacing the reference to elaboration onto French (with brief mention also of Latin, though for the moment this slips quickly out of the frame). So he comments that 'many no[ble t]hynges' have been accomplished by those who 'endyte' in Latin and French. Then there comes a 'but':

> But certes, there ben some [that] speken their poysye-mater in Frenche, of whiche speche the Frenchemen have as good a fantasye as we have in heryng of Frenchemennes Englysshe.[99]

This is cryptic: it seems to mean that there are 'some' who cast their poetry into French who do so without skill or authority, their French provoking a similar reaction among Frenchmen to that experienced among Englishmen hearing a Frenchman speaking English. He goes on to say, in another s-bend, that there are many terms in English that 'we Englyshmen' can scarcely understand. In that case, a Frenchmen would all the more be unable to follow:

> Howe shulde than a Frencheman borne suche termes conne jumpere in his mater, but as the jay chatereth Englyssh?[100]

Conversely, then, 'Englysshmen' cannot be expected to stretch to the 'privy termes in Frenche, whatsoever we bosten of straunge langage'.[101] Usk's rallying conclusion is that we should let the clerks endite in Latyn, and the Frenchmen

> in their Frenche also endyten their queynt terms, for it is kyndely to their mouthes; and let us shewe our fantasyes in suche wordes as we lerneden of our dames tonge.[102]

This is a remarkable passage, for many reasons. One conclusion I think we should not draw is the facile one that Usk is straightforwardly championing English over French. Usk is following a sinuous path between different notions of eloquence. Instead of simple assertions or justifications for his English prose, he takes his reader on an extraordinarily revealing tour of an English vernacular writer's prejudices, anxieties and ambitions. Perhaps the first point to note is the overwhelming importance of French in Usk's perception. It emerges gradually as the domineering other tongue against which he is measuring himself—hearing himself—and of course as we read a little later on, he is intensely aware of his temerity in writing on love in a language other than French. 'To ben mayster of

[99] *Idea of the Vernacular*, 30, lines 19–21.
[100] *Idea of the Vernacular*, 30, lines 22–4.
[101] *Idea of the Vernacular*, 30, lines 22–4
[102] *Idea of the Vernacular*, 30, lines 27–9.

Fraunce by myght',[103] a conquest that even Edward III did not achieve, is an aim which can only attract scornful laughter.

The second is that in working out this desire through the medium of English, Usk chooses a very strange English. When he says that a Frenchman could not follow arcane English terms, he expresses this almost incoherently: 'conne jumpere in his mater, but as the jay chatereth Englyssh'. The only other use of 'jompre' in English is in *Troilus* where again the point is to show linguistic incompetence or discordance ('Ne jompre [vr. iumpere] ek no discordant thyng yfeere,/As thus, to usen termes of phisik/In loves termes', II, 1037–9). We might compare this with a passage from Machaut's *Fonteinne amoureuse*, where, in the long central dream, Venus describes the three wrangling goddesses fighting over the golden apple of Discord as chattering like a jay:

Vous ressamblez trop bien le jay
Qui jargonne, gangle, et parole
Toute jour parmi sa gëole,
Et quant il a finé son dit,
Riens ne vaut tout ce qu'il a dit.
(1784–8)

You are just like the jay
Who jabbers, chatters and talks
All day in his cage,
But when he has finished his speech,
Everything he has said has been worthless.[104]

It is hard to follow Usk, but his explorations of these linguistic relationships are as startlingly original as they are confused. We feel we are in the presence of someone trying to think through matters of value and cultural hierarchy in a very instinctive but discerning direction. His rough articulations register a sense of English itself as a jabbering, discordant jargon struggling to compete with the smoothness of French, and the political control of Latin. But like Chaucer, perhaps, he seems all the more determined to find an articulate role for English in this subaltern position. What gives his musings a distinctive edge is the explicit way he allows them to emerge from the uneven surface of his own prose. It is also because (like Trevisa) he is so sensitive to sound and pronunciation. Usk gives us a raw and lively sense of the awkwardness of speaking and hearing other languages, and how fluency is partly a physical matter of finding a way of being at ease in another language's sounds and ways of producing those sounds.

[103] *Idea of the Vernacular*, 31, line 70.

[104] *Guillaume de Machant, Le livre de la Fontaine amoureuse*, ed. and trans. J. Cerquiglini-Toulet (Paris : Stock, 1993).

Usk seems to be trying to find an English that has its own quality of the arcane. But this is an oddly invented obscurity. He seems to want to drive forward various forms of incomprehension across the two languages in order to register difference between them. His efforts to find that difference are confused, because after all many Englishmen use French. If some 'Englysshmen' find French terms 'privy' then their best means of retaliation is to create an arcane English. Yet this is an English that the English themselves scarcely recognise. Could Usk be attempting to utter a linguistic fantasy: an English so strange to itself that it echoes a French reaction to English? Usk seems to be fantasizing—imagining, speculating, desiring and creating delusions—across cultures, trying to think and express such thoughts in that linguistic no man's land, a war zone, as he implies, in which each side tries to imagine what each other hears and understands. When he says 'let us shewe our fantasyes in suche wordes as we lerneden of our dames tonge' I think this is not so much an appeal to be 'English', as something more intractable. He wants that element of strangeness, of 'queyntness', and 'fantasye', to be part of, to be expressed by, an English that could somehow retain its strangeness to itself through capitalizing on its strangeness to the French.

MOTHER TONGUES

What then does Usk mean by 'dames tonge'? In the final part of this chapter I try to bring together the several threads of enquiry by introducing yet another. But first, to clear up a possible confusion: it is important to be aware that Usk is conducting a three-way argument between English and French, not a bipolar one. He is working with English as well as French speakers and writers (endyters) of French. Interestingly, he also seems to be assuming French speakers and hearers of English. And while he sneers at some of the French produced by the English—the 'poysye-mater in Frenche'—there is evidently plenty more that, alongside Latin, commands high respect from him and gives no impression of being confined to Frenchmen 'borne'.

The use of the term 'dames tonge' is certainly polemical; the question, as ever, is what direction the polemic is facing. Usk is early to use the phrase (1385); its most significant early context in English is undoubtedly Wycliffite, also in the 1380s, though the written copies date from the 1390s.[105] The phrase in Latin is of course much earlier, and occurs for instance in the incipit to Mannyng's *Chronicle* (1338):

Incipit prologus de historia Britannie transumpta per Robertum in materna lingua

[Here begins the prologue to the history of Britain translated by Robert into the mother tongue] (*Idea of the Vernacular*, 20)

[105] See below.

Broadening the context to Europe, well before the remarkable claims made for the vernacular in Dante's *De Vulgare eloquentia* (c.1304), there was discussion of *materna lingua* in the Council of Reims (1119):

iterum Catalaunensis episcopus . . . idem clericis et laicis materna lingua exposuit.[106]

[the bishop of Catalonia repeatedly . . . explained this to the clerks and laity in the vulgar tongue]

There are other early references to *maternus sermo* in 1108 and in the *Autobiography* of Guibert de Nogent (1115), where Guibert describes a debate in front of the pope as taking place not in the mother tongue but in Latin: 'Fiebat autem res non materno sermone sed literis' [This thing was done not in the maternal tongue but in the learned language'].[107] Vernacular German references occur from the 1300s.[108]

Looking at the phrase 'mother tongue' in both Latin and vernacular contexts reveals that it is never simply descriptive or normative. Despite the emotion that the phrase often conjures, the definition of 'mother tongue' is often far from straightforward. The language in which one lived one's childhood may not be the same as the language that one uses most in which to write, even if it is ostensibly the 'same' language. In the medieval period, there was largely a sharp disjunction between the language one spoke and the language one wrote, usually Latin. It is easy to forget that the sheer extent of Latin usage, even once French, and in due course English began to be more widely written, gave the educated much greater eloquence and indeed fluency in that language than they possessed in the vernacular. Turning one's mother tongue into a written language was thus a source of strain, a sense that there was a gulf to cross between one form of the language and the other. However artlessly oral it appears, Chaucer's English is a constructed neo-language not a 'simple' vernacular. The mother tongue, then, is a confusing phrase. It may mean just as much in Latin as it does in the vernacular.

Moreover, the figure of the mother, although it provides a deep-rooted association with naturalness, is also a disturbing element in the phrase, since it sets up doubts about what natural language use is and whether we really value it. For those many people now and then who use more than one language on a daily basis, in different contexts, deciding which more fully meets the description 'mother tongue' is often not easy or even significant.

Two of the most significant and original discussions of vernacularity and the mother tongue by Roger Bacon (1214–92) and Dante (*c.*1265–1321), illustrate

[106] K. Ahlzweig, *Muttersprache-Vaterland: Die deutsche Nation und ihre Sprache* (Opladen: Westdeutsche Verlag, 1994), 26–7.

[107] Book III, ch. IV, cited in Ahlzweig, *Muttersprache-Vaterland*, 28.

[108] Ahlzweig, *Muttersprache-Vaterland*, 30–31.

some of these points. Bacon's views on philology were brilliantly idiosyncratic. I have already mentioned in Chapter 2 his comments on dialect. Here I want to single out his uncompromising views on translation. For him there were three levels of proficiency in the acquisition of languages of high learning, namely Greek and Hebrew. The highest (first) level of skill in translation could be obtained only by someone who was as familiar with these languages as he was with his mother tongue: 'ut quilibet sciat has linguas sicut maternam in qua natus est, ut nos loquimur Anglicum, Gallicum, et Latinum . . . ' [so that anyone who knows these languages as if it was the mother tongue in which he was born, such as those we call English, French and Latin . . .].[109] In the second and third levels, respectively, one would know enough to be able to translate works written in these languages, or, most rudimentarily, would know enough to read, grasp elementary grammar, and pick up allusions to the Fathers. Bacon's own astonishing linguistic skills led him to be scornful of the inadequacies of others: yet it does not seem to be simply his own abilities that caused him to think in this way about linguistic knowledge. For him, it was clearly possible to seek fluency in a learned second or third language: and we might notice both that Latin is included with English and French as a language of mother tongue fluency, and that mother tongue fluency was (in theory at least) just as achievable with Greek or Hebrew, languages which of course, for Bacon, were long-dead witnesses to past cultures.[110]

Dante's thoughts on the vernacular in *De vulgari eloquentia* are also unexpected. It is not just that he expresses them in Latin, which gives his insistence on the natural eloquence of the vulgar tongue a slightly hollow ring, but also that he seems caught up in a contradiction. On the one hand, he wants to argue that the speech of the common people is natural, imbibed by children from their earliest imitations of their nurse, and on the other that it is noble and illustrious and fit for verse. Deschamps's *L'Art de Dictier* finds itself in a similar bifurcation, this time between speech and song (Dante's concerns, and Dante's own much acknowledged relationship with the troubadours were not far from Deschamps's), where song is cast as 'unnatural' unlike the 'natural music' of verse. It is as hard to take Dante seriously on the value of childlike approaches to language as it is to see Deschamps as having a coherent thesis of music (or its absence). For both authors, what comes naturally in language is to be valued, yet this is pronounced in elaborate, highly 'unnatural' forms, carefully wrought, especially in the case of Dante, to work their maximum rhetorical effect. When Dante playfully runs through each of the main Italian vernaculars in turn (Roman, those from the March of Ancona, Spoleto, Milan, Bergamo, Aquileia, Istria, Sardinia, Sicilian, Apulian, Tuscan, and Genoese (there

[109] R. Bacon, *The Greek Grammar of Roger Bacon and a Fragment of his Hebrew Grammar*, ed. E. Nolan and S. A. Hirsch (Cambridge: Cambridge University Press, 1902), xlv.

[110] For incisive comment on Bacon and language, see Lusignan, *Parler vulgairement*, 62–77.

are many more)), he, even more playfully, discounts each of them as having any claim to being 'illustrious' by using examples of their poetry against them.[111]

In following through further citations and argument about the *materna lingua*, we discover that this same contortion about what is desirable—the natural or the artificial—runs through it, leaving a far from clear message about vernacular values. Returning to a late fourteenth-century English context, the most extraordinary claims for English as a mother tongue are to be found in the writings of the Wycliffite Bible translators. Chapter 15 of the *General Prologue*, dated by Anne Hudson to perhaps 1395–7 and attached to some manuscripts of the late version of the Wycliffite Bible, speaks out for an English translation of the Bible by asserting that since:

> Frenshe men, Beemers and Britons han þe Bible and oþere bokis of deuocioun and of exposicioun translatid in here modir langage. Whi shulden not English men haue þe same in here modir langage?[112]

The Bible translation debate can be touched on only very briefly within the different focus of this book, but one or two issues raised by these translators of pertinence to the present discussion may be signalled. It is worth recalling that this allusion to 'modir langage' is again complex, and does not make the rhetorical concessions that we might expect. They do seek to write a 'comoun langage', but justify this by using the argument that for the Romans Latin was 'a comoun langage to here puple'. The language of simplicity, openness and brevity that is applied to English elsewhere in the Prologue is thus not claimed to be unique to English, but a property of common language. The flattening of a sense of distinction between Latin and vernacular here is highly disruptive of a learned versus lewed orthodoxy. Once Latin starts to be thought of as a mother tongue, then many assumptions about vernacularity start to look rather different. The old dichotomy between educated and uneducated apparently collapses.

Women come into the picture in a typically convoluted way. If we go back for a moment to the *Manières*, it should be pointed out that a further irony about them is the way in which the dialogues *write* about *speech*. The more they put speech into writing, the more they depart from their ostensible function, a problem faced by phrase books in all periods. Women entwine themselves into this Gordian knot by being the recipients and often also patrons of these manuals, and yet by being associated with the kind of inadequate linguistic command that requires such tutoring. I have been influenced here partly by Juliet Fleming's interesting arguments about the sixteenth- to eighteenth-century

[111] Chs X–XV. I have used the edition by P. V. Mengaldo, in *Opere minori*, II (Milan and Naples: Riciardi, 1979) and consulted the translation by S. Purcell, *Literature in the Vernacular* (Manchester: Carcanet, 1981).

[112] A. Hudson, ed., *Selections from English Wycliffite Writings*, (Cambridge: Cambridge University Press, 1978), 71, lines 165–8.

compilation of English language dictionaries. She suggests that dictionaries were written for women, but in order to exclude them from a notion of 'standard' language. In taking the issues back to the late fourteenth and early fifteenth centuries, it seems to me remarkable that women are named here too and addressed as the principal sources of social (and presumably, financial) authority for these materials, and yet that their famed eloquence is associated with French rather than English.[113]

Bibbesworth's treatise is dedicated to Dionysia or Denise de Munchensi (d. 1304). She remarried in 1235; her first husband, with whom she had two children, was a Langton, and brother of Stephen; her second, with whom she had one son, was Warin de Munchensi, from a wealthy landowning family.[114] Bibbesworth says in his prologue that he writes for a woman about to give birth:

Le tretiz ki munseignur Gauter de Bibbesweth fistt a madame Dyonise de Mountechensi pur aprise de langage.

[The treatise which monseigneur Gautier de Bibbesworth made for my lady Dionysia de Munchensi in order to learn the language.]

Femme ke aproche sun teins
De enfaunter . . .

1–2

[A woman who is approaching her time to give birth . . .][115]

The *Femina nova*, in part an adaptation of Bibbesworth, does not point to any new specific female impetus for its revised production, but the opening gloss of its title is significant:

Liber iste vocatur femina quia sicut femina docet infantem loqui maternam sic docet iste liber iuvenes rethorice loqui Gallicum provit infra patebit.[116]

[This book is called 'Femina' because just as a woman teaches a child to speak the mother tongue, so this book teaches young people to speak French with eloquence, as will be demonstrated below.]

The book, then, is a substitute for the mother: but this does not mean that it will teach at a lower level. On the contrary, the teacher wants his pupils to attain the

113 'Dictionary English and the Female Tongue', in *Enclosure Acts: Sexuality, Property, and Culture in Early Modern England*, ed. R. Burt and J. M. Archer (Ithaca and London: Cornell University Press, 1994), 290–325.

114 T. Hunt, 'Bibbesworth, Walter of (b. in or before 1219, d. in or after 1270)', *Oxford Dictionary of National Biography*, Oxford University Press, September 2004; online edn, October 2005; <http://0-www.oxforddnb.com.catalogue.ulrls.lon.ac.uk:80/view/article/2340> (accessed 6 December 2008). For more details on her life, see Haas, '*Femina*', 143–5.

115 I cite from Rothwell, ed., *Walter de Bibbesworth: Le Tretiz* (Aberystwyth: The Anglo-Norman Online Hub, 2009), 1.

116 W. A. W. Wright, ed., *Femina* (Cambridge: The Roxburghe Club, 1909), 1.

kind of eloquence that is both natural *and* rhetorically sophisticated, 'vous parlereȝ bialment/et . . . naturalment'.

In English, however, when women are associated with the mother tongue it tends to be an unflattering connection. In a fairly neutral example, the writer of a medical treatise in English remarks:

I think to..draw oute of latyn into englysh dyuerse causis of here maladyes..because whomen of oure tonge done bettyr rede and undyrstande þys langage þan eny oþer[117]

But more commonly, and particularly as the fifteenth century draws on into the sixteenth, English not only finds itself the target of attack for its rough, barbaric qualities but the notions of impurity, corruption, barbarousness, and the vulgar are often gendered; the vernacular itself or the vulgar text is figured as feminine.[118] Instances of this in relation to French in Chaucer are his sly choice of the Prioress as a representation of Stratford French and the 'maner Latyn corrupt' spoken by Custance when she arrives on the shore of Northumberland (519). Two tendencies are on the increase, the rising tenor of opprobrium, anxious self-deprecation, and hard-hitting scorn in comments about English well into the sixteenth century, as Richard Jones long ago discussed, and second, an increasing—and increasingly harsh—self-description of English as a mother tongue.[119] We not only have Caxton writing of 'rude and comyn englyshe' (1489), but many examples in the sixteenth century (as I will go on to discuss in the next chapter) of a preoccupation with the barbarousness of English compared with Latin or Greek.[120] Roger Ascham considered Latin and Greek to be the only learned tongues. 'Yet, neuerthelesse,' he wrote, 'the rudenes of common and mother tonges, is no bar for wise speaking. For in the rudest contrie, and most barbarous mother language, many be found [who] can speake verie wiselie' (Ascham, *The Scholemaster*, 1570).[121]

'Mother tongues'—are they, in short, a mixed blessing? Fleming takes this in a Lacanian direction—more prosaically perhaps, one could also remark how often the term is sentimentalized in modern as well as medieval contexts, in a way that tells us more about society's attitudes towards mothers than it does about notions of language. Anyone who has been brought up—as I have—by a mother who could not use her mother tongue in teaching her child 'her' language will realize that there is often a monolingual fantasy at work here about what constitutes a 'mother tongue'. To claim support for one's language by describing it as one's mother

[117] See *MED*: 'Langage': 1. (a) 1450: *Diseases of Women* (1) Oxford, Bodleian Library, MS Douce 37.

[118] M. W. Ferguson, *Dido's Daughters: Literacy, Gender and Empire in Early Modern England and France* (Chicago and London: University of Chicago Press, 2003), 124.

[119] R. Jones, *The Triumph of the English Language* (London: Oxford University Press, 1953).

[120] Prologue to *Blanchardyn and Eglantine*, in *The Prologues and Epilogues of William Caxton*, ed. W. J. B. Crotch, EETS, OS 176 (London: Oxford University Press, 1928), 105.

[121] Jones, *The Triumph of the English Language*, 15.

Figure 9. Christine de Pisan and her son

London BL MS Harley 4431, f.261v (1410–1411). Copyright The British Library: reproduced with permission.

tongue is both to argue for its visceral importance to oneself and yet, by that very physical and emotional bond, to imply that it is somehow primarily associated with childhood and hence with an elementary stage in one's education. To gain real cultural power, a language must be both more and less than a mother tongue. One wonders what language Christine was implicitly speaking in the portrait of her teaching her son (who incidentally was sent to England to the household of the Earl of Salisbury in 1397) shown in Fig. 9. It was unlikely to have been Italian.

CHRISTINE DE PIZAN AND CAXTON

A final, double example will serve as a conclusion since it involves a male translator responding to a female text. This is Caxton's 1489 Prologue to *The Book of Fayttes of Armes and of Chyvalrye*, a double text because it is a translation of Christine de Pizan's *Le livre des fais d'armes et de chevalerie* (1412).[122]

[122] I cite this from *Idea of the Vernacular*, 171.

Christine begins this work with a remarkable piece of self-justification. She is very conscious of her temerity as a woman in writing on a topic that is utterly remote from a woman's normal concerns (spinning and occupying themselves in household things). Her tactic is to elicit support from a female god, Minerva, the 'goddess of armes and of chyvalrye', a move which brilliantly exposes the characteristically contradictory mode of male high style, in which male virtues and preoccupations are so often figured as female. Minerva not only serves Christine's purpose here because she is a woman: the special link is that they are countrywomen, and even more so, that they therefore speak the same language. Christine thus finishes her Prologue with the following rhetorical climax:

[/haulte deesse ne te desplaise ce que moy simple femmelette sy comme neant enuers la grandeur de ton renomme scauoir ose presentement/emprendre a parler de sy magnifie office comme est celuy des armes du quel premierement/en laditte renommee contree de grece tu donnas lusage et/en tant te plaise moy estre fauourable que ie puisse estre aucunement consonante en la naction dont tu fus nee qui comme adont/feust nommee la grant/grece le pais doultre les alpes qui ores est dit puille et Calabre en Ytalie ou tu nasquis et] je suis comme toy femme ytalienne.[123]

(BL MS Royal 19 B. XVIII)

[hie Goddesse, be thou not displeased that I, symple and lytyl woman, lyke as nothyng unto the gretenes of thy renommee in cunnyng, dare presently compryse to speke of so magnyfike an offyce as is th'office of armes, of whiche fyrst, in the said renomed contree of Grece, thou gavest th'usage. And insomoche it may plaise the to be to me favorable, that I may be somwhat consonaunt in the nacyon where thou was born, whiche as thenne was named the Grete Grece, the contree beyonde the Alpes or montaygnes, whiche now is sayd Puylle and Calabre in Ytalye where thou were born, and I am, as thou were, a woman Ytalien.][124]

It is remarkable to observe Christine making a declaration of selfhood in this form: 'je suis comme toy femme ytalienne' has a ring similar to Gower's 'Jeo sui Englois'. Both search, with somewhat convoluted subtlety, for a means of asserting vernacular pride: in both, French is the medium for finding international recognition for a local linguistic identity. When we turn to Caxton, we find much the same kind of language that has become common about English by the last quarter of the fifteenth century: Christine is translated as desiring to treat the topic in the 'most plain and entendible langage that I shal mowe' (lines 26–7), and as describing herself as 'a simple and lytel woman' (*femmelette* in French). The passage in English thus resonates twice over: first of a woman, conscious of her specially vulnerable position in writing of 'the right honorable

123 Transcribed from the manuscript.
124 *Idea of the Vernacular*, 171, lines 51–9.

offyce of armes and of chyvalrye',[125] and second, being translated into English by a man, very conscious of his 'Englissh's' vulnerability in writing of such high matters. There seems to be a crucial difference between the two positions: where Christine cunningly derives Latinate eloquence from her audacious assertion of vernacular vulnerability, Caxton retreats to another kind of response, a response which cannot quite see a way of making English vernacularity seem so 'polisshed'. The declaration, in English, in a woman's voice, 'I am, as thou were, a woman Ytalien', is much more anxious than Gower's in French.

There remains one final thread to pick out: the relationship between mother tongues and orality. I suggest that this period of renewed Anglo-French hostility marks a highly volatile relationship of mutual change, even exchange between England's vernaculars. English (as we can see from so many of the fifteenth-century Prologues by such writers as John Metham and Osbern Bokenham) is writhing uneasily under its self-description as a mother tongue. Mothers are dubious models, linguistically, and perhaps offer only mirrors to self-laceration and contempt. Despite, or perhaps even because of Chaucer's extraordinary efforts at internationalization, English is not yet confident enough in its local identity to feel authorized as a written vernacular. It appeals to the notion of a mother tongue to justify its natural status but this notion confirms its vulnerability. French, on its part, revels in a more learned fantasy about female eloquence, but this association also contains the capacity to sully it. It must shake off its links with mere female orality and confirm its status of written, authoritative expression. If the *Manières* write about speaking, then the English prologues usurp the space allotted to the speaker-compiler in the prestige language texts of Latin or French and fill it instead with anxieties about *writing* English. Both vernaculars thus give voice from very different directions to the same question: how can one be both 'clene and pure' *and* eloquent?

[125] *Idea of the Vernacular*, 170, lines 17–18.

10

Betrayal and Nation

French hath long time beene termed the language of Ladies . . . as if written by men it may have a good garbe, spoken by you it hath a double grace . . . That as Tullie *averred of his Roman Ladies for Latine, so not onely for our mother-tongue, but also for the principall, Italian and French, not onely our princely Mother of Majestie, Magnificence, omnisufficiencie, but (for instance) I avowe, you my five honoured Schollers (whom as euer in heart, so would I honor now by these my laboures) are the purest, finest, and clearest speakers.*

2R2r

THE CLAIMS OF RETROSPECTION

This quotation comes from John Florio's Preface to his translation of Montaigne's *Essays*, published in 1603.[1] It is the 'Epistle Dedicatorie' to Book III. Each of the three books is dedicated to a pair of female patrons, with an elaborate inscription such as this at the start of each book, and the three of them collected together as a group after the main title page. It serves as a starting point for this final chapter for many reasons. Firstly, it takes us well beyond a period when French might have been regarded as an 'English' vernacular. In 1603 England had lost Calais for some two generations and attention had turned to Spain; an imprisoned Raleigh was beginning his *History of the World* and it was to be only four years before the founding of Jamestown in America. Henry V's obsession with claiming France for England was past history. By this time, we might think, French was truly a foreign language. So what had changed, and when? The loss of Calais in 1558 is an obvious watershed, the Reformation another. Just as Florio, cut off from his English mother tongue by being the son of a Protestant Tuscan exile who was brought up in Switzerland and schooled in Germany, asserts a new 'Mother of Majestie' for English on his return to England by 1576, so England, in exile from Rome, had cut itself off from one mother and asserted a new maternal genealogy in Elizabeth.

[1] Iohn Florio, *The essayes or morall, politike and millitarie discourses of Lo: Michaell de Montaigne* (London: Val. Sims for Edward Blount, 1603).

And yet, Florio's way of writing seems remarkably like that of his fifteenth-century Oxford predecessors. He writes as a teacher for a female audience, makes high-flown associations between his female dedicatees and the French language, and seems to feel that 'our mother tongue' needs supplementing by French. These very similarities of reference raise questions about period and change. The talk of watersheds may be misleading. Why do we presume that fundamental changes have occurred? And even if we were right to make that presumption, how would we discern, let alone locate change?

Such questions strike at the heart of nation because it is crucial to nation both to seek a moment of national creation and to look back. Any idea of nation is always looking back, seeking a long explanation of who we are. The newer the nation, as Patrick Geary reminds us, from the Normans to the modern Assembly of Kosovo, which declared its independence as the Republic of Kosovo in February 2008, the more fervent its claims to and over the remote past.[2] The paradox is the collision between newness and the past: nation, many commentators tell us, acts as the very definition of modernity and yet the precondition of its existence is a connection to the past. This forms a strange yoking, since one is a form of rejection of the past and the other a yearning to possess it in its entirety.

1603, perhaps coincidentally, acts as a stimulus to many kinds of looking back, from Elizabethan to early Tudor, from early Tudor to Lancastrian, from early modern to medieval. In thinking in this book about Chaucer, language, and nation, matters of chronology have been a constant concern. It has seemed important to begin much earlier than the fourteenth century, and now to finish much later. Although this appears to create a firmly linear narrative, the contrary purpose of this book has been to unravel the chronology of nation and its many constructions. For, as I have tried to show, 'nation' in English terms has all these chronologies and more; it also accommodates the rather different chronologies perceived of, and by, France and the French. From a current medieval literary scholar's point of view, the most powerful paradigm is that of Chaucer as father; but this is rivalled by two others, the Norman Conquest and that of Shakespeare and the birth of the modern. There are also those who want to take us back to Alfred or even earlier. The subtle and not-so-subtle collisions between these different starting points for Englishness are illustrative of certain disciplinary tensions which themselves have their own histories. The perception that Shakespeare is the fountainhead of English and Englishness sits in often oddly silent denial that Chaucer held this honorific before him; likewise the view that

[2] P. J. Geary, *The Myth of Nations: The Medieval Origins of Europe* (Princeton: Princeton University Press, 2002), 7. Yet, to reiterate, and as Geary rightly comments, many of these claims to sovereignty 'are a creation of the nineteenth century' (13); see the classic essay by E. Hobsbawm, 'Introduction: Inventing Traditions', in E. Hobsbawm and T. Ranger, eds, *The Invention of Tradition* (Cambridge: Cambridge University Press, 1983), 1–14.

Chaucer is the 'first founder of oure fair language' insouciantly ignores the pioneering translation work urged by Alfred in the ninth century.

The Norman Conquest is one of the points of origin whose occlusions have been least remarked or mourned: as we discussed in Chapter 2, turned into a boundary marker between Old English and (Early) Middle English, the twelfth century, with its paucity of texts written in English, disappears from view.[3] Yet book production in England in Latin and French reached unprecedented heights in the twelfth century.[4] As part of a story of nation, the Conquest itself, however, has been energetically painted over: the notion that patriotic Englishness in the Anglo-Saxon period lived on through the attempts of the Normans to strangle it and finally emerged, triumphant and unbowed in the time of Chaucer, is one that is determined to write out the French role in English literary history.[5] One way of correcting this prejudice is to insist that the tiny remnants of writing in English are more, not less, important than we have always thought;[6] another is to attend to the ways in which England produced so much writing (before and after the Conquest) that was not in the English vernacular.

It is this condition that seems so hard for an Anglo-centric history to imagine. Some of the cultural complexities at issue are revealed when we remember that nation does not tell itself in the same way on the other side of the Channel. Models of French nationhood have been differently constructed from those of the English. Although the same modernist arguments occur that are used of England and nation—that the idea of France is secular and republican—more commonly, French historians have been happy to locate the birth of France in the Middle Ages. As Colette Beaune puts it: 'sensitized by three wars, generations of French scholars made the medieval birth of the nation one of their grandest themes',[7] and, although she does it differently, this is no less true of her own book, *Naissance de la Nation France.* One of the ways in which this has been effected is through language: it has been important to historians as well as to historians of the language to claim an unbroken monolingual identity for French.

[3] See Chapter 2, p. 41.

[4] The standard account is N. R. Ker, *English Manuscripts in the Century after the Norman Conquest* (Oxford: Clarendon Press, 1960); for more recent comment, see E. Treharne, 'Categorization, Periodization: The Silence of (the) English in the Twelfth Century', *NML*, 8 (2006), 247–73.

[5] R. W. Chambers, *On the Continuity of English Prose from Alfred to More and His School* (London: Early English Text Society, 1932), lxxxv–lxxxvi; I cite (with a sense of how scholarly opinion changes, and will no doubt change again) from the copy he gave to my now retired colleague at UCL, Valerie Adams, and which she passed on to me.

[6] 'The care early Middle English writings demand of our formalism may not only redeem a loss by finding a literature we have not known, it should help us to see the literature we have always known much more clearly': C. Cannon, *The Grounds of English Literature* (Oxford: Oxford University Press, 2004), 49.

[7] C. Beaune, *The Birth of an Ideology: Myths and Symbols of Nation in Late-Medieval France*, trans. S. R. Huston and ed. Fredric L. Cheyette (Berkeley: University of California Press, 1991), 2.

With appropriate judiciousness Anthony Smith has rightly observed that it is both England *and* France in the very longevity of their history that have provided 'the litmus test of the antiquity of the concept of the nation and the nature of national sentiment, as well as of the historical continuity of particular nations.'[8] This book proposes further that it is this very entanglement between English and French to which we need to return in investigating pre-eighteenth-century nationhood. That we have a binary not a single model of vernacularity in these long centuries is a historical, linguistic, and cultural condition that deeply affects the sense of modernity, linguistic identity, and historical autonomy in English, and for that matter French literary history. As a concomitant to this claim, it argues that a bifurcated Anglo-French model for vernacularity is not only central to any understanding of nation but also crucially resistant to it. For once we begin to think through the implications of a double rather than a singular perception of linguistic identity, we are prevented from thinking of nation in isolationist, individualist ways. The Anglo-French culture that existed in England for several centuries prevented either English or French from being a single condition. To speak French was no less an English act than to speak English. Conversely, to speak English was to speak only one of the English vernaculars. It was a divided and unequal but shared linguistic culture.

The Familiar Enemy is an attempt to consider on the one side how a notion of Englishness copes with bi-vernacularity and, on the other, how a notion of Frenchness copes with Anglo-French. For both sides this is a dislocating exercise: it is not easy for a modern English first-language speaker to turn back the clock to a time when English was in a position of linguistic inferiority, neither for a modern French consciousness to absorb the implications of a multiple and fractured French, possessed by a people that claimed political dominance as well as kinship. This chapter explores the way in which this dislocation is part of each history. In the case of Chaucer, it is not so much that his Englishness has been overplayed—as Seth Lerer and others have shown, this was part of his history from his earliest readers on—as that his Englishness has been retrospectively defined. If we take this other vernacular seriously, as seriously as Chaucer and his contemporaries across Europe did, then English looks different. This is not merely because French influenced English as a matter of lexis or etymology, though this is important, but that its presence as Anglo-French within an English culture gave English a sibling language with which it was in uneasy competition. French was both internal and external to English, just as it was both internal and external to France and the French.

[8] A. D. Smith, *Nationalism and Modernism: A Critical Survey of Recent Theories of Nations and Nationalism* (London and New York: Routledge, 1998), 172. Taine puts forward a similar justification for his *History*, 20–1.

By moving on to a time beyond the Middle Ages it becomes easier to see how fully narratives of nation indulge in retrospect.[9] This is partly served simply by looking back, but it is also because two of the greatest instances of nation-building—as they have later come to be seen—in the histories of France and England were also exercises in retrospection: the life of Jeanne d'Arc and the *Life of King of Henry Fifth* in the Folio edition of the works of Shakespeare. This final chapter turns to these two pre-eminent mutually defining national myths, both of which raise crucial questions about chronology. They occurred within two decades of each other in two apposing battles: Agincourt (1415) and Orléans (1429). Their similarities and differences uncannily echo the larger themes of the Anglo-French relationship. Both were highly improbable and in some sense pyrrhic victories; both stimulated hugely public rewritings; both created images of defiant success that have endured over all others as ways of figuring nation. At the same time, the two stories, as they have become, naturally pull in opposing directions. Each is built upon an opposing view of how to construct the past.

JEANNE LA PUCELLE

'Je l'adveue'

The story of Jeanne d'Arc provides a compelling instance of cultural as well as personal retrospect. At first a dazzling spur to a rejuvenated French self-confidence with her defeat of the English at Orléans on 8 May 1429, once captured by the Burgundians a year later at Compiègne just outside Paris she was quickly rejected by her erstwhile advocates, publicly tried over a period of five months, and burnt as a heretic in Rouen by the English occupying enemy on 30 May 1431, only then to be reinstated over the centuries as both a French patriotic heroine and, in 1920, a saint. She is the only person in history to have been condemned *and* canonized by the Catholic Church; add to this her youth, her lack of education, her gender, and her persistent wearing of male clothes and she becomes a highly unlikely source of national identification.

The puzzle for this chapter might be expressed initially as why Jeanne becomes a national symbol in the face of so much that seems to disqualify her for this role. When we consider that, in becoming a figure of a nation, she was sacrificed to that nation, then she seems not unlikely but impossible. She seems far too unstable a figure to stand, as such, for anything: how could she, of all candidates,

[9] I would like to acknowledge a long-standing debt to Raymond Williams's powerful analysis of the process of regression in each generation's view of the relationship between city and country, working backwards from the twentieth to the eighteenth century and earlier, *The Country and the City* (London: Hogarth Press, 1985; 1st pub. 1973), 9–12.

become the blessed one who rescued 'toute France' from ruin as Christine de Pizan declared?[10] It could only be possible through a strange, even blind act of faith, or a form of suppression or radical distortion. This then is the first question: what are the forms of distortion in the records and how do we recognize and interpret them? In any life from the medieval past, the questions about 'what happened' are revealed as constrained by the distancing, even spoiling processes of time upon written records; but in the case of Jeanne the questions of 'how do we decide' and 'how do we tell it' are more than usually caught up in larger matters of national interest, and were so entangled from the earliest moments of reaction to her. For her immediate contemporaries and judges as well as those who came after to reassess those judgements, that activity of suppression or distortion becomes a means of expressing other kinds of individual and political allegiance.

My second question thus concerns the ways in which individual allegiances apparently develop into larger collective opinions. In the complicated textual forms in which it was recorded by her contemporaries, Jeanne's story gives us a means of seeing—with more than usual detail—how communal perspectives develop. One point to be drawn from the ubiquitously cited Benedict Anderson is his emphasis on the importance of the rise of journalism to any notion of horizontal communal imagining.[11] Rapid circulation of printed material enables people to have a sense of public opinion (even if to some extent this is a fictional sense) and to imagine themselves part of it. Without the availability of this kind of print it is very much harder—at times, with restricted evidence, impossible—to track the transition between locally expressed assumptions and those that suddenly become general or even universal. Jeanne is a rare medieval example of a figure who provoked not merely a public but a 'national' response. The written responses to her give us a means to observe the relation between assertion and action, between decision and public event in the workings of nation. Yet, as we will see, this is a far from transparent relationship.

The third issue concerns Jeanne's humble, uneducated relation to language. The paradox of her record is that it casts her speech into a massive, Latinate written edifice, yet it was precisely her raw illiteracy that provided the spark of contemporary reaction, later fanned into the roaring flames of a heretic's death, and later still, of national symbolism. Part of the quest here is thus to grasp something more about the way in which the vernacular, spoken by an uneducated female voice, and yet mediated by an imposing Latin legal and ecclesiastical culture, became a quite different symbol of Frenchness from the vernacular triumphs of law, bureaucracy, and secular fiction.

[10] C. de Pizan, *Ditié de Jehanne d'Arc*, ed. A. J. Kennedy and K. Varty (Oxford: Society for the Study of Mediaeval Languages and Literature, 1977), Stanza 19.

[11] B. Anderson, *Imagined Communities* (London and New York: Verso, 1983; rev. edn 1991), 61, 65.

Jeanne's trial records seem magnified as against the minor cases of public annoyance in the London civic records into much more weighty, and dark, political imaginings. In this they show us not only the pressures on the 'commun vois' but on our ability much later to recognize and isolate it. The sense of public voice so glaringly put on display in Jeanne's trial is shown to be a morass of disparate assertions subject to many factors: the unequal power of erudition over illiteracy, the imponderable quotient of belief, and the collusion between faith and worldliness. The focus in this chapter is on the quality and character of the assertions that crowd Jeanne's history. Starting with her own declarations, her short life and its much longer after-life were constructed through stringent efforts to examine these declarations, and re-examine them through new declarations. Jeanne makes us reflect on the intricate relations between personal certainty and the grounds of communal approval or persuasion. These in turn are complexly informed by two kinds of epistemology: one grounded in individual identity and the other in public meaning, one in the meaning of her words *to her* and the other in the meaning of her words contextually as they are understood *by others*. The chapter looks at some of these issues among the trial records and chronicle reports by pondering the distance between good faith and bad faith, between true and false witness, between the traitor and the person loyal to death.

Such contemplations bring us to the extraordinary divagations of retrospection that were engineered by her case. Not only do these writings provide us with perspectives on 'the relations between textuality and the political process'[12] but they give us an insight into the cunning forces of retrospection and how they shape the telling of history from more angles than we are often prepared to countenance. On one hand, then, it is a matter of observing the manner in which her story is founded on claim and counter-claim, on belief and disbelief. Jeanne's story is very heavily about turning points: moments and processes of revocation, of individual and communal changes of mind, of betrayal and stubborn assertion, of defence, denial, and restitution. On the other, it is revealing to take these moments as instances of retrospection, and observe how they have been shaped by particular desires driving the need to look back at such moments. I will trace these briefly through the different phases of her life and subsequent trials and retrials, in order, eventually, to place these statements of assertion alongside matters of political change and perception. Unsurprisingly, it is instructive to view how her life appears in the context of the long medieval history of social, political, and literary entanglements between the 'English' and the 'French'. The several ways in which she was both the subject of, and subject to, startling abjuration may offer some insights into the often-disturbing intricacies of nation and betrayal in the later Middle Ages.

[12] P. Strohm, *England's Empty Throne: Usurpation and the Language of Legitimation* 1399–1422 (New Haven and London: Yale University Press, 1998), xiii.

Forms of evasion

The surviving and in fact hugely abundant textual material works with different forms of controlling rhetoric.[13] Her trial had several stages. In brief, Jeanne was interrogated in Rouen over a three-month period from February to April 1431. The proceedings were overseen by two judges appointed by the English, Pierre Cauchon, a celebrated Parisian jurist who took the leading role, and Jean Lemaitre, local representative of the Inquisition at Rouen. Cauchon called around sixty assessors to the court, some forty of whom sat on a regular basis. From the hundreds of questions asked of Joan and her responses a list of seventy charges was compiled and read over to her during the course of a week. The list of seventy was then condensed to twelve articles, and this summary sent to the University of Paris for expert deliberation. Two judgments heavily denouncing her were eventually produced and a summary of their verdict read out to her. She was strongly advised to sign a letter of abjuration, and did so. But a little later she recanted this abjuration and insisted on the truth of her first story. This led to her excommunication and death at the stake.

This material gives a powerful impression of a rhetorically masterful, retrospective, male point of view, but its ostensible function, to reveal an illiterate female story, is sometimes strangely trumped by that story's stubborn inadequacies. Paul Strohm has well described the propensity of texts to be 'selective, diversionary, and amnesia-prone, forgetting or repressing crucial things about their own origins and those of the events with which they deal'.[14] What Strohm casts as the general disposition of a text is of course an understood precondition of a legal inquiry. As with any legal case, there is a strong awareness cutting through the hostile questions of what Jeanne is *not* saying: instead the text consists of gaps and fissures between the lines of questioning and the replies. Always having to guess at the line of supposition that any one question may be implying—and often, as the witnesses to the nullification trial attest, the questions came in a rush with interruptions from all sides of the room—Jeanne's reported answers show a wide range of responses, from confusion, denial and evasion to attempts at straightforwardness or even witty circumlocution.

The following sequence of questions and answers about her revelations (Tuesday, 27 February 1431; fourth session) is characteristically disjointed on both sides. She is asked whether the apparitions who came to her were of the same age:

[13] Philippe Contamine estimates some 2,700 pages of documentary material relating to Jeanne were printed by the mid-nineteenth century; this has risen since through the addition of much supplementary material to 4,500 pages ('Une biographie de Jeanne d'Arc est-elle encore possible?', in J. Maurice and D. Couty, eds, *Images de Jeanne d'Arc, Actes du colloque de Rouen (25, 26, 27 mai 1999)* (Paris: PUF, 2000), 1–15 (9–10).

[14] Strohm, *England's Empty Throne*, xii.

Interroguee se ilz sont d'ung mesme aage,
Respond: Je n'ay pas congié de le vous dire.
Interroguee s'ilz parlent ensemble, ou l'ung apprez l'autre,
Respond: Je n'ay pas congé de le vous dire; et toutesfoys j'en ay tous les jours conseil de toutes les deux.
Interroguee laquelle [apparust] la premiere,
Respond: Je ne les congneuz pas si tost. Et l'a bien sceu aulcunes foys, mais l'a omblié. Et s'elle a conseil, le dira voluntiers; et ce est eu registre de Poitiers.
Item, dit aussi qu'elle a eu le conseil de sainct Michel.
Interroguee lequel vint le premier,
Respond que ce fut sainct Michel.
Interroguee se il y a gueres de temps,
Respond: Je ne vous nommes point de voix de sainct Michael, mais de grant confort.[15]

[Asked whether they are the same age, she answered that she did not have leave to say.
Asked whether the saints speak together, or one after the other, she answered: 'I do not have permission to say; but in any case I always receive counsel from them both.'
Asked which one appeared to her first, she answered: 'I didn't recognize them immediately; I knew well once, but now I've forgotten. If I have leave, I'll willingly say; it is noted in the register at Poitiers.' She added that she had received counsel from Saint Michael. Asked which one came first, she answered that it was Saint Michael.
Asked if it was a long time ago, she answered: 'I am not speaking of the voice of Saint Michael, but of great comfort.']

The replies keep resorting to the formula of evasion that occurs so frequently in the record: 'Je n'ay pas congié de le vous dire'. Yet here a straight denial ('I do not have leave to tell you who came first') is followed by the concessive ('I knew well

[15] P. Paul Doncoeur and Y. Lanhers, eds, *La Minute française des interrogatoires de Jeanne La Pucelle d'après le Réquisitoire de Jean d'Estivet et les manuscrits de d'Urfé et d'Orléans* (Melun: Librairie d'Argences, 1952), 113, hereafter cited as Doncoeur; P. Tisset and Y. Lanhers, eds, *Procès de condamnation de Jeanne d'Arc,* 3 vols (Paris: Klincksieck, 1960–71), I, 72–3; hereafter cited as Tisset and Lanhers. The textual history of the Joan records is complex. Three copies remain of the official Latin version. The original 'French minute' of the trial has not survived; it exists only in the form of two later copies, the earlier of the two being incomplete at the start. The records of both the condemnation and rehabilitation trials were first fully edited by Jules Quicherat from 1841 to 1849; J. Quicherat, ed., *Procès de condemnation et de réhabilitation de Jeanne d'Arc dite La Pucelle,* Société de l'Histoire de France, 5 vols (Paris: Renquard, 1841–9), hereafter cited as Quicherat. Pierre Champion's re-edition of the condemnation in 1920–1 was completed by Pierre Tisset and Yvonne Lanhers (1960–71); the rehabilitation or nullification proceedings were re-edited by Pierre Duparc, *Procès en nullité de la condamnation de Jeanne d'Arc,* 5 vols (Paris: Klincksieck, 1977–88), hereafter cited as Duparc. A project to revise and update the remaining material in Quicherat's monumental work is currently under way in the Centre Jeanne d'Arc in Orléans. I cite here largely from the French minute as edited by Donceur, with cross-references to Tisset and Lanhers, but where appropriate include citations from the Latin for comparison. For the Latin, I use the translation from D. Hobbins's edition, *The Trial of Joan of Arc* (Cambridge, MA: Harvard University Press, 2005), hereafter cited as Hobbins; translations from the French minute are my own. An excellent selection and translation of source material from her life and trial records has recently been produced by C. Taylor, *Joan of Arc, La Pucelle* (Manchester: Manchester University Press, 2006).

once but now I've forgotten'), which modulates, through sudden lurches back into the third person, into an unforced declaration ('I am not speaking of the voice of St Michael, but of great comfort').

The passage conveys a marked sense (again, as witnesses later observed) that its disjointedness is not merely the result of jumbled copying but a representation on one side of persistent attempts to provoke naively literal, human descriptions of the visions and on the other an equally persistent desire to avoid succumbing to that provocation. The moment where Jeanne's flat statements leak something unexpected ('the great comfort' of St Michael's voice) has an almost comic force. This is certainly true of her famous retort to the later question about St Michael's nudity (1 March; fifth session):

> *Interroguee se il estoit nud,*
> Pensez vous, respond, que nostre Seigneur n'ait de quoy les vestir?[16]

[Asked whether he was naked, 'Do you think,' she answered, 'that God has nothing to clothe him with?']

Part of what is going on here is that despite these hints of self-assertion, and as the oscillation between first and third person reveals, this is an autobiography that someone else is trying to write, often in deliberate opposition to the materials being supplied. Unlike the *Book of Margery Kempe*, a rare English example of autobiography remarkably enough from the same decade, the story that is being extracted from Jeanne is not hers, because it is not produced according to her principles of selection, or any sense of order that she might have had.[17] Mixed in with this is a sense that Jeanne, too, is not necessarily a fixed point in this relationship: it is not simply that one side is trying to draw out and distort a version of the 'truth' from the other, but that Jeanne is also looking to find answers to 'subtle and captious' questions she has not yet asked herself, in terms she would never have used.[18] There are two versions of the narrative on view: the events as she remembers them, and the story the investigators are seeking to elicit under questioning. These two forms of retrospect are complexly interrelated: the urgent drive of their desire to find a certain story acts to cast doubt on her recollections and disturbs their sense of narrative and due sequence. 'What happened' becomes genuinely malleable—for her as well as for them—under the pressure of these seemingly endless, shifting, dynamic interrogations.

[16] Doncoeur, 129; Tisset and Lanhers, I, 87.

[17] See also Gerson's *De probatione spirituum* on St Bridget of Sweden (1415), discussed in D. A. Fraioli, *Joan of Arc: The Early Debate* (Woodbridge: Boydell, 2000), 12. It is interesting to compare English heresy testimonies in this regard, such as those of Richard Wyche and William Thorpe; on the ambiguities of these writings as forms of self-representation see R. Copeland, *Pedagogy, Intellectuals, and Dissent in the Later Middle Ages: Lollardy and Ideas of Learning* (Cambridge: Cambridge University Press, 2001), 151–219.

[18] The terms are Jean Massieu's, priest of Rouen and usher at the trial in his account cited by R. Pernoud, *Joan of Arc* (Harmondsworth: Penguin, 1964), 205, hereafter cited as Pernoud.

Further pressures on the shape of Jeanne's recollections are created by language and the complexity of the record itself. The one is (at least partly) related to the other. As usual in court proceedings a notary produced minutes in French, these were translated into Latin and a full record of each session drawn up. This record could include other supporting material: witness statements, letters, summons, and so on.[19] For a long time—up to and beyond the nineteenth-century edition by Jules Quicherat—it was the Latin records of the Rouen trial that held sway. For these, after all, were the official records, of which five authenticated copies were made: three for the Inquisitor, one for the King of England, and one for Pierre Cauchon. But more recently, since the re-edition of the trial documents by Pierre Tisset and Yvonne Lanhers, more attention has been given to the two copies of the French minutes originally written by the notary Guillaume Manchon; these *notula in gallico* are now valued for seeming to possess much closer access to the atmosphere of the courtroom and to the words Jeanne actually uttered than the fluent legalese of the Latin reports.[20] To have the French as well as the Latin version of events is to make plainer the chasm of language, terminology, ideology, gender, and education that—often wilfully, on both sides—separated Jeanne from her accusers. The distance—the disparities, silences, re-orderings—between the French notes and the Latin report, hints at the cultural and political differences between them.[21]

I will come back to the textual record shortly, for the intricacies go further still. But in the meantime the ebb and flow in the mass of other records that make up Jeanne's larger narrative is worth further comment. There are three main phases in the gradual construction of belief and its closely matching counterpart of accusation: it begins with the very first account Jeanne presented to the future Charles VII of her voices (by way of her first mentor Robert Baudricourt), what we could call the 'original' story and the kinds of immediate reaction it provoked. Second, comes the phase of her imprisonment, in which over a period of less than five months from the start of the trial to her death by burning she turned from a figure of miraculous faith to a heretic; and third, the astonishingly open-ended process of her retrial, begun in 1450 and not completed for another four hundred and fifty years, during which she turned again from heretic, to innocent believer, and in due course, saint. Each phase discloses different facets of the process of public assent. In its largest outline it moves from private to public in

[19] For a detailed discussion of the sources, see Tisset and Lanhers, III, 2–54; a convenient summary may be found in Contamine, 'Une biographie'.

[20] For descriptions of the manuscripts, Orléans, Bib. Mun. MS 518 ('O') and Paris BnF fonds lat. 8838 ('U'), see Tisset and Lanhers, III, xxiv–xxv.

[21] Some of these issues are investigated by K. Sullivan, *The Interrogation of Joan of Arc* (Minneapolis: University of Minnesota Press, 1999), although she does not deal closely with textual differences among the sources. Daniel Hobbins argues that the differences between the French and Latin versions have been exaggerated, and the unreliability of the official Latin translation overstated (*The Trial of Joan of Arc*, 7–13). The topic awaits further research.

ever-increasing circles, from the first private individual revelation, to Jeanne's emergence as national symbol, and finally to the ecclesiastical acclamation of sainthood played out (in Christian terms) to an eternal and infinite public. Yet each phase has its own character as a turning point, as a nexus of potential doubts, and each is coloured by the distorting processes of retrospection.

'Le retour de l'événement'[22]

Firstly, then, did Jeanne believe in her own story? If so, then for how long? The two short years of Jeanne's public activity, as readers have found throughout the centuries, are very poignant in their rapid decline from glowing assurance to wretched imprisonment. Perhaps most poignant of all is the developing suggestion (always faint, never categoric) that there might have been a reversal in her and not just in her fortunes. The stark, hard-won statements of the textual reports hint at subtle changes: her initial simple assurance combined with simple goals changes into more complex situations where she has to argue, allow changes of plan, is subjected to prolongations, vicissitudes, and overruled by 'better' military and political advice. Should she have urged an attack on Paris?

This is how the 'original' revelation has come down to us:

Second session; Thursday, 22 February 1431

Et si dist que, dez l'aage de traize ans, elle eust revelacion de nostre Seigneur par une voix qui l'enseigna a soy gouverner. Et pour la premiere foys elle avoit eu grand paour. Et dist que ladicte voix vint ainsy que a mydy, en temps d'esté, elle estante au jardin de son pere, en ung jour de jeune,[23] et si dist que ladicte voix vint au costé dextre, vers l'eglise. Et dist que ladicte voix n'est gueres sans clarté, laquelle est tousiours du costé de ladicte voix.[24]

Dit oultre que ladicte voix, apprez qu'elle l'eut ouye par troys foys, elle congneust que c'estoit la voix ange.

[22] I take the phrase from P. Nora, 'Le retour de l'événement', *Faire de l'histoire*, I (1974), 210–30.

[23] The Latin text has 'et ipsa Iohanna non ieiunaverat die precedenti' ('and Joan had not fasted the previous day').

[24] Doncoeur, 91; Tisset and Lanhers, I, 47. The Latin text adds 'Que quidem claritas est ab eodem latere in quo vox auditur, sed ibi communiter est magna claritas. Et quando ipsa Iohanna veniebat in Franciam, sepe audiebat illam vocem. Interrogata qualiter videbat claritatem quam ibi adesse dicebat, cum illa claritas esset a latere: Nichil ad hoc respondit; sed transivit ad alia. Dixit preterea quod, si ipsa esset in uno nemore, bene audiret voces venientes ad eam. Dixit eciam quod sibi videbatur esse digna vox, et credit quod eadem vox erat missa ex parte Dei; et postquam audivit ter illam vocem, cognovit quod erat vox angeli. Dixit eciam quod illa vox semper bene costodivit eam et quod ipsam vocem bene intellexit' [This light comes from the same side where she hears the voice, but all around in that place there is a great light. When she came to France, she often heard the voice. Asked how she saw the light she spoke of, since the light was at her side, she did not answer, but passed on to other subjects. She said that if she was in a wood, she would clearly hear the voices coming to her. It seemed a worthy voice, and she believed that the voice was sent by God; after she heard the voice three times, she knew it was the voice of an angel. She said that the voice always protected her well and she understood the voice well]. Hobbins, 53.

Dit ainsy que celle voix l'a tousiours bien gardee . . .

Et apprez luy dist qu'il estoit neccessaire qu'elle venist en France.

Et luy disoit deux ou troys foys la sepmaine qu'elle partist pour venir en France. Et que son pere ne sceust riens de son partement.

Avecques ce luy dist qu'il faloit qu'elle hatast de venir et qu'elle leveroit le siege de devant Orleans; et qu'elle allast a Robert de Baudricourt, capitaine de Vacoulleur; et que il luy bailleroit des gens pour la conduire.[25]

[And she said that, from the age of thirteen years, she had revelations from our Lord by a voice that taught her how to conduct herself. And the first time she was extremely frightened. And she said that this voice came like this at noon, in the summertime, when she was in her father's garden on a fast day, and she said that this voice came from the right, towards the church. And she said that this voice never came without light, light that was always by the side of the voice. She further said that, after she had heard the voice three times she knew it was the voice of an angel. She also said that this voice had always protected her well . . . And afterwards it said to her that it was necessary for her to go to France; and it told her two or three times a week that she should leave for France and that her father should not know of her departure. As well as this it told her that she must hurry to go and that she would raise the siege in front of Orléans; and that she should go to Robert de Baudricourt, captain of Vaucouleur, and that he would send men to escort her there.]

This simple paratactic report conveys the artlessness of the vocation: she heard a voice, she had to follow its instructions, she went to Vaucouleurs, and then to the dauphin.[26] Leaving aside the astonishing success she evidently had in carrying out these actually far from straightforward instructions, as more information comes in, partly through the persistence of the questioning, and partly through retrospective accounts from other witnesses, the pattern of events gains a troubling complexity. At first, the generals' doubts and uncertainties (as they themselves recount) meet with the same strong assertions:

[on the road to Rheims] The duc d'Alençon:

Post cujus eventum fuit conclusum quod fieret insultus contra villam, et clamaverunt precones: 'Ad insultum!' Ipsaque Johanna dixit loquenti: 'Avant, gentil duc, à l'assault!' Et, cum eidem loquenti videretur quod premature agebant ita cito incipere insultum, ipsa Johanna dixit loquenti: 'Nolite dubitare! Hora est parata 'quando placet Deo'; et quod oportebat operari quando Deus volebat: 'Operate, et Deus operabitur'; dicendo ulterius eidem loquenti: '*A! gentil duc*, times-tu?[27]

[After this incident, it was decided to launch the attack against the town, and the heralds cried: 'To the assault!' Then Joan said to the witness who was testifying: 'Forward, gentle duke, to the assault!' And when it appeared to the witness that they were acting

[25] Doncoeur, 93; Tisset and Lanhers, I, 47–8.

[26] An issue that cannot be pursued here is the uncanny resemblance of her untutored account to that of Augustine in his *Confessions*.

[27] Duparc, I, 384; Quicherat, III, 95–6.

prematurely in joining so quickly in the attack, Joan said to him: 'Do not hesitate! This is the hour that pleases God.' She added that it was necessary to work when God wished it: 'Help yourself and God will help you.' Later she said to the witness: 'Ah, gentle duke, are you afraid?'][28]

But on the road to Compiègne, it becomes less clear that things are happening according to a prophetic knowledge or sense of timing that Jeanne was privy to.

Tenth session, Tuesday, 13 March

Interroguee se, quant elle alla devant Paris, se elle eust par revelacion de ses voix de y aller,

Respond que non, mais a la requeste des gentilzhommes, qui vouloyent faire une escarmouche ou une vaillance d'armes; et avoit bien intencion d'aller oultre et de passer les fossez.

Interroguee aussi d'aller devant La Charité, s'elle eust revelacion,

Respond que non; mais par la requeste des gens d'armes, ainsy comme aultresfoys elle a dit.[29]

[(Asked whether, when she went to Paris, she had gone there through the revelation of her voices, she said no, she went at the request of nobles who wanted to carry out a skirmish or an assault-at-arms. She fully intended to go farther and to cross the trenches of Paris. Asked also whether she had a revelation about going to the town of La Charité, she said no, she went at the request of the men-at-arms, as she said previously.]

The relation between prophecy and success becomes tense and obscure: did these things happen because Jeanne was overruled, because she mistook her heavenly orders, or because, after all, as she later says about the capture itself, that the voices had indeed predicted it all along but not indicated the time or place? The trajectory of success or should it be 'failure' becomes very hard to read: is this a story of failing conviction? The illustrator in Paris BnF fr.5054 (Fig. 10), by contrast, shows her in the 8 September assault on Paris as a prominent dominating figure on the left-hand side of the picture, her enlarged hand outstretched commandingly towards the action. Or is imprisonment rather the sign of supreme success, of justification or even, as was claimed then and later (though never without contradiction by the Catholic Church), of martyrdom? Jeanne, caught in the temporality of a retrospective narrative, her reported words constantly used against her, seems not so much guided by God as by wayward texts. Enguerran de Monstrelet reports, rather cuttingly: 'Si y estoit Jehenne la Pucelle, tousjours ayant diverses oppinions, une fois voellant combatre ses ennemis, et aultre fois non'[30] [Thus was Jeanne la Pucelle, always having contrary opinions, now wanting to fight her enemies, and now not]. The narrative itself may be lying, but there is also the hint that her past words are becoming the fodder for immediate military action. Event and prophecy are becoming mutually

[28] Translation cited from Taylor, *Joan of Arc*, 307.
[29] Doncoeur, 169; Tisset and Lanhers, I, 140–41.
[30] Quicherat, V, 388.

Figure 10. Siege of Paris by Jeanne d'Arc (September 1429)
Paris BnF fr.5054, fol.66v. Copyright Bibliothèque nationale de France: reproduced with permission.

informing in an inhibiting way. If nothing can be done unless it has received the sanction of a divinely appointed voice, then if the voice becomes hard to hear nothing can be done. We are not surprised when her story finally grinds to a halt, since its demise has been predicted in the hobbling interrelationship between her revelations and her choices in the battlefield.

Even more intriguingly, we realize that the contours of this narrative are being drawn from a mixture of chronological standpoints. Looking back, even from the relatively short distance of the rehabilitation proceedings of 1455–6, it is obvious that Jeanne's capture makes her vulnerable to multiple possible retellings, which are themselves shaped by the new political context of the mid-1450s. The comments by Alençon, for example, gain a quite different resonance when we recall that immediately after them he was arrested on charges of treason.[31] He had been captured at Verneuil in 1424 and put on a great show of loyalty to the French crown, swearing to Bedford: 'I am unshakeable in my purpose never in all my life to take an oath against my rightful sovereign lord, Charles, king of France.' But thereafter he became one of the leaders of the Praguerie, a revolt against Charles VII, in which he worked closely with the English and tried to stir up plans with Richard, duke of York and Henry VI to invade Normandy in 1455. The news of this leaked to Charles during Jeanne's rehabilitation trial. For Alençon himself, then, matters of assault and the exact timing of a decision were also at stake even as he spoke of Jeanne's own capture. In relation to Jeanne's story, where timing became a matter of spiritual justification, the rehabilitation trial testimonies turn out to be creating that sense of timing from individuals who were caught up in various pressures to deflect the timing of their own actions by presenting a version of hers that justified theirs. In short, the trial records show the wheels of narrative time turning in contrary directions in that larger effort to turn the clock back on her first arraignment.

Vernacular moments

If it is hard to see straight in Jeanne's story, one reason is that it is told in more than one language. A full comparison of the French and Latin records would no doubt be revealing. Even a brief glance, however, gives a sense of the intricate political concerns that were just below the surface of certain linguistic clashes. Perhaps the most famous comment on language made by Jeanne herself is her response on 1 March 1431 to a question about St Margaret, one of the two female saints (the other being St Catherine) whom Jeanne identified in her vision of voices. Cauchon presses her on their physical characteristics:

Interrogata an ille sancte apparentes habent capillos:
Respondit: Bonum est ad sciendum.[32]

[31] S. H. Cuttler, *The Law of Treason and Treason Trials in Later Medieval France*, (Cambridge: Cambridge University Press, 1981), 100–6 and 210–22. Charles d'Orléans wrote a 'self-effacing, erudite, impassioned and sensitive speech' pleading for mercy on Alençon's behalf. He argues that if the king were to convict him then death would be better than imprisonment: 'Death would deliver him from the pain and sorrow of this world, for I myself know from my imprisonment in England…that to escape the affliction in which I found myself, I often wished that I had died at the battle [of Agincourt] where I was taken.' BnF fr. 5738, fol. 32v, Cuttler, *The Law of Treason and Treason Trials*, 104; the speech is also summarised in M. G. A. Vale, *Charles VII* (London: Eyre Methuen, 1974), 208–9.

[32] Tisset and Lanhers, I, 84. There is no French version surviving of this section of the record.

... Item dicit quod vox illa est pulchra, dulcis et humilis et loquitur ydioma gallicum.
Interrogata an sancta Margareta loquiturne ydioma anglicum:
Respondit: Qualiter loqueretur anglicum, cum non sit de parte Anglicorum?

[Asked if the saints who appeared to her had hair, she answered:
'It is good to know.' ...
Item, she said that the voice was gentle, soft and low, and spoke the French language.
Asked if St Margaret did not speak the English language, she answered: 'Why should she speak English when she is not on the English side?'][33]

This seems a fairly straightforward piece of anti-English sentiment from Jeanne, and is rarely discussed much in detail as a result. But it does not quite speak for itself, or rather, the issues are perhaps more intricate than they seem. Jeanne is usually taken to make a simple equation with being English and speaking English, and between speaking French and being French. Yet if we look more carefully at the dynamics of the questioning it is Cauchon who suddenly polarizes and nationalizes her earlier response. That Margaret spoke French is indeed specified by Jeanne, perhaps to emphasize that she did not speak Latin. Cauchon's deliberately provocative follow-up brings out the kind of ringing response that has given Jeanne a nationalist character. But Cauchon's question seems addressed to the wider audience in the chamber: the French and English clerics, prelates, canon and civil lawyers and local legal officials. His joke allows several kinds of response: in the pay of the English himself, and in the wake of the arguments over nation in the Council of Constance, he can properly ask why a saint should be exclusively appropriable to French interests: why should St Margaret not support the English? But others might also have appreciated the metynomic room for manoeuvre in the phrase 'speak the English tongue'. This is not a literal description of linguistic choice but a metaphorical one of political choice: Cauchon is speaking the English tongue as he prosecutes the trial in Latin and French.

In another set of questions about these two saints (17 March 1431), Jeanne's reply is carefully even-handed:

Interroguee si elle sçait point que saincte Katherine et Margueritte hayent les Angloys,
Respond: Elles ayment ce que nostre Seigneur ayme, et hayent ce que Dieu hait.

Interroguee si Dieu hait les Angloys,
Repond que, de l'amour ou hayne que Dieu a aux Angloys, ou que Dieu leur faict a leurs ames, ne sçait rien; mais sçait bien que ilz seront mis hors de France, excepté ceulx qui y mourront; et que Dieu envoira victoire aux Françoys, et contre les Angloys.

[Asked whether she knew that Saints Katherine and Margaret hated the English, she replied: 'They love what our Lord loves and they hate what God hates.' ...
Asked whether God hated the English, she answered that, of the love or hatred that God had for the English or of what he would do to their souls, she knew nothing, but she was

[33] Taylor, *Joan of Arc*, 162.

certain that they would be driven out of France, except those who would die there, and that God would send victory to the French against the English.][34]

If we take such a sequence as verbatim reporting then these are magnificently judged replies managing to be at once impartial and prophetically anti-English. It seems unlikely that Jeanne should be credited with very much here beyond her evidently strong desire to fight successfully against the English. The circumstances around the recording of her words were, however, full of tension, and the fight to take possession of what she was saying was bitter and rancorous. We learn this from comments made by the notary Guillaume Manchon in the rehabilitation proceedings. There was 'great tumult' he reported, 'and Joan was interrupted at almost every word when she was speaking about her apparitions'. He himself protested because of the presence of 'two or three secretaries of the King of England' who 'wrote down the words and the testimony of Joan as they pleased, leaving out her excuses and anything which served to exonerate her'. Manchon says he refused to continue in his job unless order was established. They changed venue and put two English guards on the door. But trouble continued as 'some were saying that she had not replied as the witness had written'. He therefore 'where it appeared to him that there was a difficulty... wrote '*Nota*' at the top'.[35]

Manchon plays honest broker here, the professional who is simply trying to do a difficult job as best as he can. But it is easy to see how his position was compromised in the retelling. Those seeking to restore Jeanne's reputation in 1452–6 were looking for ways to demonstrate that the initial trial had been conducted improperly and this makes the notary the immediate potential scapegoat. He can retaliate only by saying that he was constrained to write as he did, an answer which reveals with devastating clarity that he was *bound* to misinterpret as far as one side or the other would think. What Jeanne said was never going to be a matter of transparent record, because it was in no one's interest for it to be rendered as such.

A further example of linguistic abrasion in the trial occurs in the extraordinary clash between Jeanne and Pierre Cauchon in the 21 February session. The investigators asked her to recite the Pater Noster and Ave Maria.[36] But she will not do so unless they hear her confession. Cauchon is silent but overbearingly present in the scene: implicitly he refuses to comply with her request. He

[34] Doncoeur, 193.

[35] Taylor, *Joan of Arc*, 322. ['fuit factus maximus tumultus...et interrumpebantur quasi singula verba ipsius Johanne, dum loqueretur de suis apparitionibus, quia ibidem erant aliqui secretarii regis Anglie, duo aut tres, qui registrabant prout volebant dicta et depositiones ejusdem Johanne, omittentes excusationes ejusdem, et ea que faciebant ad sui deonerationem...et quod aliqui dicebant quod ita non responderat sicut erat scriptum per loquentum, ubi ipsi videbatur difficultas, ponebat 'Nota' in capite, ut iterum interrogaretur et cessaret difficultas. Et hoc est quid denotant illa 'Nota' in capite posita.', Duparc, I, 417].

[36] Tisset and Lanhers, I, 41.

eventually tries to find an escape by offering Jeanne the opportunity to say her confession to 'unum aut duos notabiles viros de lingua gallicana'. It is not entirely clear what this might mean.[37] As Pierre Tisset points out, early editors leapt to the nationalistic conclusion that 'de lingua gallicana' meant 'de la langue de France' or even 'de nationalité française',[38] on the assumption that her refusal was based on anti-English grounds. But of course the great majority of the interrogators were indeed French, albeit subjects of Henry VI. It is possible that this is a metaphoric usage akin to speaking 'the English tongue', meaning in reverse those on the French side; but the rub here is precisely that 'French' is divided and has no single meaning either linguistically or politically. It is probably simply a way of patronizing Jeanne by presuming her refusal to be caused by ignorance of Latin. Either way, several undercurrents are implied. There is constant awareness of the different linguistic strata present in the room, both between the uneducated Jeanne and the academic masters, and between the languages of betrayal and opposition lurking in the atmosphere amongst learned and uneducated alike, between those in the pay of the English, and those whose allegiance was to Charles or the Burgundians. 'En opposant un écrit naïf' [39] to the sophisticated legal narrative of her accusers Jeanne exposes the web of bad faiths in which they are all entangled.

[37] Serge Lusignan briefly discusses the various terms for French in medieval usage in 'Langue française et société du XIIIe au XIVe siècle', in J. Chaurand, ed., *Nouvelle Histoire de la Langue Française* (Paris: Editions du Seuil, 1999), 93–143 (113–14), and makes the interesting observation that the term *romana* (in Latin) or *roman* (in French), at first the ubiquitous description of the vernacular, later denoted a form of regional speech in contrast to *lingua gallicana* or *gallice* or *franceis* or *françois* which initially referred to the language of Paris and its immediate vicinity and later was increasingly applied to the language of the realm of Francia. However, I have some reservations over the question of how far such usage implies a national frame of reference (a question that was posed after all by l'abbé Grégoire in 1790), and what we are to deduce in general from medieval comments on the vernacular (see Chapter 2, p. 64 for a different reading of the St Louis miracle he goes on to discuss on 114). Clearly (as he remarks) this specific matter of terminology merits a full study. For a further specific example, see his *Parler vulgairement: Les Intellectuels et la langue française aux XIIIe et XIVe siècles* (Paris; Montréal: Vrin; Les Presses de l'Université de Montréal, 1986), 88, in a commentary by Aquinas on Jesus teaching in the Temple (John 7: 4–18). The Jews ask Jesus how he manages to teach with such power without having studied. Aquinas comments: 'Circa primum sciendum est, quod iudicio illus standum est, utrum aliquis bene operetur in aliqua arte, qui est expertus in arte illa: sicut an aliquis bene loquitur gallice, standum est iudicio eius qui est peritus in lingua gallica' ['It is first necessary to know that in order to determine whether one is practising an art correctly, one must appeal to the judgement of someone who is expert in that art. Thus in order to evaluate whether a person speaks French well, one must seek the judgement of someone who is competent in the French language'], Aquinas, *Super E. s. Ioannis*, VII, II, 5. See also the comments by Bacon cited in Chapter 2 above.

[38] See Tisset and Lanhers, II, 41, n. 2. References to these early editors are given on II, xv–xviii.

[39] G. Bennington and J. Derrida, *Jacques Derrida* (Paris: Éditions du Seuil, 1991), 1.7–8. This work was first published in French, and then translated into English by Geoffrey Bennington under the same title (Chicago: University of Chicago Press, 1993). The book comprises Bennington's account of Derrida's work, subtitled *Derridabase*, and Derrida's response, subtitled *Circonfession* (*Circumfession*). I expand this allusion to Derrida in 'Converting Jeanne d'Arc: *trahison* and *nation* in the Hundred Years War', *NML*, 8 (2006), ed. Rita Copeland, Wendy Scase, and David Lawton (Turnhout: Brepols, 2006), 67–97.

The many witness statements produced at the nullification trial of 1452–6 may be entangled but, along with much other writing by theologians such as Jacques Gelu and Jean Gerson, poets such as Christine de Pizan and Martin le Franc, and chroniclers such as Enguerran de Monstrelet, they demonstrate that for many of Jeanne's contemporaries the key question was her authenticity. Can she be genuine? Is she a charlatan? Is she not merely a Valois pawn? We can see in these responses various ways in which public assent sometimes gathers in support of Jeanne and sometimes conspicuously fails to do so. Mathieu Thomassin (b. 1391), a chronicler who was in service to Charles VII, remarks in a carefully worded phrase:

Et de prime face, chacun disoit que c'estoit une trufferie; et à nulle chose que elle dist l'on ne adjouxtoit point de foy.[40]

[and at first, everyone said that it was a form of trickery; and no one attached any faith to anything she said.]

He articulates the very process of putting faith in her words by which Jeanne was constantly judged. He speaks not just for himself, but rather generalizes that individual decision ('on ne adjouxtoit point de foy') into a collective view: 'c'estoit une trufferie'. Thomassin's Valois perspective wavers between clear-sighted suspicion of credulousness and a certain sympathetic credulity of his own. For instance, his mention that Jeanne was: 'de bien simple manière. Et parloit peu, sinon que on parloit à elle'[41] [(had) a very simple manner. She spoke little except when she was spoken to] prepares the reader for an allusion to that other example of female simplicity, by way of a prophecy by Merlin which was being circulated at the time as evidence of her genuineness: 'Descendit virgo dorsum sagittarii et flores virgineos obscurabit' [A virgin will descend on the back of the archer and will hide the virgin flower].[42] But he counterpoises this with a harsh comment on her lack of education, criticizing the 'gros et lourd langage' [coarse and heavy language] and poor construction of her dictated 'lettre aux anglais'.[43] Evidently, untutored roughly expressed faith pushed at the limits of an educated cleric's ability to support it: he turns with relief to Christine de Pizan, finding in her a writer's approval for Jeanne:

entre les autres une notable femme appelée Christine, qui a fait plusieurs livres en françois (je l'ay souvent veue à Paris), feit de l'advénement de ladicte Pucelle et de ses gestes ung traictié . . .[44]

[40] Quicherat, IV, 304–05.

[41] Quicherat, IV, 304.

[42] Quicherat, IV, 305; Taylor, *Joan of Arc*, 77; see also Fraioli, *Joan of Arc: The Early Debate*, 65.

[43] 'Et feit escripre des lectres qu'elle mesmes dicta, en gros et lourd langage et mal ordonné. J'en ay leu les copies dont la teneur s'en suit': Quicherat, IV, 306.

[44] Quicherat, IV, 310.

[among others a well-known woman called Christine (I have often seen her in Paris), who has written many books in French, composed an account of the arrival of this above-mentioned Pucelle and of her deeds . . .]

A woman 'qui a fait plusieurs livres en françois' makes another book on this 'simple villageoise', and thus rescues her from the poor command of language that was casting doubt on her authenticity.[45]

Dubiety about Jeanne is expressed even more violently, of course, by the English side. In a fragment of a letter from John, duke of Bedford, we see the opposite view of credulity, as a form of 'unlevefulle doubte' that takes the place of the 'sadde beleve' and betrays the easy susceptibility of people to superstition:

There felle, by the hand of God, as it seemeth, a greet strook upon your peuple that was assembled there in grete nombre, caused in grete partie, as y trowe, of lakke of sadde beleve, and of unlevefulle doubte that thei hadde of a disciple and lyme of the Feende, called the Pucelle, that used fals enchauntements and sorcerie.[46]

What makes this worthy of remark is not that Bedford was concerned simply to villify Jeanne, but rather, as he goes on to say, that he perceives she is having a profound effect on the populace:

The which strooke and discomfiture nought oonly lessed in grete partie the nombre of youre people, there, but as well withdrowe the courage of the remenant in merveillous wyse, and couraiged youre adverse partie and ennemys to assemble hem forthwith in grete nombre, etc.[47]

This is a running observation among the commentators, and clearly the reason why Jeanne mattered: she was taken seriously because she was taken seriously.[48]

Jeanne's contemporaries recognized that unusual processes were taking place in public opinion as a result of her claims. When we read through the records we find a remarkable range of positioning. It is not a straightforward matter of whether they believed her or not, but rather of the kind of pressure they seem to feel to assert one kind of view or another. Much depends on whether someone was writing before or after her death, and before or after her rehabilitation. There

[45] Other chronicles mention Jeanne's humble beginnings, such as the *Chronique de la Pucelle*, which describes her succinctly as a 'simple villageoise' and comments on people's early doubts: 'Lesquelles choses messire Robert réputa à une moquerie et derision, s'imaginant que c'estoit un songe ou fantaisie' ['these things messire Robert held to be a mockery and derision, imagining that it was a dream or delusion'] (Quicherat, IV, 205).

[46] Quicherat, V, 136.

[47] Quicherat, V, 136.

[48] The contemporary English response to Jeanne is a large and complex topic, but important contexts for it are to be found in concern about heresy and its links with political dissent, both internally with respect to the Lollards and also European controversies over the Hussites, and the debates on witchcraft at the council of Basel as well as in France. Bedford's own position (if we compare his remarks about the siege of Orléans in the Privy Council statement of 1434 to his silence about Jeanne throughout his correspondence from 1429 to 1435) is puzzling and remarkable. I am grateful to Craig Taylor for discussion of this point, and of Regnault de Chartres (see n. 49 below).

is not the space here to give a proper account of this, but it is interesting (and unsurprising) to note how much a certain type of moral language develops after the event:

Thus, in a letter to his diocese, Archbishop of Rheims, Regnault de Chartres, Chancellor of Charles VII, wrote:

Dieu avait souffert prendre Jehanne la Pucelle pour ce qu'el s'estoit constitué en orgueil, et pour les riches habitz qu'el avoit pris; et qu'el n'avoit faict ce que Dieu luy avoit commandé, ains avoit faict sa volonté.[49]

[God had allowed Joan the Maid to be taken because she had made herself full of pride and because of the rich clothing which she had worn, and because she had not done what God had commanded her, but had done her own will.]

Sometimes the language of doubt is expressed with more blatant cynicism:

Episcopus Noviomensis:

Scit tamen quod episcopus Belvacensis non deducebat hujusmodi processum suis expensis, ut credit, sed expensis regis Angliae et quod misiae quae fiebant, fiebant per Anglicos.[50]

[The Bishop of Noyon: I know, however, that it was not at his own expense that the Bishop of Beauvais held that trial, but at the expense of the King of England, and that the expenses which were incurred in it were on the account of the English.]

Discourses of secular and religious doubt are thoroughly confused in these texts. The public meaning of Jeanne depended closely on what she said; at the same time what she said was heavily subject to reconstruction. What we learn is how far people were prepared to trust to versions of events that they profoundly doubted.

Abjuration

The final twists and turns of the Rouen trial culminate in the astonishing reversals of Jeanne's abjuration. We will trace them and then compare the trial with some secular trials and tales of treachery and imposture.

Describing 'what happened' in the last few days of Jeanne's imprisonment is typically difficult.[51] The sources range from the reports of the plenary session held by the University of Paris to discuss the twelve articles of accusation formulated against Jeanne by the Rouen court; letters sent from Pierre Cauchon,

[49] Quicherat, V, 168–9. Regnault de Chartres's comments about Joan must be seen within the light of his own political position in the faction fighting at Charles's court: he was the effective leader of the group that sought to oust Joan and the Angevin clique, and then break the Anglo-Burgundian alliance by making peace with Burgundy. As such, his condemnation of Joan is not unexpected.

[50] Quicherat, III, 56.

[51] For a detailed discussion and narrative, see Tisset and Lanhers, III, 134–43.

the principal judge, from the King of England, witness statements from clerks, the various university academics and others who were present at exchanges between Jeanne and various interrogators in prison, and then at the burning itself. A scaffold and platform was erected in the cemetery of St-Ouen on 24 May 1431 and Jeanne brought out to face a crowd that included her assessors and other prelates, and to hear a sermon by Guillaume Érard, a sympathizer with the English. When this was finished, Jean Massieu, the usher, was charged with reading her a document (*cédule*) of abjuration, which she was asked to sign. This *cédule* turns out to be something of a purloined letter. In the official records, there is a very long forty to fifty-line revocation, given in French and Latin, in which Jeanne is presented as elaborately denouncing her own feigning, blasphemy, wearing of 'dissolute, illmade and immodest'[52] clothes and other crimes and errors. It contains a rough signature.[53] But those who were there at the scaffold, including Massieu himself, described the *cédule* as a short five- or six- (or eight)-line declaration.[54] Many other often-contradictory details occur in the various accounts: in some Jeanne says she would rather sign than be burnt, in others, she says she cannot read or write and draws a circle on the *cédule* 'by way of derision'.[55] In one astonishing witness statement by the assessor Guillaume du Desert, she apparently laughed aloud while uttering the words of the abjuration.[56]

I have dwelt on this because, in a way that is perhaps reminiscent of the mysterious presentation of the pardon in *Piers Plowman*, so much of Jeanne's predicament seems to turn on this evanescent text, a document whose

[52] En portant habit dissolu, difforme et deshonneste contre la decence de nature', Tisset and Lanhers, I, 389.

[53] For the long text of the abjuration, in French and Latin, see Tisset and Lanhers, I, 389–92.

[54] 'Massieu: Et est bene memor quod in eadem cedula cavebatur quod de cetero non portaret arma, habitum virilem, capillos rasos, et multa alia de quibus non recordatur. Et bene scit quod illa cedula continebat circiter octo lineas, et non amplius; et scit firmiter quod non erat illa de qua in processu fit mentio, quia aliam ab illa que est inserta in processu legit ipse loquens, et signavit ipsa Johanna': Duparc, I, 433; Quicherat, III, 156; Pernoud, 259 ['In this cédule he remembers well that there was a warning that in the future she should no longer bear arms, neither wear man's dress nor short hair, along with many other things that he does not recall. He knows well also that the cédule contained about eight lines and no more; and he knows with certainty that it was not the one mentioned in the procès, for the witness had read a different one that had been inserted into the procès and that Jeanne had signed].

[55] Haimond de Macy: 'Et tunc quidam secretarius regis Anglie, tunc presens, vocatus Laurentius *Calot*, extraxit a manica sua quamdam parvam cedulam scriptam, quam tradidit eidem Johanne ad signandum; et ipsa respondit quod nesciebat nec legere, nec scribere. Non obstante hoc ipse Laurentius Calot, secretarius, tradidit eidem Johanne dictam cedulam et calamum ad signandum; et per modum derisionis, ipsa Johanna fecit quoddam rotundum' (Duparc, I, 406; Quicherat, III, 123; Pernoud, 257) [One of the secretaries of the King of England who was present, called Laurent Calot, took out of his sleeve a little written cédule that he held out to Jeanne to sign; but she replied that she did not know how to read or write. Notwithstanding, this secretary, Laurent Calot, held out the cédule to Jeanne along with a pen to sign it; and as if in derision Jeanne drew a sort of circle].

[56] Duparc, I, 213; Quicherat, II, 338; Pernoud, 261–2.

significance seems paradoxically to lie more in its intangibility than in its material solidity. Moreover, at the time the relapse was even more important than the abjuration. This whole drama of textual recantation was but a prelude to Jeanne's recantation of her recantation, and hence to her final condemnation as a heretic and burning. Indeed, Régine Pernoud argues (in support of one of the fifteenth-century commentators) that this was precisely what Cauchon had in mind, since 'according to the rules of the Inquisition courts, none but those who, having recanted their heresy, had relapsed could be condemned to suffer death by burning'.[57] In the event, in another turn on events, the trigger and sign of Jeanne's relapse is not a document, or even a verbal utterance, but a change of clothing. As is well known, in the afternoon of the abjuration (as the Latin record relates) she is ordered to change into women's clothing, and complies, also shaving her head. But on the Monday following, they find her in prison back in male clothes.

Jeanne's cross-dressing has been much discussed, so I will add little here.[58] But it builds on my argument that the crux of Jeanne's story is less a matter of plain and stubborn assertion or conviction, but rather of change and counter-change. In particular, we might connect the uncertainty, and indeed perplexed fury that her insistence on male dress caused her interrogators with the broader unease in the period about identity and allegiance. The context of war with England might have been expected to give clarity to the sense of opposition between one enemy and the other; in reality, the identity of 'English' and 'French' was highly volatile and a source of often unspeakable tension. The courtroom struggle over private confession between Jeanne and Cauchon is one such example. That Jeanne was herself caught between 'français' and 'français' in her trial, between powerful collaborators and a weak resistance, is of far greater significance than that she was tried by 'the English'. As many have remarked, there is a great paucity of contemporary English response to Jeanne. The vast production of writing accusing and legitimizing her was French, and was stimulated by the traumatic acknowledgement that she had been betrayed by her own. Let us turn outwards from her trial to examine this briefly.

Treachery and treason

One does not have far to look for evidence of the ubiquitous culture of treachery and complex allegiance felt in France over several generations during this period. Over the course of the fourteenth century, as Edward III developed his policies of confrontation, the need to assemble armies over widely spaced regions of the

[57] Pernoud, 264.

[58] For a recent sensitive account, see S. Crane, *The Performance of Self: Ritual, Clothing, and Identity During the Hundred Years War* (Philadelphia: University of Pennsylvania Press, 2002), ch. 3, 'Joan of Arc and Women's Cross-Dress', 73–106.

French-speaking continent from Flanders to the Guyenne meant that pressure was applied not only to feudal obligations, but to the practice of drafting mercenaries. Given the rich pickings available to those engaged in Edward's 'chevauchees', there was a considerable incentive for people to travel long distances to be conscripted who would follow the course of war as it ebbed and flowed in different locations. Those fighting on the 'English' side might include peoples as diverse as the Gascons, Bretons, Normands, Picards, Flamands, and Genoese. Higher up the social ladder, during the course of the complex negotiations between (principally) English, Flemish, Breton, and Burgundian landed interests, key figures would pass from one side to another as the balance of power shifted.

Geoffroi d'Harcourt is one such: found a traitor to the king of France for attacking the bishop of Bayeux, Guillaume Bertran, who was under royal protection, he was banished on 3 April 1344 'pour pluseurs conspiracions, aliances, traïsons, machinations, monopoles et crimes de majesté royal blecié et autres excès' ['for many conspiracies, alliances, betrayals, plots, cabals, crimes of lese-majesté and much else'].[59] In 1345 he went to England and paid liege homage to Edward III with whom he stayed until the siege of Calais. Then he left the English camp to serve Philippe VI, who pardoned him. But as a result of this double betrayal Edward confiscated his goods and imprisoned his men and servants.[60] Olivier de Clisson, who brokered Jean de Montfort's alliance with Edward, had a more summary fate. Philip ordered him to be arrested in Paris as a traitor when he came for the jousting and he was executed 'pour pluseurs traîsons et autres crimes perpetrez par lui contre le roy et la coronne de France, et aliances qu'il avoit faites au roy d'Angleterre, anemi du roy et du royaume de France' [for several acts of treason and other crimes perpetrated by him against the king and the crown of France, and alliances that he had made with the king of England, enemy of the king and of the realm of France].[61] The records of the Parlement de Paris reveal repeated attempts by king and parlement to round up and punish traitors. Yet circumstances were such that it was often more politic to pardon, or at least ignore, especially if it might be important to secure someone's services in the future. As Yvonne Lanhers wryly remarks, 'Tout au cours du XIVe et du XVe siècle, les rois avec sagesse et patience pardonnèrent aux villes, aux seigneurs et aux roturiers qui les trahissaient' [Throughout the course of the fourteenth and fifteenth centuries, kings with wisdom and patience pardoned the towns, lords and captains who betrayed them].[62]

The Burgundian chronicler Enguerran de Monstrelet writes perceptively about some of these fraught relationships between king and 'traitor'. The

[59] *Confessions et jugements de criminels au Parlement de Paris (1319–1350), Archives Nationales, $X^{2a}4$,* ed. M. Langlois and Y. Lanhers (Paris: Archives Nationales, 1971), 151.

[60] E. Deprez, 'La double trahison de Godefroi d'Harcourt', *Revue Historique,* 99 (September–December 1908), 32–4.

[61] *Confessions et jugements,* ed. Langlois and Lanhers, 151.

[62] *Confessions et jugements,* ed. Langlois and Lanhers, 25.

following story, which Enguerran places at the time of the Treaty of Melun,[63] concerns 'ung gentil homme de l'ostel du roy d'Angleterre, nommé Bertran de Caumont' [a young nobleman of the household of the King of England, named Bertran de Caumont]. In a subtle and far-reaching phrase, he describes him as someone who, on the very day of the battle of Agincourt, 'estant françois se rendit anglois' [being French gave himself as English]. Bertran was from Guyenne, and therefore was under fealty for his land to the English king. 'Pour sa vaillance' [For his valour], writes Enguerran, 'estoit de lui moult amé' [he was greatly loved by him]. But the relationship turns sour when Bertran 'par convoitise de pécune qu'il en eut' [through envy because of the penury he was in] decides to help a certain Amenon de Lau who had been charged with murdering Jean, duc de Bourgogne. When this came to Henry's knowledge, 'grandement il fut troublé' [he was greatly troubled] and ordered Bertran to be decapitated. The dukes of Clarence and Burgundy try to dissuade him, but Henry refuses to pardon him, saying that he would not have any traitors in his army. Enguerran adds drily that Henry's desire to make Bertran an example cost him 50,000 nobles, even though Bertran 'n'eust onques fait ceste desloyaulté contre lui' [had never committed this disloyalty against him].[64] The position of a chronicler writing for a lord who himself 'estant françois se rendit anglois' causes him to write with both sympathy and sharp honesty. The very closeness of the feudal bond provokes the harshness of the king's response, and yet Bertran seems to have had much more uncertainty about where his loyalties lay. He makes a grand gesture at Agincourt (although this is also a double about turn), and then looks around for further pecuniary advantage.[65]

Treason was applied extremely widely as a legal term during the course of the war—we may recall that Charles VI branded his own son a traitor—and it clearly came to be viewed by Charles VII as a useful means of confiscating property. Actions that were considered treasonable included the violation of truces, desertion, the sending or selling of provisions to the enemy, espionage, illicit convocation of assemblies, and scandalous speech. It even applied (with often lucrative consequences) to Englishmen who held lands in France and in reverse, to Frenchmen who had property in Normandy.[66]

Comments about the fickleness of the Gascons are frequent among chroniclers of different political persuasions. Froissart (Book III, ch. 21), writing of the mid-1380s, gossips snidely as follows:

[63] This story of Caumont takes place after the capture of Melun in 1420; for another account, see *Oeuvres de Georges Chastellain*, ed. Kervyn de Lettenhove, 8 vols (Brussels: F. Heussner, 1863–6), I, 184–5.

[64] *La chronique d'Enguerran de Monstrelet*, ed. Louis Douët d'Arcq, 6 vols (Paris: Renouard, 1862), IV, ch. CCXXXI, 14–15.

[65] On the case of Arnaud Foucaut, an adventurer in the pay of the English who came up before the Parlement in 1345, and of Richard Langlois, see my 'Converting Jeanne d'Arc', 91–2.

[66] Cuttler, *The Law of Treason and Treason Trials*, 34–41.

le seigneur de Labreth se repentoit assez pres de ce qu'il estoit devenus françois, ainsi que le sire de Moucident, Gascon, qui fu prins à la bataille d'Aimet, et jura en la main du duc d'Anjou qu'il vendroit à Paris et se tourneroit bon François, et demourroit à tousjours mais. Voirement vint il à Paris, et il fist le roy Charles tres bonne chiere, mais il ne lui sceut onques tant faire que le sire de Moucident ne s'emblast du roy et s'en retournast sans congié prendre en son païs, et devint angloiz et rompi toutes les couvenances que il avoit au duc d'Anjou. Aussi fist le sire de Rosem, le sire d[e] Duras et le sire de Langurant. Tele est la nature des Gascoings: ilz ne sont point estable, mais encores aiment ilz plus les Angloiz que les François, car leur guerre est plus belle sur les François que elle ne soit sur les Angloiz, c'est li uns des plus principaulx incidences qui plus les y encline.

[the lord d'Albreth strongly repented his having turned to the French, as did the lord de Mucident, a Gascon, who, when taken prisoner at the battle of Aimet, swore on the hand of the duke of Anjou that he would set out for Paris and become ever after a good Frenchman. He did go to Paris where the king warmly received him; but he did not know at all what to do when the lord of Moucident stole away from the king and returned to his country without leave, where he again became an Englishman, and broke all his covenants with the duke of Anjou. The lords de Rosem, de Duras, de Langurant, did the same. This is the character of the Gascons: they are very unsteady, but they still love the English more than the French, for the war against France is sweeter than it would be against the English, and this is one of the most important factors that attracts them there.][67]

The position of the Gascons as 'English' was evidently disturbing for many; perhaps this was less to do with a sense that they should have supported the French king—after all Aquitaine had been 'English' for several centuries—than that they showed up all too clearly how frail some of the claimed loyalties were amongst other more obviously 'French' regions. Conversely, in a double twist, Charles VII had a Scots bodyguard; but in the siege of Caen in 1450 they allowed themselves to be bribed by Edmund Beaufort, duke of Somerset, to help capture the king. Charles had them tried as traitors, then drawn, beheaded, and quartered.[68]

One builds up a picture quite quickly from these and other examples of a prevailing atmosphere of uncertainty and lack of confidence in the process of public allegiance. In the complexities of war, carried out fitfully with a mixture of soldiers drawn from old feudal ties from all over the French-speaking continent and others hired as mercenaries, the question of who belonged to whom could become tense and changeable:

[67] Jean Froissart, *Chroniques, Livre III (du Voyage en Béarn à la campagne de Gascogne) et Livre IV (années 1389–1400)*, ed. P. Ainsworth and A. Varvaro (Paris: Librairie Générale Française, 2004), 312.

[68] Cuttler, *The Law of Treason and Treason Trials*, 30.

Et furent les Gascons qui étaient bien montés, et la greigneure partie de leur gent, ordonnés encontre les arbalétriers et archers et compagnons de Paris, et les Écossais contre les Anglais, la grosse bataille contre la grosse bataille.[69]

[The Gascons, who had good horses, together with the larger part of their forces, were over against the archers, crossbowmen, and men of Paris, the Scots opposite the English, their main body opposite ours.][70]

One of the most interesting sources in this respect (from which I have just quoted) is the so-called *Journal d'un bourgeois de Paris*, written by an anonymous cleric associated with the University of Paris, during the years of the English occupation (1405–49). At the start of the narrative, he is often virulently Burgundian (and hence pro-English); but as the work proceeds, doubts creep in and his sympathies fluctuate and become more Armagnac. But whatever his feelings about the English, he dislikes the Picards more.[71] Once again, this text is witness to a turning point: the author finds himself (not very consciously) over a period of several years shifting ground, shifting loyalties.

The language of bad faith, of changing allegiances and doubts over identity that is characteristic of many such testimonials and chance remarks in chronicles of the Hundred Years War fits all too well with Jeanne's trial records. The process of interrogation is itself often devious and insidious; when one turns to the supporting material, especially in the *procès de nullification*, then the backbiting, flurries of allegation and partisan invective are rampant.[72] Jeanne herself seemed not above slinging some mud against the Burgundians and English: conspiracy stories circled widely. Jeanne's case does not, in this respect, stand apart from contemporary partisan warfare created by the presence of the English in the French-speaking continent, but is utterly within it and a by-product of it.

This may seem an obvious point, yet the modern reception of Jeanne has been reluctant to admit it. There have been two main acts of retrieval: in the first Jeanne has been converted back into a simple folk figure, illiterate, of peasant stock, female and faithful. In the other, not always connected act, Jeanne has of course been turned into a national emblem, where again she has been presented in the simplest terms possible, as an unwavering beacon of national pride. The intricacies of Jeanne's textual record in the fifteenth century may give the lie to this, but it has not prevented such singular images from developing. One of the

[69] *Le Journal d'un Bourgeois de Paris de 1405 à 1449*, ed. C. Beaune (Paris: Librairie Générale Française, 1990), 251.

[70] *A Parisian Journal*, trans. Shirley, 228–89.

[71] Some pro-Dauphin chroniclers make a point of mentioning that Jeanne was captured by a Picard. See, for instance, Martial d'Auvergne (1440–1508), *Vigiles du roi Charles VII*, in Quicherat, V, 51–78: 'Lors au conflict et par surprinse | Comme chascun tiroit arrière, | Ladicte Pucelle fut prinse | Par ung Picart' (73); or Le Hérault Berri, 'et y fut prinse laditte Pucelle d'ung Picart; et depuis la vendit messire Jehan de Luxembourg aux Anglois' (Quicherat, IV, 50).

[72] On the legal context of the trial, see H. A. Kelly, 'The Right to Remain Silent: Before and After Joan of Arc', *Speculum*, 68 (1993), 992–1026.

most extraordinary simplifications of her actions which nonetheless possesses remarkable historical power is enacted in the 8 May festival at Orléans, the date when the siege was lifted and the townspeople welcomed in the royal army.[73] The year after, a magnificent commemorative procession was organized in celebration, and in 1435 a play performed.[74] This *Mystère* re-enacts the events of the day and finishes with a triumphal entry into the city by Jeanne herself who then asks the town citizens to establish this processional festival as an annual event. Even the dramatic character Jeanne could not have predicted that 8 May was to be the same date as France's liberation from Germany in 1945. The same festival which continued unchanged through the centuries until it was revised in 1855 (during the Crimean War), 1921 (after her canonization), 1929 (the quincentenary) and in 1947, was thus able to collapse the two liberations into one memory and indeed collapsed Jeanne into playing the same saviour in each story. It was not the only example of its kind (Paris and Dieppe had similar doublings) but it stands as the most extravagant public enactment of the principle of retrospection that I have been tracing throughout the chapter. The needs of memory create new forms of history on top of the old not to supplant the past but rather, in the stimulus of each new commemorative present, to rewrite it and realign it.

HENRY V

Shakespeare's Joan and Olivier's *Henry V*

The Orléans festival in its 1947 guise is not straightforwardly commemorative, however. If the original 1435 impulse was to celebrate the town's liberation from English occupation, then it doubles oddly as a celebration in 1947 of the English as liberators from German occupation. In that sense it has a chiasmic relationship with a celebrated instance of English commemoration: Laurence Olivier's playing of Henry V in the 1944 film he also directed and produced. As the American critic James Agee wrote for its US premier in 1946, 'the man who made this movie made it midway in England's most terrible war, within the shadows of Dunkirk. In appearance and in most of what they say, the three soldiers with whom Henry talks on the eve of Agincourt might just as well be soldiers of World War II.'[75] But Agee did not remark on the oddity of a re-enactment of the defeat of the French serving as a glorious and stirring study of a war in which the French were the close allies of the English rather than the enemy. Both instances taken together seem to show how each side needs the other to create a sense of aggressive opposition to an enemy: their old contest is the deepest figure of enmity. Yet one can also see it more positively as a

[73] Beaune, *The Birth of an Ideology*, 143–4.

[74] V. L. Hamblin, ed., *Le mistère du siège d'Orléans*, TLF 546 (Geneva: Droz, 2002).

[75] *Time Magazine*, 8 April 1946 from *Agee on Film* (New York: McDowell, Obolensky 1958).

strangely mutual false imagining: as allies they imagine themselves to be enemies, for as enemies they never quite succeeded in shaking off their profound cooperation.

The reduction and clarification of Jeanne as a symbol for nation speeds up as the centuries pass, but the process began early. Shakespeare's Joan in his *Henry VI, Part One* has become a vulgar, assertive Amazon heavily touched up with witchcraft very much on the model of Bedford's 'disciple and lyme of the Feende, called the Pucelle, that used fals enchauntements and sorcerie'. It is as if the abandoned victim of Anglo-Burgundian politics, scorned and ignored by the English in the fifteenth century, begins to assume a stronger outline in the sixteenth now that the English have properly lost. *Henry V,* I would argue, is different, and for the view that the play is 'an intensely masculine, simple, sanguine drama of kinghood and war', Olivier and the sentiments he was able to stir up at a time of modern war is largely responsible.[76] To make my case I will first discuss Gaunt's speech in *Richard II,* Act II, Scene 1.

Countless histories of England juxtapose Gaunt's 'This royal throne of kings, this scept'red isle' with *Henry V's* St Crispian's speech, 'we few, we happy few, we band of brothers', as resonant ways of articulating a vision of Englishness, perhaps the most resonant in English. Yet it is less often remarked that Gaunt's speech is reworked from a French poem. Even more disruptive to the notion that this is a purely English moment, the work in question, the second part of the creation poem *Le Seconde Sepmaine* (1584) by Guillaume de Salluste du Bartas, is an ecstatic response to the French recovery of Calais in 1558:

> Ha, France . . .
> O mille et mille fois terre heureuse et feconde!
> O perle de l'Europe! ô paradis du monde!
> France, je te salue, ô mere des guerriers,
> Qui jadis ont planté leurs triomphans lauriers
> Sur les rives d'Euphrate, et sanglanté leur glaive
> Où la torche du jour et se couche et se leve.[77]

There is an English translation of this passage in John Eliot's *Ortho-Epia Gallica or Eliot's Fruits from the French* (1593), a teaching dialogue whose title recalls Florio's first Italian-English teaching publication, *Florio his Firste Fruites* (1578):

> O Fruitfull France! most happie Land, happie and happie thrice!
> O pearle of rich *European* bounds! O earthly Paradise!
> All haile sweet soile! O France the mother of many conquering knights,

[76] *Time Magazine*, 8 April 1946, from *Agee on Film*, 1958.

[77] Peter Ure among modern editors offers the most detailed discussion of the relationship between du Bartas, Sylvester's translation, Eliot and *Richard II.* See his detailed notes in *King Richard II,* 2nd Arden edn (London: Routledge, 1961), 50–53, echoed in C. R. Forker, ed. *Richard II* (The Arden Shakespeare, Third Series, 2002), 487–8. I cite the French passage from *The Works of Guillaume de Salluste Sieur Du Bartas*, ed. U. T. Holmes, J. C. Lyons and R. W. Linker, 3 vols (Chapel Hill: University of North Carolina Press, 1935–40), III, 169–70.

> Who planted once their glorious standards like the triumphing wights
> Upon the banks of *Euphrates* where *Titan* day-torch bright
> Riseth[78]

Gaunt's speech thus turns out to be a French lesson, and one full of irony on both sides. French relief and pride at gaining Calais, so long in English hands, is particularly high-pitched because it is less of a recovery than a conquest; the tone is a backhanded acknowledgement, in short, of the extended duration of English power in France. Gaunt's speech, in translating this pride back into English, becomes a mournful picture of loss, although one that becomes progressively more defiant in its depiction of 'dear' insularity. The sea is a moat, a defensive wall against 'less happier lands', which seems a pointed echo in reverse of Eliot's thrice happy France, itself a slightly more sober version of Du Bartas's excitable 'mille et mille fois terre heureuse', and not so remote from Deschamps's eulogies discussed in Chapter 4: 'O doulz pais, terre tres honourable'. That this picture of rich fecundity should be informed by the country England has now lost, is doubly poignant. England's fecundity is indeed French in inspiration, and it clearly takes a great effort of rhetorical will to present 'this England' as newly self-sufficient in its 'reputation through the world'.

Henry and Catherine

Rereading *Henry V* from the perspective of the fifteenth century I am struck likewise by how little jingoism is the issue and how much the balance of linguistic power between French and English. From II.4 onwards the play is set entirely in France and it culminates not in Agincourt but in that famous sparring Anglo-French enactment of war's cultural legacy in the dialogue between Henry and Catherine. Language is constantly held up for inspection, through dialect, comic pronunciation, class, gender and, yes, nation. A whole scene (II.3) takes place in French (unimaginable without translation in early twenty-first-century Britain), though the French lords are all presented as speaking English, showing that the point is to appose French-English with the English-French of the final scene. The climax of the play is thus an intensely focused display of cross-lingual wordplay that dazzlingly comprehends and adds its own twist to a long history of Anglo-French power politics.

Shakespeare, perhaps unsurprisingly, explores this political history through many of the ways we have seen explored by earlier writers, both French and English, in French and in English. One of the largest frameworks, stretching from the opening discussion in I.1 by the Archbishop of Canterbury and the Bishop of Ely, of a parliamentary bill to absorb Church possessions into the royal coffers, to the final 'Amen' sealing the marriage contract between Henry and Catherine, is that of sharp commercialism. The appropriation of property and

[78] *King Richard II*, ed. Ure, Appendix III, 206.

the sale of royal women, as we have discussed, funded several large war efforts. Its larger significance as a representation of how people deal with their differences is underscored in two moments in the play: the angrily eloquent response by Henry to the gift of tennis balls from the Dauphin and the sudden moment of quiet nastiness when Pistol cuts the throat of his French prisoner at the end of IV.6. The 'tun of treasure' as the French insultingly call the balls throws Henry's claim to 'certain dukedoms' back in his face, and acts as a slow-burning stimulus to Henry's far from jocular order to his men to kill the prisoners when he fears another French attack. For Pistol, the action costs him two hundred crowns, the huge sum that he was promised by the soldier as a ransom if he had kept him alive. In both cases, the bargain appears to be set up as a joke, but turns into the violent prosecution of war.[79]

The trading of Catherine, at least, is softened by the language of love ('this day / Shall change all griefes and quarrels into loue', Sc.27.2874–5, p.667 (V.2.19–20)); but Shakespeare gives great depth to this language by layering it with Anglo-French references throughout the play. One prominent thread is the use of jargon: continuing in the tradition we have observed going back to the late twelfth or early thirteenth century, Shakespeare's characters act out several kinds of French, including more than one form that is specially contrived to be comic. The central scenes work as a sequence of carefully juxtaposed linguistic encounters, starting with the English lesson in III.4. The central joke of this scene is that it is a *manière de langage* in reverse. The learning of vocabulary in Bibbesworth, the *Femina nova*, Kingsmill, and the more recent *Ortho-Epia Gallica* is translated back both verbally and culturally, so that we are presented with the spectacle of a French queen trying to learn English, because she must ('*il faut que ie apprene a parler*', Sc.12.1273–4, p.651 (III.4.4–5)). But of course this would never happen except in a play: no one in fifteenth-century France was seeking to learn English at all formally, and even Charles d'Orléans was only doing so as a prisoner based in England. Like the English interlocutor in the dialogue with a Parisian who compliments him on his French accent, Alice is praised for her English accent by Catherine: '*Alice, tu as este en Angleterre, & tu bien parlas le Language*' (Sc.12.1270–1, p.651 (III.4.1–2)). But Catherine is hardly in the best position to judge, and for an English audience the praise backfires when it hears Alice's strong French accent: '*Le main il & appelle de Hand*'. This fairly simple humour moves into another gear with the word 'bilbow'. Working her way from her fingertips to her upper arm and face, Catherine is trying to say 'elbow'. Alice warns her of its difficulty, but from now on each word gains in its mispronunciation a punning sexual overtone: nick (for neck), sin (for chin) and later foot (les pieds), and cown (la robe). Oblivious to these escalating *faux pas*, Alice absurdly compliments her mistress on her pronunciation: '*en verite vous pronouncies les mots ausi droict, que les Natifs d'Angleterre* (Sc.12.1303–4, p.652 (III.4.34–5))'

[79] Citations to *Henry V* are to *William Shakespeare: The Complete Works Original-Spelling Edition*, gen. eds. S. Wells and G. Taylor (Oxford : Clarendon Press, 1986). I also refer to *Henry V*, ed. G. Taylor, The Oxford Shakespeare (Oxford: Clarendon Press, 1982).

Like *Des Deus Anglois et de l'Anel*, the scene revolves cleverly around matters of orthography and sound: her words only sound crude and obscene to French ears or to English ears used to hearing continental French. As she learns to speak these English words through the standard pedagogic technique of repetition, she gradually learns to speak a false English that turns out to be vulgar French in disguise: as Gloucester finds in reverse in *Jehan et Blonde*:

> Si vaut qa lui parler françois,
> Mais sa langue torne en Englois.[80]
>
> [And so he wanted to speak French to him
> But his language turns into English.]

Her new English turns and betrays her through its resemblance to French.

It is easy to forget that the scene works linguistically through a French matrix: the English audience, in other words, is expected to take French as the base language and English only as a translated tongue. The next scene, and the one after a Welsh interlude, provides another reversal by presenting French lords speaking 'natif' English, albeit with French tags for colour. But Shakespeare uses their English as a thoroughgoing species of fighting talk: from the chiasmic 'Normans, but bastard Normans, Norman bastards' (Sc.13. 1335, p.652 (III.5.10)), a brilliantly compressed one-line history of post-Conquest England, they run through most of the standard insults: about the weather ('Is not their Clymate foggy, raw, and dull?', Sc.13.1341, p.652 (III.5.16)), the English preference for beer over wine, and in scene 7, their association with dogs, in this case a liking for mastiffs. Intriguingly, two references even recall Philippe de Vitry: the duke of Bourbon starts boasting of his horse as '*le cheval volant*, the Pegasus' which almost makes him the modern sixteenth-century butt of Philippe's scornful comment aimed at Jehan de le Mote:

> Com tu, qui ne vaulz une mite
> A Pegasus faire voler
> En Albion de Dieu maldicte.[81]
>
> [Like you, who are not able one whit
> To make Pegasus fly
> In Albion cursed by God.]

A few lines later, when the levels of banter have risen further, Bourbon quotes the same proverb, 'Le chien est retourné à son propre vomissement', used by Philippe in his motet *Phi millies/O Creator/Iacet granum/Quam sufflabit*. It would be remarkable indeed if Shakespeare had read Philippe de Vitry, but it does seem to suggest that a specific discourse of Anglo-French invective had a long-running circulation.

[80] See Chapter 3 above pp. 76 and 84.
[81] See Chapter 4 above, p. 124. The proverb below is not in the 1600 quarto, used in the Original Spelling Edition: I cite here from Taylor (1982).

Shakespeare keeps the sense of English as foreign-sounding by the very different ploy in the intervening scene of introducing the Welshman Fluellen. Often played as an instance of snobbish English caricature, along with the portrayals of the Irishman (Captain MacMorris) and the Scot (Captain Jamy), heard against the different kinds of French in the play these characters can be interpreted rather differently as Shakespeare's recognition, born once more from a long history of such recognition, that English and French are equally engaged in issues of diversity. Gower the Englishman's reproof of Pistol after the incident of the leek is a rebuke to such English snobbery, not an expression of it:

> You thought, because he could not speake English in the natiue garb, he could not therefore handle an English Cudgell: you finde it otherwise, and henceforth let a Welsh correction, teach you a good English condition, fare ye well.
>
> (Sc.26.2841–5, p.667 (V.1.68–72))

The distance between Catherine's 'natif' pronunciation of English and Fluellen's is not far: both speak true in their false English, and both teach English foreign manners. More than that, the strong presence of French in the play inverts any expectation that French is necessarily more foreign than Welsh, Irish, or Scots. That Henry succeeds in winning Agincourt but immediately has to deal with fighting in his own ranks implies that the strangers at home may be harder to control than the family over the Channel, and their speech harder to understand. The respect they command because of their difference from English is, in that sense, greater than that commanded by the French, who (at least in this play) can be suborned like a truculent relative through the pressure of marriage.

Pistol's scene with the French soldier is perhaps the funniest and cleverest of all these cross-linguistic encounters. Here Pistol takes on the role of derisory speaker of Anglo-French jargon, earlier played by Gloucester in *Jehan et Blonde*, Renart *jongleur* and, nearer to Shakespeare's time, by Herod in the Corpus Christi play cycle. Another play with even closer comparison is *Le Mystère de Saint Louis* (*c.*1470), which contains pseudo English as well as *franco-anglais.* Talbot, the fifteenth-century English commander (anachronistically transplanted into the time of Louis) exclaims: 'Sy non fait, je coupy son gorg' ['if he doesn't do it I will cut his throat'] (p. 59). He and the other English characters, especially the king and the duke of Gloucester, constantly swear by 'Saint Joan' or 'Bi Saint Gorg!'[82] But like these earlier examples, more is going on than crude linguistic chauvinism. Shakespeare sets up (at least) four linguistic levels: the 'natif' French of the soldier, Pistol's mongrel Anglo-French jargon (wonderfully mixing with an Irish refrain), the boy's unremarked good French and finally the English exchanged between Pistol and boy (itself wildly fluctuating and of mixed register). Pistol's attempt to sound like a schoolteacher continues the general theme of cultural

[82] F. Michel, ed., *Le Mystère de Saint Louis* (Westminster: Roxburghe Club, 1871), 55–74. See also Rickard, *Britain in Medieval French Literature*, 175.

education: 'Perpend' he says, like Touchstone, Feste, and Polonius. He has the attitude of a long-suffering culturally superior native who patiently tries to make sense of a dim-witted foreigner, and all this in a barbarously hybrid response to the lucid French of the soldier:

> French Souldier: *O prennes miserecorde aye pitiez de moi.*
> Pistoll: Moy shall not serue, I will haue fortie Moyes:
> Or I will fetch thy rymme out at thy Throat,
> In droppes of Crimson blood.
> French Souldier: *Est il impossible d'eschapper le force de ton bras.*
> Pistoll: Brasse, Curre? thou damned and luxurious Mountaine Goat,
> Offer'st me brasse?
>
> (Sc.20.2294–301, p.661 (IV.4.12–18))

Pistol's misunderstandings and mispronouncings touch on comically raw places in the Anglo-French linguistic relationship that have persisted over the centuries, as modern editorial concerns over the text even now demonstrate. The final (and medial) French 's' is traumatic for the English: the *Femina nova* has a long list of words where the consonants should not be pronounced, such as draps (dras), mesmes (memez), porks (pors), corps (cors), clerkys (clers), where the latter three are particularly 'English' examples. Pistol's taking of 'bras' as 'brass' is amusingly mentioned in a note in Furnivall's discussion of a book on Chaucer by the French scholar E. G. Sandras. In case you were wondering, Furnivall notes helpfully: 'Sound the final *s*, says a distinguished French editor: *sans draps* means 'without sheets'. Follow the same rule in M. Paulin Paris's name.'[83] Not one to pass over a detour, Furnivall follows this up with a passage from Etienne Pasquier:

> Voyant le monde par un jugement délicat *mots proferez avec toutes leurs lettres* estre un peu trop rudes au son des aureilles, on reforma au long aller cette grossiere façon de parler en une plus douce, et au lieu d' *eschole, establir*, &c., *avec prononciation de chaque lettre* et element, l'on s'accoustuma de dire *école, etablir*, &c., vray que tousjours est demeuré l'ancien son en ces mots *espese* et *esperer*, mais peut estre que quelque jour viendront-ils au rang des autres, aussi bien que *de nostre* temps ce mot d' *honneste* (auquel en ma jeunesse j'ay veu prononcer la lettre de S) s'est maintenant tourné en vne E, fort long.
>
> (*Pasquier: Recherches de la France*, 1633)[84]

Seeing that society through delicate judgement finds words presented with all their letters to be a little too coarse in sound to the ears, we have taken the lengthy journey and reformed this gross way of speaking into one more sweet, and instead of *eschole, establir*,

[83] Review of E. G. Sandras, *Etude sur Chaucer considéré comme imitateur des trouvères* (Paris: Durand, 1859) by Professor Ebert, trans. J. W. Van Rees Hoets, in *Essays on Chaucer*, Part 1, The Chaucer Society (London: Trübner, 1868).

[84] Cited by F.J. Furnivall, in Hoets, *Essays on Chaucer*, 1, n. 1.

&c., where each letter and element is pronounced, we have got used to saying *école, etablir*, &c.. It is true that the former sound has remained in such words as *espese* and *esperer*, but perhaps one day they will reach the rank of the others, just as in our own time the word *honneste* (of which in my youth I had expected to pronounce the letter s) is now turned into a very long E.]

The passage is pertinent for its revelation, a generation after *Henry V*, of the snobberies and vagaries *inside* French of the pronunciation of 's': it reminds us of what we know perfectly well within our own languages that pronunciation is not a linguistic constant but a social weapon.[85] Modern Shakespeare editors have also stumbled into these traps in their attempts to correct the French of the Quarto and Folio versions of the play. The problem is, how do we know whether Shakespeare had 'good French'? Used to making certain kinds of orthographic distinction between dialectal and 'standard' English, modern English editors of the French in Shakespeare find themselves on uncertain ground: are the compositors making mistakes, or presenting a dialectal or comic error, or simply rendering the multiple orthographies of a non-standard sixteenth-century English perspective of French?[86] The contrast between Pistol's extravagant misunderstandings of the soldier and the boy's ability to translate him fluently[87] suggests that the scene is not interested so much in correct or incorrect French but in the edgier and less easily rectifiable issues of speaking over a sword.

When we come finally to the Henry–Catherine scene, French is in a complex condition for the audience: a familiar language, spoken fluently by French and English characters alike; a language of flamboyant and learned reference spoken by the enemy ('le cheval volant'); and a common vernacular like any other, liable to be misunderstood by those from another region. English, likewise, has been defamiliarized: it has been presented as Irish, Scots, and Welsh as well as English and taught by one Frenchwoman to another as a foreign language. Catherine, having learnt her English so well in III.4, is now asked by Henry to teach him. But the question of linguistic competence has become very tense and full of bluffs and double bluffs. The audience has learnt, through the display of multiple kinds of French and English, not to assume that linguistic knowledge is either easily defined or articulated.[88] Had Shakespeare read the passage of Froissart cited in Chapter 5 on the subtlety of the French in matters of diplomatic negotiation?

[85] There are some very funny nineteenth-century instances of French attempts to pronounce English cited by Daniel Karlin, including comic tricks played by the French on one another's efforts. Remy de Gourmont claims to have asked several of his compatriots to pronounce 'plum-pudding', and gives the following results: 'plum, pleum, plome, ploume; poudigne, poudinègue, poudine, poudingue' (*Proust's English*, [Oxford: Oxford University Press, 2005], 131).

[86] See, for instance, Gary Taylor's comments on 'qualité' and 'seigneur' in *Henry V*, IV.4, p.234.

[87] Taylor remarks that 'in productions the boy's French is usually halting and mispronounced' but that 'there is no evidence of this in the text', note to l.23, 235.

[88] On the legal implications of the use of French in this scene, see B. Cormack, '"If We Be Conquered": Legal Nationalism and the France of Shakespeare's English Histories', in his *A Power to Do Justice: Jurisdiction, English Literature, and the Rise of Common Law, 1509–1625* (Chicago and

Car en parlure françoise a mots soubtils et couvers et sur double entendement, et les tournent les François, là où ils veulent, à leur prouffit et avantage: ce que les Anglois ne sçauroient trouver, ne faire, car euls ne le veulent entendre que plainement.[89]

Again, at first sight, all is reversed. English brute force has rendered French eloquence mute and stumbling. Henry goads Catherine into English, pretending throughout (though with the occasional deliberate slip into competence) that his French is halting; she in a matching battle of wits plays on her alleged ignorance of this barbarous tongue to prove her cultural superiority, if she cannot prove her political supremacy:

I cannot speake your England.
(Sc.27.2957, p.668 (V.2.102–3))

But Henry, half cruelly, half tenderly teases her into linguistic submission:

if you will loue me soundly with your French heart, I will be glad to heare you confesse it brokenly with your English Tongue.

(Sc.27.2959–61, p.668 (V.2.104–6))

And finally absorbs her utterly into English through the ancient Latin-vernacular pun angle/angel:

An Angell is like you *Kate*, and you are like an Angell.
(Sc.27.2964, p.668 (V.2.109–10))

She *must* speak English, she must become an English pun, and this is expressed in an instance of English eloquence that shows English in its oldest foreign characterization. This is a densely intra-lingual moment. As Bede tells it, when St Gregory sees boys from the island of Britain in the marketplace in Rome he is struck by 'their fair complexions, handsome faces, and lovely hair' ['candidi corporis ac uenusti uultus, capillorum quoque forma egregia']. Informed that the race they belong to is called 'Angli' he replies with rapturous wordplay that they have the face of 'angeli' or angels ('nam et angelicam habent faciem').[90] Employing chiasma once more, Henry's neatly performative compliment makes Kate both English and 'fair'; she is also now being exchanged from one currency to

London: University of Chicago Press, 2007), 177–223 (219). See further David Womersley's argument that *Henry V* is deeply engaged with Henri IV's claim to the English throne, one taken very seriously in the England of 1599: 'France in Shakespeare's Henry V', *Renaissance Studies*, 9/4 (1995), 442–59; R. Cotterill, 'The Structural Role of France in Shakespeare's First and Second Historical Tetralogies', *Renaissance Studies*, 9/4 (1995), 460–76; and Leah Marcus's connection of *1 Henry VI* to the English protestants' participation in the French wars of the 1590s, *Puzzling Shakespeare: Local Reading and its Discontents* (Berkeley: University of California Press, 1988), 51–105.

[89] KL, *Livre IV (1392–1396)*, 15, 114. See Chapter 5 above, pp. 154 and 165.

[90] Bede, *Bede's Ecclesiastical History of the English People*, ed. B. Colgrave and R. A. B. Mynors (Oxford: Clarendon Press, 1979; 1st pub.1969), 132–5.

another, from French franc to English angel. We are also reminded of Deschamps's *calembour* on Anglux, Angela, and Angleterre: it is as if certain key Anglo-French encounters draw on much larger and longer memories of linguistic exchange that surface with sudden specificity.

Catherine's cultural role models are nonetheless too powerful to ignore entirely. In asking her whether she likes him (and whether Shakespeare knew it or not) Henry, like Edward III before him, is falling into the role of the knight in the genre of the *pastourelle* who is often, though not always, bested by the superior cleverness of Marion the humble *bergiere*. Marion, in the most famous instance of a dramatised *pastourelle*, Adam de la Halle's late thirteenth-century *Le Jeu de Robin et de Marion*, uses punning replies to discomfit the knight by pretending to be ignorant of his use of language. Yet each mocking repetition of his words (*oisel, ane, hairon* [bird, ass, heron]; vv. 25–27, 34–35, 40–41), serves to draw attention to the erotic subtext of his questions.[91] Catherine, similarly, by asserting 'I cannot tell vat is "like me"' succeeds in mocking Henry's language, even in her broken English: it is precisely the fact, in other words, that she does not need to know English that trumps his knowledge of French:

Sauf vostre honeur, le Francois ques vous parleis, il & melieur que l'Anglois le quel Ie parle.
(Sc.27.3043–4, p.669 (V.2.183–4))

This is a subtle insult rather than a compliment, a boast rather than an admission of weakness.

As the dialogue proceeds, however, Henry becomes more eloquent in French and English. He does not merely parade his plain English as a 'plain king' victorious over 'fausse' French, but gives up on the pretence that she cannot understand him and bursts into long wooing speeches, as carefully crafted in their rough simplicity as Criseyde's to Troilus. Using Alice not as an interpreter but as a mere device to delay and draw attention to his own wordgames, Henry bears down on Catherine in both languages. For the idea is not for English to triumph, but for English to become French, and French English:

That English may as French, French Englishmen,
Receiue each other.
(Sc.27.3222–3, p.671 (V.2.352–3))

This is a view of nation that is remarkably free from brute conquest: reflecting the spirit of Troyes, Shakespeare's Henry has a whole vision of two nations coming together, not of one nation overmastering the other. But this also makes it unlike 'nation' in the way that the play was reinterpreted in the 1940s. The mutuality, the linguistic enmeshing, the sheer as yet uncontrollable diversity of English means that Henry's desires in that final scene are always self-deprecating even at

[91] See Chapter 4, n. 15.

their most assertive. Plain English is not necessarily a source of unequivocal pride, and ladies, after all, prefer to speak French.

ASSERTING DIVERSITY

When we look back at Shakespeare's version of the Hundred Years War, and at the case of Jeanne d'Arc, the two forms of retrospect are not equivalent. It may partly be because it is very hard to perform two forms of cultural retrospect with equal breadth of perspective; the genuinely bicultural, bilingual approach is no doubt illusory. But perhaps it is possible to see that if the two histories are not taken together then even larger distortions take place. One common connection is the atmosphere of uncertainty and instability brought about by the vacuum left after war trickled to its end. On the French side, the fall of Jeanne d'Arc left the English very much in control for at least two more decades, and even her rehabilitation did not signal a new form of French national consciousness so much as another period of bitter recrimination and feuding. In England, the later fifteenth century ranks as one of the most violently conflicted internally of any before the Tudors, and not therefore a model for national unity. Yet there seems to be an irresistible modern urge to claim that the war created two nations. Putting the two great nation-building stories together helps us see that there is a similar degree of modern denial and construction in each. A language of national assertiveness develops in modern commentaries: the conflict was 'despite everything . . . essential in the awakening of French national consciousness'.[92] In England, if nation has not been claimed as happening earlier, then two responses are common, both of which tend to leave the later fifteenth century out of count: an 'aggressive national culture' is located either in the early decades of the fifteenth century or else in the sixteenth.

Both Jeanne and Henry V suggest that the problems here are to do with constructing models of assertion. Of these there are no shortage in modern or medieval discussions of nation. One might even say that ringing generalization is the characteristic mode of national discourse. But I have been arguing that the complex linguistic environment traced by this book over several centuries questions the assertiveness that is so characteristic of the critical as well as political language of nation. As many citations have already indicated, the dominant discourse of nation amongst modern commentators is positivist and assertive. So many of us are looking for a moment when, *the* moment when nation can be claimed or located, usually *avant la lettre*. We champion isolated instances of nationalist invective or self-description that then act for us as signs of a larger national impulse. In this I find myself unable to share the perspective of Thorlac

[92] The phrase is Philippe Contamine's, 'Mourir pour la patrie', in P. Nora, ed., *Lieux de mémoire*, II: *La Nation*, III, 11–43 (19).

Turville-Petre, much as I have gained from his pioneering work in detail. He notably finds Englishness in Robert Mannyng's *Chronicle* (completed in 1338), and aggressive Englishness even earlier in the *Cursor Mundi* (*c.*1300). He concludes on the latter as follows: 'The language unites author and audience as a single community and one nation.'[93] What is at issue here is not his analysis of this individual work, but the much wider crux of how we generalize outward from any particular author or work. Turville-Petre makes clear that he is talking about an audience that is being constructed by the *Cursor Mundi* author, not necessarily one that really existed, but he still picks it out as an instance of linguistic assertion that he wants us to read cumulatively and hence in some sense literally. The last sentence of his whole book thus looks forward: 'nothing in English of this date (early fourteenth century) sees itself as national literature, but in their context in the manuscript the Harley lyrics point the way ahead.'[94] One might have sympathy with this remark yet feel uncertain that this single manuscript can really speak for the nation, even, or perhaps especially, proleptically.[95]

Despite its subtlety, Turville-Petre's book, in short, amongst many others, wants to find nation. Much of my effort has been to turn this approach around and rather than assert nation, ask what it means to construct difference as opposed to unity. My more local question is not about 'the date of commencement' of nation but about what it means to call something or someone else foreign.[96] In the context of this book and of English's double vernacular culture this is about what it means to call French foreign. The act of assertion is so much part of nation that it becomes suspect: we always need to ask who is making the assertion and why, and—very often—who in the process is being excluded, denied or ignored. More modern (post-1880) efforts to found nations or to assert independence are of course genuine performative acts with very serious repercussions; but they are also acts of imaginative assertion. This makes them vulnerable and fragile. In looking back even further, I suggest we keep in mind that fragility is always part of any claim to unity. Part of this fragility is that any assertion about English has English's other vernacular in the shadows.

In brief, *Femina* and a range of other teaching manuals and documents are evidence that the bicultural Anglo-French condition did not slide into antique oblivion in the fifteenth century in the way that arguments tracking English and nation often assert. How could it in the decades when England was most fully confident of its political and military power on the French mainland? And,

[93] T. Turville-Petre, *England the Nation: Language, Literature and National Identity 1290–1340* (Oxford: Clarendon Press, 1996), 40.

[94] Turville-Petre, *England the Nation*, 217.

[95] In his 'Afterword' to K. Lavezzo, ed., *Imagining a Medieval English Nation* (Minneapolis: University of Minnesota Press, 2004), 340–46, while Turville-Petre comments that the nationalism he located in the period of his book was 'quite specific to this period', goes on to give even more proleptic force to such nationalism (341).

[96] A. Hastings, *The Construction of Nationhood: Ethnicity, Religion and Nationalism* (Cambridge: Cambridge University Press, 1997), 9. See Ch.1, 30 above.

as I have argued, the notion that a 'standard English' developed in the fifteenth century, usually attributed to the influence of Chancery practices, is far from straightforward. It is an intriguing education to follow through linguistic tropes of self-deprecation into a period well after Chaucer's supposedly transforming effect on the English tongue. Indeed, as Richard Jones in his classic study and, more recently, Paula Blank has demonstrated, the anxieties increase rather than diminish. It is the recognition of *diversite* that triumphs rather than English itself.[97]

Wyatt, for instance, in his 1529 Prologue to his translation of Petrarch's *Boke of the Quyete of Mynde* makes a complaint about the 'defaute of tonge' familiar from Chaucer: as he worked,

> the labour began to seme tedious/ by superfluous often rehersyng of one thing. which tho parauenture in the latyn shalbe landable (sic)/ by plenteous diuersite of the spekyng of it . . . yet for lacke of suche diuersite in our tong/ it shulde want a great dele of the grace.[98]

But here Wyatt's use of *diversite* has more in common with Bibbesworth's delight in lexical variety: *diversite* is 'faire' and is a sign of the copiousness of Latin as opposed to the narrowness of English.

Two further passages, one by the evangelical William Turner (1548) and the other by Thomas Wilson, Cambridge humanist and later lawyer, whose *Art of Rhetorique* was published in 1553, show that a direct and continuing engagement with French are central to English language treatise writing. Both are contributors to a vehemently expressed debate about the use of neologisms. Ostensibly, they seek to purify the English language from 'straunge ynkehorne termes':

> Among all other lessons this should first be learned, that wee neuer affect any straunge ynkehorne termes, but to speake as is commonly receiued: neither seeking to be ouer fine, nor yet liuing ouer-carelesse vsing our speeche as most men doe, and ordering our wittes as the fewest haue done. Some seeke so far for outlandish English, that they forget altogether their mothers language . . .[99]

But their protestations belie their practice, and reveal that the border between *straunge* and familiar is far from agreed or fixed. Wilson wants to argue that there is a right sort of neologism as well as a wrong sort:

> Now whereas wordes be receiued, aswell Greeke as Latine, to set forth our meaning in the English tongue, either for lacke of store, or els because we would enrich the language: it is well doen to vse them, and no man therein can be charged for any affectation, when all other are agreed to followe the same waie . . . the Communion is a fellowship, or a comming

[97] R. Jones, *Triumph of the English Language* (London: Oxford University Press, 1953); P. Blank, *Broken English: Dialects and the Politics of Language in Renaissance Writings* (London and New York: Routledge, 1996).

[98] *The Quyet of Mynde*, in *Collected Poems of Sir Thomas Wyatt*, ed. K. Muir and P. Thomson (Liverpool: Liverpool University Press, 1969), 440–63 (440).

[99] G. H. Mair, ed., *The Art of Rhetorique* (Oxford: Clarendon Press, 1909), 162–5, cited in Jones, *Triumph of the English Language*, 101.

together, rather Latin then English: the kings prerogatiue declareth his power roiall aboue all other, and yet I know no man greeued for these termes, being vsed in their place, nor yet any one suspected of affectation when such generall wordes are spoken.[100]

If a word has a Greek or Latin root then suddenly it becomes 'generall' and understood by 'all men'. French 'affectations' are quite another thing:

Some farre iourneyed gentleman at their returne home, like as they loue to goe in forraine apparell, so thei wil pouder their talke with ouersea language. He that commeth lately out of Fraunce, will talke French English and neuer blush at the matter.[101]

This wonderful oxymoron 'French English' which Turner embellishes as 'newe french englishe blossomes' keeps cropping up with a regularity that suggests that it expresses a more intrinsic condition of English than either writer cares to admit. Part of what is going on here is a battle between the status of current, contemporary, spoken vernacular and the written language of the ancients. French is awkwardly placed, for English, as an authoritative vernacular which it has helped to create in precisely that form, and this lies at the bottom of these heartfelt linguistic posturings. (Although it is important to remember that Du Bellay in his nearly contemporary *Deffence et Illustration de la Langue Françoyse* of 1549 has just as great an anxiety to prove French's worth against Greek and Latin.) The *diversite* of which Trevisa wrote has not vanished into a smooth upward path towards 'clene and pure' English, but become a reinvigorated Babel of tongues in an English more fragmented than ever.

Shakespeare shows us a double chronology in action: his assigning of a national moment to the battle of Agincourt and his desire to revalue that moment from his own turn of the century perspective. It is revealing to see how much he saw Agincourt as a way of representing issues about language that he was intensely involved in on his own account. English, even a hundred years on, is still attempting to assert its own character as a vernacular and is still finding French there in the shadows, or on the other side of the bed. Shakespeare confirms how far language is involved in making history, and how languages reveal history in their own convolutedly shared structures and lexis. As the thirteenth-century fabliau authors were keenly aware, asserting linguistic identity can be a richly comic and self-mocking undertaking. For that reason languages give the lie to attempts to create national beginnings. Their entanglements are a counter-plot to national histories; they show how national histories are strange, wilful distortions made to create very specific narratives. What role do authors play in these shapings? They encourage us to read back, reread, reinvent in and out of time, to upset the chronologies that make literary as well as national histories. Nation, as we are now realizing in our own time, has no need to be tied to a single narrative, or a single beginning.

[100] Cited in Jones, *Triumph of the English Language*, 101–2.
[101] Jones, *Triumph of the English Language*, 101.

Conclusion

There is a lyrical description of ships coming in to harbour in Lydgate's *Troy Book*, where Jason's ship arrives at Troy:

> Whan Hercules and Iasoun on his hond,
> Out of her schip taken han þe lond,
> And with hem eke her kny3tes euerychon,
> Þat fro þe see ben to lond[e] goon,
> For-weried after her trauaille;
> And þei in sothe come to arivaille
> At Symeonte, an hauene of gret renou*n*,
> þat was a lyte by-syde Troye town —
> And þei wer glad to ben in sikirnesse
> From storm and tempest after werynesse;
> For þei ne ment tresou*n*, harm, nor gyle,
> But on þe stronde to resten hem a while
>
> (723–34)[1]

The weary Greeks are glad to find shelter, a safe haven 'from storm and tempest'. But they are immediately under suspicion as strangers and that, perhaps unjust, 'spark of lytel enmyte' (line 792) grows soon enough into war. Lydgate starts by trying to defend the arrivals from such slanderous imputation, claiming them to be friendly guests, but, in implicitly admitting defeat, turns the case round to say that the destruction of Troy after all led to the founding of Rome. Put this alongside the entrancing description of a fleet in full sail in the Prologue to *Henry V*:

> . . . O do but think
> You stand upon the rivage and behold
> A city on th'inconstant billows dancing —
> For so appears this fleet majestical,
> Holding due course to Harfleur. Follow! Follow!
> III, Prol.13–16
>
> (pp.155–6)

With typical Shakespearean compression, the ships embody the city they are sailing towards: they bring their city with them, dancing 'on th'inconstant billows'. Once again, however, there is menace in the air: the shimmering, graceful motion presages a straight course to the destruction of Agincourt and the occupation of Paris. Yet Shakespeare manages to leave an abiding impression

[1] *Lydgate's Troy Book*, ed. Henry Bergen, EETS, 2 vols (London: Kegan Paul &c, 1906), I, 32–3.

of extraordinary adventure, summed up in the talismanic image of England's king setting sail across the waves.

These two passages evoke many of the entanglements between peoples, cultures, histories, and languages that this book has explored. In a sense, their ships are in contrasting phases of movement: Jason's ships are putting out their anchors, Henry's are in mid-sail. The first is ostensibly the more aggressive location: the invading fleet has landed; the conquest is about to spring into action. Lydgate, following Guido delle Colonne's *Historia Destructionis Troiae*, shows a different possible history. If only they had been recognized for what they were, simply tired voyagers in need of refreshment and respite from the stormy seas, then the Trojan war might never have happened. Instead, goaded by Fortune, the Trojans assume and take offence. The poignant hint at the base of the story is that Greeks and Trojans are not so far apart. Troy is actually very close to Greece; it is just across the Aegean. Neither is as foreign to the other as they claim. They have the same gods, and if they speak a different language they also seemingly share one. In the bewildering number of histories of this founding story, authors are able to take constant advantage of the confusions of lineage at the heart of it. In the *Brut*, Brutus is driven from Rome to live with the Greeks, where he finds disaffected Trojans. They and Brutus 'spoken to-gedre of kynrede & of lynage & of Aqueyntaunce'.[2]

Through Brutus and his displaced Trojans the story of Troy comes to Britain and becomes part of the history of Britain. We remember Wace telling it: the fleet arrives through sunlight and starlight, full of great joy at the prospect before them. It has been a circuitous route. Jason and his Argonauts represent not so much the start of the Trojan war but a literary trope for the beginning of the war: it is still some time into the future before their arrival on the shores 'by-side Troye' is realized retrospectively to have been the trigger for the longer, larger animadversions between Trojan and Greek. The Trojan war is in fact cyclical, rather than a single cataclysmic event; a story that repeats its trajectory many times in its own Aegean location, and in the many other locations across Europe to which it is brought. Its future in Britain is likewise both cyclical and circuitous. In history as well as romance, in action as well as writing, the arrival of guest-strangers signals the constant cycles of friendship and violence that were much later to characterize the Hundred Years War. Lydgate, writing at the request of Prince Henry, soon to be the king sailing his fleet to Harfleur, seems sensitive to this link between the modern war and the ancient myth. He, and perhaps his patron, is sensitive, in other words, to the ways in which aggression and friendship, the kinsman staking claims, the family returning from abroad, are all fundamental elements in the current hostilities. In this way his *Troy Book*

[2] *The Brut, or The chronicles of England. Edited from Ms. Raw. B171, Bodleian Library, &c.*, ed. F. W. D. Brie, EETS, 2 vols (London: Kegan Paul,1906, 1908), I.

participates in a new cycle marking a new claim for kingship and conquest, but one that is keenly aware of its place in a long, turbulent, and far from progressive history of such claims.

Anyone who has stood on the Cap Gris Nez on a fair day and gazed out across the Channel can see the English shore. The Chorus in the Prologue to Act 1 of *Henry V*, speaking to its audience in the 'wooden O' of the Globe, urges it to look in the other direction across the 'perilous narrow ocean' and see 'the vasty fields of France' (12). If it takes an effort of imagination to do this standing in the Globe, it is perfectly possible to go to the coast and see it for oneself. The sleeve of sea is so thin that each side is able to share each other's landscape by looking across. There have been several images of standing on the shore in this book: one of the most evocative is that created by Machaut of the duc de Berri waiting for his ship to take him to the English coast as a hostage. Hostility and hospitality, Jacques Derrida points out, share the same root; the *hôte* (in the sense of 'guest') is also an *otage*, he is in hostage to his host's grace.[3] Many writers discussed in this book have found this to be a vital, agonizing, but also creative means of representing the Anglo-French relationship. The stranger as house-guest who turns out to be the enemy, or worse, the family member who becomes an all too familiar enemy: these are the deep-seated causes of affiliation and hatred, death-defying loyalty and miserable treachery that often permeate literary exchanges.

They also permeate the language. But this gives cause for hope. With this ominous but strangely heart-hearth-warming pun—*hostis-hospes*—deep within the language they share, English and French throughout many centuries have no straightforward structure of dominance as a model for nation. I do not see a language of imperialism in Shakespeare's fleet-city: it is easy to forget that this is an image he is projecting *after* the loss of Calais. Modern readers have been too ready to assume a politics of nationhood, especially through language. The deeply entwined linguistic histories of English and French are full of complex, prevaricating, and spontaneous moments that we misjudge if we read them backwards as actual or proleptic claims for the imagined mother tongue of nation. In that way they argue against single, assertive models for nationhood. A double vernacular history may at times be double-tongued, but it is also unable to deny the other for long. More importantly, the gifts of exchange are enduring. It remains to be seen whether this can ever be reciprocated, but for the English, French has undoubtedly been its richest source of vernacular power. Neither coastline, then, offers a final perspective on the other; it is always possible to travel between the two. *The Familiar Enemy* has tried to sketch an imaginary bridge between island and continent, where the locus for imagining difference is to be found somewhere on the voyage rather than at the journey's end.

[3] Derrida lists the following (incomplete) semantic chain '*hostis, hospes, hosti-pet, posis, despotes, potere, potis sum, possum, pote est, potest, pot sedere, possidere, compos,* etc. —)', in his *Le monolinguisme de l'autre ou la prothèse d'origine* (Paris: Galilée, 1996), 32.

Bibliography

PRIMARY SOURCES

Allmand, C. T. and C. A. J. Armstrong, eds, *English Suits before the Parlement of Paris 1420–1436*, Camden Fourth Series, 26 (London: Offices of the Royal Historical Society, 1982).

The Anonimalle Chronicle 1333–1381, ed. V. H. Galbraith (Manchester: Manchester University Press, 1927).

Aspland, C. W., *A Medieval French Reader* (Oxford: Clarendon Press, 1979).

Atchison, Mary, ed., *The Chansonnier of Oxford Bodleian MS Douce 308: Essays and Complete Edition of Texts* (Aldershot: Ashgate, 2005).

d'Aumale, S.A.R. le duc, [Henri d'Orléans, duc d'Aumale], 'Notes et documents relatifs à Jean Roi de France et sa captivité en Angleterre', *Miscellanies of the Philobiblon Society*, II (London: Charles Whittingham, 1855–6), item 6, 1–190.

——, 'Nouveaux documents relatifs à Jean roi de France, communiqués par M. Leon Lacabane', *Miscellanies of the Philobiblon Society*, V (London: Charles Whittingham, 1858-9), item 2, 1–24.

Bacon, Roger, *The Greek Grammar of Roger Bacon and a Fragment of his Hebrew Grammar*, ed. Edmond Nolan and S. A. Hirsch (Cambridge: Cambridge University Press, 1902).

——, *Opus majus*, ed. J. H. Bridges, 2 vols (Oxford, 1897).

Baker, J. H. ed., *The Reports of John Spelman*, ed. J. H. Baker, Selden Society 93–4, 2 vols (London: Selden Society, 1978).

Barbazan, Etienne [de], ed., *Fabliaux et contes des poëtes françois des xii, xiii, xiv, xves siècles, tirés des meilleurs auteurs*, 3 vols (Paris, Amsterdam, 1756).

Beauvillé, V. de, *Recueil de documents concernant la Picardie*, 5 vols (Paris, 1860).

Bede, *Bede's Ecclesiastical History of the English People*, ed. Bertram Colgrave and R.A.B. Mynors (Oxford: Clarendon Press, 1979; 1st publ. 1969).

Boccaccio, Giovanni, *Chaucer's Boccaccio: sources of 'Troilus' and the Knight's and Franklin's tales*, ed. and trans. N. R. Havely (Cambridge: D. S. Brewer, 1980).

Bonet, Honoré, *The Tree of Battles*, trans. G. W. Coopland (Liverpool: Liverpool University Press, 1949).

Boogaard, Nico H. J. van den, ed., *Rondeaux et refrains du XIIe siècle au début du XIVe* (Paris: Klincksieck, 1969).

A Book of London English 1384–1425, ed. R. W. Chambers and Marjorie Daunt (Oxford: Clarendon Press, 1931).

Boswell, Jackson Campbell and Sylvia Wallace Holton, eds, *Chaucer's Fame in England: STC Chauceriana, 1475–1640* (New York: MLA, 2004).

Brand, Paul, ed., *The Earliest English Law Reports*, Selden Society 111–12, 122–23, 4 vols (London: The Seldon Society, 1996–2007).

——, ed., *Curia Regis Rolls* (Woodbridge: Boydell Press, 1999).

——, ed., *Plea Rolls of the Exchequer of the Jews* (London: Jewish Historical Society of England, 2005).

Breuil, A., 'La Confrérie de Notre-Dame du Puy, d'Amiens', in *Mémoires de la Société des antiquaires de Picardie*, 2e série, III (1854), 485–680.

Buik of Alexander, ed. Graeme R. L. Ritchie, Scottish Text Society, New Series 17, 12, 21, 25, 4 vols (Edinburgh: Blackwood, 1921–9).

Calendar of Letter-Books preserved among the Archives of the Corporation of the City of London at the Guildhall, ed. Reginald R. Sharpe, 11 vols (London: J. E. Francis, 1899–1912).

Calendar of Select Pleas and Memoranda of the City of London Preserved among the Archives of the Corporation of the City of London at the Guildhall, ed., A. H. Thomas, 3 vols, I: *Rolls A1a-A9, a.d.1323–1364;* II: *A.D.1364–1381*; III: *A.D.1381–1412* (Cambridge: Cambridge University Press, 1926, 1929, 1932).

Caxton, William, *Dialogues in French and English by William Caxton*, ed. Henry Bradley, EETS, ES 79 (London: Kegan Paul, Trench, Trübner, 1900).

Caxton, William, *The Prologues and Epilogues of William Caxton*, ed. W. J. B. Crotch, EETS, OS 176 (London: Oxford University Press, 1928).

La Chanson de Roland, ed. F. Whitehead (Oxford: Blackwell, 1946).

Chaplais, Pierre, ed., *Some Documents Regarding the Fulfilment and Interpretation of the Treaty of Brétigny 1361–1369*, Camden Miscellany, XIX (London: Offices of the Royal Historical Society, 1952).

Charles d'Orléans, *Fortunes Stabilnes: Charles d'Orléans's English Book of Love*, ed. Mary-Jo Ann (Binghamton, NY: Medieval and Renaissance Text Society, 1994).

——, *The English Poems of Charles d'Orléans*, ed. Robert Steele and Mabel Day, 2 vols, EETS, os 215 (London: Oxford University Press, 1941).

Chartier, Alain, *Fifteenth-Century English Translations of Alain Chartier's Le Traité de l'esperance and 'Le Quadrilogue invectif'*, ed. Margaret S. Blayney, EETS 270, 2 vols (London: Oxford University Press, 1974–1980).

——, *Le Quadrilogue Invectif*, ed. E. Droz (Paris: Champion, 1950).

——, *Le Quadrilogue Invectif*, trans. Florence Bouchet (Paris: Champion, 2002).

Chastellain, Georges, *Oeuvres de Georges Chastellain*, ed. Kervyn de Lettenhove, 8 vols (Brussels: F. Heussner [etc.], 1863–66).

'*Le Chastiement des clers*: a *dit* concerning the Nations of the University of Paris, edited from Paris, Bibliothique Nationale, MS fr.837', ed. Daron Burrows, *Medium Aerum*, 69(2000), 211–26.

Chaucer, Geoffrey, *Geoffrey Chaucer: The Minor Poems*, ed. George B. Pace and Alfred David (Norman, OK: University of Oklahoma Press, 1982).

——, *The Riverside Chaucer*, gen. ed. Larry D. Benson, 3rd edn (Oxford: Houghton Mifflin, 1987; pbk repr. Oxford University Press, 1988).

Chaucer's Boece: A Critical Edition Based on Cambridge University Library, MS Ii.3.21,ff. 9r–180v, ed. Tim Machan (Heidelberg: Winter, 2008).

Christine de Pizan, *The Book of Fayttes of Armes and of Chyualry. Translated and Printed by William Caxton from the French Original by Christine de Pizan*, ed. A.T.P. Byles, EETS, OS 189, rev.edn (London: Oxford University Press, 1937; 1st publ.1932).

——, *Ditié de Jehanne d'Arc*, ed. Angus J. Kennedy and Kenneth Varty (Oxford: Society for the Study of Mediaeval Languages and Literature, 1977).

Chronicles of London, ed. C. L. Kingsford (Oxford: Clarendon Press, 1905).

Condé, Baudouin de, and Jean de Condé, *Dits et contes de Baudouin de Condé et de son fils Jean de Condé*, ed. A. Scheler, 3 vols (Brussels: Devaux, 1866–7).

Cosneau, Eugène, *Les grands traités de la guerre de cent ans* (Paris: Picard, 1889).

La Cour amoureuse dite de Charles VI, ed. Carla Bozzolo and Hélène Loyau, 2 vols (Paris: Léopard d'Or, 1982–92).

Creton, Jean, *Metrical History of the Deposition of King Richard II*, ed., J. Webb, *Archaeologia*, 20 (1824), 1–423.

Martin M. Crow and Clair C. Olson Chaucer Life-Records, ed. (Oxford: Clarendon Press, 1966).

Curtis, Richard, 'The Skinhead Hamlet' in *The Faber Book of Parodies*, ed. Simon Brett (London: Faber, 1984), 316–20.

Dante Alighieri, *De vulgari eloquentia*, in *Opere minori*, ed. P. V. Mengaldo, II (Milan and Naples: Riciardi, 1979).

——, *Literature in the Vernacular*, trans. Sally Purcell (Manchester: Carcanet, 1981).

Le Débat des hérauts d'armes de France et d'Angleterre suivi de The Debate between the Heralds of England and France by John Coke, ed. L. Pannier, SATF (Paris: Firmin–Didot, 1877).

Deschamps, Eustache, *Oeuvres Complètes de Eustache Deschamps*, ed. le Marquis de Queux de Saint–Hilaire and Gaston Raynaud, SATF, 11 vols (Paris: Firmin Didot, 1878–1903).

——, *L'Art de dictier*, ed. and trans. Deborah M. Sinnreich-Levi (East Lansing: Colleagues Press, 1994).

——, *Eustache Deschamps: Selected Poems*, ed. Ian S. Laurie and Deborah M. Sinnreich-Levi, trans. David Curzon and Jeffrey Fiskin (New York and London: Routledge, 2003).

Diekstra, F. N. M., 'The Poetic Exchange between Philippe de Vitry and Jean de le Mote: a New Edition', *Neophilologus*, 70 (1986), 504–19.

Dobson, R. B., ed., *The Peasants' Revolt of 1381* (London: Macmillan, 1970).

Donait soloum douce franceis de Paris, ed. Brian Merrilees, in *Anglo -Norman Anniversary Essays*, ed. Ian Short, ANTS (London: ANTS, 1993), 273–91.

Doss-Quinby, Eglal, and Samuel N. Rosenberg, eds, with Elizabeth Aubrey, *The Old French Ballette: Oxford Bodleian Library, MS Douce 308* (Geneva: Droz, 2006).

Dryden, John, *Of Dramatic Poesy and Other Critical Essays*, ed. George Watson, 2 vols (London: Dent, 1962–8).

Du Bellay, Joachim, *The Regrets: A Bilingual Edition*, ed. and trans. R. Helgerson (Philadelphia: University of Pennsylvania Press, 2006).

Faral, Edmond, ed., *Mimes français du XIIIe siècle* (Paris: Champion, 1910).

——, ed., *Le Manuscrit 19152 du fonds français de la bibliothèque nationale. Reproduction phototypique publiée avec une introduction* (Paris: Droz, 1934).

Fisher, John H., Malcolm Richardson and Jane L. Fisher, eds, *An Anthology of Chancery English* (Knoxville: University of Tennessee Press, 1984).

Florio, Iohn, *The essayes or morall, politike and millitarie discourses of Lo: Michaell de Montaigne* (London: Val. Sims for Edward Blount, 1603).

Fortescue, John, *A learned commendation of the politique lawes of Englande newly translated into Englishe by Robert Mulcaster* (London: Richard Tottell, 1567).

——, *De Laudibus Legum Anglie*, ed. Stanley B. Chrimes (Cambridge: Cambridge University Press, 1942).

Froissart, Jean, *Oeuvres de Froissart: Chroniques*, ed. Kervyn de Lettenhove, 25 vols in 28 (Brussels: V. Devaux, 1867–77).

——, *Oeuvres de Froissart: Poésies*, ed. A. Scheler, 3 vols (Brussels: V. Devaux, 1870–2).

Froissart, Jean, *Chroniques, Livre I*, ed. S. Luce, I–VII, SHF (Paris: Renouard, 1869–88), *Livre II*, ed. G. Raynaud, IX–II (Paris: Renouard, 1894–9), *Livre III*, ed. L. and A. Mirot, XII–XV (Paris: Champion, 1931–75).

——, *Jean Froissart, L'Espinette amoureuse*, 2nd rev. edn (Paris: Klincksieck, 1972).

——, *Chroniques, début du premier livre. Edition du manuscript de Rome Reg.lat.869*, ed. G. T. Diller, TLF, 194 (Geneva: Droz, 1972).

——, *Le Joli Buisson de Jonece*, ed. A. Fourrier (Geneva: Droz, 1975).

——, *Ballades et Rondeaux*, ed. Rae S. Baudouin (Geneva and Paris: Droz, 1978).

——, *'Dits' et 'débats'*, ed. A. Fourrier (Geneva: Droz, 1979).

——, *Le Paradis d'amour, L'Orloge amoureus*, ed. Peter F. Dembowski, TLF, 339 (Geneva: Droz, 1986).

——, *Chroniques. Livre I. Le manuscrit d'Amiens*, ed. G. T. Diller, 5 vols (Geneva: Droz, 1991–8).

Gace Brulé, *The Lyrics and Melodies of Gace Brulé*, ed. and trans. Samuel N. Rosenberg and Samuel Danon, music ed. Hendrik van der Werf (New York and London: Garland, 1985).

Gace de la Buigne, *Le Roman des deduis*, ed. A. Blomqvist (Karlshamm: E. G. Johansson, 1951).

——, *Chroniques, Livre III (du Voyage en Béarn à la campagne de Gascogne) et Livre IV (années 1389–1400)*, ed. Peter Ainsworth and Alberto Varvaro (Paris: Librairie Générale Française, 2004).

Geoffrey of Monmouth, *Historia regum Britanniae/The History of the Kings of Britain*, ed. Michael D. Reeve and trans. Neil Wright (Woodbridge: Boydell, 2007).

Gildas, *De Excidio Britonum*, ed. and trans. Michael Winterbottom (Chichester: Phillimore, repr. 2002; 1st publ. 1978).

Gilles li Muisis, *Poésies*, ed. Kervyn de Lettenhove, 2 vols (Louvain: Lefever, 1882).

Gower, John, *The Complete Works*, ed. G. C. Macaulay, 4 vols, (Oxford: Clarendon Press, 1899–1902).

——, *Cinkante Ballades* and *Traitié*, trans. R.F. Yeager (Kalamazoo, MI.: TEAMS, forthcoming).

Grandson, Othon de, *Oton de Grandson: sa vie et ses poésies* (Lausanne: Librairie Payot, 1941).

La Guerre de Cent Ans vue à travers les registres du parlement (1337–1369), ed. Pierre-Clément Timbal (Paris: CNRS, 1961).

Guillaume Guiart, *Branche des Royaux Lignages, Chronique métrique de Guillaume Guiart*, ed. J. A. Buchon, Collection des chroniques nationales françaises, 7 (Paris: Verdière, 1828).

Hardt, Hermann von der, ed., *Magnum oecumenicum Constantiense Concilium*, 6 vols in 4 (Frankfurt, 1700).

Henry of Lancaster, *Le Livre de Seyntz medicines: the unpublished devotional treatise of Henry of Lancaster*, ed. E. J. Arnould (Oxford: Basil Blackwell, 1940).

Higden, Ranulf, *Polychronicon Ranulphi Higden monachi Cestrensis*, ed. Churchill Babington and J.R. Lumby, 9 vols, Rolls Series 41 (London: Longman, Green, Longman, Roberts, and Green, 1865–86).

——, *John Trevisa's Translation of the Polychronicon of Ranulph Higden (Book VI)*, ed. Ronald Waldron (Heidelberg: Heidelberg University Press, 2004).

Hobbins, Daniel, ed. and trans., *The Trial of Joan of Arc* (Cambridge, MA: Harvard University Press, 2005).

Holinshed, Raphael, *The Third volume of Chronicles* (London: Henry Denham, 1586).

Horstmann, Carl, ed., *Yorkshire Writers: Richard Rolle of Hampole* (London: Swan Sonnenschein; New York: Macmillan, 1895).

Hudson, Anne, ed., *Selections from English Wycliffite Writings* (Cambridge: Cambridge University Press, 1978).

Hugo, Victor, *Les Travailleurs de la mer, précédé de l'Archipel de la Manche*, ed. David Charles (Paris: Librairie Générale Française, 2002).

Hunt, Tony, ed., *Teaching and Learning Latin in Thirteenth-Century England*, 3 vols (Cambridge: D. S. Brewer, 1991).

Janequin, Clément, *Chansons polyphoniques*, ed. A. Tillman Merrit and François Lesure, 6 vols (Monaco: Editions de l'oiseau-lyre, 1956).

Jacques de Longuyon, *Les Voeux de paon*, in *Buik of Alexander*, ed. Ritchie, II–IV.

Jean le Court dit Brisebare, *Le restor du paon*, ed. Richard J. Carey (Geneva: Droz, 1966).

Jean Brisebarre, *Le Restor du paon*, ed. Enid Donkin (London: MHRA, 1980).

Jean de le Mote, *Le Parfait du Paon*, ed. Richard J. Carey (Chapel Hill: University of North Carolina Press, 1972).

Jean le Seneschal, *Les Cent Ballades*, ed. Gaston Raynaud, SATF (Paris: Firmin-Didot, 1905).

Jeffrey, David L. and Brian J. Levy, eds, *The Anglo-Norman Lyric: An Anthology* (Toronto: Pontifical Institute of Mediaeval Studies, 1990; 2006).

Jehan le Bel, *Chronique de Jean le Bel*, ed. Jules Viard and Eugène Déprez, 2 vols, SHF (Paris: Renouard, 1904–5).

Jenkins, Atkinson, T., 'Deschamps' Ballade to Chaucer', *Modern Language Notes*, 33 (1918), 268–78.

Joinville, Jean de, *Jean de Joinville: Mémoires ou Vie de saint Louis*, ed. J. Monfrin (Paris: Garnier Flammarion, 1998).

Journal d'un bourgeois de Paris, 1405–1449, ed. A. Tuetey, Société de l'Histoire de Paris (Paris: Nogent-le-Rotrou, 1881).

Le Journal d'un Bourgeois de Paris de 1405 à 1449, ed. Colette Beaune (Paris: Librairie Générale Française, 1990).

Langland, William, *Langland, Piers Plowman: The Prologue and Passus I–VII*, ed. J. A. W. Bennett (Oxford: Clarendon Press, 1972).

——, *The Vision of Piers Plowman: A Critical Edition of the B-Text Based on Trinity College Cambridge MS B.15.17*, ed. A. V. C. Schmidt (London: J. M. Dent, 1995).

Langlois, Monique and Yvonne Lanhers, eds, *Confessions et jugements de criminels au Parlement de Paris (1319–1350), Archives Nationales, X2a4* (Paris: Archives Nationales, 1971).

Langtoft, Pierre, *The Chronicle of Pierre de Langtoft*, ed. Thomas Wright, 2 vols (London: Longmans, Green, Reader, and Dyer, 1866).

Le Grand d'Aussy, ed., *Fabliaux ou Contes du XIIe et du XIIIe siècle, fables et roman du XIIIe, traduits ou extraits d'après plusieurs Manuscrits... nouvelle édition, augmentée d'une dissertation sur les Troubadours*, 3 vols (Paris: Eugène Onfroy, 1781).

Legge, M. Dominica, ed., *Anglo-Norman Letters and Petitions from All Souls ms. 182*, Anglo-Norman Texts 3 (Oxford: Blackwell, 1941).

Liber donati: A Fifteenth-Century Manual of French, ed. Brian Merrilees and Beata Sitarz-Fitzpatrick, ANTS, Plain Texts Series 9 (London: ANTS, 1993).

Le Livre des Mestiers: Dialogues Français-Flamands composés au XIVe siècle par un maître d'école de la ville de Bruges, ed. Henri-Victor Michelant (Paris: Tross, 1875).

Lydgate, John, *Lydgate's Troy Book*, ed. Henry Bergen, EETS, 2vols (London: Kegan Paul &c., 1906).

Machan, Tim, ed., *Sources of the Boece* (Athens and London: University of Georgia Press, 2005).

Machaut, Guillaume de, *Poésies lyriques*, ed. V. Chichmaref, 2 vols (Paris: Champion, 1909; repr. Geneva, 1973).

——, *La Louange des Dames by Guillaume de Machaut*, ed. Nigel Wilkins (Edinburgh: Scottish Academic Press, 1972).

——, *Le Confort d'ami (Comfort for a Friend)*, ed. and trans. R. Barton Palmer (New York and London: Garland, 1992).

——, *Le Livre de la Fontaine amoureuse*, ed. and trans. Jacqueline Cerquiglini-Toulet (Paris: Stock, 1993).

——, *Le Livre du Voir Dit*, ed. P. Imbs and J. Cerquiglini-Toulet (Paris: Librairie Générale Française, 1999).

——, *La Prise d'Alixandre (The Taking of Alexandria)*, ed. and trans. R. Barton Palmer (London and New York: Routledge, 2002).

Manières de Langage (1396, 1399, 1415), ed. Andres M. Kristol (London: ANTS, 1995).

Mezières, Philippe de, *Le Songe du Vieil Pèlerin*, ed. and trans. G. W. Coopland, 2 vols (Cambridge: Cambridge University Press, 1969).

——, *Epistre au Roi Richart/ Letter to King Richard II*, ed. and trans. G. W. Coopland (Liverpool: Liverpool University Press, 1975).

Le mistère du siège d'Orléans, ed. V. L. Hamblin, TLF 546 (Geneva: Droz, 2002).

Monstrelet, Enguerrand de, *La chronique d'Enguerran de Monstrelet*, ed Louis Douët d'Arcq, 6 vols (Paris: Renouard, 1862).

Montaiglon, Anatole de, and Gaston Raynaud, eds, *Recueil général et complet des fabliaux des XIIIe et XIVe siècles*, 6 vols (Paris: Librairie des bibliophiles, 1872–90).

Munimenta gildhallae Londoniensis, ed. H. T. Riley, Rolls Series, 3 vols (London: Longman, Brown, Green, Longmans, and Roberts, 1859–62).

Le Mystère de Saint Louis, ed. Francisque Michel (Westminster: Roxburghe Club, 1871).

Nennius, *Historia Brittonum*, in *British History and the Welsh Annals*, ed. and trans. John Morris, Arthurian Period Sources, 8 (London: Phillimore, 1980), 50–84.

Nicole de Margival, *Le Dit de la Panthère*, ed. Bernard Ribémont, CFMA, 136 (Paris: Champion, 2000).

Nithard, *Nithard: Histoire des fils de Louis le pieux*, ed. and trans. Ph. Lauer, Les Classiques de l'Histoire de France au moyen âge, 7 (Paris: Les Belles Lettres, 1926).

Noomen, Willem, and Nico van den Boogaard, eds, *Nouveau Recueil complet des fabliaux*, 10 vols (Assen: Van Gorcum, 1983–8).

A Parisian Journal (1405–1449), trans. Janet Shirley (Oxford: Clarendon Press, 1968).

Porter, Lambert C., ed., *La Fatrasie et le fatras, essai sur la poésie irrationnelle en France au Moyen Age* (Geneva: Droz, 1960).

Procès de condamnation de Jeanne d'Arc, ed. Pierre Tisset and Yvonne Lanhers, 3 vols (Paris: Klincksieck, 1960–71).

Procès de condemnation et de réhabilitation de Jeanne d'Arc dite La Pucelle, ed. Jules Quicherat, Société de l'Histoire de France, 5 vols (Paris: Renquard, 1841–49).

Procès en nullité de la condamnation de Jeanne d'Arc, ed. Pierre Duparc, 5 vols (Paris: Klincksieck, 1977–88).

Pour ce que plusieurs, Debating the Hundred Years War: Pour ce que plusieurs (la loy salique) and a declaracion of the trew and dewe title of Henry VIII, ed. Craig Taylor, Camden Fifth Series, 29, Royal Historical Society, UCL (Cambridge: Cambridge University Press, 2006).

Récits d'un bourgeois de Valenciennes (XIVe siècle), ed. Kervyn de Lettenhove (Louvain: Lefever, 1877).

Reid, T. B. W., ed., *Twelve Fabliaux from MS f.fr.19152 of the Bibliothèque Nationale* (Manchester: Manchester University Press, 1958).

Remi, Philippe de, *Jehan et Blonde, Poems, and Songs, edited from Paris BNF fr.1588, Paris BNF fr.24006, and Paris BNF fr.837 by Barbara N. Sargent-Baur*, Faux Titre, Etudes de langue et littérature françaises publiées, no.201 (Amsterdam and Atlanta: Rodopi, 2001).

Richard II, *The Diplomatic Correspondence of Richard II*, ed. Edouard Perroy, Camden Third Series, 48, Royal Historical Society (London: Offices of the Society, 1933).

Rigg, A. G., ed., *A Book of British Kings* (Toronto: Pontifical Institute of Medieval Studies, 2000).

'*La Riote du monde*', ed. J. Ulrich, *Zeitschrift für romanische Philologie*, 8 (1884), 275–89.

Rivière, Jean-Claude, ed., *Pastourelles: Introduction à l'étude formelle des pastourelles anonymes françaises des XIIe et XIIIe siècles*, 3 vols, TLF, 213, 220, 232 (Geneva: Droz, 1974–6).

Le Roman de Renart, ed. Mario Roques, CFMA (Paris: Champion, 1948).

Shakespeare, William, *The Complete Works: Original-Spellings Edition*, gen. eds. Stanley Wells and Gary Taylor (Oxford: Clarendon Press, 1986).

——, *Henry V*, ed. Gary Taylor, The Oxford Shakespeare (Oxford: Clarendon Press, 1982).

——, *King Richard II*, ed. Peter Ure, 2nd Arden edn (London: Routledge, 1961).

——, *Richard II*, ed. Charles R. Forker (The Arden Shakespeare, Third Series, 2002).

Short, Ian, and Roy Pearcy, eds, *Eighteen Anglo-Norman Fabliaux*, ANTS 14 (London: ANTS, 2000).

Le Songe du Vergier, édité d'après le manuscrit royal 19 C IV de la British Library, ed. Marion Schnerb-Lièvre, 2 vols, Sources d'Histoire Médiévale publiées par l'Institut de Recherche et d'Histoire des Textes (Paris: Editions du CNRS, 1982).

Symons, Dana M., ed., *Chaucerian Dream Visions and Complaints* (Kalamazoo, MI.: TEAMS, 2004).

Taylor, Craig, trans. and annot., *Joan of Arc, La Pucelle* (Manchester: Manchester University Press, 2006).

Tennyson, Alfred, *The Poems of Tennyson*, ed. Christopher Ricks (London and Harlow: Longmans, 1969).

Thomas, *Les fragments du Roman de Tristan: poème du XIIe siècle*, ed. Bartina H. Wind (Leiden: E. J. Brill, 1950).

Thomas, *The Romance of Horn by Thomas*, ed. Mildred K. Pope and T. B. W. Reid, Anglo-Norman Texts, 9–10, 12–13, 2 vols (Oxford: Blackwell, 1955–64)

Le Trésor amourenx, in Froissart, *Oeuvres*, ed. Scheler III, 52–305.

Trevisa: see Higden.

Vitry, Jacques de, *The Historia Occidentalis of Jacques de Vitry: A Critical Edition*, ed. John Frederick Hinnesbusch, Spicilegium Friburgense, 17 (Fribourg: The University Press, 1972).

Les Voeux du héron, ed. Wright, *Political Poems*, I, 1–25.

Wace, *Le Roman de Rou de Wace*, ed. A. J. Holden (Paris: Picard, 1970–3).

——, *Wace's Roman de Brut: A History of the British*, ed. and trans. Judith Weiss, rev. edn (Exeter: University of Exeter Press, 2002).

——, *The History of the Norman People: Wace's Roman de Rou*, trans. Glynn S. Burgess (Woodbridge: Boydell, 2004).

Walter of Bibbesworth, *Le Tretiz*, ed. William Rothwell (Aberystwyth: The Anglo-Norman Online Hub, 2009).

Waterschoot, W., *Lodewijk van Velthem, De Guldensporenslag. Een fragment uit de voortzetting van de Spiegel Historiael* (The Hague: Martinus Nijhoff, 1979).

White, E. B., *Here is New York* (New York: The Little Bookroom, 1999; 1st publ. 1949).

Wilson, Thomas, *The Art of Rhetorique*, ed. G. H. Mair (Oxford: Clarendon Press, 1909).

——, *Chaucer and the Poems of 'Ch' in University of Pennsylvania MS French 15* (Cambridge: D. S. Brewer, 1982).

Wimsatt, James I., *Chaucer and the Poems of 'Ch' in University of Pennsylvania MS French 15* (Cambridge: D.S. Brewer, 1982)

Windeatt, B. A., ed. and trans., *Chaucer's Dream Poetry: Sources and Analogues* (Cambridge: D. S. Brewer, 1982).

Wogan-Browne, Jocelyn, Nicholas Watson, Andrew Taylor and Ruth Gvans, eds., *The L'den of the Vernacular: An Anthology of Middle English Literary Theory 1280–1520* (Exeter: University of Exeter Press, 1999).

Wright, Thomas, ed., *Political Poems and Songs relating to English History*, Rolls Series, 2 vols (London: Longman, Green, Longman, and Roberts, 1859–61).

Wyatt, Thomas, *Collected Poems of Sir Thomas Wyatt*, ed. Kenneth Muir and Patricia Thomson (Liverpool: Liverpool University Press, 1969).

Year Books of Edward II, ed. F. W. Maitland, Selden Society 17 (London: Quaritch, 1903).

SECONDARY SOURCES

Adams, J. N., *Bilingualism and the Latin Language* (Cambridge: Cambridge University Press, 2003).

Aers, David, 'A Whisper in the Ear of Early Modernists; or Reflections on Literary Critics Writing the "History of the Subject"', in *Culture and History 1350–1600: Essays on English Communities, Identities and Writing*, ed. David Aers (London and New York: Harvester Wheatsheaf, 1992), 177–202.

——, '*Vox populi* and the literature of 1381', in Wallace, ed., *Cambridge History*, 432–53.

Agee, James, *Agee on Film* (New York: McDowell, Obolensky 1958).

Ahlzweig, Klaus, *Muttersprache-Vaterland: Die deutsche Nation und ihre Sprache* (Opladen: Westdeutsche Verlag, 1994).

Ainsworth, Peter F., *Jean Froissart and the Fabric of History* (Oxford: Clarendon Press, 1990).

Akehurst, F. R. P., and Stephanie Cain Van D'Elden, eds, *The Stranger in Medieval Society* (Minneapolis: University of Minnesota Press, 1997).

Albert, Hermann, *Mittelalterlicher englisch-französischer Jargon*, Studien zur englischen Philologie, 63 (Halle: M. Niemeyer, 1922).

Allen, Rosamund S., 'John Gower and Southwark: The Paradox of the Social Self', in Boffey and King, eds, *London and Europe*, 111–47.

Allmand, Christopher, *Lancastrian Normandy, 1415–1450: The History of a Medieval Occupation* (Oxford: Clarendon Press, 1983).

——, *The Hundred Years War: England and France at War c.1300–c.1450* (Cambridge: Cambridge University Press, 1988).

——, ed., *War, Government and Power in Late Medieval France* (Liverpool: Liverpool University Press, 2000).

Anderson, Benedict, *Imagined Communities* (London and New York: Verso, 1983; rev. edn 1991).

Angers, Denise, 'La guerre et le pluralisme linguistique: aspects de la guerre de Cent Ans, *Annales de Normandie*, 43 (1993), 125–39.

Arn, Mary-Jo, 'Two Manuscripts, One Mind: Charles d'Orléans and the Production of Manuscripts in Two Languages (Paris BN MS fr.25458 and London, BL MS Harley 682)', in Arn, ed., *Charles d'Orléans in England*, 61–78.

——, ed., *Charles d'Orléans in England* (Cambridge: D. S. Brewer, 2000).

Ascoli, Georges, *La Grande-Bretagne devant l'opinion française depuis la guerre de cent ans jusqu'à la fin du XVI siècle*, 3 vols (Paris, 1927, 1930; repr. Geneva: Slatkine, 1971), I.

Asperti, Stefano, *Carlo I d'Angio e i trovatori: componenti 'provenzali' e angioine nella tradizione manoscritta della lirica trobadorica* (Ravenna: Longo, 1995).

Avril, François, *Manuscript Painting at the Court of France: The Fourteenth Century (1310–1380)*, trans. Ursule Molinaro and Bruce Benderson (London: Chatto & Windus, 1978).

Ayres-Bennett, Wendy, *A History of the French Language through Texts* (London: Routledge, 1996).

Baker, Denise N., ed., *Inscribing the Hundred Years' War in French and English Cultures*, SUNY series in Medieval Studies (Albany: State University of New York Press, 2000).

Bakhtin, Mikhail, *Rabelais and his World*, trans. H. Iswolsky (Bloomington and Indianapolis: Indiana University Press, 1984).

Balibar, Renée, 'National language, education, literature', in *Literature, Politics and Theory: Papers from the Essex Conference 1976–1984*, ed. Francis Barker, Peter Hulme, Margaret Iversen, Diana Loxley (London: Routledge, 1986; new edn, 2003), 126–47.

Barron, Caroline 'London 1300–1540', in Palliser, ed., *The Cambridge Urban History*, 395–440.

——, *London in the Later Middle Ages: Government and People, 1200–1500* (Oxford: Oxford University Press, 2004).

——, and Nigel Saul, eds, *England and the Low Countries in the Late Middle Ages* (Stroud: Alan Sutton, 1995).

Bartlett, Robert, *The Making of Europe: Conquest, Colonization and Cultural Change, 950–1350* (Princeton: Princeton University Press, 1993).

——, *England Under the Norman and Angevin Kings 1075–1225* (Oxford: Clarendon Press, 2000).

Baswell, Christopher, 'Multilingualism on the Page', in Strohm, ed., *Middle English*, 38–50.

Beaune, Colette, *Naissance de la nation France* (Paris: Gallimard, 1989); *The Birth of an Ideology: Myths and Symbols of Nation in Late-Medieval France*, trans. S. R. Huston and ed. Fredric L. Cheyette (Berkeley: University of California Press, 1991).

Becker, Karin, *Eustache Deschamps: L'État actuel de la recherche* (Orléans: Paradigme, 1996).

Becker-Ho, Alice, *L'Essence du Jargon* (Paris: Gallimard, 1994).

Beidler, Peter G., 'New Terminology for Sources and Analogues', *SAC*, 28 (2006), 225–35.

Bennett, Philip, 'Le normand, le picard et les koïnés littéraires de l'épopée aux xiie et xiiie siècles', in *Picard d'hier et d'aujourd'hui, Bien Dire et Bien Aprandre: Revue de Médiévistique*, 21, ed. Jacques Landrecies and Aimé Petit (Lille: Université Charles–de-Gaule, 2003), 43–56.

Bennington, Geoffrey and Jacques Derrida, *Jacques Derrida* (Paris: Éditions du Seuil, 1991); *Jacques Derrida*, trans. Geoffrey Bennington (Chicago: University of Chicago Press, 1993).

Bent, Margaret, 'Words and Music in Machaut's Motet 9', *Early Music*, 31 (2003), 363–88.

—— and Andrew Wathey, 'Vitry, Philippe de', *Grove Music Online*, ed. L. Macy (Accessed 30 January 2008), <http://www.grovemusic.com>.

Berndt, Rolf, 'The Period of the Final Decline of French in Medieval England (Fourteenth and Early Fifteenth Centuries)', *Zeitschrift für Anglistik und Amerikanistik*, 20 (1972), 341–69.

Bischoff, Bernhard, 'The Study of Foreign Languages in the Middle Ages', *Speculum*, 36 (1961), 209–24.

Blank, Paula, *Broken English: Dialects and the Politics of Language in Renaissance Writings* (London and New York: Routledge, 1996).

Bloch, R. Howard, '842: The First Document and the Birth of Medieval Studies', in *A New History of French Literature*, ed. Denis Hollier (Cambridge, MA: Harvard University Press, 1989), 6–13.

——, *The Scandal of the Fabliaux* (Chicago and London: University of Chicago Press, 1986).

Blockmans, Wim and Walter Prevenier, *The Promised Lands: The Low Countries Under Burgundian Rule, 1369–1530*, trans. Elizabeth Fackelman, rev. and ed. Edward Peters (Philadelphia: University of Pennsylvania Press, 1999).

Boffey, Julia and A. S. G. Edwards, 'Middle English Verse in Chronicles', in *New Perspectives on Middle English Texts. A Festschrift for R. A. Waldron*, ed. Susan Powell and Jeremy J. Smith (Cambridge: D. S. Brewer, 2000), 119–28.

Boffey, Julia, A. S. G. Edwards, and Pamela King, eds, *London and Europe in the Later Middle Ages*, (London: Centre for Medieval and Renaissance Studies, Queen Mary and Westfield College, University of London, 1995).

Bombarde, Odile, ed., *Froissart dans sa forge. Colloque réuni à Paris, du 4 au 6 novembre 2004, par M. Michel Zink, professeur au Collège de France, membre de l'Académie des Inscriptions et Belles-Lettres* (Paris: Académie des Inscriptions et Belles-Lettres, 2006).

Boogaart, Jacques, 'Encompassing Past and Present: Quotations and their Function in Machaut's Motets, *EMH*, 20 (2001), 1–86.

Boogaard, Nico van den, 'Le Fabliau anglo-normand', in *Nico H. J. Boogaard autour du XIIIe siècle-études de philologie et de littérature médiévale*, ed. Sorin Alexandrescu, Fernand Trijkoningen and Willhem Noomen (Amsterdam: Rodopi, 1985), 179–89.

Boudet, Jean-Patrice and Hélène Millet, eds, *Eustache Deschamps en son temps* (Paris: Publications de la Sorbonne, 1997).

Boulton, M. B. M., *The Song in the Story: Lyric Insertions in French Narrative Fiction, 1200–1400* (Philadelphia: University of Pennsylvania Press, 1993).

Bowers, John M., 'Three Readings of *The Knight's Tale*: Sir John Clanvowe, Geoffrey Chaucer, and James I of Scotland', *JMEMS*, 34 (2004), 279–307.

Braddy, Haldeen, *Chaucer and the French Poet Graunson* (Baton Rouge: Louisiana State University Press, 1947).

Branca, Vittore, *Giovanni Boccaccio: profilo biografico* (Florence: G. C. Sansoni, 1977).

Brand, Paul, *The Making of the Common Law* (London: Hambledon, 1992).

——, 'The Languages of the Law in Later Medieval England', in *Multilingualism in Later Medieval Britain*, ed. D. A. Trotter (Cambridge: D. S. Brewer, 2000), 63–76.

——, *Kings, Barons and Justices: The Making and Enforcement of Legislation in Thirteenth-Century England* (Cambridge: Cambridge University Press, 2003).

Braudel, F., 'Comment l'Angleterre devint une île', in *Le Temps du monde*, 3 vols (Paris: Armand Colin, 1979), III, 302–4.

Breuilly, John, *Nationalism and the State* (Manchester: Manchester University Press, 1982).

——, 'Changes in the Political uses of the nation: continuity or discondinuity?' in *Power and the Nation in European History*, ed. Len Scales and Oliver Zimmer (Cambridge: Cambridge University Press, 2005), 67–101.

Brewer, D.S., ed., *Chaucer: The Critical Heritage*, 2 vols (London: Routledge & Kegan Paul, 1978).

Brownlee, K. S., *Poetic Identity in Guillaume de Machaut* (Madison: University of Wisconsin Press, 1984).

——, 'Fire, Desire, Duration, Death: Machaut's Motet 10', in Clark and Leach, eds, *Citation and authority*, 79–93.

Brubaker, Roger, *Nationalism Reframed: Nationhood and the national question in the New Europe* (Cambridge: Cambridge University Press, 1996).

Brunot, Ferdinand, *Histoire de la langue française des origines à 1900, I: De l'époque latine à la Renaissance* (Paris: Armand Colin, 1905).

——, *La réforme de l'orthographe: Lettre ouverte à Monsieur le Ministre de l'Instruction publique* (Paris: Armand Colin, 1905).

Brusegan, Rosanna, 'Le *Jeu de Robin et Marion* et l'ambiguïté du symbolisme champêtre', in *The Theatre in the Middle Ages*, ed. Herman Braet, Johan Nowé and Gilbert Tournoy (Leuven: Leuven University Press, 1985), 119–29.

Bullock-Davies, Constance, *Professional Interpreters and the Matter of Britain* (Cardiff: University of Wales Press, 1966).

Burke, Peter and Roy Porter, eds., *Languages and Jargons: Contributions to a Social History of Language* (Cambridge: Polity Press, 1995).

Burnley, J. D., 'Sources of Standardisation in Later Middle English', in *Standardizing English*, ed. J. B. Trahern, Jr, (Knoxville: University of Tennessee Press, 1989), 23–41.

Burroughs, Charles, 'Spaces of arbitration and the organization of space in late medieval Italian cities', in *Medieval Practices of Space*, ed. Barbara A. Hanawalt and Michal Kobialka (Minneapolis: University of Minnesota, 2000), 64–100.

Burrow, J. A., *Ricardian Poetry: Chaucer, Gower, Langland and the 'Gawain' Poet* (London: Routledge and Kegan Paul, 1971).

——,'The Portrayal of Amans in *Confessio Amantis*', in *Gower's Confessio Amantis: Responses and Reassessments*, ed. A. J. Minnis (Cambridge: D. S. Brewer, 1983), 5–24.

——, 'The Shape of the Vernon Refrain Lyrics', in *Studies in the Vernon Manuscript*, ed. Derek Pearsall (Cambridge: D. S. Brewer, 1990), 187–99.

——, 'The Languages of Medieval England', in *The Oxford History of Literary Translation in English*, vol. 1: *To 1500*, ed. Roger Ellis (Oxford: Oxford University Press, 2008), 7–18.

Burrows, Daron, *The Stereotype of the Priest in the Old French Fabliaux: Anticlerical Satire and Lay Identity* (Bern: Peter Lang, 2005).

Busby, Keith, *Codex and Context: Reading Old French Verse Narrative in Manuscript*, 2 vols (Amsterdam and New York: Rodopi, 2002).

Buschinger, Danielle, ed., *Autour d'Eustache Deschamps: Actes du Colloque du Centre d'Études Médiévales de l'Université de Picardie-Jules Verne Amiens, 5–8 Novembre 1998* (Amiens: Presses du Centre d'études médiévales, Université de Picardie-Jules Verne, 1999).

Butterfield, Ardis, 'Puy', *Medieval France: An Encyclopaedia*, gen. ed. W. W. Kibler (New York: Garland Press, 1995).

——, '*Mise-en-page* in the *Troilus* Manuscripts: Chaucer and French Manuscript Culture', in *Reading from the Margins: Textual Studies, Chaucer, and Medieval Literature*, ed. Seth Lerer (San Marino, CA: Huntington Library, 1996), 49–80; [published simultaneously as *Huntington Library Quarterly*, 58 (1995), 49–80].

——, 'French Culture and the Ricardian Court', *Essays on Ricardian Literature in Honour of J. A. Burrow*, ed. Alistair Minnis, Charlotte C. Morse, and Thorlac Turville-Petre (Oxford: Clarendon Press, 1997), 82–121.

——, *Poetry and Music in Medieval France from Jean Renart to Guillaume de Machaut* (Cambridge: Cambridge University Press, 2002).

——, 'Articulating the Author: Gower and the French Vernacular Codex', *The Yearbook of English Studies*, 33, Special Number: *Medieval and Early Modern Miscellanies and Anthologies*, ed. Phillipa Hardman (MHRA, 2003), 80–96.

——, 'The Art of Repetition: Machaut's Ballade 33 "Nes qu'on porroit"', *Close Readings: Essays in Honour of John Stevens and Philip Brett*, ed. Tess Knighton and John Milsom, Special Issue of *Early Music*, 31 (2003), 346–60.

——, '*Confessio amantis* and the French Tradition', in *A Companion to Gower*, ed. Echard, 165–80.

——, 'Le tradizioni della canzone cortese medievale', in *Enciclopedia della musica (The Einaudi Encyclopedia of Music)*, gen. ed. Jean-Jacques Nattiez with Margaret Bent,

Rossana Dalmonte and Mario Baroni, 4 vols, IV: *Storia della musica europea* (Turin: Einaudi, 2004), 130–51; translated as 'Les traditions du chant courtois médiéval', *Musiques: Une encyclopédie pour le XXIème siècle*, gen. ed. Jean-Jacques Nattiez, Histoires des musiques européennes, 4 (Paris: Editions Actes Sud / Cité de Musique, 2006).

——, ed., *Chaucer and the City* (Cambridge: D. S. Brewer, 2006).

——, 'Converting Jeanne d'Arc: *trahison* and *nation* in the Hundred Years War', *NML*, 8 (2006), ed. Rita Copeland, Wendy Scase, and David Lawton (Turnhout: Brepols, 2006), 67–97.

——, 'English, French and Anglo-French: Language and Nation in the Fabliau', Special Issue of *Zeitschrift für deutsche Philologie*: '*Mittelalterliche Novellistik im europaïschen Kontext*', ed. Mark Chinca, Timo Reuvekamp-Felber, and Christopher Young (Berlin: Erich Schmidt, 2006), 238–59.

——, 'The Musical Contexts of *Le Tournoi de Chauvency*', in *Autour du Tournoi de Chauvency*, ed. Mireille Chazan and Nancy Regalado, Publications romanes et françaises (Geneva: Droz, forthcoming).

——, 'Guerre et paix: l'anglais, le français et "l'anglo-français"', *Journée d'études anglo-normande, organisée par l'Académie des Inscriptions et Belles-Lettres, Palais de l'Institut, 20 juin 2008*: *Actes*, ed. André Crépin and Jean Leclant, Académie des Inscriptions et Belles-Lettres (Paris: De Boccard, 2009), 7–23.

——, 'Chaucerian Vernaculars', *SAC*, 31 (2009), forthcoming.

Calin, William, *A Poet at the Fountain: Essays on the Narrative Verse of Guillaume de Machaut* (Lexington: University Press of Kentucky, 1974).

——, *The French Tradition and the Literature of Medieval England* (Toronto: University of Toronto Press, 1994).

——, 'Deschamp's 'Ballade to Chaucer' Again, or, The Dangers of Intertextual Medieval Comparatism', in Sinnreich-Levi, ed., *Eustache Deschamps, French Courtier-Poet*, 73–8.

Camera, Matteo, *Annali delle due Sicilie*, (Naples, 1860).

Camille, Michael, 'The Dissenting Image: a Postcard from Matthew Paris', in *Criticism and Dissent in the Middle Ages*, ed. Rita Copeland (Cambridge: Cambridge University Press, 1996), 115–50.

Cannon, Christopher, *The Making of Chaucer's English* (Cambridge: Cambridge University Press, 1998).

——, *The Grounds of English Literature* (Oxford: Oxford University Press, 2004).

Carlin, Martha, *Medieval Southwark* (London: Hambledon Press, 1996).

Catto, Jeremy, 'Written English: The Making of the Language 1370–1400', *Past and Present*, 179 (2003), 24–59.

Cayley, E., *Debate and Dialogue: Alain Chartier in his Cultural Context* (Oxford: Oxford University Press, 2006).

Cerquiglini, Bernard, *La naissance du français* (Paris: PUF, 1993).

——, *Le Roman de l'orthographe: au paradis des mots, avant la faute 1150–1694* (Paris: Hatier, 1996).

——, ed., *Les Langues de France* (Paris: PUF, 2003).

Cerquiglini, Jacqueline, 'Le lyrisme en mouvement', *Perspectives médiévales*, 6 (1980), 75–86.

——, *'Un Engin si Soutil': Guillaume de Machaut et l'écriture au XIVe siècle* (Paris: Champion, 1985).

Cerquiglini-Toulet, *The Colour of Melancholy: The Use of Books in the Fourteenth Century*, trans. Lydia G. Cochrane (Baltimore and London: Johns Hopkins University Press, 1997).

——, 'Démembrement et dévoration: une structure de l'imaginaire poétique de Jean Froissart', in Bombarde, ed., *Froissart dans sa forge*, 91–103.

Chakrabarty, Dipesh, *Provincializing Europe: Postcolonial Thought and Historical Difference* (Princeton: Princeton University Press, 2000).

Chalon, L., 'La scène des bourgeois de Calais chez Froissart et Jean le Bel', *Cahiers d'analyse textuelle*, 10 (1968), 68–84.

Chambers, R. W., *On the Continuity of English Prose from Alfred to More and His School* (London: EETS, 1932).

Chaplais, Pierre, *English Diplomatic Practice in the Middle Ages* (London and New York: Hambledon and London, 2003).

Chaurand, Jacques, ed., *Nouvelle Histoire de la Langue Française* (Paris: Editions du Seuil, 1999).

Chaytor, H. J., *From Script to Print* (Cambridge: Cambridge University Press, 1945).

Clanchy, M. T., *From Memory to Written Record: England 1066–1307*, 2nd edn (Oxford: Blackwell, 1993; 1st edn 1979).

Clark, Alice, 'Machaut reading Machaut: Self-Borrowing and Reinterpretation in Motets 8 and 21', in Clark and Leach, eds, *Citation and authority*, 94–101.

Clark, Cecily, 'The Myth of "the Anglo-Norman scribe"', in *History of Englishes: New Methods and Interpretations in Historical Linguistics*, ed. Mattio Rissanen, Ossi Ihalainen, Terttu Nevalainen, and Irman Taavitsainen (Berlin: Mouton de Bruyter, 1992), 117–29.

Clark, Suzannah and Elizabeth Eva Leach, eds, *Citation and authority in Medieval and Renaissance musical culture: learning from the learned* (Woodbridge: Boydell, 2005).

Clemen, Wolfgang, *Chaucer's Early Poetry*, trans. C. A. M. Sym (London: Methuen, 1963).

Cobby, Anne E., 'Understanding and Misunderstanding in *La Male Honte*', in *France and the British Isles in the Middle Ages and Renaissance: Essays in Memory of Ruth Morgan*, ed. Gillian Jondorf and David N. Dumville (Woodbridge: Boydell, 1991), 155–72.

Cohen, Jeffrey Jerome, ed., *The Postcolonial Middle Ages* (Basingstoke: Macmillan, 2000).

Coldiron, A. E. B., *Canon, Period, and the Poetry of Charles of Orleans: Found in Translation* (Ann Arbor: University of Michigan Press, 2000).

Cole, Andrew, 'Chaucer's English Lesson', *Speculum*, 77 (2002), 1128–1167.

——, 'Heresy and Humanism', in Strohm, ed. *Middle English*, 421–37.

Coleman, Janet, *Medieval Readers and Writers: English Literature in History 1350–1400* (London: Hutchinson, 1981).

Coleman, Joyce, 'Strange Rhyme: Prosody and Nationhood in Robert Mannyng's Story of England', *Speculum*, 78 (2003), 1214–38.

——, 'The Flower, the Leaf, and Philippa of Lancaster', in *The Legend of Good Women: Context and Reception*, ed. Carolyn P. Collette (Woodbridge: D. S. Brewer, 2006), 33–58.

Colley, Linda, *Britons: Forging the Nation 1707–1837* (New Haven and London: Yale University Press, 1992).

'Colloquium: Chancer and the future of Language Study', *SAC*, 24 (2002), 299–354.

'Colloquium: The Afterlife of Origins', *SAC*, 28 (2006), 217–70.

Contamine, Philippe, *War in the Middle Ages*, trans. Michael Jones (Oxford: Blackwell, 1984; repr. Barnes & Noble, 1998; 1st publ. *La Guerre au moyen âge*, 1980).

——, 'Mourir pour la patrie', in Nora, ed., *Lieux de mémoire*, II: *La Nation*, III, 11–43.

——, 'Une biographie de Jeanne d'Arc est-elle encore possible?', in *Images de Jeanne d'Arc, Actes du colloque de Rouen (25, 26, 27 mai 1999)*, ed. Jean Maurice and Daniel Couty (Paris: PUF, 2000), 1–15.

Cooper, Helen, *Shakespeare and the Middle Ages* (Cambridge: Cambridge University Press, 2005).

——, 'London and Southwark Poetic Companies: 'Si tost c'amis' and the Canterbury Tales: Appendix: An Edition and Translation of Renaus de Hoiland, 'Si tost c'amis'', music edn by Helen Deeming, in Butterfield, ed., *Chaucer and the City*, 109–25.

Cooper, Lisa H., 'Urban Utterances: Merchants, Artisans, and the Alphabet in Caxton's Dialogues in French and English', *NML*, 7 (2005), 127–61.

Copeland, Rita, *Rhetoric, Hermeneutics, and Translation in the Middle Ages: Academic Traditions and Vernacular Texts* (Cambridge: Cambridge University Press, 1991).

——, *Pedagogy, Intellectuals, and Dissent in the Later Middle Ages: Lollardy and Ideas of Learning* (Cambridge: Cambridge University Press, 2001).

Cormack, Bradin, *A Power to Do Justice: Jurisdiction, English Literature, and the Rise of Common Law, 1509–1625* (Chicago and London: University of Chicago Press, 2007).

Cotterill, Rowland, 'The Structural Role of France in Shakespeare's First and Second Historical Tetralogies', *Renaissance Studies*, 9.4 (1995), 460–76.

Coulter, Cornelia C., 'The Library of the Angevin Kings at Naples', *Transactions and Proceedings of the American Philological Association*, 75 (1944), 141–55.

Crane, Susan, 'Anglo-Norman cultures in England, 1066–1460', in Wallace, ed., *The Cambridge History of Medieval English Literature*, 35–60.

——, *The Performance of Self: Ritual, Clothing, and Identity During the Hundred Years War* (Philadelphia: University of Pennsylvania Press, 2002).

Crépin, André, 'Chaucer et Deschamps', in *Autour d'Eustache Deschamps*, ed. Buschinger, 37–43.

——, 'Quand les anglais parlaient français', Séance publique annuelle du 26 novembre 2004, *Comptes Rendus de l'Académie des Inscriptions et Belles-Lettres*, 4 (2004), 3–22.

Croenen, Godfried, 'Latin and the Vernaculars in the Charters of the Low Countries: The Case of Brabant', in Goyens and Verbeke, eds, *The Dawn of the Written Vernacular*, 107–25.

——, 'Froissart et ses mécènes: quelques problems biographiques', in Bombarde, ed., *Froissart dans sa forge*, 9–32.

Curry, Anne, *Agincourt: A New History* (Stroud: Tempus, 2005).

——, 'Languages in the Military Profession in the Later Middle Ages', paper presented at *Language Over Time: A Symposium On Anglo-Norman In The Context Of Medieval French Language Use*, Birmingham City University, 19 January 2008.

Cuttler, S. H., *The Law of Treason and Treason Trials in Later Medieval France*, (Cambridge: Cambridge University Press, 1981).

Davies, R. R., *The First English Empire: Power and Identities in the British Isles 1093–1343* (Oxford: Oxford University Press, 2000).

Davis, Steven, 'Guillaume de Machaut, Chaucer's *Book of the Duchess*, and the Chaucer Tradition', *Chaucer Review*, 36 (2002), 391–405.

Dean, Ruth, and M. B.M. Boulton, *Anglo-Norman Literature: a guide to texts and manuscripts* (London: ANTS, 1999).

Dees, Anthonij, 'Dialectes et scriptae à l'époque de l'ancien français', *Revue de linguistique romane*, 49 (1985), 87–117.

——, 'Propositions for the Study of Old French and its dialects', in *Historical Dialectology: Regional and Social*, ed. Jacek Fisiak, Trends in Linguistics, Studies and Monographs, 37 (Berlin: Mouton de Gruyter, 1988), 139–48.

——, 'La reconstruction de l'ancien français parlé', in *New Methods in Dialectology*, ed. M. E. H. Schouten and P. T. van Reenen (Dordrecht: Foris, 1989), 125–33.

——, Marcel Dekker, Onno Huber and Karin H. van Reenen-Stein, *Atlas des formes linguistiques des textes littéraires de l'ancien français*, Beiheft zur Zeitschrift für romanische Philologie, 212 (Tübingen: Niemeyer, 1987).

De Grazia, Margreta, 'The Modern Divide: From Either Side', in J. Summit and D. Wallace, eds, *Re-Thinking Periodization*, Special Issue of *Journal of Medieval and Early Modern Studies*, 37/3 (2007), 453–67.

Delachenal, R., *Histoire de Charles V*, 5 vols (Paris: Picard, 1909–31).

DeMarco, Patricia, 'Inscribing the Body with Meaning: Chivalric Culture and the Norms of Violence in *The Vows of the Heron*', in Baker, ed., *Inscribing the Hundred Years War*, 27–54.

Deprez, E., 'La double trahison de Godefroi d'Harcourt', *Revue Historique*, 99 (September–December 1908), 32–4.

Derrida, Jacques, *La Carte postale: de Socrate à Freud et au-delà* (Paris: Flammarion, 1985); *The Post Card from Socrates to Freud and Beyond*, trans. Alan Bass (Chicago and London: University of Chicago Press, 1987).

——, *Le monolinguisme de l'autre ou la prothèse d'origine* (Paris: Galilée, 1996); *Monolingualism of the Other, or, the Prosthesis of Origin*, trans. Patrick Mensah (Stanford, CA: Stanford University Press, 1998).

Devaux, Jean, 'From the Court of Hainault to the Court of England: The Example of Jean Froissart', in Allmand, ed., *War, Government and Power*, 1–20.

Deviosse, Jean, *Jean le Bon* (Paris: Fayard, 1985).

Dictionnaire du Moyen Français (ATILF / Nancy Université – CNRS), <http://www.atilf.fr/dmf>.

Diller, George T., '"Pour la cause de ce que j'estoie François." Langue(s) et loyauté(s) dans les *Chroniques* de Froissart', *Le Moyen Age*, 104 (1998), 461–71.

Doss-Quinby, Eglal, *Les refrains chez les trouvères du XIIe siècle au début du XIVe* (New York: Peter Lang, 1984).

Dragonetti, Roger, *La Technique poétique des trouvères dans la chanson courtoise* (Geneva: Slatkine, 1979; 1st publ. Bruges, 1960).

Duchet-Suchaux, Gaston, 'Emergence d'un sentiment national chez Eustache Deschamps', in Buschinger, ed., *Autour d'Eustache Deschamps*, 73–77.

Dulac, Liliane, 'La representation de la France: Eustache Deschamps et Christine de Pizan', in Buschinger, ed., *Autour d'Eustache Deschamps*, 79–92.

Dwyer, Richard A., *Boethian Fictions: Narratives in the Medieval French Versions of the Consolatio philosophiae* (Cambridge, Mass: Mediaeval Academy of America, 1976).

——, 'Je meurs de soif auprès de la fontaine', *French Studies*, 23 (1969), 225–8.

Earp, Lawrence, 'Lyrics for Reading and Lyrics for Singing in Late Medieval France: The Development of the Dance Lyric from Adam de la Halle to Guillaume de Machaut', in *The Union of Words and Music*, ed. Rebecca A. Baltzer, Thomas Cable, and James I. Wimsatt, (Austin: University of Texas Press, 1991), 101–31.

Earp, Lawrence, *Guillaume de Machaut: A Guide to Research* (New York and London: Garland, 1995).

Ebert, Prof., Review of E. G. Sandras, *Etude sur Chaucer considéré comme imitateur des trouvères* (Paris: Durand, 1859), trans. John W.Van Rees Hoets, in *Essays on Chaucer*, Part 1, The Chaucer Society (London: Trübner, 1868).

Echard, Siân, 'Gower's 'bokes of Latin': Language, Politics, and Poetry', *SAC*, 25 (2003), 123–56.

——, ed., *Companion to Gower* (Cambridge: D. S. Brewer, 2004).

——, 'Gower in Print' in Echard, ed., *Companion to Gower*, 115–35.

Elliott, Emory, ed., *Columbia Literary History of the United States* (New York and Guildford: Columbia University Press, 1988).

Ellis, Roger and Ruth Evans, eds, *The Medieval Translator* (Exeter: University of Exeter Press, 1994).

Evans, Ruth, 'Translating Past Cultures?', in Ellis and Evans, eds, *The Medieval Translator*, 20–45.

——, 'The Afterword of Origins: A Response', *SAC*, 28 (2006), 263–70.

Everist, M., 'Motets, French Tenors, and the Polyphonic Chanson ca.1300', *The Journal of Musicology*, 24 (2007), 365–406.

Ewert, Alfred, *The French Language* (London: Faber and Faber, 1933).

Faraglia, N. F., 'Notizie di molti libri scrittori alluminatori ecc. della Biblioteca del re Roberto', *Archivio storico italiano*, 5th series, 3 (1889), 357–59.

Farber, Lianna, *An Anatomy of Trade in Medieval Writing: Value, Consent, and Community* (Ithaca and London: Cornell University Press, 2006).

Favier, Jean, *La Guerre de Cent Ans* (Paris: Fayard, 1980).

Fein, Susanna, ed., *Studies in the Harley Manuscript: The Scribes, Contents, and Social Contexts of British Library MS Harley 2253* (Kalamazoo: Western Michigan University, Medieval Institute Publications, 2000).

Ferguson, Margaret W., *Dido's Daughters: Literacy, Gender and Empire in Early Modern England and France* (Chicago and London: University of Chicago Press, 2003).

Figg, Kristen Mossler, *The Short Lyric Poems of Jean Froissart: Fixed Forms and the Expression of the Courtly Ideal* (New York and London: Garland, 1994).

Fisher, John H., *John Gower: Moral Philosopher and Friend of Chaucer* (London: Methuen, 1965).

——, 'Chancery and the Emergence of Standard Written English in the Fifteenth Century', *Speculum*, 52 (1977), 870–99.

——, 'A Language Policy for Lancastrian England', *PMLA*, 107 (1992), 1168–80.

Fisher, Ruth M., 'Cosyn and Cosynage: Complicated Punning in Chaucer's 'Shipman's Tale'', *Notes and Queries*, 210 (1965), 168–70.

Fleischman, Suzanne, 'Methodologies and Ideologies in Historical Grammar: a Case Study from Old French', in *Medievalism and the Modern Temper*, ed. R. Howard Bloch and Stephen G. Nichols (Baltimore and London: John Hopkins University Press, 1996), 402–38.

Fleming, Juliet, 'Dictionary English and the Female Tongue', in *Enclosure Acts: Sexuality, Property, and Culture in Early Modern England*, ed. Richard Burt and John Michael Archer (Ithaca and London: Cornell University Press, 1994), 290–325.

Forde, Simon, Lesley Johnson and Alan V. Murray, eds, *Concepts of National Identity in the Middle Ages* (Leeds: School of English, University of Leeds, 1995).

Fraioli, Deborah A., *Joan of Arc: The Early Debate* (Woodbridge: Boydell, 2000).

François, Alexis, *Histoire de la langue française cultivée des origines à nos jours*, 3 vols (Geneva: Jullien, 1959).

Franklin, A., *Les rues et les cris de Paris au XIIIe siècle* (Paris: L. Willem, P. Daffis, 1874).

Franzten, Allen J., *Desire for Origins: New Language, Old English, and Teaching the Tradition* (New Brunswick and London: Rutgers University Press, 1990).

Freeman, M. A., *The Poetics of 'Translatio Studii' and 'Conjointure': Chrétien de Troyes's 'Cligés'* (Lexington, KY: French Forum, 1979).

Galbraith, V. H., 'Nationality and Language in Medieval England', *Transactions of the Royal Historical Society*, 23 (1941), 113–28.

Galloway, Andrew, 'Latin England', in Lavezzo, ed., *Imagining a Medieval English Nation*, 41–95.

Geary, Patrick J., *The Myth of Nations: The Medieval Origins of Europe* (Princeton: Princeton University Press, 2002).

Gellner, Ernest, *Nation and Nationalism* (Oxford: Blackwell, 1983).

——, *Encounters with Nationalism* (Oxford: Blackwell, 1994).

Georgianna, Linda, 'Periodization and Politics: The Case of the Missing Twelfth Century in English Literary History', *MLQ*, 64 (2003), 153–68.

Gilbert, Jane, 'Men Behaving Badly: Linguistic Purity and Sexual Perversity in Derrida's *Le Monolinguisme de l'autre* and Gower's *Traitié pour essampler les amantz marietz*', *Romance Studies*, 24 (2006), 77–89.

Gillespie, Vincent, 'Vernacular Theology', in Strohm, ed., *Middle English*, 401–20.

Gillingham, John, *The English in the Twelfth Century: Imperialism, National Identity and Political Values* (Woodbridge: Boydell, 2000).

Godefroy, Frédéric, *Dictionnaire de l'ancienne langue française, et de tous ses dialectes du IXe au XVe siècle*, 10 vols (Paris: F. Vieweg, 1881–1902 [1826–1897]).

Goodman, Anthony, *John of Gaunt: The Exercise of Princely Power in Fourteenth-century Europe* (Harlow: Longman, 1992).

Goodrich, Peter, 'Literacy and the Languages of the Early Common Law', *Journal of Law and Society*, 14 (1987), 422–44.

Goyens, Michèle, and Werner Verbeke, eds, *The Dawn of the Written Vernacular in Western Europe* (Leuven: Leuven University Press, 2003).

Gransden, Antonia, *Historical Writing in England II c.1307 to the Early Sixteenth Century* (London: Routledge & Kegan Paul, 1982).

Green, Dennis, *Medieval Listening and Reading: The Primary Reception of German Literature 800–1300* (Cambridge: Cambridge University Press, 1994).

Green, Richard Firth, *A Crisis of Truth: Literature and Law in Ricardian England* (Philadelphia: University of Pennsylvania Press, 1999).

——, 'Palamon's Appeal of Treason in the *Knight's Tale*', in Steiner and Barrington, eds, *The Letter of the Law*, 105–14.

Greenfield, Liah, *Nationalism: Five Roads to Modernity* (Cambridge, MA and London: Harvard University Press, 1992).

Gros, Gérard, *Le Poète, la Vierge et le prince du Puy. Etude sur les Puys marials de la France du Nord du XIVe siècle à la Renaissance* (Paris: Klincksieck, 1992).

Grossel, Marie-Geneviève, 'Trouvères du Hainaut', in *Image et Mémoire de Hainaut Médiéval*, ed. Jean-Charles Herbin (Valenciennes: Presses Universitaires de Valenciennes, 2004), 85–98.

Guenée, Bernard, *L'Occident aux XIVe et XVe siècles: Les Etats* (Paris: PUF, 1971).

——, 'Les Tendences actuelles de l'histoire politique du moyen âge français', *Actes du 100e Congrès National des Sociétés Savantes, Paris, 1975*, 2 vols (Paris: Bibliothèque nationale, 1977), I, 45–70.

——, 'Des limites féodales aux frontières politiques', in Nora, ed., *Les Lieux de mémoire*, II: *La Nation*, ii, 'Le Territoire', 11–33.

——, *Un roi et son historien: Vingt études sur le règne de Charles VI et la Chronique du Religieux de Saint-Denis*, Mémoires de l'Académie des Inscription et Belles-Lettres, nouvelle séries, vol.18 (Paris: Boccard, 1999).

Haas, Renate, '*Femina*: Female Roots of "Foreign" Language Teaching and the Rise of Mother-Tongue Ideologies', *Exemplaria*, 19 (2007), 139–62.

Hahn, Thomas, 'Money, Sexuality, Wordplay, and Context in the *Shipman's Tale*', in *Chaucer in the Eighties*, ed. Julian N. Wasserman and Robert J. Blanch (Syracuse, NY: Syracuse University Press, 1986), 235–49.

Haines, John, *Eight Centuries of Troubadours and Trouvères: The Changing Identity of Medieval Music* (Cambridge: Cambridge University Press, 2004).

Hanawalt, Barbara A., and Michal Kobialka, eds., *Medieval Practices of Space* (Minneapolis: University of Minnesota, 2000).

Hanly, Michael, 'Courtiers and Poets: An International Network of Literary Exchange in Late Fourteenth-Century Italy, France, and England', *Viator*, 28 (1997), 305–32.

Hanna III, Ralph, 'Presenting Chaucer as Author', *Medieval Literature: Texts and Interpretation*, ed. Tim W. Machan (Binghamton: Medieval & Renaissance Texts & Studies, 1991), 17–39.

——, 'Chaucer and the Future of Language Study', *SAC*, 24 (2002), 309–15.

——, *London Literature: 1300–1380* (Cambridge: Cambridge University Press, 2005).

Harding, Vanessa, 'Cross-Channel Trade and Cultural Contacts: London and the Low Countries in the Later Fourteenth Century', in Barron and Saul, eds, *England and the Low Countries*, 153–68.

Hardy, B. C., *Philippa of Hainault and her Times* (London: Long, 1910).

Harriss, Gerald, *Shaping the Nation: England 1360–1461* (Oxford: Clarendon Press, 2005).

Hassell, James W., *Middle French Proverbs, Sentences and Proverbial Phrases* (Toronto: Pontifical Institute of Mediaeval Studies, 1982).

Hastings, Adrian, *The Construction of Nationhood: Ethnicity, Religion and Nationalism* (Cambridge: Cambridge University Press, 1997).

Hellinga, Lotte and J. B. Trapp, eds., *The Cambridge History of the Book in Britain: Vol.3: 1400–1557* (Cambridge: Cambridge University Press, 1999).

Herbin, Jean-Charles, ed., *Richesses médiévales du Nord et du Hainaut* (Valenciennes: Presses universitaires de Valenciennes, 2002).

Herman, József, *Vulgar Latin*, trans. Roger Wright (1st publ. as *Le Latin Vulgaire*, 1967; rev. edn, 1997; trans. University Park: Pennsylvania State University Press, 2000).

Hobsbawm, Eric, 'Introduction: Inventing Traditions', in *The Invention of Tradition*, ed. Eric Hobsbawm and Terence Ranger (Cambridge: Cambridge University Press, 1983), 1–14.

——, Nations and Nationalism Since 1780 (Cambridge: Cambridge University Press, 1990).

——, *The Age of Extremes: The Short Twentieth Century, 1914–1991* (London: Michael Joseph, 1994).

Hollier, Denis, ed., *A New History of French Literature* (Cambridge, MA, and London: Harvard University Press, 1989).

Horobin, Simon, 'A New Fragment of the Romaunt of the Rose', *SAC*, 28 (2006), 205–15.

——, and Linne Mooney, 'A *Piers Plowman* Manuscript by the Hengwrt/Ellesmere Scribe and its Implications for London Standard English', *SAC*, 26 (2004), 65–112.

Howard, Jean E., and Paul Strohm, 'The Imaginary 'Commons'', *JMEMS*, 37 (2007), 549–77.

Howlett, David, *The English Origins of Old French Literature* (Dublin: Four Courts, 1996).

Hsy, Jonathan, 'Polyglot Poetics: Merchants and Literary Production in London, 1300–1500' (unpublished doctoral dissertation, University of Pennsylvania, 2007).

Hudson, Anne, *The Premature Reformation: Wycliffite Texts and Lollard History* (Oxford: Clarendon Press, 1998).

Hunt, Tony, 'Insular trilingual compilations', in *Codices Miscellaneaum, Brussels Van Hulthem Colloquium 1999*, ed. R. Jansen-Sieben and H. Van Dijk, Archives et Bibliothèques de Belgique (Brussels: Archives et Bibliothèques de Belgique, 1999), 51–67.

——, 'Bibbesworth, Walter of (b. in or before 1219, d. in or after 1270)', *Oxford Dictionary of National Biography*, Oxford University Press, Sept 2004; online edn, Oct 2005, <http://0www.oxforddnb.com.catalogue.ulrls.lon.ac.uk:80/view/article/2340>, accessed 6 December 2008.

Huot, Sylvia, *From Song to Book: The Poetics of Writing in Old French Lyric and Lyrical Narrative Poetry* (Ithaca and London: Cornell University Press, 1987).

Ingham, Richard, 'Syntactic Change in Anglo-Norman and Continental French Chronicles: Was There a 'Middle' Anglo-Norman?', *French Language Studies*, 16 (2006), 25–49.

James, M. R., *A Descriptive Catalogue of the Manuscripts in the library of Trinity Hall, Cambridge* (Cambridge: Cambridge University Press, 1907).

Janson, Tore, 'Language Change and Metalinguistic Change: Latin to Romance and Other Cases', in *Latin and the Romance Languages*, ed. Wright, 19–28.

Jones, Michael, '"Gardez mon corps, sauvez ma terre"—Immunity from War and the Lands of a Captive Knight: The Siege of Orléans (1428–29) Revisited', in Arn, ed., *Charles d'Orléans in England*, 9–26.

——, ed., *The New Cambridge Medieval History, VI c.1300–c.1415* (Cambridge: Cambridge University Press, 2000).

——, and Malcolm Vale, eds., *England and her Neighbours 1066–1453: Essays in Honour of Pierre Chaplais* (London: Hambledon, 1989).

Jones, Richard, *The Triumph of the English Language* (London: Oxford University Press, 1953).

Joseph, G., 'Chaucer's Coinage: Foreign Exchange and the Puns of The Shipman's Tale', *Chaucer Review*, 17 (1983), 341–57.

Justice, Steven, *Writing and Rebellion: England in 1381* (Berkeley: University of California Press, 1994).

Kabir, A. Jahanara and Deanne Williams, *Postcolonial Approaches to the European Middle Ages: Translating Cultures* (Cambridge: Cambridge University Press, 2005), 205–26.

Karlin, Daniel, *Proust's English* (Oxford: Oxford University Press, 2005).

Kean, P. M., *Chaucer and the Making of English Poetry*, 2 vols (London: Routledge & Kegan Paul, 1972).

Kedourie, Elie, ed., *Nationalism* (London: Hutchinson, 1960).

Keen, Maurice, 'Brotherhood in Arms', *History*, 47 (1962), 1–17.

Kelly, Douglas, '*Translatio Studii*: Translation, Adaptation, and Allegory in Medieval French Literature', *Philological Quarterly*, 57 (1978), 287–310.

Kelly, Henry Ansgar, *Chaucer and the Cult of Saint Valentine* (Leiden: Brill, 1986).

——, 'The Right to Remain Silent: Before and After Joan of Arc', *Speculum*, 68 (1993), 992–1026.

Kelly, Henry Ansgar, 'Joan of Arc's Last Trial: The Attack of the Devil's Advocates', in *Fresh Verdicts on Joan of Arc*, ed. Bonnie Wheeler and Charles T. Wood (New York: Garland, 1996), 205–36.

Kendall, Elliot, 'The Great Household in the City: the *Shipman's Tale'* in Butterfield, ed., *Chaucer and the City*, 145–61.

Ker, N. R., *English Manuscripts in the Century after the Norman Conquest* (Oxford: Clarendon Press, 1960).

Keymeulen, Jacques Van, 'Geographical Differentiation in the Dutch Language Area during the Middle Ages', in Goyens and Verbeke, eds, *The Dawn of the Written Vernacular*, 391–404.

Kibbee, Douglas A., *For to Speke Frenche Trewely: The French Language in England, 1000–1600: Its Status, Description and Instruction* (Amsterdam and Philadelphia: John Benjamins, 1991).

Kinoshita, Sharon, *Medieval Boundaries: Rethinking Difference in Old French Literature* (Philadelphia: University of Pennsylvania Press, 2006).

Kosta-Théfaine, Jean-François, ed., *Othon de Grandson, chevalier et poète: Etudes*, Medievalia, 63 (Orléans: Paradigme, 2007).

Kristol, A. M., 'L'enseignement du français en Angleterre (XIIIe-XVe siècles): Les sources manuscrites', *Romania*, 111 (1990), 289–330.

——, 'La prononciation du français en Angleterre au XVe siècle' in *Mélanges de philologie et de littérature médiévales offerts à Michel Burger*, ed. J. Cerquiglini-Toulet and Olivier Collet (Geneva: Droz, 1994), 67–87.

Krynen, J., *Idéal du prince et pouvoir royal en France à la fin du Moyen Âge (1380–1440)* (Paris: Picard, 1981).

Lacy, Norris J., 'Warmongering in Verse: *Les Voeux du Héron*', in Baker, ed., *Inscribing the Hundred Years War*, 17–26.

Laidlaw, James, 'L'Innovation métrique chez Deschamps', in Buschinger, ed., *Autour d'Eustache Deschamps*, 127–40.

Lalou, Elisabeth, 'Les textes en jargon franco-anglais du XIIe au XIVe siècle' in *La "France Anglaise" au moyen âge: Actes du 111e Congrès national des sociétés savantes (Poitiers, 1986)* (Paris: Comité des Travaux Historiques et Scientifiques, 1988), 543–62.

Lambley, Kathleen, *The Teaching and Cultivation of the French Language in England During Tudor and Stuart Times* (Manchester: Manchester University Press/ London: Longmans, 1920).

Lassabatère, Thierry, 'La Cité des Hommes. La vision politique d'Eustache Deschamps' (unpublished doctoral dissertation, Paris IV—Sorbonne, 2002).

Latham, R. E., *Revised Medieval Latin Word-List from British and Irish Sources* (London: Oxford University Press, 1965).

Latré, Guido, 'But What Does the Fleming Say?: The Two Flemish Proverbs and their Contexts in Chaucer's Canterbury Tales', *Leeds Studies in English*, 32 (2001), 255–73.

Laurie, Ian S., 'Eustache Deschamps: 1340?–1404', in Sinnreich-Levi, ed., *Eustache Deschamps, French Courtier-Poet*, 1–72.

Lavezzo, Kathy, ed., *Imagining a Medieval English Nation* (Minneapolis: University of Minnesota Press, 2004).

——, *Angels on the Edge of the World* (Ithaca and London: Cornell University Press, 2006).

Lavisse, Ernest, *Histoire de France*, 9 vols (Paris: Hachette, 1900–1911).

Lawton, David, 'Dullness and the Fifteenth Century', *English Literary History*, 54 (1987), 761–99.

Le Nouveau Littré: Le dictionaire de référence de la langue française, gen. ed. Clande Blum (Paris: Garnier, 2005).

Le Saux, Françoise H. M., ed., *A Companion to Wace* (Cambridge: D. S. Brewer, 2005).

Leach, Elizabeth Eva, 'Fortune's Demesne: The Interrelation of Text and Music in Machaut's *Il Mest Avis* (B22), *De Fortune* (B23) and Two Related Anonymous Balades', *EMH*, 19 (2000), 47–79.

——, 'Learning French by Singing in 14th-century England', *Early Music*, 33 (2005), 253–270.

——, *Sung Birds: Music, Nature and Poetry in the Later Middle Ages* (Ithaca: Cornell University Press, 2007).

Leech-Wilkinson, Daniel, '*Le Voir Dit*: A Reconstruction and a Guide for Musicians', *Plainsong and Medieval Music*, 2 (1993), 103–40.

Lees, Claire, 'Analytical Survey 7: Actually Existing Anglo-Saxon Studies', *NML*, 7 (2005), 223–52.

Legge, M. Dominica, *Anglo-Norman in the Cloisters* (Edinburgh: Edinburgh University Press, 1950).

——, *Anglo-Norman Literature and its Background* (Oxford: Clarendon Press, 1963).

Lehoux, Françoise, *Jean de France, Duc de Berri: Sa Vie, son action politique (1340–1416)* (Paris: Picard, 1968).

Lerer, Seth, *Chaucer and His Readers* (Princeton: Princeton University Press, 1993).

——, ed., *The Yale Companion to Chaucer* (New Haven and London: Yale University Press, 2006).

Lettenhove, Kervyn de, *Histoire de Flandre*, 6 vols, III, *époque communale 1304–1384 depuis le traité d'Athies jusqu'à la bataille de Roosebeke* (Brussels: Vandale, 1847).

——, 'Notes sur quelques manuscrits des bibliothèques d'Angleterre, part 1', *Extraits des Bulletins de l'Académie royale de Belgique*, 2nd series, No.12, Vol. 20 (1868), 3–22.

Lewis, C. S., *De descriptione temporum* (Cambridge: Cambridge University Press, 1955).

Lindenbaum, Sheila, 'London Texts and Literate Practice', in Wallace, ed., *Cambridge History*, 284–309.

Littré, Emile, *Dictionnaire de la langue française*, 7 vols (Paris: J. J. Pauvert, 1956–58).

Lloyd, T. H., *Alien Merchants in England in the High Middle Ages* (Brighton: Harvester, 1982).

Lodge, R. Anthony, *A Sociolinguistic History of Parisian French* (Cambridge and New York: Cambridge University Press, 2004).

——, 'The Sources of Standardisation in Medieval French: Written or Spoken?' paper presented at *Language Over Time: A Symposium On Anglo-Norman In The Context Of Medieval French Language Use*, Birmingham City University, 19 January 2008.

Loomis, Louise R., 'Nationality at the Council of Constance: An Anglo-French Dispute', *The American Historical Review*, 44/3 (1939), 508–27.

Loomis, Roger Sherman, 'Edward I, Arthurian Enthusiast', *Speculum*, 28 (1953), 114–27.

Lot, Ferdinand, 'A quelle époque a-t-on cessé de parler latin?', *Archivum latinitas medii aevi*, 6 (1931), 97–159.

Lusignan, Serge, *La langue des rois au Moyen âge: le français en France et en Angleterre* (Paris: PUF, 2004).

——, *Parler vulgairement: Les Intellectuels et la langue française aux XIIIe et XIVe siècles* (Paris; Montréal: Vrin; Les Presses de l'Université de Montréal, 1986).

Lusignan, Serge, 'Langue française et société du XIIIe au XIVe siècle', in Chaurand, ed., *Nouvelle Histoire de la Langue Française*, 93–143.

——, 'Les Langues vernaculaires écrites dans le domaine roman', in Goyens and Verbeke, eds, *The Dawn of the Written Vernacular in Western Europe*, 469–72.

——, 'Parler français: les enjeux linguistiques des négociations entre Français et Anglais à la fin du Moyen Âge', in *Zwischen Babel und Pfingsten: Sprachdifferenzen und Gesprächsverständigung in der Vormoderne*, ed. Peter von Moss (forthcoming).

—— and Stéphanie Brazeau, 'Étude diachronique d'un exemple de la graphie picarde: les chirographes de l'échevinage de Douai (1223–1500)', paper presented at *Language Across Time: A Symposium on Anglo-Norman in the Context of Medieval French Language Use*, Birmingham City University, 19 January 2008.

Lynch, Kathryn, 'Dating Chaucer', *Chaucer Review*, 42 (2007), 1–22.

McDonald, Nicola, 'Doubts about Medea, Briseyda and Helen: Interpreting Classical Allusion in the Fourteenth-Century French Ballade *Medee fu en amer veritable*', in *Studies in English Language and Literature: 'Doubt wisely' Papers in Honour of E. G. Stanley*, ed. M. J. Toswell and E. M. Tyler (London and New York: Routledge, 1996), 252–66.

McFarlane, K. B., *Lancastrian Kings and Lollard Knights* (Oxford: Clarendon Press, 1972).

McHardy, A. K., 'The Alien Priories and the Expulsion of Aliens from England in 1378', *Studies in Church History*, 12 (1975), 133–41 [=*Church, Society and Politics*, ed. Derek Baker, published for The Ecclesiastical History Society (Oxford: Blackwell, 1975)].

McIntosh, Angus, Michael Samuels, and Michael Benskin, eds, *A Linguistic Atlas of Late Mediaeval English*, 4 vols (Aberdeen: University Press of Aberdeen, 1986).

McKitterick, Rosamond, 'Latin and Romance: An Historian's Perspective', in Wright, ed., *Latin and the Romance Languages*, 130–45.

Machan, Tim W., *Techniques of Translation: Chaucer's Boece* (Norman, OK: Pilgrim Books, 1985).

——, *English in the Middle Ages* (Oxford: Oxford University Press, 2003).

McNeill, William H., *Polyethnicity and National Unity in World History, The Donald G. Creighton Lectures, 1985* (Toronto: University of Toronto Press, 1986).

Marchello-Nizia, Christiane, 'L'Historien et son prologue: forme littéraire et stratégies discursives', in *La Chronique et l'histoire au moyen âge: colloque des 24 et 25 mai, 1982*, ed. Daniel Poirion, Cultures et civilisations médiévales II (Paris: Presses de l'Université de Paris-Sorbonne, no date given), 13–25.

Marcus, Leah, *Puzzling Shakespeare: Local Reading and its Discontents* (Berkeley: University of California Press, 1988).

Margherita, Gayle, *The Romance Origins: Language and Sexual Difference in Middle English Literature* (Philadelphia: University of Pennsylvania Press, 1994).

Matthews, David, *The Making of Middle English, 1765–1910* (Minneapolis: University of Minnesota Press, 1999).

Matzke, John E., 'Some Examples of French as Spoken by Englishmen in Old French Literature', in *Modern Philology*, 3 (1905–06), 47–60.

Meale, Carol M., 'Patrons, Buyers and Owners: Book Production and Social Status', in *Book Production and Publishing in Britain 1375–1475*, ed. Jeremy Griffiths and Derek Pearsall (Cambridge: Cambridge University Press, 1989), 201–38.

Merrilees, Brian, 'Donatus and the Teaching of French in Medieval England', in *Anglo-Norman Anniversary Essays*, ed. Ian Short, ANTS Occasional pubns, 2 (London: ANTS, 1993), 273–91.

——, 'John Gower's French Vocabulary', paper presented at 'Gower and the hypertext', Senate House, University of London, 28–30 July 2003.

Middleton, Anne, 'The Idea of Public Poetry in the Reign of Richard II', *Speculum*, 53 (1978), 94–114.

Minnis, Alastair, 'A Note on Chaucer and the *Ovide Moralisée*', *Medium Aevum*, 48 (1979), 254–57.

Moeglin, Jean-Marie, *Les Bourgeois de Calais: Essai sur un mythe historique* (Paris: Albin Michel, 2002).

Moran, Jo Ann Hoeppner, *The Growth of English Schooling, 1340–1548: Learning Literacy and Laicization in Pre-Reformation York Diocese* (Princeton: Princeton University Press, 1985).

Mühlethaler, Jean-Claude, ed., *Charles d'Orléans: Ballades et Rondeaux: édition du manuscrit 25458 du fonds français de la Bibliothèque Nationale de Paris*, 2nd edn (Paris: Livre du Poche, 1992).

Muscatine, Charles, *Chaucer and the French Tradition: A Study in Style and Meaning* (Berkeley: University of California Press, 1957).

Newton, Stella Mary, *Fashion in the Age of the Black Prince: A Study of the Years 1340–1365* (Woodbridge: Boydell, 1999; 1st publ. 1980).

Nicholas, David, *The Van Arteveldes of Ghent: The Varieties of Vendetta and the Hero in History* (Ithaca: Cornell University Press, 1988).

——, *Medieval Flanders* (London: Longman, 1992).

——, *The Later Medieval City, 1300–1500* (London and New York: Longman, 1997).

Nicolas, Sir Nicholas Harris, *History of the Orders of Knighthood of the British Empire* (London: John Hunter, 1842).

Nijsten, Gerard, *In the Shadow of Burgundy: The Court of Guelders in the Late Middle Ages* (Cambridge: Cambridge University Press, 2004).

Nolan, Barbara, 'Anthologizing Ribaldry: Five Anglo-Norman Fabliaux', in Fein, ed., *Studies in the Harley Manuscript*, 289–327.

——, 'Usage' in *Troilus and Criseyde*: A Literary Lineage' (unpublished paper).

Nora, Pierre, 'Le retour de l'événement', *Faire de l'histoire*, I (1974), 210–230.

——, ed., *Les Lieux de mémoire*, 7 vols (Paris: Gallimard, 1984–92).

Norberg, Dag, 'A quelle époque a-t-on cessé de parler latin en Gaule?', *Annales*, 21 (1966), 346–56.

Nykrog, Per, *Les fabliaux* (Geneva: Droz, 1973).

Olson, Glending, 'Making and Poetry in the Age of Chaucer', *Comparative Literature*, 31 (1979), 272–90.

——, 'Geoffrey Chaucer' in Wallace, ed., *Cambridge History*, 566–88.

Orme, Nicholas, *Medieval Schools from Roman Britain to Renaissance England* (New Haven, Conn.: Yale University Press, 2006).

Ormrod, W. M., 'The Use of English: Language, Law, and Political Culture in Fourteenth-Century England', *Speculum*, 78 (2003), 750–87.

Page, Christopher, *Voices and Instruments of the Middle Ages* (London: Dent, 1987).

——, 'Court and City in France, 1100–1300', in *Antiquity and the Middle Ages from Ancient Greece to the 15th century*, ed. James McKinnon (Basingstoke and London: Macmillan, 1990), 197–217.

Painter, George D., *William Caxton: A Quincentenary Biography of England's First Printer* (London: Chatto & Windus, 1976).

Palliser, D., ed., *The Cambridge Urban History of Britain*, vol. 1: *600–1540* (Cambridge: Cambridge University Press, 2000).

Palmer, J. J. N., ed., *Froissart: Historian* (Woodbridge: Boydell, 1981).

——, 'Book I (1323–78) and Its Sources', in Palmer, ed., *Froissart: Historian*, 7–24.

Patterson, Lee, *Chaucer and the Subject of History* (London: Routledge, 1991).

Pearcy, Roy J., 'Punning on 'cosyn' and 'cosynage' in Chaucer's *Shipman's Tale*', *American Notes and Queries*, 17 (1979), 70–1.

——, 'Anglo-Norman Fabliaux and Chaucer's Merchant's Tale', *Medium Aevum*, 69 (2000), 227–60.

Pearsall, Derek, *The Life of Geoffrey Chaucer: A Critical Biography* (Oxford: Blackwell, 1992).

——, 'Strangers in Fourteenth-Century London', in Akehurst and D'Elden, eds, *The Stranger in Medieval Society*, 46–62.

Pearsall, Derek, 'Chaucer and Englishness', *Proceedings of the British Academy*, 101 (1999 for 1998), 77–99.

——, 'The Idea of Englishness in the Fifteenth Century', in *Nation, Court and Culture: New Essays on Fifteenth-Century English Poetry*, ed. Helen Cooney (Dublin: Four Courts Press, 2001), 15–27.

Pernoud, Régine, *Joan of Arc* (Harmondsworth: Penguin, 1964).

Petit, Ernest, *Séjour du Jean II (1350–1356)* (Paris: Imprimerie Nationale, 1896).

Pettegree, Andrew, 'Centre and Periphery in the European Book World', *Transactions of the Royal Historical Society*, 18 (2008), 101–28.

Phillips, Helen, '*The Complaint of Venus*: Chaucer and de Graunson', in Ellis and Evans, eds, *The Medieval Translator*, 86–103.

Piaget, Arthur, 'La Cour amoureuse dite de Charles VI', *Romania*, 20 (1891), 417–54.

Plumley, Yolanda, 'Citation and Allusion in the late *Ars nova*: The Case of *Esperance* and the *En attendant* songs', *EMH*, 18 (1999), 287–363.

——, 'Intertextuality in the Fourteenth-Century Chanson', *Music and Letters*, 84 (2003), 355–77.

——, 'Playing the Citation Game in the Late-Fourteenth Century', *Early Music*, 31 (2003), 20–39.

——, 'Crossing Borderlines: Points of Contact between the Late-Fourteenth Century Song and Lyric Repertories', *Acta Musicologica*, 76 (2004), 201–21.

Pognon, E., 'Ballades mythologiques de Jean de le Mote, Philippe de Vitry, Jean Campion', *Humanisme et Renaissance*, 5 (1938), 385–417.

Poirion, Daniel, *Le Poète et le prince* (Paris, 1965; repr. Geneva: Slatkine, 1978).

Pope, M. K., *From Latin to modern French with especial consideration of Anglo-Norman phonology and morphology* (Manchester: Manchester University Press, 1934).

Posner, Rebecca, *The Romance Languages* (Cambridge: Cambridge University Press, 1996).

'Les premiers assises nationales des langues de France', Dossier, Ministère de la culture et communication, No.109, September 2003. <http://www.culture.gouv.fr/, 'Publications'>/

Previté-Orton, Charles W., *The Shorter Cambridge Medieval History*, 2 vols (Cambridge: Cambridge University Press, 1952).

Rashdall, H., *The Universities of Europe in the Middle Ages*, rev and ed. F. M. Powicke and A. B. Emden, 3 vols (Oxford: Oxford University Press, 1936).

Reaney, Gilbert, 'Guillaume de Machaut: Lyric Poet', *Music and Letters*, 39 (1958), 38–51.

Reicher, Stephen and Nick Hopkins, *Self and Nation: Categorization, Contestation and Mobilization* (London: Sage, 2001).

Reynolds, Susan, *Kingdoms and Communities in Western Europe 900–1300*, 2nd edn (Oxford: Oxford University Press, 1997).

Ribard, Jacques, *Un Ménestrel du XIVe siècle: Jean de Condé* (Geneva: Droz, 1969).

Richards, Earl Jeffrey, 'The Uncertainty in Defining France as a Nation in the Works of Eustache Deschamps', in Baker, ed., *Inscribing the Hundred Years' War*, 159–75.

Richardson, H. G., 'An Oxford Teacher of the Fifteenth Century', in *Bulletin of the John Rylands Library*, 23 (1939), 436–57.

——, 'Business training in Medieval Oxford', *The American Historical Review*, 46 (1941), 259–79.

——, 'Cistercian Formularies', in *Formularies which Bear on the History of Oxford c.1204–1420*, ed. H. E. Salter, et al., 2 vols (Oxford: Clarendon Press, 1942), II, 281–327.

——, 'Letters of the Oxford Dictatores', in *Oxford History Society*, New Series, 5 (1942), 360–416.

Richardson, Malcolm, 'Henry V, the English Chancery, and Chancery English', *Speculum*, 55 (1980), 726–50.

Rickard, Peter, 'Anglois coué and l'Anglois qui couve', *French Studies*, 7 (1953), 48–55.

——, *Britain in Medieval French Literature 1100–1500* (Cambridge: Cambridge University Press, 1956).

Rigg, A. G. and Edward S. Moore, 'The Latin Works: Politics, Lament, Praise', in Echard, ed., *Companion to Gower*, 153–64.

Robertson, Kellie, 'Common Language and Common Profit', in Cohen, ed., *The Postcolonial Middle Ages*, 209–28.

Rosser, Gervase, *Medieval Westminster: 1200–1540* (Oxford: Clarendon Press, 1989).

Rothwell, William, 'Of Kings and Queens, or Nets and Frogs: Anglo-French Homonymics', *French Studies*, 48 (1994), 257–73.

——, 'The Trilingual England of Geoffrey Chaucer', *SAC*, 16 (1994), 45–67.

——, 'The Place of Femina in Anglo-Norman Studies', *Studia Neophilologica*, 70 (1998), 55–82.

——, 'Anglo-French and Middle English Vocabulary in *Femina Nova*', *Medium Aevum*, 69 (2000), 34–58.

——, 'English and French in England after 1362', *English Studies*, 6 (2001), 539–59.

——, 'The Teaching and Learning of French in Later Medieval England', *Zeitschrift für französische Sprache and Literature*, 111 (2001), 1–18.

——, 'Henry of Lancaster and Geoffrey Chaucer: Anglo-French and Middle English in Fourteenth-Century England', *MLR*, 99 (2004), 313–27.

Rouse, Richard and Mary Rouse, 'The Goldsmith and the Peacocks: Jean de la Mote in the Household of Simon de Lille, 1340', *Viator*, 28 (1997), 281–303.

Russell, Joycelyne G., *Diplomats at Work: Three Renaissance Studies* (Stroud: Alan Sutton, 1992).

Rychner, Jean, *Contribution à l'étude des fabliaux: variantes, remaniements, dégradations*, 2 vols, Université de Neuchâtel: Recueil de travaux publiés par la Faculté des lettres, 28 (Neuchâtel: Faculté des Lettres, 1960).

Sabatini, Francesco, *Napoli angioina: cultura e società* (Naples: Edizioni Scientifiche Italiane, 1975).

Salter, Elizabeth, *English and International: Studies in the Literature, Art and Patronage of Medieval England*, ed. Derek Pearsall and Nicolette Zeeman (Cambridge: Cambridge University Press, 1988).

Saunders, Corinne, Françoise Le Saux and Neil Thomas, eds, *Writing War: Medieval Literary Responses to Warfare* (Woodbridge: D. S. Brewer, 2004).

Scanlon, Larry, 'King, Commons and Kind Wit: Langland's National Vision and the Rising of 1381', in Lavezzo, ed., *Imagining a Medieval English Nation*, 191–233.

Scase, Wendy, *Literature and Complaint in England, 1272–1553* (Oxford: Oxford University Press, 2007).

Scattergood, V. J. and J. W. Sherborne, eds, *English Court Culture in the Later Middle Ages* (London: Duckworth, 1983).

Scattergood, [V.] John, 'Chaucer's *Complaint of Venus* and the 'Curiosite' of Graunson', *Essays in Criticism*, 44 (1994), 171–89.

——, 'The Short Poems', in *Oxford Guides to Chaucer: The Shorter Poems*, A. J. Minnis, V. J. Scattergood and J. J. Smith (Oxford: Clarendon Press, 1995), 483–503.

——, 'Literary Culture at the Court of Richard II', in Scattergood and. Sherborne, eds, *English Court Culture in the Later Middle Ages*, 29–43.

Schofield, John and Geoffrey Stell, 'The Built Environment 1300–1540', in Palliser, ed., *The Cambridge Urban History*, 371–93.

Schulze-Busacker, Elizabeth, 'French Conceptions of Foreigners and Foreign Languages in the Twelfth and Thirteenth Centuries', *Romance Philology*, 41 (1987), 24–47.

Sinnreich-Levi, Deborah M., ed., *Eustache Deschamps, French Courtier-Poet: His Work and his World* (New York: AMS Press, 1998).

Shepherd, Geoffrey, 'Early Middle English', in *The Middle Ages*, ed. W. F. Bolton (London: Barrie & Jenkins, Sphere, 1970), 81–117.

Short, Ian, 'On Bilingualism in Anglo-Norman England', *Romance Philology*, 33 (1979–80), 467–79.

—— and R. Pearcy, eds, *Eighteen Anglo-Norman Fabliaux*, ANTS 14 (London: ANTS, 2000).

——, *Manual of Anglo-Norman* (London: ANTS, 2007).

Simoni-Aurembou, Marie-Rose, 'Le français et ses patois', in Chaurand, ed., *Nouvelle Histoire de la Langue Française*, 547–80.

Simpson, James, *Reform and Cultural Revolution* (Oxford: Oxford University Press, 2002)

——, 'Chaucer as a European Writer', in Lerer, ed., *Yale Companion*, 55–86.

Smith, Anthony D., *Nationalism and Modernism: A Critical Survey of Recent Theories of Nations and Nationalism* (London and New York: Routledge, 1998).

Smith, D. Vance, 'Chaucer as an English Writer' in Lerer, ed., *Yale Companion*, 87–121.

Spearing, A. C., *Textual Subjectivity: The Encoding of Subjectivity in Medieval Narratives and Lyrics* (Oxford: Oxford University Press, 2005).

Spivak, Gayatri Chakravorty, *Outside in the Teaching Machine* (New York and London: Routledge, 1993).

Sponsler, Claire, 'Alien Nation: London's Aliens and Lydgate's *Mummings* for the Mercers and Goldsmiths', in Cohen, ed., *The Postcolonial Middle Ages*, 229–242.

——, 'The Captivity of Henry Chrystede: Froissart's Chroniques, Ireland, and Fourteenth-Century Nationalism', in Lavezzo, ed., *Imagining a Medieval English Nation*, 304–39.

Spurgeon, Caroline F. E., ed., *Five Hundred Years of Chaucer Criticism and Allusion 1357–1900*, 3 vols (Cambridge: Cambridge University Press, 1925).

Staley, Lynn, *Languages of Power in the Age of Richard II* (Pennsylvania: Pennsylvania State University Press, 2005).

Stanbury, Sarah, 'Vernacular Nostalgia and the Cambridge History of Medieval English Literature', *Texas Studies in Lit and Lang*, 44/1 (2002) 92–107.

Stein, Robert M., 'Multilingualism', in Strohm, ed., *Middle English*, 23–37.

Steiner, Emily and Candace Barrington, eds, *The Letter of the Law* (Ithaca and London: Cornell University Press, 2002).

Stewart, L., 'The Chant-royal, A Study of the Evolution of the Genre', *Romania*, 96 (1973), 431–96.

Strohm, Paul, *Hochon's Arrow: The Social Imagination of Fourteenth-Century Texts* (Princeton: Princeton University Press, 1992).

——, *England's Empty Throne: Usurpation and the Language of Legitimation 1399–1422* (New Haven and London: Yale University Press, 1998).

——, *Theory and the Premodern Text* (Minneapolis: University of Minnesota Press, 2000).

——, *Politique: Languages of Statecraft between Chaucer and Shakespeare* (Notre Dame, IN: University of Notre Dame Press, 2005).

——, ed., *Middle English*, Oxford Twenty-First century Approaches to Literature (Oxford: Oxford University Press, 2007).

Strohm, Reinhard, 'The *ars nova* Fragments of Ghent', *Tijdschrift van de Vereniging voor Nederlandse Musiekgeschiedenis*, 34 (1984), 109–31.

——, *Music in Late Medieval Bruges*, rev. edn (Oxford: Clarendon Press, 1990).

——, *The Rise of European Music 1380–1500* (Cambridge: Cambridge University Press, 1993).

Studd, Robin, 'England and Gascony 1216–1337', *England in Europe 1066–1453*, ed. Nigel Saul (London: Collins and Brown, 1994), 97–107.

Suchier, Hermann, *Le français et le provençal*, trans. P. Monet (Paris: Émile Bouillon, 1891).

Suggett, H., 'The Use of French in England in the Later Middle Ages', *Transactions of the Royal Historical Society*, 28 (1946), 61–83.

Sullivan, Karen, *The Interrogation of Joan of Arc* (Minneapolis: University of Minnesota Press, 1999).

Summerfield, Thea, 'The Political Songs in the *Chronicles* of Pierre de Langtoft and Robert Mannyng', in *The Court and Cultural Diversity*, ed. Evelyn Mullally and John Thompson (Woodbridge: D. S. Brewer, 1997), 139–48.

Sumption, Jonathan, *The Hundred Years War*, 2 vols (London: Faber, 1990 and 1999).

Sutton, Anne F., 'Merchants, Music and Social Harmony: the London Puy and its French and London Contexts, circa 1300', *The London Journal*, 17 (1992), 1–17.

——, 'The *Tumbling Bear* and Its Patrons: A Venue for the London Puy and Mercery', in Boffey and King, eds, *London and Europe*, 85–110.

Symes, Carol, *A Common Stage: Theater and Public Life in Medieval Arras* (Ithaca: Cornell University Press, 2007).

Taine, Hippolyte A., *History of English Literature*, trans. H. Van Laun, 2 vols (Edinburgh: Edmonston and Douglas, 1871).

Taylor, Craig, 'War, Propaganda and Diplomacy in Fifteenth-Century France and England', in Allmand, ed., *War, Government and Power*, 70–91.

Taylor, Karla, 'Social Aesthetics and the Emergence of Civic Discourse from the *Shipman's Tale* to *Melibee*', *Chaucer Review*, 39 (2005), 298–322.

Taylor, Jane, *The Making of Poetry: Late-Medieval French Poetic Anthologies* (Turnhout: Brepols, 2007).

Thomas, Brook, 'National Literary Histories: Imagined Communities or Imagined Societies?', in *MLQ: Special Issue: National Literary Histories*, ed. Brook Thomas and Marshall Brown, 64 (2003), 137–52.

Tobler, Adolf, and Erhard Lommatzsch, *Altfranzösisches Wörterbuch*, 10 vols (Berlin: Weidmannsche Buchhandlung, 1925–1976).

Torraca, Francesco, 'Giovanni Boccaccio a Napoli (1326–1339)', *Archivio storico per le provincie napoletane*, 39 (1914), 420–23.

Tout, T. F., *Chapters in the Administrative History of Mediaeval England: The Wardrobe, The Chamber and the Small Seals*, 6 cols (Manchester: Manchester University Press, 1920–33).

——, *France and England in the Middle Ages: their relations in the Middle Ages and Now* (Manchester: Manchester University Press, 1922).

Townend, Matthew, 'Contacts and Conflicts: Latin, Norse, and French', in *The Oxford History of English*, ed. Lynda Mugglestone (Oxford: Oxford University Press, 2006), 61–85.

Treharne, Elaine, 'Categorization, Periodization: The Silence of (the) English in the Twelfth Century', *NML*, 8 (2006), 247–73.

Trigg, S., *Congenial Souls: Reading Chaucer from Medieval to Postmodern* (Minneapolis: University of Minesota Press, 2002).

Trotter, D. A., 'Anglo-Norman', in *Languages in Britain and Ireland*, ed. Glanville Price (Oxford: Blackwell, 2000), 197–206.

——, ed., *Multilingualism in Later Medieval Britain* (Cambridge, 2000).

——, 'L'Anglo-Norman: variété insulaire, ou variété isolée?', *Médiévales*, 45 (2003), 43–54.

——, 'Not So Eccentric as It Looks: Anglo-French and French French', *Forum for Modern Language Studies*, 39 (2003), 427–38.

——, 'Language Contact, Multilingualism and the Evidence Problem', in *The Beginnings of Standardization: Language and Culture in Fourteenth-Century England*, ed. Ursula Schaefer (Frankfurt: Peter Lang, 2006), 73–90.

——, 'Witnesses to spoken Anglo-French? Evidential problems and documentary transmission', paper presented at *Language Over Time: A Symposium On Anglo-Norman In The Context Of Medieval French Language Use*, Birmingham City University, 19 January 2008.

Tucoo-Chala, Pierre, 'Froissart dans le Midi Pyrénéen', in Palmer, ed., *Froissart: Historian*, 118–31.

Turville-Petre, Thorlac, *England the Nation: Language, Literature and National Identity 1290–1340* (Oxford: Clarendon Press, 1996).

Turner, Marion, *Chaucerian Conflict: Languages of Antagonism in late Fourteenth-Century London* (Oxford: Clarendon Press, 2007).

Uitti, Karl D., 'From Clerc to Poète: The Relevance of the *Romance of the Rose* to Machaut's World', in *Machaut's World: Science and Art in the Fourteenth Century*, ed. M. P. Cosman and B. Chandler, Annals of the New York Academy of Sciences, 314 (New York: New York Academy of Sciences, 1978), 209–16.

Vale, Malcolm, *English Gascony 1399–1453: A Study of War, Government and Politics during the later stages of the Hundred Years' War* (London: Oxford University Press, 1970).

——, *Charles VII* (London: Eyre Methuen, 1974).

——, 'England, France and the Origins of the Hundred Years War', in *England and her Neighbours 1066–1453: Essays in Honour of Pierre Chaplais*, ed. Michael Jones and Malcolm Vale (London: Hambledon, 1989), 199–216.

——, *The Princely Court: Medieval Courts and Culture in North-West Europe* (Oxford: Oxford University Press, 2001).

Varvaro, Alberto, 'Latin and Romance: Fragmentation or Restructuring?', in *Latin and the Romance Languages*, ed. Wright, 44–51.

——, 'La condamnation du sire de Clary: Froissart entre code chevaleresque et loi du roi', *Actes du colloque international 'Jehan Froissart' (Lille 3—Valenciennes, 30 sept.—1er oct. 2004)*, ed. Marie-Madeleine Castellani and Jean-Charles Herbin, *Perspectives Médiévales*, Supplément au n°30, mars 2006 (Paris: Société de Langues et et Littératures Médiévales d'Oc et d'Oïl, 2006), 277–87.

Vising, Johan, *Anglo-Norman Language and Literature* (London: Oxford University Press, 1923).

Waldron, Ronald, 'Trevisa, John (b. c.1342, d. in or before 1402)', *Oxford Dictionary of National Biography*, Oxford University Press, 2004 <http://0-www.oxforddnb.com.catalogue.ulrls.lon.ac.uk:80/view/article/27722> (accessed 3 December 2008).

Walker, Simon, *The Lancastrian Affinity, 1361–1399* (Oxford: Clarendon Press, 1990).

Wallace, David, 'Chaucer and the European Rose' in *SAC. Proceedings, No. 1 1984: Reconstructing Chaucer*, ed. Paul Strohm and Thomas J. Heffernan (Knoxville, Tenn., 1985), 61–7.

——, *Chaucerian Polity: Absolutist Lineages and Associational Forms in England and Italy* (Stanford, CA: Stanford University Press, 1997).

——, ed., *The Cambridge History of Medieval English Literature* (Cambridge: Cambridge University Press, 1999).

——, 'Chaucer's Italian Inheritance', in *The Cambridge Companion to Chaucer*, ed. Piero Boitani and Jill Mann, 2nd edn (Cambridge: Cambridge University Press, 2003), 36–57.

——, *Premodern Places: Calais to Surinam, Chaucer to Aphra Behn* (Oxford: Blackwell, 2004).

Wallace-Hadrill, J. M., *Bede's 'Ecclesiastical History of the English People': A Historical Commentary* (Oxford: Clarendon Press, 1988).

Warren, Michelle R., 'Post-Philology', in *Postcolonial Moves: Medieval Through Modern*, ed. Patricia Clare Ingham and Michelle R. Warren (Basingstoke: Palgrave Macmillan, 2003), 19–45.

Wathey, Andrew, 'The Peace of 1360–1369 and Anglo-French Musical Relations', *EMH*, 9 (1990), 129–74.

——, 'The Marriage of Edward III and the Transmission of French Motets to England', *Journal of the American Musicological Society*, 45 (1992), 1–29.

——, 'European Politics and Musical Culture at the Court of Cyprus', in *The Cypriot-French Repertory of the Manuscript Torino J.II.9* (Stuttgart: Hänssler, 1995), 33–53.

——, 'Philippe de Vitry's Books', in *Books and Collectors 1200–1700: Essays Presented to A. G. Watson*, ed. J. P. Carley and C. G. C. Tite (London: British Library, 1997), 145–52.

——, 'Myth and Mythography in the Motets of Philippe de Vitry', *Musica e storia*, 6 (1998), 81–106.

Watson, Nicholas, 'Censorship and Cultural Change in Late-Medieval England: Vernacular Theology, the Oxford translation debate, and Arundel's Constitutions of 1409', *Speculum*, 70 (1995), 822–64.

Watts, John, *Henry VI and the Politics of Kingship* (Cambridge: Cambridge University Press, 1996).

Whiting, B. J., 'The Vows of the heron', *Speculum*, 20 (1945), 261–78.

Wilkins, Nigel, 'Music and Poetry at Court: England and France in the Late Middle Ages', in Scattergood and Sherborne, eds, *English Court Culture in the Later Middle Ages*, 183–204.

Williams, Raymond, *The Country and the City* (London: Hogarth Press, 1985; 1st publ. 1973).

Wilson, Geoffrey, *A Medievalist in the Eighteenth Century: Le Grand d'Aussy and the 'Fabliaux ou Contes'* (The Hague: Martinus Nijhoff, 1975).

Wilson, R. M., 'English and French in England: 1100–1300', *History*, 28 (1943), 37–60.

Wimsatt, James I., *Chaucer and the French Love Poets: The Literary Background of 'The Book of the Duchess'* (Chapel Hill: University of North Carolina Press, 1968).

——, 'Guillaume de Machaut and Chaucer's *Troilus and Criseyde*', *Medium Aevum*, 45 (1976), 277–92.

——, 'Collections of French Lyrics Chaucer May Have Known', in *L'Imagination médiévale: Chaucer et ses contemporains: Actes du Colloque en Sorbonne*, edited by André Crépin, Publications de l'Association des Médiévistes Anglicistes de l'Enseignement Supérieur, 16 (Paris: Publications de l'AMAES, 1991), 33–51.

——, *Chaucer and His French Contemporaries: Natural Music in the Fourteenth Century* (Toronto: University of Toronto Press, 1991).

Wogan-Browne, Jocelyn, *Saints' Lives and the Literary Culture of Women, c. 1150–c. 1300: Virginity and its Authorizations* (Oxford: Oxford University Press, 2001).

Womersley, David, 'France in Shakespeare's Henry V', *Renaissance Studies*, 9/4 (1995), 442–59.

Woodbine, George, 'The Language of English Law', *Speculum*, 18 (1943), 395–436.

Wright, Craig, *Music at the Court of Burgundy 1364–1419: A Documentary History* (Henryville, PA: Institute of Mediaeval Music, 1979).

Wright, Laura, 'Trade between England and the Low Countries: Evidence from Historical Linguistics', in Barron and Saul, eds, *England and the Low Countries*, 169–79.

——, *Sources of London English: Medieval Thames Vocabulary* (Oxford: Clarendon Press, 1996).

——, 'The Records of Hanseatic Merchants: Ignorant, sleepy or degenerate?', *Multilingua*, 16 (1997), 339–50.

Wright, Roger, ed., *Latin and the Romance Languages in the Early Middle Ages*, (London and New York: Routledge, 1990).

——, *A Sociophilological Study of Late Latin* (Turnhout: Brepols, 2002).

Yeager, R. F., *John Gower's Poetic: The Search for a New Arion* (Cambridge: D. S. Brewer, 1990).

——, 'John Gower's French', in Echard, ed., *A Companion to Gower*, 137–51.

——, 'John Gower's Audience: The Ballades', *Chaucer Review*, 40 (2005), 81–105.

Young, Christopher and Thomas Gloning, eds, *A History of the German Language through Texts* (London and New York: Routledge, 2004).

Zink, Gaston, *Phonétique historique du français* (Paris: PUF, 1986).
Zink, Michel, *Froissart et le temps* (Paris: PUF, 1998).
Zumthor, Paul, *Essai de poétique médiévale* (Paris: Éditions du Seuil, 1972).
——, 'Le Carrefour des rhétoriqueurs: Intertextualité et Rhétorique', *Poétique*, 27 (1976), 317–37.

Index

Printed in Great Britain
by Amazon.co.uk, Ltd.,
Marston Gate.